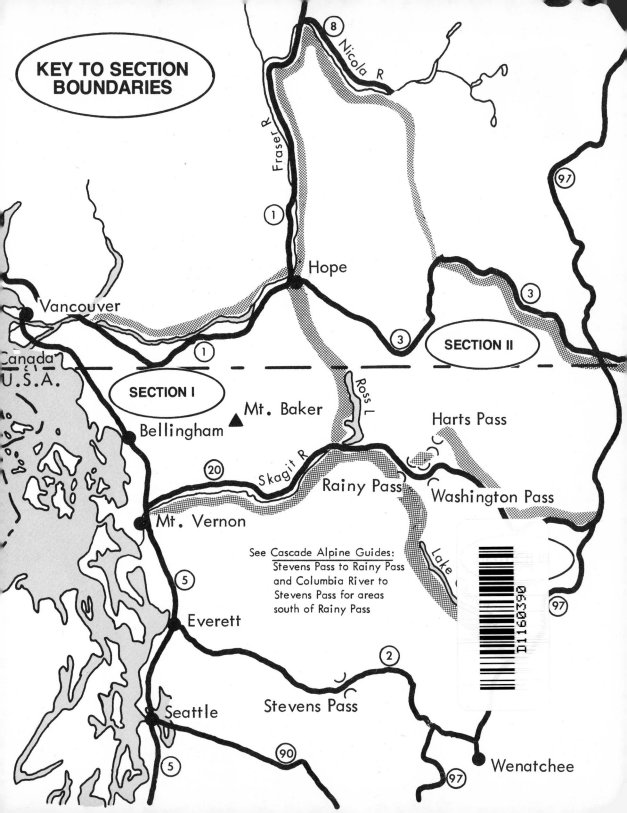

KEY TO SECTION BOUNDARIES

8

Nicola R

Fraser R

97

1

Hope

Vancouver

3

3

SECTION II

1

Canada
U.S.A.

SECTION I

Ross L

Mt. Baker

Harts Pass

Bellingham

20

Skagit R

Rainy Pass

Washington Pass

Mt. Vernon

See Cascade Alpine Guides:
Stevens Pass to Rainy Pass
and Columbia River to
Stevens Pass for areas
south of Rainy Pass

Lake

5

97

Everett

2

D1160390

Seattle

Stevens Pass

90

5

97

Wenatchee

CASCADE ALPINE GUIDE

CASCADE ALPINE GUIDE

CLIMBING AND HIGH ROUTES
Rainy Pass to Fraser River

by FRED BECKEY

THE MOUNTAINEERS *Seattle*

THE MOUNTAINEERS

Organized 1906

To explore and study the mountains, forests and watercourses
   of the Northwest;

To gather into permanent form the history and traditions of
   this region;

To preserve by the encouragement of protective legislation
   or otherwise the natural beauty of Northwest America;

To make explorations into these regions in fulfillment of the
   above purposes;

To encourage a spirit of good fellowship among all lovers of
   outdoor life.

First Edition 1981

The Mountaineers,
719 Pike Street, Seattle, Washington 98101

Manufactured in the United States of America

Published simultaneously in Canada by Douglas and McIntyre, Ltd.,
1615 Venables Street, Vancouver, B.C.   V5L 2H1

Photo overlays by Lucy Lark

Maps and topographic sketches by Mary-Ann Ciuffini

Other sketches by Susan Marsh

Design by Marge Mueller

Title Photo: Challenger Glacier on Mt. Challenger. Mt. Shuksan in distance.
Photo by Bob and Ira Spring

Library of Congress Cataloging in Publication Data

Beckey, Fred W., 1921-
     Cascade alpine guide.

     Includes bibliographical references and index.
     1. Mountaineering — Cascade Range — Guide-books.
2. Cascade Range — Description — Guide-books.   I. Title.
GV199.42.C37B417   1981   917.95   81-2335
ISBN 0-89886-002-4   AACR2

Contents

ACKNOWLEDGEMENTS   8

PREFACE   9

INTRODUCTION   10

SECTION I. NORTHWESTERN CASCADE RANGE:
Skagit River to Fraser River   15
Notes   139

SECTION II. NORTHEASTERN CASCADE RANGE:
Harts Pass, Washington, to Nicola River, British Columbia   146
Notes   203

SECTION III. NORTHEASTERN CASCADE RANGE:
Lake Chelan and Rainy Pass to Methow River and Harts Pass   213
Notes   278

APPROACHES   283

INDEX   317

Acknowledgements

No treatment of this nature could be presented without the benefit of modern maps, aerial photography and library resources. To a great degree, this guide represents the secondary resources of these invisible assistants, and the knowledge of hundreds of individual contributors. Librarians and archivists at several institutions graciously assisted in historical research. I wish in particular to thank the staffs of the Archives of the Canadian Rockies, Banff; Bancroft Library, University of California; Special Collections Division and Regional Manuscripts Collection, University of Washington; Washington State Library, Olympia; Oregon State Historical Society, Portland; and Stanford University Libraries. Access to cartographic archives was courteously afforded me by the National Archives and Records Service, Washington, D.C., and the U.S. Forest Service, Portland.

Certainly this volume is enhanced by the many excellent photographic contributions, and as in the two previous volumes, I wish to thank Austin Post for selecting special images from his marvelous aerial obliques taken during U.S. Geological Survey glacier study flights. The guidebook is patently enriched by the numerous photographic contributions.

Proud as the author and publisher are to present this book, the third in the *Cascade Alpine Guide* series, we are also humbly aware of the many talents and contributions needed to make this publication a reality. Many persons reviewed climbing and hiking routes or otherwise made helpful suggestions on introductory material. In particular I wish to thank Vic Adams, Alex Bertulis, Paul Binkert, Van Brinkerhoff, Les Davenport, Scott Davis, Pete Doorish, Joan Firey, Bill Fix, Brad Fowler, Dallas Kloke, Greg Markov, Don McPherson, George Mustoe, Jim Nelson, Roy Ratliff, Peter Renz, Karl Ricker, John Roper, Eric Sanford, Mickey Schurr, Don Serl, Bryce Simon, Gordon Skoog, Frank Tarver, Reed Tindall, Joseph Vance, Glenn Woodsworth, and John Young. A review of logging access roads and mountain trails, both in Washington State and British Columbia, was only possible with the time and special maps provided by Jim Vickerson and the Chilliwack Mountain Rescue group, Barrie Richardson of Cattermole Timber Co., Winton Wefer of Georgia-Pacific Corporation, rangers Bill Howard and Glen Bertram of the B.C. Forest Service, and the staffs of Mt. Baker-Snoqualmie National Forest and North Cascades National Park.

In addition, Glenn Woodsworth, Rowland Tabor, Karl Ricker, and Richard B. Waitt, Jr. generously reviewed portions of my rough drafts of material on geology and geomorphology, and made useful suggestions from their wealth of knowledge of the North Cascade terrain and rock structures. The loan of Will F. Thompson's positive contact transparencies made the analysis of mountain terrain more reliable.

Much appreciation is expressed to Edwin H. Brown, of Western Washington University in Bellingham, for review of regional geology and for the courtesy of providing office space in which to prepare the manuscript.

To the capable staff of The Mountaineers • Books, directed by John Pollock, I owe my appreciation not only for supporting this project, but for coordinating the complexities of publishing. Here the comprehensive planning and preparation for production by Donna DeShazo and editing by Peggy Ferber were important factors in making this guide attractive, yet practical for its purpose.

Also, for different reasons, I am indebted to the patience of numerous restaurant proprietors, at whose establishments I often worked late into the night, probably more often giving the illusion of being an overworked school teacher than a profitable customer.

FRED BECKEY

Preface

The mountains are here interpreted through word portrait, camera, artistry, and maps. This guidebook is in part an encyclopedia of natural features, but it can only give a brief image of a region or a peak, sometimes with emphasis applied to a feature of specific interest. An attempt to provide the same criterion of significance has been applied to climbs, yet some imbalance appears because of popularity or available knowledge. Some of the detailed information collected here has existed for some time, but has not been integrated into a single format to produce a digest of physical geographic features and human history on a regional scale.

While the author and publisher are both anxious to describe the safest, shortest, and most sensible routes to summits, this is not always possible because of lack of documentation or direct experience. Some of the research involved locating a wide variety of sources, and the consequent writing required the integration of a mass of detail, with some conflicting interpretation.

This guide is dedicated to Pacific Northwest outdoor users with the hope that it will enhance appreciation of the natural world of our mountains, and stir a response to its environmental challenges. All too often the factual foundation for leisure-time decisions and public decisions affecting our lives is only available to the selected few — usually those living in the nearby geographic region. In the belief that our mountain wildlands belong to all the citizenry, and not only to those who feel a proprietary interest, this guide seeks to fairly portray some of their visitation opportunities. It is hoped that as a consequence, some of these new visitors will become friends of the wilderness.

"The Cascade mountains north of Mount Rainier present, from the Sound, the same difference from the southern, in the character of the scenery, as that noticed on the eastern side, arising from a difference in geologic character. Seen from the lower end of Whidby's island, the more distant range is a bare and ragged sierra, some of the peaks of which rise to the limits of perpetual snow. Mount Baker, which terminates the view, has a sharp and precipitous outline more resembling that of Mount Hood than the regular forms of Rainier, St. Helens, and Adams. The fact of an interior mountain basin, inferred during the examination of the country on the Okinakane, seems to be confirmed. In this, then, appears to be a wide entrance through the gap of the Samish river. Mount Baker, it should be mentioned, has during this winter, been in action, throwing out light clouds of smoke. The last eruption of any note is said to have been in 1843, when a slight shock of an earthquake was felt at Fort Langley."
GEORGE GIBBS, 1854
Olympia, Washington Territory

Introduction

GEOLOGY OF
THE NORTH CASCADES

Although the present landscape is young, the complex geologic history of the North Cascades goes back well over a billion years. It is only within the last dozen years that unified hypotheses of the evolution of the North Cascades and the margin of the broad cordillera have been formulated, and these proposals are constantly changing. Anything written in the geologic history of this region must be considered as simply the best present approximation, rather than fact.

Most geologists now accept the theory that the earth's crust (the outer 10-50 km of the earth) consists of a number of relatively rigid plates. Although internally relatively coherent, the plates can slide past (or under) one another on great faults; it is the interactions of these plates that are thought to drive the geologic forces that have produced the North Cascades and other mountains. Blocks of continental crust, too light to dive into the mantle, collide and produce great chains of fold mountains.

Plates consist of both relatively light granitic crust about 35 km thick under the continents, and denser basaltic crust about 10 km thick under the oceans; the heavier ocean crust may dive beneath continental crust along a subduction zone and chains of volcanic arcs form above the downgoing slab. From about 20 to 0 m.y. before present local volcanoes in Washington, southwestern British Columbia, and southeastern Alaska formed above downgoing slabs of oceanic crust: examples are Mt. Baker and Mt. Garibaldi.

One deduction from the plate tectonic theory is that the rocks that now constitute the North Cascades probably formed in widely separated places, hundreds or thousands of miles from their present position, and that probably the older the rocks the more displacement they have undergone. Faults moved slivers of continental shelf northward at different speeds. (Major faults are breaks along which blocks slid past one another.) These blocks or fragments moved along great faults such as the Straight Creek Fault (one of the great structural features of the entire Cordillera) which now separate areas of greatly different geology. Accretion of these crustal fragments to the main North American plate probably took place over at least one hundred m.y.; probably only the youngest rocks, such as the Chilliwack Batholith and the great Cascade volcanoes, were formed in their present positions.

Most of the fragments of plates that form the North Cascades probably formed well S of their present position, possibly even in the southern hemisphere. Ancestral North America may have moved N across the equator more than 200 m.y. ago. Just as rocks W of the San Andreas Fault in California (the Pacific plate) are moving N with respect to the rest of the state (and may eventually relocate in Alaska), so the various fragments of the Cascades moved N at various times into their present positions. The Cascades were probably built up jigsaw fashion over several hundred m.y.

Nearly everyone is familiar with the "layer cake" appearance of the Rocky Mountains; this type of layering is generally absent from the Cascades. The Rockies are composed largely of sediments such as quartzite, shale, and limestone that were deposited along the margin of the ancient North American continent. Most of these sediments were derived from the erosion of highlands in the interior of North America. The Cascades, on the other hand, are composed largely of volcanic rocks, sediments derived from the erosion of these volcanics, and granitic and metamorphic rocks. Volcanism, heat, and pressure have been much more important in the Cascades than in the mountains to the E.

The North Cascades, then, were built by the slow, forceful collision of plates, with attendant heat and incalculable pressures, the accumulation of sediments deposited in an ancient sea, and the upwelling of molten magma — which helped lift them. Rising bedrock eventually pushed the ocean waters westward.

During the Mesozoic orogeny (100-150 m.y. ago) when the major rock units were formed and brought together, the region may have been impressively mountainous, judging by the amount of crustal shortening which the thrust faults indicate. Erosion beveled the landscape shortly thereafter, and the Chuckanut Formation was deposited in broad stream valleys coursing across the present Cascades.

The mountains of today have resulted from relatively young (10 m.y. to present) uplift of the ancient rocks and erosive carving by alpine streams and glaciers. Cascade volcanoes are an impressive final addition built upon an already rugged mountain range.

Selected references to the geology of the North Cascades are:

Easterbrook, Don J. and Rahm, David A. *Land-forms of Washington*. Bellingham, 1970.

Holland, S.S. "Landforms of British Columbia," *B.C. Dept. Mines and Petroleum Resources Bull.* 148 (1964).

Huntting, M.T., Bennett, W.A.G., Livingston, V.E. Jr., and Moen, W.S. Geologic Map of Washington. Wash. Div. Mines and Geology (1961).

McKee, Bates. *Cascadia: The Geologic Evolution of the Pacific Northwest*. New York, 1972.

Misch, Peter. "Geology of the Northern Cascades of Washington," *The Mountaineer* 45 (1952): 3-22.

LAND ADMINISTRATION

Virtually the entirety of the North Cascades in Washington State is administered federally (and in British Columbia, provincially). As trustee of the Mt. Baker-Snoqualmie and Okanogan National Forests, the U.S. Forest Service is responsible for management of much of the mountain region. Since 1968 the National Park Service has administered the North Cascades National Park and Ross Lake National Recreation Area in this section (the latter is essentially a part of the Park, but permits certain activities such as motor boating and hunting). Most of the Park is covered by the Wilderness Act of 1964, giving the highest available degree of protection to the terrain included between Skagit River and the International Boundary.

In the specially dedicated lands each overnight party must obtain and carry a Wilderness Permit (Forest Service) or Backcountry Permit (Park Service) which must be shown on request to a ranger. Permits may be obtained by mail from headquarters or at ranger stations. Where a planned itinerary crosses both Forest Service and Park Service lands, either agency can issue a single permit covering the entire itinerary.

Regulations are subject to change because of difference in localities, seasons, ecosystem carrying capacity and park visitation pressures; to avoid conflict and fines, plan on obtaining and following current regulations.

To protect the wilderness quality of our precious mountain resources, it is imperative to close all entry trails to vehicles, to close off the last miles of many logging and other access roads to vehicles both in Washington and British Columbia, to permit hiker and horseman to enter the high regions, and any wilderness, free of unrelated sound and visual impact.

Resource protection should be a major criterion in regulating ORV travel. The 1977 plan for Wenatchee National Forest would still permit motor vehicle usage on 99½ trail miles. Such usage should be abolished on high-altitude trails and major hiker valley entry routes in the Chelan and Methow mountains.

NOTES TO THE READER

Various routes on a mountain are listed in clockwise direction, following the most popular route as known. Directions such as "left" or "turn left" are used in the sense of direction of movement.

The principal mountain trails and many connections which apply to alpine areas are listed at the end of the volume; some cross-country routes are shown, but many are left for the reader to discover. The road, trail, and cross-country information is signaled in the text by the symbol ♦. Each section is prefaced by map references and ranger station locations. However, it should be noted that Forest Service roads will be renumbered in about 1981, and new maps issued accordingly.

Some locations are defined only by elevation as shown on the most recent topographic map, pending a possible later naming. When a height is not shown as triangulated, it is given as the altitude of the highest contour of the most recent topographic map, with a plus (+). Some altitudes between contour lines are defined as estimated ("est.").

"Peak" used before a numerical altitude designates a summit without a local name, the height taken from the most recent topographic map, or height indicated by approximate (est.) altitude; allow some tolerance for this estimate.

On the easier peaks and routes, first ascent claims should be regarded as provisional. Certainly the recorded history of climbing in the North Cascades is far from complete, and the best current information may need occasional revision when new data is acquired.

The reader may notice what appear to be inconsistencies in usage throughout this volume. For example, *measurements of distance* are given sometimes in miles, and sometimes in metric measurements. Ultimately, these will all be metric, both in the United States and Canada, but during the period of transition, when maps and road signs have not all been changed, it seemed best to reflect as accurately as possible the current practice at time of publication.

Fractions and decimals will also be found intermixed: when distance is not exact, fractions are used; decimals indicate a more precise statement.

Canadian and American *spellings* of certain common features differ, e.g., Okanogan and Okanagan, Hozomeen and Hozameen.

Features on a mountain may appear for example, as West Ridge (indicating that there is in the text a route described on the ridge on the west side of mountain) or W ridge (indicating that there simply is a ridge on the W side of the mountain).

AERIAL PHOTOGRAPHY AND SKETCHES

Special interpretive problems arise in the use of both orthographic sketches and aerial oblique photography. Oblique photographs cannot be accurately scaled but are useful in emphasizing landforms, studying the vertical dimensions of terrain, and for a variety of interpretation. The aerial photographs have the advantage of excellent resolution, but do not produce distortion-free orthographic views. It is difficult to compute angles off aerial photographs because of divergence of view in expanding toward a horizon, and the image distortion arising from converging meridians. Distortion is due to tilt of the camera's optical axis, and the usual radial distortion of the wide angle is given an altitude dimension. It should be remembered that photos are printed as a rectangle, but the ground area is a trapezoid: distortion increases toward the edges of a photograph.

TECHNICAL CLIMBING RATINGS

Grades reflect judgement of the original or subsequent parties in the N.C.C.S. and Yosemite decimal system. Varying climbing standards and route conditions have a bearing on interpretation of difficulties.

The rating evaluation number cannot alone be responsible for conveying the total difficulty of the experience in a particular environment. A rating would be ambiguous if one tried to incorporate all other factors that constitute difficulty, so some narrative describing relevant factors such as exposure, lack of protection, sustained nature, looseness, etc., is necessary.

Numerical grading systems have limited application on ice. Grading of ice climbs is subject to many relevant and changing factors, and therefore very problematic. The prevailing condition of snow or ice, local changes in glacier characteristics, and in fact the detailed line taken, have made noticeable differences in the difficulty — all this assuming the climbing party is using modern and accepted technical equipment.

Knowledge and understanding of the mountains are prerequisites for competent and intelligent off-trail travel. Understanding the geography and local terrain can help prevent miscalculations in planning and timing of summit ventures.

SAFETY AND BACKCOUNTRY USE

Responsible alpine hikers and mountaineers, recognizing the problems of adverse impact in the mountains caused by increased visitation, exercise much care and self-restraint to prevent environmental degradation, and wherever possible adopt minimum impact attitudes and techniques. Many of the cherished practices of earlier years must be set aside if the remaining wilderness is to survive the enormous number of people who are discovering it. Backcountry administrative regulations and permit systems gall those who are used to camping wherever and whenever the mood strikes, but these must be adhered to for the sake of fairness and protection of wilderness. The days of the casual wood fire at higher elevations are gone in the Cascades, and light portable stoves are essential for cooking. In campsites where wood fires are specifically permitted, use only dead twigs and boughs for fires; do not cut green materials, which won't burn well anyway. Campfire permits are required in most Washington State areas, but not in British Columbia ATP. Forest closures during summer dry spells must be respected.

The problem of litter is a world-wide one, calling for personal self-control: do not bury refuse or secretly stow it under boulders, down crevasses, or in backcountry latrines. *CARRY IT OUT.* Where and when a wood fire is available, burn all paper, but carry out tins, plastics, and foil.

Leave pets at home.

When rock climbing use restraint in use of climbing aids such as pitons and bolts, which can permanently deface the rock and degrade the route for others. A recent and specialized abuse of the rock climbing environment is the use of chalk, whose mark makes an aesthetic insult. Certainly its use diminishes the pleasure of others, and interferes in the discovery of a route's secrets. Other abuses, such as trampling, graffiti, and removal of fixed pitons are perpetrated by individuals, sometimes without negative intent, but certainly with cumulative effect.

Weather in the Cascades is actually highly predictable: either it is raining or it will be shortly. Always take some form of weather protection. On long climbs it is advisable to take a bivouac sack or protective tarp cover, and always take wool clothing, hat, and gloves.

During hunting season wear bright red or yellow clothes, or join the animals in areas where hunting is not allowed.

Forest roads in British Columbia are subject to continual changes due to logging operations; closures are always possible. Some roads may be gated and/or open at irregular intervals, sometimes weekends.

In the forest, do not blaze trails, or mark routes with ribbon or tape. Above timberline stay on trails when possible, and when no trail exists in meadow areas, walk on rocks rather than vulnerable vegetation. Help prevent trail erosion by avoiding duplicate paths and cutting switchbacks. Watch for cracks in snowfields and for weak surfaces above gullies and streams. Belay on steep or dangerous slopes and couloirs.

When fording streams, keep boots on for more secure footing, loosen the waist belt of the pack, and use an ice axe or long pole for support. In glacier-fed streams the amount of water and current strength may vary over a rather short period of time, depending on the time of day and temperature. Sometimes a short wait pays enormous dividends in ease of crossing.

Should help in effecting a rescue be required in Washington State, call the nearest county sheriff, or North Cascades National Park Ranger Station if the accident is within the Park. In British Columbia call the nearest unit of the R.C.M.P., or the Provincial Emergency Program (Search and Rescue; Hope and Chilliwack), or Mountain Rescue Group, P.O. Box 764, Vancouver, B.C.

ABBREVIATIONS

hwy	highway
Crest Trail	Pacific Crest Trail
ATP	at time of publication
r.t.	round trip
ft	feet (altitude)
m.y.	million years
B.P.	before present time (geology)
est.	estimated altitude
m	meters
km	kilometer (glacier length)
km²	square kilometer (glacier area)
KB, LA	knife blade, lost arrow
C.A.J.	*Canadian Alpine Journal*
A.A.J.	*American Alpine Journal*
B.C.M.	*British Columbia Mountaineer*

LEGEND FOR PHOTOS

route — — — — — —

variation —.—.—.—

hidden route ·········

campsite ▲

LEGEND FOR SKETCHS AND MAPS

trail or route — — —

route ···············

major summit △

minor summit ⊙

campsite ▲

campground ⋀

ridge ▰▰▰▰▰

road ═══

mine ⚒

structure ■

MT. SHUKSAN – Price Glacier
NATIONAL PARK SERVICE

SECTION I

Northwestern Cascade Range

SKAGIT RIVER TO FRASER RIVER

(Skagit River, Diablo Lake, Ross Lake, Klesilkwa River, Silverhope Creek, Fraser River)

GEOGRAPHY

At the turn of the century general usage had not firmly fixed the northern limits of the Cascade Range. Some atlases extended the name along the Canadian Coast Mountains, but the master trench principle clearly makes the Fraser River the obvious boundary. The basis for mountain grouping is purely topographical and generally founded on established usage. As a result of their explorations in 1901 George Otis Smith and Frank Calkins declared the "Skagit Mountains" (the eastern portion of the section) "include the wildest and most rugged country in the whole Cascade Range."[1] The geologists named the mountain mass extending S from the International Boundary Custer Ridge in admiration of Henry Custer's crossing from the headwaters of Chilliwack River in 1859. A deeply isolated extension of these mountains is now famed as the Picket Range.

In any event the natural boundaries are obvious. The Hope Mountains portion of the Skagit Range is separated on the W by the southward-flowing Klesilkwa River and N-flowing Silverhope Creek. The Skagit Range forms the divide between the latter streams and Chilliwack River; the unit N of the Chilliwack is the Cheam Range. The Picket Range, Cheam Range, and peaks along the Nesakwatch-Sleese divide are examples of highly developed secondary ranges surpassing the main watershed in height and relief. Besides the Mt. Baker region there are a Boundary subrange (Nooksack-Chilliwack), Baker River subrange (Baker Lake to Goodell Creek), Skagit-Chilliwack subrange (Picket Range and Chilliwack Group), and a Chilliwack-Fraser subrange (Cheam Range).

The sharply defined topography and character of individual formations are principal characteristics of the North Cascades landscape diversity. There is evoked an impression of lush evergreen forests, and high snow-covered peaks — a diverse collection of mountainscapes. Even though alpine glaciation was the primary sculptor of the landscape, the features developed largely from stream erosion, interrupted by formation of Pleistocene ice. Vigorous dissection by the denuding agencies has removed a vast volume of rock from the structurally complex range. The abundance of water tends to increase weathering rates, the breakup of bedrock into smaller fragments forming the soil.

The range is distinctive for the number of hanging (slope) glaciers lying on alp slopes, which it is believed have largely formed by mass wasting above timberline to now form the slopes at timberline. The alp slopes of the North Cascades are generally made up of floors of small or moderate sized cirques lying side by side along mountain flanks. Timberline meadows are everywhere in striking contrast with steep canyon and valley walls.

Cirque floors, at the level of ancient orographic snowlines, often hold small lakes as a consequence of ice scouring. Reginald A. Daly applied the expressive term "tandem cirques," then added "Many of the corries in the belt are of extreme picturesqueness." But the largest body of water within the section, Chilliwack Lake, owes its existence to an end moraine. The boulder moraine holding the lake, evidently formed during a long halt in the recession of ancient glaciers, has a notch where Chilliwack River rushes on its torrential way to the flats of the lower Fraser.

It is difficult to think of the Cascade Range without the long valley of the Skagit, which drains a region from Monte Cristo on the S to Manning Park on the N. In peculiar headwater relationships, the Skaist, Sumallo, and Klesilkwa gather their waters across the Boundary in Canada. The acute angle of the SE-flowing Sumallo tributary (which separates the Skagit and Hozameen ranges) is matched westward by Klesilkwa River, which is flowing the same direction. From here the Skagit turns SE to enter the United States near longitude 121°00'. Ross Lake, located along a structural break, is now a dilation of the river, which lies N-S with little trend to the confluence of Ruby Creek.

The remarkable course of the Skagit River can hardly escape comparison with that of the greater Columbia and the Kootenay, which together constitute the vast Rocky Mountain Trench. The captured waters of the Skagit have reversed courses of some streams (e.g., Suiattle River, Klesilkwa River) and certain branches run in opposite directions (Little Beaver Creek, Baker River). The river predates the Pliocene uplift (during the uplift of the Interior Plateau the Fraser River entrenched itself; the Skagit kept its course across the Skagit Range).

Downstream from Big Beaver Creek the Skagit cuts across the crystalline rock core through a deep gorge having a V-shaped cross-profile and overlapping spurs.[2] For about 25 mi. above the mouth of Diobsud Creek the river course is in a steep-gradient, narrow, steep-walled gorge that shows little effect of glacial erosion. The geologic features along the length of the canyon carry names that stimulate visions of early history. Devils Elbow was named during the heavy backpacking of the gold stampede. The gravel bars of Ruby Creek, alluvium-rich with placer deposits, was near the site of the old Ruby Inn, which stood until the valley was flooded.

The broad valley of Baker River was carved by a glacier, but the subsequent history of the valley includes river erosion, sedimentation in an ancient lake, and lava flows from Mt. Baker.

The united waters of the three forks of Nooksack River, which discharges into tidewater just NW of Bellingham, are the principal drainage of the Mt. Baker-Mt. Shuksan area. In its upper reach the North Fork is flowing on alluvium and is not entrenched, but near Wells Creek the river enters a gorge cut into the volcanic valley floor. Upper Chilliwack River is a glacial torrent that flows for 18 mi. down a deep, wide valley from its headwaters at Hannegan Pass to join Chilliwack Lake by an estuary on the SE corner. The lake, with its bold shores, is somewhat crescentic in shape, with the deepest bay on the N side. Bauerman considered "The Chilekweyuk . . . is the most rapid of all the streams in the country,"[3] and the growth of the river's fan near the Fraser River caused formation of Sumas Lake.[4]

Small streams of snowfield and glacier meltwater typically coalesce into watercourses that tumble down canyons or narrow V-shaped side-valleys to join large streams or rivers. Many of the deep stream gorges of this section are caused by the erosion of joint planes. The most primitive, trail-less and roadless valleys in the North Cascades are located in this section: Bacon Creek and its East Fork, Baker River and its Pass, Bald Eagle, and Picket Creek forks, Stetattle Creek, Goodell Creek, McMillan Creek, Luna Creek, and Silesia Creek.

This cirque and canyon landscape, with its angular peaks, largely owes its present form to the plucking and grinding of ice. The U-shaped valleys with hanging tributaries that head in cirques, and truncated valley spurs, speak of lengthy and repeated episodes of valley and cirque glaciation. When rock was too massive to be quarried (as on Mt. Terror, Mt. Triumph, Twin Spires, and Mt. Slesse), the glaciers only ground and polished, instead of effectively excavating. Reginald A. Daly, studying the Chilliwack valley at the turn of the century, noted that "Glaciers occupying the valleys of Depot, Silver, Middle, Slesse, and Tamihy creeks, have similarly driven back the lateral spurs, greatly steepened the valley walls, and reduced intervening ridges to razor-back profiles."[5]

The range has been repeatedly sculptured by glaciation during Pleistocene time; landscapes have been affected by both alpine and continental glaciation. Once there were integrated systems of immense valley glaciers, some of which merged into piedmont ice in Puget Sound Basin. Despite the more recent event of ice sheet glaciation, the nonglacial and alpine glacial landscape was largely retained.

Daly saw one of the most noteworthy effects of this ice activity in regional landscape evolution, still to be observed in Chilliwack Lake: "This sheet of water must, for the grandeur of its setting, rank among the finest in the Dominion. It has some resemblance to Lake Lucerne, but, in the larger features of colour and form in forest, crag, and glacier, the panoramas on the Canadian lake are certainly the superior."[6]

In Pleistocene time continental ice sheets moved S from Canada irregularly in lobes, a broad front creeping southward and submerging the lower mountains and local glaciation. The last ebb and flow of the ice sheet was the Wisconsin stage, a cycle lasting an estimated 50,000 years.[7] In the glacial maximum the Fraser and Chilliwack ice sheets became confluent and formed part of an immense piedmont glacier.[8]

Ice masses tended to form in pre-existing wide, deep valleys, particularly in the Skagit, where rocks were less resistant than in some other troughs of the greater region. Ice sheet glaciation in this valley may have been very brief and have rapidly disappeared from the North Cascades by downwasting.[9]

The Little Ice Age terminated in the mid-19th century. The majority of low-altitude temperate glaciers have only existed precariously since this time. On volcanoes, glaciers now located in deep canyons are generally failing to expand, even when conditions are favorable. The fact that the Coleman, Roosevelt and Easton glaciers on Mt. Baker are not deeply entrenched has a bearing on their activity pattern. Present glacier types in this section include small valley glaciers (Deming Glacier), icefall (slope) glaciers (Price Glacier), cirque glaciers (McMillan Creek cirque), hanging and cliff glaciers (Hanging Glacier). Except on Mt. Shuksan, the Cascades do not have icefall glaciers derived from high plateaus.

The climate of this section is strongly influenced by alternating semipermanent high and low pressure cells over the North Pacific which control airflow across the coastal margin from Oregon to the vicinity of Prince William Sound in Alaska. The distinct rainy season in autumn and winter is caused by domination of the Aleutian low pressure system that reaches its maximum intensity then and produces a powerful southwesterly flow of moist maritime air. During the summer, the low pressure cell generally weakens and moves N, and a high pressure system intensifies over much of the North Pacific. Clockwise circulation around this system tends to bring a northwesterly flow of relatively cool, dry air during summer months.

Although portions of this section extend leeward of the main orographic barrier and are subject to some continental control, most of the mountains are within the seaward slope of heavy precipitation and equitable temperatures. This is evident by annual precipitation figures for the following locations: Baker Lake — 150 inches, Chilliwack — 120 inches, Beaver Pass — 70 inches, Ross Lake — 50 to 75 inches.

The winter snowpack averages 18 ft annually at higher elevations, resulting in heavy depths in many localities until late spring. By June 1 elevations below 3500 ft are usually snow-free and some southern exposures are free well above that level.

The seaward slope has a snowline relatively low in relation to timberline. The firn limit is a reflection of changes in several climatic variables — temperature gradient, amount of snow accumulation, and thermal effectiveness; these determine the height to which the annual snowline will migrate each year.[10]

Nature in this region has chosen to create some of her whimsical feats. In the diversity of ecological zones, the creative span runs from great fluted-buttress western red cedars at about 2000-ft altitude to miniature phlox plants in hidden rock pockets as high as 7000 ft. Within the general theme of wetness,

there is a great climatic diversity caused by elevation differences. The tall dense conifer forest of the low Skagit Valley once contained giant cedars pictured as 17½ ft in diameter. The Nooksack valleys are dominated by Douglas fir; trees here are up to 200 ft tall and over 500 years old. Other trees and shrubs of the lower regions include white fir, bigleaf maple, black cottonwood, red alder, vine maple, Oregon crabapple, and devil's club — a native shrub of extreme flexibility, large leaves, and creeping stems that covers an average of 15 square ft.[11] In the forest shade it is common to see skunk cabbage, bearberry, salmonberry, sword fern, lady fern, deer fern, and bracken fern.

In the Canadian zone Pacific silver fir (lovely fir) grows to 4000 ft, western hemlock is profuse, mountain hemlock begins to appear, as does the subalpine fir (balsam) — the *Abies lasiocarpa,* with its conical crown. Alaska yellow cedar and the huckleberry bushes are seen on slopes. In the Hudsonian zone, the belt of more open forest, life forms are sensitive to disturbance and have a slow recovery time. Clumps of alpine fir and mountain hemlock are the dominant species, with much shrub understory.

The timberline marks the disappearance of some tree specimens or their change into deformed krummholz forms. As the higher altitudes are reached, dwarf evergreens predominate; the spire shape typified by one dominant stem is replaced by a more branched appearance, the main stem tending to bear lateral branches on the leeward side. Heather may form extensive mats with a variety of herbaceous plants. Delicate wildflowers and patches of evergreen, sometimes clinging to exposed rocks, are often found together.

Two animals of the high belt are singled out for observation. The mountain goat (*Oreamnos americanus*), who homes in high crags and favors the practice of climbing above the intruding human, is not a true goat, but a relative of the European chamois and Asiatic goat-antelope. The hoary marmot, which sets off a chain of whistling, can often be seen on protruding rocks near its hole.

For those willing to persevere the approaches, there are many classic alpine climbs. Some, such as the Nooksack and Price glaciers on Mt. Shuksan are not difficult of access. Climbing on Shuksan or in the more remote Picket Range can be anything from nearly all ice to all rock, but inevitably, many climbs turn out mixed. This is particularly true of N faces, where all but the steepest rocks are often snow or ice-covered. Since conditions vary from year to year, distinctions between ice and mixed routes are interwoven. Route descriptions therefore vary according to complexity. They are intended to keep a climber on route, but not bare every climbing detail or be a substitute for route finding skills.

With the limits of weather and daylight most of the longer alpine climbs demand confidence and fitness rather than technique. The exceptions where all factors are important are obvious, such as certain ice climbs or routes on long faces, such as on Mt. Slesse. While traveling along brushy and avalanche-scarred valley slopes, it is often worth a wide detour to get into tall timber.

General references to this area are: Easterbrook and Rahm, *Landforms of Washington; Challenge of the North Cascades,* pp. 231-56; *Mountaineer,* 1916, pp. 62-63; 1969, pp. 39-44; *A.A.J.,* 1969, p. 318.

GEOLOGY

Rocks of the northwestern North Cascades are mostly metamorphic and igneous types typical of orogenic zones resulting from plate convergence. From Church Mountain on the W to the Skagit River on the E and Fraser River on the N, the region includes rocks that range in age from hundreds of millions of years to glacial deposits still in the process of formation. Old metamorphic rocks and young volcanic and sedimentary rocks are intruded by granitic plutons that together form a complicated and diverse geology.

The principal rock units in the region of interest are the Skagit Suite, Shuksan Suite, Yellow Aster Complex, the Chilliwack Group of sediments and volcanics, Nooksack Group, Chuckanut Formation, the granitic intrusives of the Chilliwack Batholith, and Mt. Baker volcanic rocks.

The Skagit Suite makes up the crystalline core of the range. This Cretaceous-age metamorphic complex is composed of the Skagit gneiss (Custer gneiss) and Cascade River schist. It lies to the E of the Straight Creek Fault and W of Lake Chelan, extending northwesterly into Canada.[12] The gneiss usually consists of alternate layers of dark and light-colored minerals, commonly highly contorted. Generally these crystalline igneous and metamorphic rocks are relatively resistant to erosion and tend to persist as the steepest cluster of peaks. They include gneissic types such as the Picket Range, Mt. Triumph, Mt. Redoubt, Twin Spires, and peaks E of Chilliwack Lake in British Columbia.

The Shuksan Suite is an enormous thrust sheet of greenschist and carbonaceous phyllite (150-200 m.y.

old) now located on the W side of the metamorphic core. Notable peaks developed in greenschist of this rock unit are Mt. Shuksan, Mt. Hagan, Mt. Watson, Bacon Peak, Diobsud Buttes, and Sauk Mountain.

Relict premetamorphic features of the greenschist indicate that it originated as basaltic lava on the ocean floor. Metamorphism occurred 120 m.y. ago at high pressure, some 25 km below the earth's surface, possibly in a subduction zone (Edwin H. Brown, personal communication).

The Yellow Aster Complex consists of fragments of old crystalline rock that have been carried into the overlying younger rocks by thrust faulting. These rocks make up only a small fraction of the bulk of the mountain surfaces, where they are exposed as "tectonic slices" (carried upward) along fault zones on the flanks of Tomyhoi Peak, Mt. Larrabee, and the Border Peaks. This complex is one of the oldest rock units in the Pacific Northwest.

The Chilliwack Group is a thick section of ancient marine sediments extending from the Fraser and Chilliwack River area in British Columbia S to the Skagit River. Fossils from limestone beds within the group indicate the rocks were deposited from 250 to 350 m.y. ago. The Chilliwack Group occurs abundantly at higher altitudes near the International Boundary and also N of Chilliwack River, comprising the bulk of the peaks from Tomyhoi Peak-Mt. Larrabee to the Cheam Range. These rocks comprise a thrust sheet underlying the Shuksan Suite and overlying the Nooksack Group.

The Nooksack Group is a marine accumulation of siltstones and sandstones, locally with abundant fossils, deposited about 120-150 m.y. ago in association with a volcanic island arc. The lower slopes of Mt. Baker above Kulshan cabin (N side of the mountain) are Nooksack rock.

The Chuckanut Formation consists of stream-deposited sandstones with interbeds of shale and coal largely confined from Bellingham eastward into the foothills near Nooksack River. It has abundant plant fossils, some of which are fragments of palm trees, indicating a tropical climate in the Cascades 50-60 m.y. ago.

The final important unit of the region is the Chilliwack Batholith. Not related to the sediments and volcanics of the much older Chilliwack Group, the batholith originated from several masses of granitic magma that invaded the overlying crust beginning approximately 30 m.y. ago. This batholith forms the impressive peaks bordering Ruth Creek valley,

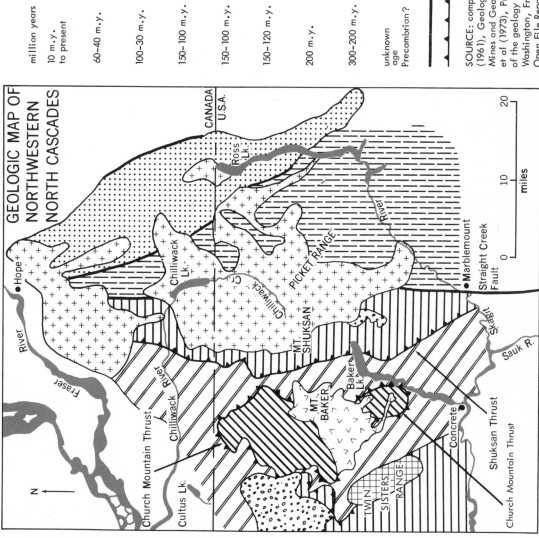

LEGEND

million years

Mt. Baker volcanic rocks	10 m.y. to present
Chuckanut Formation	60–40 m.y.
Granitic rock – Cretaceous and Tertiary (including Chilliwack Batholith)	100–30 m.y.
Skagit Suite	150–100 m.y.
Shuksan Suite	150–100 m.y.
Nooksack Group	150–120 m.y.
Hozomeen Group	200 m.y.
Chilliwack Group (including Cultus Formation)	300–200 m.y.
Twin Sisters Dunite	unknown age Precambrian ?

fault

thrust fault

SOURCE: compiled from Huntting, M.T., et al (1961), Geologic map of Washington: Wash. Div. Mines and Geology map and O'Kulitch, A.V., et al (1973), Preliminary draft of Compilation of the geology of parts British Columbia and Washington, Fraser River: Geol. Survey Canada, Open File Report.

GEOLOGIC MAP OF NORTHWESTERN NORTH CASCADES

CANADA
U.S.A.

Ross Lk.

Hope

Fraser River

Chilliwack River

Cultus Lk.

Chilliwack Lk.

Chilliwack Cr.

Chilliwack R.

PICKET RANGE

River

MT. SHUKSAN

MT. BAKER

Baker Lk.

Skagit

Sauk R.

Marblemount

Straight Creek Fault

Concrete

TWIN SISTERS RANGE

Church Mountain Thrust

Church Mountain Thrust

Shuksan Thrust

N

0   10   20

miles

Silesia-Slesse Creek, Nesakwatch Creek, the basin of Chilliwack Lake, and lower Silverhope Creek valley (including Bear Mountain, Mt. Slesse, Mt. Rexford, and Mt. Lindeman).[13]

The Twin Sisters dunite, made up of olivine, pyroxene, and chromite, is a sheetlike mass thought to have been emplaced as a type of metamorphic rock; however, details of its source are unknown.

The recent Mt. Baker volcanic rocks were superimposed on an existing topography similar to that of the present relief. Mt. Baker presently has active steam vents and is monitored by volcanologists seeking signs of impending magmatic activity. Its formation and present activity are probably the result of subduction along the Washington coast.

Although much is known about the various rock types in the North Cascades and the ages of rock formation, geologists are yet far from understanding the geologic history of the region. The nature and degree of mobility of the earth's crust in the region are the topics of greatest mystery. Some researchers speculate that rock units such as the Skagit, Shuksan, Chilliwack and others formed in diverse locales around the Pacific Ocean, and have been plastered onto the edge of the continent by sea-floor spreading as a geological "collage." This hypothesis is supported by the existence of seemingly profound faults which separate the rock units: the Nooksack, Chilliwack and Shuksan rocks are all separated by major thrust faults; these rocks in turn are separated from the Skagit Suite by the Straight Creek Fault, which bears evidence suggestive of hundreds of miles of right-lateral strike-slip offset. A contrary view is that the rocks formed essentially in place, along the Paleozoic and Mesozoic continental margin of North America, and that the faults represent displacements of only a few tens of miles at most.

Mineralization of the region is related to the emplacement of granitic rocks of the various intrusions, especially the Chilliwack Batholith. The most famed mine is the Lone Jack, near Twin Lakes, discovered on August 23, 1897 by Jack Post. In 1900 a 15-stamp mill using a steam donkey and horses was erected near Silesia Creek; a 4000-ft aerial tram was constructed for mine-to-mill transport.[14] The mill was later destroyed by fire, but the mine produced $550,000 in gold from 1902 to 1924. Ore at the Lone Jack in 1901 was valued at up to $30 per ton.[15]

The Boundary Red lode (between Mt. Larrabee and Silesia Creek) was discovered in 1898. Six patented claims were located between 4000 ft and 5500 ft, which ultimately resulted in gold and silver production of $947,579 between 1913 and 1946.[16] In the mid-1950s a steep road was roughed in to the Boundary from Canada, but the mill and bunkhouse at the mine were destroyed by avalanches.

Selected references to the geology of this area are:

Daly, Reginald A. "Geology of the North American Cordillera," Canada Dept. of Mines, *Geological Survey Memoir 38* (1912).

McTaggart, K.C. and Thompson, R.M. "Geology of Part of the Northern Cascades in Southern British Columbia," *Canadian Jour. Earth Science,* vol. 4, no. 6 (1967), pp. 1199-1228.

Misch, Peter. "Tectonic Evolution of the Northern Cascades of Washington State," *Canadian Inst. Mining and Metallurgy Spec.* vol. 8, H.C. Gunning, ed., pp. 101-48.

Monger, J.W.H. "Hope Map-Area, West Half, British Columbia," *Canada Geol. Survey,* paper 69-47 (1970).

Smith, G.O. and Calkins, F.C. "A Geological Reconnaissance Across the Cascade Range near the forty-ninth parallel," *U.S. Geol. Survey,* Bull. 235 (1904).

Staatz, M.H., et al. "Geology and Mineral Resources of the northern part of the North Cascades National Park, Washington," *U.S. Geol. Survey,* Bull. 1359 (1973), 132 pp.

HISTORY

Indians of the region were tied to a local habitat and did not exploit the landscape. They led the simple life of food collectors, and in their religious ceremonies revered animals and the salmon. The Nooksack tribe may have settled as early as 5000 years ago in the lower Nooksack and Fraser region. Their language is different from Salish-speaking coastal tribes, such as the Lummi, and there are important cultural differences. Their mode of travel was by canoe and foot. The Nook-sa-ak tribe takes its name from the bracken fern, whose root was its major staple.[17]

Part of the early exploration of this region was done by trappers for Hudson's Bay Company, which by royal charter in 1670 took possession of the territory then called "Rupert's Land." Fort Langley was the lowest company post on what was then known as Fraser's River. The North West Company was formed in 1787 and these two became great rivals until their merger in 1821. Although each company had scouts watching Indian movements and to obtain furs, little history of individual travels was recorded.

The first Hudson's Bay trail to Chilliwack Lake, in 1855, followed an old Indian route. The Fraser River mining boom spurred interest in renewing this abandoned route. Because Governor James Douglas issued a proclamation requiring miners to obtain British permits to take boats up the river, merchants in Whatcom proposed the building of a cross-mountain route to link with the brigade route near Tulameen. In 1858 Captain W.W. DeLacy cut a trail beyond the lake along Depot Creek; he eventually got through to the Brigade Trail but the route was never used much.[18] Very difficult travel, then the inception of steamships on the river to Fort Hope, doomed the project.

At the beginning of the 19th century the region scarcely had a name, other than that bestowed by Sir Francis Drake, who called it New Albion. Names appeared on contemporary maps for a time and then were forgotten. Before the first explorations of the Boundary Survey, there was a concept of a large interior mountain basin. The sketch of A.C. Anderson, a knowledgeable Hudson's Bay Company officer, gave the impression that the Nooksack River headed with a branch of the Okanogan.

The boundary line at the 49th degree parallel was easy to define on paper but not easy to locate; it followed no natural features. Both American and British parties surveyed and marked the boundary from Point Roberts to Montana from 1857 to 1862. The original survey was reasonably accurate, but a second survey between 1901 and 1908 became necessary.[19]

At the beginning, Lt. John G. Parke was chief astronomer and surveyor for the United States and Col. John S. Hawkins of the Royal Engineers headed the British contingent.[20] Semiahmoo Bay was the main base for mountain camps. Early in 1858 the U.S. party used Indian horses on the Whatcom Trail to reach Chilliwack Lake; pack saddles had been received from the quartermaster department of the Army. One of the first ventures was by Gardner and Peabody in exploring the valley of Klahaihu (upper Chilliwack) Creek to find a good point for an astronomical station.[21] George Gibbs, an explorer, geologist, and ethnologist who had been hired by Archibald Campbell in 1857, was at Chilliwack Lake in the fall of 1858; he was one of the first to reach the pass to the Skagit River drainage (Chuch-che-hum Pass), which was lower and SE of the Whatcom Trail summit.[22]

Henry Custer, a topographer during the seasons from 1857 to 1864, had charge of the reconnaissance party that crossed from near the head of Chilliwack River to Little Beaver Creek in 1859. The magnitude of Custer's pioneering becomes almost overwhelming when we take in consideration the circumstances of time, as well as the rudimentary techniques of the day.

As is frequently the case, the "inaccessibilities" of the late 19th century were alleviated as time went on. Members of the surveys climbed Mt. Spickard and Larrabee, but it is apparent that Smith and Calkins did not retrace Custer's tracks. In 1901, because of misunderstandings of the boundary location at Silesia Creek, parties from both governments met. Because of the 40-year time interval, new foot trails had to be cut up most of the streams leading to the boundary. In 1908 a joint inspection party visited each monument and marked them eastward.

The noted Ruby boom on Skagit River began in 1872 when John Sutter found a ruby stone while panning for placer gold. After N.E. Goodell came to the area in 1879 and built a roadhouse near Goodell Creek, he became the pioneer trader of the mining district. The 20-mi. section of trail from Goodell's to the mouth of Ruby Creek, known as the "Goat Trail," became famed because of a rocky corner known as Devil's Elbow; this bad spot had an overhanging rock and steep drop to the canyon (located just below Gorge Dam).[23] Travel was hazardous and sometimes impossible. A bridge across the Skagit River at Cedar Bar was destroyed when a fire to get rid of hornets went out of control. Costs of packing loads to Ruby became so high that offers to take loads from Fort Hope from British Columbia became cheaper. When the Forest Homestead Act was passed in 1906 it was possible to apply for land patents (one such location was Cedar Bar near Stetattle Creek, where the roadhouse of Mrs. Lucinda Davis became a popular rest stop for tired prospectors on the trail).

Some of the feature names of today are reminders of important pioneers of the upper Skagit Valley. Albert and Hughey Bacon trapped along Bacon Creek in the 1880s. John and N.E. Goodell built the trading post at the end of canoe travel on Skagit River in 1880. John McMillan, a miner and trapper who came from Canada in 1884, settled at a ranch location in Big Beaver Creek. Tommy Rowland came to the area in 1895, then built a cabin and barn opposite the Big Beaver; his renown comes from the announcement that he was the prophet Elisha, a belief some financiers shared with him.

There is some confusion about the early explorations of the upper Nooksack River North Fork. In

1891 Banning Austin, Charles Bagley, and Hamilton C. Wells explored to its head, then in 1896 a party of six under Austin crossed Hannegan Pass to Chilliwack Lake, reaching Hope in 28 days from Whatcom. In this same decade Bert Huntoon, C.W. Root, W.E. Garrett, and Harry Wellman explored E of Baker Lake, apparently to the Bacon Creek divide.

The pioneers who explored and climbed on Mt. Baker and Mt. Shuksan, and some of the exploits of prospectors are discussed elsewhere. But little is known concerning the first explorations between Baker River and the Skagit River aside from those of the pioneer trappers. It is known that a party under J.E. Blackburn of the U.S. Geological Survey were on a high ridge E of Bacon Creek July 15, 1909. In 1915 Anthony Arntson reached the divide of Bacon Creek, probably by way of Noisy Creek. In 1922 Ernest Kobelt and Jim Jaeger hiked far up Baker River, then crossed to the divide of Bacon Creek in visiting Berdeen Lake.

Most of the first mountain trails, such as that over Hannegan Pass, were those of the Indians, who used them for goat hunting. Miners followed these and other routes in the Skagit and Nooksack River drainages. Pioneers such as Joe Morovits built over 40 mi. of trail, including his route from Skagit River to near Baker Lake. The trail to Heliotrope Ridge on Mt. Baker was constructed by the Mt. Baker Club in 1912 to promote the marathon. The Wells Creek Trail was built in 1906 for the summer outing of the Mazamas, and a similar trail to the foot of Boulder Glacier was built in 1908 for The Mountaineers. Later, under the administration of the Forest Service, the principal trails of the area were completed, such as the trail along Swift Creek (1904), over Whatcom Pass (1908), and around Table Mountain (1925).

By the year 1901 there was a prospecting trail up Swamp Creek to the Lone Jack Mine: a trail continued down Silesia Creek to the Boundary. Miners also made use of the trail to Mamie Pass, continuing around Goat Mountain beyond the Lone Jack.

When miners began to explore the upper Skagit Valley, there was little in the way of maps to guide them. Typical was a map dated 1867, for the Northern Pacific Railroad, showing a "Skatchet River" in the position of the Nooksack; railroad surveys blandly proposed routes across the mountain divide, using a Skagit route S of Mt. Baker. One map showed the Skagit originating in a "Garden of Eden."

As shown on the General Land Office Map of 1909,

the most important nomenclature then was Mt. Baker, Mt. Shuksan, Glacier Creek, Beaver Creek, Custer Ridge, Twin Lakes Pass, Chilliwack River, Hannegan Pass, Silicia Creek, Mt. Watson, Tummeahai Creek, and Cowsap Creek. The first Forest Service maps showed little more, but by 1922 and 1926 most of today's features were shown. The Picket Range and its summits was one of the notable later entries.

From 1890 to 1937 some 5000 or more claims were staked in the Mt. Baker district. Sumas became the main outfitting center for argonauts going to the gold fields. The most famous claim became the Lone Jack, a gold mine in the isolated wilderness. Located on the steep eastern slopes of Bear Mountain (SE of Twin Lakes), the property discovered by Jack Post in 1897 was most easily reached by trail up Slesse Creek in British Columbia. Development began in 1900 with a 3000-ft aerial tramway and a 15-stamp mill packed in on mules. The mine produced considerable gold until 1906, when fires and avalanches helped destroy it. The mine was an occasional producer of gold until 1924; in 1950 a mine-to-market road was completed along Swamp Creek, a road which brought much damage to the fragile area of the high lakes.

In 1916 the Boundary Red Mine was the most important gold property in Western Washington. The approach was also from Chilliwack, taking a 40-mi. pack trail to the International Boundary. But the Boundary Red Mine declined, for after World War II the cost of gold and silver was not high enough to make the re-opening of most mines worth while.

The district also had mines along the North Fork Nooksack, where such camps as Excelsior, Hill City (Shuksan), and Gold City sprang up. In 1908 Joe Morovits and others located a group of claims near the head of Swift Creek; Morovits moved a stamp mill here alone from Birdsview. The wilderness struggle of the miners is captured by a quotation given in 1897: "Only in Washington are there such terrible forests and gulches intermingled and distorted, as if especially to retard the progress of mankind. Giant trees fallen and broken across each other and grown over with an impenetrable thicket of underbrush; gulches that seemed like gigantic wounds in the bosom of nature . . . . It was too much! I gave a man $20 to pilot me back the three miles to the trail."[24]

In British Columbia the pack trail and later wagon road to Chilliwack Lake opened claim development; the ranch of Charles Thurston, opposite Slesse Creek, was an important way stop.

A notable alpine operation was the Lucky Four Mine, where a drilling outfit was installed on the glacier of Foley Peak; there was great difficulty of working under the ice with a drill and gas engine.[25]

The property on Silver Peak (near Hope) was discovered by an Indian while goat hunting; ore from the Eureka and Van Bremer mines here was packed by Indians and horses to the valley.

As part of the Washington Forest Reserve, Mt. Baker National Forest was established by proclamation in February 1897. The Forest Service built ranger stations at Bacon Creek, Babcock Creek, Backus, Reflector Bar, Ruby Creek, and Boundary; the Rowland and McMillan homesteads were taken over as guard stations. To spot many fire problems, various lookouts were built at high observation points. These included Sauk Mountain (1928), Church Mountain (1928), Copper Mountain (1934), Winchester Mountain (1935), Anderson Butte (1936), and Park Butte (1936).

When the land was a frontier wilderness, the government first allowed exploitation by anyone. After the decision was made that water riches would be developed by a large publicly owned company, the Department of Agriculture gave Seattle City Light rights to develop Skagit Valley in 1917. The first dam to be completed was the wood crib at Gorge Creek (1924); the eventual new dam, completed in 1961, cost $29 million. Diablo Dam and its powerhouse was completed in 1929. Projects such as this 389-ft dam converted a remote mountain gorge to a very accessible stairway of dams and reservoirs. The largest project, Ross Dam, was begun in 1937 and built in steps. After timber clearing and removal, Ross Lake reached Canadian soil in 1953, with a water height of 1600 ft at the dam. When the structure was completed in 1950, the concrete rose 545 ft above the river bed. At the time there was little opposition by state residents, but when the raising of Ross Dam was planned in 1970 the proposal became a public issue.

Transportation has changed notably in Skagit Valley since the use of canoes by early explorers. During the hectic mining times, steamers plied the Skagit River, often racing each other with much excitement and some feuds. Trails and then the wagon road were improved late in the century. The steam engine followed, with the Great Northern Railroad reaching Rockport in 1901 and Goodell (Newhalem) in 1921. The railroads did not fulfill the ambitions of road builders, who contemplated a cross-state highway. In the steep canyon above Gorge Reservoir, a new road between Newhalem and Diablo was finished in 1957. Pushing eastward, the North Cascade Highway construction between 1961 and 1968 proceeded past the S side of Diablo and Ross lakes, once the route of the "Goat Trail." However, to see and learn the backcountry, one must still do as the pioneers did: travel on foot.

LAND MANAGEMENT
North Cascades National Park
Headquarters:

> 800 State St.
> Sedro Woolley, WA 98284
> (206) 855-1331
> Hours: 8:00 am to 4:30 pm weekdays

Ranger Stations:

> Skagit District: Marblemount, WA 98267
> (206) 873-4590
> Hours: winter: 8:00 am to 4:30 pm (daily)
> summer: 7:00 am to 8:00 pm (daily)
> (mid-June to Labor Day)

Backcountry use permits for park visitors can be obtained at Marblemount, Stehekin, and Chelan, and also at Early Winters, Winthrop, Twisp, Glacier, and Concrete ranger stations for those entering through National Forest lands.

Written backcountry permits are required for overnight stay. Permits are issued on an arrival basis and can be issued the day before departure.

Permits are issued on a individual camp basis for which maximum use levels have been designated. Groups larger than 12 in number are not permitted to travel or camp as a unit. Restrictions apply to camping in certain subalpine passes and meadows.

Cross-country camping: To protect the fragile environment, wood fires are not permitted in areas of cross-country travel. One must camp over ½ mi. from maintained trails and 1 mi. from designated camps. No route markup is permitted.

Trail camping: Hikers must camp only in camp areas which are designated with trailside posts. Wood fires are permitted only in camps where iron fire grates have been installed.

Climbers are asked to register.

Pets are prohibited in the backcountry of the National Park.

Mt. Baker-Snoqualmie National Forest

Headquarters:

1601 Second Avenue, Seattle, WA 98101
(206) 442-5400

National Park Service-Forest Service Information
Center

Room 110
915 Second Ave., Seattle, WA 98174
(206) 442-0170
442-5542

Ranger Stations:

Baker River (24.5 mi. from Burlington on Hwy
No. 20)
Concrete, WA 98234
(206) 853-2851

Glacier
Glacier, WA 98244
(206) 599-2714

Heather Meadows Recreation Area
Summer season and winter weekends. Radio
contact.

Komo Kulshan Guard Station (Baker Lake)
14.5 mi. from North Cascades Hwy
June 1 to September 15

Avalanche warning (Glacier)
(206) 599-2714

British Columbia

Field Station:

Hope
(604) 869-9961

Note: Information ATP indicates the Cultus Lake
Ranger Station will be closed at the end of 1981
and the district will be consolidated with offices near
Rosedale.

District Office of B.C. Forest Service
57 Kipp Ave., Chilliwack, B.C.
(604) 792-8664

Restrictions and closures may occur during high fire
hazard periods. Otherwise campfires may be lighted
unless posted prohibited or by general fire restrictions.
Fires must not be located within 10 ft of a tree, stump,
log, and 50 ft of slash or structures.

Fires must be attended at all times and completely
extinguished when leaving area.

MAPS
Washington State Maps
U.S. Geological Survey (topographic)

Mt. Challenger (1953)	1:62,500
Marblemount (1953)	1:62,500
Lake Shannon (1952)	1:62,500
Mt. Shuksan (1953)	1:62,500
Mt. Baker (1952)	1:62,500
Hamilton (1952)	1:62,500
Wickersham (1951)	1:62,500
Hozomeen Mountain (1969)	1:24,000
Mt. Spickard (1969)	1:24,000
Pumpkin Mountain (1969)	1:24,000
Mt. Prophet (1969)	1:24,000
Ross Dam (1963)	1:24,000
Diablo Dam (1963)	1:24,000
Kendall (1972)	1:24,000
Maple Falls (1972)	1:24,000
Deming (1972)	1:24,000
Canyon Lake (1972)	1:24,000
North Cascades National Park (1974)	1:100,000 metric
Concrete (1955)	1:250,000
Victoria (1957)	1:250,000

Topographic maps can be ordered by mail, prepaid:
Distribution Section — U.S. Geological Survey, Denver Federal Center — Bldg. 41, Denver, CO 80225.

Mt. Baker-Snoqualmie National Forest (planimetric) maps are available from forest headquarters and
ranger stations.

British Columbia
Federal Maps

Victoria-Vancouver   92 S E (1973) 1:500,000
Vancouver   92 G 1:250,000
    (122°00' to 124°00' and 49°00' to 50°00')
Hope   92 H (1970) 1:250,000
    (120°00' to 122°00' and 49°00' to 50°00')
Skagit River   92 H/3 (1975) 1:50,000
    (121°00' to 121°30' and 49°00' to 49°15')
Chilliwack   92 H/4 (1975) 1:50,000
    (121°30' to 122°00' and 49°00' to 49°15')
Hope   92 H/6 (1976) 1:50,000
    (121°00' to 121°30' and 49°15' to 49°30')

Provincial Maps

Chilliwack Lake   92 H/SW (1972) 1:126,720
    (121°00' to 122°00' and 49°00' to 49°30')

"Part of the way the guide (Joe Morovits) went strait (sic) up the sides of the cliffs grown over with shrubs and moss, and we followed him, although it took the last bit of energy we could muster . . . . There was one plant which was the bane of the trip. This is popularly known as, and the title is exceedingly appropriate, the 'devil's club.' It has a thick fleshy stem and a large flat leaf, both of which are set with sharp, stinging nettles. It grows to a height of seven or eight feet in some places. One would almost rather slip than lay hold upon it, for it means torture to grasp it."

R.B. VAILE, 1900
On ascent of Mt. Baker

MT. BAKER   10,778 ft/3285 m

Mt. Baker is the northernmost of the Quaternary stratovolcanoes of the Cascade Range of northern California, Oregon, and Washington, standing 15.5 mi. S of the United States/Canada boundary, and 30.5 mi. (49 km) from Bellingham Bay at tidewater. The actual summit (Grant Peak) is a 35-acre nearly level ice mound which hides the 1300-ft ice-filled summit crater; at a distance of 0.7 mi. is Sherman Peak (10,000 ft+), a southeastern remnant of a larger crater rim.

By an accumulation of andesitic lavas and breccias the young, relatively smooth volcano has built to its present height, about 2 km above a very dissected basement complex of metasedimentary rocks of Paleozoic and Mesozoic age.[26] These ancient platform rocks were already carved into valleys when the first eruptive lavas forming the cinder cone poured into them during Pleistocene time.

To the W of the present summit are the older Black Buttes, the old eruptive vent now extensively dissected; new lavas built a cone that overshadows the original one: on Mt. Baker one can see great overlapping layers of lava from various overflow periods. Owing to the high annual precipitation and its latitude, the mountain is almost completely covered by glaciers which flow radially from the central summit. The mountain's large glacier system feeds three important rivers (Baker, Middle and North Fork Nooksack) and is indirectly the source of hydroelectric power. The ponderously advancing and retreating glaciers record a history of rhythmic change, as centuries of successive ice ages have alternated with periods of mild climate. Here is a record of life processes against the ice frontier: the extinction of forests, then recovery in the wake of diminished glaciers.[27] Particularly wide glacier valleys and broad cirques have been carved into the W flank of the volcano by an ancient series of valley glaciers which originated near the mountain's summit.

With an ice volume of about 20 sq mi, the largest glaciers are the Coleman and Roosevelt, fed by an accumulation area which extends from Heliotrope Ridge on the W to Bastile Ridge on the E. Apparently both glaciers respond rapidly to minor climatic changes. The Coleman has exhibited a generally advancing trend since 1947 and in the decade of the 1950s advanced over 0.5 mi. into Glacier Creek;[28] the Roosevelt subsequently advanced and the result today is two very crevassed ice tongues, nearly touching between 4300 and 4400 ft.

The recency of the summit cone is shown by the lack of vast glacier erosion as in the case of Mt. Rainier and Mt. Adams, which are much more deeply amphitheatered. The crater, which has been discharging steam and gases for over a century, was the most thermally active in the Cascade Range until the 1980 eruptions of Mt. St. Helens. Fumaroles, thermal springs, and areas of warm ground, some of which are subglacial, are concentrated here. Because much of the ground on Sherman Peak contains clay-rich material which results from hydrothermal alteration, major causes of instability are water saturation of this material as well as lubrication at the ground-firn interface.[29] The combination of these factors plus a large annual quantity of snow accumulation has led to periodic release of snow, firn, and a surface layer of rock and mud from Sherman Peak. Avalanches of snow, firn, rock, and mud have been released six times in the last two decades from Sherman Peak, tracking nearly identical paths 2.0-2.6 km down Boulder Glacier.

The 4.7-km Deming Glacier could be considered the most interesting ice display on the mountain. Its tongue flows into a deep rock chasm at the southern base of the fort-like Black Buttes. The 3.7-km Easton Glacier, on the broad and low-gradient S slope, heads on Sherman Peak.[30] The Boulder Glacier flows on the ESE flank of Mt. Baker, with snow of the summit crater its source; ice extends downvalley 2.4 km to an elevation of 4800 ft. The present glacier is a remnant identifiable by well defined moraines and trimlines which represent ice fluctuations below timberline. The magnificent Park Glacier, on the NE flank of the volcano, terminates partly in Park Cliffs, a spectacular wall of ice and rock above the flat terminus of the glacier. Easton wrote of this scene: "the icebergs go over like the waters of Niagara."

The discovery of Mt. Baker by white man is shrouded in some mystery. Whether or not Apostolos

Valerianos, the Greek pilot known as Juan de Fuca, actually saw the ice-clad volcano in 1592 is highly debatable. If he did enter the strait named for him and spent 20 days there, the probability that he sighted the mountain is high.[31] Numerous ships passed within sight of the volcano from 1580 to 1780, but the white landmark is not mentioned.[32] In all events, these did not amount to effective historical discoveries, an event usually credited in 1790 to Manuel Quimper, the Spanish navigator stationed at Nootka Sound on Vancouver Island.[33] Quimper placed the volcano on his maps as La Gran Montaña del Carmelo.[34]

While near New Dungeness on April 29, 1792, Captain George Vancouver's cartographer Joseph Baker sighted the white-hued volcano, which Vancouver then named for him. "From this direction round by the N and NW the high distant land formed, as already observed, like detached islands, amongst which the lofty mountain, discovered in the afternoon by the third lieutenant and in compliment to him called by me Mount Baker, rose a very conspicuous object, bearing by compass N 43 E apparently at a very remote distance."[35]

To the Lummi Indians of Puget Sound, the volcano was Koma Kulshan, meaning broken or damaged,[36] although some versions give the latter word as "Great White Watcher." When haze, clouds, or smoke shrouded the lower levels, Mt. Baker had been likened to a colossal island of ice and snow floating on denser air. An early Oregon immigrant, in fact, exclaimed that Baker was higher than Mt. Rainier.[37] The most astute geographic observer of the period of early settlement in Washington Territory, George Gibbs, contributed this opinion: "Seen from the lower end of Whidby's Island, the more distant range is a bare and ragged sierra, some of the peaks of which rise to the limits of perpetual snow. Mount Baker, which terminates the view, has a sharp and precipitous outline, more resembling that of Mount Hood than the regular forms of Rainier, St. Helens, and Adams."[38]

Certainly the mountain's awesomeness was compounded by eruptions and volcanic steam. Gibbs wrote, "Mount Baker . . . has, during this winter, been in action, throwing out light clouds of smoke. The last of the major eruptions occurred about 15,000 years ago; the most recent in 1843."[39] Other accepted dates of historic eruption activity were 1854, 1858, 1859, and 1870.[40]

Man's association with Kulshan came first with the British, not from those within the Territory. Edmund

Thomas Coleman, an Englishman who had some mountaineering experience in the Alps,[41] after settling in Victoria and often confronted with the spectacle of Mt. Baker, resolved to set his foot on the volcano, whose beauty he compared to the Jungfrau in the Bernese Oberland. In 1866 he made two attempts to reach the mountain, nearly succeeding to the summit on the second of these.[42] First his party proceeded by canoe up the Skagit River to "Tukullum" (Baker River), where the Koma Indians declined to let the party proceed. Then with John Tennant and John Bennett, Coleman took a route which led via the North Fork Nooksack River, then up the Coleman Glacier to the saddle between Colfax Peak and the true summit. To Coleman and Bennett an overhanging cornice of ice near the foot of Roman Wall proved an overwhelming problem.

In April 1868 the persistent adventurer made another attempt, again solving the logistical obstacle by hiring Nootsac Indians Squock and Talum with their canoes to travel the Nooksack River and its middle fork. Coleman's men, Tennant, David Ogilvy, and Thomas Stratton, were not alpinists, but they were accustomed to pioneering and wilderness travel, which here consisted of trackless forest that included huge fallen logs and dense underbrush. Finally emerging to open ground, they reached Marmot Ridge, W of the Black Buttes, which Coleman termed Lincoln and Colfax.[43] On August 17 in clear weather, the intrepid group, paced by Stratton, traversed and climbed the Coleman Glacier to the high saddle[44] and continued via the Upper Deming Glacier to the summit. With the aid of specially-made ice creepers (crampons), they climbed the final slope in two hours, with some step cutting. A somewhat embellished account of this pioneering ascent was later provided by Coleman, who pointed out, "As precipices extended downward from our feet, a single false step would have been fatal."[45]

The second ascent of the mountain was made by Valentine V. Lowe and L.L. Bales (from Whatcom) via the South Fork Nooksack River. They apparently climbed Easton Glacier, getting to within 150 yards of the true summit on June 29, 1884.[46]

The year 1891 began the popular ascents: the third ascent, led by Lowe, was made July 3 via Coleman Glacier; one source reported the steepness reached an angle of up to 80 degrees.[47] The SE flank of Mt. Baker was climbed August 24 by a party of seven, led by J.O. Boen of La Conner (party included the first woman to ascend), beginning at Baker Lake. In the third successful ascent of the year, Major Edward S. Ingraham and party climbed via the Coleman Glacier, a venture in September marked by a three-day snowstorm. J.M. Edson and Beverley B. Dobbs reached the summit in July 1892 via Coleman Glacier, after an unsuccessful attempt at bypassing Pumice Stone Pinnacle (The Cockscomb). That year also saw an ascent by the Whatcom Street Car Brigade.

On August 7 of that year Joe Morovits boldly accomplished a solo climb of the mountain via the Rainbow and Park glaciers. The choice of the difficult Northeast Ridge was by chance: ascending with six others, all of whom halted at Pumice Stone Pinnacle, Morovits cut foot notches in the final ice slope with his rifle, later admitting he had placed himself in a very precarious position on his first real snow and ice experience. Morovits became a regional legend through his exploits in packing, pioneering enterprise, climbing, and guiding on Mt. Baker in his 27 years alone.[48]

In 1906, the Mazama summer outing (the first of the large club outings) visited the Mt. Baker region, traversing Ptarmigan Ridge to establish Camp Kiser as part of a major exploration and glacier mapping program. In an exception to the efforts of organized groups bent on avoiding the steeper routes, a large party under F.H. Kiser attempted the Northeast Ridge; 32 members reached Pumice Stone Pinnacle, which they failed to turn. Then Kiser, Asahel Curtis, C.E. Forsyth, L.S. Hildebrandt, Martin Wanlich, and C.M. Williams were successful on August 7, climbing essentially the way of Morovits and his "rifle ascent" of 1892.[49]

In 1908, historian Charles F. Easton made his first climb of the volcano, but in planning a summit camp had not anticipated high winds: the party had to carve out an ice cave between the lava cliff and glacier, and in attempting to descend the Boulder Glacier in a storm the next day, were forced to spend another night out on a snow block wedged in a crevasse.

The year 1911 witnessed the first Mt. Baker Marathon, a summit race from Bellingham conceived to promote business and draw attention to scenic wonders.[50] The 118-mi. round trip through Glacier involved 24 mi. on foot, the remainder by auto and railroad. Contestants had to be checked by referees stationed in blankets and furs at the summit area to register arrivals. It was the danger of the hidden crevasse, causing a nearly fatal accident to a competitor (who spent 6 hours in an "ice trap"), which led to cancellation of the marathon after 1913.

Despite all its pedestrian qualities, perhaps Mt. Baker has a subtle but compelling challenge. The traditional competitions of the marathons, and the Coleman, Morovits, and Mazama climbs provide further evidence of the mountain's stimulating influence.

To underscore the dangers of unroped glacier travel, it is said that at least one early prospector who traveled the glaciers of Mt. Baker fell into a hidden crevasse. The president of the B.C. Mountaineering Club, J.C. Bishop, lost his life in 1913 through falling into a hidden crevasse on the Coleman Glacier. The continuous change of glacier features adds greatly to the fascination which the mountain holds: small crevasses crossed by narrow snow bridges one season become yawning chasms the next. As a grim reminder of crevasse dangers on Mt. Baker, an accident summary published for 1979 listed four separate accidents, all from collapsing snow bridges or direct falls into crevasses, resulting in serious injuries and two deaths.

Other tragedies have resulted from inadequate precaution, and one fatal hypothermia case resulted when a climber undertook the summit ascent in cotton jeans. This accident, in 1973, underlines the harsh realities of climbing in stormy conditions. If the weather becomes threatening, turning back is no disgrace. The thermal effect on the mountaineer on an unprotected, high summit such as Mt. Baker in rapidly increasing wind can be insidious.

That the mountain can have dangerous snow conditions during midsummer, even on rather gentle slopes, was tragically demonstrated on July 22, 1939, when a college group was struck by an avalanche on the upper Deming Glacier (normal route). Snow, followed by rain and very warm days contributed to snow surface instability. The ½-mi. slide took six lives. Beware of very hot temperatures; climb at night or in the very early morning.

There is also a potential hazard from lahars (mud and debris flows) resulting from volcanic activity. The most immediate threat has been a promontory of decomposed rock to the E of Sherman crater, where debris avalanches could reach climbers on Boulder Glacier.[51] Another timely warning: Do not venture into steam vents in the Sherman crater area.

The first winter ascent of the volcano was made by four members of the Mt. Baker Club on December 27, 1925: W.L. Cochran, Clarence A. Fisher, Louis Gilfilen, and Jerry V. Smith. In the first known ski ascent of a major Northwest summit, Ed Loness and Robert B. Sperlin skied to and from the summit on May 4, 1930.

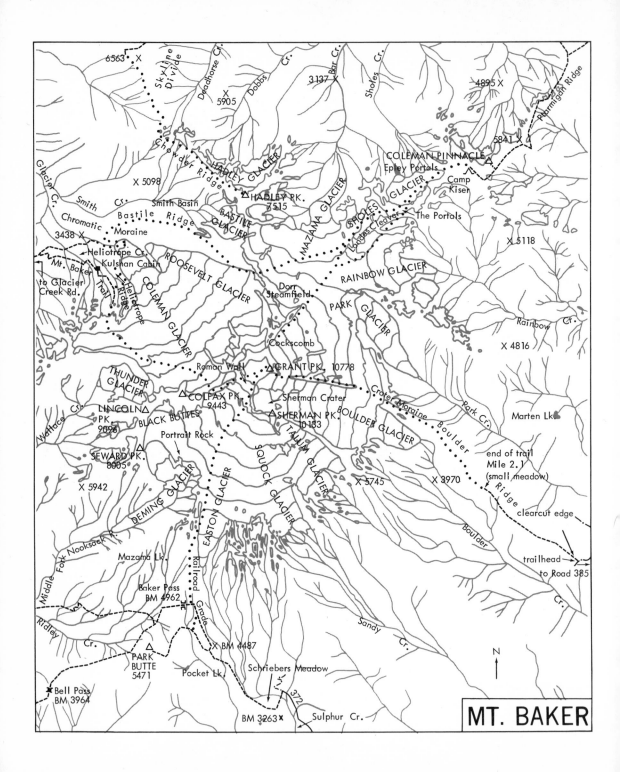

6563 X

Skyline Divide

Deadhorse Cr.

Dobbs Cr.

Bar Cr.

Sholes Cr.

X 5905

3137 X

4895 X

Ptarmigan Ridge

5841 X

COLEMAN PINNACLE

Epley Portals

Camp Kiser

Chowder Ridge

HADLEY GLACIER

MAZAMA GLACIER

SHOLES GLACIER

X 5098

HADLEY PK. 7515

The Portals

Glacier Cr.

Smith Cr.

Smith Basin

Bastile Ridge

BASTILE GLACIER

Lasdes Cleaver

X 5118

Chromatic Moraine

RAINBOW GLACIER

3438 X

Heliotrope Cr.

Kulshan Cabin

ROOSEVELT GLACIER

Mt. Baker Trail

Heliotrope Ridge

COLEMAN GLACIER

Dorr Steamfield

Rainbow Cr.

to Glacier Creek Rd.

PARK GLACIER

X 4816

Cockscomb

Roman Wall

GRANT PK. 10778

THUNDER GLACIER

COLFAX PK. 9443

Sherman Crater

Crater Moraine

Boulder

Park Cr.

LINCOLN PK. 9098

BLACK BUTTES

SHERMAN PK. 10183

BOULDER GLACIER

Marten Lk.

Portrait Rock

TALUM GLACIER

SEWARD PK. 8005

X 5745

X 3970

end of trail Mile 2.1 (small meadow)

Ridge

X 5942

SQUOCK GLACIER

clearcut edge

DEMING GLACIER

EASTON GLACIER

Boulder

trailhead to Road 385

Middle Fork Nooksack R.

Mazama Lk.

Railroad Grade

Baker Pass BM 4962

Cr.

Ridley Cr.

Sandy Cr.

N

PARK BUTTE 5471

X BM 4487

Pocket Lk.

Schriebers Meadow

372

Bell Pass BM 3964

BM 3263 X

Sulphur Cr.

MT. BAKER

MT. BAKER from northwest
AUSTIN POST, U.S. GEOLOGICAL SURVEY

A ski traverse was made in spring 1932 by Darroch Crookes, Don Henry, and Benton Thompson. A ski traverse from Kulshan cabin to the summit, then descending via The Cockscomb to Epley Portal was made by Andy Hennig, Erick Larsen, and Dwight Watson on May 13, 1939.

Selected references to the Mt. Baker region include: *Mountaineer,* 1916, pp. 26-35, 38-64; 1964, pp. 41-53, 75-83; *Mazama* 3, no. 1 (1907); 5-26; vol. 6 (1920): 3-16, 23-53; vol. 12, no. 12 (1930): 7-19; vol. 35 (1953): 5-19; vol. 53, no. 13 (1971): 12; Percival R. Jeffcott, *Chechaco and Sourdough,* Ferndale; Percival R. Jeffcott, *Nooksack Tales and Trails,* Ferndale, 1949; Charles F. Easton, *Mt. Baker – Its Trails and Legends,*

Whatcom Museum of History and Art (Bellingham).

Some of the more rewarding and available accounts of early climbs of Mt. Baker are: *Mazama,* 3, no. 1 (1907): 31-48; vol. 12, no. 12 (1930): 34-43; vol. 6, no. 1 (1920): 3-16, 26-53; *Canadian Alpine Journal* 3 (1911): 174; *Mountaineer,* 1908, pp. 87-99; 1919, pp. 42-44; 1928, pp. 15-18; 1937, p. 33 (glaciers), 1941, p. 8; *Sports Illustrated,* January 7, 1963 (Joe Morovits); *Accidents in North American Mountaineering,* 1974, pp. 17-19; *Off Belay,* August 1976, pp. 6-29; C.E. Rusk, *Tales of a Western Mountaineer,* Seattle, 1978, pp. 117-35; Stephen L. Harris, *Fire and Ice,* Seattle, 1976, pp. 223-51; Fred Beckey, *Challenge of the North Cascades,* Seattle, 1969, pp.

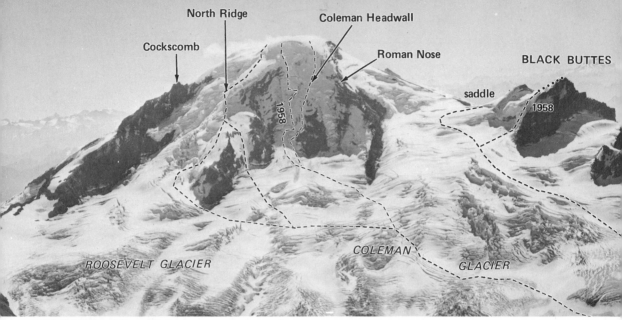

MT. BAKER — *Coleman Glacier*
AUSTIN POST, U.S. GEOLOGICAL SURVEY

189-96; Jack H. Hyde and Dwight R. Crandell, "Postglacial Volcanic Deposits of Mt. Baker, Washington, and Potential Hazards from Future Eruptions," U.S. Geol. Survey, *Prof. Paper 1022 C* (1978).

COLEMAN-DEMING GLACIER: First ascent by the 1868 Coleman party (see history). Take Mt. Baker Trail◆ for approach to the Coleman Glacier. Because of the popularity of Kulshan cabin, some parties make camp on The Hogback, at about 6000 ft, close to the glacier. Snowfields blend into the glacier above this altitude: parties should always be roped for travel here, both on the ascent and descent (two fatalities when descending in 1979).

Ascend snow and firn slopes toward the Black Buttes before altering the route bearing toward the broad ice saddle between the East Butte (Colfax Peak) and the summit cone. There are numerous large crevasses on the Coleman Glacier, sometimes requiring minor detours (watch for hidden crevasses). From the saddle (9000 ft+) ascend the pumice ridge about 300 ft (summit bearing is 50 degrees magnetic from top of pumice), then diagonal S to where the slope gradient lessens; one may arrive at another pumice slope (depending on snow cover) between the old crater and the true summit. Bear left and ascend directly to the highest point. Time: 8 hours from road (6 hours from Kulshan cabin). Reference: *Accidents in North American Mountaineering,* 1979, pp. 51-53.

ROMAN NOSE: This feature is a 2000-ft snakelike cleaver between Coleman Glacier Headwall and the Roman Wall (a large cliff of unstable andesite). Early season climbs are safest (minimize danger of falling and loose rock). First ascent by Ed Cooper, Don Ihlenfeldt, Mike Swayne, and Gordon

Thompson on June 27, 1960. First winter ascent by Anton Karuza and Greg Thompson January 9, 1977.

Begin as per Coleman-Deming Glacier route. Gain the crumbling lava crest of the nose by a snow finger on the W. The lower crumbly, narrow ridge includes a 20-ft vertical step. Then traverse steep snow slopes just below and E of the crest; after 1000 ft one reaches the first vertical step (150 ft). Follow a ledge leading right (possible ice), then loose rock. From the base of the 200-ft second step follow a ledge rightward (possible ice traverse); in 200 ft climb back to the crest by a short rock pitch. The rock ridge merges into a snow ridge leading onward toward the summit.

Note: The winter party followed the crest entirely, beginning on the W side, using chocks for protection (to 5.6). Ramps and crack systems were climbed when off the crest; a snow bypass was made E of the great rock buttress, then a face was climbed to the crest, continuing on ramps and snow to the summit. Grade II or III. References: *Mountaineer,* 1961, p. 100; 1977, p. 106; *A.A.J.,* 1961, p. 360; *C.A.J.,* 1961, pp. 63-64.

COLEMAN GLACIER HEADWALL: This is the steep headwall consisting of a series of short ice cliffs bound by Roman Nose on the right and a rock face and ice rim on the left. The route has become a popular one, not necessarily technically difficult, but the key to the ascent often lies in the nature of snow conditions. First ascent by Ed Cooper, Phil Bartow, Donald Grimlund, and David Nicholson on August 18, 1957.

Ascend per Coleman-Deming Glacier route to 8100 ft, then bear left through crevasses to the headwall base (8500 ft). Follow an avalanche cone between two prominent rock islands to a series of short, steep ice cliffs. Ascend these rightward, then continue on 45-50-degree firn or ice slopes to beneath the upper cliffs. Contour right until blocked by crevasses, then ascend beside a narrow rock outcrop to the summit plateau (rightward). Grade II or III. Time: 7-8 hours. Note: Some parties climb the first portion between the right-hand rock island and Roman Nose. This was done on the second ascent, a few weeks after the original climb. References: *Mountaineer,* 1958, pp. 101-2; 1977, p. 72; *A.A.J.,* 1959, p. 305.

COLEMAN GLACIER HEADWALL DIRECT: This route leads in a straight direction to the summit. First ascent by Les MacDonald and Henryk Mather in April 1958. Begin in an avalanche gully below the center of the face. Move up over steep snow and ice until a rock and ice pillar blocks the route. Traverse right one lead (ice screws) over very steep ground, then climb again, avoiding overhanging ice lips by keeping left of them. At about 4/5 of the height of the face, ascend between seracs to reach the break in the summit cap; one pitch over a chimney or other weakness should lead to easy firn slopes. Grade III or IV. Time: 6 hours. Reference: *A.A.J.,* 1959, p. 305.

NORTH RIDGE: This feature of Mt. Baker has become a classic moderate route, although the ice wall at 9600 ft

MT. BAKER from northeast
AUSTIN POST, U.S. GEOLOGICAL SURVEY

MT. BAKER – *upper Park Glacier*
AUSTIN POST, U.S. GEOLOGICAL SURVEY

becomes more technical in late summer. First ascent by Fred Beckey, Dick Widrig, and Ralph Widrig on August 7, 1948.

Begin as per Coleman-Deming Glacier route, then make a rising traverse to the prominent arete at the NNW foot of the upper face. Ascend the NW slope of the latter to the ice wall on the crest where it points downward; possible need for ice screws. At the final bergschrund make a leftward oblique traverse to the summit plateau. Grade II. Time: 8 hours from camp. References: *Mountaineer*, 1948, p. 50; *Appalachia*, December 1948, p. 229; *A.A.J.*, January 1949, p. 219; *Challenge of the North Cascades*, pp. 196-200.

ROOSEVELT GLACIER: This very crevassed N-side glacier is best done in late spring or early summer. First ascent by Fred Beckey, Don (Claunch) Gordon, and John Rupley on June 22, 1958. Begin as per Coleman-Deming Glacier route, then traverse the glacier to an obvious corridor leading eastward below the NW face of Mt. Baker. Continue on an ascending traverse to the headwall of the Roosevelt Glacier, which steepens W of The Cockscomb at about 9500 ft. Ascend a corridor and moderately steep firn and ice for 800 ft to a large bergschrund dividing the face. Cross seracs and a possibly difficult schrund, then ascend 40-degree firn to the summit. Take ice screws. Grade II. Time: 8-10 hours from camp. References: *Mountaineer*, 1959, p. 105; *Mazama* 53, no. 13 (1971): 13-15.

Variation: From about 9500 ft the climbing route has been made very close to The Cockscomb, with a completion above the latter.

THE COCKSCOMB ROUTE: This climb features the tottering crag on the NE flank of Mt. Baker, once more aptly called Pumice Stone Pinnacle, that thwarted the Mazama climbers of 1906. Prior to this date the pinnacle was a double formation; one of two pillars fell away at an unknown time, hurling tons of rock onto Roosevelt Glacier. Two cleavers at a lower altitude join to form the Cockscomb Ridge: one is located between Roosevelt and Mazama glaciers; the other is between the Mazama and Park glaciers. The first ascent of the route was made by Charles Murley, John Musser, and Klindt Vielbig on July 4, 1960.

Several beginnings can be made: per Roosevelt Glacier to Cockscomb Ridge at about 7800 ft. Occasional traverses to the E may be necessary on the ridge below the crag to avoid bergschrunds. One also can reach the northern of the lower cleavers from Landes Cleaver; from about 7800 ft follow the cleaver, then cross to the E side about 9000 ft. This approach can also be begun via Ptarmigan Ridge and Mazama Glacier (see Park Glacier Headwall).

The 300-ft Cockscomb can be turned closely on the E; here is steep snow and ice, with potential avalanche danger. Higher, the ridge merges into the summit ice plateau. Take ice screws. Time: 12 hours from camp. References: *Moun-*

MT. BAKER from east
U.S. FOREST SERVICE

taineer, 1961, pp. 99-100; *A.A.J.,* 1959, p. 306; 1961, p. 360.

PARK GLACIER HEADWALL (Northeast Ridge): This challenging route on the NE flank of the volcano and E precipice of the Northeast Ridge, is the one originally done by Joe Morovits in 1892, then repeated by the Mazama party of 1906. The climb should be done before August to ensure that the schrund exit is in condition.

See Table Mountain-Ptarmigan Ridge♦ for the route to Camp Kiser. Continue W to Epley Portals (5900-ft+ saddle) and the left (S) side of gentle Sholes Glacier; one can leave the glacier through The Portals (6100-ft+ saddle between Points 6517 and 6949 on Landes Cleaver). Proceed on

a S-slope traverse, keeping above the icefall of Rainbow Glacier at the cleaver's last rock wall; crevasses may become a problem after mid-summer. Distance from Camp Kiser to the cleaver end at about 6500 ft (water and campspot) is about 2.5 mi.; 6 hours from road.

The alternative is continue on Sholes Glacier in a SW direction, keeping closely under the N side of the rock crest to reach the Mazama Glacier at about 6400 ft. Ascend Rainbow, then Park Glacier in a SW direction toward the summit, keeping left of the cleaver joining The Cockscomb (there are large crevasses at about 8000 ft on Park Glacier). The ice slope alongside The Cockscomb has a large bergschrund at 10,000 ft, where the slope inclination is 45

LINCOLN PEAK SHERMAN PEAK COLFAX PEAK GRANT PEAK

Sherman Crater

BOULDER GLACIER

MT. BAKER — summit and Sherman Crater; fumaroles and steam, March 1978
AUSTIN POST, U.S. GEOLOGICAL SURVEY

degrees for 400 ft. It is usually best to bypass the first main schrund on the left, then climb steeply right as necessary to get through the second schrund and crevasse configurations to the corniced, narrow ridge beyond the Cockscomb. The crest is then followed to the summit. General variations include crossing diagonally from Mazama to the upper Park Glacier, and even to the Boulder Glacier, but this is an escape from the route. Variations are sometimes made ascending the rightmost part of the face, close to the Cockscomb, where the slope is shorter and not so corniced. Take ice screws or snow flukes, depending on season. Time: 6 hours from camp at W end of Landes Cleaver. References: *Mazama* 3, no. 1 (1907): 17-19; vol. 18, no. 12 (1936): 36; Dorothy Pilley, *Climbing Days* (London, 1935), p. 299.

Variation (Park Glacier Headwall): By Norman Bodine, Jim Friar, and Tim Keliher July 5, 1970. From the large schrund at the center of the headwall, pass near the left edge of a group of small midface rocks. Access across the large overhanging schrund was gained by means of a steep firn/ice ramp which came to 60 degrees. The steep upper face had three-four leads, followed by a cornice. Reference: *A.A.J.*, 1971, p. 349.

BOULDER GLACIER: This is one of the more popular routes on Mt. Baker, one done by numerous variations and some oblique traverses. There is a lahar warning on the route. In early times a large bergschrund near the summit proved a dangerous snow bridge (called "The Cornice"; Easton, p. 107). One version of this glacier route was climbed during the first ascent on August 24, 1891 by S.W. Bailey, Alex and Charles Beilenberg, J.O. Boen, William Lang, Sue L. Nevin, and Robert Woods.[52] The variation using the Boulder-Park Glacier cleaver (to the N) was first led by Joe Morovits on July 2, 1894. His party included Alex and Charles Beilenberg, Mr. Gaetzman, J. Mounts, and Robert Woods. Morovits repeated the route in 1895, 1896, and 1900 (see note 48). Claude E. Rusk and George Cantwell erroneously claimed a first ascent on September 3, 1903, and while they may have kept farther N on the eastern slope of the final summit, they largely repeated the Morovits route.

See Boulder Creek Trail♦ for approach; keep on the S side of the main ridge to a small meadow (timberline camp at 5000 ft). Keep right of a ravine bearing NW and follow the snowfield in the same direction to Boulder Glacier. The

MT. BAKER *from southeast*
U.S. FOREST SERVICE

simplest route is to ascend the Boulder-Park cleaver, although the crevassed glacier can be taken directly. At about 10,000 ft bear left of steep upper rocks and an ice slope reaching the ridge between Sherman crater and the true summit (at NE end of rim). Time: 7 hours from camp. Reference: *A.A.J.*, 1945, pp. 437-38 (regarding 1944 accident on ice sheet above final bergschrund).

EASTON GLACIER: This S flank route, the most moderate on Mt. Baker, is a good ski trek in spring. For approach see Baker Pass Trail♦. Continue up the moraine of Railroad Grade to timberline (good camp at 5500 ft; 3 mi., 4 hours). Continue up the well defined moraine and bear onto the glacier almost due N, keeping left (near Deming Glacier) of a small icefall at 7000 ft. Generally it is best to stay to the left side of the glacier, then bear directly to the summit on the Deming-Easton. Pass Sherman crater and the rock wall above on the W, but keep right on Roman Wall while ascending the final ice crown slope on the SW. Time: 8 hours from road.

Variation (Crater Route): Done July 9, 1961. This was reported as a detour route via the 9700-ft Sherman crater notch, involving a 1/4-mi. steep descending traverse before continuing N to the true summit. References: *Mountaineer*, 1962, pp. 100-101; *A.A.J.*, 1962, p. 200.

HADLEY PEAK   7515 ft/2291 m

This is the high point of Chowder Ridge, located where Dobbs Cleaver joins on the northern slope of Mt. Baker. The peak is rocky on the N, but there is only a short slope above the Hadley Glacier; this broad glacier is almost 2 mi. wide (drains to Dobbs Creek); a segment near the NW edge of Mazama Glacier is to its SE. The Bastile Glacier, which connects with the Mazama, is located S of Hadley Peak.

ROUTE: See Bastile Ridge Route♦. The short volcanic spur on the S is a trek; ascend from the E edge of Bastile Glacier. Note: There is an easy connecting ridge between Hadley and Peak 7842.

COLEMAN PINNACLE   6414 ft/1955 m

This is a small volcanic pinnacle at the SW end and high point of Ptarmigan Ridge, 2.3 mi. SW of Table Mountain. The upper N flank of the formation holds a small glacier. The apparent first climb was made by the Mazama outing party in 1906.

From the trail on the SE flank hike to the shoulder of the final summit; there is some 150 ft of scrambling.

The peak is of more interest as a viewpoint than a climb, and offers a good ski tour to the base of the rock. Floral exhibits in summer include the monkey flower and mertensia.

LOOMIS MOUNTAIN   5587 ft/1703 m

This is a bulky mountain 3.2 mi. S of Baker Pass at the head of the upper forks of the South Fork Nooksack River. The first ascent was made by B.W. Huntoon and H.M. Wellman in 1894 during their road survey; they traveled along the Nooksack South Fork to Baker Pass, then SE to Baker River, then N over Austin Pass.
ROUTE: See Baker Pass Trail◆. The best way to reach the summit without entering the brush zone is to hike S along the South Fork divide.

BLACK BUTTES

Located between Mt. Baker's summit cone and the Middle Fork Nooksack River, the Black Buttes are the remains of an andesitic cone formed before the volcanic cone shifted to the present site. Flows here were apparently very viscous, for they show a steep dip. The Buttes were deeply eroded by glaciation to a maze of jagged pinnacles and sheer walls, now roughly flanked by the Coleman, Deming, and Thunder glaciers. Located 1¼ mi. W of Mt. Baker's true summit, the East Butte (Colfax Peak) is the higher of the two principal summits. There is a small icecap on its eastern shoulder, extending to the Coleman-Deming glacier saddle, and a hanging ice cliff on the North Face; the remainder of the peak is formed from very steep rock walls.

The West Black Butte (Lincoln Peak) is located 0.7 mi. to the W. This peak is the most inaccessible, being very craggy and pinnacled; there is a sheer 1000-ft N face (above Coleman Glacier), and a longer 1500-ft wall on the E. The western end of the peak drops steeply into the cirque of Thunder Glacier; even the most hospitable flank, the S and SW, is corrugated with gullies and ridges. Of the other summits and crags, only Seward and Lee have been given provisional names.

Through a clearing in the fog during his historic climb of Mt. Baker, Edmund T. Coleman sighted and named the main summits Lincoln and Colfax. On August 14, 1868, Coleman described the Black Buttes: "Thousands of feet above the snow-field, rose on every side black, jagged, splintered precipices. Of these the Lincoln Peak is the most prominent."[53] Historian Charles Easton described the summits as "a solid, homogeneous mass of black basalt . . . minareted at the summit," and likened them to a Chinese wall. When in the area between 1907-1909 surveyor Thomas Gerdine called the Buttes "Sawtooth Rocks," a name which appeared on some early maps.

COLFAX PEAK   9443 ft/2878 m
First ascent by David Anderson, Clarence A. Fisher, and Paul Hugdahl about 1921.
ROUTE: Approach the Mt. Baker saddle via Coleman Glacier route. The climb is over easy firn slopes to the first summit (keep left of a schrund); make a short descent, then follow a lava ridge (if uncovered) or the final snow slopes to the summit. Time: 1 hour. References: Easton, p. 228, note 31; *B.C.M.*, September 1933.
NORTH FACE: First ascent by Ed Cooper and Fergus O'Conner on May 4, 1958. The route climbed the ice wall between the main (E) and lower summit, and was only possible because of snow cover on avalanched blocks, which permitted the ascent of an overhanging ice cliff; the blocks bridged the schrund and formed a slot in the cliff. The remainder of the route is steep, but has no special problem (recommend doing route before June). Take ice screws. Reference: *A.A.J.*, 1959, p. 302.
NORTH FACE-WEST SIDE: First ascent by Paul Johanson and S. Reilly Moss in late September 1974. This 800-ft route climbs the right margin of the hanging ice, not far from the 1958 line of ascent. Ascend a steep ice sheet (gully) to the ice cliff; the best route is to keep right. On the original, there was some bridging between ice and the rock on the right. Take ice screws. Time: 4 hours.

LINCOLN PEAK   9096 ft/2773 m
First ascent by Fred Beckey, Wesley Grande, John Rupley, and Herb Staley on July 22, 1956. The character of the climb is described in the account written by Staley: "the West Butte presented a vast forest of lava rock in various stages of decay."
SOUTH FACE: Take Middle Fork Nooksack River Road◆ to its end near Ridley Creek, then drive or hike the steep switchbacks through the clearcut. Above, one can hike N a short distance to two small lakes in an alpine setting at near 5100 ft; good camp here or just above (2 hours). Ascend past flowery slopes, moraine, and snow toward the small cirque on the objective's S flank, then taking the largest gully here (it is directed toward a crown-shaped tower — the second from the left). Ascend the glacier to rock; here climb a rounded rock step with 100 ft of exposure because of a moat beneath. Traverse up and left over loose slabs and steps to a second gully. Ascend this 50-degree gully aout 1000 ft (snow or rock) to a notch above the N face. Then turn left. From here, blocks, a chimney, and an exposed crack were climbed on the original ascent; at a crag 80 ft lower than the true summit, a 40-ft rappel was made into a notch next to the final lead. Note: Variations are possible on the upper

portion of the route. The second ascent party climbed a gully which ends only 30 ft W of the summit, with no need for a rappel. Time: 6 hours from camp by lakes; 9 hours from Kulshan cabin. References: *Mountaineer*, 1956, p. 121; *A.A.J.*, 1957, pp. 146-48; *Appalachia*, December 1956, p. 240.

Approach Variation: Done on original climb. From Kulshan cabin ascend moraine and snow bordering the Coleman Glacier, then cross the divide and descend 1500 ft to Thunder Glacier. Make a long snow (or moraine) traverse beneath the W face of the peak, then turn the corner of the wall and head for the large gully.

SEWARD PEAK   8005 ft/2440 m

This third summit of Black Buttes is located 0.7 mi. W of Lincoln Peak, a pointed peak flanked by Deming Glacier. First ascent by Dallas Kloke and Bryce Simon on July 11, 1973.

ROUTE: This is not a technical ascent, but enjoyable because of the setting and generally firm rock. Approach as for Lincoln Peak, then hike up easy heather and snow slopes to the lower W face of the SW ridge. Climb easy rock and a prominent snowpatch to the ridge crest (one short awkward move just below crest is class 4). Ascend the ridge to the top of a step before descending on right side on easy ledges to the small snowfield which leads to a saddle just W of a false summit. Climb a 100-ft rock band (solid and knobby), then take easy snow and rock to the summit. Class 4. Time: 4 hours from camp. Reference: *Mountaineer*, 1973, p. 82.

TWIN SISTERS RANGE

Standing as a high western outlier of the North Cascades, the Twin Sisters Range is located SW of Mt. Baker, only 21.5 mi. (34.6 km) from tidewater at Samish Bay. While the name is derived from the two highest peaks (separated by 0.9 mi.) on the 6 mi. NW-SE trending range, there are a considerable number and variety of smaller summits, towers, and crags, many of which have taken provisional names along a feminine theme.

The distinctive reddish brown coloring of Twin Sisters Range makes a remarkable contrast with the glaciers of Mt. Baker and the dark rock of the Black Buttes and the lower coniferous forest zone. Indians of the region noted the reddish color (due to presence of iron) and called the range "Kwik-kwek Smanik." The peridotite making up the range weathers to a very rough textured surface, providing some of the best climbing rock in the Cascades, rock not smoothed by the ice sheet above the level of 5300 ft (1738 m).[54] The elliptical-shaped dunite of the range is the largest body of exposed olivine in the Western Hemisphere,

emplaced from distant origins in Early Tertiary time by faulting into sedimentary rocks of the Chuckanut Formation as a solid mass.[55] Aside from the great variety of established climbing routes, the solidarity of the rock provides endless opportunities for variations of all difficulty, and also excellent places for practice climbing in a lovely alpine setting. The views of Mt. Baker, Border Peaks, Cheam Range, Picket Range, Cascade Pass area, Whitehorse Mountain area, Olympic Mountains, San Juan Islands, and Vancouver Island can be magnificent.

The range is the site of two significant glaciers: Sisters Glacier is the largest (1 km in width), draining into Sisters Creek; two lesser glaciers are located in the basin of Green Creek, the larger being on the W side of Little Sister. These glaciers are on the NE flank of the range, in the Middle Fork Nooksack River drainage. There are numerous other small ice remnants, usually in sheltered pockets under the crest.

With the vast hinterland of peaks, dominated by Mt. Baker, few early settlers of the Puget Sound Trough even noticed the Twin Sisters Range, even though they stand out on the horizon as seen from the San Juan Islands. Interestingly, the first known mention (by an Englishman) compared the range with a group of peaks in the Alps: from near the Black Buttes while en route to Mt. Baker, Edmund T. Coleman on August 16, 1868 commented on the "Red Ridge with its glaciers cradled in its arms," which greatly resembled in outline the Aiguilles Rouges as seen from "the north side of the valley of Chamounix." A passage in *The Mountaineer* of 1916 related how the morning sun "shoots its rays upon the jagged, rocky tops of the Sisters Range, flooding them in a rich mellow light." The first map provided by the Forest Service (1913) identified the range as "Sawtooth Rocks," an appellation fortunately not perpetuated.

Since the South Twin is the higher of the two principal peaks, the first mountaineering ambitions turned here. Its first ascent was made by J.M. Edson, E.A. Hegg, and P.J. Parris on August 1, 1891, through trackless forest via South Fork Nooksack River and Skookum Creek. Describing their adventure, a newspaper reported, "Unlike all the neighboring mountains, this range is of bare rocks, with too little soil, even at its base, for any growth of vegetation but stunted and scattering trees and shrubs. Its sides are very precipitous and they only found one place where it was practicable to ascend."[56] In August 1898 the companion North Twin was climbed by a party of nine, who described the wilderness adventure as very

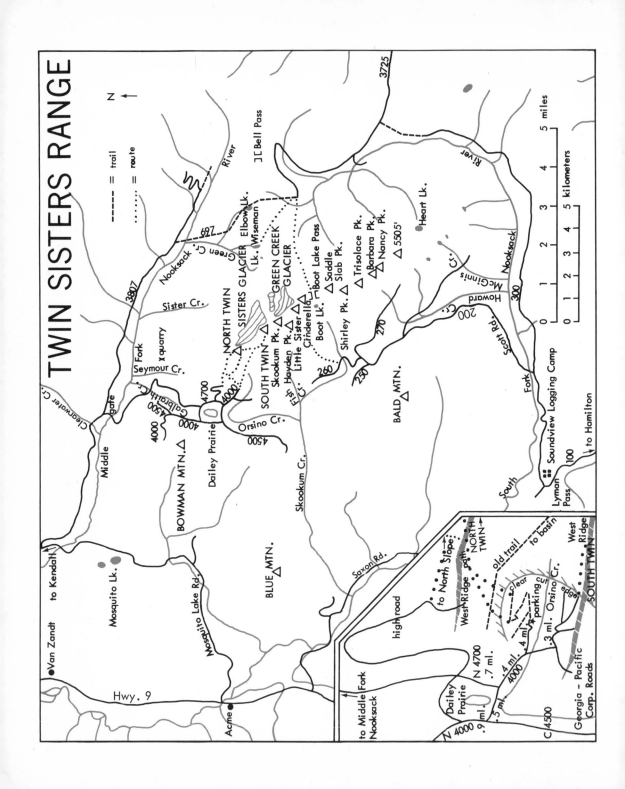

TWIN SISTERS RANGE

N ←

- - - - = trail
.... = route

Van Zandt • to Kendall

Hwy. 9

Acme •

Mosquito Lk.

Cleerwater Cr.

Middle

Fork

3807

Nooksack

Green Cr.

627

River

][Bell Pass

3725

gate

Galbraith Cr.

x quarry

Sister Cr.

Seymour Cr.

4700

4000

4000

4500

4000

4500

Orsino Cr.

Dailey Prairie

BOWMAN MTN. △

Mosquito Lake Rd.

Mosquito Lk.

NORTH TWIN △

SISTERS GLACIER

Elbow Lk.

Lk. Wiseman

GREEN CREEK GLACIER

SOUTH TWIN △

Skookum Pk. △

Hayden Pk. △

Little Sister △

Cinderella

Boot Lake Pass

Saddle

Boot Lk. •

Slab Pk. △

Shirley Pk. △

Trisolace Pk. △

Barbara Pk. △

Nancy Pk. △

△ 5505'

Heart Lk. •

260

250

270

200

300

McGinnis Cr.

Howard Cr.

Nooksack

Scott Rd.

South Fork

Lyman Pass

100

Soundview Logging Camp

to Hamilton

Skookum Cr.

BALD MTN. △

BLUE MTN. △

Saxon Rd.

to Middle Fork Nooksack

5 miles

5 kilometers

0 1 2 3 4 5

Inset map (lower right)

high road

to North Slope

West Ridge path

NORTH TWIN

old trail

to basin

West Ridge

SOUTH TWIN

clear cut

parking cut

.3 ml. Orsino Cr.

edge

.4 ml.

.4 ml.

N 4700 .7 ml.

Dailey Prairie .5 ml.

C 4500

N 4000 .9 ml.

.3 ml.

Georgia - Pacific Corp. Roads

Hayden Peak · Skookum Peak · South Twin · North Ridge · North Twin

SISTERS GLACIER

GREEN CREEK GLACIER

Green Creek valley

TWIN SISTERS from east
AUSTIN POST, U.S. GEOLOGICAL SURVEY

difficult ("It was awful work").[57] Several years before 1916 the party of Carl E. Bell, J.W. Sandison, and Fred W. Weil approached via the Middle Fork and apparently climbed South Twin from that flank.[58]

Approaches: See Dailey Prairie Road♦, Scott Paper Road♦, Baker Lake Hwy♦ (Loomis-Nooksack Road is a possible alternative when fire closes other routes).

References: Easton, pp. 50-51, 58, see note 31; *Mountaineer*, 1916, pp. 59-62; 1974, pp. 62-63; *Summit*, November 1961, pp. 12-13; *B.C.M.*, April 1975.

NORTH TWIN   6570 ft/2003 m

Although lower than South Twin, this peak is not less spectacular. Particularly from the W and SW it presents a pyramidal, sharp rock horn form, and on its opposite flank (Middle Fork Nooksack River) there is rugged glacierized alpine terrain. There is a distinct rock wall on the E and NE. Both the West Ridge and the South Face routes have been climbed in winter. An ascent of the North Twin has become a popular one-day climb, especially by the enjoyable West Ridge.

The usual climbing approach is via Dailey Prairie, where road spurs ascend to 3600 ft and 4000 ft only 1.0 and 1.3 mi. from the summit.

NORTH SLOPE: This is the easiest summit route. There may be avalanche conditions in early summer, but this is generally a good early season climb. A road fork SE of Dailey Prairie is a good approach to the lower West Ridge, from where one can make a hiking traverse to the North Slope (see Dailey Prairie Road♦), or use the higher northern roadway via N 4700 if snowfree and open. Hike or drive one of the roads to the timbered portion of the West Ridge (see map: Twin Sisters Range). From about 5000 ft on the ridge (where path fades at scrub trees) make an easy heather-boulder traverse northward. A diagonal traversing ascent continues through scattered firs to a low-gradient slope (usually snow) below the NW rock face. Keep left and below cliffs while making a traversing ascent to the final N slope, which until late summer is usually a snow face (not difficult) of only moderate angle (35 degrees). This leads directly to the summit. Time: 3 hours. Take ice axe.

Note: If the higher spur road is open for driving one can approach the route more directly by beginning N of the West Ridge, thus avoiding traversing.

NORTH TWIN

SOUTH TWIN

West Ridge

West Ridge

North Slope

col

to Dailey Prairie

TWIN SISTERS from west
HAROLD WOLLACK

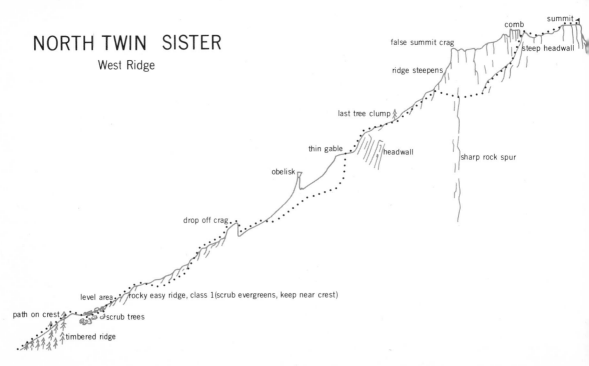

NORTH TWIN SISTER
West Ridge

summit

comb

false summit crag

steep headwall

ridge steepens

last tree clump

thin gable

headwall

sharp rock spur

obelisk

drop off crag

level area

rocky easy ridge, class 1 (scrub evergreens, keep near crest)

path on crest

scrub trees

timbered ridge

This route is frequently used to descend the peak since it is much faster than downclimbing the West Ridge or other routes. However, the snowfield can be hazardous in early season.

SOUTH FACE: The broad pyramid-shaped face of North Twin overlooking the cirque between Twin Sisters offers numerous possibilities for serious scrambling, but the most popular line is up a long narrow gully that leads from the base of the mountain to the lower E summit knob. The start of the gully can be found by hiking to the back of the cirque, where a large talus cone (or snow) marks the beginning of the route. A small cliff midway involves about 20 ft of class 4, the remainder of the climbing being class 3. In early spring the route is a steep snow climb. At the top climb steeply on rock left to the summit. Time: 1-1/2 hours from the cirque.

For climbers intent on climbing both Twin Sisters in a day, the South Face gully provides an efficient way to descend from the North Twin to reach the base of South Twin, which can then be climbed via the Northeast Ridge. From the summit of North Twin, descent of the gully begins immediately SE of the summit knob.

Variations: The South Face offers numerous route possibilities, involving scrambling to class 5, on numerous gullies and ribs. The SE ridge is one alternative and offers pleasant climbing on superb rock.

WEST RIDGE: This is a splendid climb, hard to equal in its difficulty rating; the rock is superb. There is easy scrambling at first, but the ridge narrows and steepens during the final 300 ft to the false summit.

From the highest (northern) road spur (from N 4700) ascend open timber eastward near the crest of the wooded lower ridge (or approach via steep path from end of switch-backs above Orsino Creek, farther SE, per South Twin-West Ridge). Follow a path on the ridge until the terrain becomes bouldery; at the area of small scrub-trees here keep either on the crest or its right (class 1 and 2) to the top of a prominent crag on the crest which has a 30-ft dropoff. (Here one can see the false summit area clearly; it appears to be the summit. The Obelisk tower is ahead on the ridge.) Continuing, the best progress is made about 100 ft right of the crest. At about 800 linear ft from the dropoff crag, climb left on solid rock (class 3) to the short thin walking gable to reach a small headwall just right of the crest. Begin this section on the left and in about 200 ft (distance) reach the final clump of seven trees on the crest.

From here one can continue directly over the false summit crag (with craggy yellow overhang on right), about 600 ft distance away (steep class 3). When taking this line it is best to keep slightly on the N side of the crest and take a broken exposed chimney. The alternative is to traverse right about 100 ft to a narrow SW ridge spur (skyline seen from dropoff crag). Traverse easily around the corner here (well below the overhang) to an easy rock and gully system that merges into a steeper face capped by a light yellow rock comb. Climb steep rock with bucket holds (class 3) closely right and below a ridge comb. About 700 ft of nearly level easy scrambling and

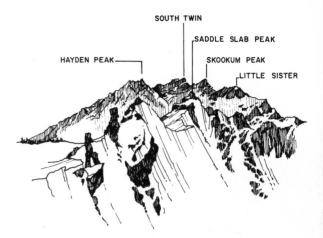

TWIN SISTERS RANGE from south

boulder hopping on the crest leads to the summit (at far E end of ridge). Class 3-4. Time: 3-4 hours from road; 2 hours down. Prior to July take ice axe.

Variation: From the timberline basin between Twin Sisters one can diagonal left on talus and gullies to the West Ridge just above the tree line.

SOUTH TWIN   6932 ft/2113 m

The South Twin, the highest peak in the range, is located between Sister and Green Creek forks of Middle Fork Nooksack River and upper Skookum Creek (a South Fork tributary). The Sisters Glacier is located on the NE slope. Below the small pocket glacier on the NW face is a 19th century moraine.

For early climbs, see history. First winter ascent by Fred Beckey, Tony Hovey, Vic Josendal and Roe D. Watson on January 26, 1963 (via West Ridge).

WEST RIDGE: See Dailey Prairie Road◆. This is the most popular climbing route. Drive to the logging area SE of the Prairie and N of Orsino Creek (see North Twin). There are two standard ways to reach the cirque between Twin Sisters:

(1) The best is to hike directly upslope (steep path) from the end of the eastern logging spur switchbacks (see map) to an intersection with an old trail in the forest. Follow this right to basin (1 hour, car to cabin at edge of basin).

(2) From first hairpin switchback of this spur hike on path through clearcut eastward into forest, then continue to prominent rockslide. Ascend, then traverse up and right to another rockslide, leading into cirque basin.

Strike for the large snow basin between the Twins by bearing right; the talus slope leading to the basin is usually snow-covered until midsummer. Get into the West Ridge low down (easiest) or higher up by penetrating to the far right end of this basin floor and a steep broken rock slope (40 degree snow until late summer) to a high notch about 400 ft below the summit. Make a traversing ascent on the S flank of the ridge, then ascend gullies to the summit (a broad rock plateau). Class 2-3. Time: 3 hours. Note: There are good rock climbing opportunities along the final portion of the ridge (class 4 and 5).

Variation: By taking a higher and more southern spur of the logging road, the West Ridge can be followed entirely. The route is long but not difficult, though narrow in spots.

NORTHWEST FACE: This 800-ft rock face leads from the SE corner of the central basin directly to the summit. First ascent by Dallas Kloke and Reed Tindall on June 13, 1967. First winter ascent by Jack Bradshaw and Tom Falley in January 1972 or 1973.

Begin just left of center-face and diagonal right before bearing directly for the summit. One pitch of 60 ft about three-quarter height involved very steep snow on original climb; the rock is loose in places. In early summer some steep snowpatches will be encountered, especially near the top. Grade I-II; class 4 (to 5.2). Time: 6 hours. Reference: *A.A.J.,* 1968, p. 139.

Variation: North Face of West Ridge: By Dave Davis and Greg Markov, November 1973.

NORTH RIDGE: Approach via the cirque basin between the peaks, scrambling over the headwall at its lowest point (at the 5800-ft+ col) to arrive at Sisters Glacier on the E side. Then traverse S briefly on the glacier to the bergschrund to gain the crest of the North Ridge. The route can be done mostly on snow; the crest of the ridge is reportedly somewhat crumbly, sometimes with steep snow.

NORTH FACE: Reach as per North Ridge, then continue ascending S to 6000 ft (15 minutes on glacier). Usually there is a bergschrund problem here, advising an early season ascent. Climb a short, quite steep snow slope on the left side of the face directly to the summit. Watch for avalanche danger. Take snow flukes or crampons, depending on season. Time: 5 hours.

Note: This is a good descent route in early season.

NORTHEAST RIDGE: Approach as per North Ridge, but traverse farther on the glacier to the first rock spur striking the ice. An easy scramble is then taken to the crest (beware of loose boulders, but rock is generally solid). Then follow the ridge about 500 ft to the broad summit plateau. Class 2-3. Time: 4 hours.

SOUTH GULLIES: There are several moderate gullies on this flank of South Twin of no special difficulty (use hands, and scrambling; some loose rock). The first ascent of the peak was probably done in this area. Now this route is seldom done unless a traverse is made from Skookum Peak. A winter climb (South Face Couloir) was done by Jack Bradshaw and Tom Falley in January 1974.

ARROWTIP TOWER est. 6250 ft/1905 m

This is the northern of two similar rock towers, about 400 ft apart on the crest of the North Ridge of South Twin. The tower stands about 75 ft above Sisters Glacier and appears as a sharp tooth. First ascent by Dave Litke, Doug McKeever, and George Mustoe on October 15, 1971.

The best approach is from the glacier. Climb directly from here or by the short connecting ridge with Block Tower. The final 25-ft section of the objective is on the SE (class 4).

There is also a W face route (details unknown). A route via the N face was done by Jerry King and Richard Rossiter in June 1972. From the basin headwall slightly left of the tower, do two leads on steep rock to a platform below the N face. Gain the summit via a crack system (one lead); class 5.

BLOCK TOWER est. 6250 ft/1905 m

This is a 40-ft squared block perched on the ridge adjacent to Arrowtip Tower, closely above the glacier on the E. First ascent by Doug McKeever and George Mustoe on October 15, 1971.

Climb to a large step on the S side of the tower, then up to a small ledge on the E face; make a 15-ft traverse on a narrow ledge to a step on the N side just below the top (two mantles here). Class 5.3 (one chock and runner).

The "Toe Jam" on the E face was done by Joe Ford and Richard Rossiter on July 8, 1973 (5.8).

The W face was climbed by a 400-ft route to the ridge connecting to the towers (ending nearest Block Tower) by Mike Berry, Dallas Kloke, George Neibel, and Scott Masonholder on October 17, 1976. From the broken rock at the base ascend a gully which leads up slabby rock (two leads) to the base of a prominent, broad dihedral; ascend this pitch (75 ft of class 5). The rock is quite solid except on ledges. Class 5.5. Time: 2 hours.

SKOOKUM PEAK   6500 ft+/1981 m+

This is the third peak of note in the range, a sharply pointed rock summit located 0.4 mi. from South Twin, at the very head of Green Creek and the glacier in its cirque. First ascent by Dave Dixon and Dallas Kloke on May 31, 1969 (via Northwest Ridge). Reference: *A.A.J.,* 1971, p. 348.

From Dailey Prairie Road♦ climb from over the wooded lower West Ridge of South Twin, then descend into a small basin; cross a spur ridge to the lower part of a larger talus basin below objective. The apparently easiest route is to circuit around to the S side (gulley scrambling on firm rock).

NORTHWEST RIDGE: This route begins via 150 ft of easy rock to the notch adjacent to Jaw's Tooth. Ascend the 300-ft ridge on good rock for three short leads involving a few easy class 5 moves (mostly easier). Class 5.4 (several chocks).

WEST RIDGE: First ascent by Dave Dixon and Dallas Kloke on September 14, 1975. Ascend the basin to the NW base of objective; scramble easy rock to the ridge crest. Keep on the ridge the entire distance (four leads of class 3-4); the final 300 ft of rock is easier. A few chocks and slings are useful; rock is excellent. Class 4. Time: 5 hours from road.

JAW'S TOOTH   est. 6400 ft/1951 m
This 65-ft pinnacle is located adjacent to Skookum Peak on its N side. First ascent by West Ridge Skookum party. From the dividing notch ascend the S side along first the left edge, then up and around the right side of the final summit horn (one lead, class 5.2, several chocks). Time: 1 hour.

HAYDEN PEAK   6400 ft+/1951 m+
Hayden is a prominent off-ridge summit located 1 mi. S of South Twin, slightly W of the main Twin Sisters crest. Hayden Creek drains its S flank. First ascent by Dave Dixon and Dallas Kloke on September 30, 1972.
SOUTHWEST ROUTE: Approach via Scott Paper Road♦. Follow Hayden Creek tributary northward, then up a wooded ridge to the base of the peak. The easy SW slope and ridge are taken to the summit. Class 2-3. Time: 4 hours from road. Reference: *Mountaineer,* 1972, p. 86.

LITTLE SISTER   6524 ft/1989 m
This is a prominent summit located 1 mi. from South Twin. On its W there is a large talus basin which makes a horseshoe-shaped connection with Hayden Peak; to the SW there is a long ridge trending parallel to Hayden. There is a prominent right-slanting couloir on the S face. On the N flank is the second largest glacier in the range ("Green Creek Glacier"). First ascent by Harte Bressler, Ken Hunich, Tom Meland, and Harry Wollak on June 1, 1969.

The best approach is via Scott Paper Road♦ (see Shirley Peak). Ascend the short SW ridge (class 2) or climb snow gullies on the S side, then do a short rock section. The other approach is via Loomis-Nooksack Road (see Baker Lake Hwy♦), then hiking W via the slope of a ridge along a western fork of the upper Nooksack South Fork, to cross the Twin Sisters divide at Boot Lake. From the basin here traverse NW to beneath Little Sister and Cinderella.

CINDERELLA PEAK   6400 ft+/1951 m+
This peak is closely SE of Little Sister; it is a broad summit, divided by a prominent snow gulley on the SW flank. First ascent by Sue Beske, Rob Cockerham, and Jim Diehl on July 28, 1972. The summit can easily be reached from the SW gully or the N via the notch adjacent Little Sister; a prominent buttress on the SE presents a long rock climb of 1000 ft to connect with the S ridge of the peak.

SHIRLEY PEAK   5836 ft/1779 m
Upper Hayden Creek drains the W side of this small

pointed summit with a steep E face on the crest, 2.4 mi. from South Twin.
ROUTES: The peak is an easy scramble up the ridge from the S or via the NW slope. One can traverse the high W slope S of Little Sister across the basin of Boot Lake.

The approach is via Scott Paper Road♦ to the road's horseshoe bend at Hayden Creek (3000 ft). Follow an overgrown logging spur E to its end. Ascend logged area to shallow gully section which is taken to the end of the ridge from the peak. Stay N and below the ridge on snow or talus to the peak. Time: 3 hours from road.

A western route was done by Dallas Kloke, George Mahler, Lee Mann, and Reed Tindall in May 1963. The route ascends an easy W rock face left of the SW gully (class 2-3).

SADDLE SLAB PEAK
5700 ft+/1737 m+
Distinctive for its W-dipping rock strata, this small rock peak 0.3 mi. N of Shirley Peak, has blocky rock formations on its faces. First ascent by Lee Mann, George Mahler, Dallas Kloke, and Reed Tindall in May 1963 (via West Ridge).
WEST RIDGE: Approach as per Shirley Peak (from Hayden Creek). The route takes ascending ledges from the S side of the objective ridge. There are two short summit blocks. Time: 4 hours from the road.
NORTHEAST ROUTE: First ascent by Dallas Kloke and Lou LaMay on September 16, 1976. Ascend to the NE side of the summit about 100 ft below the summit; climb a 20-ft slab, making a short friction move diagonally left (5.6 — use small protection chock). Follow the ridge crest easily to the top.

PEAK 5800+   5800 ft+/1768 m+
This twin-crested small summit is located NW of Saddle Slab Peak, closely SE of Boot Lake; the South Peak is easily climbed from the N on mostly snow, or up the S ridge by rock scrambling. The North Peak can be easily ascended by the W slope or the E ridge.

TRISOLACE PEAK   5800 ft+/1768 m+
This formation is a row of small crags between Shirley and Barbara peaks. The N ridge was done by Mike Berry, Dave Dixon and Dallas Kloke on January 9, 1977. Class 3-4. Time: 5 hours.

BARBARA PEAK   5902 ft/1799 m
This is a small rock peak located 3.2 mi. from South Twin. Barbara and Nancy peaks are the last two notable summits on the range. First ascent by Tom Meland and Harry Wollak on June 4, 1969.
ROUTES: From the Scott Paper Road♦ make an ascent on the right side of the plunging creek draining between Bar-

bara and Nancy peaks (bypass at right of a wooded buttress at 3800 ft). From the saddle between them both summits can be attained.

To climb Barbara take a steep gully on the SW side for 300 ft, then continue on excellent rock to the pyramidal summit. Class 3.

The S face was climbed by John Brantley and Dallas Kloke in June 1971. From a broad ledge 100 ft above the talus-snow, take an obvious corner; the hardest portion is a 20-ft jam crack (class 5.5). Total three solid rock leads. Time: 5 hours from road. Reference: *Mountaineer,* 1971, p. 84.

NANCY PEAK   5900 ft+/1798 m+

The last summit of note in the range, closely SE of Barbara Peak at 3.6 mi. N of South Fork Nooksack River, the peak has a distinct long E ridge. First ascent by Barbara Peak party.

ROUTES: From the central saddle one could approach the top of a rock shelf, then climb directly up a rock shoulder to the summit.

From the W base of the peak, ascend a snow finger on the right for several hundred ft, then traverse left to the shelf.

CHURCH MOUNTAIN   6315 ft/1925 m

Church Mountain is a popular trail trek, but is also a fine mountain viewpoint for perspectives of Mt. Baker and the Fraser River Valley. See Church Mountain Trail◆. Early Nooksack Valley settlers named the mountain for its spired summit shape. On the long S slope of the mountain are massive Chilliwack Group volcanics resting on Nooksack Group strata, visible from the highway above the timber level.

TOMYHOI PEAK   7451 ft/2271 m

Tomyhoi is an attractive alpine peak with a high bench glacier and culminating in a rock summit horn 1.6 mi. from the Boundary on the Tomyhoi-Damfino Creek divide (2.8 mi. W of Mt. Larrabee). The glacier, which cascades waterfalls over cliffs fringing upper Tomyhoi Creek, has an unusually level upper portion (resting on a plateau), and is quite visible from Chilliwack in the Fraser Valley. Basement crystalline rocks and overlying metamorphic rocks are spectacularly exposed around the peak.[59] The higher portion of Tomyhoi consists of slightly metamorphosed marine sediments and volcanics of the Chilliwack Group. Slices of the Yellow Aster Complex crystalline basement are exposed on the flanks (and on the normal route approach) along with remnants of the green-schist of the Shuksan thrust fault.

During the first Boundary Surveys the peak was referred to as "Put-lush-go-hap," and was possibly climbed by the reconnaissance leader Henry Custer.[60] George Gibbs, geologist with the survey, described Tomyhoi Lake: "there the mountain overhangs the water in an almost perpendicular bluff of 1,000 ft.; cascades, some of them nearly half that height, fall in spray from its sides, the lake itself, towards the end of June, was still sheeted in ice and snow, and its outlet was a continuous fall of nearly 1,000 ft. in half a mile."

Various manuscript maps and journals from the survey refer to "Put-lush-go-hap" as the name for the lake and an associated mountain. Although the name Tomyhoi is not mentioned in early mining stories, versions of the name (including Tommy High) originated with the first gold seekers; the true derivation may mean "tammiax" or "deformed" from native language; the caption Tamihi is given for Slesse Mountain in a report of the International Boundary Survey, and Tomyhoi has been applied to the Border Peaks in the past. A map drawn in the notebook of geologist George Otis Smith in 1901 identifies the summit as "Needle Pk." If the peak was not climbed by Americans from the first survey, the first climb may have been done by Lage Wernstedt about 1927, or by Ben Thompson or Clarence A. Fisher in the early 1930s. The peak and its locale were practically unknown to climbers before 1935, despite the fact it is prominent from the area of Austin Pass. References: Baker, Bull. 174, pp. 46-47 see Section II, note 63; Sixth Report of U.S. Board on Geographic Names (refers to former spellings Put-hish-go-hap and Tummeahai); *B.C.M.,* May 1949, August 1950, December 1970.

SOUTHEAST ROUTE: See Keep Kool Trail◆ for approach to Yellow Aster meadows. From the upper pond area (5500 ft) hike toward a long broad ridge rising and trending NNW; this culminates in Tomyhoi Peak in about 2½ mi. This route is first meadowy ridge-slope hiking. When the heather cover gives way to rock, cross a hump, then make a descent of about 200 ft to a rounded col (6300 ft). Continue upward as the ridge broadens again. Later a narrowing rocky section of the ridge can be hiked to above the edge of the glacier, but it is easier to bypass this section by traversing an expansive bench system on the N flank. Avoid several rock pinnacles by traversing the top edge of the glacier on snow or firn, then climb over a rocky hump (false summit). Descend 100 ft to a notch (7250 ft). Climb moderately steep but firm rock along the left edge of the ridge (160 ft), then cross a narrow 50-ft level gable. Follow a ledge W for 30 ft to a broad corner; turn right and take easy scree-rock ledges W of the crest to the summit. Class 3. Time: 4 hours from meadows; 10 hours r.t. from road. Note: There is an emergency shelter cabin in trees on the saddle separating the North Butte Yellow Aster from the Tomyhoi ridge.

NORTH ROUTE: From Tamihi Creek Road (see Chilliwack River Road♦) near the Boundary descend to the creek and cross a log, then to a large slide area N of the peak. Aim for the western edge of the glacier on the NE shoulder: ascend a boulder field and terminal moraine, bearing right along the timber edge above the glacier (campsite at 5200 ft). Traverse left on the glacier and climb to the base of summit cliffs. One can avoid these to the left (normal route) or make a direct completion on the N ridge (broken ledges and face climbing; class 3-4). Time: long day r.t. There was an accident on this route during the snow traverse (*B.C.M.*, March 1968).

AMERICAN BORDER PEAK
8026 ft/2446 m

This imposing rock massif, such an outstanding sight on the northern skyline from the Heather Meadows area of Mt. Baker, is located barely 0.3 mi. S of the International Boundary between Tomyhoi and Silesia (Slesse) creeks, rising some 6500 ft from the latter's valley.

Personnel of the American Boundary Survey 1859-61 called the Border Peak-Mt. Larrabee ridge the "Tum mea hai Mountains." Both American and Canadian Border peaks have had various names, successively and simultaneously, including American and Canadian Tomyhoi, and Boundary Red and Canadian Red, until the name Tomyhoi was officially mapped for the peak W of Tomyhoi Lake. Barnard called American Border "Glacier Peak" and "Silicia Peak" and the Larrabee-Border Peak ice valley "Glacier Basin."

As a climb, American Border Peak is not nearly as difficult as it appears, but both summit routes have long approaches, each with some complications, and the rock tends to be gritty and exposed. The first ascent was made by Alec Dalgleish, Tom Fyles, Stan Henderson and R.A. (Gus) Fraser on September 14, 1930, climbing from Twin Lakes by the Southeast Face Route. The first winter climb was made by Henryk Mather and Hans Starr in March 1958, beginning from Red Mountain Mine (skis to glacier, then SE route). References: *C.A.J.*, 1930, pp. 98-100; *B.C.M*, November, 1971.

SOUTHEAST FACE: The tedious approach over loose talus and scree makes this route long, but the climb provides the rewards of a spectacular location. The usual approach is made by Gargett Mine Trail♦ (can camp at High Pass or mine). From about 200 ft below the mine begin a long "footsore" traverse. Take scree slopes across a minor (wooded) ridge (SW rib of Larrabee), then cross a broad shallow basin (red scree) to the very sharp, craggy reddish rock and tree buttress (NW rib); reach rib at brushy tree area about ½ mi. from mine, descending about 200 ft on the traverse. Turn the corner in tree area, where a steep slope leads to next basin. In about ¼ mi. gain 200-300 ft. Toward the N end of the open basin is a boulder jumble (water, camping). Note: Parts of this traverse are tedious and slippery.

Alternative: When in large basin beyond SW rib, make a rising traverse and climb the gully against the NW rib (last gully on N side basin — total 500 ft rise). Cross a notch in rib and then do sharp reverse, descending gully (500 ft down — maybe some snow).

Then climb N and up (aim for timber belt), then up grassy gully through tree belt (rocky stream bed). Take shallow ribs and gullies (grey rock area) toward main ridge-crest notch closest to peak at 6800 ft+ (the final part is 200-300 ft of game trail on bare scree rib); 4 hours to here.

Scramble NE up on sloping easy slab terrain above the glacier on the Slesse Creek slope to SE rib of objective peak (rock changes to white-tan) for about 100 ft (red rock area). Traverse several hundred ft E, gaining little elevation. Before terrain gets steep, scramble N and up about 150 ft to the crest of the yellowish SE rib. Cross the rib, then walk-scramble about 100 yards (gaining 100 ft) to an obvious broad, right-slanting gully; this short, steep gully is usually snow-filled. Climb to the notch at its top (50-100 ft), then traverse N across grassy-mossy ledges for several hundred feet (some looseness) towards the "Great Chimney" (it faces S and is mostly invisible until nearby). Make a short descent (est. 100 ft) into gully running perpendicular to it. Either scramble around up and right, then back left into chimney or climb directly up into it (20 ft — 5.3). Walk up inside chimney to the big chockstone and climb the E (right) wall of the chimney past the stone (class 4 — 30 ft), then scramble the boulders up and through a cannonhole (natural tunnel). From the notch platform area atop chimney follow the gully 100-150 ft up and W to the ridge crest. Scramble and boulderhop N along the wide final crest; the last and minor obstacle is a pyramidal tower. At its far side is a flat area separated from the true summit. Class 3 (possibly class 4 at exposed spots). Time: 7 hours from Gargett Mine.

Approach Variation: From Red Mountain Mine via bush, slab, and glacier (see Slesse Creek Road; Chilliwack River Road♦). This is a much more difficult approach.

NORTHEAST FACE: First ascent by Dwight Baker, Fred Beckey, and John Dudra on September 21, 1952. On the original climb a glacier descent was made from the col S of the peak, then the E face was skirted to ice and snow fingers to the NE. The best approach now is via Slesse Creek Road, per the wooded spur used to reach Canadian Border Peak.

Descend SE into the basin and skirt its rock walls on snow and talus. Ascend beyond cliffs (but left of waterfalls) via short rock walls and snowpatches (about 100 ft of class 4; otherwise class 3). Keep on rock right of the hanging pocket glacier, which has ice fall danger. Easy rock, a snow gully

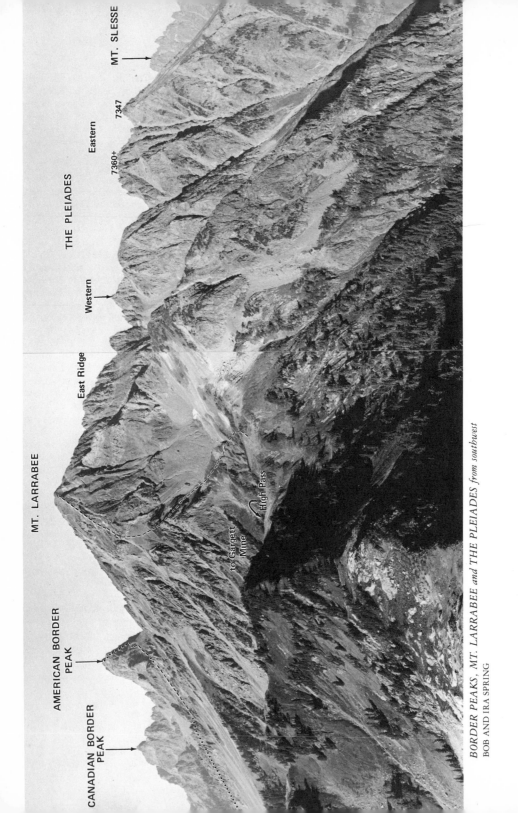

CANADIAN BORDER PEAK

AMERICAN BORDER PEAK

MT. LARRABEE

THE PLEIADES

MT. SLESSE

East Ridge

Western

Eastern

7360+

7347

to Gargett Mine

High Pass

BORDER PEAKS, MT. LARRABEE and THE PLEIADES from southwest
BOB AND IRA SPRING

and heather can be climbed to the glacier above the lower ice fall. Higher, cross left onto the glacier to gain the mixed rock and snow of the upper NE face or first climb to near the col NW of the objective. A key feature on the face is a large 45-degree snow gully reached by a traverse onto the rock face. Move S occasionally on pleasant rock pitches of only moderate difficulty (class 4 but mostly class 3); occasional snowpatches are encountered until late summer. Take ice axe and crampons. References: *Mountaineer,* 1952, p. 83; *Appalachia,* June 1953, p. 401; *A.A.J.,* 1953, p. 540; *B.C.M.,* December 1956. Time: 6 hours from camp.

MT. LARRABEE (Red Mountain)
7868 ft/2398 m

The largest massif of reddish rock in the North Cascades, Mt. Larrabee is located on the Tomyhoi-Silesia Creek divide 1.4 mi. S of the Boundary and 10.4 mi. NNW of Mt. Shuksan. The mountain is dominant on the skyline looking northward from the Heather Meadows area of Mt. Baker. Its greatest relief is from the valley of Silesia Creek, where it rises 5800 ft from the boundary line. Larrabee and the Border Peaks are characterized by highly fractured rock of the Chilliwack Group, consisting of interbedded and interfolded phyllites and greenstone; some basement crystalline rocks are also present.

Traditionally known as Red Mountain, the name was changed to honor Charles F. Larrabee, member of a prominent Bellingham family. On at least one old claim map the mountain is called "Tomyhoy." Miners early in the century found the mountain a familiar sight. One report states "Red Mountain forms one of the most picturesque and prominent landmarks in the whole district, because of the rich and red colouring of its sides and from the oxidation of the iron in the country rock, the bluish colouring of the glaciers in the crevasses on the northern slope" (Minister of Mines, 1915 Annual Report). There is a possibility that the mountain was climbed by Henry Custer during the first years of the Boundary Survey (1858-61), but evidence is lacking. Probably the first ascent was made by the J.J. McArthur-led Canadian party (station "Red" was marked by a bronze disc); in 1935 a 5-ft cairn was erected by surveyors. About 1900 Thomas Braithwait and a partner pushed around the mountain's N side on a goat hunt and discovered gold. This site ultimately became the Boundary-Red gold mine ledge, which resulted in Red Mountain Mine, 1.3 mi. NE of the summit. The Gargett Mine on the SW slope near High Pass has workings up to 6800 ft. Climbing routes have been done on various flanks and the North Face offers ice climbing possibilities. A winter ascent

from Red Mountain Mine and the East Buttress was done by Henryk Mather and Elfrieda Pigou in March 1958. Reference: *Joint Report,* p. 88 (photo), 415.

SOUTHWEST ROUTE: Approach via High Pass (see Gargett Mine Trail♦) S of objective; follow heather slopes leftward at the foot of the basin to reach a minor southern rock spur. Ascend scree and easy rock of this spur to a little cliff (est. 7000 ft); a minor gully left of the rib breaks the cliff band. Ascend this, then continue to scramble up easy talus slopes and minor gullies. One of several dikes of firmer rock forms a corner spur that can be taken for a distance; this is followed by a mixture of loose rock and dirt with some poor footing, but the route is not difficult partly because of moderate angle. Time: 5 hours from Twin Lakes.

Variation (Southeast Ridge): This is a craggy rock ridge beginning on the right side of the first scree basin. Climbing history and quality of rock are unknown.

Approach Variation: From Red Mountain Mine (see Chilliwack River Road♦-Slesse Creek Road) cross snow and glacier to the crest of the main ridge between Larrabee and American Border peaks (6800 ft+). Then proceed around to the SW side of the mountain for the final ascent (numerous gullies and ribs to traverse).

NORTH FACE: This reddish alpine face features gullies, snow and ice patches, and loose rock, but a grey-colored buttress leading to the upper E ridge provides some firmness. The route can have glacier problems if done in late summer. First ascent by Fred and Jim Douglas in 1968. The route from Red Mountain Mine (4000 ft) traverses to the northern glacier, then ascends this to the buttress on the face. Cross the moat (can be difficult) and ascend several leads of rock (class 4) to the buttress. The climbing then becomes easier: the buttress merges into the face, which here is loose rock. Grade III; time: 9 hours from mine.

EAST BUTTRESS: Climbed in winter in completing a traverse over The Pleiades. This very long alpine route has commitment, considerable exposure, and continual rock climbing.

THE PLEIADES   7360 ft+/2243 m+

This is a constellation of jagged rock spires on the ridge trending E from Mt. Larrabee, at 1.2 mi. S of the Boundary. Four principal summits span ½ mi; the eastern two are highest (from W to E: 7280 ft+, 7200 ft+, 7360 ft+, 7347 ft). There are steep ice fragments and couloirs on the North Face; here a narrow glacier descends to broaden and end near Boundary Red Mine. Below the Chilliwack Group of slates and phyllites on The Pleiades one can see light-colored Yellow Aster basement crystallines, introduced by thrust faulting. This rock makes for occasional delightfully solid sections in the midst of an area noted for loose rubble. The first ascents and traverse of all summits (W to E) were made by Dwight Baker, Fred Beckey, and John Dudra on September 20, 1952. The first

THE PLEIADES   MT. LARRABEE

Western   Eastern

to American
Border Peak

Mine

MT. LARRABEE from northeast
DICK CULBERT

winter ascent was made by Henryk Mather and El-frieda Pigou in March 1958 (from mine via NE ridge of East Peak; the party continued on a 2-day traverse of the peaks and to Mt. Larrabee). The name was given by the first ascent party. Interestingly, a chart of the Pleiades in stereographic projection and adapted to Bessel's positions of the principal stars of that group for 1840 was used for astronomy studies during the North West Boundary Survey. References: *Mountaineer*, 1952, p. 83; *A.A.J.*, 1953, p. 540.

SOUTHWEST ROUTE (original): From Gargett Mine Trail♦ cross the basin NE from the shoulder of Larrabee. A loose gully gives access to the main notch (6900 ft+) E of the western summits. Either the E or W group of peaks is scramble-climbing (class 3) from here. There is a snow and ice patch beneath the two W summits: it is best to climb the far-W summit from its W, and the pointed second summit (firm rock) from its E. One can reach the eastern summits from the notch via the narrow loose gully on the S side of the divide.

WEST PEAK VIA NORTH RIDGE: First ascent by Dick Culbert, Bruce McKnight, and Glenn Woodsworth on September 17, 1961. From Red Mountain Mine (see Chilliwack River Road♦-Slesse Creek Road) ascend easy rock in the basin to gain the prominent ridge dropping from the western peak. The ridge is mostly class 3, but there is one upper class 4 notch. Rock is firm; there is also some snow on the climb.

EAST PEAK VIA NORTH RIDGE: From Red Mountain Mine ascend easy slopes and gain the North Ridge of the most eastern peak. This ridge is a long scramble, with one class 4 notch in the upper part (loose rock here).

NORTH FACE COULOIRS: Three snow/ice couloirs on the North Face are reasonable routes (reach from Red Mountain Mine); some brush is encountered on the slope to the glacier. The snow tongue (central couloir) above the N-side glacier which divides the E and W summit groups has ice cliffs; huge crevasses and a bergschrund may be a problem. A bypass may be done on rocks to the left. There is a long snow couloir from near the mine extending via the glacier to between the two eastern summits.

TRAVERSE ROUTE: Best done W to E as by 1952 and 1961 parties, this alpine route offers a long day of class 3 and 4 on indifferent rock. Ascend the North Ridge of the West Peak, then traverse the other summits; just beyond the main notch use a gully on the S face. One can descend by the North Ridge of the East Peak. Time: 10 hours from mine.

BIG BOSOM BUTTES   6521 ft/1988 m

These are a pair of rocky, bosomy-shaped summits on the ridge between Silesia Creek and its West Fork (ridge is incorrectly called Skagit Range on maps — should be Silesia Ridge). The S butte (6521 ft/1988 m), the one with the best form, is 3.3 mi. S of the International Boundary. The lower N butte (6384 ft/1946 m) is located 0.6 mi. to the N. A southern point (6400 ft+/1951 m) has a sheer, though short wall on its E. Rock on the Buttes is breccia of Hannegan volcanics; these overlap the granodiorite of Chilliwack Batholith. The imaginative name was bestowed by geologist Rowland Tabor, who with Doug McKeever made the first ascent of the S summit on August 2, 1967.

ROUTES: Approach from Twin Lakes, via Silesia Creek Trail♦. Follow the latter upstream to near the first large stream heading into the ridge E (about 1.5 mi. SE of Silesia forks). Then climb W to bypass a large cliff (est. 4800 ft) on its S side; this is on E side of the S butte. The slope is brushy and timbered. Climb steep debris-laden ledges to reach the S ridge of objective, then traverse up and N (scree) on a W-side ledge; class 2. Time: 6 hours from trail.

The N butte is harder to reach: one can probably continue NW to the S summit ridge, or ascend directly from Winchester Creek to gain the N ridge at about 6000 ft (some brush and steep cliffs). One can readily traverse the ridge southward over Peaks 6839 and 7035, then continue to Mamie Pass.

GOAT MOUNTAIN   6891 ft/2100 m

Goat is a massive, though not regionally important mountain N of lower Ruth Creek and S of Twin Lakes in the area between Mt. Shuksan and Mt. Larrabee. Goat has two principal summits (E and W); the E peak has a short rock horn; the lower W peak (6721 ft/2049 m) and a more distant N peak (6509 ft/1984 m) are closely SW of Lone Jack Mine. The mountain is composed of Darrington Phyllite (part of the Shuksan Suite). There is an old mine at 5000 ft on the N slope of the mountain; a trail was once built from Swamp Creek. The old Silver Tip Mine, at 3600 ft on the S slope, was discovered by H.C. Wells in 1896; a 1000-ft tram was built to the adit in 1945.

Written material from the Boundary Survey 1859-61 describes a summit they visited between Slesse Creek and a tributary of the Nooksack River. Calculated at 6117 ft, this could have either been Goat or Winchester Mountain. Geologists Frank Calkins and George Otis Smith were definitely atop one of Goat's summits on September 23, 1904, giving the height as 6300 ft, and referring to the Swamp Creek Glacier just S of West Twin Lake.[61] Miners referred to the summit above Lone Jack as "Bear."

SOUTHWEST ROUTE: Goat Mountain Trail♦ extends high on the S shoulder of the W peak. Continue on meadowed slopes to this summit or bear NE to the broad saddle between the summits to reach the heather ridge extending to the E peak. This approach is easy but long, involving an elevation gain of 4400 ft.

NORTHWEST ROUTE: Follow Twin Lakes Road (see Mt. Baker Hwy♦) ½ mi. beyond the Tomyhoi Lake trailhead; here a faint mining spur descends to Swamp Creek. Hike close to the creek bank to reach the basin NW of Goat (some brush and high water in the gorge but travel is not difficult). Ascend gentle glacier and snow slopes to the main saddle between the peaks.

Variations: From the same basin a diagonal snow/icefield on the upper NW face of the E peak provides a pleasant and moderately steep climb; the snow becomes a narrow and steepening finger at its top, ending the route just W of the summit point.

From the basin it is also possible to ascend to the N ridge; here a direct finish can be made by 200 ft of steep rock climbing (class 4).

Another start to both of these routes can be made directly from Twin Lakes. Hike S over the first knoll, then drop to a saddle; keep high on a traverse of the upper W slope of "Bear" to the N ridge of Goat (moderately steep at times; beware of avalanche danger in early summer). From here one can continue the traverse easily to the diagonal snowfield.

GRANITE MOUNTAIN   6124 ft/1867 m

This is a summit of Chilliwack Batholith, with a long granitic western face closely SE of Mamie Pass. Geologists Smith and Calkins in the summer of 1901 climbed mountains S of their camp near Lone Jack Mine (September 21; Calkins journal 1926, p. 13). They probably climbed "Bear," Goat Mountain, and Granite Mountain, and perhaps also the 6688-ft summit marked "Granite" on current maps: one of the summits described was called "Root."

ROUTE: From Mamie Pass (see Hannegan Pass Trail♦) follow the divide to the 6124-ft summit. A higher peak (7035 ft/2145 m) on a spur between the forks of Silesia Creek is located about 1.2 mi. NE of Mamie Pass; one can probably reach this summit from the connecting ridge.

MT. SEFRIT   7191 ft/2192 m

Sefrit is a craggy fore-peak flanking the upper valley of North Fork Nooksack River, one with a sharp rock summit, the first on Ruth Ridge. Despite its proximity to roads, the mountain is infrequently climbed, the lower flanks being protected by brush as well as a formidable band of cliffs on the N side. All routes are avalanche prone early in the season, and the presence of several false summits can confuse route finding.

Sefrit is on the contact of the Shuksan greenschist and Chilliwack Batholith: the flanks of the mountain are of greenschist while the upper elevations are granodiorite and quartz diorite. The pinnacled summit ridge is badly weathered on the E, but solid on the NW flank. The broad, steep rock wall above the glacier NW of the summit is carved from the batholith. The rocky peaks to the SE, on Ruth Ridge, are lower than Sefrit; the highest of these is Peak 6966, 1 mi. distant.

At first the mountain was called Ruth (for Grover Cleveland's daughter), per the 1913 Forest Service map, but at some time after 1930 this name was transferred to the peak near Hannegan Pass. The present name is for Frank I. Sefrit, Bellingham civic leader.

The first ascent may not have been done prior to early summer, 1930, when Jim Irving and Brick Spouse made the ascent, probably from the NW, taking a glacier, snow and ridge route. References: *B.C.M.*, July 1930, June 1932, July 1940, July 1954, August 1961, August 1968.

SOUTHEAST RIDGE: Follow Hannegan Pass Trail◆ 1.5 mi. to where a prominent couloir, snow-filled until late summer, can be seen on the S side of Ruth Creek. This couloir provides a direct route through the lower cliffs to the broad glacierized snow basin 2000 ft higher. Take care crossing the creek: in early season avalanched snow may simplify the crossing. Some parties have climbed mossy slabs and brush right of the stream through cliff bands in the bowl. The best access to the Southeast Ridge is to bear slightly left from the upper snowfield, but the ridge climbing can be reduced by bearing rightward and climbing steep snow to the crest. The shattered crest is followed to the summit (generally best to keep slightly on opposite side). The narrow ridge is mainly an exposed scramble, but a few moves are class 4. Time: 5 hours. Note: The descent can offer good glissading in late spring and early summer.

WEST ROUTE: At about 1 mi. up the North Fork Nooksack Road (from Hannegan Road fork; see Mt. Baker Hwy◆) ascend a forest slope to a broad heather belt; keeping left will avoid lower gullies and slide alder, then ascend rightward to below upper craggy area. Ascend a gully (may be snow-filled) to the ridge crest, which is taken to the summit. The nearby NW pinnacle, which is solid rock, can be reached as a minor objective (climbed 1930).

SEFRIT (NORTHWEST) GLACIER: This glacier is an elongate NW-SE trending body of ice flanked by the steep rock wall of the NW ridge, and reaches to a terminus at about 5000 ft. The 1930 party likely climbed the glacier to near its head, then a flanking high slope and couloir to reach the NW ridge near the summit. The E face of the summit

pyramid was first climbed by Steve Erickson and George Mustoe on June 3, 1972.

Leave Hannegan Road◆ just before a large avalanche scar at 4.3 mi. from Mt. Baker Hwy◆. Bushwhack to Ruth Creek, then cross on logs to reach the conspicuous slide fan on Sefrit's lower N slope. Ascend the fan slope to gain a steep couloir (snow until late), which is followed 2000 ft to the glacier. Ascend the gradual slopes 1500 ft to the col (est. 6700 ft+) E of the summit pyramid. Continue upward along a snow arete to reach the foot of the pyramid's E face; the face tapers down in height to the SE and is intersected by heather ledges. Climb four to six pitches of rock, the exact route being determined by where the moat beneath the face can be crossed. Class 5 (moderate) with some class 4 at top. Time: 7 hours. Reference: *Mountaineer*, 1972, p. 86. Note: The route start is very brushy after mid-June.

Variation: Instead of climbing the rock pyramid's face, continue a traversing ascent on snow to the upper Southeast Ridge; this route has not been verified, but appears feasible. The alternative, keeping N of the summit pyramid by taking the steep glacier and snow couloir, may have been the route of parties in 1930 and 1932, for they describe the long and pinnacled summit ridge and long glissades.

Variation: The glacier/snow col can be reached from the ½-mi. point of the trail by ascending cliffs, gullies, and steep snow on the NE face of the mountain.

RUTH MOUNTAIN   7106 ft/2166 m

Ruth is a broad pyramidal mass located 3.7 mi. NE of Mt. Shuksan at the head of North Fork Nooksack River, Ruth Creek, and the upper Chilliwack River. The scenic glacier on the N slope, with its uniquely triangular shape, is 2.3 km wide, and extends downward to 6000 ft. Tertiary Hannegan volcanics form Ruth Mountain. The old granodiorite topography was buried beneath volcanics in Pliocene time. Henry Custer of the first Boundary Survey called the mountain by its Indian name, "Nu qu oi chum." The name Ruth is for Ruth Cleveland, daughter of President Grover Cleveland, but there is a question of impropriety in its application: the name was definitely meant for the first peak of Ruth Ridge (now Mt. Sefrit), then later applied to the higher ice-clad summit at the head of Ruth Creek.[62]

The mountain was prospected in 1896, but it is not known if an ascent was made; the first written material on a climb was related to the Mountaineer outing of 1916. The first ski ascent was done by Calder Bressler and Ray Clough in the late 1930s. References: *Mountaineer*, 1916, p. 13; *Mazama* 6 (1920): 21-23.

ROUTE: For approach see Hannegan Pass Trail◆. Above heather slopes E of Hannegan Pass a path leads E and S from beyond a pond, bearing around the cliffs of a shoulder. A traverse S leads to a ridge, which is taken to the glacier on the

RUTH MOUNTAIN labels: MT. BLUM, ICY PEAK, 7060, CLOUDCAP PEAK, SPILLWAY GLACIER, RUTH GLACIER, to Hannegan Pass, Nooksack cirque

RUTH MOUNTAIN and ICY PEAK
AUSTIN POST, U.S. GEOLOGICAL SURVEY

N slope (one can also bypass the rocky shoulder on the W). The ascent from here is very simple, but it may be necessary to avoid crevasses on the W side of the false summit. Ruth is a good ski climbing objective. The ascent can be combined with that of Icy Peak. Time: 5 hours from road.

MINERAL MOUNTAIN
6781 ft/2067 m

This is a high massif rising between Chilliwack River and the upper Baker River, 3.3 mi. E of Ruth Moun-

tain. The slightly lower S peak (6720 ft+) is 1.1 mi. along the N-S summit ridge. The Baker River is only 1200 ft in altitude at the southern foot of the S peak, and the slabby rock flanks here present very complex terrain, with very steep side streams. On the SW flank (Pass Creek) there are great granitic slab walls. Rock is intrusive of the Chilliwack Batholith. Reference: *Mountaineer,* 1963, p. 87.

ROUTES: See Chilliwack River Trail♦-Mineral Mountain High Route for the western approach.

Another way to the summit is to leave the valley trail at Easy Creek; cross the Chilliwack River and follow a game path and brush along Easy Creek to the pass (4640 ft+) at the valley head. Now ascend W over moderately steep snow and rock to the summit (not technical).

ICY PEAK   est. 7070 ft/2155 m

Icy Peak is a good name for a sprawling, moderate-altitude massif, which is almost ice-covered by four glaciers. The peak is located at the head of North Fork Nooksack River and Pass Creek fork of Baker River, E of Mt. Shuksan, between Ruth Mountain and Cloudcap Peak. Three small and closely spaced rock points emanate from the broad upper level of the peak. Observers agree that the NW peak is highest, although the map suggests the S peak (listed at 7060 ft/2152 m); there is also a broader E (SE) peak with a glacier broadly sloping on the Pass Creek flank. Exposed rock on the peak is Chilliwack Batholith.

The two glaciers on the upper western slope of Icy Peak are broad and low-gradient, draining on slabs toward the Nooksack cirque (these glaciers are 0.5 km² in area and separated by a minor rock divider). But it is the Spillway Glacier, which flows through a narrow breach in the NE slope of the peak, that is interesting. This is a true icefall glacier, 1 km in length, but with an area of only 0.3 km², and with an unstable flow mode, periodically breaking apart and advancing almost as an ice avalanche.[63] The first ascent of the peak is unknown; when Hermann Ulrichs climbed the peak in 1935 there was a rusty tin on the summit. References: Austin Post and E.R. LaChapelle, *Glacier Ice*, (Seattle: The Mountaineers, 1971) p. 35; *B.C.M.*, February-March 1970; *Mazama* 35 (1953): 14-15.

WEST ROUTE: See Nooksack Trail♦. From the boulder camp near the head of Nooksack cirque ascend gradually SE on morainal debris and snowfields, keeping right of the first cliffs. When close to the cirque walls bear left, keeping below a brush patch, then climb up talus into a fairly steep gully in the upper cliffs (extreme left of cirque in view) that leads to the upper firn and glacier slopes. Follow the ridge divide between glaciers (or keep on firn) to the summit pinnacle (NW peak); a steep gully scramble (class 3) leads to the top from the SW.

NORTH ROUTE (via Ruth Mountain): Climb to the first notch right (NW) of Ruth Mountain's summit (within 500 ft), then cross a W-facing snow slope to the S-facing ridge leading to the Ruth-Icy saddle. A gully, scree, and open rock lead to the saddle area at about 5800 ft. Climb the gradual glacier on Icy's NW slope. Bear to the W of the true summit, to reach rock on its final SW side. Time: 3 hours from Ruth.

OTHER ROUTES: The Spillway Glacier was climbed via a very circuitous approach by Grant and Tim Benedict, and Gary Jones July 30, 1972, crossing E to the glacier from the Icy-Ruth saddle. Many crevasse jumps were made, and an ice cliff was climbed; the jumble of seracs make this a potentially dangerous climb. Easier glacier travel at the upper end led to the small col between the E and S summits. (*Mountaineer*, 1972, p. 85).

A climb was made on the E peak by Elfrieda Pigou in 1958. The western face of the S peak was climbed August 1973 by Lynn Householder, Richard Rossiter, and Gary Thompson (two leads of loose rock, 5.2; *Mountaineer*, 1974, p. 64). The NE side of the true (NW) summit was climbed by Al Errington and Ray Smutek on August 22, 1970 (200 ft of moderately loose rock).

MT. SHUKSAN   9127 ft/2782 m

Mt. Shuksan epitomizes the jagged alpine peak like no other massif in the North Cascades. Here is something of the character of the Swiss Weisshorn, uniquely set in Western Washington, rising in a spearhead of dark-hued rock, (greenschist) carved by elements into deep cirques and ragged aretes, adorned with chaotic hanging glaciers, frosted and tiered with snow plaques and ice patches.

Shuksan has no equal in the range when one considers the structural beauty of its four major faces and five ridges, and the variety of routes they provide. There is no other sample in the American West of a peak with great icefall glaciers derived from a high plateau, and in the Pacific Northwest it is the only non-volcanic peak whose summit exceeds timberline by more than 3000 ft. Shuksan's satellite bastions — Nooksack Tower, Jagged Ridge, and Cloudcap Peak — also form a most impressive alpine retinue.

The distortion of Shuksan by a foreshortening effect increases as one comes close to the mountain's walls on the N, for here it rises 7700 ft in just 3 mi. from the valley of North Fork Nooksack River. The oft-seen NW face is its showpiece, known for the elegance and beauty of crevassed, steep glaciers and the great surmounting summit rock pyramid. While the ice-clad, fluted faces and cirques of Shuksan facing from E to N to W, high above their low valley footings give the mountain an immediate distinction of steepness and ferocity from the human standpoint, it is the well defined aretes — the SE (Jagged Ridge), the SW (Curtis-Sulphide), the NW (Shuksan Arm), and the NE (Nooksack Ridge) — which rise as short subsidiary chains to the summit pyramid or its ice plateau, that seal Shuksan's final stamp of magnificence. Perched above two cascading glaciers in the midst of two of these gigantic random forms of great beauty and mystery rises the nearly perpendicular shaft of Nooksack Tower, almost seeming to defy the laws of gravity. The mass of these geometric complexities consist of submarine basalt flows metamorphosed to greenstone. This rock, called greenschist, is displayed on Shuksan and aretes such as Jagged Ridge, but below the Sulphide Glacier exposed granodiorite is visible. The greenschist on Nooksack Tower has been affected by contact metamorphism of the Chilliwack Batholith.

Sometimes popular interest has a way of underlying the really outstanding mountains, and here the prestige of Mt. Shuksan is derived as much from its aesthetic qualities as its immensity. Shuksan deserves the attention it has received, for it has emerged as a mountain that captures the imagination of both the climbing and sightseeing public. Possibly the mystique of the mountain is partially due to its invisibility to the tourist from the classic view until Heather Meadows is reached (although Shuksan can be seen from Alderbrook to White Rock on the U.S.-Canada border). Despite the multiplicity of the classic image, Shuksan periodically appears displayed backwards on calendars and recently so on the cover of a paperback book.

Shuksan's summit is notable as a large three-sided rock pyramid standing 500 ft to 1200 ft above four encircling glaciers. The most visible of these, the Hanging Glacier, flanks the N shoulder on its W, and from 8400 ft under the steep summit wall plunges to ice cliffs at various intermediate levels. Joining it on the W is the more moderate White Salmon Glacier, which continues as the NE ice flank of Shuksan Arm.

A comparatively low intermediate ridge below the great N shoulder of the mountain divides the Price and White Salmon basins into two nearly parallel halves. While the eastern half of this basin is filled by Price Glacier and associated ice remnants, the western basin falls almost without a break from the base of the summit pyramid and northern flank of Shuksan Arm, the 3-mi. W-NW-trending barrier that divides White Salmon Creek from Shuksan Creek, drainages that find their way to Puget Sound in quite opposite routes.

The Price Glacier is the steepest and most tumbled of those on the mountain.[64] This very crevassed glacier discharges as an icefall of great height into the main catchment basin on the NE flank of Shuksan. Here formidable Nooksack Tower and Nooksack Ridge form the southern barrier of the glacier, and keep a high-level profile between the summit ice

plateau and the ice plunging toward Price Lake. The southern wall of Nooksack Ridge is in opposition to the spine of Jagged Ridge, which descends E-SE for over 2 mi. in a slight curve from the summit ice plateau to Cloudcap Peak, then continues in outline to Icy Peak. Between these great rock ramparts is the spectacular Nooksack Glacier and its magnificent wide arcuate cirque of rock walls, ice and denuded slab. When members of the Mountaineer outing in 1916 saw the cirque from Ruth Mountain, their words reflected amazement: "The great glacier in the center is made up of myriads of shapeless ice masses clinging in unaccountable fashion to their rock bed. No approach to the mountain seems possible on this side."[65] The 2.6-mi. (4.2 km)-wide glacier begins from a narrow col (8000 ft+) on the summit icefield, then descends in an ice chute to the great cirque where crevassed ice fans on bedrock slab. An interesting geologic observation is that above the glacier (on Jagged Ridge and Cloudcap Peak) the rock is greenschist while below the ice level is exposed granodiorite. Below the lowest rock cliff is a segment of avalanched residual ice, mantled by a broad band of ablation drift. A short distance beyond the margin of the glacier are fresh, bouldery, unstable, horseshoe-shaped moraines which indicate greater ice volume in the recent past. Here in the upper valley of North Fork Nooksack River the dynamic nature of the alpine environment is demonstrated in active erosive forces of streams and glaciers, climate, and the ongoing processes of plant colonization and succession.[66]

On the broad southern flank of Shuksan the combined Sulphide-Crystal Glacier system, the mountain's largest ice mass (5.5 km^2) is a high firn shelf which discharges gradually into the broad cirque of Sulphide Lake and Creek, where portions of these glaciers lie below the regional snowline (to 1130 m). Downwasting has exposed bedrock at ice margins and has separated the glaciers into distinct parts. Separating the Sulphide Glacier from Shuksan Creek, a lengthy divide trends first SW from the summit pyramid, then S, presenting a rock skyline. This divide crowns Shuksan's extensive western face, which contains the two-section Curtis Glacier, forming a curious pattern between its upper connection with the Sulphide Glacier to ice-cliff termination at the head of Shuksan Creek. Various smaller ice sections are joined to the major glaciers, and others exist as individual patches no longer connected.

The earliest appearance of the mountain's name in print is in the journal of Henry Custer, at the time he was reconnaissance leader for the North West Boundary Survey in 1859, and on Custer's manuscript map which identifies "Tsuskan" well E of Mt. Baker.[67] The sound of avalanches apparently inspired the name; pioneer miner R.S. Lambert related that Shuksan was "Roaring Mountain" to the Nooksack Indians.

Shuksan is one of the finest mountaineering objectives in the North Cascades and its reputation as a compound of alpine problems is certainly deserved; a wide variety of challenges can be encountered on this quite complex mountain. The climber has the choice of rock walls, moderate firnfields, steep ice, and easy scrambling. Despite a sometimes-forbidding appearance, Shuksan has yielded 14 routes, numerous variations, and impressive subsidiary climbs, including some directly up dangerous ice cliffs.

To the mountaineers who first endeavored to reach the mountain and had the choice of five glacier basins from which to commence their attempts, it was immediately apparent that the southern glacier provided one easy gradient to the sharp, pyramidal summit. The mountain's formations easily show why first the Sulphide Glacier, and later the Curtis and White Salmon glaciers were used to reach the summit, and also explain the delay in finding what became the most efficient route to the summit.

Whether or not Joe Morovits climbed Shuksan about 1897, a date accepted by pioneer mountaineer Claude Rusk, is debatable: at all events, it did not amount to an effective record. We may fairly credit Morovits with pre-1900 exploration high on the S slope, but there is no indication that he climbed to the top of the summit pyramid.[68] The accepted first climb was made by Asahel Curtis and W. Montelius Price on September 7, 1906. The climbers, both of whom are now commemorated by mountain nomenclature, first tried a route via Shuksan Arm, then finally gained Sulphide Glacier via the far southwestern face.

The complexity of most of Shuksan's routes requires some navigational skills, as demonstrated by the discovery of Fisher Chimneys in 1927 by Clarence A. Fisher and Dr. E.P. Spearin. The access and configuration of Shuksan Arm easily explains the protracted history of the Lake Ann basin and upper Shuksan Creek as a way to the summit, and also various early failures to reach the peak more directly. The history differs from that of the Nooksack and Price Glacier cirques. After the latter facades were appraised as uninviting in 1916, 24 years elapsed before an attempt here was made in 1940. The era of modern climbing began in 1939, when the ascent of the Hanging Glacier was made by Andy Hennig and Otto Trott, both with European experience, a bold effort that did not spur imitators for some years. Until then climbers were restrained by the idea that a successful route to the summit must be one that could be descended again the same day. But only five years after the first party entered Nooksack cirque, the headwall of Price Glacier was climbed, followed by the climb of Nooksack Tower.

The climbing history of Shuksan is in marked contrast with that of Mt. Baker, its western neighbor; the difference is probably due to the visibility of the latter from the Puget Sound Trough, and the gradual obvious nature of its glacier climbing slopes. One is tempted to preserve the myth that Shuksan is an enormous climb, when in reality a competent party should have no trouble climbing most of the routes, and returning to camp, well within one day. But the dangers of exposure well above timberline were demonstrated as early as 1929 when two climbers were killed by a severe summer snowstorm, and the serious accident in 1940 on the N face of the summit pyramid.

References: *Mazama* 3, no. 1 (1907): 27-30; vol. 6 (1920): 17-20; vol. 12 (1930): 21-28; vol. 35 (1953): 7-11, 17; *Mountaineer*, 1907, p. 52; 1916, pp. 7-25; 1928, pp. 25-28; 1955, pp. 52-54; *Overland Monthly*, n.s. 50 (August 1907): 110-118; *B.C.M.*, August, 1927; October 1928; *Summit*, December 1960, pp. 14-17; January-February 1963, pp. 19, 22-25 (glaciers); *Challenge of the North Casacdes*, pp. 99-112.

FISHER CHIMNEYS: This route, for many years established as the traditional way up Mt. Shuksan, climbs a series of complex gullies, rock chimneys, ramps and ledges on the S flank of Shuksan Arm, then crosses to the upper edge of White Salmon Glacier before continuing to Upper Curtis Glacier, then to the Sulphide Glacier. It is a clever and tortuous route, not technically difficult, yet involving stimulating route finding. Clarence A. (Happy) Fisher had done explorations near the Curtis and Hanging glaciers prior to his discovery of the system of chimneys above Lower Curtis Glacier. After a final reconnaissance with Dr. Emmons Spearin, the complete ascent was made on July 3, 1927 with Esther Buswell, Paul Hugdahl, Lars Loveseth, Winnie Spieseke, and Harriet Taylor.

From Lake Ann♦ follow the trail eastward est. 1½ mi. to the first large rockslide (est. 5200 ft); this is near the trail's high point just past a small gorge, several hundred yards before reaching Lower Curtis Glacier. Continue on the same level immediately below the rock cliff (obvious tread), then where cliffs end into scree and a small right-slanting draw ascend about 300 ft to a grassy, rocky knoll (this is part of a broad meadowed bench with talus above; cliffs drop to the

RUTH MTN.   ICY PEAK   CLOUDCAP PEAK

summit

CRYSTAL GLACIER

UPPER CURTIS GLACIER

SULPHIDE GLACIER

HANGING GLACIER

Southwest Face

Winnie's Slide

ice fall

1962

second travesrse

slab bypass

first traverse

1951

1962

Fisher Chimneys

Shuksan Arm

1963

1907

LOWER CURTIS GLACIER

o Lake Ann

trail

MT. SHUKSAN from west
U.S. FOREST SERVICE

glacier beneath). Bear E along the talus slope to the bottom of the deepest gully, which is the beginning of Fisher Chimneys. Note: On this early portion of the route it is important to keep right and get above the glacier cliffs, then generally continue on a rightward tack.

At the end of the long traverse the route passes near a giant boulder as one begins the steep rightward gully-chimney ascent of about 300 ft through broken cliffs. Turn right again on a slanting grassy ramp into the next gully; follow a meager path worn into succeeding gullies to the crest of Shuksan Arm (est. 6720 ft). Note: About the only tricky spot in the chimneys is where early climbers made a crawl (Fat Man's Misery) under a wall; once around this spot, the route is a scramble to the top of the Arm. Now diagonal E on firn of the upper edge of White Salmon Glacier (keep just below ridgetop but above a rock outcrop). Climb directly to

55

Scree

FISHER CHIMNEYS

the steepest portion of Winnie's Slide, which after one pitch of 40 degrees flattens to the crossing of a narrow rock rib (end of Arm) to the western edge of Upper Curtis Glacier. Climb right on the glacier, keeping left of the steep crevasse field, as necessary, toward the summit pyramid (to about 7350 ft), then bear sharply S on a slight glacier descent beneath the upper rock wall for about ¼ mi. At the base of the wind cirque (est. 6950 ft) climb up and left in a half circle on the broad and moderately steep passage of Hells Highway to the edge of Sulphide Glacier (7600 ft+). Travel NE across the firn to near its highest point at the center of the summit rock pyramid, which is 600 ft high here (the highest snowpatch indents the pyramid). Here are a series of steep parallel rock gullies which lead to the summit (class 3). Some climbers prefer a gully near the SW side of the pyramid, but the more central one is standard. Note: Beware of party-inflicted rockfall; the summit slabs dip downward and are precarious when wet. There are numerous variations. Time: 6 hours from Lake Ann.

Descent: Allow 4 hours. In Fisher Chimneys beware of getting close (left) near cliffs that drop to the lower glacier.

Variation: Southeast corner of summit pyramid: A more sporting, but not difficult alternative on the summit section is to climb the corner-ridge which begins at the far right corner of the glacier edge; the pyramid here toes down to the Crystal Glacier. This class 3-4 variation avoids typical gully rockfall.

Variation: Hour Glass Couloir: This is a more direct way

through the Upper Curtis-Sulphide Glacier rockwall, closely SW of the summit pyramid. This variation may have first been done by Clarence A. Fisher and party in the late 1920s. The 400-ft couloir can save time for a small, fast party under good conditions, but has the disadvantages of a bergschrund crossing, greater difficulty and loose rock not experienced on Hells Highway; rockfall danger can be minimized by keeping on rock just right of the couloir. The general opinion is that the variation seldom has the advantage of shortness.

SUMMIT PYRAMID ROUTES

NORTHWEST FACE-LABOR DAY ROUTE: This route is W of the 1939 route and E of the Hour Glass. First ascent by Michel Castro, Les and Monique MacDonald on Labor Day, 1956. At 300 ft N of the Hour Glass climb a clean, continuous crack for 100 ft, turning the slightly overhanging portion near its top by a lieback. Traverse 30 ft right and upward into a wide chimney. At its top, traverse a heather ledge leftward into the original crack (above an overhanging portion). Climb 40 ft of good rock to a left-slanting overhanging flake; this leads to a steep wall. Climb a jam crack 15 ft to where it broadens; ascend to the ridge on the left-hand wall. The hardest portion of the route is near the exit on the summit ridge. Grade VI British (hard class 5); used four pitons. Rock is sound.

THE DIRITISSIMO: This route is near the 1939 completion on the summit pyramid, and is probably partly the same; the route was reported by Les MacDonald and Gerard McGill in 1960, stating the rock was mostly a steep jumble, with some looseness.

EASTERN ROUTE: First ascent by Keith Apps, John Boylan, Les and Monique MacDonald, and Jack Stewart in 1966. The route is largely a steep jumble, with the bergschrund being the most difficult portion; the finish is at the notch on the NE ridge of the summit pyramid. Grade IV British.

Variation (White Salmon Glacier): This route is one of the shortest to the summit, but the advantage is gained only when the valley slope is snow-covered; the route has been done on skis. The first ascent was made by Dorothy E. Pilley, I.A. Richards, and Benton Thompson on September 9, 1926. From the road spur into White Salmon Creek valley (est. 3200 ft) a path descends gradually through forest; follow the right side of the creek (some brush) about 1½ mi. Near the valley head bear left to the lower fan of the glacier, then right on firn to a moraine campsite (est. 4800 ft). The route up the glacier to Winnie's Slide is generally straightforward, the line between crevasses being quite obvious. Generally it is best to keep to the right side of the glacier, bypassing small rock cliffs (lower angle and no avalanche hazard from the NW face). It should be pointed out that in winter and spring this entire area can be in an avalanche zone, and there is annually evidence of snow debris in the upper valley. References: Dorothy Pilley, *Climbing Days* (London, 1935), p. 299; *B.C.M.*, June 1962 (ski).

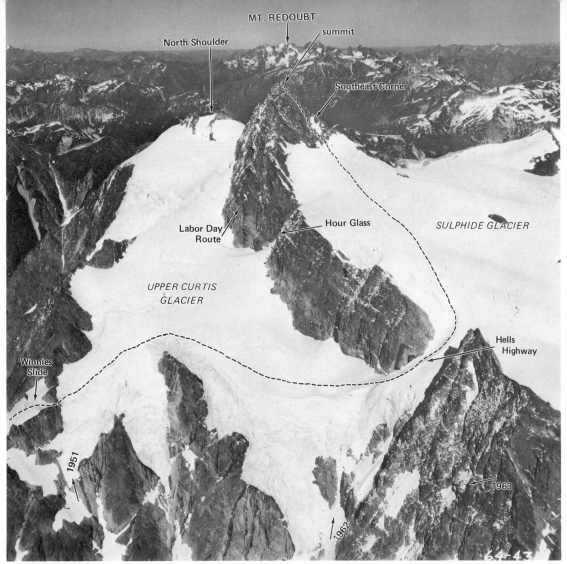

MT. SHUKSAN *from west*

Variation (Lower Curtis Glacier): By Dave Collins, Donald (Claunch) Gordon, and Maury Muzzy on September 23, 1951. From the N (left) flank of Lower Curtis Glacier climb a rocky trough through the cliff NE to the westernmost ice tongue of the upper glacier. The route consists of alternating rock ribs in a snow gully (class 3-4); a sheet of very steep blue ice got the original party over the icefall near the top of the variation. This is a long and more arduous route than the Fisher Chimneys; watch for falling debris.

Variation (Shuksan Arm): By Paul and Ralph Engburg, Clarence A. Fisher, Fairman B. Lee, and Morgan Van Winkle on July 4, 1926 (seventh ascent of Shuksan). The route follows near the crest of the Arm, obviously a scenic but very irregular route (see Shuksan Arm Route◆). There is some possibility that this party climbed the Hour Glass, for they reported an ice chute and snow roof on the ascent.

NORTHWEST RIB: This is the narrow rock spur which separates White Salmon and Hanging glaciers; the route crosses the 1939 ascent line. First ascent by Pat Cruver and Dave Davis in July 1974. Use the White Salmon approach (see Fisher Chimneys). The original party kept mostly on the rib's crest, but many variations are possible. The climb joined the Northwest Face Route at the summit pyramid and completed by the 1939 finish.

MT. SHUKSAN from north
AUSTIN POST, U.S. GEOLOGICAL SURVEY

Grade III; class 5.7 (one pitch); the climb is mostly class 4 easy class 5 on sound rock. Reference: *Mountaineer,* 1974, p. 64.

HANGING GLACIER (Northwest Face): This broad rock, ice, and snow face, seen directly from Heather Meadows, was the scene of the first technical alpine route on Mt. Shuksan. Its ascent was made by Andy Henning and Otto Trott on September 3 and 4, 1939.

The original route traversed gullies and ribs from Shuksan Arm, crossed the tongue of the White Salmon Glacier, then reached the rock at the right side of the main tongue of Hanging Glacier (for the best approach see Fisher Chimneys route-White Salmon Glacier variation; one can camp just below and W of White Salmon Glacier). Here, between the lowest rock wall on this flank and the Hanging Glacier, ascend to a "greenish" bench that has a right to left trend, then traverse rock toward the glacier tongue. Then ascend the glacier: ice screws may be needed on slopes that may be very steep for short distances. The original party made a bivouac on the rock below the summit pyramid, then entered its northern rock wall at a marked yellow area; they climbed to the right side of a deep couloir, later climbing in it or on its left side. About midway on the summit pyramid leave the couloir and climb slightly right. Grade III or IV; take crampons, rock and ice protection. Time: 6-10 hours. References: *Mountaineer,* 1939, p. 51; *Seattle Times,* August 7, 1940 (serious accident on N face of summit pyramid).

Variation: By Donald Gordon and Layton Kor, September 1 and 2, 1960, via the dihedral beneath the glacier tongue (subject to stonefall and hard to protect during some 500 ft of steep slabby rock; class 4 and 5).

HANGING GLACIER ICE CLIFF: This route begins at the toe of the easterly protrusion of Hanging Glacier and ascends the rock and ice wall directly to the glacier above. The cliff at the glacier front creates an unstable, hazardous situation; its risks should be understood. First ascent by Donald A. Anderson and Greg Markov about July 15, 1972.

Approach as per Hanging Glacier route. Climb several hundred ft of rock slabs (from class 3 to easy but unbelayable class 5) to the ice toe at the base of the wall. Climb two leads of 45 degrees up and right along a ramp that traverses the face. Climb several short leads, then steep seracs which hang on the upper face (aid screws used on a bulge); this leads to a serac enclosure surrounded by a smooth crevasse wall (in 1972 two large crevasses ran the entire glacier width). Find ice chimneys, bridge, or flake to gain upper glacier access. From here a variety of lines of varying difficulty can be followed. The original route worked near the glacier center, bearing right around a steep wall and then up a moderate 40-degree ice slope before exiting onto the N shoulder (North Face). Grade III. Reference: *Mountaineer,* 1972, pp. 84-85.

NORTHWEST ARETE: This crest stands out distinctly from the remainder of the Northwest Face; it borders the W side of the Northwest Couloir and terminates on Hanging Glacier. First ascent by Hans Baer and Alex Bertulis in October 1965.

Reach the base of the arete via the White Salmon approach. Traverse across the lower slopes of the Northwest Couloir and reach the arete. Keep on the crest: most of the climbing is easy class 4, but some upper portions involve some class 5 maneuvers. On the original climb the upper glacier was crossed to the N face of the summit pyramid; the latter climb involved continuous climbing rated class 5.3 to 5.6. Grade III; class 5.6; rock is excellent. Take 15 items of protection up to 1 inch, and crampons. Time: 8 hours camp to summit.

NORTHWEST COULOIR: This snow and ice couloir, E of Hanging Glacier and the Northwest Arete, averages 40 degrees in steepness for over 2000 ft. It extends from about the lower eastern residual portion of the glacier to the upper part of the arete near the ice beneath the summit pyramid. First ascent by Ed Cooper and Robert Working on July 20, 1957.

Approach as per North Face route, then ascend through the bottleneck of the prominent couloir to where it splits. The original party took the right slope here to the edge of the arete, then ascended rock (class 3 and 4) until it was feasible to cross to the left edge of the glacier (the route turned the skyline to go between rock and glacier). A 150-ft exposed ice cliff led to the upper glacier. Grade II or III; take crampons. Note: There can be rockfall danger in the couloir. The schrund where the couloir narrows is steep and may have to be turned on rock to the left. Reference: *Mountaineer,* 1958, pp. 100-101.

NORTH FACE: This is a splendid, scenic and only moderately technical route on firn and ice leading to the summit ice plateau. The first ascent was made by Rex Fassett, Elsa Hanft, and Benton Thompson in August 1927.[69] Not knowing of the ascent, Fred Beckey and Bob Craig made the ascent in September 1947, and completed the climb via the E face of the summit rock pyramid; the first winter ascent (to N shoulder) was done by Bruce Blume and Dave Seman on December 23, 1975.

An approach can be made as per White Salmon Glacier cirque (see Fisher Chimney route), but it is easier travel to descend directly to the creek from the road end, then ascend right through deep timber to more open slopes of the N ridge; possible bivouac above timberline on the divide E of the upper valley (snowmelt water about 5500 ft). Make a leftward climbing traverse on the hanging glacier above Price Lake, and in about 500 ft climb rightward on firn or ice to reach the crest of the face through an ice finger. (This places one above the first rock barrier.) Ascend steeply to the shoulder NE of the summit pyramid, then traverse the ice plateau to the E face of the summit; ascend the rock directly (class 4) or traverse around to the S side normal completion. Grade II or III; take crampons. Time: 6 hours from White Salmon divide. References: *Mountaineer,* 1947, p. 52; 1959, pp. 105-106; *A.A.J.,* 1948, p. 102; *B.C.M.,* March 1975.

Variation: One can continue traversing nearly to the far upper end of the hanging glacier, then climb ice patches through rock breaks near the NE rib to the shoulder.

NORTH RIB: This rib is a distinct feature on Mt. Shuksan between the North Face and Price Glacier (rib actually faces NE), and leading to the N shoulder of the summit. First ascent by Dan Davis, Jerry Feucht, John Holland, and Steve Marts on August 18, 1963; a bivouac was made about 500 ft below the N shoulder.

Reach the rib as per the North Face route; after traversing E across the hanging glacier route, cross a rock outcrop, passing about 200 ft below a prominent rock pinnacle. Then angle left on a portion of the Price Glacier to the bottom right side of the North Rib. Climb and bear left to the rib

BACON PEAK   MT. WATSON

MT. SHUKSAN

Baker
Lake

JAGGED
RIDGE

Hells Highway

North Rib

Winnies Slide

PRICE
GLACIER

HANGING
GLACIER

1939

North
Face

Northwest
Couloir

△ camp

White Salmon
Creek

MT. SHUKSAN from north
U.S. FOREST SERVICE

crest, then climb rock and snow to the base of a gendarme (pass it on left). Above its notch climb right of the steep rib to the obvious snow crest: this is followed by mixed climbing (on the crest) to the N shoulder, passing gendarmes en route on their right. The original party climbed the NE ridge of the summit pyramid. Grade III; class 3 and 4 — some poor rock and rockfall; take crampons and ice screws. Time: minimum 6 hours from White Salmon divide. References: *Mountaineer,* 1963, p. 132; *A.A.J.,* 1964, p. 174; *B.C.M.,* March 1975.

PRICE GLACIER: This glacier and its magnificent ice cascades are described in the introduction to Mt. Shuksan. First ascent by Fred Beckey, Bill Granston, and Jack Schwabland on September 9, 1945 on a traverse of the mountain.

For approach see Price Lake Route♦. An easy continuation leads SE near the subalpine divide to rock slabs at the

glacier's eastern edge (camp spots). Ascend the left side of the glacier below the bergschrund of Nooksack Tower. The top of the long rock rib (6600 ft) dividing the E and main portions of the glacier provides a narrow ice entry to the steep, crevassed section of the upper ice cirque. The original party crossed onto the middle here, angled left above a rock island, then back right through a corridor above the upper ice cliffs; some parties have first ascended to about 7800 ft before making an oblique traverse. A bergschrund series usually blocks direct access to the final 55-degree ice chute: either ascend the chute or climb along the right rock wall (class 5); one may find a cornice beneath the ice plateau. Complete the summit pyramid by the E face or SE ridge, or the normal S side. Grade III or IV. Time: 8-10 hours from timberline. References: *Mountaineer,* 1946, p. 45; *A.A.J.,* 1946, pp. 46-47; 1978, p. 523; *Challenge of the North Cascades,* pp. 104-108; Steve Roper and Allen Steck, *Fifty Classic*

Labels on image: JDCAP PEAK · JAGGED RIDGE · NOOKSACK TOWER · summit pyramid · PRICE GLACIER · North Face · NOOKSACK GLACIER · Price Lake · sack ue

MT. SHUKSAN — eastern faces
PHILIP LEATHERMAN

Climbs of North America, San Francisco, 1979, pp. 119-22.

   Variation (Northeast Chute): This is a 40-degree firn chute which bears from the upper glacier to near the top of the N shoulder; first climbed by Don Russell, Reed Tindall, Don Williamson, and one other in 1971. This 500-ft variation is useful when crevasses block the final portion of the normal route. The most difficult part may be crossing steep avalanche flutings (snow flukes recommended).

NOOKSACK RIDGE: This is the serrate ridge between Nooksack Tower and the summit ice shoulder. The probable first ascent was made by Fred Beckey and Ronald Niccoli on August 7, 1960. After a rappelling descent of Nooksack Tower, a traverse of this ridge was also made in early August 1960, by Les MacDonald and Gerard McGill. Begin as per Price Glacier route, then climb 2000 ft of moderately steep firn and ice fingers to the notch W of the Tower (varying steepness and crevasses). Then climb along the rickety ridge crest (class 4); the perspective here is sensational, but the rock quality is inferior. Grade III. Time: 9 hours from timberline to summit. References: *A.A.J.,* 1961, pp. 364-65; *Mountaineer,* 1961, p. 99.

NOOKSACK GLACIER: This glacier (East Nooksack Glacier on maps) increased greatly in the late 1940s and early 1950s. An active ice tongue flowed over the cirque threshold nearly to the valley floor. Because the lower fringe of the glacier is active and thin, there tends to be much breakup of ice by midsummer. Beware of unstable seracs and slabs of ice here. Early season climbs are recommended.

   The original climbing party had to cut through the climax cornice, and because of the late hour and poor visibility, ended the route on the summit ice plateau. What was intended to be only a scouting mission succeeded in establishing the new route. First ascent by Helmy Beckey and Lyman Boyer on May 31, 1941.

   From the head of Nooksack cirque ascend steep rock slabs southward 500 ft or more to the main body of the glacier;

MT. BAKER

Landes Cleaver   Coleman Pinnacle

RAINBOW GLACIER

Ptarmigan Ridge

MT. SHUKSAN
Summit Pyramid

SULPHIDE
GLACIER

North Shoulder

CRYSTAL GLACIER

Northeast Chute

Nooksack Ridge

Nooksack Tower

PRICE GLACIER

NOOKSACK GLACIER

MT. SHUKSAN — summit area from east
U.S. FOREST SERVICE

generally the ascent is best done on the left (E) fringe of ice. Make a long climb toward the right side of the glacier through the crevassed areas to meet the steep final ice chute leading to the summit plateau (may have to keep close to wall of Jagged Ridge for a distance). This 500-ft chute is 55 degrees at the top; there are possible bergschrund problems at the base and usually a cornice at the top; the schrund pattern has been such that it is most feasible to turn lower crack on right and then make exposed up and left traverse to bypass the key cliff and final schrund. Beware of falling ice and avalanches here. The summit pyramid is about 0.6 mi. westward. Bear rightward on upslope to the E face of the pyramid (across Crystal Glacier) to foot of rock, then contour left to SE corner (ridge) to bypass ice cliff breakup separating the Crystal from the Sulphide. Time: 8-10 hours. References: *Mountaineer*, 1941, pp. 32-33; *A.A.J.*, 1959, pp. 306-7; *Challenge of the North Cascades*, pp. 108-10.

SULPHIDE GLACIER: This is the least technical, and now perhaps the fastest route to the summit; it is the ideal route for a winter or spring ski ascent. Drive via Shuksan

MT. SHUKSAN from south
U.S. FOREST SERVICE

AMERICAN BORDER PEAK

MT. SHUKSAN

Nooksack Tower

to
Hells
Highway

SULPHIDE GLACIER

CRYSTAL GLACIER

Sulphide Lake

Lake Road (see Baker Lake Hwy♦). In 500 yards make the first right fork and then switchback 3 mi. to a junction; take right fork D into Shannon Creek drainage and drive about 1.5 mi. in the E fork drainage (road impassible). Hike the road about 1 mi., then find Shannon Ridge Trail No. 742 in old clearcut. Hike into thick timber (NW) to the ridge top at about 4600 ft.; then follow the flat wooded crest about 1 mi. (meadow campsites). The N end of the ridge joins a cliffy slope on the E below a ridge col. Climb the steepish bare slope NE to this col; cross it and contour NNE on a talus shelf between two cliff bands (keep close to base of upper cliff). Beyond the cliff the slope broadens and fans to the low-gradient terminus of Sulphide Glacier. Campsites before glacier; 3-4 hours (route has been cairned). Ascend the latter, which steepens at about 6400 ft. Above this rise, skirt crevasses on the left, as necessary, then aim toward the summit pyramid (see Fisher Chimneys route for detail). Time: 4-5 hours from foot of glacier to summit.

Winter or Spring Variation: When the road is snow covered, from the upper junction, follow the road ¾ mi. to the crossing of Shannon Creek's W fork; keep E of the creek and climb NW to a low saddle (est. 3300 ft) in the timbered ridge, then hike the ridge upslope.

Shuksan Creek Variation: From Shuksan Creek S of Lake Ann♦, a long sloping shelf bears SE, gradually narrowing to a shoulder with small trees near the edge of the Sulphide Glacier (est. 6500 ft).

A variation of this route was done by the Mazama outing in 1920: climb eastward from the creek to Curtis Falls (bench camp), then S on benches and rock to reach the glacier.

SOUTHWEST FACE: This route ascends a rectangular-shaped precipice which rises 1800 ft above Lower Curtis Glacier. The first third is extremely steep rock, clashing with the nearby icefalls and snowpatches to give this flank of Shuksan a wild, sculptured look. First ascent by Dave Beckstead and Donald (Claunch) Gordon on July 29, 1963. This party virtually climbed the initial difficulties without packs for reconnaissance purposes, then with protection pitons in, returned to the climb. Approach via Lake Ann♦.

Begin at the center of the precipice and climb slightly rightward to the perpendicular wall. Then climb left beneath this dark precipice on an exposed traverse. The crux is a delicate slab bypass pitch where the ramp climbs sharply at its terminus under a whitish bullet-shaped rock (smooth rock and difficult). Now ascend a gully for about 150 ft to reach the next rising traverse, which is easier; this ends at the snowpatch on the left end of the wall, about 600 ft up the route. Angle right to a rib near the center of the face (class 3 and 4), then ascend this rib to the top of the face, which leads to the edge of Sulphide Glacier at 7600 ft+. Grade III; class 5 (original used 10 pitons). Time: 10 hours from camp. Reference: *A.A.J.*, 1965, p. 412.

WEST FACE: This route connects the Lower Curtis Glacier with Hells Highway of the Fisher Chimney route. As a climb, the rock is solid with favorable strata dips, but instability of the upper icefall can make this route very

dangerous. First ascent by Mike Forney, Tony Hovey, Don Keller, and Eric Zahn on August 27, 1962. Approach via Lake Ann♦. Move over the lower rocks to the face directly under the center of the upper glacier's ice cliff. Ascend leftward on a ledge to a short vertical wall and then to a good belay (class 4). The route then generally works upward: at about 100 ft below the ice cliff bear right through a stream and up rock to the ice; ascend along the ice base to a corner just above a prominent pinnacle. Several ice pitches lead over the first cliff section; on the original ascent an area of easy but shattered ice led to the final wall, which was climbed to the Upper Curtis Glacier. Grade II or III; take crampons and ice screws. References: *A.A.J.*, 1962, p. 206; *Mountaineer*, 1962, p. 105.

NOOKSACK TOWER   8268 ft/2520 m

This mammoth rock tower is one of the most difficult summits in the Cascade Range; this fact, together with the commitment of time, descent, and varying ice conditions, makes it a serious objective at any time. The geography of the Tower is described in the Mt. Shuksan introduction. First ascent by Fred Beckey and Clifford Schmidtke on July 5, 1946.

Follow the Price Glacier route to the double bergschrund at about 6600 ft at the northern base of the Tower. Cross this steep entry barrier area, then ascend 800 ft up the narrowing 50-degree ice couloir left of the main N buttress. Just below where the couloir narrows to a thin ice ribbon, climb obliquely right onto the rock, then climb 800 ft along the left side of the corner buttress (class 3). The final 400 ft beneath the summit are steeper and more difficult (class 4 or 5). Grade III; take crampons and some rock protection. Watch for loose rock.

Descent: Can use rock anchors alongside couloir; do not rappel into the E summit notch and descend upper couloir.

Time: 4-6 hours from schrund (original was 5½ hours from timberline). References: *A.A.J.*, 1947, p. 436; *Mountaineer*, 1946, p. 46; *Summit*, April 1961, pp. 16-17.

NORTH FACE: First ascent by Alex Bertulis and Scott Davis on September 2, 1973. The route, while termed a face, is really so narrow laterally that it can also be described as a ridge because there is a distinct corner. The three most prominent features on the face/ridge are two overhanging walls at the start of the ridge and the upper headwall. One begins at the ridge center. Note a good bivouac ledge at 6500 ft exists at head of long narrow rock rib just below the base of the Tower.

From the head of the rock rib climb to the head of the firn slope connecting to the vertical Tower face. Just left of the crest, the first lead starts with a strenuous jam crack and short, narrow chimney. Continue over low-angle slabs rightward several pitches to under the major overhanging (yellow) wall. The next pitch traverses left just under a small overhang and reaches the E flank to the ridge crest. Continue upward, keeping mostly on the crest of the North Ridge/

NOOKSACK TOWER

PHILIP LEATHERMAN

Nooksack Ridge

PRICE GLACIER

1945

North Face

1946

Face, passing small towers until eventually the vertical headwall is reached (about 12 leads from start). To avoid aid climbing on the headwall, traverse up and around to the W side (involving strenuous lieback crack and delicate face climbing) to a semi-hanging belay on a small sloping ledge. The fourteenth pitch starts with a delicate short traverse (5.9) across vertical rock, then continues with a difficult and long reach around the corner. When the headwall is turned proceed directly up to the ridge crest. Another pitch surmounts the last real difficulties by a short, difficult traverse to the left and up; the summit is reached shortly.

Grade IV; class 5.9. There are 16 pitches with about 7 pitches being 5.7 or harder. The climbing is mostly sustained moderately difficult free climbing: because of the effort required, overall exposure, and difficulties of descent, the grade is greater than a typical Yosemite overall rating. The rock is generally solid. Time: 3 days r.t. from road. Reference: *A.A.J.,* 1974, pp. 55-57.

JAGGED RIDGE

Various traverses have been made along the crest, or high on its S flank, between Cloudcap Peak and the summit ice plateau of Mt. Shuksan. A traverse was made beginning at Cloudcap Peak by Tony Hovey, John Meulemans, and Irene Meulemans on July 12 and 13, 1959. Along Jagged Ridge they descended slabs and gullies to a knob protruding from the snow (bivouac), then across a small glacier; one should keep as high as possible here. Then traverse some 2 mi. of rocky buttresses under various small summits (rock is solid, class 3); a slanting snow finger and steep rock scrambling lead to the upper Crystal Glacier. The first W-E traverse was part of a two-day alpine traverse over Nooksack Tower and Ridge to the summit, then SE along Jagged Ridge to the Nooksack cirque by Gerard McGill and Les MacDonald in August 1960.

Another party traversed the entire ridge from W to E, touching all the main summits, and claimed the first climb of the W ridge of Cloudcap (Joan Firey, Joe Firey, Tony Hovey, John Meulemans, and Irene Meulemans, on July 2 and 3, 1967). One should allow 8-10 hours from summit to summit, and expect constant class 3 and 4 rock climbing and a few intervals of snow and ice. References: *A.A.J.,* 1960, pp. 118-19; *Mountaineer,* 1960, pp. 81-82; 1968, p. 204.

CIRQUE TOWER est. 7700 ft/2347 m. This is a small but prominent tower about one-third of the distance from Crystal Glacier to Cloudcap Peak. The first ascent was made by Fred Beckey, Bob Lewis, and John Parrott on July 12, 1953 via a descending traverse of upper Crystal Glacier. Class 4. Several small summits on the W were also climbed. Reference: *Mountaineer,* 1953, p. 67.

NOOKSACK CIRQUE WALL: This route climbs a 1200-ft ice face from the upper edge of Nooksack Glacier to the W portion of the crest of Jagged Ridge. The face is easily identified as the largest ice section on the ridge. To get on the main glacier it is best to climb before late summer (see Nooksack Glacier). First ascent by Dusan Jagersky and Jim Wickwire in September 1973.

A 100-ft ice hose was climbed to get onto the face, which averages 45 to 55 degrees. The route then follows an obvious rib of ice; the finish bears leftward, where there is a narrow twisting gully. Time: 3-4 hours on the wall, depending on conditions. Descent: made via Jagged Ridge to upper Sulphide Glacier. Reference: *A.A.J.,* 1974, p. 144.

CLOUDCAP PEAK (Seahpo Peak)

7429 ft/2264 m

Located 2½ mi. SE of Mt. Shuksan's summit at the termination of Jagged Ridge, Cloudcap is an extremely rugged peak of rock and ice, one without an easy ascent route. The setting in the Nooksack cirque and the peak itself form one of the alpine climaxes of the North Cascades (see Mt. Shuksan). From the opposite Baker River flank, where there is a local relief of 6500 ft, Cloudcap resembles a steep gothic rock shape of nearly perfect proportions. The name is to symbolize a local lenticular cloud, which often envelopes a summit in this maritime range, and is caused by high winds which rise over the peak. The term Seahpo was originated by the Forest Service and placed on their maps after the first ascent party had named the peak and published an account in accepted priority. First ascent by Fred Beckey and Helmy Beckey on June 27, 1941.

EAST RIDGE: From the Nooksack cirque (see Icy Peak) ascend ground moraine, snowfields, and glacier S to the Icy-Cloudcap ridge. From a notch at the toe of Cloudcap's East Ridge, ascend the rock spur briefly, then make leftward oblique traverse and climb to the apex of a small glacier to just below the second notch; one could vary the route and climb along the rock ridge to the notch. Gain the rock here (solid) and climb vertically slightly left of the ridge into a shallow gully that ends in 50 ft at a small tree (exposed class 4); in 50 ft the climbing eases in angle and becomes class 3. Note: Some parties have experienced difficulty crossing the notch where ice melts out after July, forcing difficult rock climbing; the ledge here generally has 8 to 10 ft of ice.

Climb on the ridge crest (steep heather), then bear left across a steep gully which may be snow-filled or icy. Traverse left more on heathery ledges to the next rib, then scramble to the summit. Time: 5½ hours from cirque. Descent: two rappels may be needed; possible problem in getting over schrund. References: *Mountaineer,* 1941, pp. 32-33; *B.C.M.,* October 1967.

WEST ROUTE: See Jagged Ridge, W to E traverse.

CLOUDCAP PEAK from east
NATIONAL PARK SERVICE

LAKE ANN BUTTRESS

The buttress is the 1000-ft rock wall immediately above Lake Ann.

CENTER ROUTE: By Fred Beckey and Tom Stewart on September 19, 1965. Three slab pitches of good rock are taken on a shallow open book near the center of the buttress. A short aid section is taken to exit onto the upper face, and aid was used again 300 ft higher. Grade III; class 5.5 to 5.8 on many pitches; rock is rather friable and cracks generally marginal. Reference: *A.A.J.*, 1966, pp. 135-36.

CENTER-WEST ROUTE: One of two routes done on the western part of the buttress-face; by Les MacDonald and Elfrieda Pigou in 1960. This quite hard route reaches to the slight depression W of the buttress summit. The climb is mostly free (British Grade V; difficult; about 20 pitons used on original).

    Yellow Slab Variation: By Les MacDonald and Peter Taylor in 1964 or 1965. This route is on the westerly side of

the buttress, and reaches to the W side of the western sub-point. MacDonald related that the climb's name is for a route on Scawfell Pike in the English Lakes District: "We Britishers never give up — importing ideas, tea, and sentimental names of climbs." The climb is slightly more difficult than the Center-West route.

SAUK MOUNTAIN   5537 ft/1688 m

Sauk is a small but remarkable summit located 2.6 mi. N of Rockport in the Skagit Valley; there is a 5300-ft direct rise on this slope. Sauk Mountain offers training for hikers, joggers, and even good winter climbing. There are small cliffs on the S, W, and NW flanks, with steep and rocky areas. There can be ice climbing given the right conditions. It is known that G.O. Smith, the geologist, visited the summit in 1895. Bailey Willis, A.H. Sylvester and John Charlton (U.S.

Geological Survey) triangulated from the summit in August 1897, finding Sauk a useful survey station. Earlier names noted for the mountain are "Mt. Gweht" on a map drawn by George Gibbs and "Mt. Pantalonah" in the account of Otto Klement.
ROUTE: See Sauk Mountain Trail♦.

DIOBSUD BUTTES   5893 ft/1796 m

These summits are a series of moderate-altitude, but very rough and rocky peaks of the Shuksan Metamorphic Suite located 4 mi. NW of Skagit River at Bacon Creek. The first Diobsud Butte (5871 ft/1790 m) has a very sheer SE face, quite impressive from Marblemount. The second summit (NW butte) is also a very rocky and dominant formation, and generally considered the main Diobsud Butte. The third summit ("Logger" — 6080 ft+/1853 m) is a broad rock mass located about midway between the main Butte and "Electric," between upper Diobsud Creek and the central fork of Falls Creek; it has a very rocky E flank. The highest summit in the grouping ("Electric" — 6365 ft/1940 m), is 2 mi. N of the main Butte, at the head of Falls Creek branch of Bacon Creek. From the E this summit is rocky with small glaciers located below the upper face. Small glaciers decorate the northern flank.

The entire area of the Buttes is very cliff-laced, subject to avalanches in spring and brushy terrain when snow is melted. A major fire burned much of the lower area in 1925. Complex gullies and rock barriers make through-hikes taxing; the area is a haven for goats, who thrive in such locales. Some early settlers apparently called the group Diabase Buttes. The first ascent of the main peak was probably by Albert H. Sylvester and a survey party some time between 1907 and 1909.
ROUTE: Take Diobsud Creek Road♦. From the end of the logging road at the far right side of cutting, hike into timber; one can take a gully to the ridge, then follow (good travel) WNW to Diobsud Buttes. The rock faces and fringing slabs of the first Butte make its bypass a problem. One can travel over or around the main Butte (scrambling and brush).

"Logger Butte" was first climbed by Ron Aronoff, Kent Crites, Stuart Ferguson, John Roper, and Reed Tindall on May 6, 1978. This party had spring snow conditions, so traversed around the E and N slopes of the first two Buttes (would be much brush by summer). The traverse around a basin takes one to a very prominent snow couloir on the E face; the last portion is rock or very steep snow to the saddle (5600 ft+) N of the main saddle N of the main (second) Butte. Cross the saddle to the W side to make the final ascent on the S ridge (not difficult).

"Electric Butte" was first climbed by Carla Firey, Joan Firey, Jim McCarthy, and Irene Meulemans in September 1976 as part of a traverse of Bacon Creek rim. The party descended "Diobsud Glacier" on the SE flank of Bacon Peak; they then skirted below an ice cliff and then descended a valley SW for about ½ mi. (Diobsud Creek flank). The route here turned SE, ascending easterly via a long 1200-ft snow couloir slope to a plateau area NW of the summit (est. 5400 ft) with a small glacier surrounded by crags and pinnacles. The final climb was on the W face; after some scrambling there was about 100 ft of class 4 rock. The descent was made eastward over the summit, then a traverse made S, with a contour along the Bacon-Diobsud Creek divide. The crossing of N-side couloirs, with gains and losses, and some brush, was done to bypass the first two Buttes.

MT. WATSON   6234 ft/1900 m

Watson is located between Noisy, Anderson, and Diobsud creeks E of Lake Shannon. The eastern and more pointed of twin summits is higher; there is also a lower E rock crag/tower. There are two noticeable ramps on the SE flank and a small glacier on the N slope. Greenschist is well exposed on the mountain. The mountain is a scenic snow climb and rock scramble — an easy day tour. Reference: *Mountaineer,* 1967, pp. 119-20.
NORTHWEST ROUTE: From near the saddle crossing to Watson Lakes (see Anderson Lakes Trail♦), about ¼ mi. before the trail reaches Watson Lakes, where it crosses a brushy slope beneath a large slab, leave it and ascend gradually S to the skyline; follow a way-trail S of Little Watson Lake to upper Anderson Lakes. From the N end of the first lake, follow an easy gully E to the skyline ridge, then ascend this S to the edge of the large firnfield on the E side of the ridge. Climb SE up the firn toward the saddle between the E and W summits. Just below the top of the snowfield, bear right to an obvious "reverse Z" ledge system. Climb the ledges to the skyline (one long lead), then scramble to the W summit; the E summit is a pleasant scramble from the saddle. Class 3-4. Time: 3-4 hours from road.

Note: The gullies on the S slope are steep, loose, and not recommended.
Variation: Follow the NW ridge from beyond Anderson Lakes; make a short rock scramble at the summit.
NORTH FACE: First ascent by Dave Dixon and Dallas Kloke in September 1970. From the NW shoulder make a short descent to the small glacier on the N slope. Ascend to the base of the NE rock wall, then climb easy slabs; there are two leads on steeper, solid slab to the summit. Class 4. Reference: *Mountaineer,* 1971, p. 84.

BACON PEAK   7066 ft/2154 m

Bacon is a quite massive summit located between the upper portions of Bacon, Noisy, and Diobsud creeks. Rock on the peak is of the Shuksan Metamorphic

Bacon Creek · "Electric Butte" · DIOBSUD BUTTES · DIOBSUD CREEK GLACIER · BACON PEAK · HELEN BUTTES · GREEN LAKE GLACIER · NOISY CREEK GLACIER · Green Lake · Noisy Creek

BACON PEAK from northwest
AUSTIN POST, UNIVERSITY OF WASHINGTON

Suite; the W face of the mountain at the head of Noisy Creek is steep, with much exposed rock. Arkose interbedded with beds of black argillite of the Chuckanut Formation make up the N side of the mountain.[70] The notable feature of Bacon Peak is its glaciers, which total over 3.2 km² in area. The largest of these (Diobsud Glacier, trending SE and draining to Diobsud Creek) has a 2.5 km E-W width from the summit to the eastern fringe. This glacier almost interconnects N of the summit with the northeastern glacier ("Green Lake Glacier") which is 1.5 km in length and 2.1 km in width; this glacier has a curious rock divider (a break) trending to the E. Near Bacon's summit there is a great wind cirque formed from the glacier firn. The third glacier of importance — about 1.4 km in length — is on the NW flank, draining to Heather Creek fork

(Noisy Creek).

The first ascent was made by Edward C. Barnard's party in 1905, using a route from the West Fork of Bacon Creek. The summit was re-visited for triangulation by the U.S. Coast and Geodetic Survey in 1926. References: *Joint Report,* p. 336; *Mountaineer,* 1967, p. 120.

SOUTHWEST ROUTE: From near the base of the Mt. Watson N-slope glacier (est. 5000 ft) bypass a small rock divider and then traverse SE along the base of a lesser glacier; continue to the low divide (a saddle in the fault line) between Diobsud and Noisy creeks (4900 ft+); can camp on the S side. Traverse E into the basin SW and S of Bacon Peak (basin drains to Diobsud Creek); basin contains some snow much of the season but is a good route. Continue to make a logical ascent to the summit area; follow the snow ridge to the highest point. Time: 4 hours saddle to summit. Note: One

69

MT. HAGAN *from northwest*
ROWLAND TABOR, U.S. GEOLOGICAL SURVEY

can make a more direct route by descending into the head of Noisy Creek, then climbing the W slope of the peak, but parties have reported this to be quite brushy.

NOISY CREEK ROUTE: Take Noisy Creek Trail♦ and continue 2 mi. beyond its end to the mouth of "Heather Creek," the stream flowing W from the 5100-ft+ pass above Green Lake. Ascend deep forest steeply along the N bank (some game trails can be found, generally 100-200 ft above creek). At about 4700 ft the valley levels to a meadow and offers a campsite (9 hours). Ascend along the left side of the stream cascades to heathery slopes at the pass above Green Lake (at 2.2 mi. N of Bacon Peak). Hike S along the open divide to a small glacier. Cross its upper left portion, then cross snow and small rock ribs to the "Green Lake Glacier" (on NNE slope). Make an ascending glacier walk southward. Time: 2 hours from pass. Note: One can combine the climbs of Bacon Peak and Mt. Hagan.

Approach Variation: From about 2 mi. in the valley of Noisy Creek ascend a spur ridge eastward, then take the high ridge SE to near Green Lake.

PEAK 6561 6561 ft/2000 m. Located E of Bacon Peak and W of Bacon Creek. This minor summit is nearly glacier-surrounded.

MT. HAGAN 6800 ft+/2073 m+

This mountain is a cluster of small, attractive rock summits E of Baker Lake and 4.2 mi. NNE of Bacon Peak. There are three main summits of almost equal height, with the southern being the true summit. Hagan has a number of satellite summits, mainly to the NW and SW. Rock is of the Chuckanut Formation, intruded by Chilliwack Batholith. The principal

MT. HAGAN

South Crags South Peak → Middle Peak North Peak

col

← to Green Lake

Berdeen Lake

MT. HAGAN from east
BOB AND IRA SPRING

glacier is on the N slope of the summits and drains to Blum Creek; extensive barren slabs are exposed below the ice margin. The western cirque (Hidden Creek drainage) has a glacier of very pleasing shape; the summit rock peaks cradle the glacier in a long arc. The first ascent was made by Fred Beckey, Melvin Marcus, Martin Ochsner, Keith Rankin, and Herb Staley on August 16, 1945. References: *A.A.J.*, 1946, pp. 45-46; *Mountaineer*, 1946, p. 45.

ROUTE: See Bacon Peak for the approach to the pass near Green Lake. Contour a broad heather bench on the E side of the divide (N above the lake) and in about ½ mi. reach a saddle in the divide; here is a small lake (4500 ft+), 1.4 mi. from the 5100-ft+ pass. Ascend northward on a long ridge, bearing rightward at 5500 ft and ascending a shallow basin via gullies and rockslides. Bypass a rock peak to the right and cross a col (6320 ft+) to the western glacier. Traverse the glacier briefly to the N side of the summit rock pyramid, which is the S peak. Ascend its N side to a notch on its upper E side. Traverse on the S face, on the summit ridge; work up a spur on the E, then bear around to the S, where slabs lead to the summit (class 3).

The middle summit is an easy scramble from the S side (same notch).

The N peak (same first ascent party) is a more serious undertaking, having a steep 50-ft pitch on its S face (class 5.5). The problem is an exposed move over a bulge; a lichened (dark) crack area is taken through a light-colored lateral bulge (can protect with three chocks).

Approach Variation: The approach to the various rock summits from the E (Berdeen Lake side) appears simple. The respective notches can be reached by taking snowfields.

BERDEEN PEAK   6484 ft/1976 m

This is a small peak located SE of Berdeen Lake, between main and E forks of Bacon Creek; the peak looks like a flattop with a small glacier on the NW flank. The peak is very rugged and rocky on the S and E flanks, above the Bacon Creek forks.

ROUTE: Take the approach for Mt. Hagan, then from the E flank of the latter hike ridges along the rim of Berdeen Lake. Keep high on the glacier slope or along the ridge crest; do not descend into cliffy locales. The ascent is not technical, but is a long trek.

MT. BLUM   7680 ft/2341 m

Mt. Blum is an unusually massive hulk for its altitude, the depth of its valley footings (Baker River and branches) giving an impression of volume. The mountain has a rounded shape, not particularly distinctive, yet alpine with its firm granitic rock and sequence of small glaciers on every flank. Blum is a dominant mountain, and its form fits the North Cascades: it is the most prominent mountain between Mt. Shuksan, Whitehorse Mountain, and the Picket Range. The precise location is 4 mi. from Baker Lake and 7½ mi. SE of Shuksan.

The mountain was once called "Old Baldy" or "Bald," then formally named for John Blum, a Forest Service fire patrol pilot who crashed near Snoqualmie Pass in 1931. The first ascent may have been made by the U.S. Geological Survey at an unknown date, or it may have been the climb of Ernest Kobelt and companion in the mid-1920s.

WEST ROUTE: From about 0.3 mi. upstream from Greiner's shelter (see Upper Baker River Trail♦) ford the river and hike about ¼ mi. through jungle to heavy timber which forms the first spur ridge E (left of) Blum Creek. Note: Cross river in mid to late summer and early in day. Ascend a very steep but good climbing ridge (mostly big open timber) to just N of Blum Lakes; when near the huckleberry area the ridge turns E and comes out just above the third Blum Lake; descend to the second lake (largest is at 4960 ft+), then ascend SE up-valley. Note: There is a camp area at 600 ft above the lower lakes. Chutes lead to the small glacier (some minor cliffs); a snow gully leads to the S shore of the glacier-fed upper lake. The large firn-snowfield S of Mt. Blum leads to a broad saddle (6560 ft+). From here the final S ridge takes a low-gradient rock spur (not technical). More direct routes can be made to the summit from Blum Lakes, but they are likely no time advantage.

NORTH RIDGE: This sharp rock crest between two glaciers offers a good alpine rock climb on firm granite. First ascent by Dave Hutchinson, Phil Leatherman, and Mark Weigelt on September 16, 1971. At about ½ mi. along the trail ford the river to the opposite bank. Then ascend 5000 ft of waterless steep forest ridge (campspot at small lake below terminus of North Ridge). The ridge begins near 5700 ft above snow and talus slopes (possible moat problem to gain ridge crest). The original party was forced to use a 20-ft gully at the ridge base with an overhanging chockstone (bypass this on right wall). Several difficult pitches continue to the ridge crest, where the climbing becomes generally easier. Grade III; class 5.9. References: *Summit,* January-February 1972, pp. 8-11; *A.A.J.,* 1972, p. 115; *Mountaineer,* 1971, p. 85.

NORTHEAST SPUR: This is more of an extended spur than a ridge, and except for the summit crag area, it is largely ice-covered. The setting is very alpine. First ascent by Russell Smith and Rowland Tabor in 1966. See Upper Baker River Trail♦-Mt. Blum Route. Traverse the S side of the ridge, which includes snow and glacier slopes, then attain the steep, loose Northeast Spur via the glacier on its

N. Scrambling near the summit easy, but exposed; class 3. Time: 10 hours from Bald Eagle Creek.

SOUTH ROUTE: See Bacon Peak and Mt. Hagan for approach to small divide lake. From alp slope benches above Berdeen Lake ascend NW to the ridge, then cross the snow saddle N of Mt. Hagan (6400 ft+) to the opposite glacier. Descend the wide, open basin, angling right to cross an obvious notch in the NW-descending spur ridge dividing this from a smaller basin to the N (Blum Lakes). To reach the objective make a short snow descent (can cross below upper lake or keep higher), then cross a W-facing basin to its opposite slope, then climb gullies to the large snowfield S of the summit (see West Route). Reference: *Mountaineer,* 1967, pp. 121-23.

LONESOME PEAK   6720 ft+/2048 m+
This is the provisional name for a small but rugged summit between the western terminal forks of Lonesome Creek fork of Bald Eagle Creek, located 1 mi. N of Berdeen Lake. Rock is granodiorite, part of the underlying Chilliwack Batholith. There is an attractive higher hornlike peak about 0.4 mi. to the NW (at 6800 ft+). First ascent by Doug McKeever and Rowland Tabor on August 4, 1967 during a ridge traverse from Mt. Despair to Berdeen Lake.

PEAK 6585   6585 ft/2007 m. Located between Lonesome Creek and the East Fork Bacon Creek, 2.3 mi. WNW of Mt. Despair (Point 6514 is the western summit); climbed by the 1967 party.

PIONEER RIDGE   7020 ft/2140 m
This ridge is a massive area midway between Mt. Blum and the northern Picket Range, extending from low cliffy footings of Baker River and Picket Creek; here is a formidable barrier of cliffs and slabs with great local relief, one of the roughest spots in the North Cascades. The highest summit is at the SE end of the Ridge, near Jasper Pass. There is a small glacier (facing NE) on Point 6944 (the second highest summit). Rock of the ridge is light-colored granodiorite with volcanic remnants at the eastern summit (Hannegan volcanics overlie the Skagit gneiss). Reference: *Routes and Rocks,* p.23, see note 72.
ROUTE: See Upper Baker River Trail♦-Pioneer Ridge Route.

MT. CROWDER (Old Brownie)
                                    7082 ft/2159 m
This peak is an area of very remote access, 1.7 mi. SW of Mt. Fury, the high point of a ridge trending S from Phantom Peak, between upper Goodell and Picket creeks. There is a steep rock face on the N (Picket

MT. DESPAIR *from east*
PHILIP LEATHERMAN

Creek flank) but the W and SW slopes are moderate. The first ascent was made by Jack Ardussi, Cal Magnusson, Don Mech, and Don Schmechel in 1962. Reference: *Mountaineer,* 1963, pp. 86-87.

ROUTE: Approach as for the W side of Phantom Peak, then continue S (see Easy Ridge Trail♦). Traverse to the col between Phantom and Crowder (6000 ft+). Climb SW over a sub-summit (7020 ft) to the base of the summit formation; a rib of solid rock leads to the top. An easy slope can be taken on the SW flank to the base of Pioneer Ridge. (One could approach via Pioneer Ridge High Route; see Upper Baker River Trail♦).

MT. DESPAIR   7292 ft/2223 m

Despair is a very prominent mountain of granitic rock 6.8 mi. NW of Newhalem on the Skagit River and closely W of Goodell Creek. It is quite isolated from its neighbors. From Mt. Triumph, Despair appears pyramidal in shape, but there are two distinct summits, with the southern being slightly higher. Jasper Pass, a low divide between Goodell and Bald Eagle creeks, is located N of the mountain. On the alpine E slope of Despair there are two glacier cirques divided by a precipitous rock pyramid. Slabs of granite above Goodell Creek feature a local relief of 4500 ft. The southern of two glaciers has an avalanche ice accumulation extending down to 2700 ft altitude. The relief on the W (Bacon Creek East Fork) is similar.

The names Despair, Triumph, along with the Picket Range, were first shown on Forest Service maps dated 1931, leading to the suspicion that these names were derived by Lage Wernstedt of the Forest Service. First ascent by Lloyd Anderson, Fred Beckey, and Clint Kelley July 2, 1939. Reference: *Mountaineer,* 1939, p. 28.

SOUTHEAST ROUTE: From Triumph Pass (see Triumph Pass Route♦) descend the glacier to about 200 ft above a small lake, then continue on the alp slope on the E ridge shoulder about 2 mi. N to the pocket lake (4960 ft+) immediately S of Despair. Follow around the right side of the cirque, ascend a ridge, ascend through cliffs onto the upper snowfield (45 degrees) and broken rock of the final portion of the SE face; easy climbing — firm rock. Time: 3-4 hours from the pass.

MT. TRIUMPH from northwest
ROLAND AMUNDSEN

Variation: By Carla Firey, Joan Firey, David Knudson, and Peter Renz in 1970. The approach was from Jasper Pass and a camp at 6100 ft on the glacier E of the North Peak. Traverse the glacier to the high col (where the two E side glaciers meet). From the far glacier take a steep slanting snow couloir to the E ridge.
SOUTH FACE: First ascent by Doug Barrie, Dave Laster, and Cliff Lawson on July 24, 1962. Begin the route via the midface S-face gully; follow rightward until this ends in a grassy platform. Then climb a rock rib (short solid leads over steps). Gullies are then taken rightward to join the Southeast Route. References: *Mountaineer*, 1963, p. 93; *A.A.J.*, 1963, p. 474.

NORTH PEAK   7200 ft/2134 m+
This peak is closely NNW of the main summit. First ascent by Doug Barrie, Ken Hunich, Cliff Lawson, Marilyn Loranger, Mike Swayne, and Gordon Thompson on July 6, 1963. Approach per Southeast Route, then contour the SW flank at about 5600 ft (some slab). Begin the climb in a snow couloir on the W side of the objective. When this intersects with a snow face at 6900 ft, follow a gully system to the notch dividing the summit (the northern block is higher). Reference: *Mountaineer*, 1964, p. 133.

The N ridge offers a straightforward snow-ice climb from the vicinity of Jasper Pass (no technical difficulties); possibly first climbed by Ron Johnson and party on August 1, 1968.

MT. TRIUMPH   7270 ft/2216 m
Mt. Triumph is one of the outstanding sights in the North Cascades despite its moderate altitude. The symmetry of its isolated rock horn is seen to advantage from the highway 1 mi. W of Marblemount, where the great local relief from low valley footings can be appreciated. The low flanking valleys of Bacon and Goodell creeks provide Mt. Triumph space laterally from competing high summits of the Bacon Peak-Mt. Blum ridge on the W and the Picket Range on the E. Triumph is located 5 mi. NW of Newhalem; rock is the Skagit gneiss, in some places (particularly the N face) very ice-polished. There are small glaciers below the E and N faces.

The first ascent was made by Lloyd Anderson, Lyman Boyer, Dave Lind, Sig Hall, and Louis Smith on July 31, 1938 during somewhat of an explorative milestone in the then-unknown area N of Skagit River. An early attempt to reach Triumph was halted by vertical ridge cuts near Thornton Peak; the original climbing party approached from Thornton Creek, then when near the mountain had problems with both brush and group separation. Route finding on the mountain was baffling until a goat tread was located in a cliff barrier; the climbers followed five goats along a

MT. TRIUMPH from east
PHILIP LEATHERMAN

bench, and in defiance the animals rolled rocks on them. References: *Mountaineer,* 1938, p. 26; 1939, p. 28.

WEST ROUTE: Take Triumph Pass Route◆ to the S edge of the steep rock rampart on the W side of objective. Ascend a left-slanting gully to a sloping bench. Ascend heathery rock nearly to the Northwest Ridge — to a level with a great rightward-sloping bench (note: one can ascend to here directly from Triumph Pass). Follow the bench to a notch on the peak's SW corner, then continue for a short distance to the SE shoulder (large step/ledge feature of Triumph). For the final 200 ft of climbing, take a shallow rock gully directly to the summit on moderately steep rock; part of this section is in a chimney. Class 4. Warning: Triumph can be a very treacherous climb when wet. Time: 3 hours from near Triumph Pass.

Descent: good rappel horn near summit.

NORTHWEST RIDGE: First ascent by Joan Firey, Joe Firey, Peter Renz, and Frank Tarver in July 1969. From near Triumph Pass climb the spur to a small col (6320 ft+) on the objective ridge, crossing the ridge diagonally. Climb to a ledge under the large impressive step on the ridge (class 4); the next lead bears right and up to a steep rib with firm holds (favorable dip). The final 400 ft from the top of the step to the summit is scrambling. Grade II; class 5.3 (mostly class 4 and 5; several pitons and chocks sufficient). Reference: *Mountaineer,* 1970, pp. 102-3.

NORTHEAST RIDGE: This is reported as a noteworthy climb on generally firm rock; the climb is impressive because of its alpine setting and the fact that much of the flanking E face is overhanging. First ascent by Natalie Cole, Joan Firey, Joe Firey, and Frank Tarver in August 1965. Approach by Thornton Lakes Trail◆. Traverse the lower lake on its W, cross the main stream beyond, pass the middle lake on its E. Here ascend a talus cone and a left-slanting grassy (snow) ravine that leads to the prominent notch (5760 ft+); can camp here, 3 hours. Here is easy access to the E-facing glacier filling the basin between Thornton Peak and Mt. Triumph. Traverse the glacier and gain the objective ridge via up-sloping ledges on its lower S flank. Generally climb the narrow crest, but on the final third there are two difficult steeper steps with problems: at the first step traverse on the N flank (class 5) until a great notch is reached, then ascend the N face. At the final step, traverse leftward on a ledge, then when the angle permits climb easy slabs to the summit. Grade II or III; class 5.5. Time: 6 hours from notch above middle lake. Reference: *Mountaineer,* 1966, p. 199.

SOUTH RIDGE: First ascent by Lou Dangles, Doug Martin, John Streich, and Bill Sumner on July 23, 1972. Approach as per Northeast Ridge; gain the South Ridge from the glacier. The ridge and various chimneys involve much scrambling with occasional class 5 pitches (some of this is poorly protected) to eventually meet the broad platform of the SE shoulder. Class 5.6. Reference: *Mountaineer,* 1972, p. 84.

THORNTON PEAK   6911 ft/2106 m

This is the unofficial name for a sharp rock horn located closely NW of Upper Thornton Lake (Triumph-Goodell Creek divide) and ¾ mi. S of higher Mt. Triumph; the name is for William T. Thornton, pioneer of the upper Skagit in the early 1900s. The first ascent was made by Lloyd Anderson, John James, and David Lind on June 27, 1938; they called it Damnation Peak (but this summit as shown on maps of the time is in the drainage of Damnation Creek, some 2½ mi. to the SW). The original party attempted to reach Mt. Triumph from the summit, but were thwarted by steep ridges and a gorge. Reference: *Mountaineer*, 1938, p. 24.

SOUTHEAST RIDGE: See Triumph Pass Route♦. From the col at 6000 ft+ NW of Thornton Lakes hike N along the ridge until an easterly snow traverse can be made into a shallow basin beneath the summit. A break in the rock structure offers a route angling up and right on snow to the SE summit ridge. Ascend the broken slabs of the final 200 ft of rock (class 3) or take snow on the E side. Time: 3 hours from Thornton Lake.

TRAPPERS PEAK   5964 ft/1818 m

A small peak very close to the NE side of Lower Thornton Lake.

ROUTE: Take Thornton Lake Trail♦. From where the trail crosses the divide to the lakes follow the easy S ridge.

DAMNATION PEAK   5635 ft/1718 m

A rocky summit of moderate altitude, N of Oakes Peak, and between Bacon and Triumph creeks, 3.7 mi. from the Skagit River. Here rock of the Chilliwack Batholith is largely covered by brush and forest. The name Damnation was used on a 1938 ascent which took place on Thornton Peak to the NE.

ROUTE: The logical approach would be from the road in the valley of Damnation Creek (see Thornton Creek Road♦), which extends to within about 1 mi. SE of the summit. There will be some bush and possible easy scrambling.

MT. ROSS   6052 ft/1845 m

This is a small frontal summit, a high point of the rocky ridge between Goodell Creek and the narrow gorge of Skagit River; relief from the latter is 5500 ft. The summit is located about 2½ mi. NE of Newhalem. The name is for James D. Ross, long the supervisor of the Skagit's Seattle City Light operation. Some pioneers called the peak Goodell Mountain.

ROUTE: Avoid any ascent of the cliffy Skagit gorge area. The best way to begin is near Newhalem, sorting out the best method of ascending the rocky mountain slopes, first in

a NE direction, then northerly on a spur. Complete the final portion by the SW ridge. The trek will be brushy, with rock outcrops; allow a full day for the ascent. The climb is not technical, but do not expect an easy trip.

THE ROOST   6705 ft/2044 m

Visible from the highway W of Newhalem, this small, rocky ridge summit is located at the head of Jay Creek, 1 mi. N of Mt. Ross and directly E of the Goodell-Terror Creek junction. There is a very steep rock face on the N, some 400 ft or more in height (granodiorite). First ascent by John Roper and Taffy Roper on July 12, 1966.

ROUTE: From the end of the overgrown logging road of Goodell Creek (see Goodell Creek Route♦) follow a scant path to 3200 ft, then climb directly up the hillside cross-country (some brush) to reach a talus tongue and open meadows at about 5200 ft. Continue to the ridge trending N off the objective, then follow this to the summit (not technical). Time: 6 hours from Newhalem.

PEAK 7200+   7200 ft+/2194 m+

This is a hornlike ice-shaped summit located 1 mi. S of Azure Lake on the Terror-Stetattle Creek divide. The peak is nearly surrounded by glacier fragments.

ROUTE: Reach the peak from the high traverse above Terror Creek (not difficult); See Goodell Creek Route♦.

DAVIS PEAK   7051 ft/2149 m

This is a very rugged rock summit 2 mi. N of Gorge Dam, deeply entrenched on the E and N sides by Stetattle and Jay creeks. From the E side, the peak has a horn shape, with deep footings on the Skagit and Stetattle Creek valleys. The North Face is a steep rock wall of Skagit gneiss, nearly a mi. in width. There is a glacier below the face, draining to Stetattle Creek. The peak is seldom visited because of the very rugged approach and rocky flanks. The name was given by the Reaburn climbing party for Lucinda Davis and family, pioneer homesteaders of the area. It had previously been known as Stetattle Peak. First ascent by David Ledgerwood and W.A. Reaburn, surveyors for the U.S. Geological Survey in 1904. The ascent was described as a hard climb from the Davis ranch. The route taken was up the spur and SE ridge from near where the third highway tunnel is now located. Survey parties climbed Davis again in 1905 and 1906. Reference: *Joint Report*, pp. 336-37.

SOUTH RIDGE: This is a strenuous cross-country route from North Cascades Hwy♦ just E of Gorge Creek (N of Gorge Dam), climbing directly up the steep, cliffy and bushy mountainside. Keep E of a prominent tributary gully of Gorge Creek in order to reach a broad rib at about 4500 ft (rib leads onto the S ridge of Davis Peak). From a saddle at 5720 ft+ climb 200 ft of slab to the sharp ridge leading to the peak. Time: 8 hours or more. Note: One could also make the ascent from near midway along Gorge Lake, about the original climbing route.

NORTH FACE COULOIR: First ascent by Dallas Kloke and Bryce Simon on July 12, 1976. From 2 mi. up Stetattle Creek Trail♦ cross the creek, then make a brushy ascent. Climb a cliff of about 500 ft (class 2 to 4) to reach the small glacier beneath the face (4400 ft). Ascend the right side of the glacier to the lower wall of the NW side of the North Face. Climb several rock pitches to ledges, where one can traverse left to the beginning of the couloir; the last pitch leading into the couloir is followed mostly on 40- to 45-degree snow to the ridge crest a short distance E of the summit. Grade III; class 5.6. Time: 14 hours r.t. Reference: *A.A.J.*, 1971, pp. 170-71.

ELEPHANT BUTTE   7380 ft/2249 m

This is a large granitic massif, the highest point on Stetattle Ridge, 7¼ mi. W of Ross Lake. The N and E flanks of the mountain are quite steep, and there are small glaciers on the NW flank. See Stetattle Creek Trail♦ and Stetattle Ridge Route♦; the summit is an easy, scenic hike from the W.

PEAK 6914   (6914 ft/2107 m), located 1.3 mi. W of Elephant Butte, is a similar ridge hump; the S slope and SW ridge offer simple ascent routes.

MT. PROPHET   7640 ft+/2329 m+

The name Prophet is for Tommy Rowland, prospector and religious fanatic of Skagit Valley 1895-1900.

The Mt. Prophet group is a small subrange W of Ross Lake, following the NW-trend of Big Beaver Creek, between the latter and Arctic Creek. Rock is Skagit gneiss. Ancient glaciers have carved some nine cirques along the S and SW flanks of this extensive ridge, and carved broader, deeper ones on the northern flank. The mountain and its long ridge have several small glaciers in these cirques. The chief body of glacier ice on the mountain is the Arctic Glacier (flows to Arctic Creek), which becomes quite crevassed in late summer; the glacier is 0.6 km in length. A glacier in a narrow corridor of Arctic Creek basin, to the E of the true summit, becomes an ice finger in its upper portion; the glacier ranges from 6150 ft to 4800 ft.

The true summit crag of Mt. Prophet is flanked high by the Arctic Glacier, so has no real rock walls; however some of the slightly lower peaks on the ridge have distinctive rock faces. There is a near NW peak (7524 ft/2295 m), with a very steep N face, continu-ing to 5800 ft above a small glacier; from here a short steep wall continues over 1 mi. on the NE flank of the ridge. Another peak, at 7185 ft, located 2.2. mi. NW of the true summit, has a very steep NE face, with a narrow glacier on its E. At 0.7 mi. NW of the latter summit is a 7035-ft peak, with a very steep, short N face. Point 6910 is steep on the NE flank. At the farthest NW end of the ridge is a 6872-ft peak, with a steep 2000-ft NW face, only 1 mi. from Little Beaver Creek.

ROUTE: A timbered ridge trends eastward from Big Beaver Creek Trail♦. This appears to be the most feasible route, although it is a long ascent (begins near the 2000-ft level) and involves some light bush travel.

ARCTIC GLACIER: A route on this glacier to the col just SE of the summit was done by Mark Allaback, Steve Allaback, Peter Eckman, Alex Medlicott, Jr., and John Roper on July 28, 1978. The final part of the route to the col consists of firn-ice patches and rock.

GENESIS PEAK (7244 ft/2208 m) is 2.2 mi. SE of the true summit and 3.3 mi. from Ross Lake; it is the prominent summit at that end of the ridge, ¾ mi. from Skymo Lake. The peak has a fairly steep N face above a small glacier.

There are rock summits of note on two other supporting ridges: the row of peaks W of No Name Creek and E of East Fork Arctic Creek culminates in Peak 6688, at 2.2 mi. NE of Mt. Prophet. Peak 6254, which has a steep N face, is located on a spur between Arctic and Mist creeks, 1 mi. NE of Peak 7185.

Genesis Peak was first climbed by Norman Burke, Cliff Lawson, Ed Lebert, and Dan Sjolseth on September 13, 1975. The best route appears to be from the Big Beaver Trail, by heading up the forest spur NE of Thirtynine Mile Creek, (the S and W slopes are gradual). Peak 7185 was climbed via its SW ridge by the Arctic Glacier party on July 29 (an easy ascent), and Peak 7035 was climbed on July 30 (via NW ridge to notch at summit). The summit of Peak 6872, when climbed (1978), was found to have garbage remaining from an unidentified government agency's helicopter visit.

THE PICKET RANGE

The Picket Range is a physiographic subsection of the North Cascades, a remarkably linear NW-SE chain of sharp gneissic rock peaks N of Newhalem on the Skagit River, and about 13 mi. E of Mt. Shuksan, between Goodell Creek, upper Baker River, Big Beaver and Little Beaver creeks. In the two serrate main crests, popularly divided as the northern and southern groups, there are eight surveyed peaks from 7053 ft to 8292 ft in height in a 7-mi. span, but in the additional jumble of summits there are at least 21 peaks from 7500 ft to 8200 ft in altitude. The extreme compactness of the range and regional unity is more evident when it is understood that the range is less than 6 mi. long.

The high peaks of the Picket Range retain ridge continuity. The nearly even summit altitudes now isolated by erosion strongly suggest they are remnants of much more extensive even-crested ridges dismembered by erosion, largely in the form of intense alpine glaciation, to form the present topography: the well defined peak level and continuity of the crestline in the Picket Range lends strength to the theory that alp slopes at higher levels during Pleistocene interglacial time truncated alpine summits at those levels. The Picket Range and rugged crests to the W are very deeply dissected by steep-walled glacial gorges. Six low-gradient valleys enter the northern and southern groups below an altitude of 3000 ft, and one (Goodell Creek) enters at 1000 ft only 4 mi. from Mt. Terror. The principal cirques have floors at about 3500 ft (although McMillan Creek cirque has a floor of about 2800 ft, with local relief over 1 mi.). Double cirques typical of the range are very evident in the heads of both McMillan and Luna creeks. Stemming from these origins, valley glaciers once filled the whole Big Beaver Creek drainage and its awesome erosive powers created the broad U-shaped cross profile.

Mt. Challenger, the northernmost Picket Range summit, has the largest glacier (3.4 km²),[71] and is the northern hinge of a splendid continuity of hanging glaciers that ring the Luna Creek cirque, with the only separations being several steep rock buttress dividers emanating from high peaks. This same glacier continuity is apparent in the McMillan Creek cirque of the Southern Picket Group, where the peaks and rock walls are an even more closely knit unit.

There is a prevalance of glaciers at timberline in the Picket Range. At this level avalanches tend to accumulate on timberline benches. Erosion of mass-wasting, much more vigorous above timberline than below, has formed extensive alp slopes at timberline. The only broad alp slopes in the entire range are those at the head and E flank of Terror Creek, in Crescent Creek basin, and on Challenger Arm. On the periphery of the range, Easy and Stetattle Ridges demonstrate the extent of alp slopes and mass-wasting at timberline.

Both the northern and southern groups have a remarkably similar map outline, with magnificent amphitheaters and hanging glaciers in the inside (NE) arcs. The Northern Picket Group is shaped as a great horseshoe about upper Luna Creek with Luna Peak and the Luna Creek-Little Beaver Creek ridge being the outliers. But from the W the overall impression is a repetition of steep craggy rock peaks and long rugged buttresses that descend into lower U-shaped valleys. Small pocket glaciers and steep moraine/talus slopes have prohibited formation of a continuous timberline here. The group's culmination is Mt. Fury, with its two high summits, although the mountain is challenged by asymmetrical Luna Peak, a geographic anomaly because of its disjointed location to the E.

In both groups of the Picket Range the biotite gneiss, the metamorphic backbone of the North Cascades, is well displayed on ridges and in the cirques of Terror, Crescent, and Luna creeks. In places the gneiss, formed by metamorphism of sedimentary and volcanic rocks about 100 m.y. ago, has many tight folds and contortions. Many intrusive dikes have been formed (some crisscrossed) of several types and ages. Many breccias of shattered and cemented rocks are found throughout both groups of peaks. The considerable exposures of shattered gneiss breccia (silica-cemented fragments) may represent a violent eruption of gases from the once-molten intrusion of the underlying Chilliwack Batholith.[72] The western contact of Skagit gneiss and large granitic bodies at its margins is intrusive material, clearly seen at Mt. Hagan, Berdeen Lake, and the North Fork Nooksack River cirque. Whatcom Peak and Mt. Challenger are composed entirely of the batholith.

During Cretaceous time there was strong deformation here. Rocks E of the Straight Creek Fault were metamorphosed to schist and gneiss, and intruded by igneous rocks. Contact metamorphism has indurated the pre-existing sedimentary and volcanic rocks so that they stand up as the higher peaks. The strike and dip of bedding and foliation in the metamorphic rocks is reflected in the shape of evolved land forms. Frost shattering is aided by greater accessibility of water into rock along foliation planes.

Pleistocene and recent glaciation has been especially vigorous at cirque heads. Upper Luna Creek originates in a steep-walled cirque carved in granitic rocks below Mt. Challenger, Phantom Peak, and Mt. Fury. Here is a special example of a glacial cirque: a complex of hanging glaciers and ice patches with a combined area of 3.8 km², some fed by avalanches. The remnant glacier at the cirque head portrays textbook examples of a bergschrund where a deep crevasse separates the active glacier body from the steep headwall of its

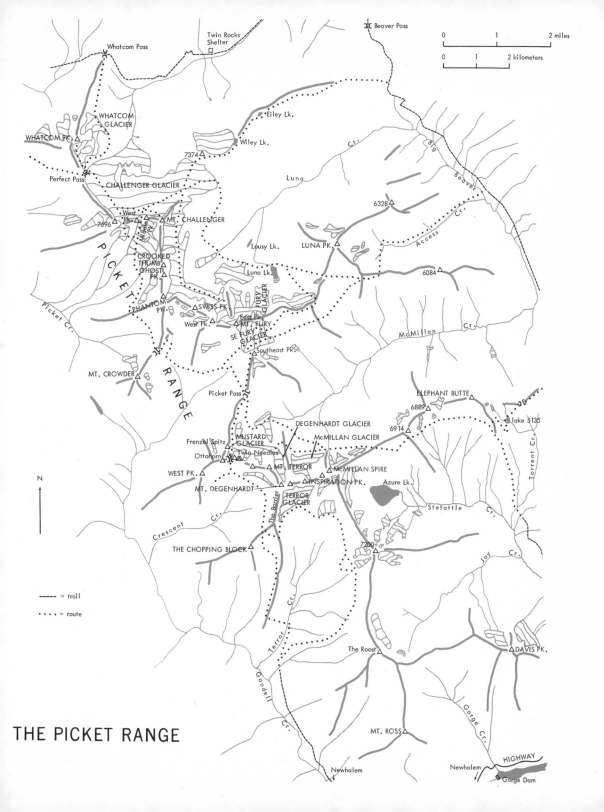

THE PICKET RANGE

----- = trail

•••• = route

Beaver Pass

0   1   2 miles

0   1   2 kilometers

Twin Rocks Shelter

Whatcom Pass

WHATCOM GLACIER

WHATCOM PK.

Eiley Lk.

Wiley Lk.

7374

Perfect Pass

CHALLENGER GLACIER

Luna

Cr.

Big Beaver

Cr.

Access Cr.

6328

West Pk.

7696

Mc.Pk.

MT. CHALLENGER

Lousy Lk.

LUNA PK.

6084

P I C K E T

CROOKED THUMB

GHOST PK.

Luna Lk.

PHANTOM PK.

SWISS PK.

FURY GLACIER

West Pk.

East Pk.

MT. FURY

SE FURY GLACIER

McMILLAN Cr.

MT. CROWDER

R A N G E

Southeast Pk.

Picket Cr.

Picket Pass

ELEPHANT BUTTE

lake 5135

6889

DEGENHARDT GLACIER

Frenzel Spitz

MUSTARD GLACIER

McMILLAN GLACIER

6914

Torrent Cr.

Ottohorn

Twin Needles

WEST PK.

MT. TERROR

McMILLAN SPIRE

Azure Lk.

MT. DEGENHARDT

INSPIRATION PK.

N

TERROR GLACIER

Stetattle Cr.

Crescent Cr.

The Barrier

THE CHOPPING BLOCK

7200+

Joy Cr.

Terror Cr.

The Roost

DAVIS PK.

Goodell Cr.

MT. ROSS

HIGHWAY

Newhalem

Newhalem

Gorge Cr.

Gorge Dam

cirque container.

The entire area is very active with large rockfalls. Cone-shaped residual ice masses have built up on the cirque floor, an area on the way to becoming a debris-covered glacier. The stagnant terminal zone is manifested by a dismal appearance: rock rubble cascading onto ice aids in shielding it from solar radiation (such moraines with fossil ice date from 1880). There are two moraine-locked lakes in the area of ground moraine in the upper valley. End moraines (debris ridges, climax of 19th century glaciation) which mark the former position of the Challenger Glacier on the Luna cirque slope are also evident. Lower, valley-train outwash flats reach to massive moraines built during earlier centuries (11th to 18th; Will F. Thompson). Here the outwash body with organic-rich silt beds have allowed a vegetation mat to grow; this mat thickens downvalley and Englemann spruce begins to appear. On the eastern ridges of the Picket Range larches begin to occur, proof of diminishing moisture.

In the Southern Picket Group the steep escarpment of N faces, with several extremely steep and badly crevassed glaciers which divide individual peaks, competes as one of the several grandest scenes in the North Cascades. Characteristically, rock walls rear abruptly from glaciers in convoluted topography. The narrow serrate ridge crests here are being sculptured by glacial ice cutting and moving along flanks of peaks and bases of ridges. Snow avalanches on steep slopes combine with rock weathering at high altitudes where there are frequent diurnal temperature changes, imperceptibly modifying the steep terrain. Lower in the McMillan Creek valley, and on ridge flanks where glaciers are gone, their work is seen in rounded knobs and polished slope surfaces, smoothed and striated rock bosses, long lateral moraines running downvalley, and fresh barren terminal moraines spread in the flat valley reach.

The southern flanks of the group are shaped in two expansive alpine cirques at the head of Terror and Crescent creeks. While ice has virtually vanished in the latter cirque, 1.5-km wide Terror Glacier consumes most of the basin between The Barrier and the ridge overlooking Azure Lake. The ring of rock above the Terror Glacier, highlighted by Inspiration Peak and McMillan Spires, reaches the scenic climax of the group. The Barrier, a long, narrow rock ridge (300 ft to 500 ft high and 1 mi. long) which has been honed asymmetrical by the ancient Terror Glacier, separates the two ice-smoothed cirques. Crescent Creek cirque is headed by an amazing array of steep rock peaks and pinnacles, of which Mt. Terror reaches the highest altitude. Standing as a lone sentinel SW of The Barrier, The Chopping Block forms an outpost to the group, now abandoned by the glaciers which once carved its lopsided horn.

Despite all we know, despite pictures, and maps, the range is bound to remain full of dazzling surprises. In a sense it is today's version of the remaining exploration left on Earth.

Because of the primitive terrain, the Picket Range has remained the wildest and most unexplored region in the North Cascades. It is not an area for the wilderness novice; its brushy valleys and jagged ridges are a test for the most seasoned mountaineers. The length of climbs, combined with steep mixed terrain and variable conditions demand all-around competence and fitness. The rewards of the range include spectacular alpine climbs on generally solid rock.

It should be noted that routes up the creek beds of Luna and McMillan valleys are definitely not recommended (for established routes, see Approaches-Trails). When traversing ridges and glaciers, one is likely to be dismayed at the appearance of deep gorges, serrate crests, and crevassed icefalls, often very difficult for backpacking. Always take ice axe and crampons.

The remarkable likeness of this subrange to a picket fence is especially apparent from a western view of the southern group. This unique resemblance, not the name of Captain George E. Pickett of the U.S. Army, in charge of Fort Bellingham in 1856 and who later gained fame in the Civil War, is the origin of the range's title. The very names of some of the peaks — Challenger, Fury, Terror, and Phantom — betray something of their flavor. Mapping done by Lage Wernstedt for the Forest Service in the mid-1920s is apparently responsible for name and summit identities first shown on 1931 maps (the Forest Service map of 1922 does not even hint at a name for the range).

Although a reconnaissance party from the Boundary Survey in 1859 was close to Whatcom Pass and a road survey party crossed the pass in 1896, the Picket Range remained the most isolated sector of the North Cascades. The difficulties of approach discouraged closer investigation. The geologists Smith and Calkins in 1901 noted that granitic rock appeared to extend W of Skagit River; in his journal for September 8 George Otis Smith wrote: "it apparently occurs west of the river and is believed to make up the very rugged peaks at the head of Beaver and Little Beaver creeks." Because of the brush-thick stream valleys, ridge exploration logically came first. As early as 1905 Glee Davis and Burton Babcock climbed to the crest of the Goodell-Stetattle Creek divide S of McMillan Spire. Davis ventured along Stetattle Ridge (from Sourdough Mountain) as did Lage Wernstedt later. Gaspar Petta, for whom Jasper Pass is named, trapped in the valleys of Goodell and Bacon creeks in the 1920s.

Not until 1931 did William Degenhardt and Herbert V. Strandberg make their enterprising trek from Goodell Creek along a stream W of Terror Creek to Pinnacle Peak (The Chopping Block), resulting in the first alpine ascent in the Picket Range. They then descended The Barrier in darkness, and crossed Terror Glacier and the cirque of Terror Creek to the ridge above Azure Lake; it is interesting to note that when descending toward the valley of Goodell Creek the party used the rope on some subalpine cliffs. In 1932, with James Martin, they continued into the high basin of Crescent Creek to climb Mt. Terror, but were unsuccessful in crossing The Barrier. Not until the 1950s did ventures to the southern group begin in earnest, aided by a logging road into the valley of Goodell Creek.

The first men into the headwaters of Luna Creek in the northern group probably were Bill Cox and Will F. Thompson; soon after leaving the Big Beaver Creek Trail in the summer of 1937 they found "a broad flood plain laced with small willows as blindly dense as an old laurel hedge." After ½ mi., the travel improved slightly through spruce forest and along gravel bars, but much impeding alder intervened; the best route was found to be along the apex of talus cones on the northern slope frontage. In 1962 both the Degenhardt Glacier and the glacier reaching to the notch just W of Mt. Terror were climbed, offering problems similar to those encountered earlier on Mt. Fury and Phantom Peak by Cox, Thompson, Fred and Helmy Beckey during pioneering climbs. These glaciers are becoming more broken, and may be impossible without direct aid during certain times, or resorting to cliff bypasses. In August 1963 Alex Bertulis and Half Zantop made the first alpine traverse of the Picket Range, a 10-day trek beginning from the S; the crux of this effort was rappelling on the N face of Mt. Terror in a steep fault between the main and lower summits to reach the cirque of McMillan Creek.

Approach route connections: Big Beaver Creek Trail◆-Luna Lake High Route, Challenger Arm Route, Challenger Arm to Luna Lake and Picket Pass; Chilliwack River Trail◆-Whatcom Pass-Challenger Glacier Route; Easy Ridge Trail◆-Perfect Pass Route

and Picket Pass Route; Goodell Creek Route◆ and The Barrier-Crescent Creek Route; Stetattle Creek Trail◆; Stetattle Ridge Route◆.

References: *Mountaineer,* 1931, pp. 38-40; 1932, pp. 21-26 (southern group); 1950, p. 39 (northern); 1952, p. 12 (geology); 1958, pp. 99-100 (northern); 1959, pp. 102-4; 1962, pp. 75-83; 1963, pp. 57-62, 84-87 (northern) and p. 93 (southern); 1964, pp. 93-97; 1968, pp. 163-67; 1974, pp. 17-22 (traverse); 1977, pp. 25-29; *Appalachia,* December 1944, pp. 205-16; June 1952, pp. 101-2 (northern); *Mazama,* 1966, pp. 40-42 (southern); *A.A.J.,* 1959, p. 208; 1962, pp. 65-68 (southern); 1963, pp. 475-76 (northern); 1964, p. 174 (traverse); 1971, pp. 347-48 (traverse); *Routes and Rocks* (see note 72), pp. 27-35, 41-45; *National Geographic,* May 1968, pp. 642-43 (southern); *Summit,* January-February 1961, pp. 20-23 (northern); January-February 1971, pp. 6-10 (northern); *Challenge of the North Cascades,* pp. 71-80.

McMILLAN SPIRE   8000 ft+/2438 m+

McMillan Spire, with its two pyramidal rock summits, is the eastern and one of the dominant features of the Picket Range. The Spire is located 1 mi. E of Mt. Terror. Both summits rise off an eastern segment of Terror Glacier less steeply than nearby Inspiration Peak. But on the North Face the summits form magnificent alpine rock buttresses rising 2400 ft above the main portion of the McMillan Creek glacier. The name, as McMillan Creek, is for John McMillan, early Skagit trapper and packer. First ascent (West Spire) by Fred and Helmy Beckey on August 29, 1940. A winter ascent was made by Mike Colpitts and Jaerl Secher-Jensen in March 1976. References: *Mountaineer,* 1940, p. 38; 1952, p. 13; *Appalachia,* December 1944, p. 215; June 1952.

WEST RIDGE: Use Goodell Creek Route◆ to Terror Creek basin. Ascend the Terror Glacier, polished slabs, and some snowpatches to the broad Inspiration-McMillan col (7280 ft+). The ridge from here is moderately easy climbing (maximum class 3). Time: 3 hours from basin camp.

NORTH FACE: First ascent by Fred Beckey and Jerry Fuller on July 16, 1966. By taking Stetattle Creek Trail◆ and climbing to Stetattle Ridge◆ one can make a 1000-ft traversing descent on snow and glaciers to beneath the main face. Here climb ice segments to below the summit, then follow crack systems, ribs, and assorted slabs. The route begins above the bergschrund near the lowest main rock toe and head directly for the summit; some snowpatches on route. Rock is generally firm. Grade III; class 4 and 5 (18 roped pitches). References: *Mountaineer,* 1966, p. 199; *A.A.J.,* 1966, p. 135; *Summit,* December 1966, pp. 24-27.

EAST PEAK   WEST PEAK

North Face

North Buttress

McMILLAN SPIRE from north
DAVID KNUDSON

SOUTHEAST FACE: First ascent by Dick Benedict, Earl Hamilton and Jim McCarthy on July 16, 1970. From the notch between the Spires (see East McMillan Spire) climb around the N side of a small gendarme (awkward). Do about 200 ft of class 4 to the S corner of the vertical E face. Make a 40-ft rising traverse into an obvious major diagonal crack-chimney system which cuts across the Southeast Face. Then climb the exposed face (5.4); after a good belay (with chock) continue the same system to a ledge. Make a short traverse left; here is a difficult exposed and unprotected move around a bulge (5.7). Then the climbing becomes moderate, ending about 100 ft W of the summit. Grade II; class 5.6 or 5.7 (two leads of class 5). Reference: *Mountaineer,* 1971, p. 55.

SOUTH FACE: First ascent by Dave Collins, Donald (Claunch) Gordon, and Paul Salness in June 1951. This 1000-ft rock route begins under the summit on the S face and veers right to the upper E ridge (possibly crossing or intersecting the Southeast Face route). There are some difficult

Labels on image: McMILLAN SPIRE, INSPIRATION PEAK, West Peak, East Peak, Little Mac Spire, MT. DEGENHARDT, The Pyramid, Southeast Face, West Ridge, East Ridge, West Ridge, towers, South Face, South Face, South Face, Southwest Arete, ROR CIER

SOUTHERN PICKET RANGE from south
DAVID KNUDSON

sections, topped by a very wide chimney. Class 4 and 5.

EAST McMILLAN SPIRE   7920 ft+/2415 m
First ascent by Dave Collins, Donald (Claunch) Gordon, and Paul Salness in June 1951, via the West Ridge. Traverse the glacier around the cirque rim and ascend to cross a wide bergschrund. Climb the steep, slanting 1000-ft snow finger on the S face to the notch dividing the Spires. Continue up the West Ridge — about 450 ft of climbing (class 3-4). Note: The schrund can be a problem in late summer. Reference: *Appalachia*, June 1952, p. 103.

NORTH BUTTRESS
This imposing 2300-ft buttress is the eastern rock rampart of the Southern Picket Group, and is one of the grand rock bastions in the Picket Range. Rock is firm gneiss, but tends to slabbiness (sometimes hard to protect and poor in cracks; rock best near bottom and becomes slabbier and looser high on route). First ascent by Doug McNair and Bryce Simon on September 18-19, 1976 (one bivouac). The party made the approach from Terror Creek basin by a traverse of a shelf system above Azure Lake, then a sharp ridge descent to the edge of the McMillan Creek glaciers. The route begins at the right edge of the buttress center, slightly above the lowest toe. Follow the right side and gain the sharp crest just below the summit. Grade IV (30 pitches); class 5.7 and A1 (minor aid); thin pitons are most useful. Time: 1½ days. Reference: *A.A.J.*, 1977, pp. 170-71.

LITTLE MAC SPIRE   est. 7600 ft/2317 m
The summit is a pyramidal appendage on the E side of East McMillan Spire; the E face drops abruptly to Azure Lake; the S face is about 500 ft in height, at the edge of Terror Glacier basin. First ascent by Michael Heath and Bill Sumner on June 19, 1969 (via S face).

The route consists of broken rock and ledges from the glacier to the steep central section. A large heather-rock ledge is followed left for about 100 ft. Then climb steep cracks and projections to a pedestal top (belay). Make a short right traverse, then a vertical crack leads to a belay where the angle lessens. Then traverse across a steep slabby area to a good ledge on the upper face (200 ft below summit). Climb steep loose rock (5.8), then make a short lead around a block

South Face

Variation

West Ridge

INSPIRATION PEAK from west
DAVID KNUDSON

INSPIRATION PEAK
7840 ft+/2390 m+

Inspiration is a thin wedge of rock with a high crown. The Terror Glacier flanks its S face and glacier ice of the McMillan Creek cirque foots the northern face. The peak is located about 0.6 mi. ESE of Mt. Terror, between The Pyramid and McMillan Spire. Its rock is Skagit gneiss that has acquired a granodiorite composition here and on McMillan Spire. The best description of the peak is that given by the 1932 climbing party in the range, who wrote that the Terror-McMillan divide peaks have "only two dimensions — width and height." The term "impossible" was added for the human viewpoint. First ascent by Fred and Helmy Beckey on August 29, 1940. References: *Mountaineer,* 1940, p. 38; *Appalachia,* December 1944, pp. 215-16.

WEST RIDGE: From Terror Basin slabs and the crevassed glacier are taken to broken rock of the low toe spur SW of the summit. Ascend the steep, major rock couloir, bypassing a large chockstone on the left (about 600 ft to the West Ridge). The final ridge (similar to the inclined edge of a book) begins by climbing slabby rock (a snowpatch may be on the slab) from the ridge notch. Much of the 500-ft corner is slabby and exposed 70-degree rock, but higher the ridge is well broken and firm. The critical spot is low down, where the overhang on the left has eroded the ridge/arete to a narrow and very steep pitch (next to South Face). Class 4 and 5. Time: 5 hours from basin.

Variation: By D. McKay and Joe Quigley in 1957. Make a traverse under the white overhanging wall to turn the corner on the N. Proceed onto the North Face, which is well broken (class 3-4); there may be some snow on the traverse.

Variation: From Crescent Creek basin and The Barrier one can reach the ridge crest above the W couloir by traversing snow-boulder slopes on the S face of Mt. Degenhardt, and ledges on the S face of The Pyramid (some snowpatches on ledges).

NORTH FACE; This steep 1500-ft rock face is located above the main glacier segment of McMillan cirque, and because of its position is usually in the shade. Reach the face as per the North Buttress of McMillan Spire, then climb the crevassed glacier to the right; the glacier's apex can be a problem. First ascent by Alex Bertulis, Sergei Efimov, Mark Fielding, and Alexei Lebedehin on June 19, 1977.

Begin climbing on the right third of the face. Ascend a crack which slants slightly left (belay from holds part way up); continue up the crack, then climb right on difficult rock (minimal protection), then directly up to a ledge. Climb left to small snowpatch, ascend left and up to the tip of ice tongue, then up and right to a belay on a small ledge beneath overhangs. Climb up and left on small holds, then straight up on easier rock to a ledge. The next pitch involves rock and ice in a big corner on the right, then traverses left from top of

and up a narrow chimney to the summit. Grade III; class 5.8 (used 20 pitons and chocks). Time: 6 hours up; 4 hours down. References: *Mountaineer,* 1970, pp. 101-2; *A.A.J.,* 1970, p. 122.

Descent: Rappel into notch W of summit.

SOUTHWEST ARETE: First ascent by Art Huffman and Don Williamson on August 15, 1970. This route follows a well defined crest (firm rock); the East McMillan-Little Mac gully is just W of the arete (three nearly vertical steps on the arete). There are eight enjoyable leads (class 4 and 5). Grade II; class 5.4. Time: 4 hours on rock. Reference: *A.A.J.,* 1971, p. 348.

INSPIRATION PEAK   The Pyramid   MT. DEGENHARDT   MT. TERROR

DEGENHARDT GLACIER

North Face

McMILLAN CREEK GLACIER

SOUTHERN PICKET RANGE from north
AUSTIN POST, UNIVERSITY OF WASHINGTON

ice to a ledge. Another pitch straight up leads to a lower angle area where ledge system leads right on easier rock to the base of a steep crack system. The last five pitches lead up steep cracks and chimneys to the final chimney, which comes out on the West Ridge one easy pitch below the summit (final chimney had waterfall on original). Grade IV; class 5.9 (12 pitches); two pitches in the 5.8-5.9 range, with most being mid-fifth. Take chocks from small wired to 3 inches. Reference: *A.A.J.*, 1978, p. 524.

Descent: Via East Ridge (several rappels), then scrambling to steep icefields W of the eastern towers, then to glacier; bivouac made during descent.

EAST RIDGE: First ascent by Fred Beckey, Dave Collins, and Ed Cooper early October 1958. From slabs in upper Terror Creek basin climb the edge of the glacier arm under the South Face. Traverse the upper glacier segment to the first diagonal gully series to the East Ridge (between the main face and the first of the East Towers). Climb 400 ft of very steep granite on the ridge crest (two 70-ft pitches are class 5; the higher of these pitches is 150 ft below the E summit and is 85 degrees in angle). Bypass a small overhang near the summit on its N. The remainder of the ridge to the E summit and onward to the highest point is much easier. References: *Mountaineer,* 1959, pp. 104-5; *A.A.J.*, 1959, pp. 302-3.

SOUTH FACE: This 800-900-ft-high face would appear

improbable, but there are a surprising ramp and inside gash. The rock is firm, with nice exposure; a challenging but never severe climb. First ascent by Michael Heath and Bill Sumner on June 18, 1969.

Begin at the far left corner of the face, where the lowest rock spur meets the glacier (one lead of 5.7). This is followed by several hundred ft of scrambling, in order to reach the diagonal right-slanting ramp system that cuts across the center of the face. Follow this system for three leads to where it forks (upper and lower). At about 50 ft beyond this fork a great gash meets the upper ramp and ascends the vertical face 400 ft to the skyline closely W of the summit. Enter the gash by climbing past its start along the ramp 40 ft, then double back up and around a corner (5.6). Three leads of face climbing and chimneying — to 5.8 — inside the gash brings one to under a chockstone just below an easy summit pitch. Grade III; class 5.8 (used 20 pitons and chocks). Time: 12 hours r.t. to basin camp. References: *Mountaineer,* 1970, p. 101; *A.A.J.,* 1970, pp. 121-22.

EAST TOWERS   7600 ft+/2317 m

Five small rock towers crest the steep rock and ice ridge immediately E of Inspiration Peak. Generally reach the climbs by climbing S face gullies from Terror Glacier.

Don Tower (on the far E) was first climbed by Dave Collins, Donald (Claunch) Gordon, and Paul Salness in 1951. The route is a clockwise spiral, beginning on the E ridge (5.5 — with 30 ft of exposed climbing). The next tower to the W can be circled on the N side in the ice slope moat; then ascend a rib to a secondary pinnacle on the W side. A short knifed ridge turns back to the top. Towers three and four were first climbed by Graham Mathews and David Michael in 1951; the fourth tower is done on the low-angle W side. The fifth tower (on the W) was done by D. McKay and J. Quigley in 1957 via its NW corner. References: *Mountaineer,* 1953, p. 68; 1978, p. 108.

THE PYRAMID   7920 ft+/2414 m+

This pyramidal-shaped summit is almost a satellite of Mt. Degenhardt, on the high ridge connecting the latter with Inspiration Peak. The name's origin is apparent from Mt. Triumph, but from the NE flank, where the Degenhardt Glacier slopes steeply to McMillan Creek cirque, the peak appears as a small rock point above a steep rock face (this face rises steeply above the largest glacier in the cirque); on the main ridge there is a small ice saddle connecting The Pyramid with Mt. Degenhardt. First ascent by David Collins, Donald (Claunch) Gordon, and Paul Salness, June 1951. References: *Appalachia,* June 1952, p. 102; *Mountaineer,* 1963, p. 93.
ROUTE: From The Barrier or Crescent Creek basin take the

route to the S ridge of Mt. Degenhardt. Climb and cross heathery ledges (snow in early summer) to the base of The Pyramid, then climb its left profile. Here is about 250 ft of class 3 rock scrambling (slabs and steep, broken blocks). The 1951 party climbed directly from Terror Glacier, up moderately steep rock and a snow couloir to the saddle.

MT. DEGENHARDT
8000 ft+/2438 m+

This is the second highest summit in the Southern Picket Group, located at the junction of Crescent Creek and Terror Creek ridges, SE of Mt. Terror. The mountain first appears in history on August 7, 1931 when William Degenhardt and Herbert Strandberg climbed it from a western and northern route, then again in 1938 when four members of the Ptarmigan climbing club, traversing the ridge form the S, mistook the objective for Mt. Terror.[73] Reference: *Mountaineer,* 1931, pp. 39-40.
ROUTE: See Goodell Creek Route♦-Barrier-Crescent Creek Route. Traverse and rise on snow below The Barrier into the high bowl between Terror and Degenhardt; snow gullies then lead to both N and S of the summit rock area. The best route has proven to be directly to the left (NW) summit ridge, then around an obvious ledge behind the N skyline (a rising ramp) to finish by rock climbing on the E or SE face of the summit; class 3-4.

An alternative completion is to traverse from the upper end of The Barrier via a steep ridge (part of the route is by a snow gully and ramp). Keep right of a gendarme on the final S ridge (this is closely beneath the summit). The 1938 party apparently completed this route.

A variation of this finish was done by Pete Schoening and Phil Sharpe (June 1951), completing the climb via broken rock on the E face.
DEGENHARDT GLACIER: First ascent by Joan Firey, Joe Firey, Tony Hovey, Ken Hunich, Don Keller, John and Irene Meulemans on July 9, 1962. The best access to upper McMillan cirque (see Stetattle Creek Trail♦), after descending the glaciers and moraine slopes below McMillan Spires, is to make an ascending NW traverse of the terminal moraine toward outlet of a small lake (crossing over moraine where brush dwindles). A more direct alternative is to do an ascending steeper gully at the S border of the moraine, where it joins the ridge of the "Barricade." Note: The traverse on slabs under the McMillan Glacier calls for alertness because of potential ice activity (called a "bowling alley" by original party).

Ascend the snow fan and ridge (above "Barricade") to E of the main icefall of Degenhardt Glacier. From the highest part of the ridge traverse below the E side of icefall on small rock ledges above the "Barricade" (the traverse is under an area of active icefall and presents some hazard). From the highest obvious rock ledge step onto the glacier. The ascent is generally straightforward through the lower area, but long

Labels on image: MT. TRIUMPH, Northeast Ridge, Northwest Route

THE CHOPPING BLOCK
ED COOPER

crevasses may totally block the route in some years (has appeared impossible in some seasons). The upper area is steep but generally passable by gaining its eastern edge. A steeper ice section near the E margin may require belaying. Ascend to the ice saddle between The Pyramid and the objective to join the route from opposite flank. References: *Mountaineer,* 1963, p. 95; photo 1962, p. 22.

BARRIER PINNACLES The pinnacles SW of Mt. Degenhardt were climbed by Graham Matthews and David Michael in 1951; some of them may possibly have been climbed by the 1938 party.

THE CHOPPING BLOCK (Pinnacle Peak)   6805 ft/2074 m

This unusually shaped rock summit crowns the rugged ridge between Terror and Crescent creeks, its rocky flank high above the wilderness valley of Goodell Creek at 6.2 mi. NW of Newhalem. The peak looks like a squared-off sentinel, isolated from the main jagged ridge of the southern Picket Range. Local residents once called it Babcock's Chopping Block and Stump Mountain (because there are two other summits called "Pinnacle" in Washington, an

effort will be made to adopt a new name). Pioneer climber Herbert Strandberg aptly described the peak: "it has the appearance of a huge cone, having its top lopped off at an angle of about twenty-five degrees." The steepest profile, therefore, faces the Picket group, and when the peak has a patch of snow near the summit, it resembles an ice cream cone, the least steep face being the SW. The peak is very visible from the highway at the crossing of Goodell Creek because of its frontal position. The first ascent was made by William Degenhardt, James C. Martin, and Herbert V. Strandberg on August 9, 1932. Reference: *Mountaineer,* 1932, p. 22.

SOUTHEAST FACE: For approach see The Barrier route (Goodell Creek Route♦-Barrier-Crescent Creek Route). This is the 1932 route, which begins from the side facing The Barrier. Traverse beneath the steep E face to the SE side of the peak. Climb a 200-ft chimney, then a slabby face. There may be minor difficulties just below the summit slab; the route is partially a face and a ridge climb. Class 3-4. Time: 3 hours from timberline.

NORTHWEST ROUTE: First ascent by Ed Cooper and Glen Denny September 9, 1961. Begin from saddle NE of the peak. The route ascends lower rock of NE ridge (a few snowpatches here). Below midway on the climb make a diagonal rightward traverse onto the N to NW face (steep class 3), then reach the summit via the W ridge or slightly behind (steep grassy rock). Class 3-4. Time: 2 hours. Reference: *A.A.J.*, 1962, p. 68.

NORTHEAST RIDGE: First ascent by Carla Firey, Joan Firey, David Knudson, and Peter Renz on July 12, 1970. Begin as above. Bypass an initial overhanging section (first ridge step) by ascending ledges on the N face (right; class 3) and then return to the ridge. Ascend this directly (class 3-4), then complete the climb on the N side of the ridge; class 5.4. Descent: via S side, then along SE ridge face. Reference: *Summit,* April, 1971.

MT. TERROR   8151 ft/2484 m

Terror is distinctive as the highest peak in the Southern Picket Group, a S-slanting pyramidal rock formation located 7.3 mi. N of Newhalem, between Crescent Creek and the head of McMillan Creek. Terror rises picturesquely 950 ft above a remnant glacier of Crescent Creek basin, but it is on the E face that the mountain presents a truly impressive bastion of rock and ice. Here a great buttress and face of gneiss rears 2550 ft above the Degenhardt Glacier and its fringing ice connections from the spectacular cirque of McMillan Creek.

Early Forest Service maps showed Mt. Terror at the present location of McMillan Spire, but on newer editions this error has been corrected to the rightful position farther W. The ambiguity of the correct location for Mt. Terror dates to before the 1930s, when the precise nomenclature of the peak grouping was nebulous. Lage Wernstedt had apparently provided the name, but because of loosely applied map lettering, the 1931 climbing party concluded the name "Terror" meant the entire grouping. A year later they made its first ascent, having by then decided the name only applied to their objective. This first climb was made by William Degenhardt, James Martin, and Herb Strandberg on August 18, 1932. The second ascent was not done until July 31, 1960 (Vic Josendal, Gibson Reynolds, Phil Sharpe, Warren Spickard, Jay Todd, Roe D. Watson). The first winter ascent was made by Paul Ekman, Roy Farrel, Joan Firey, and Joe Weis in February 1977. Reference: *Mountaineer,* 1932, p. 25.

WEST RIDGE: This is the normal route from Crescent Creek basin (see Goodell Creek Route♦) and the one done on the first ascent. One can also make the approach from Terror Glacier, then crossing The Barrier for a traverse and descent into the upper basin of Crescent Creek. Climb the 400-ft-deep slot on the S face below the deep notch W of the summit (some steep snow — take crampons). The easiest

way to handle the next portion is to climb a few ft behind the corner (class 4); the original party spent many hours trying to get up the class 5 pitch directly above the notch. Climb the long rock ridge slope to the first summit horn (class 3); traverse high around its right side (S) into the final notch. Here the climb to the summit is moderately steep, but provides firm rock (class 3 — belay optional). For descent: There is a rappel anchor above notch.

NORTH FACE: First ascent by Charles Bell, Ed Cooper, David Hiser, and Mike Swayne on July 8-11, 1961. Approach via Stetattle Ridge♦, then descend to McMillan cirque for the traverse beneath the hanging shelf-glaciers (9-14 hours: see Mt. Degenhardt). Cross "The Barricade" by traversing snow and a deep prominent gully, then a short face to gain the glacier. Cross and ascend the glacier to reach the buttress face of Mt. Terror via a steep glacier slope several hundred ft high on the NE side of the rock face. Climbing is on firm gneiss (mostly class 3 and 4 with only one class 5 pitch); follow the buttress to meet the West Ridge route below the first summit horn (original party made a bivouac on the face). Grade III; class 3-5. References: *Mountaineer,* 1962, p. 95; *A.A.J.,* 1962, p. 67.

EAST RIDGE (East Edge of Southeast Face): The first ascent was made by Carla Firey, Joan Firey, David Knudson, and Peter Renz on July 13, 1970. Rock is quite solid when climbing was the hardest and most exposed — as on the steep part of the first pitch and the strenuous part of the last pitch — but slightly loose near the middle of the route. It is now apparent that the route described earlier as the SE face of Mt. Terror, credited to a 1938 party, was done on the southerly ridge of Mt. Degenhardt.

From Crescent Creek basin the route is gained via the level southeasterly ridge connecting Mt. Degenhardt and Mt. Terror. Access may be from the former directly or via class 3 slabs from the basin. From where the flat ridge abruptly joins the Terror ridge corner proceed up large broken (unstable) blocks. Move right up a diagonal ledge. Then climb directly up a short steep section to easier rock. The route continues in zigzag fashion, connecting ledges and bearing left toward the E skyline and finally rightward toward the summit. A short, strenuous pitch leads directly into a broken chimney (route crux) on the E side of the summit. Class 5.5 (four to five pitches of class 4 and 5). Time: 12 hours r.t. from camp below The Chopping Block. Reference: *A.A.J.,* 1975, p. 128.

THE RAKE (The Blob)   est. 7700 ft/2347 m

This is the first distinct rock formation W of Mt. Terror, consisting of a narrow crest with several sharp points; the map's contour of 7840 ft appears too high in relation to flanking summits. The first ascent was made by Pete Schoening and Phil Sharpe on Labor Day 1951, when they erroneously termed this formation Twin Needles. It is still uncertain exactly where the route lies, but the line taken was apparently the ridge

Himmelhorn

Twin Needles

The Rake

MT. TERROR

The Chopping Block

MT.
DEGENHARDT

The Pyramid

INSPIRATION
PEAK

McMILLAN
SPIRE

Terror Creek Basin

cross

The Barrier

cross

Crescent Creek Basin

SOUTHERN PICKET RANGE from southwest
DAVID KNUDSON

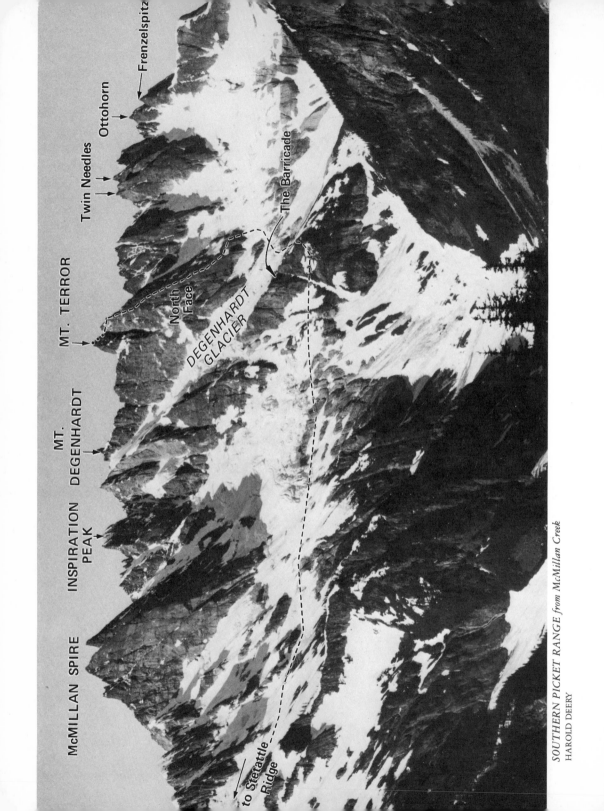

McMillan SPIRE

INSPIRATION PEAK

MT. DEGENHARDT

MT. TERROR

Twin Needles

Ottohorn

Frenzelspitz

North Face

The Barricade

DEGENHARDT GLACIER

to Stetattle Ridge

SOUTHERN PICKET RANGE from McMillan Creek
HAROLD DEERY

SOUTHERN PICKET RANGE from west
NATIONAL PARK SERVICE

next to the Crescent Creek basin couloir nearest the E end of the glacier. Follow the couloir edge, then cross it to gain the summit ridge (apparently the E ridge); class 3 and 4. There is some speculation that the gully taken may be the second from the right. Reference: *Appalachia,* June 1952, p. 103.

The lower W summit was climbed in 1962.

The N buttress, via a steep ice and glacier couloir from McMillan Creek cirque, was climbed to the W summit point by Carla Firey, Joan Firey, Joe Firey, David Knudson, Frank de Saussure, and George Wallerstein in July 1974. Most of the rock climbing was class 4 and easy class 5 (firm); the party was stopped by time and a slab problem continuing to the true summit. The descent was made from the W notch on very steep snow.

TWIN NEEDLES   7840 ft+/2390 m+

These are two slender rock spires (Crescent Creek Spires) 0.6 mi. W of Mt. Terror. On the NE face the needles stand among the sentinels high above McMillan Creek cirque. Both the West Needle (7840 ft+/2390 m+), which is the highest point W of Mt. Terror, and the East Needle (7760 ft+/2366 m) have vertical E faces with short summit overhangs. The present topographic map errors in the name placement location.

WEST TWIN NEEDLE: The first ascent was made by William Degenhardt, James Martin, and Herb Strandberg on August 17, 1932. The party took six hours from Crescent Creek basin to the summit, using tennis shoes the last 800 ft on the S face. The route consists of steep scrambling, gullies, grass on rock, and a diagonal chimney (class 3 and 4).

Himmelhorn

MT. TERROR

HIMMELHORN from north
DAVID KNUDSON

Reference: *Mountaineer,* 1932, p. 25.

The N face, approaching from McMillan Creek cirque and "Mustard Glacier," was first climbed by Larry Clark, Joan Firey, Joe Firey, and Peter Renz in July 1968. The glacier problems include crevasses and perhaps a moat. The route takes the steep snow ramp that lies at the angle of westerly rock dip, under Himmelhorn (there are some awkward slabby rock and snow sections). The final part of the route joins the 1932 line. Gain the notch between the Twin Needles by a descent of the S side, then make a ledge system traverse, crossing several minor gullies.

EAST TWIN NEEDLE: First ascent by West Twin Needle 1968 party. The party continued the route from the dividing notch with a difficult pitch, some 50 ft in height to a good belay stance. The pitch began by diagonalling right, then left again (piton protection and one aid chock to avoid

danger of rock pulling out). The next pitch (class 4) ends on the knifed summit ridge. Class 5.6 and aid. References: *Mountaineer,* 1969, pp. 113-17 (error p. 116 on naming sequence); *A.A.J.,* 1969, pp. 388-89.

The Blip: This is a minor pinnacle adjacent East Needle, climbed by Jim Lucke, Gary Mellom, and John Roper on July 7, 1973 (S couloir and W ridge; class 3). Reference: *Mountaineer,* 1973, p. 82.

HIMMELHORN   est. 7800 ft/2377 m
The most spectacular of the Crescent Creek Spires is the second highest summit W of Mt. Terror. The peak is located just W of West Twin Needle, and is very slightly lower; the E face is particularly vertical. First ascent by Ed Cooper, Glen Denny, Joan Firey, Joe Firey, and George Whitmore on September 8, 1961.

From Crescent Creek basin take a steep couloir (some snow) and bypass a chockstone on the left, to reach the Himmelhorn-Ottohorn notch (about 500 ft above the basin). Traverse on an ascending ledge around the N face. Climb a steep, broken rock depression, which tops out just W of the summit; the hardest part is just after leaving the ledge (one lead of moderate class 5; the remainder is class 4). Time: 4 hours from basin (long day from Chopping Block camp). Reference: *A.A.J.,* 1962, p. 67.

Dusseldorfspitz is a spectacular thumb jutting E of Himmelhorn; climbed by original party, going over summit.

OTTOHORN   est. 7700 ft/2347 m
This is the next rock summit W of Himmelhorn. The "Mustard Glacier" on the McMillan Creek cirque heads at the notch between these two summits, and is quite steep and crevassed, although providing a possible backpacking crossing of the Southern Picket Group. The first ascent was made by the Himmelhorn party, taking the E ridge from the notch (class 3). Reference: *A.A.J.,* 1962, p. 68.

FRENZEL SPITZ   est. 7450 ft/2271 m
This summit is a solitary rock pyramid below the Crescent Creek Spires, closely under the N face of Ottohorn. First ascent by Himmelhorn party, September 10. Route: see Goodell Creek Route♦-The Barrier and Crescent Creek Route. The descent of 400 ft, and traverse to the objective requires crampons. The final route is via the S ridge (class 4). References: *A.A.J.,* 1962, p. 68; *Mountaineer,* 1963, p. 93.

WEST PEAK   7053 ft/2150 m
The far-western rock peak facing the Crescent Creek basin is 1.3 mi. W of Mt. Terror on a massif extending into Goodell Creek; there is long western rock face here, some 3800 ft in height, with a very slabby lower area. The first ascent of the peak was made by William Degenhardt, James Martin, and Herb Strandberg on

West Peak   Southeast Peak   LUNA PEAK

Goodell-McMillan
Creek divide

MT. FURY from south
KEN HUNICH

August 16, 1932. The route climbs the slabby SE face (two pitches on solid rock — class 4). Reference. *Mountaineer*, 1932, p. 24.

MT. FURY   8292 ft/2527 m

More than any other peak, Mt. Fury epitomizes the grand alpine wilderness of the amazing Picket Range. Like many peaks of the range, Mt. Fury has no really easy summit route, but provides reasonable alpine climbing and a wide span of difficult challenges on its northern ice and rock faces. Fury is a great rock wedge of ancient gneiss trending E and W between McMillan Creek, the Luna Creek cirque, and the head of Goodell Creek, almost exactly 2 mi. SE of Mt. Challenger. There are two distinctly main summits, 0.5 mi. apart, so closely aligned in altitude that the human eye cannot detect the difference.

The rock walls of the northern faces are clad by a series of spectacular hanging glaciers which are among the steepest and most chaotic in the North Cascades; the western glacier makes a complete horseshoe-shaped connection in the Luna Creek cirque with Challenger Glacier. But the largest segments of glacier ice are "Fury Glacier," SW of Luna Lake, and the unnamed southeastern glacier, located between Fury's East Peak and the slopes of McMillan Creek.

Skagit gneisses on Mt. Fury are banded and have been formed from ancient sediments and volcanics by strong metamorphism with granitization. Intense deformation and compression are commonly evident.[74] The structure and erosion of this rock are particularly apparent on the northern walls of both the East and West Peaks.

When the first ascent of the East Peak was made by Bill Cox and Will F. Thompson in early September 1937 they found no sign of human visitation anywhere in Luna Creek valley. On Fury Glacier they took to the moat to avoid seracs and avalanches, then worked through the glacier. At the final steep couloir leading to the E summit ridge, they moved onto adjacent cliffs, spending 2 hours of intense rock climbing before moving back into the couloir and cutting through the cornice. On the second ascent of the peak in July 1940, Fred and Helmy Beckey kept in this couloir the entire distance. But the route done in 1958, via the Luna-Fury ridge col, has become the standard to reach both peaks of Fury. Take ice axe, rope, and crampons on all routes. References: *Appalachia,* December 1944, p. 212; *Mountaineer,* 1958, p. 100.

MT. FURY *from northeast*
NATIONAL PARK SERVICE

EAST PEAK   8288 ft/2526 m

EAST ROUTE: The route from Luna Lake to the ridge crossing at 7040 ft+ was first done by Tim Kelley, Dale Kunz, Tom Miller and Franz Mohling in 1958. First hike up moderately angled moraine and snow (SE), then a small glacier to the ridge crest (the crossing is left of the continuous rock rim extending from Fury); en route avoid two ice cliff sections on the glacier. Cross to the S slope, turn a small spur, then contour talus and snow of the shallow open cirque, then a slabby section above the lower cliffs. This leads to the edge of the large SE glacier; some parties elect to descend beneath the cliffs to reach the foot of the glacier, but this is normally not necessary. The glacier slopes in a moderate gradient toward the summit, and has only one steep section and bergschrund to pass. At the end, follow an arete to the far snow point. Time: 4-6 hours from lake.

For the route on the NE (Fury) Glacier, done in 1937 and 1940, see introduction to Mt. Fury.

Variation (East Ridge): By Alan Fries and Anthony Mendoza on September 13, 1975. From the lowest col on the standard route follow the ridge and the rock edge; there is one exposed 25-ft step (solid, class 5). Reference: *Mountaineer,* 1975, p. 102.

SOUTHEAST ROUTE: First ascent by Alex Bertulis and Half Zantop in August 1963 during the S to N Picket Range traverse. From McMillan Creek cirque follow the Goodell Creek divide and ascend the Southeast Peak of Fury (Outrigger Peak — 7680 ft+/2341 m; 0.6 mi. SSE of the East Peak) over its somewhat crumbly S or W flank. Descend some to the col (7280 ft+) at the western edge of Fury's SE glacier; ascend the latter, which becomes steeper toward the middle elevations. Time: 6 hours from cirque.

NORTH BUTTRESS: This major rock and ice feature on the N face of Fury's East Peak provides an elegant alpine route, one of the select group of classic mixed climbs in the North Cascades. It is a superb route with a variety of climbing and route finding problems. First ascent by Fred Beckey and Dan Davis on July 15, 1962. The original party traversed Luna Creek cirque glaciers from Challenger Arm. At the end of this long traverse, cross under the hanging ice

Southeast Peak

East Peak

icket Pass

SOUTHEAST
GLACIER

to Luna Lake

MT. FURY from southeast
ROBERT J. DeWITZ, U.S. FOREST SERVICE

cliff of Fury (avalanche chute danger) to a steep snow finger which slants toward a notch on the objective buttress. Climb left of the snow finger to the crest, then follow the well broken but steep rock to its final headwall above a short band (usually keep slightly right of crest; various snowpatches, gullies, one deep notch and localized route finding problems). Atop the headwall climb between two slender rock pinnacles, then climb the long final narrow firn arete between two hanging glaciers in a classic completion; a short rock pitch along the crest W of the summit leads to the highest point. Grade III or IV; class 4 and 5. Time: 9 hours from Challenger Arm. References: *A.A.J.,* 1963, p. 474; *Mountaineer,* 1963, p. 90; *Summit,* July-August 1963, p. 27.

Descent: Made via standard route to Luna Lake, then northward across cirque.

NORTHEAST FACE: First ascent by Andy Carson, Martin Epp, and Ernst von Allman on August 1, 1968. This route ascends the long ice shield of the steep, broken "Fury Glacier" between the rock fin and crag of Fury's East Peak and the North Buttress. First climb the lower snow accumulation slopes, then climb onto slabby rock of the jumbled crest left of the right lobe of the glacier. When this ridge

terminates below the headwall of the East Ridge, cross glacier segments under the rock wall to the ice shield. The original party encountered continuously hard snow. The face is 45 to 50 degrees, steepening at the top. Grade III. Time: allow a long day.

Descent: Via upper part of North Buttress, then down a steep snow gully to the broken lower glacier. The party climbed the two pinnacles on the buttress; the upper one was harder (some aid).

WEST PEAK   8292 ft/2527 m

First ascent by Vic Josendal, Maury Muzzy, Phil Sharpe, Warren Spickard, and Roe (Duke) Watson on August 19, 1958 via the West Ridge route. The Ptarmigan climbing club party of 1940 (Calder Bressler, Ray Clough, and Will Thompson) who tried the peak, went part way but ran out of time after climbing the East Peak.

EAST RIDGE: First ascent by Joan Firey, Joe Firey and Don Keller in 1961 (second ascent of peak). This has now become the standard route, traversing from the East Peak. There is much exposed class 3 and 4 rock climbing, with some poor

MT. FURY from southwest
ROWLAND TABOR, U.S. GEOLOGICAL SURVEY

rock. One must climb over or around some of the ridge towers, the net result being a long and tedious alpine round trip (one should be prepared for possible bivouac). Time: 6-8 hours r.t. from East Peak. References: *Summit,* January-February 1961, pp. 20-21; *A.A.J.,* 1962, p. 201.

WEST RIDGE: Reach as per Phantom Peak-North Route. There is a good campsite at Picket-Goodell Creek Pass, SW of the objective. From here ascend the ridge until it meets the cliffs of a southern buttress of Swiss Peak. Make a steep heather traverse, then climb 1000 ft of easy rock. Then traverse E over several snowfields. The original party made a 200-ft descent of cliffs to gain the small glacier just W of Fury's West Peak at about 6800 ft. Note: It appears feasible to make a much lower traverse of this cirque on the Goodell Creek flank, crossing and ascending snow and slabs to reach the foot of the glacier more directly.

Ascend the glacier tongue to a col at about 7500 ft (crampons); here are two notches which overhang the N face. Climb the more northerly of two gullies on the W side of the summit; the climbing is steep and loose. A 120-ft

chockstone pitch is a problem (class 5); this section involves 400-ft of gully climbing and two pitches of face climbing to reach the West Ridge. Traverse eastward on the N face some 200 ft or more (loose rock) to an obvious gully. Ascend this to the summit ridge, bypassing the summit on the N. Turn back W for a short summit scramble. Time: 10-12 hours (original party made bivouac on descent). References: *Mountaineer,* 1959, pp. 102-3; *A.A.J.,* 1959, p. 209.

SOUTHEAST PEAK (Outrigger Peak)
7680 ft+/2341 m+

First ascent by Joan Firey, Joe Firey, Don Keller, and Irene Meulemans in 1962. See East Peak-Southeast Route. Reference: *Mountaineer,* 1963, p. 93.

LUNA PEAK   8285 ft/2525 m

In addition to having a somewhat crescent-shaped ridge connecting it with the main ridge of the northern Picket Range, the satellite position of Luna Peak

LUNA PEAK *from north*
NATIONAL PARK SERVICE

makes its name especially appropriate. Located 2.6 mi. NE of Mt. Fury (which is barely higher), this isolated peak has doubtful claim for a true brotherhood with the range, yet the high ridge connection seals its association. Luna is largely of topographic, not mountaineering interest, for despite its height and bulk, the peak lacks the compelling appeal of attractive alpine climbing problems. The NE point of the nearly leaning summit crest is the highest on the peak, but because of the highly sheared rock, few parties scramble beyond the first summit point. The long SW slope (McMillan Creek flank) is very gradual compared to the opposite Luna and Big Beaver Creek faces. The first ascent was made by Bill Cox and Will F. Thompson in early September 1937.

SOUTHWEST RIDGE: Approach from Luna Lake or Luna Lake High Route (see Big Beaver Creek Trail◆). From the ridge saddle to the first summit point the route needs no description. The last portion and continuation to the final summit point is a precarious scramble over broken and creaking rock (class 3 and 4). Time: 3 hours from lake. References: *Appalachia,* December 1944, p. 211; *Mountaineer,* 1971, p. 87.

SWISS PEAK   7840 ft+/2390 m+

This is the nearly level-topped summit between Mt. Fury and Phantom Peak, distinctive because of its 1900-ft face above the glacier in Luna Creek cirque. The peak is located 0.4 mi. NW of Mt. Fury. The broad S slope is headed by a distinctive, glacier-patched, scooped rock cirque at the very head of Goodell Creek. The original ascent was done via the face by Andy Carson, Martin Epp, and Ernst von Allman on July 28-29, 1968. Reference: *A.A.J.,* 1969, p. 389.

NORTHEAST FACE: The route ascends the conspicuous central pillar on the face, following the line of the pillar when it fades out in the upper face. At about 11 rope lengths of the climbing the original party made a bivouac, then completed the climb and descended the next day. Reach the face as per Phantom Peak, and begin directly from the pillar base, with the first pitch ascending near its center. Succeeding pitches (5.6) angle slightly right and lead to a large grass and scree ledge at the base of the vertical yellow wall. Traverse beneath this wall (right side of pillar) to the base of "Pudding Chimney." Climb two leads (very loose and difficult — unprotected 5.8) to an adequate ledge on the right.

LUNA CREEK CIRQUE
AUSTIN POST, U.S. GEOLOGICAL SURVEY

Traverse left to a narrow and difficult chimney which leads to a large platform in the middle of the pillar. From here, ascend the chimney formed by a huge flake to a ledge (used for bivouac). Make a left traverse onto the center of pillar. Ascend here for continuity, climbing about 10 leads (moderate 5 to 5.7). Near the summit the route fades into towers.

Keep left to avoid loose sections. Grade IV or V; class 5.8 (27 pitches).

Descent: Traverse crest W toward Phantom Peak. Make rappels (loose rock) to the glacier arm below the latter (some crevasse problems).

PHANTOM PEAK 8045 ft/2452 m

Phantom is located about midway between Mt. Fury and Mt. Challenger, where the northern Picket Range makes a right angle in outline. The glacier E of the peak, above the cirque of Luna Creek, creates a most spectacular scene with its crevasse and icefall patterns. The opposite W face is almost devoid of ice; here is a steep 1500-ft rock wall, with buttresses beginning at 6400 ft in altitude. The summit is a small tower perched on a rugged crag directly on the main crest. Nearly horizontal joints are filled with white dikes. The joints and planes of weakness in the gneiss influence the shape and form of the ridge. First ascent by Fred Beckey and Helmy Beckey on July 11, 1940. References: *Appalachia,* December 1944, pp. 212-13; *Mountaineer,* 1940, p. 39; 1959, p. 103; 1968, p. 166; *A.A.J.,* 1959, pp. 209-10.

SOUTHWEST ROUTE: It is not certain who made the first ascent of this route; it may have been the Larry Lewin party in 1968. From an alp campspot W of Crooked Thumb (see North Route) traverse around the lower western cliffs of Phantom, then ascend the small pocket glacier on the SE flank. Continue up a 1000-ft snow gully to the notch (7760 ft+) at its head; here meet the original route. Time: 5 hours. Reference: *Mountaineer,* 1968, p. 166.

NORTH ROUTE: First ascent by Vic Josendal, Phil Sharpe, and Warren Spickard on August 21, 1958. From a camp at the alp W of Crooked Thumb cross slabs and a small glacier to the outlet (6800 ft) of a long, loose gully leading to the N ridge of Phantom; some of the climbing is done via ledges on the left side. From the ridge notch (7600 ft+) climb firm rock over the first false summit (est. 7800 ft) to meet a sheer 130-ft cliff. Make a 110-ft rappel down the E side of the ridge to the top edge of the high glacier-snowfield climbed on the original route; the 1958 party climbed along the awkward snow-rock moat because they had only rock-climbing shoes. Climb steep but solid slabs to the 7760-ft+ notch between the true summit and the SE crag (here join the original route). On descent the moat problem was avoided by rappels on the sheer cliff. Class 4-5. Time: 6 hours. References: *Mountaineer,* 1959, pp. 103-4; *A.A.J.,* 1959, pp. 209-10; *Summit,* January-February 1961, pp. 21-22.

EAST ROUTE: This is the original route, from Luna Creek cirque. The difficulty and time required will depend partly on snow conditions and the nature of the numerous crevasses; there may be some problem and even danger in ascending the polished slabs to the lowest part of the central glacier; beware of unstable seracs and ice blocks which may slide loose. Ascend through the complex crevasse system to the steeper portion of the glacier where it flows from a high col, then narrows between two great rock walls at about 6800 ft. At the large bergschrund leave the ice and climb rightward over broken rock to the highest glacier-snowfield.

Ascend this steeply to the notch directly SE of Phantom's summit (7760 ft+). From the notch climb the SE face over clean, solid slab for several hundred ft (class 4) to the final ridge. Turn left and make a short traverse S on the ridge (pass several small gendarmes) to the summit block. Ascend this 25-ft block on its SE face. Class 4. Time: 6 hours.

CROOKED THUMB 8120 ft/2475 m

This spectacular peak on the main ridge 0.6 mi. S of Mt. Challenger has one of the largest E faces in the range, with a segment of the Challenger Glacier extending beneath it in Luna Creek cirque. Badly weathered gneiss with quite a variation in its degree of firmness overlies a large mass of quartz diorite. Some nearly vertical joints are now filled with quartz veins. The vertical joints on the Crooked Thumb-Phantom Peak ridge erode out to make pinnacles and chimneys. First ascent by Fred and Helmy Beckey on July 10, 1940. References: *Routes and Rocks,* pp. 28-29; *Appalachia,* December 1944, pp. 210-11; *Mountaineer,* 1940, p. 39; 1962, p. 82; 1963, p. 85; *Summit,* January-February 1961, p. 22.

NORTHWEST ROUTE: Approaching from Challenger Glacier, one can descend from the 7520-ft+ notch between the West and Middle Peaks of Mt. Challenger to the glacier at about 6900 ft (steep snow descent). Ascend and traverse this glacier about 600 ft in height to the base of the rock. A hidden snow finger (deep narrow couloir) is the key to the route on the Northwest Face. Most parties ascend the gully to the N summit ridge notch (then follow the latter); the original party ascended the gully about 300 ft, then climbed a 100-ft face to a whitish ledge on the right, which was then traversed to a rock bowl; this was climbed (loose rock) to the ridge crest N of the summit thumb. Note: Some parties have taken ledges and steps leading SW to almost under the summit; a pitch rated 5.4 can be done to the ridge 20 ft S of the summit thumb. The exposed finish on the thumb is done on a spiral from the E to S. Grade II; class 4 and 5. Time: one-half day.

Note: If the entire N ridge crest is followed, considerable loose, crumbly and exposed rock work is encountered, but the various small gendarmes are not difficult to pass.

Approach Variation: By Joan Firey, Joe Firey, Don Keller, Tony Hovey, and Frank de Saussure in 1960. A slanting glacier arm on the E face was taken to the N ridge (the final part may be an ice chute or loose rock gully); 3 hours to notch. From here, follow the ridge to the summit (4 hours).

NORTHEAST FACE: First ascent by Jack Ardussi, Cal Magnusson, Don Mech, and Bob Swanson on July 31, 1962. Begin near the right edge of the East Face, where the glacier arm makes a small indentation. Climb up and left on steep rock to the right edge of the prominent ice patch. Climb a diagonal gully and chimney system to the first notch N of the summit; there was a difficult overhang in this section

Labels on image: Stetattle Ridge, MT. FURY - East Peak, MT. TERROR, PHANTOM PEAK, MT. CROWDE, MT. CHALLENGER, Middle Peak, West Peak, 7696, CHALLENGER GLACIER, WHATCOM PEAK, Perfect Pass, traverse, WHATCOM GLACIER, to Whatcom Pass

MT. CHALLENGER from northwest
AUSTIN POST, U.S. GEOLOGICAL SURVEY

(class 3 to 5). Time: 11 hours from camp. Reference: *Mountaineer,* 1963, pp. 85-86.

EAST FACE: First ascent by Roger Jackson, Stan Jensen, Steve Marts, and Don Schmechel on July 31, 1962. From the glacier on Luna Creek cirque begin the rock climbing S of the major gully on the East Face (gully directed toward Ghost-Crooked Thumb notch). Ascend steep slabby rock for several leads (class 5); poor protection on first 80-ft pitch above moat. A dike forms an ascending ledge which crosses

the gully and a minor ridge on the face, then steepens and leads to easier climbing 500 ft below the summit. The remainder of the route, which ends at the summit, is class 4. Reference: *Mountaineer,* 1963, pp. 85-86.

GHOST PEAK   7840 ft+/2390 m+

Really a southern summit, almost a horn of Crooked Thumb, this peak with a very sheer E rock face above Luna Creek cirque is located on the very narrow crest of

CROOKED THUMB

notch

1960

Waiting Tower

1952 1968

MT. CHALLENGER

Middle Peak

CHALLENGER GLACIER

MT. CHALLENGER from northeast
AUSTIN POST, U.S. GEOLOGICAL SURVEY

the range. First ascent by Carla Firey, Joan Firey, David Knudson, and Peter Renz on July 17, 1970. Reference: *Mountaineer,* 1971, p. 85.

ROUTE: From a camp near the W side of Phantom Peak, the original party made a westward traverse of the lower S face (about 300 ft; easy). Climb rock steeply upward (class 3-5), taking the right-hand ridge crest (S arete) on the middle section, then slightly left near the summit (slightly on the W face). The rock is generally solid; two pitches of class 5 (chocks useful). Time: 15 hours r.t.

MT. CHALLENGER   8236 ft/2510 m

Challenger, with its provocative name, consists of a series of rock-horn summits which anchor the NW end of the Picket Range. The principal feature of the mountain is that it holds the largest glacier in this area of the North Cascades. This broad glacier on the N slope of the summit row (4 km wide), a result of a high sloping N-facing rock plateau in a heavy snow belt, was noted by the first Boundary surveyors[75] and is indeed a great display of ice (ranging in height from 8000 ft to 4800 ft).[76] The main body of the glacier at its eastern portion turns S to form a long ice segment on the bedrock of Luna Creek cirque; this portion of

the glacier, sloping beneath the steep eastern rock walls of Mt. Challenger and Crooked Thumb, is a very impressive sight. Here is the northern bastion of a continuous rock barricade extending 1½ mi. S to Phantom Peak, one of the great rock barriers in the North Cascades. Above the main northern slope of Challenger Glacier and the principal accumulation basin, the row of rock peaks generally increases in height eastward to the true summit. Rock on Mt. Challenger is firm quartz diorite of the Chilliwack Batholith. The first ascent was one of the early climbs in the Picket Range, made by Philip Dickert, Jack Hossack, and George MacGowan on September 7, 1936. A winter ascent of the mountain was done in February 1977. References: *Mountaineer,* 1936, pp. 9-11; *Appalachia,* December 1944, pp. 209-10; *B.C.M.,* July 1974; *Summit,* January-February 1963, pp. 18-19, 21.

CHALLENGER GLACIER: From near Perfect Pass (see Easy Ridge Trail◆) ascend the glacier, taking a logical route SE between crevasses. At about 7000 ft there is a 45-degree firn slope leading to near the crest of the summit ridge; to the E is another steep slope which must be climbed before making an easterly traverse to the rock tower. Pass the various sub-summits, and the true summit rock tower comes into view (it is the farther of two outcrops). The climb is some 50 ft of solid rock (easy class 5). Time: 3 hours.

Variation: From Challenger Arm ascend firn, keeping right of a rock cliff face. Find an area to proceed between crevasses and head for the ice saddle between the summit (left) and the next rock point on the right.

NORTHEAST SPUR-EAST FACE: There is a broad, very steep rock face E of Challenger's summit, a maximum of 1000 ft in height above the glacier arm extending across Luna Creek cirque. There are many ribs, buttresses and gullies on this face; the routes climbed in 1962 and 1968 appear to be nearly identical, beginning from behind a small rock tower ("Waiting Tower"), then climbing the 700-ft E face of the Northeast Spur to the glacier snow dome (upper level). The first ascent was made by Jack Ardussi, Roger Jackson, Stan Jensen, Cal Magnusson, Steve Marts, Don Mech, Don Schmechel, and Bob Swanson on July 30, 1962. The route begins from a rock tower extending into the glacier edge. Climb a dark brown dike to a series of steep right-bearing ledges. Then climb directly to the spur's crest at the glacier; traverse the ridge to join the normal route closely below the rock summit. Class 5 (first two leads used protection). References: *Mountaineer,* 1963, p. 85; *A.A.J.,* 1963, pp. 475-76.

Variation: By Andy Carson, Martin Epp, and Ernst von Allman on July 27, 1968. This six-pitch climb appears to be very close, perhaps slightly N of the 1962 route. The party also began behind the rock tower, taking a yellow open book, then traversing right (flakes) to avoid an overhang. From a long ledge a pillar was climbed to a prominent horizontal dike (two leads, 5.6). Traverse left on the dike, then ascend a short pedestal; then climb up and right to a grassy ledge, then to the glacier. Grade II; class 5.6. Time: 4 hours. Reference: *A.A.J.,* 1969, pp. 389-90.

SOUTH RIDGE: This is the ridge connecting Challenger with Crooked Thumb. The rock is very loose in places, but the summit block is quite firm on this flank. First ascent by Joan Firey, Joe Firey, Don Keller, Tony Hovey, and Frank de Saussure in 1960. The approach was made from the W, taking the chute between Crooked Thumb and the objective. From the col on the ridge (7600 ft+) there are some four pitches (class 4). The climb is reported as pleasant and airy; one piton was used on the W side of the summit block. Time: 5 hours from below peak. References: *Mountaineer,* 1963, p. 82; *A.A.J.,* 1962, p. 201.

MIDDLE PEAK   7920 ft+/2415 m+
This is a pyramidal rock peak, on the glacier fringe, the first obvious one W of the true summit. First ascent by Cal Magnusson and party in 1962. From the glacier climb the firn tongue and finger to rock on the W face, then climb steep but broken rock (class 3). References: *Mountaineer,* 1963, p. 86; *A.A.J.,* 1963, p. 475.

WEST PEAK   8000 ft+/2439 m+
This is the round-shaped summit 0.4 mi. W of the true summit of Challenger. First ascent by Fred Beckey, Dan Davis, and Eleanor Street on July 14, 1962. From the glacier saddle W of the peak climb loose rock on the W ridge crest to the notch atop a snow finger; rappel into the notch, then cross a knifed and loose rock ridge to firmer rock of the main objective; continue on the W face (class 3). Note: The notch problem can be reduced by circling the W side of the peak on snow, to where a gully leads to the notch. References: *A.A.J.,* 1963, p. 475; *Mountaineer,* 1963, p. 85.

The crag farther W (7696 ft/2346 m) was climbed by Alex Bertulis and Helmut Geldsetzer in September 1962, an easy scramble from the N (1 hour from Perfect Pass). References: *A.A.J.,* 1963, pp. 65-68; *Mountaineer,* 1963, pp. 58-60.

WAITING TOWER
This is a small rock spire atop the rock toe outcrop at the very base of the Northeast Spur. First ascent by Roger Jackson and Steve Marts in 1962. Begin the two-pitch climb on the SW face, then work to the S, then finally spiral to the upper E face. Class 5 moves; one hour.

WHATCOM PEAK   7574 ft/2309 m
Whatcom is an outstanding, glacier-smoothed peak 1.4 mi. SW of Whatcom Pass and 2.1 mi. NW of Mt. Challenger in the Picket Range. Whether Whatcom Peak is a portion of the latter subrange is a matter of opinion. Like Luna Peak, it is an outlier, and is distinctly separated from the Challenger Glacier by the depression of Perfect Pass. The peak has its own steep hanging glaciers; East Whatcom Glacier drains to the upper cirque of Little Beaver Creek, and on the N a spectacular, crevassed hanging glacier drains to Brush Creek. Rock is the sheared quartz diorite of the Chilliwack Batholith.

The first ascent was apparently done in September 1936 by Fred J. Berry and Lawrence Buchanen, probably by the North Ridge.[77] Reference: *Mountaineer,* 1936, pp. 10-11.

SOUTH ROUTE: From Perfect Pass (see Easy Ridge Trail♦ and Chilliwack River Trail♦-Whatcom Pass-Challenger Glacier route) the S slope is an easy snow and broken rock ascent (1 hour); the bald summit is at the W end of several rock points.

NORTH RIDGE: This is probably the original route, and

certainly the most direct from a trail. The first 0.7 mi. of the route is along a subalpine spur (trees and heather); this is followed by a dip, then a prominent, rounded rock ridge leading directly to the summit. For most of the summer portions of this ridge are snow-covered; because of the exposure ice axes should be taken. Some of the route is scrambling along slabs of the ridge.

RED FACE MOUNTAIN   7174 ft/2187 m
This is a moderately sized pyramidal peak that trends E and W. The high point is just NE of Tapto Lakes (only 1.1. mi. N of Whatcom Pass). The peak is an easy climb and a good viewpoint for sights of the Picket Range and Chilliwack Group. Red Face derives its name from the iron oxide-stained zone 0.4 mi. wide and 1.4 mi. long that caps the peak. The N side is generally precipitous, but the S flank is gentler, with several tarns scattered along a discontinuous bench on the side of the ridge. Reference: U.S.G.S. Bull. 1359, p. 62; see note 70.
ROUTE: From Whatcom Pass (Chilliwack River Trail♦ and Little Beaver Creek Trail♦) hike N to Tapto Lakes (5680 ft+) on a timberline bench. Then ascend NE up talus between rock outcrops to the E ridge; follow this gradual crest. Time: 2 hours.

INDIAN MOUNTAIN   7131 ft/2174 m
This peak is located 2 mi. NW of Whatcom Pass, and is connected to Red Face Mountain.
ROUTE: From Tapto Lakes (see Red Face) hike W over open parkland, reaching the ridge at the W end of Red Face when this trends N toward Indian Mountain. First follow the W side of the ridge, then the broad crest; class 2.

An alternative approach can be made via Indian Creek and Lake Reveille. Climb W upstream to the Indian-Red Face saddle.

BEAR MOUNTAIN   7942 ft/2421 m
Bear Mountain, one of the most rugged "under 8000 ft" peaks in the North Cascades, rises on the Indian-Bear Creek spur, off the main divide of Custer Ridge, and E of upper Chilliwack River. Rock is part of the Chilliwack Batholith, generally firm, but tending to be altered toward the NE, where there is a contact with the gneiss of the area. The mountain's North Face has a wide reputation: the direct wall is some 2500 ft in height, with the final portion overhanging perhaps 1000 ft. Flanking this narrow precipice are four distinct buttresses, two on each side of the overhanging wall. The glacier beneath this face has a very steep reach to within 1500 ft of the summit, its final section being thin, broken, and narrow.
Boundary Survey records and a James Alden paint-

ing apply the Indian name "Klahaihu." The first ascent of Bear was made by Calder Bressler and Will F. Thompson in August 1939.
NORTHWEST RIDGE: This is now considered the most direct approach from Chilliwack River Trail♦ and is also the easiest climbing route. At 200 yards E of Bear Creek shelter find an old fire path climbing steeply to timberline. Do not follow quite to its end, but where path bears S (est. 4500 ft) continue up the forest divide. Ruta Lake (5040 ft+) is a good campsite — 4 hours. Continue along the divide, sometimes S of the crest. The final granitic blocks of the summit ridge have some steep moves, but are well broken (class 4 — rope optional); there are a number of self-evident possibilities, slightly S of the crest.
Approach Variation: From the base of the South Face route (Indian Creek), traverse and climb NW (forest and talus) to moderately steep rock below the objective ridge. One can also reach this position from about 3 mi. on the trail by ascending a timber cone.
NORTH FACE (West Buttress): This is a steep, very prominent buttress, somewhat rounded in form, located 0.3 mi. NW of the summit of Bear. The ascent of the buttress is enjoyable, with firm rock and reasonable protection. First ascent by Alan Kearney, Shari Kearney, Ed Newville, and Jeff Thomas on September 11, 1977. See North Face route for approach. The original party made a bivouac some 400 ft up the buttress, then bore up and left to a chimney. Climb this feature, then cracks and face problems to the left edge of the buttress; from here 17 pitches continue to the upper Northwest Ridge. Grade IV; class 5.9. Reference: *A.A.J.,* 1978, p. 522.
NORTH FACE (North Buttress): This route is an exceptional alpine rock climb, with a purity of position and a unique aspect. Most of the route above the central glacier is on the steep buttress, and climbing is in the 5.3 to 5.7 range. First ascent by Fred Beckey and Mark Fielding on July 14-15, 1967. The original party reached the face by traversing from the fire path to Bear Creek, but the descent from the saddle beyond Ruta Lake is more suitable; a traverse across scree and snow leads to the glacier beneath the face. The ice becomes steep and possibly dangerous near its head, where it narrows (watch for pieces breaking off).

Immediately above the ice climb a steep slabby pitch, hard to protect (uncomfortable). Then traverse rightward easily on a ledge beneath the great wall; here a ramp slants sharply to the corner of the crest (class 4 and some short moves). The serious climbing begins on the buttress, which keeps mostly on the exposed crest to the ridge W of the summit. The most strenuous pitch is reached in several leads: this a deep squeeze chimney just left of the corner. Grade V; class 5.8 and A4 (44 pitons and one bolt used on original; one bivouac made). References: *Challenge of the North Cascades,* pp. 247-56; *Mountaineer,* 1968, pp. 202-3; 1973, p. 33; *A.A.J.,* 1968, pp. 67-72.
EAST RIDGE: First ascent by Roger Fahy, Dan Hendricks, Marilyn Loranger, Stan Jensen, John Stout, Alfred Tatyrek,

East Ridge

North Face — West Buttress

Bear
Creek
cirque

Bear Creek

BEAR MOUNTAIN — north face
KEN HUNICH

and Bill Van de Graff on August 14, 1964. Reach the long E ridge from upper Indian Creek (Indian-Bear Creek saddle). The route keeps partly on the ridge crest and partly on a long, narrow ledge system which allows easy bypassing of various towers. At the V-shaped notch between the highest summits the route meets the variation of the South Route; then traverses left 20 ft to the base of a very steep narrow gully, then one lead to the top (four pitons used). Time: 5 hours. References: *Mountaineer,* 1965, p. 86; *A.A.J.,* 1965, p. 411.

SOUTH ROUTE: This is approximately the line of the first ascent route, except that the 1939 party went up the very deep obvious couloir which is snow-filled much of summer. They then climbed slabs, using tennis shoes, and when high on the crags traversed about 200 yards W to just beneath the notch at the true summit.

The best beginning is about 4 mi. along Indian Creek Trail (see Chilliwack River Trail♦) at 4000 ft, directly S of Bear's summit (just E of the first gravelly creek). Ascend a long wooded ridge between two prominent gullies that lead to slabs beneath the summit rocks (2 hours). From here the true summit has a boxlike shape with a pointed crag to its right. Climb a shallow gully with two steep pitches. Cross a rib leftward to another gully, climbing this toward the notch

between the summit and the pointed crag. At about 200 ft beneath the notch, make a tricky move out of the gully (leftward) and climb a 150-ft vertical face; easier climbing continues to the summit. Class 4 and 5. Time: 6 hours.

Variation: By Fred Beckey, Helmy Beckey, and Louis Graham in June 1941. From 20 ft below the described notch, climb W up a steep 100-ft face. The first part is a V-shape (open book) to a piton belay on a narrow ledge at the very edge of the North Face. Traverse left 20 ft across a difficult section to the base of a steep, narrow gully; then one lead completes the climbing.

From the belay spot above the open book one can climb 30 ft of vertical rock via a strenuous crack which leads to the top of a large flake (5.5); by Ted Carpenter, Steve Moore, Joe Vance, and Bill Weitkamp in 1970.

RUSTIC PEAK 7732 ft/2357 m

This summit is a high point on the Pass Creek-Redoubt Creek ridge at 2.9 mi. SE of Bear Mountain. The long ridge trending SE of Bear is informally called "Rusted Ridge" for its stained coloring. Here red pinnacles of biotite and hornblende schist contrast with white ribs of marble, a metamorphosed limestone once deposited on the ocean floor. Rustic Peak has a long rock face on its SW, where it stands out to best advantage. There is a small glacier on its E flank, part of a series of glaciers on the Redoubt Creek slope. First ascent by Stan Jensen, Ruth Ittner, Marilyn Loranger, John Stout, and Alfred Tatyrek on August 10, 1964. References: *A.A.J.,* 1965, p. 411; *Mountaineer,* 1965, p. 86; *Routes and Rocks,* p. 38.

ROUTE: Approach via Indian Creek Trail (see Chilliwack River Trail♦). From the Bear-Redoubt Creek saddle traverse the easy NE slopes along the base of the small glacier series (keep below rock ribs), then up the NE snow chute (and rock) to a notch on the E ridge (6800 ft). Make a short traverse across SE-facing snowfields, then make a moderately steep snow ascent on the southern exposure to the crest of the final SW ridge; an easy scramble leads to the summit.

Alternative Approach: From the open basin W of the peak the ascent seems feasible by using gully systems (see Pass Creek Route-Little Beaver Creek Trail♦).

Northeast Variation: By Jim Lucke and John Roper on July 6, 1978. The ascent was made from Redoubt Creek up the N side of a stream draining E of the summit, then to the S slope; no difficulties.

Summits on Rusted Ridge of note include Point 7360 ft+ (2244 m+; the farthest NW summit); a probable new route via the NW ridge was done by Mark and Steve Allabach, Joe Medlicott, and John Roper on August 13, 1979 (short class 4). Point 7440 (2268 m), the nearest summit to Rustic Peak has an extensive glacier and short, sheer E face.

TWIN SPIRES (Mox Peaks)

The dark rock and remarkably steep profiles of Twin Spires add a special blend of rugged form to the Custer Ridge area of the North Cascades. Their bold distinctive outlines attract the eye from three directions, and in their locale are only overshadowed by Mt. Redoubt and Mt. Spickard. The Spires are located 1.8 and 2.2 mi. SE of Mt. Redoubt, at 3.7 mi. S of the Boundary.

Rock of the Spires is ancient gneiss, which tends to be friable; fracture/shear zones dip sharply N. Great walls are found on both Spires, with the longest faces being the E wall of the Southeast Spire and the S and W faces of the Northwest Spire (and W side of its sub-summit). The SW flank of the Southeast Spire has a "bowl-like" glacier and firn slope located between the summit walls and Ridge of Gendarmes, very like a horseshoe in shape. Also on the Perry Creek drainage is an impressive small glacier located between the high walls of both spires. The large Redoubt Glacier flanks the NW side of the Northwest Spire (see Mt. Redoubt).

The name Twin Spires was used informally by mountaineers previous to 1939, but the Forest Service,

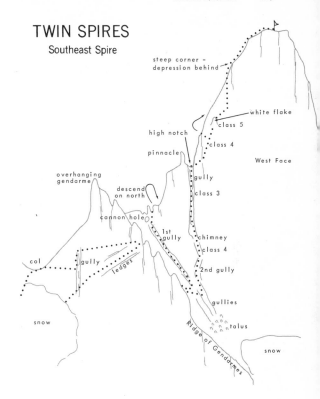

TWIN SPIRES
Southeast Spire

in disregard to tradition, applied the name Mox Peaks. The whimsy of this appelation is not clear to those who know the area. Both Spires provide challenging and seldom-done ascents, and the summit of the Southeast Spire is one of the most difficult to attain in the range.

The first climbing was done in 1939 when Bill Cox and Will F. Thompson went onto the Ridge of Gendarmes about 1 mi. from the Southeast Spire. Fred Beckey and Helmy Beckey made the first ascent of the Northwest Spire on June 21, 1941 and that of the Southeast Spire on June 22, 1941. References: *Mountaineer,* 1941, pp. 31-32; 1973, p. 30; *Summit,* June 1960, pp. 22-23; August 1960, pp. 20-21; September 1970, pp. 11-12.

NORTHWEST SPIRE   8320 ft+/2535 m+

NORTH RIDGE: The Depot Creek Route♦ is the most direct. If the approach is made from the basin of Bear Creek continue to the 7200-ft level of Redoubt Glacier E of Mt. Redoubt. From here traverse eastward about 1½ mi., keeping below two small rock tongues to where the glacier makes a small circular indentation in the N rock ridge of the

JACK MOUNTAIN MT. PROPHET Southeast Spire Ridge of Gendarmes Northwest Spire

erry
reek
basin

TWIN SPIRES from north
NATIONAL PARK SERVICE

objective; here the intervening span to the ridge is shortest. Bear toward a low point in the ridge, where there is a snow-capped section. This climbing involves a 45-degree snow finger, then a slabby rock pitch (some blocks); class 4. Follow the narrow ridge to a level section 200 ft from the summit. Make an exposed traverse to the left (E face) to directly beneath the summit, then climb 80 ft of vertical rock (awkward but solid) to a tiny notch on the N side of the highest block. A short, steep exposed pitch completes the route. Class 4 and 5. Time: 5 hours from Redoubt-Depot Creek divide.

SOUTHEAST FACE: First ascent by Dave Adams and Donald Goodman on July 28, 1980. From the NW edge of the col between the Northwest and Southeast spires scramble up a prominent gully 30 ft to a belay ledge. Continue to ascend the loose gully to the left of a prominent gendarme (80 ft, class 5).

From the top of this gully traverse right (NE) on a ledge for 40 ft then cut back left (W) for 80 ft to a prominent gully (class 3). Ascend this gully 300 vertical ft (class 3 slab) to below the NE ridge. From here scramble to the NE ridge, picking up the standard route. A possible variation would be to ascend directly to the right of the summit from the top of the slabby gully (est. 130 ft of low class 5). Time: 6 hours round trip from the col. This is a good route for those interested in also climbing the Southeast Spire, as both routes start at the central col.

WEST RIDGE: First ascent by Dan Hendricks, Stan Jen-

sen, Marilyn Loranger, and Bill Van de Graff on August 12, 1964. Begin from the glacier at the W of the Spire's large western subsidiary tower. Climb to the top of a broad snow finger above a wide bergschrund. A relatively easy rock traverse (class 3) is made across the N face of the tower to gain the notch at the base of the final West Ridge. The ascent from here is exposed, with several pitches of class 4 and 5. Time: 5 hours from Redoubt-Bear Creek saddle. References: *Mountaineer,* 1965, p. 86; *A.A.J.,* 1965, pp. 411-12.

SOUTHEAST SPIRE 8480 ft+/2585 m+

To begin this climb one can camp on the 7200-ft divide at the head of Depot Creek or at timberline near the upper basin center of Redoubt Creek (reach from Bear or Depot Creek divide). See Depot Creek Route◆ and Chilliwack River Trail◆-Indian Creek Trail and Bear Creek High Route. Ascend eastward along heather slopes and moraine to the remnant glacier between the Spires. There are several routes to a notch in the Ridge of Gendarmes. Note: This pinnacled ridge trends SW, then S and SE in a horseshoe outline from the W wall of the Spire at about 8250 ft. One can ascend snow or rock gullies from about 200 ft below the 7760-ft+ col between the Spires; the original party crossed the ridge just W of the fourth gendarme (8000 ft+). Alternatively, from the col one can obliquely climb ledges southward to an E-W rock gully, ascend to its head, then cross a rib and climb broken rock S to an obvious notch on the jagged ridge.

Descend two pitches on the opposite side for a traverse leftward to the loose gully descending from the notch right of the large overhanging gendarme (distinct gap where ridge veers sharply up to W face). Ascend a gully to the notch adjacent to a cannonhole (keep right of two sharp pinnacles in notch). Cross and descend about 100 ft in a steep gully (possible snow); belay stances are poor and rock is dangerously loose on down-sloping ledges. Make an exposed rightward traverse on these ledges for about 250 ft. Then climb about 200 ft directly upward, keeping right of a white overhang. A long, exposed lead follows near the corner between the N and W faces: instead of continuing up a sharp arete, traverse to a shallow rock gully above the white overhang, then climb a nearly vertical 80-ft whitish trough (5.5 or 5.6); above the climbing is broken and eases to the nearby summit. Grade II or III; class 5.5 or 5.6. Time: 6 hours r.t. from col.

Variations: From the notch on Ridge of Gendarmes work obliquely down and E about 200 ft (toward a snow-filled gully); descend this gully another 100 ft (or less if route can be found), then crossing a ledge to the next gully to the E, at the base of two gullies between the Gendarmes and the main W face of the Spire. Climb the right-most gully, which is first a chimney with blocks (class 3 and 4), then a loose gully, to the high notch immediately against the face. Make a short right traverse (5.5), then climb about 80 ft directly upward to the right side of a detached whitish horn (belay behind). One can continue on the exposed and somewhat loose left side of the steep corner above (165-ft lead; this was done by Tim Place and Bryce Simon in 1974). Other variations of this finish have deen described; from about 60 ft above the high notch, one can traverse left around a corner on a ledge to the depression (at white trough) of the original route, as done by Jim Price and Steve Swenson in 1973. From the original route below the white overhang a variation is to traverse 100 ft onto the W face, ascend a gully to an exposed ledge between overhangs, then make a crawl back N to reach the corner (Stan Jensen and party, 1978). Medium-sized chocks have been used on the route and these variations for protection.

The descent can be made by three rappels on the Spire itself and one in the gully.

Approach Variation: From the upper basin of Perry Creek, ascend to the bowl-shaped glacier SE of the Spire (keep right of icefall). Ascend to snow fingers at its head, then take the left-hand gully-chimney to the cannonhole notch (done on second ascent of Spire by Brad Fowler and Dave Leen).

PERRY-REDOUBT CREEK RIDGE

Three summits stand out on the ridge trending SE from the Southeast Spire, all located on the divide between Perry and Redoubt creeks and the Perry-Little Beaver divide. These peaks have steep rock walls on the Perry Creek faces, but have moderate gradients on the opposite flank.

Peak 7648 (2331 m), which is 0.7 mi. from the Spire, and on the Ridge of Gendarmes, has a bowl-shaped glacier under its northern rock face. "Consolation Gendarme," the highest of these summits (7740 ft/2359 m) is directly S of Mt. Spickard, and 1.1 mi. from the Spire; this summit has an especially sheer E face. A known climb was done by Jim Lucke and John Roper on July 4, 1978, via gullies facing SSW (class 3) and a descent to the NW. "Tranquility Gendarme" (7374 ft/2248 m) is the next in importance (0.7 mi. farther E). Possible first ascent by John Roper on same date, via W ridge

MT. SPICKARD   8879 ft/2706 m

Called Glacier Peak by early surveyors and mapping agencies, this highest peak on Custer Ridge (Chilliwack group of peaks) is an ice-clad, towering hulk of complex shape, associated with rugged sub-peaks and connecting ridges. Mt. Spickard is closely S of Silver Lake, 2 mi. S of the Boundary and 6½ mi. W of upper Ross Lake. There is a great vertical relief (up to 7100 ft) from the Skagit Valley (Ross Lake) to the summit. The eastern face of the mountain and sub-peak 8824 on this flank have a great rock wall, a long rock buttress, and crevassed glacier, above Silver Creek's S fork. The western face of the mountain is steep, loose rock, but two major gullies provide breaks. This face corners at the long, jagged Northwest Ridge, where steep rock walls stand on both flanks. The broad N flank of the mountain cradles Silver Lake Glacier, the ice sloping steeply between flanking ramparts and sub-peaks. One of the main topographic features of the mountain is the 1.7-mi. ridge connecting with the Northwest Peak of Twin Spires; on this ridge is Point 8405 (actually on the SW ridge of Spickard), which itself has a rugged W face. It is only the South Slope (Perry Creek drainage) which is of moderate angle. Here a sharp SE ridge divides the slope from the precipitous E face. Rock on these faces and ridges is volcanic breccia, but there are both granitics and volcanics in the area. Custer gneiss is overlain by Skagit volcanics (Tertiary age), which extend E to the Skagit River. Rock W of the mountain is the gneiss complex.

Continental ice once reached to about 7000 ft on the mountain. But the great cirque of Silver Lake apparently was carved out by alpine glaciation. Filling much of the southern portion of the cirque is the Silver Lake Glacier, (1.8 km long and 0.9 km² area) extending from the summit of Mt. Spickard into the waters of the lake. Beneath the E face there is a significant

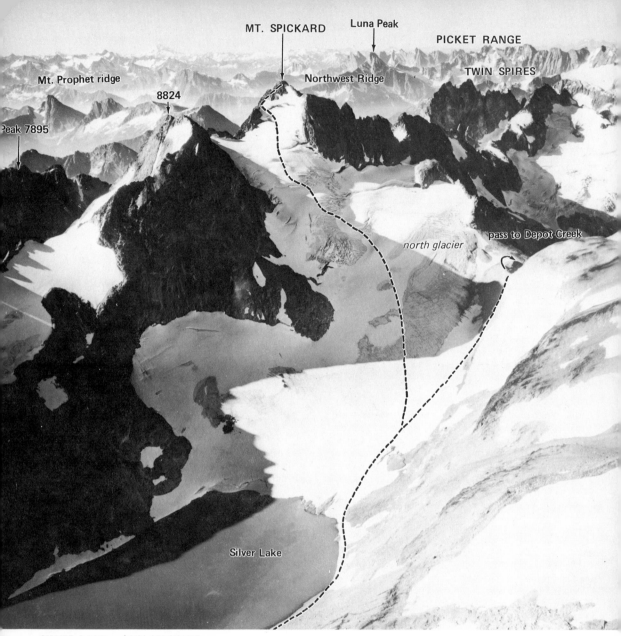

MT. SPICKARD   Luna Peak   PICKET RANGE

Mt. Prophet ridge   8824   Northwest Ridge   TWIN SPIRES

Peak 7895

pass to Depot Creek

north glacier

Silver Lake

SILVER LAKE and MT. SPICKARD
AUSTIN POST, UNIVERSITY OF WASHINGTON

glacier (8200 ft to 6200 ft); there is a small glacier at the foot of the Southwest Face and high on the Perry Creek slope.

British geologist Hilary Bauerman referred to the mountain in his comment, "The mountains on the west side of the [Skagit] river rise to a height of nearly 9,000 feet. Their sides show seven small glaciers" (*Report,* p. 13B). Later Reginald A. Daly, who in 1902 and 1906 studied the volcanics here, wrote "Glacier Peak and its neighbours are, indeed, among the most inaccessible summits in the whole Boundary belt west of the Flathead river" (Daly, pt. 1, p. 528). Survey reports indicated the mountain "is difficult and dangerous to climb" (*Joint Report,* p. 336). Little is known about the first ascent in 1904, except that American surveyor W.A. Raeburn was involved (possibly alone), and that he slept on the mountain two nights. Thomas Riggs, Neuner, and Beall in 1905, exploring the high country from Whitworth to the N, crossed the ridge into Silver Lake, then began to explore routes on the mountain, not aware of the method Raeburn had used to gain the summit. First they were stopped by crevasses on the glacier route above the lake, then found the W flank a precipice "which did not even have a roosting place on it for a bird." After traversing down and around the rugged, brushy E flank of the mountain, they made the ascent on the S side, via a glacier, various cliffs, and a "hogback" that connected a high cliff with the main mountain. Only Riggs and Beall completed the climb (August 19), at one point straddling the summit ridge, and carrying surveying instruments. Noel J. Ogilvie and a Canadian party climbed the mountain again in 1906, but by a different route. The name Glacier Peak was changed to Mt. Spickard for Warren Spickard, who met tragedy during a descent of nearby Northwest Peak of Twin Spires. References: *A.A.J.,* January 1949, pp. 160-64; *Mountaineer,* 1973, pp. 27-33; *Summit,* August 1960, pp. 18-21; *Routes and Rocks,* pp. 36-37.

SOUTH SLOPE: This route, or one of its variations, is likely the way all early surveying parties climbed; it is the least technical way to reach the summit, for the mountain here features a long sloping face of talus and snowfields, with only a small glacier and a moderate summit rock face. The normal approach is from the head of Perry Creek (see Little Beaver Creek Trail♦). Ascend heather and talus slopes of considerable height on the upper left side of the basin, then angle rightward in a gully through a break in cliffs (there are several ways to get through this barrier), then climb rightward. Cross the small slope glacier below the col (8000 ft+) in the SW ridge, then climb the glacier and snow to the final summit rock slope. A shallow gully on its upper right side, and minor gullies continue. This is not really a difficult route, but does involve some scrambling and exposure; the logical time is early summer, when the tedious lower slopes are covered by snow.

Variation: From just S of the Southwest Couloir climb the glacier arm southward to the 8000-ft+ ridge col. Here cross to the Perry Creek approach or follow the moderately easy rock of the ridge to the summit.

SOUTHWEST COULOIR: This route can be approached from Depot Creek, (see Depot Creek Route♦) or the Redoubt-Depot Creek divide, then making a long glacier traverse below the steep cliffs of the Twin Spires-Spickard ridge. Ascend the glacier below the Southwest Face to the

central, narrow snow couloir (40-degree angle); from a minor notch on the upper Northwest Ridge at about 200 ft below the summit, a short rock scramble continues to the top (may be forced to N flank part of the climb here). Time: 5 hours from camp. Note: The couloir is free of snow and full of debris in late season.

NORTHWEST RIDGE: This extended, craggy rock protrusion of the mountain divides the Southwest Face from the North Face. One can reach the route from Silver Lake, but it usually has been done from the upper basin of Depot Creek. Hike NE toward the obvious moraine, then left, then bear around it to the right. Traverse to a steep 500-ft snow gully, a feature which leads left again to a small notch in the Northwest Ridge. Traverse the crest to the top of the Southwest Couloir; during the first portion there is a 100-ft pitch (class 4) and one 50-ft rappel. The ridge route generally keeps on the SW side, below the crest (some loose rock). Time: 4 hours from Silver Lake or Depot Creek camp. Reference: *B.C.M.,* March 1975.

NORTH FACE (Silver Lake Glacier): The best time to make this climb is in early summer, when sufficient snow covers crevasses and ice. Apparently the first ascent was made by Paul Binkert party of five on May 17, 1959. Approach via Silver Lake Route♦ or Depot Creek Route♦. From the lake outlet note that steep terrain on the SE side may require a steep snow or ice crossing of the pocket glacier; it is better to keep on the opposite side of the lake. Ascend the glacier in a SW direction, then enter the cirque on the North Face of the mountain. Make an ascending leftward traverse across the moderately steep glacier and gain the NE ridge about 200 ft below the summit. Take crampons. References: *B.C.M.,* June 1959; *A.A.J.,* 1965, p. 412; 1968, p. 139.

PEAK 8824   8824 ft/2690 m
This is a high northeastern summit, more of a rock spur, 0.4 mi. from the true summit. The peak has a very rugged E face and also very precipitous NE-facing rock walls S of the eastern end of Silver Lake. First ascent by Dick Culbert in 1961. From the SE corner of the lake scramble to scree and slabs above the first line of cliffs. Traverse SW toward the peak until able to climb ice to a small col at the base of the final NE ridge (crampons). A shattered knife-edge (class 3-4) continues to the summit. Time: 4 hours.

PEAK 7895   7895 ft/2406 m
Located 0.9 mi. SE of Spickard, on the Perry Creek slope. There is a very rugged and steep N face on the flank toward Silver Creek's S fork; a steep glacier ice couloir separates this peak from Spickard. The easiest ascent route appears to be the SE flank, beginning in the cirque of Perry Creek.

PEAK 7153   7153 ft/2180 m
This small summit, 1.9 mi. ESE of Mt. Spickard,

MT. SHUKSAN
MT. BAKER
MT. REDOUBT
BEAR MTN.
Peak 7680
TWIN SPIRES
MT. SPICKARD
Peak 8824
MT. CUSTER
pass
southeast face
MT. RAHM
Silver Lake
Toothpick
Devils Tongue
Silver Creek
McNaught Creek Cirque

between Perry and Silver creeks, is the highest of a number of small points where the ridge begins to taper eastward. A route from upper Perry Creek appears to have no technical problems; largely a series of gullies and bouldery slopes on this flank.

MT. RAEBURN   6863 ft/2092 m

Although not a high regional summit, the mountain is a notable landmark from Ross Lake, since it is only 1.9 mi. from the western shore. The summit is midway between Silver and Little Beaver creeks, E of Mt. Spickard. The provisional name is for surveyor W.A. Raeburn, who was not only a veteran of early Cascade Range summit surveys (Spickard, Davis, Jack), but also took part in the survey of the Alaska-Canada boundary early in the century. The first ascent was probably made by a B.C. Mountaineering Club party led by Frank H. Dawes on June 5, 1960. Reference: *B.C.M.,* August 1960.

NORTHEAST RIDGE: From the entrance of Silver Creek at Ross Lake (see Silver Lake Route♦) cross near the stream's mouth and take a distinct forest ridge SW. This steep ridge is followed, and at a rocky area it may be best to contour under cliffs; on original ascent snow was taken on the edge of summit basin. The final rocky ridge is a steep scramble; belaying is advised on a short section. Class 3 or 4. Time: 6 hours from lake.

Note: The slope from lower Perry Creek is probably a shorter route to the summit, but has little appeal.

DEVILS TONGUE   8048 ft/2453 m

This is a rocky pyramid with very steep N and NE rock faces, located ½ mi. NE of the NE end of Silver Lake, just S of the Boundary. The peak is 0.6 mi. E of Mt. Rahm, and connected to it by a serrated ridge. The broad and rocky S face, above upper Silver Creek, is also steep and corrugated. The "International Glacier" below the N face drains to McNaught Creek in British Columbia. A narrow couloir of this glacier reaches to the notch just W of Devils Toothpick. First ascent by Don Cowie and Don Thom in 1957.

EAST FACE: From camp near Galene Lakes (see Galene Lake Trail♦) traverse a meadowed ridge SW and descend to beyond the 5720-ft+ col at the head of International Creek. Traverse W to a higher col (Silver-McNaught divide), and follow the dividing ridge W for 1.3 mi. to a col (6160 ft+) 1 mi. ENE of objective. Climb the ridge with a steep N face westward, then SW to a sub-peak (7103 ft). Traverse the rocky ridge W 0.4 mi., then climb on a leftward tangent onto the E rock face of the narrowing summit pyramid. This is a long route with route finding and considerable scrambling. Class 3, but could be more difficult. Time: 5 hours from camp.

SOUTHWEST FACE: This route has been descended (uncertain if climbed). From NE of the lower end of Silver Lake (see Silver Lake Route♦) gullies on the face appear to offer a feasible rocky route (est. class 3-4); one should expect a moderately long climb.

Devils Toothpick (7720 ft+/2354 m) is the narrow, steep tower just W of Devils Tongue.

MT. RAHM (International Peak)
8478 ft/2584 m

This is the central rock summit on the local transverse ridge between Silver Lake and the International Boundary. The mountain's rugged and very steep 1500-ft NE face flanks the W side of mi.-wide "International Glacier" in the cirque of McNaught Creek. This glacier, which descends to an altitude of 5500 ft, extends to beyond the rock walls of Devils Tongue; a narrow apex of the glacier reaches steeply to a gap on the connecting ridge between the peaks, on the divide with Silver Lake. The S flank of the mountain, which rises in a slope of scree, snow and cliff 1700 ft above the lake, is of less visual interest. This face becomes increasingly steep toward Devils Tongue. Rahm's N face is indented by a narrow couloir-glacier extending to the summit, just 0.2 mi. S of the Boundary. The long and broad NW flank of the mountain, which faces the E terminal fork of Maselpanik Creek, forms part of the rockwall barrier ridge extending from Rahm to Mt. Custer. Beneath the steep rock face of the mountain and ridge, the mi.-wide "Maselpanik Glacier" fills the upper portion of the creek's cirque. The name was choosen for geologist David A. Rahm. First ascent by Joe Hutton and Peggy Hutton and Roy Mason on August 5, 1955. Reference: *B.C.M.,* February 1956.

SOUTHWEST ROUTE: From the rock-slab slopes above Silver Lake (see Silver Lake Route♦ or Depot Creek Route♦) take advantage of a break in the short cliffs at 7600 ft above midway on Silver Lake. Take a rightward ascent up talus, easy scrambling, snow, and finally a small glacier bowl; a final talus slope leads to the summit. Note: The 1971 party on nearby Mt. Custer reached the cliffs by traversing the firn and ice segments NE closely under the ridge connecting the peaks.

NORTH ROUTE: As done by the original party, the route takes the McNaught-St. Alice Creek divide from Skagit River (boat crossing suggested); party reached the ridge at 5700 ft. Above the lower forested portion, the long SW-trending divide affords easy, open travel; there are attractive campspots 2 mi. from the Boundary at 6200 ft (4 hours taken on ridge).

A shorter approach is from Maselpanik Creek Road (Silver-Skagit Road♦): ascend the E fork and avoid waterfalls to the right. Cross a cirque and part of International Glacier

SILVER LAKE AREA from northeast
NATIONAL PARK SERVICE

CUSTER RIDGE from north
AUSTIN POST, U.S. GEOLOGICAL SURVEY

to gain the objective's N buttress near its base (this position can also be reached by continuing along the divide taken on original or from the road by ascending steep timber to the open Maselpanik-St. Alice divide). The final ascent is done by climbing the steep glacier. At 500 ft from the summit is a wide schrund; the original party climbed into the schrund and escaped via rocks of the buttress (on E). The eastern of two minor points is the true summit.

See Mt. Custer for traverse route connecting the mountains.

PEAK 8200+   8200 ft+/2499 m+
This is a crag 0.3 mi E of Rahm's summit on the main ridge. Its N and E rock faces above the International Glacier are extremely sheer. The first ascent of the peak was made by Jack Bryceland and Gordon Longmuir in 1965 by scrambling along the exposed connecting ridge (45 minutes). Reference: *B.C.M.*, March 1958.

CAMP PEAK   7700 ft+/2347 m+
This summit is just on the International Boundary, 1.1 mi. NW of Mt. Rahm, between the headwater forks of Maselpanik Creek; the highest point of the peak is in British Columbia, as shown clearly in sketches made during the first surveys of the Boundary belt.

MT. CUSTER   8630 ft/2630 m
This is the provisional name for a high, reddish rock peak 0.5 mi. NW of the upper end of Silver Lake, closely S of the Boundary. There is a long ridge trending NW to Mt. Rahm, one that forms a broad cirque above Silver Lake; the entire ridge has a short upper rock wall steepened by erosion above a former glacier. There is a steep glacier on the N face of the mountain (0.6 km long, drains to Maselpanik Creek); the glacier has an arm which reaches to the ridge crest just W of

MAD EAGLE PEAK — col — MT. REDOUBT — MT. CUSTER — MT. SPICKARD — TWIN SPIRES — R.MTN. Ridge — Bear Creek basin — Indian Creek

CHILLIWACK GROUP from south
BOB AND IRA SPRING

the summit. There is also a hanging ice segment that reaches to the summit ridge just E of the highest point. George Gibbs, when writing about the geography of the region as learned from experience with the Boundary Survey, mentioned the glacier at the head of Maselpanik Creek; he estimated it at ½ mi. in extent (Gibbs, *Physical Geography;* see Sec. II, note 21). Note: Custer Ridge as a locale is misnamed on the U.S.G.S. topographic map: the name applies to the entire Chilliwack-Skagit River watershed in the area. The first known ascent of the mountain is that of Frank Dawe, Roy Mason, and Karl Teichman in 1958 (it is not known if any survey parties made an earlier ascent).

SOUTH RIDGE: From the SW end of Silver Lake (see Silver Lake Route◆) ascend the glacier SW to near the pass (7360 ft+) to get above a rock barrier. Ascend gentle snow and rockslide slopes N to reach the rocky South Ridge of the mountain. There is some scrambling up loose sections (pass one gendarme), but the final part is easier than it appears. Time: 4 hours from lake.

Variation: One can reach the latter part of the ridge from a base in Depot Creek; the approach is via a large snow-bowl cirque.

SOUTHEAST FACE: First ascent by Greg Rice, John Roper, and Reed Tindall on August 10, 1971. From the lake climb easy slabby cliffs, then small gullies, snow, then a scree gully to a notch in the E ridge close to the summit. There are a few rock moves on the route, but the climbing is largely scrambling.

A traverse along the entire E ridge of Mt. Custer was made to Mt. Rahm by Dick Cagle and Russ Krocker in July 1979.

MT. REDOUBT   8956 ft/2730 m

Redoubt is one of the several highest and most prominent peaks in this section, and is a distinctive land-mark from most high peaks in the North Cascades, and even those N of the Fraser River in British Columbia. Its precise location is 3 mi. S of the Boundary at Monument 66, between upper Chilliwack River and upper Ross Lake in the Chilliwack group of peaks. The craggy mountain is comprised of Skagit gneiss, often very shattered. This rock, with its striking bands, is much in evidence in the form of steep, discontinuous cliffs at the head of Bear Creek (S face), the most prominent feature being a sheer and distinct flying buttress. But Redoubt's most impressive facade is the northern one, facing Depot Creek, where a great bastion of rock walls form the headwall of Depot Glacier. On this flank of the mountain, the combined area of the Redoubt and Depot glaciers totals some 5.1 km²; the larger of these very crevassed glaciers (the Redoubt) extends E to the flank of Mt. Spickard, and has formed conspicuous 19th century moraine ridges along the broad cirque.[78]

American Boundary Survey explorer Henry Custer, from a peak N of Depot Creek on August 2, 1859, wrote of "sharp, frightful, fantastic" peaks, which must have included Mt. Redoubt as the center of attention. The first ascent was made by Canadian climbers Jimmie Cherry and Bob Ross in 1930 during a rather unknown venture. Bill Cox and Will F. Thompson climbed the mountain again in September 1937, approaching by Bear Creek, completing the summit rock crest on the SW (W of the gullies normally used). References: *Mountaineer,* 1950, p. 39; *B.C.M.,* February 1973.

SOUTH ROUTE: For approach see Chilliwack River Trail◆-Indian Creek Trail or Bear Creek High Route. The entrance to the upper, craggy rock face is guarded by three

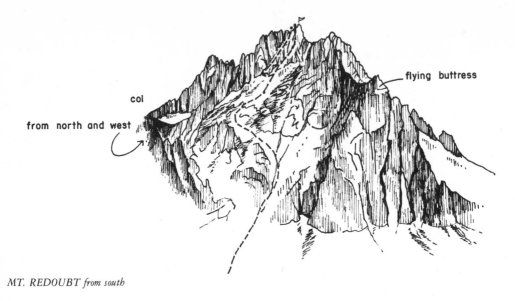

col

flying buttress

from north and west

MT. REDOUBT from south

large rock buttresses (gates) above the gradual slopes by Bear Lake; the plan is to climb into the wide depression between the higher (western) two. Hike N along the Bear-Redoubt Creek divide, then make a rising leftward tack for the gap left of the sheer flying buttress (or ascend directly from Bear Lake). Ascend a narrow steep couloir into the S face depression, then scramble left onto a snow-scree shoulder. Opinions vary as to the best route for completion: one established route is to reach the best of several continuing gullies from the obvious ledge on the right. Before the gully, cut back on a steep rock ramp (class 3), which is followed into an easier gully leading to the notch beside the main peak. A scramble, on or near the rock crest, leads to the summit.

From the scree shoulder it is also quite feasible to move left to the adjoining rock. Here traverse a ledge into a rock gully (exposed dropoff below). The first 20 ft in the gully are best done roped, but climbing then becomes a scramble; at the last portion one can climb leftward and follow a ragged ridge crest. Time: 4 hours from Bear Lake.

Approach Variations: From a camp at about 7200 ft on the Depot-Redoubt Creek divide (see Depot Creek Route♦) cross the glacier westward through the high broad gap (7680 ft+) under the flying buttress of Redoubt (above Point 8080 ft+). Time: 4 hours to summit.

From West Depot Glacier (½ mi. NW of the summit) one can climb directly to the high col (7600 ft+) on the divide with Bear Creek (adjacent to Mad Eagle Peak). Descend the opposite slope and circle beneath the western cliffs of Redoubt, then make a traversing ascent of snow and ledges to the scree shoulder. It should be noted that the glacier tends to be badly crevassed in late summer. An alternative approach to the foot of the glacier is via the lake fork variation of the Depot Creek entry.

WEST FACE: This rounded rock face has a rather broken appearance, with a final short steep section at the summit structure. First ascent by Alex Bertulis, Victor Lapatinskas, and Peter Nalis in July 1973. Reach the upper face directly from Bear Lake or from the arm of Depot Glacier. The route taken is class 3 except for the vertical notch of the final ridge crest (aid used here); rock is generally shattered. Reference: *Mountaineer,* 1973, p. 32.

NORTHEAST FACE: The major portion of this spectacular and very steep face is a N- and NE-facing rock wall varying from 1000 to 1700 ft above Depot Glacier. A high, crevassed arm of the glacier extends onto a slightly protruding spur of the face, its apex forming a very steep ice apron that becomes a narrow snow/ice rib E of the summit. First ascent by Fred Beckey and John Rupley on July 23, 1971; a winter ascent was made by Robin Barley and Peter Rowat in February 1977.

The most direct approach is Depot Creek Route♦, but another method is to take the route into the lake fork of Depot Creek (see Mad Eagle Peak); if taking the Indian Creek or other approaches one must descend to 6300 ft on Redoubt Glacier to bypass a rock arm and reach Depot Glacier. The problem on the route is to climb through intricate crevasse patterns to reach the ice apron. It has proven best to cross the first bergschrunds on the right, then climb near the left edge of the ice to the sharp ice crest. Continue to the rock rib above. After climbing the rock some distance it is possible to traverse left to a steep couloir leading to a notch SE of the summit. Grade III; take cram-

MT. REDOUBT — north face
PHILIP LEATHERMAN

pons, ice screws, and snow flukes. References: *A.A.J.,* 1972, pp. 115-16; *C.A.J.,* 1978, p. 81.

EAST FACE: It is not certain if this route has been completed; it is certainly feasible to ascend Redoubt Glacier into the cirque between the E and SE ridges, but the steep rock of the eastern summit headwall is an uncertain aspect; probably class 4. The narrow arete could be continued to the main summit.

POINT 8080 ft+   8080 ft+/2463 m+
This crag is a frontal spur of Mt. Redoubt, 0.6 mi. SSE of the summit at the SW edge of Redoubt Glacier; the glacier extends into the broad saddle between the crag and Redoubt. The summit of this crag is on the Redoubt-Bear Creek divide; there is a short but sheer rock face on the Bear Creek flank. A known ascent from the glacier divide was made by Mark Allabach and John Roper, August 12, 1979. There is a short scrambling section (class 3), then a talus jungle toward the summit.

MAD EAGLE PEAK   8080 ft+/2463 m+
This is the double-rock peak 2.4 mi. S of the Boundary and 0.5 mi. NW of Mt. Redoubt on the Bear-Depot Creek divide. The pointed W summit peak which inspires the name is 5 to 10 ft lower than the E peak. The S faces of both summits are quite steep and are broken by a slanting couloir. There are two small glaciers flanking the peak on the Depot Creek side. The first ascent was apparently made by Mark and Steve Allabach, Joe Medlicott, and John Roper on August 11, 1979.

ROUTE: From Redoubt High Route (see Chilliwack River Trail♦) or Depot Creek Route♦-Lake Fork cross through the 7120-ft+ col NW of the summit (the original party reached the col from a traverse of Peak 7680 ft+). From the col make a descending traverse across the northern glacier, keeping below the steep dirty ice. Ascend polished slabs and scree to left of the glacier to reach the N ridge. Rocky scrambling leads to the summit (class 3).

PEAK 7680+   7680+/2341 m+

This summit is 1.1 mi. NW of Mt. Redoubt, on the Bear-Depot Creek divide. A small snowfield-glacier rests in the cirque between the summit and Peak 7365, draining to the lake on the Depot Creek flank. The first ascent was apparently made by Roman Babicky, John Bates, Brian Nuttall, Bill Hobeck, and John Stinson on September 22, 1974; they approached the peak on snow from the 6960-ft+ col between the objective and Peak 7365. Reference: *B.C.M.,* June 1975.

ROUTE: Approach from Redoubt High Route or the Lake Fork variation of Depot Creek Route♦. In ascending from the lake, scramble up moraine, then ascend the small glacier to its W to the col on the main ridge. The W ridge is taken to the summit (not technical); crampons may be useful. The 1974 party also climbed Peak 7365, from the col via the S shoulder (not difficult).

   The SE ridge of Peak 7680+ is a feasible route (descended in 1979). When ascending from the lake climb the left edge of the western glacier to the right portion of the glacier between the objective and Mad Eagle Peak.

NODOUBT PEAK   7290 ft/2222 m

A small summit from the elevation standpoint, but a quite massive pyramidal formation, with low footings; altitude on the Chilliwack River, just W, is 2000 ft. The peak is on the rugged Bear-Depot Creek divide, 3 mi. NW of Mt. Redoubt. The first ascent appears to have been made by D.J. Fraser in 1935 when establishing "Station M" on the ridge SE of Monument 64; the provisional name was originated by geologists who climbed the peak in 1967. Point 6404, to the SE of the summit, was climbed by Francis Herbst while surveying in 1859.

ROUTE: See Redoubt High Route (Chilliwack River Trail♦). The completion to the summit from the W is not technical; the low-gradient S ridge is also a simple route, and could be used as part of a traverse.

   An alternative, but now much longer approach would be to ascend the forested hillside from the trail on the N side of Bear Creek, to reach the S ridge at 6700 ft; this would be a brushy slog.

MT. EDGAR (B.C.)   6500 ft+/1981 m+

This is the high point of the Depot-Paleface Creek ridge, 2.5 mi. E of Chilliwack Lake and about 2 mi. N of the Boundary. Surveyors occupied various summits on this ridge in 1859-61, as well as in later years. Map: Skagit River 92 H/3.

ROUTES: Maps once marked a trail from Depot Creek toward the summit, but it certainly must now be vanished in the logging slash and new growth. The summit can be reached from either the lower portion of the road in Depot Creek or from the road in Paleface Creek's valley (see Chilliwack River Road♦).

THOMPSON PEAK (B.C.)   7000 ft+/2134 m+

This summit is on Custer Ridge 4.7 mi. E of Chilliwack Lake and 3.6 mi. N of the Boundary, between Paleface and Maselpanik creeks, an area of fine high meadowland noted by parties of the first Boundary Survey. Another summit of about the same altitude (7000 ft+) and closer to the Boundary (at 1.8 mi. S of Thompson) was apparently climbed by the U.S. party some time between 1858 and 1861.[79] The first ascent of Thompson was made by Roy Mason and Donald MacLaurin in 1961. This party also climbed a summit to the E (slightly lower) and probably climbed the summit to the S. References: *B.C.M.,* April and May, 1962. Map: Skagit River 92 H/3.

ROUTES: The original party climbed from a pass at the head of Paleface Creek's South Fork, then followed ridges northward. It is now more feasible to approach from Paleface Creek Road (see Chilliwack River Road♦) and a spur to about 4000 ft (W of the peak), then find a suitable route (some brush).

   The most direct route appears to be from Maselpanik Creek Road; at the side valley about 6½ mi. take the road spur W and ascend to the divide S of the peak (likely some brush).

   An old trail route once extended from Depot Creek NE to the lake at 5900 ft+; this is a possible route to the S portion of Custer Ridge, but still a long way to Thompson.

WHITWORTH PEAK (B.C.)   7525 ft/2294 m

A prominent, gently sloped summit 5½ mi. N of the International Boundary, between Klesilkwa River and Maselpanik Creek. The N peak is highest; the S peak is 7273 ft (2217 m) and nearby *Finlayson Peak* is 7236 ft (2206 m). The peak appears to be composed of volcanic rocks, chert, and shale of the Triassic-Jurassic Hozameen Group. The first ascent was probably made by Thomas Riggs and party (surveyors) in 1905; earlier surveyors were nearby, perhaps on the ridge or a high point to the S of the true summit. Map: Skagit River 92 H/3.

ROUTE: From Maselpanik Creek Road spurs (see Silver-Skagit Road♦). Take the highest E spur (hiking) to 4800 ft and continue to the ridge about 2 mi. S of the summit. Merely trek along the open, scenic ridge (pass over the minor summit of Finlayson). The main rewards of the ascent are the views of upper Skagit Valley, Silvertip Peak, and Hozomeen Mountain.

MT. LOCKWOOD (B.C.)
6700 ft+/2042 m+
Located 1.3 mi. W of Maselpanik Creek and 2.5 mi. S of Klesilkwa River on a N-S trending ridge. Map: Skagit River 92 H/3.

ROUTE: See Silver-Skagit Road♦. The best approach appears to be via Maselpanik Creek Road at about 2½ mi., then ascend W to the summit (apparently simple). One can also gain the divide to the N from a short distance up the Maselpanik Road. Time: 6 hours from road.

KLESILKWA MOUNTAIN (B.C.)
6800 ft+/2073 m+
On the main divide of Custer Ridge between upper Klesilkwa River and upper Silverhope Creek at 3½ mi. E of Chilliwack Lake. The ascent was likely made by early survey parties. Map: Skagit River 92 H/3.

ROUTES: It is an easy ascent from the North Fork of Paleface Creek (see Chilliwack River Road♦) S of the objective. One can hike the road spur off the North Fork to 4400 ft below the mountain; expect some brush.

Approaches are also possible from the NE and W. The N ridge may be an easy ascent.

PALEFACE MOUNTAIN (B.C.)
5800 ft+/1767 m+
MT. MERONUIK (B.C.) 5900 ft+/1798 m+
Both peaks are 1.2 mi. E of Chilliwack Lake; Paleface is .8 mi. N of Meronuik.

ROUTE: Reach both peaks from the N branch of Paleface Creek Road (see Chilliwack River Road), by climbing slash and brush on the E flank.

MT. WITTENBERG (B.C.)
6100 ft+/1859 m+
Between Hicks Creek and upper Silverhope Creek at 3 mi. NE of Chilliwack Lake. Map: Skagit River 92 H/3.

ROUTE: The shortest approach is from Flora Creek W of the mountain; there will be some brush in the cross-country

travel. Take the Post Creek Trail♦ (Lindeman Lake) to the W end of Greendrop Lake.

MT. NOWELL (B.C.)
6000 ft+/1829 m+
This is a minor summit 3.3 mi. E of Mt. Northgraves and about 2½ mi. W of Silverhope Creek, on the NE end of the divide between Hicks and Yola creeks. Map: Skagit River 92 H/3.

ROUTE: See Silver-Skagit Road♦. A logging spur from Yola Creek Road climbs the W slope of Nowell and bears up near a lake (5300 ft+) to W of the summit (less than an hour via open forest and meadows).

A rocky summit at 6500 ft+ is S of the head of Yola Creek; one can apparently reach this peak by traversing the heathery divide, or directly from the head of the road.

JEFFREY PEAK (B.C.)   6729 ft/2051 m
Jeffrey is a bulky, moderately prominent summit of the region located SW of the Yola-Cantelon Creek junction 4 mi. from Silverhope Creek. The first ascent was made by surveyors. Map: Skagit River 92 H/3.

ROUTE: A spur W of the Yola Creek Road (see Silver-Skagit Road♦) at about 3400 ft cuts across the mouth of the basin holding the lake (3900 ft+) SE of the objective; one may need to hike over 2 mi. up the road from the junction. Ascend W to open slopes SE of the summit. The alternative approach is directly from the lake through meadows and cliffs.

MT. NORTHGRAVES (B.C.)
6900 ft+/2103 m+
This is a steep peak with granitic walls, located between upper Yola and Cantelon Creek branches of Silverhope Creek and 5.5 mi. E of Welch Peak. Rock is partly granitic and partly volcanic, very sheared and mixed. First ascent by Ashlyn-Armour Brown, Dick Culbert, and Bruce McKnight in 1960.

SOUTHWEST ROUTE: From the end of the road in Yola Creek (see Silver-Skagit Road♦) hike through forests on the NW side of the valley. Bear across a rockslide at the cirque mouth below the South Face of objective and into the basin beyond. Easily gain the pass (6100 ft+) on the Yola Creek divide, then take the divide (heather) some distance to the summit (keep left of difficulties). Time: 5 hours.

SOUTH FACE: This face (about 1200 ft in height) is composed of metavolcanic rock, which is sound but difficult to protect. The route climbed is a serious one; there are other possibilities. First ascent by Jack Bryan, Dick Culbert, Fred Douglas, and Paul Starr in 1972. The cirque beneath the face is reached in 2 hours (see Southwest Route). Avoid the lowest part of the face by climbing the left edge (class 4); then climb onto the prominent central nose where this feature takes shape. Ascend on cracks and corners for seven leads of difficult climbing. Climb an obvious large white corner (one aid piton); another corner higher was avoided by climbing left. Grade III; class 5.8 and A1. Time: long day. References: *B.C.M.*, November 1972; *C.A.J.*, 1973, p. 62, and photo p. 61.

MT. LING (B.C.)   6472 ft/1973 m
Midway between Wahleach Lake and Silverhope Creek, 2½ mi. W of Jeffrey Peak (between Cantelon and Foley creeks).
ROUTE: Use the Cantelon Creek Road (see Silver-Skagit Road♦-Yola Creek branch) to 3300 ft E of the objective; hike up easy slopes to the summit.

SILVER PEAK (Eureka Peak) (B.C.)   6400 ft+/1951 m+
Directly E of Isolillock Mountain, this peak is prominent from Hope; it has three minor summits on a N-S crest. While the Chilliwack Batholith extends from Hope through Klesilkwa River, the upper part of Silver Peak is composed of Eocene conglomerate which forms the roof of the youngest part of the batholith. Map: Hope 92 H/6.
ROUTE: See Isolillock Mountain. From the col one can ascend 600 ft easily to the S summit point; one can also do the climb from the cirque at the valley head: ascend rockslides to the right of the old tram route into the cirque. Reference: *B.C.M.*, April 1963.

ISOLILLOCK MOUNTAIN (Holy Cross Mountain) (B.C.)   6810 ft/2076 m
This is a prominent summit 5½ mi. SW of Hope and W of Silver Lake in the Silverhope Creek valley. A cross of snow on its N face (toward the Eureka Mine) has long given it the name of Holy Cross. Granitic rocks 70 to 80 m.y. old here are cut by the Chilliwack Batholith. There is a great local relief on this mountain, for the altitude at Silver Lake is only 500 ft. The ascent was done by Roy Howard and E.E. Smith in August 1936, but they believed that a survey party may have preceded them. References: Cairnes, Memoir 139 — see Sec. II, note 5; Bauerman, Report of Progress — see Sec. II, note 2; *B.C.M.*, December 1936, July 1949, July 1952, June 1957. Map: Hope 92 H/6.
ROUTES: Reach from Silver-Skagit Road♦ and Eureka Creek branch. An abandoned mining road climbs to about 4500 ft in the valley N of the objective and Silver Peak before bearing 500 ft onto the N ridge of the latter. The snow col (5800 ft+) between the peaks is easily reached from the road's end or from where it leaves the valley. The final ascent is an easy rock scramble.
From the road at about 4700 ft, one can climb to the N

ridge of Isolillock, taking a gully of about 800 ft (snow) through a step in the ridge. Continue up the ridge and scramble over the false summit to the peak. Note: Rocks and grass on these routes can be slippery. Time: 1 day r.t. from valley (long day if necessary to hike entire distance).

MT. BARR (B.C.)   6228 ft/1898 m
A minor peak 2½ mi. E of the N end of Wahleach Lake. There is an unnamed summit slightly higher (6300 ft+/1921 m) 1.8 mi. to the E. Map: Harrison Lake 92 H/5.
ROUTE: Logging roads reach the S side of the mountain from the N end of Wahleach Lake (see Jones Lake Road♦); a hiking spur may go to 3600 ft.

CHEAM RANGE (B.C.)
The Cheam Range is one of the most important subranges in this section, and is unusual for being aligned E to W. Located between the Fraser and Chilliwack rivers (E of Chilliwack) for a span of some 8 mi., the peaks of the range are very visible from such towns as Abbotsford, Sumas, and Lynden. The four eastern peaks (Foley to Knight) are often called the Lucky Four Group because of their proximity to the mine of that name. The Cheam Range is high and rugged, with very low footings; there are several outstanding glaciers, but rock quality is generally poor. The Chilliwack Batholith is exposed at lower levels on the NE side, but the peaks themselves are of the volcanic Chilliwack Group.
The early history of the Cheam Range relates mostly to the Lucky Four Mine near the glacier of that name on Foley Peak. The mine is near the geologic contact; its site was produced by volatiles, heat and metals emanating from the cooling batholith. Miners built a trail up Wahleach Creek and began activity in this copper prospect during World War I. By easy corruption the name Wahleach was altered to Welch for the range's highest summit; the names Foley and Stewart were given for contractors on the Canadian Northern Railway. Mountaineers first visited the range in 1888-1889 when Cheam and Lady peaks were climbed. The first traverse of the peaks (from Cheam Peak on the W end to Foley Peak) was done by Jack Bryan and Jim Craig in the summer of 1961. The standard approaches are Lucky Four Mine Trail♦, Mt. Cheam Trail♦, and Williamson Lake Trail♦. Map: Chilliwack Lake 92 H/4. References: *B.C.M.*, October 1924, July 1925, November 1933, May 1962; *Avalanche Echoes (A.C.C.)* February, March,

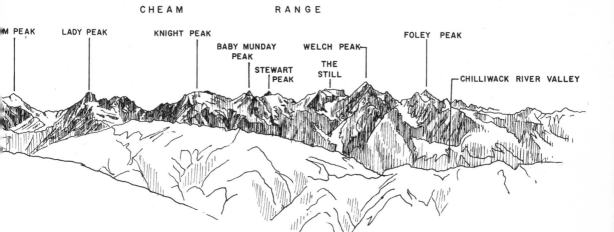

CHEAM   RANGE

M PEAK   LADY PEAK   KNIGHT PEAK   BABY MUNDAY PEAK   WELCH PEAK   FOLEY PEAK   STEWART PEAK   THE STILL   CHILLIWACK RIVER VALLEY

CHEAM RANGE from south

and April 1943; *C.A.J.*, 1949, pp. 93-98; *Mountaineer*, 1951, p. 31.

CHEAM PEAK (B.C.)   6913 ft/2107 m

Cheam is the western summit of the range, rising abruptly on the S rim of Fraser Valley. Located only 12 mi. from the city of Chilliwack, the peak's steep valley slope and profile are eye-catching from the Trans-Canada Hwy. The steep Mt. Cheam Trail♦ is the usual route, the final part being the SW ridge of the summit. The hike is a popular one, almost a conditioning pilgrimage, but one should plan a long day return if the roads are walked. The steep upper slopes and cornices on the summit ridge can be dangerous in the spring season. The apparent first ascent was by A.O. Campbell, Ebe R. Knight, Popcum Sawmill, Mr. Thompson, and two Indian packers in September 1888. References; *B.C.M.*, October 1924, May 1928, October 1938, October 1953, August 1957, September 1957, June 1959, September 1962, May 1964, November 1969; British Columbia Monthly, August 1924, p. 5.

NORTH FACE: First ascent by Don Heppner, Doug Herchmer, Don Serl, and Kurt Ulmer on June 30, 1975. From Trans-Canada Hwy♦ climb a trail beginning 2.7 mi. E of Bridal Falls (or drive? a rough road beginning at 4 mi. E of the falls) to the 4300-ft knoll just above small lakes 1½ mi. NE of Cheam Peak; there is a campsite at about 4200 ft. Traverse W and descend a snowy gully to runouts below the face. Climb easy snow slopes up and right to the tiny pocket glacier below the North Face. From the top of the glacier climb a rock wall (class 5) and 250 ft up steep snow to the base of the triangular upper rock face. Traverse right along the top edge of snow for 400 ft to the NW corner of the pyramid, then climb directly up the ridge and gullies bounding the face on the right (about 800 ft of class 3 and 4); the route exits onto the SW ridge several hundred ft from the summit. Class 3 to 5. Time: 8 hours camp to summit.

NORTHEAST RIDGE: This route climbs a series of slabs and short walls (1500 ft of rock climbing) above logging areas; the route is behind the highway's view. First ascent by Eric Larsson and Henning Von Have in 1966. From the campsite area described for North Face route ascend steep forest and windfalls. The lower half of the climbing is easy and pleasant scrambling, but later the route steepens and becomes somewhat loose. Keep left of the crest, then take the obvious narrow gully through a cliff band at several hundred ft left of the ridge corner (about 300 ft below the summit). Class 4. Reference: *B.C.M.*, June 1970.

LADY PEAK (B.C.)   7100 ft+/2164 m+

This prominent peak is located 1 mi. SE of Cheam Peak. From most vantages Lady appears flat-topped, with steep rock wall flanks. The largest face rises above Wahleach Lake; from the E the peak features a very rectangular wall; the SE ridge appears to provide a pleasant rock climb. The coordinates given by Henry Custer of the Boundary Survey (American party 1858-61) for "Klehtlakeh Mountain" come close to

Lady Peak; possibly Custer made the first ascent. More likely the first climb was by a Fraser Valley party consisting of Isaac Henderson, Ebe B. Knight, and John R. Smith in September 1889. The approach was from the W side of Wahleach Lake southward to the Lady-Cheam col. References: *B.C.M.*, August and September, 1957; British Columbia Monthly, August 1924, p. 5.

WEST ROUTE: From about 5500 ft on the SW ridge of Cheam Peak traverse E to the Lady-Cheam col (5800 ft+). Make an easy scramble up the objective's W slope (keep high); 1 hour from the trail.

Western Approach: From Chipmunk Creek Road (see Chilliwack River Road♦). This may be a suitable ski tour approach.

KNIGHT PEAK (B.C.)
7200 ft+/2195 m+

Knight is a quite massive summit, located 2½ mi. SE of Cheam Peak. The glacier on its NW flank is one of the major ones in the Cheam Range; there is also a glacier on its NE side. There was a commercial airplane crash on the S slope of the peak in 1941. The first ascent was made by Ebe B. Knight and David Walker in September 1892. The approach was possibly by the glacier between Lady and Knight. Reference: British Columbia Monthly, August 1924, p. 5.

ROUTES: From a camp at about 5100 ft on the slope above Airplane Creek (see Airplane Creek Trail♦) ascend NW (around Baby Munday Peak) to the saddle E of Knight Peak (6700 ft+). The summit portion is merely a trek.

Another approach is to scramble the easy divide from the W, crossing through the Lady-Knight col (5800 ft+).

BABY MUNDAY PEAK (B.C.)
7200 ft+/2195 m+

This is a spectacular, hornlike rock peak located very closely SW of Stewart Peak and 0.4 mi. SE of Knight Peak. The short E face is quite steep. Despite its appearance, the ascent of the peak is not particularly difficult. A.S. Williamson, in charge of operations at the Lucky Four Mine in 1923, whimsically applied the name in honor of the Mundays' daughter. The first ascent was by Bill Dobson and Bill Henderson on July 23, 1933. They described the climb as "a very narrow ridge of tottering rock with numerous perpendicular pitches over a tremendous drop." References: *B.C.M.*, May 1962, September 1968, September 1973.

SOUTHEAST RIDGE: Take Airplane Creek Trail♦, then ascend the SE face of the objective to just S of the summit horn; then climb the exposed ridge-face to the summit. Class 3 (loose rock, one exposed spot). Note: This ridge may also be reached farther S over ledges.

Approach Variation: By taking Lucky Four Mine Trail♦ one can cross the glacier and alpine slope N of Welch Peak to the Still-Stewart col (6600 ft+); cross to the lake at 6400 ft+ in the cirque E of the peak.

NORTH FACE: First ascent by Jack Bryan and Jim Craig, 1961. The climb was done from the ridge on the N via the deep notch between the S (main) and middle peak of Baby Munday. From the latter the party made one rappel, then continued up the face to the highest summit. Solid rock (two class 4 pitches).

STEWART PEAK (B.C.)
7300 ft+/2225 m+

Stewart is a glaciated summit of the Lucky Four Group, located 1.3 mi. NW of Welch Peak; the main glacier (Stewart Glacier) is SE of the summit. The first ascent was claimed by C. Chapman, H.C. Lewis, Don and Phyllis Munday in 1923, but probably was done by Ebe B. Knight and David Walker in September 1894. The two made a climb that they later probably misinterpreted as Foley, but reason dictates that the summit they climbed was Stewart. References: *B.C.M.*, September 1968; British Columbia Monthly, August 1924, p.5.

SOUTHEAST RIDGE: Take the Airplane Creek Trail♦, then from the 6400-ft+ lake continue to the Stewart-Still col (6600 ft+). Then ascend over heather and rock ledges of the Southeast Ridge (not difficult).

A variation from the col is to climb the shorter SW ridge. A longer and much more alpine approach is to take the Lucky Four Mine Trail♦, then reach the col by bearing N of Welch Peak.

NORTH FACE: This is the face/buttress descending from the summit toward Wahleach Lake; the face steepens at 5500 ft and has a glacier to its W. First ascent by Adolf Bitterlich and Henryk Mather in July 1967 or 1968. Logging roads extend to about 3300 ft S of the lake; a cross-country trek (some brush) was taken to the foot of a gully (2 hours). Midway up the gully (some snow) climb rightward, where there is good rock on the face; class 5.

THE STILL (B.C.)   7500 ft+/2286 m+

This small massif SE of Stewart and ½ mi. NW of Welch Peak was given this name because of vapor steaming on gullies of the N face. The summit area is an E-W ridge, somewhat loose. The first ascent was made by the Welch Peak party (1924), via the icefall of the Stewart Glacier to the Still-Stewart col. From this col (6600 ft+) ascend the W face or the NW ridge (easy).

WELCH PEAK (B.C.)
7800 ft+/2377 m+

Welch is the dominating and highest peak in the Cheam Range, located 3.2 mi. SE of the S end of

FOLEY PEAK and WELCH PEAK
WALTER CADILLAC

Wahleach Lake and 4 mi. N of the Chilliwack Valley; the summit is 4 mi. ESE of Cheam Peak. Welch is generally visible from the peaks of the Chilliwack Group, Border Peaks, and summits N of the Fraser River. A smaller S summit is 7333 ft (2236 m). The largest glacier (Wahleach) is N of the mountain (from 6500 ft to 5100 ft); the Foley Glacier is located on the NE slope, and extends to 5500 ft.

The first ascent was made by Arthur Cooper, Fred Smith, and Brick Spouse in May 1924 via the Wahleach Glacier and Foley-Welch col. The party found the E ridge steep, narrow and corniced, so they made an icy rock traverse to the S portion of the ridge, then reached the final summit rocks. References: *B.C.M.*, August 1923, September 1956, July 1957, September 1960.

SOUTHEAST FACE: The best approach is via Williamson Lake Trail♦ and continue to the Welch-Foley col (6800 ft+).

Climb the lower E ridge (loose rock), passing a prominent gendarme by a 50-ft descent and traverse on the S face. Scramble the broken rock of the summit slope (class 3; possibly a few snowpatches). To avoid the short wall ringing the summit structure on its E side, at about 100 ft below the top turn this feature on the S. Time: 3 hours from Williamson Lake. Note: One can climb a slabby gully below the S peak's notch (the gully trends right to the notch); then follow the South Ridge or keep on a right bypass.

Approach Variation: From Conway Camp on Lucky Four Mine Trail♦ traverse about ½ mi. to the crevassed Foley Glacier, then climb to the col; it is usually best to first keep left on the glacier. Time: 4 hours camp to summit.

SOUTH RIDGE: First ascent by Esther and Martin Kafer in October, 1965; first winter ascent by Don Serl on February 25, 1978. This ridge is accessible from Williamson Lake. Make a heathery approach via the top of a prominent shoulder; the route provides class 3-4 climbing on moderately firm rock. One can traverse rightward around any difficulties on the ridge. Time: 4 hours from lake.

FOLEY PEAK (B.C.) 7500 ft+/2286 m+

Foley is a steep rock pyramid, smaller but equally impressive as Welch Peak, to which it is connected by a col on the W. It is the eastern summit of the Cheam Range, and the small glacier on its NE flank (Lucky Four Glacier) is the farthest one in the range; the Foley Glacier, just W of the summit is the larger of the two. Foley Peak has a SW summit (7300 ft+/2226 m+) along the narrow ridge from the col. First ascent by Beverley Caley, Dudley Foster, Eric Fuller, Harold O'Conner, Don Munday, Phyllis Munday, and Bill Wheatley in May 1924 (via Northeast Face). First winter ascent by Paul Berntsen, Ken McComber, and Paul Stolliker in December 1974 (via Southeast Ridge). References: *B.C.M.*, May 1924, July 1929, August 1938, September 1956, July 1957, October 1963, January 1970, April 1970.

SOUTHEAST RIDGE: From Lucky Four Mine◆ cross the small glacier and snowfields below the eastern rock face. Make a traversing ascent to a broad notch in the left skyline (Southeast Ridge), then cross to the SE side. Climb rightward slanting gullies on the S face onto the upper SE ridge. Class 3.

Alternative Approach: From the Welch-Foley col (see Welch Peak) contour the N side of the sub-peak to Foley's SW col (7100 ft+). Descend and contour below Foley's S face (snow possible) and into the basin SE of the objective (2 hours from lake); then continue to the Southeast Ridge crest through a loose gully.

SOUTHWEST RIDGE: First ascent by Gernot Walter and Ed Zenger in 1970 or 1971. From the final SW col (reached by a traverse on the S) climb the ridge and face; class 5.4 (rock generally sound). Time: 2 hours.

NORTHWEST RIDGE: First ascent by "J" Fairley, Tom Fyles, and Ed Otten in the early 1930s. This loose ridge is a steep route (low class 5). Begin by a snow couloir from N of the Welch-Foley col. Time: 4 hours from col.

NORTHEAST FACE: (Original route) From the Lucky Four Glacier climb (snow or firn) and some rock to the eastern arete at about 300 ft below the summit. The original party found steep snow here (the climb would be easier later in the season).

GOETZ PEAK (B.C.)

6600 ft+/2012 m+

This summit is located 1.3 mi. N of higher Williams Peak.

ROUTES: Goetz is reached easily from Williams Peak by traversing around its W slope; hike the final open divide.

Another approach is to hike E from the spur at 6 mi. on the Foley Creek Road (see Chilliwack River Road◆).

WILLIAMS PEAK (B.C.)

6965 ft/2123 m

A granitic rock horn of very pyramidal form 4 mi. NW of the lower end of Chilliwack Lake and 4.8 mi. SE of Welch Peak. The first ascent was made in 1908 by the Canadian Boundary Survey, under J.J. McArthur; in the report the peak was termed Silver Peak. References: *B.C.M.*, November and December 1961; *Joint Report*, p. 415. Map: Skagit River 92 H/3 and Chilliwack H/4.

ROUTE: Reach from the top of Williams Ridge Trail◆. Ascend the W slope and face until reaching the base of a chimney-groove system at about 6300 ft. Traverse right, contouring to the SW ridge. Ascend here easily. A climb of the direct W side is class 4. Time: 2 hours ridge to summit.

MT. WEBB (Radium Peak) (B.C.)

7097 ft/2163 m

Rising steeply 1½ mi. from Chilliwack Lake, this peak is 2.6 mi. N of Mt. Lindeman.

ROUTE: See Radium Creek Trail◆. The S ridge is a trek. The NW ridge can also be done directly from the cabin (easy route).

MACDONALD PEAK (B.C.)

7300 ft+/2225 m+

This triangular-shaped summit 1.7 mi. N of Mt. Lindeman, closely W of the shore of Chilliwack Lake, may have been first climbed by a party from the Boundary Survey. Henry Custer in 1859 almost certainly climbed Mt. Webb, just NE of Macdonald. Reference: *B.C.M.*, December 1974.

ROUTES: Take Centre Creek Road (see Chilliwack River Road ◆) to the last junction (est. 4000 ft), then drive or hike a spur to about 5000 ft. Ascend a stream valley to about 5900 ft, then hike S to a flowery spur ridge. This leads to a rocky spine bearing the summit (2-3 hours).

A northern approach uses Radium Creek Trail ◆ to the 6200-ft+ col between Macdonald and Webb. Either summit can be reached easily from here. Both peaks provide magnificent views of the Chilliwack peaks and Cheam Range.

MT. LINDEMAN (B.C.)   7578 ft/2310 m

This massive peak is only 0.9 mi. from the International Boundary and less than 2 mi. from the S end of Chilliwack Lake. Hilary Bauerman, geologist for the British party during the Boundary Survey 1859-61 referred to the "highest granite peak in the mountains surrounding Chilukweyuk Lake . . . the summit presenting a nearly vertical cliff-face of about 1,200 ft . . . "[80] Reginald A. Daly was somewhere on the mountain, but probably did not make the summit

to Centre Creek

upper lake

Hanging Lake

MT. LINDEMAN from south
ROWLAND TABOR, U.S. GEOLOGICAL SURVEY

ascent; there is also the possibility that Henry Custer and party made the ascent of Lindeman or Macdonald Peak about 1859. Custer's sketch labels Lindeman as "High Lake Mountain." On a field survey map it is called "Sien-i-tic" and the name Chilowheyuck appears for Chilliwack Lake. The reference from the Marcus Baker *Joint Report* citing an altitude of 7244 ft is almost certain proof of the ascent of one of the two peaks by a United States survey party. Map: Skagit River 92 H/3.

SOUTHWEST ROUTE: From the highest road on Centre Creek (see Chilliwack River Road ◆) ending at about 4200 ft, follow the timber slope SE up the broad stream valley. The route breaks into meadowland (one swamp area) and continues to the col (6500 ft+) between Lindeman and a

subsidiary peak to the W. Cross and ascend into the snow basin on the upper SW face of the mountain; keep right of a cleft in the summit ridge while climbing eastward during the short summit scramble (class 3). Time: easy day r.t.

Variation: From the summit of Macdonald Peak descend along the broad connecting ridge to the dividing col (5900 ft+), then traverse slopes to the W col (some snow travel — crampons may be helpful). Time: 3½ hours from Macdonald.

Variation: Approach from Hanging Lake (see Hanging Lake Trail◆). Getting above the lake will be a minor encounter with Alaska cedar, but should prove no problem for the hardy in reaching the upper lake. Continue to the SW face of the mountain. With the greater gain in altitude from Chilliwack Lake, the rewards of the fine summit view should be greater.

NORTH FACE: This is a 3500-ft climb on a steep granitic face, first made by Alice Culbert, Dick Culbert, and Fred Douglas in October 1971. Take a boat or canoe to cross the lake, then ascend to the cirque floor (about 3300 ft) — some bush; it is advisable to keep in old forest to the right of the stream here as far as feasible. The cirque is double; keep right and avoid the difficulties of the dividing area. The route then takes the prominent central buttress. The lower part is class 4. Where the buttress fades into a face transfer left into the far gully; ascend this until it ends in a chimney. Climb right around a large white protrusion and continue to the ledge above. On the original climb, darkness caught the party near the exit chimney; total of five leads of class 5, minor aid, and some poor rock in gullies; most of the climb is class 3 and 4. References: *C.A.J.,* 1972, p. 72; *B.C.M.,* April 1972.

MIDDLE PEAK   7464 ft/2275 m
Of more historic than topographic interest, this summit is located just 0.3 mi. S of the International Boundary near Monument 60. The peak overlooks Hanging Lake on its E, and is on the divide between Chilliwack Lake and Centre Creek. Henry Custer, a companion named Mitchly, and an Indian likely made the ascent on July 17, 1859 while making a reconnaissance for the Boundary Survey. From the peak or nearby, Custer wrote: "Toward the East the Mountains reach a considerable altitude, and for the first time glaciers . . . were seen to cover the mountains to a considerable extent." Custer probably saw the Challenger Glacier. J.J. McArthur of the British Boundary Survey definitely climbed to the summit in the season of 1908. References: *Joint Report,* pp. 86, 416; *Mountaineer,* 1950, p. 39; *A.A.J.,* 1951, p. 175.
ROUTES: See Mt. Lindeman, starting via Radium Creek Trail ◆. After traversing past Lindeman, it is best to get just barely W of Monument 60, and follow the open divide. See Middle Peak High Route (Chilliwack River Trail ◆) for the eastern route. One could also make the climb via Hanging Lake Trail ◆.

COPPER MOUNTAIN   7142 ft/2177 m
Copper Mountain is the high point of a very extensive meadow-covered ridge W of upper Chilliwack River, located from 3½ to 5 mi. S of the Boundary. The ridge seems misplaced in the generally much rougher terrain of the Chilliwack group of alpine peaks. Rock here is of the Chilliwack Batholith; exposed rock includes small outcrops, summit crags, and basin rims. A group from the American Boundary Survey, possibly Henry Custer in July 1859, probably reached the summit; their altitude figure of 6856 ft fits one of the northern of Copper's points.
ROUTE: See Copper Ridge Trail ◆.

MT. REXFORD (B.C.)
7600 ft+/2317 m+
Rexford, earlier known as Ensawkwatch, is a prominent hornlike granitic summit of the Chilliwack region, being the highest point on the Centre-Nesakwatch Creek divide (between Chilliwack River and the International Boundary).

Rock is the Chilliwack Batholith, a very young intrusion tending toward straight cleavages here. Rexford, its flanking lesser summits, and the nearby Illusion Peaks provide interesting climbing on various faces, where there is an abundance of cracks, pillars, and slabs of firm rock.

Various early Boundary surveyors were near Rexford, and during the 1906 field season a United States party reached a high point somewhere on the ridge SE of the summits. The absence of a trail up Nesakwatch (Middle) Creek until logging took place perhaps explains why the peak was neglected by climbers until the 1950s. First ascent by Herman Genschorek and Walt Sparling in July 1951; the approach was made cross-country along Nesakwatch Creek. First winter ascent by Steve Fuller, Blair Griffiths, Bob Kandiko, and Don Serl on March 11, 1979.
WEST APPROACH: See Mt. Rexford Route ◆. This is the new trail which leads to the basin NW of a major cirque on Rexford.

The trail contours at about the 2500-ft level to a prominent creek descending from the SW corner of the mountain (watch for aluminum markers on opposite sides of open patches). At 3800 ft the trail crosses the top arm of a "Y" gully which comes from the summit bowl (the most prominent on W flank of Rexford) and cuts across to "Y" fork to reach the right arm. After trail crosses Y at 4300 ft (possible camp), there is no more water in summer for 2000 ft. After crossing gully continue 1200 ft more to camp in meadow area (5500-5900 ft). Map: Chilliwack 92 H/4. References: *B.C.M.,* September 1962, May 1963, June 1963, April 1968, May 1968, September 1972.
WEST RIDGE: This route, done by the original and most summit parties, climbs the lower ridge (which actually trends SW) to the final summit pyramid, and here traverses a ledge to the upper NW face. From beyond the end of the trail make a long southward traverse (from above a knoll at est. 6100 ft) across meadows, at one place following a grassy ledge at the foot of a cliff to an open area. Cross a boulder slope (scree bowl) to the base of the objective ridge, then climb a gully (possible snow) or broken rock onto its lower shoulder.

Follow the broken rock of the ridge (leftward) several hundred yards to the base of the triangular summit tower (class 3) bypassing isolated pinnacles of rock on the left (class 3). Note: A reason for some route confusion is that the true

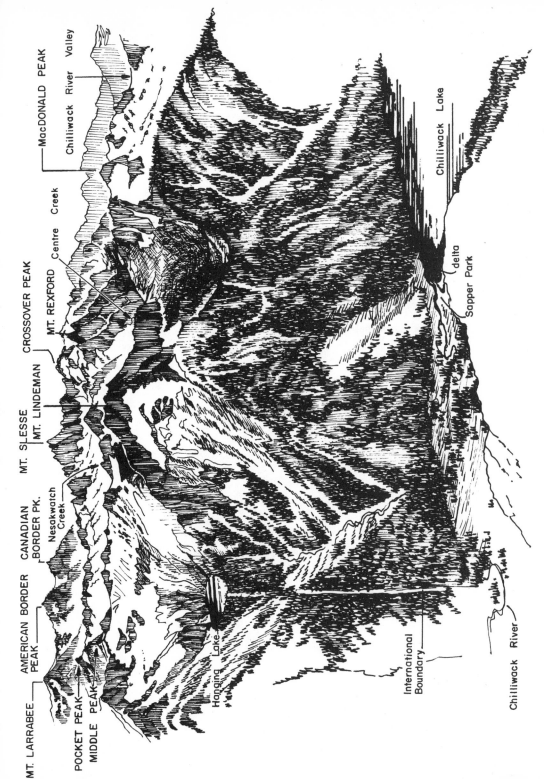

MT. LARRABEE

AMERICAN BORDER PEAK

CANADIAN BORDER PK.

MT. SLESSE

CROSSOVER PEAK

MacDONALD PEAK

POCKET PEAK

MIDDLE PEAK

Nesakwatch Creek

MT. LINDEMAN

MT. REXFORD

Centre Creek

Chilliwack River Valley

Chilliwack Lake

delta

Sapper Park

Hanging Lake

International Boundary

Chilliwack River

CHILLIWACK PEAKS from east

summit is invisible from the ridge until one is in close proximity.

Make a walking-scramble traverse of the prominent ledge-ramp below the final summit tower wall to its exposed NW corner (above the small NW notch).

Climb cracks and chimneys, bearing slightly left (class 4) onto the N face. A loose gully leads to a minor gap between the first and true summits. Climb to the summit 50 ft directly (class 4) or traverse 100 ft farther onto the N face. Rock is solid. Class 4. Time: 3-4 hours from campsite.

Variation: One can reach the final NW face from the small notch directly from either flank. The climbing is class 5 on the NW face, and if an eastern approach is made, the ice gully is climbed.

Variation (Upper West Face): By Einar Hansen and Brian Howard on September 24, 1967. This enjoyable route ascends directly to the summit on the West or SW face; some of the route is on or near a corner. There are about five leads, clean rock, with excellent belay stations on ledges. One feature of the route is a major jam crack high on the face or ridge. Ascend a crack and lieback the final pitch to the summit. Class 5.6. Reference: *B.C.M.,* May 1968.

NORTHEAST RIDGE: This is the first prominent buttress of Rexford rising from Centre Creek. The climb is very long, alpine and mixed (take crampons and ice axe), with mostly solid rock up high, but some bushes on the small steps of the lower portion. First ascent by Hugh Burton, John Burton, Colin Oloman, and Steve Saba in May 1969. First winter climb by John Arts, Scott Flavelle and Dick Mitten on January 1, 1978.

Take the Centre Creek Road and the branch which keeps on the W side of the creek to its most southerly point (est. 3000 ft). Locate the large avalanche fan and ascend this into the basin on the N side of the mountain (some bush; best when snow-covered). It may be best to ascend to a steepening area, then bear left to the next gully; follow to camp area below the face (3 hours).

A gully leads to the Northeast Ridge; a left traverse here is exposed and slippery (may have snow). Gain the ridge via a prominent chimney and follow it until the profile steepens. A leftward traverse is made (loose) on the E face, where the climb is completed. Most of the route is class 3-4, but some class 5 should be anticipated. Time: 4 hours. Reference: *B.C.M.,* November 1969.

Note: The winter ascent encountered mostly snow with two mixed pitches and two ice pitches; a bivouac was made at the base of the ridge and again at the notch between the main and Southeast Peaks. A descent was made E from this notch (potential avalanche hazard).

Variation (Upper Direct): This direct three-pitch finish is done mostly just right (N) of the crest. By Peter Stange and Gernot Walter in 1970. There is a good crack to follow near the summit. Class 5 and aid.

EAST RIDGE: This first ridge S of the Northeast Ridge has similar climbing features, although the steep portion is shorter. First ascent by Jack Bryan and Bill McNeil in July

1973. From the upper portion of Centre Creek Road opposite the East Ridge descend to the stream. Cross, then ascend (only about ½ hour of brush reported) to about 5500-ft level. The climb begins slightly above and right of the ridge toe. Follow a diagonal line up and left, heading for the ridge prow (easy class 5). From the prow there are about five leads of climbing on or near the crest (class 3-4); avoid difficulties to right.

High on the ridge there is a thin (flamelike) pinnacle; several leads above this the ridge becomes more difficult. Here cross to the S side and traverse to easier terrain. Scramble the final 300-400 ft to the summit. There are 10-12 leads of roped climbing, never over mid-class 5. Time: allow a long day from road.

SOUTHEAST ARETE: Although the easiest route to Rexford's summit, this is circuitous and involves a loss of altitude when approaching from the NW (the normal way). The plan is to get to below the notch between the true summit and lesser Southeast Peak. An easy large S gully (class 3) can be climbed to the summit (it is located S of the arete, and descends from it). To approach from the shoulder of the lower West Ridge make a long diagonal descent to beneath the notch dividing the main and Southeast Peaks; it may be necessary to ascend some brush and traverse left before working up and left to the gully. From near the SE notch climb up and left through a gully system to a broad rock couloir which is followed to the summit (class 3). Class 3 or 4, depending on route or variations taken. Time: 4 hours from camp. Reference: *B.C.M.,* May and June, 1963; also 1972.

Variation: Climb the S face to the prominent shoulder below the summit: walk around a gendarme and gain the highest point by climbing along a crack on the N side or partly up a chimney on the W side of the summit edge. There are several class 4 pitches. Time: 5 hours.

Approach Variation: The notch between Rexford and its Southeast Peak can be gained by starting from Centre Creek as per the East Ridge. The final 1000 ft is a narrow snow couloir up to 50 degrees; reported as a good route; 4 hours to notch (take crampons if in late summer). This would also be a feasible way to reach the Southeast Peak.

SOUTHEAST PEAK   7300 ft+/2225 m+

This is a sharp, triangular peak 0.4 mi. from the true summit; on its N ridge is Pi Pillar, the curious immense block (est. 7000 ft) supported by two columns. First ascent by Tony Ellis and Glenn Woodsworth on September 8, 1963. In 1935 J.H. Kihl (Boundary Survey) occupied "Station G," 2 mi. N and slightly E of Monument 58; this position is near or part of Rexford's Southeast Peak.

The peak is reached by Rexford's West Ridge, then traversing into the basin beyond. From a position 400 ft below the gap NW of the peak traverse SW across a

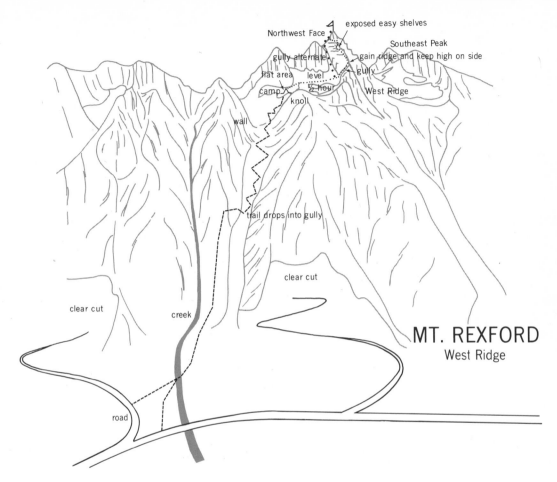

exposed easy shelves
Northwest Face
Southeast Peak
gully alternate
gain ridge and keep high on side
flat area
level
gully
camp
½ hour
West Ridge
knoll
wall
trail drops into gully
clear cut
clear cut
creek
clear cut
road

MT. REXFORD
West Ridge

ledge system to gain the SW ridge; follow this to the summit (not difficult).

PI PILLAR

First ascent by Bob Cuthbert and Geoff Mellor in 1967. Make the approach per Southeast Peak and climb to the gap adjoining Rexford. Rappel 60 ft on its E side into a rotten gully, then climb this to the ledge between the pillars. Squeeze through the hole atop, climb the N block — short aid section on obvious crack, then 20 ft of hard class 5, and step across to the top.

An alternative approach is to climb the Southeast Peak, rappel and downclimb into the notch by Pi Pillar. Reference: *B.C.M.*, May 1968.

REXFORD-ILLUSION CRAGS

There are two steep, small crags on the knife-edge ridge between Rexford and the Illusion Peaks. A route has been done via the E buttress of the southern crag, starting from the basin NE of Rexford (class 5 — firm rock); the simplest route to the summit points of the crags appears to be from the W.

An E-face ice gully NE of the gap dividing the crags and Rexford was done by Robert Coupe and Leslie Priest in 1970 (class 4); possible crevasse problem near bottom.

ILLUSION PEAKS (B.C.)
6900 ft+/2103 m+

These are two very real bald and massive slabby-granite peaks located on the Nesakwatch-Centre Creek divide 1 mi. NE of higher Mt. Rexford. The South Peak is higher; the nearby North Peak is esti-

ILLUSION PEAKS

notch

North Peak   South Peak

MT. REXFORD

West Ridge

Nesakwatch Creek

ILLUSION PEAKS and MT. REXFORD
ROBIN BARLEY

mated to be about 6850 ft (2088 m). Because of the descending altitude of the valley floor, the relief is as great as at Rexford. First ascent by Dick Culbert, Ronald Hatch, Monte Lasserre, and Arnold Shives in September 1962. Map: Chilliwack 92 H/4.

CENTRE CREEK ROUTE: This is a physical workout, but an enjoyable climbing trek with a variety of maneuvering and route finding problems; there is some scrambling and a short section of rock climbing (very firm rock). Take the main branch of Centre Creek Road which switchbacks W up the hillside; the highest S fork (may have to walk) extends almost to timberline in the basin NE of the Illusion Peaks (4900 ft). From the S-turning spur climb from burn southward through slash, and follow a minor spur ridge; traverse S off the latter to open meadows in a basin (5300 ft — camping; 4 hours). Hike W to gain the divide saddle NW of Illusion Peaks (5700 ft+), follow SE to the first subsidiary summit (6500 ft+). This point is easily traversed to the far gap. Descend to W of the gap, climb several hundred ft of rock and bush (class 3) to the summit ridge of the North Peak. Then traverse down the rock ridge with abrupt steps (there is a final horizontal cheval) rappel 40 ft into the intervening gap of the isolated South Peak (drop right down gully, and take prominent ledge out onto the face). There is one rock pitch (5.5) in regaining the first point out of the gap; climb up and slightly left around a corner (two leads),

then back right behind a protruding finger to the easy summit ridge. Time: long day r.t. Reference: *B.C.M.*, February 1964.

SOUTH ROUTE: From camp on W side of Mt. Rexford ascend to the col one hump SE of Illusion Peaks. Cross this feature and climb down ledges beyond (rock ledges on left are best way). From here the highest summit point is easy to reach; keep right to avoid bush (class 2 and 3).

NORTH PEAK-WEST FACE: This is a very long day, with a variety of climbing problems, some of them subalpine (brush reported to be minor). First ascent Dick Culbert, Fred Douglas, Paul Starr and Ross Wyborn in 1972. From the left edge of logging spur and clearcut (Nesakwatch Creek Road) a deep rocky gully leads to the gap N of the Illusion Peaks (very obvious). Ascend this, then climb right on a steep ramp under the W face until meeting the nose crest. Here is the route, which involves several leads of class 4 and 5, mostly cracks (tree ledges reduce the aesthetics, but the rock is firm). The one fearsome wall is turned on its right (climb over a flake and around a corner; 5.6). Descend via the gully.

RAPID PEAK   7059 ft/2152 m

This summit, 1.9 mi. S of the Boundary between Rapid Creek fork of Silesia Creek and the head of Nesakwatch Creek, is a small peak, but the highest in its locality. There is a moderately steep rock face on the N. The first ascent was likely made by John Handley and Rowland Tabor in August 1967.

ROUTE: See Silesia Creek Trail♦ and Chilliwack River Trail♦. Take Middle Peak High Route and make an ascent along the easy E or W ridge; one can backpack over the summit along the high route. The rewards are scenic views of the Border Peaks and Chilliwack group of summits. Time: 6 hours from Silesia Creek.

POCKET PEAK   7040 ft+/2146 m+

A rugged peak of blocky form 0.7 mi. S of the Boundary, between Silesia and Ensawkwatch creeks and NW of Pocket Lake. The peak appears very pointed from the W, and is generally horn-shaped with long faces on the W and N. Rock is well jointed quartz monzonite (Chilliwack Batholith). The first ascent was made by Doug McKeever and Rowland Tabor on July 28, 1967.

ROUTE: See Silesia Creek Trail♦. Take the Middle Peak High Route (see Chilliwack River Trail♦) to where it reaches the main ridge E of Silesia Creek near Point 6521. Descend N over meadow and snow to the saddle at the base of the objective. Keep on the ridge and climb steep heather, brush (small trees), and granite slabs to a final exposed S face rib. Here climb slabs and cracks on moderately angled firm rock. Class 4. Time: 5 hours from Silesia Creek.

One can descend the N side over steep snow and exposed blocks.

SLESSE MOUNTAIN (B.C.)
7800 ft+/2377 m+

Slesse is one of the grand sentinels of the North Cascades, rearing its rock crown closely N of the International Boundary NW of Mt. Baker and Shuksan. From the W Slesse's summit horn resembles a square-topped turret with very sheer N edge, and craggy pointed South Peak, a gunnery station. The farther Southeast Peaks appear much lower. The WSW face, which is of principal interest to climbers, begins from steep alp slopes at about 7000 ft. This face is bounded on the N by a prominent slanting couloir leading to the Slesse-Nesakwatch Creek divide closely N of the summit. On the SW side of the summit is a major gully marked by a giant gendarme jutting from a spur crag. A shelf system runs from the divide at the base of NW face clear across to near the gendarme. There is also a shallow rock couloir leading up center of lower SW face.

The immense Northeast Buttress, one of the greatest rock pillars carved by the forces of nature in western North America, begins at 5500 ft; the steep narrow North Face also begins at that altitude.

The summit ridge and W face of Slesse are Darrington Phyllite, formed by contact metamorphism with Chilliwack Batholith. The rock was baked by intrusion of granodiorite (Slesse is located between volcanics of Chilliwack Group on the Border Peaks and the batholith on Rexford). Granitic rock of Slesse is characterized by long transverse ledges (from jointing) and locally by rounded holds. A large proportion of the rock climbing on routes is on grey diorite.

The name "Slesse" is "fang" in Salish tongue; some Boundary Survey sketches labelled the peak "Turret," although another early name was Tomahi (Indian for "high places"). [81]

Even in early survey times Slesse came to epitomize the savage rock fang of North Cascades. The geologist Daly, who made a reconnaissance onto the Nesakwatch Creek slope of the mountain, admired the defiance of Slesse, for he wrote, "The inaccessible horn of Slesse mountain, 7700 feet in height, is the loftiest peak in the belt." [82] Local settlers regarded Slesse as unclimbable and legend states a survey offer of $25.00 for placing a summit flag was unclaimed. The first attempt appears August 1925 by E.A. Fuller and R.A. Fraser of Vancouver. They climbed Pierce Mountain and probably Mt. MacFarlane but were barred by another summit (Crossover); it became apparent that a direct route from Slesse Creek was the proper approach. In June and September 1926, Brick Spouse and Bill Dobson approached via Slesse Creek, and though the elements foiled them, they did climb some lower rock sections. The first ascent was made August 10, 1927 by Stan Henderson, Mills Winram and Fred Parkes. They took the northernmost couloir, which they used to turn rightward and reach a col about 200 ft below the summit. They tried a couloir farther S, encountering cliffs and finally connected ledges that led onward. Their description tells of a sheer rock face at 7500 ft where they found a chimney that provided the route solution. The second ascent was made the same month by Bill Dobson, Jim Irving, Don (Dan?) McRae, and Spouse. Then the third ascent was made in 1931 by A.A. Austin with Henderson and Winram. First winter ascent by Fips Broda and John Dudra February 1955.

The air age made a most tragic impact on Slesse the night of December 9, 1956, when a TCA North Star crashed at 7600 ft, within 100 ft of clearing a notch: 62 died in then one of the world's worst air disasters. Material from the crash is still imbedded in rock and can be found in the cirque below the E face. Map: Chilliwack 92 H/4.

Selected references include: Daly, Memoir 38, pt 2 (photograph); see note 5; *B.C.M., November 1926,*

October 1929, August 1941, July 1959, October 1960, September 1965; September 1969, November 1971, February 1974; *Avalanche Echoes (A.A.C.)*, March 1941; *C.A.J.*, 1942, pp. 274-75; *V.O.C.J.*, 1963; *Summit*, January 1964; Fred Beckey, *Challenge of the North Cascades*, Seattle: The Mountaineers, 1969, pp. 238-47; Steve Roper and Allen Steck, *Fifty Classic Climbs in North America*, Sierra Club, 1979, pp. 123-27; Paddy Sherman, *Cloud Walkers*, Seattle: The Mountaineers, 1979, pp. 60-91.

Note: Some references call Slesse Tomahi and Canadian Tamihi.

SOUTHWEST ROUTE (standard): From camp at the 5800 ft alp (see Slesse Mountain Trail ♦) follow the rocky evergreen-covered ridge up and right to the small snow/scree bowl at the northern foot of the summit rock wall. Traverse up the bowl near its western rim, then climb into the prominent gully adjacent to the main summit face nearly to the narrow left-hand notch. Climb the right-hand wall on an ascending traverse (small class-3 rock steps) to a sharp corner (with a horizontal block at corner edge); two class-3 pitches to here. Make a slightly downward 150-ft traverse (grassy slope) into a broad slabby gully. This gully continues 180 ft onto the next terrace (class 4). Traverse this distinctive sloping terrace S toward the "giant gendarme." From the end of the terrace climb to a small (40-ft) rock step on the WSW corner (class 4).

Traverse and downclimb into the bed of the next gully (this is the scree gully between the main peak wall and the giant gendarme; climb easily to the skyline at its top (est. 300 ft) to reach a small crest (behind giant gendarme); here one is nearly on the S side of the true summit. Scan the rock face for the easiest way: one can climb upward on a firm little wall; this is steep for 50 ft, with good holds — class 4 or easy class 5. Another method is to climb slightly leftward on steep broken rock. The last portion to the summit area notch is in a large sandy gully. Grade I-II; class 4 and 5. Time: camp to summit — 4 hours (14 hours r.t. from road).

Note: If approaching from the higher (6800-ft) camp, keep right of a snowfield and ridge cliff, then cross a spur to the route into the scree bowl.

Variations: There are several feasible variation gullies and ledge connections on the lower SW face which can be used to meet the normal route. The first of these begins right of the narrow notch gully and climbs the complete broad slabby gully. The second of these begins at the S end of the W face basin and is marked by the "giant gendarme" on its S side. This obvious gully (class 3-4) terminates on a small shoulder/crest above the lower SW face (watch for rockfall); the summit route continues beyond.

One can also climb the gully system leading to the high Main-South Peak notch. This is the longest possible route on this face — generally broken rock with a zigzag route pattern; class 4. One can move from this gully at several hundred ft below its top, crossing a ledge left to the gully

adjacent to the "giant gendarme," then continuing upward.

Approach Variation: This is an old alternative, not favored now, but still a suitable route to the ridge points and crags SE of the South Peak. The route ascends the steep bank and slope S of the tributary creek from Slesse (windfalls). Bear slightly right, keeping right of cliffs and climb a minor wooded ridge to a boulderfield (5000 ft). Ascend two-thirds of it, then hike right (light brush) to the prominent rock spur and high sloping meadows below the southern ramparts of the mountain's ridge; possible water shortage on meadows.

Another way to the meadows is to take the gravel bed of a stream farther S, then keep in brush on the left until the stream divides. Climb the burnt crest between the forks for 2000 ft. Just below timberline contour left across a talus basin and cross a spur ridge to the alp slopes.

Descent: Downclimb a distance; halfway down a sandy gully traverse S out of it. Continue down to the steep wall 150 ft above the crest of the "giant gendarme" (behind it) and find a rappel sling block. Downclimb again (watch rockfall); perhaps do a 40-ft rappel on the "step." Just below the top of the open gully find a great block: rappel 150 ft to the terrace.

WEST PILLAR: This is a recent route done on the upper W summit section between the normal route and Northwest Face. First ascent by Malcom Allen, Simon Tooley, and Larry Zecchel on July 24, 1977. The route is directly up from the corner where the normal route crosses into the loose gully behind the gendarme. The second pitch, which has a flaring corner topped by a roof, is the crux. There are five pitches, mainly cracks. Grade II; class 5.8.

NORTHWEST FACE: This is a steep but direct six-pitch route with mostly very firm rock. As seen from the col on the N side of Slesse, the route keeps just right of the near skyline. First ascent by Fred Beckey, Ed Cooper, and Don (Claunch) Gordon on June 21, 1959. The original party began at the highest notch against the objective face; most parties begin from the top of the open gully (est. 7200 ft) past the horizontal block of the normal route. From the left side of the large ledge here climb up and left toward the NW corner, then up the slight depression of the route; the third pitch is recalled as having small holds, and rather difficult. The easiest line is a slightly zigzag course via steep cracks and diagonal ramplike features. At the head of the depression, closely under the summit, a headwall forces a left traverse (this exposed pitch is the hardest and was described on the original as a wall of loose bricks). Grade II; class 5.6. Time: 4 hours on rock. References: *Mountaineer*, 1960, pp. 86-87; *A.A.J.*, 1960, pp. 134-35.

NORTH FACE: First ascent by Perry Beckham, Don Serl, and John Wittmayer January 27, 1980. This climb was done in 21 rope-lengths to the N notch; because of the season most of the climb was 50-degree hard-frozen snow and ice, with two 65-degree pitches half way up the lower face where a gully breaks through a slab band, and two pitches of thin ice where a couloir begins and at a "kink" about two-thirds of the way up it. The 20th pitch climbed left onto the crest of

MT. SLESSE *from east*
STEVE MARTS

MT. SLESSE — northwest face
ED COOPER

the North Rib, where the cornice had to be cut on the exposed crest. Eventually the main couloir between the rib and main mass of Slesse is gained for an excellent piton belay. The top lead was increasingly steep unconsolidated snow, with progress being made by trenching, chimneying, and tunneling a cornice for 25 ft. Time: 12 hours to bivouac on ridge.

NORTH RIB: This is the narrow rib and face between the Northeast Buttress and the NW corner of Slesse; the route is located on a slight rib about 200 ft N of a deep gully-gash. The rib is prominent for most of its length, but fades out near the notch below the upper NW corner. The climb is fairly consistently in the class 5.6-5.7 range with just a move or two of 5.8, on generally good rock; the lower portion of the 27 pitches is sometimes difficult to adequately protect. First ascent by Rob Kiesel and Jeff Lowe in July 1972.

After two leads directly above the glacier segment, traverse right one lead; this puts one on the left edge of a depression which drains a large snowfield. Then follow leftward-trending dihedrals for three or four leads back to the rib crest. Climb many leads to an 80-ft headwall with only a single crack breaking its smoothness. It is possible to bear left here on ledges and ramps for one-half lead; connect with another ramp system that leads diagonally up and right to a flat ledge above the headwall. Then climb just right of the rib crest until just below the notch which is the top of the North Face couloir. Climb left into the couloir and follow its rotten rock trough one lead to the notch (top of 22nd pitch); an escape can be made here. To complete: start from the highest ledge 50 ft right of the NW corner and climb steep, shallow dihedrals for a pitch, then go left for 50-60 ft to the very corner (edge of North Face). Follow the edge several more leads to the summit. Grade V; class 5.8 (20 chocks and three horizontal pitons adequate). Time: (original) 13 hours from base. Reference: *A.A.J.,* 1973, p. 447.

NORTHEAST BUTTRESS: This feature of Mt. Slesse is a flying buttress of nearly perfect proportions, and a unique feature of such size in western North America. The lower part of the buttress is clearly ice sculptured, smoothed and polished. This portion is quite narrow, trending NW before the crest angulates W to form a deep pocket cirque of the very sheer E face. Of the eastern protrusions of Slesse, the Northeast Buttress toes down farthest. It is very steep at its base, here flanked by small pocket glaciers (the one to the S recently cascaded away); there is a deep gash N of the buttress, adjacent to the North Face.

The largest glacier on Slesse sprawls under the SE face, heading with a high arm and narrow glacier-couloir that extends to a gap in the main SE crest of the mountain. This glacier terminates above cliffs at the lower edge of the East Buttress; between the two main buttresses a remnant of the main glacier is now mostly isolated; the ice here is very thin and its current status is in question (much of it may have cascaded away). There is a completely separate ice remnant directly beneath the North Face, and several small ice sections northward, beneath Crossover Peak.

The early climbs of the buttress were considered to be rigorous achievements because of the commitment to the climb and difficulty in retreat, as well as the length and technical problems of the route. But as knowledge and standards increased, confidence grew among climbers. An ascent may now have less historic value, but the rewards are still there. Reports from the first three ascents indicated that there were from 30 to 34 pitches, of which 25 involved class 5 climbing. A bypass of the lowest portion of the buttress (the toe), climbing the remnant pocket glacier and slabs to its S, was popular for a time because it reduced time usually spent on direct aid; but this variation is not currently recommended because of slab-climbing problems and an accident record. In August 1980 a climber was killed by falling ice debris from the pocket glacier under the E face. One report from the 1970s indicated that by making a timberline bivouac and the higher-start variation, only 13 hours were spent on the climb. This conditional approach may be nearly impossible now except possibly in early season. The disappearance of the pocket glacier combined with the challenge of the full route has now led most climbers to start at the buttress toe (1963 start); the original start is safer than in earlier years, because the considerable retreat of the pocket glacier NE of the buttress has lessened danger of falling ice from that source.

Climbers still find the steep section at mid-height the crux, with a very strenuous pitch just right of the crest. It is best to minimize the N-side traverses and climb as near the crest as feasible here. The final pitches of the route are pure joy and in a distinctly alpine exposure, bringing home the feeling this is one of the most unusual routes of its standard in the greater region. A number of parties are making the ascent annually, but the length of the climb and feeling of insecurity gives it a serious air. The buttress should only be attempted in settled weather; rain will likely start stonefall, ordinarily not a problem. A danger difficult to predict is the stability of ice blocks and seracs on the pocket glaciers. By careful route choice, this hazard can be avoided more than in previous years.

The first attempt on the face, by Fred Beckey and Steve Marts in 1963, reached the crux area above midway on the buttress when dense clouds blotted out visibility and brought the threat of rain. The first ascent was made by Beckey and Marts, with Eric Bjornstad on August 26-28, 1963. The second ascent was made by Hans Baer and Jack Bryan in 1965 and the third by Eryl Pardoe, Ian Patterson, and Paul Starr in 1970.

Begin the climb approach from Nesakwatch Creek Road (see Chilliwack River Road♦) at the 5-mi. spur, then drive W to about 3800 ft where there is a sharp bend overlooking the main basin (new logging ATP may change the spur complex). Ascend into the basin draining the eastern cirque glaciers; small trees grow almost to the old moraine near the foot of the E face. A good method to reach the buttress is to ascend old ground moraine in the cirque floor. Follow the basin to its head (just right of buttress toe) and scramble ramps and slabs back up and left. Note: The 1963 start crossed slabs from the SE to reach a flat ledge near the toe, but the lower approach is now considered better.

The climbing on the toe involves climbing an open book, then bearing slightly left up short pitches with minor overhangs and mossy cracks (a few bushes); this was originally class 5 and some aid, but now has been done free (5.10). Then climb a slab with a ribboned moss and cedar "magic carpet." A long lead on slabs is followed by one up the rounded buttress in a sloping open book (lieback). Climb left out of the book, then ascend a long slab face: there is a lower angle section here (class 4) for several leads; minor brush on route (the variation joins here). Note: Original party bore onto the N flank via steep ramps above here; one can keep right for four leads, with up to 5.7 climbing. The alternative is to stay on or near the crest (as done by third party and many others); this involves 5.8 and minor aid (has been done free). This section gives a quite steep crux for about 150 ft. Climbing here is poorly protected (chocks better than pitons). The midsection of the buttress (about 500 ft of height) is quite easy and holds snow much of the year (water and possible bivouac area).

The final 700-ft section is steep and solid, providing generally rewarding climbing (up to 5.8); the rock remains good until near the summit area. There are four hard leads, generally somewhat right of the crest; the second and third parties kept left of the original line, nearer to the crest here, and this is now the favored line to use until the wall steepens considerably. There is a good ledge, then a leaning pillar with a white base which forms the corner of the buttress. The original party climbed grooves just right of the pillar crest; from a hanging belay traverse 50 ft right (5.8 at traverse start), then climb 80 ft of difficult, steep wall to a grassy belay ledge. After the wall pitch one can climb right-slanting grooves and ramps to the base of a vertical wall. Here cracks lead past the bolt of the original climb, through a small overhang and out onto a narrow belay ledge. An easier pitch leads to a cave belay (loose), and a short lead above the cave ends on a sandy terrace (original bivouac).

Most parties continue up the crest above, toward the summit. The option is to traverse left into a depressed, broken-rock area that is shattered, sandy, poorly protected but not difficult climbing to the summit. Grade V; class 5.8 and A2; the original party used 63 pitons; about 30 chocks and a few pitons will now suffice. If using the higher conditional bypass, only about 16 roped pitches are necessary, and six or less points of aid. In late summer, it is best to carry water, for the small snowpatches on the route may be gone. References: *Fifty Classic Climbs in North America*, pp. 123-27; *Summit*, January-February 1964, pp. 30-31; *C.A.J.*, 1965, pp. 152-54; 1971, p. 66; *V.O.C.J., p. 120; A.A.J.*, 1964, pp. 66-67.

Descent: Allow part of a day to descend normal route, then traverse back over the ridge of Crossover Peak for a descent to the E glacier cirque.

Variation: This conditional beginning once traversed to the lower SE side of the buttress across the glacier above the seracs, crossing the schrund here via ice blocks. But this area is all slab now except for the extreme S end. In early season the approach may still be snow-covered. If the variation is planned it is best to follow the basin past cliffs on the left, then climb an obvious gully and scramble leftward (class 3) to get above this blockade; do not get under any active ice. A parallel approach can be used by following the wooded ridge crest to the left of the basin to below the E face. Then traverse any remaining ice and snow rightward, then climb and cross slabs (possibly wet and dangerous). Make several diagonal leads of mid-class 5 onto the shrubby section of the buttress.

EAST BUTTRESS: This buttress is located about 200 yards S of Slesse's Northeast Buttress (across an ice pocket), beginning as a sharp, low crest, and remaining quite narrow for half its height; higher it steepens into a face before becoming more broken SE of the summit. First ascent by Dennis Mullen and John Stoddard August 5-7, 1977.

Make the approach and summit descent per Northeast Buttress. The best approach is the wooded ridge left of the main basin (below E face) to reach the glacier and cirque on left of the East Buttress. Angle up and right across the cirque to a series of dihedrals which give access to the buttress crest. Climb broken rock along the crest to headwall (junction of buttress and left side of the great E face). The first pitch (leftward) here required some aid (small nuts and hooks); may go free but not if done wearing a pack; protection is marginal. Angle left from the base about 30 ft, then right 60 ft, then left to a belay on a rotten rib at the top of an obvious wide chimney to the left of the route (5.8-A3). Proceed up steep ramp to left, around corner into crack system which fades after about 20 ft (5.8). Climb on aid for about 20 ft (A3 — hooks and stoppers), where cracks open up again and lead into a series of left-leaning ramps/dihedrals leading to a wide ledge. Here is an excellent bivouac site, complete with running water and trophy-size rodents.

A steep corner just right leads up and left for a long pitch (5.9-A1) to easier ground at the left side of the lower small snowpatch. Work up its left side about halfway and exit up greasy low-angle rock (5.6-A1). Climb two nondescript

pitches up and left to base of upper snowpatch (5.5-5.7) where diorite changes to orange-white granodiorite. Climb two class-4 pitches of lower angle around right side of snowpatch to a sharp arete which provides an enjoyable 5.7 pitch. Continue in corners for 20 ft, then angle rightward over a series of rounded bulges with nice unprotected buckets, then traverse left to a dihedral/chimney system which exits on the summit ridge 200 ft above (as viewed from below, this is just left of a prominent owl-shaped pinnacle); the last pitch is an interesting 5.8 because of a couple of chockstones and some loose rock. Three pitches of moderate class 5 and some class 4 lead to the area of the South Peak notch and the summit route completion (en route are spectacular views of the South Peak). Grade V; class 5.9-A3; take 15 hexcentrics with duplicates of smaller sizes, hooks, crack "n" ups, wired stoppers, runners, 30 carabiners. Time: 2 days from road to summit.

SOUTH PEAK   7700 ft+/2346 m+
This subsidiary peak of Slesse is of a curious tilted horn shape. The summit seems to lean toward the notch connecting the main summit. First ascent by Fred Beckey, John Dudra, and Herb Staley on August 3, 1952.

NOTCH ROUTE: There are two ways to reach the N notch: (1) From the thin crest by the great gendarme of Slesse's normal route, rappel and downclimb S, then make an easterly traverse into the notch; keep W of the crest. (2) Climb directly up loose gullies from the base of walls between Slesse's peaks. Climb one lead up the divide, then keep to the right (loose class 4). Traverse right (steep but good holds — 5.5). Then climb directly upward. References: *Appalachia*, June 1953, p. 401; *Mountaineer*, 1952, p. 80.

SOUTHEAST BUTTRESS: This is the obvious buttress on the South Peak, rising from the eastern cirque just N of the glacier segment which incises Slesse's walls. The buttress appears steep and rounded on its lower sections, then becomes more craggy. There are 20 pitches on the climb. First ascent by Scott Flavelle and Keith Nannery June 18-19, 1977. For best approach see East Buttress — Main Peak. Climb to top of pocket glacier (est. 6000 ft) below the E face of South Peak. About 200 ft right of the drainage from the gully bounding the southern side of the South Peak climb directly up and then left and up steep very solid light-colored granite. Three pitches (to 5.7) lead to grassy terraces. Follow these left to the base of the aforementioned gully (est. 300 ft). Climb the gully to its forks (three leads), and then climb the ridge rising to the right, staying left of the crest for about the first eight leads (short steep walls alternate with sandy ledges). When further progress left of the crest is barred by a vertical black wall, step down and around buttress crest at base of wall and continue up grooves, slab, and walls for four pitches to sandy terraces. Here cross W into scree bowl and either (1) follow South Ridge to top or (2) climb depression between South and SE

MT. SLESSE from west
DICK CULBERT

West Pillar

Northwest
Face

to notch

South Peak

(behind)

gendarme

Ridges (four leads to summit). Grade IV; class 5.7. Reference: *C.A.J.*, 1978, p. 81.

Alternative start: By Philip Kubik and Len Soet in August 1978. Begin in the couloir S of the Slesse massif, then cross rib and ledges right to join the route at gully forks.

SOUTH RIDGE: First ascent by Paul Binkert, Jack Bryan, Fritz Gechter, and Esther Kafer in June 1961. From the broad gully at the beginning of the main summit alternative route, ascend a system of gullies, always taking the right fork. This system leads to a prominent notch in the ridge adjacent to the squarish tower hit in the aircraft disaster. Ascend a steep 40-ft pitch to a scree bowl. Then traverse left and climb a wall until a slanted chimney leads back to the summit ridge. Class 4. Time: 5 hours from camp.

SOUTHEAST PEAKS

There is a series of lesser points and crags trending SE of the South Peak. The first isolated point is the 7100-ft+ peak located just S of the deep glacier-gully arm S of the Slesse massif. Farther SE, at about 0.5 mi. from the South Peak, there are two craglike summits (6800 ft+) with eastern faces. All of these rock points are easiest to climb from the SW side. One of these summits was reached by J.H. Kihl in 1935 during survey work (termed "Station D"); he also occupied Point 6200 ft+ at 120 m N of Boundary Monument 56 and a point 1 mi. W of Monument 57, closely S of the line near Pocket Peak (*Joint Report*, p. 415, see Section II, note 64).

LABOR DAY BUTTRESS: The NE buttress of the eastern summit of the 6800 ft+ summits forms the S end of the cirque E of Slesse. Located about 1 mi. from the true summit, this buttress is about 1000 ft in height; it can be reached by a logical traverse of the cirque. The first ascent was made by Dick Culbert, Fred Douglas, and Paul Starr on Labor Day, 1969. The climb is rated a pleasant effort (class 5.4), taking some 3 hours.

CROSSOVER PEAK (B.C.)
7172 ft/2186 m

This is the bald summit 2.3 mi. NE of Mt. Slesse on the Slesse-Nesakwatch divide. Possibly the 1971 ascent was the first climb (uncertain). The peak makes for a pleasant traverse between Mt. Slesse and Pierce Lake, but route finding takes some skill. Map: Chilliwack 92 H/4.

SOUTH ROUTE: From Slesse Mountain's northwestern base traverse the first two ridge humps on their W sides, then drop slightly to the E (steep grassy traverses en route) and work through a steep gully to the foot of Crossover; one can make a climbing and rappel descent to the Slesse basin from here. Ascend Crossover on somewhat poor rock (class

2-3), then descend to upper Pierce Lake. An alternative descent is over the SE flank to the easy E ridge; one can also gain the latter route on ascent from the cirque NE of Mt. Slesse (see North Ridge).

NORTH RIDGE: First ascent by Paul Binkert and Virginia Moore on September 19, 1971. At the beginning of the Mt. Rexford Trail♦ hike up the S side of the tributary stream into the bowl below the NE face of Mt. Slesse (or reach from logging spurs — see Slesse Mountain Northeast Buttress). The route then ascends the E ridge of Crossover, then to the saddle N of the summit. The first gendarme is circled on the E; then ascend a serrated summit ridge (exposed; class 3 and 4). Descent: Make best via South Ridge (loose), then W down gully and scree to the base.

MT. MacFARLANE (B.C.)
6885 ft/2099 m

The summit, on the Slesse Mountain ridge 1 mi. SW of Mt. Pierce, was occupied by a survey party in 1935, but may have been climbed earlier (*Joint Report*, p. 80, 415; see Section II, note 64).

ROUTE: Take Pierce Lake Trail♦ to the N side of the upper lake. Ascend a rocky but easy NW spur to the summit.

MT. PIERCE (B.C.)   6426 ft/1959 m

Pierce is minor summit 2 mi. S of Chilliwack River and 2.7 mi. NNW of Slesse Mountain; it is the northernmost summit on the Slesse ridge. The mountain is chiefly of interest as a hiker's viewpoint, for vistas of Slesse Mountain and the Cheam Range. The first climb may have been made by R.A. Farmer and E.A. Fuller in 1925. Map: Chilliwack 92 H/4.

ROUTE: See Pierce Lake Trail♦. From the upper lake ascend to the SW ridge of the objective, then follow this easily to the summit. Time: one day r.t. from road.

CANADIAN BORDER PEAK (B.C.)
7400 ft+/2256 m+

This is a precipitous rock summit rising 0.4 mi. N of the International Boundary and 0.9 mi. NW of its counterpart, American Border Peak on the Slesse-Tamihi Creek divide. The craggy summit structure, which is a narrow wedge-like shape appearing to lean E, has several high points, with the true summit on the NW extremity. The flanking NE and SW walls become steep at the 6800-ft level. The peak is composed of ancient sediments and volcanics of the Chilliwack Group, metamorphosed to phyllites, slates, and greenstones. Geologists Smith and Calkins show on their map that "Canadian Tomyhoi" was their interpretation of the name for this peak at the turn of the century (G.O. Smith notebook 1322, p. 6; also *Mountaineer*, 1916, p. 9). The first ascent was made by

AMERICAN BORDER PEAK

from Gargett Mine

Northeast Face

CANADIAN BORDER PEAK

Northeast Rib

Northwest Route

shoulder

to Slesse Creek

BORDER PEAKS from northeast
DICK CULBERT

Tom Fyles and Stan Henderson in the summer of 1932, possibly via the SW face. References: *B.C.M.*, February 1962, December 1968, September 1970. Map: Chilliwack 92 H/4.

NORTHWEST ROUTE: At about 3.8 mi. on Slesse Creek Road (see Chilliwack River Road♦) a right fork and bridge give access to the stream descending from the valley N of Canadian Border Peak. Take the road up this valley, keeping on the steep spur along the creek to a ridge at about 3500 ft; one may need to hike some or all of this roadway (can only drive to 1200-ft altitude, requiring a 3-mi. walk ATP). Follow the road spur to about 4100 ft, then hike cross-country up the wooded ridge to the open shoulder at 5600 ft beneath the N face of the objective (can camp here). Cross into the shallow cirque between the main summit and a spur shoulder on the NW (watch avalanche danger in spring). From partway up this cirque (draw) angle right, scrambling up onto the shoulder, then up this to the main divide NW of the peak. A steep step where the divide abuts with the peak is passed on the right by a traverse into a large, shallow gully (somewhat loose); the gully faces NW and is not visible on the approach. Additional rock climbing leads to the summit. Several pitches of class 4. Time: 4 hours from camp; very long day r.t. from Slesse Creek. Note: It is not certain if the first ascent party did this route; the description fits the "shallow loose gully" of an ascent by Herman Genschorek, Alan Melville, Fred Rogers, and Walt Sparling on August 27, 1950.

Approach Variation: Take a spur off Tamihi Creek Road (see Chilliwack River Road♦) to about 4500 ft near the Boundary. Ascend through forest and open meadow (bear slightly right) to the divide NW of objective.

NORTHEAST RIB: This is a long rock climb, some of it loose; one should camp high for an early start. First ascent by Dick Culbert in 1963. Make the same start as per Northwest Route; from the shoulder below the N face, traverse S under the wall to a prominent rib which descends from the divide just S of the summit. Begin this on the left, and ascend; follow near the crest most of the way. On reaching the divide, traverse gendarmes or bypass them on the W. The summit pyramid is climbed just to the right of the divide. Class 3 to 5. Reference: *B.C.M.*, December 1965.

Possible routes on the SE and S side of the peak can be approached from the shoulder of the Northwest Route. Make a long traverse S across basin and snowfield under the face, then ascend rock wall to reach summit ridge E of the summit; it is not certain the route has been completed.

MT. McGUIRE (B.C.)   6620 ft/2018 m

McGuire is a bulky mountain located 2.6 mi. N of the Boundary and 1.5 mi. NE of Tamihi Creek; its W slope plunges 6000 ft. The mountain is crowned by massive limestone (Carboniferous), below which are great thicknesses of other sediments; examples of overturned folds occur in the limestone units here and on

Church Mountain. Reginald A. Daly may have climbed the mountain in 1901 during a geologic study. The climb was definitely made by J.J. McArthur and party in 1906 (while surveying); the route was from the SE, where a narrow nose of jagged rock connects the summit with the lower ridge. A station mark was placed on the summit; in 1935 another survey party made the ascent from Tamihi Creek. References: Daly, pt. 1, p. 512, see note 5; *Joint Report*, p. 415; *B.C.M.*, July 1950, January 1956, December 1960, December 1970. Map: Chilliwack 92 H/4.

EAST ROUTE: Take Borden Creek Road (see Chilliwack River Road♦) to about 4500 ft E of the mountain; take the left branch (southerly) of the road, which bears SW up the main Borden Creek valley (one may have to hike from 3300 ft). A short section of slash, a section of brush, then open timber travel reaches the E shoulder. One can bear toward the N ridge, where terrain is open, then follow the slope. Time: 4 hours from road.

Variation: Detour around the SE side of the summit to the crest on the S (1906 route).

Variation: Take the N road fork (est. 3400 ft) and follow it N over 1 mi., then up to the NE ridge of McGuire at est. 4500 ft (will probably have to walk the road); distance to the summit from here is 1.2 mi., with easy open terrain.

NORTHWEST ROUTE: Take Tamihi Creek Road S about 1½ mi., then an old logging spur to about 2500 ft, where it rounds the lower NW ridge. This is an easy trek, though some bush will be encountered; above about 4400 ft there are acres of pleasant meadows. The summit portion is not difficult.

LIUMCHEN MOUNTAIN (B.C.)
6000 ft+/1829 m+

Liumchen, sometimes called "Lihumitsa" or "Layomesun" in Boundary Survey times, is located just 241 m from Monument 48, on the Boundary 7 mi. SE of Cultus Lake. The mountain is a high ridge, actually crossing the Boundary, and characterized by rolling subalpine ridges with great floral variety. Henry Custer (1859) probably made the first climb for surveying purposes; the summit was also occupied by the Canadian survey party of 1906, under J.J. McArthur. References: *Joint Report*, p. 415; *B.C.M.*, February 1962. Map: Chilliwack 92 H/4.

ROUTE: See Liumchen Ridge Trail♦. The trail climbs over Windy Knob, then Old Baldy (5659 ft/1725 m) at the junction with the Church Mountain spur.

CHURCH MOUNTAIN (5531 ft/1686 m) rises just E of the divide from Liumchen (see above route). An easy gully, which is snow in spring, is another route to the peaks from the road on the N side.

NOTES — SECTION I

[1] G.O. Smith and F.C. Calkins, "A Geological Reconnaissance Across the Cascade Range near the forty-ninth parallel," *U.S. Geol. Survey,* Bull. 235 (1904): 16.

[2] Richard B. Waitt, Jr., "Evolution of Glaciated Topography of upper Skagit Drainage Basin, Washington," *Arctic and Alpine Research* 9, no. 2 (1977): 185. The Skagit gorge probably lies at or near the downvalley limit of early Fraser and older alpine glaciers (pp. 183, 190).

[3] Bauerman, p. 11B; see Section II, note 2. In Canadian geography this word has settled to Chilliwack after some fluctuations in use. In the times of the early Boundary Survey, the Chilliwack River was taken to begin in Chilliwack Lake and the stream above was called Klabneh, Klahaihu, and Dolly Varden Creek.

[4] Sumas Lake, which emptied into Fraser River, was once a very shallow 4½-by-10-mi. lake. When the Fraser rose in spring Sumas Prairie was covered by water; Sumas River revised its course from the overflow and carried water back to the lake. To prevent flooding of lower regions the lake was drained between 1920-1924 and dikes erected along the Fraser.

[5] Reginald A. Daly, "A Geology of the North American Cordillera," Canada Dept. of Mines, Geological Survey Memoir 38 (1912), pt. 2, p. 595. Daly believed that although the Skagit Range did not bear a continuous icecap in Pleistocene time the effects of powerful glaciation were manifest, and that the valley ice moved at a gradient of over 1000 ft per mi. "There is little wonder that the longest of the sheets occurring in the Boundary belt — the Chilliwack glacier — has produced a long, continuous U-shaped trough."

[6] Reginald A. Daly, "The Geology of the Region Adjoining the Western Part of the International Boundary," *Summary Report, Geol. Survey Canada* 14, pt. A (1901): 44-45.

[7] Fraser glaciation, the last lowland glaciation, played a major role in the topographic development of the region. As the ice thickened and moved farther southward, it inundated large areas of the North Cascades near Mt. Baker and filled the lowland near Chilliwack and Bellingham with ice more than a mi. thick. The glacier crossed the Boundary some time after 19,000 years ago. The eastern margin of the ice banked against the Cascades and extended up river valleys to build large moraines which effectively blocked drainages and formed large ice-marginal lakes. Impounded lakes included those found in Skagit Valley and Baker River valley.

[8] Daly, Memoir 38, p. 596; see note 5. Daly found erratics of Chilliwack granite at an elevation of 4700 ft on ridges S of Cultus Lake. More recently, granite boulders derived from Canada were found stranded at altitudes of 5700 ft in this area. Ice occupying Chilliwack Valley near Cultus Lake shed outwash gravel S down Columbia Valley into Nooksack drainages, a now-abandoned channel.

[9] Waitt, 1977, p. 190; see note 2. Ice-deranged drainage, streamlined topography, drift, and abandoned ice-marginal channels clearly are products of the Cordilleran ice sheet (p. 188).

[10] Firn is snow which has survived at least one season of ablation, and therefore has become denser and granular through a process of metamorphism. The word firn only refers to the substance of the material. The geographical term névé refers to the area covered by perennial snow or firn, the area lying entirely within the zone of accumulation.

[11] From its original home in Asia it probably reached the Pacific Coast during the period of Indian immigrations (*B.C.M.,* May 1940). Its dense covering of spines gives it a unique position in our native flora. Norman Collie, (1901), while in the Interior Ranges of British Columbia, revealed that the spikes, "when they enter the flesh, break off, producing poisoned wounds which fester, and whilst cutting trail it is impossible to prevent the long twisted roots flying up occasionally."

[12] Daly, pt. I, pp. 523-26; see note 5.

[13] Daly, pt. I, pp. 534-35; see note 5.

[14] Wayne S. Moen, "Mines and Mineral Deposits of Whatcom County, Washington," Division of Mines and Geology, Bull. 57 (1969): 88-89.

[15] Smith and Calkins, p. 96; see note 1.

[16] Moen, pp. 79-82; see note 14.

[17] Dr. Charles M. Buchanen studied the culture of these Indians (see *The Canoe and The Saddle,* p. 279; see note 36). Members of the first Boundary Survey found that the Indians knew trail routes into and through the mountains, but had no real curiosity to explore the country, which was mostly "terra incognita to them" (Report of Henry Custer, National Archives, R. G. 76). Thiosolac, a chief of the Samonas, a tribe living along Chilliwack River, drew an accurate map showing rivers between the Skagit and Fraser. The Steetathls were a mysterious and feared wild tribe living in the upper Skagit. A war between these Indians and "King George" Indians is described by Nels Bruseth in "Indian Stories and Legends of the Stillaguamish, Sauks, and Allied Tribes," Arlington Times Press, 2nd ed., 1950, pp. 14-15. See also Marian W. Smith, "The Nooksack, the Chilliwack, and the Middle Fraser," *Pacific N.W. Quart.* 41, pp. 330-41.

[18] H.L. Reid, "Whatcom Trails to Fraser River Mines," *Wash. Hist. Quart.* 18. DeLacy was a self-styled surveyor who largely exploited the A.C. Anderson map beyond the Skagit; his reports of the "new trail" inspired a boom in Whatcom. One party took eight weeks to reach Kamloops, showing the exaggerations about the route's condition. (J.H. Stewart Reid, *Mountains, Men, and Rivers,* New York: 1954, p. 138).

[19] Division of land by square mile originated with the Puritan settlers of New England, who liked straight lines and right angles. From the point of view of topography, of course, the straight line is absurd, since it ignores natural features and drainage patterns. Yet it became the standard

method of dividing up public domain and devising national boundaries.

[20] John Grubb Parke later became a general. At the time of the Boundary Survey he was a lieutenant in the Corps of Engineers and had worked in 1853 as head of railroad surveys on the 32nd parallel. George Clinton Gardner was assistant to Parke. The first survey party included Joseph S. Harris, Charles T. Gardner, Dr. C.B.R. Kennerly, R.V. Peabody, Henry Custer, John J. Major, George Gibbs, F. Hudson, and Francis Herbst. The party had a Zenith telescope of 32-inch focal length and a 24-inch transit (a sextant to determine latitude gives a high degree of probable error). The British party immediately encountered many delays in 1858 because of the gold frenzy. In the next season they had mishaps with horses falling off cliffs between the Chilliwack and Skagit rivers, and with river crossings. The British claimed a fire W of Chilliwack Lake was set off by the U.S. party (George F.G. Stanley, *Mapping the Frontier: The Diary of Charles William Wilson,* Seattle, 1970, p. 65).

[21] George Clinton Gardner, journal, vol. 2, Bancroft Library, University of California. Gardner and R.V. Peabody crossed the Skagit Range in late September 1858. From the ridge above Maselpanik Creek they saw the "grandeur of Chuchchehum Mountain."

The two descended directly to the Skagit River, perhaps via St. Alice Creek, while the remainder of the party went via the trail in Maselpanik Creek. Later that fall Henry Custer was engaged in a survey of the Klahaihu and the lake.

[22] The Whatcom Trail summit was about 5800 ft in altitude; the lower pass was estimated by Gibbs as 4533 ft and near level (about correct). Harris and Peabody found this lower gap which saved some 800 ft of altitude gain. The labors of Gibbs in the Cascade Range included sketching and mapping, and comparative study of Indian languages. His research and travels resulted in significant contributions in several fields in 19th century America. Gibbs saw the glacier at the head of "Manselpannik" and McNaught creeks, describing this ice as occupying "a walled basin." Survey parties occupied the ridge N of Depot Creek (now called Mt. Edgar). Point 6044 was their "Lake Hill station." Custer made sketches from the peak N of the trail summit; surveyors were on the 6500-ft summit between upper Paleface and Maselpanik creeks and reached the ridge crest S of Depot Creek.

[23] The general verdict was that this was one of the worst trails in the world (*Bellingham Bay Mail,* April 24, 1880, p. 3). Avalanches were common in winter; one man was swept into the river by the force of the wind (April 10, p. 4). At some of the rocky areas horses had to be belayed. A bridge was built to avoid the bad cliff trail at Devils Elbow in 1892, but this crossing to the S side washed out in two years. In 1895 money was raised to do some blasting and other trail improvements. Numerous maps marked the canyon and the trail features. One such was the Asher and Adams' 1874 map, which showed "Grand Rapids."

Because of the poor trail route up the Skagit Canyon, in the winter of 1879-80 several hundred men went through Hope to Ruby placer diggings (Minister of Mines, 1910 annual report, p. 131).

[24] E.W. Saportas as quoted by L.K. Hodges in *Seattle Post Intelligencer,* September 25, 1897.

[25] Minister of Mines, annual report for 1919, pp. k288, k312.

[26] H.A. Coombs, "Mount Baker, a Cascade Volcano," *Geol. Soc. Am. Bull.* 50, no. 10 (1939): 1493-1510. All the higher lava flows on the cone appear to have originated from an area now covered by the summit ice dome. Most of the material that issued from the central vent was in the form of flows (dark grey, black, red). Columnar jointing is often pronounced. The longest flows followed the course of Sulphur Creek to its confluence with Baker River. The dormant volcano is believed to have formed as a result of subduction near the present continental margin. Mt. Baker, like other local volcanoes in Washington, southwestern British Columbia, and southeastern Alaska, formed above downgoing slabs of ocean crust 20-0 m.y. ago.

[27] In general, North Cascade glaciers experienced a period of glacier rejuvenation in the decade beginning 1945 (Austin Post and Edward R. LaChapelle, *Glacier Ice,* Seattle: The Mountaineers, 1971, p. 37). The season 1973-1974 was the snowiest on Mt. Baker and in 1974 glaciers showed the largest advance since measurements began in 1948.

[28] Some forest was recently crushed by advancing ice. Trees beyond the trimline indicate a Neoglacial advance as early as the 16th century, with two younger moraines present, one being mid-19th century (Easterbrook). See A.E. Harrison, "Short Notes on Fluctuations of Coleman Glacier, Washington, U.S.A.," *Jour. Glaciology,* 9 (1970): 393-396 and K.E. Bengston, "Activity of the Coleman Glacier, Mt. Baker, Washington, U.S.A., 1949-1955," *Jour. Glaciology* 2 (1956): 708-713. See also *Mountaineer,* 1935, pp. 22-23; 1937, p. 33; 1951, pp. 36-37.

[29] David Frank, Austin Post, and Jules D. Friedman, "Recurrent Geothermally Induced Debris Avalanches on Boulder Glacier, Mount Baker, Washington," *Jour. Research, U.S. Geol. Survey* 3, no. 1 (1975): 85. At Lahar Lookout, on the E rim of Sherman crater, steam has caused rapid melting of snow and ice, and probably weakening of large rock outcroppings in the crater area, greatly increasing the hazard of rock and mudslides. Volcanic glass ejected from steam vents appears to be freshly made; this could mean heat beneath Mt. Baker is sufficient to melt rock. Volcanic activity has now shifted nearer the W rim.

[30] Below Easton Glacier the Neoglacial maximum is dated as early as the 16th century by trees growing inside a trimline, but a mid-19th century moraine is absent. The well defined W lobe of the glacier ends at about 5400 ft and the E lobe at 6000 ft. The Easton and Deming glaciers merge and form a continuous ice expanse covering the entire S and SW slopes of Mt. Baker; only at the lower margin, where ice tongues

extend short distances into the valleys, with bare bedrock ridges in between, is the ice mass separated into two distinct glaciers (see W.A. Long, "Mt. Baker's Disappearing Glacier," Summit, July-August 1966, pp. 4-7). In the 18-year period ending in 1952 the Easton had receded 123 ft per year (Long, p. 7). See also W.A. Long, "Recession of Easton and Deming glaciers," *Sci. Amer.* 39, pp. 931-40. Deming Glacier now occupies an ancient crater, as evidenced by remains of the Black Buttes. Squak (Squock) Glacier, 2.7 km in length, and descending to 5500 ft, heads at Sherman Peak and trends S between the Easton and Talum glaciers on the S slope (named for one of E.T. Coleman's Indian guides). The Talum is a very crevassed small glacier on the SE flank of Sherman Peak, with a sharp edge on the N dividing it from the Boulder Glacier. The terminus is well defined at about 6000 ft.

[31] Charles F. Easton, "Mt. Baker — Its Trails and Legends," *Northwest Jour. of Educ.* XXV, no. 5, p. 201. The Easton book probes the possibility at length and provides an interesting study of early regional navigators. Easton believed that Mt. Baker was seen not less than 13 times prior to the factual Vancouver sighting. The book is an unpublished 262-pp. compilation of documentation and manuscripts commissioned in 1911 by the Mt. Baker Club, and archived at the Whatcom Museum of Art and History, Bellingham. De Fuca's sole account for the discovery is related in the account of Michael Lok, a noted English geographer, published in 1625 as part of a book on world exploration and discoveries by Reverend Samuel Purchas. Lok claimed he obtained a report from Valerianos while in Venice in 1576.

[32] Juan Perez in 1774 was probably not far enough into the strait to see the volcano, and similar explorations by Bodega y Quadra and Ensenada de Heceta (1775) are inconclusive. The visible horizon on the strait is near Pillar Point, about 17 mi. E of Cape Flattery (Easton, p. 1, note 31). In 1778 the famed navigator James Cook named Cape Flattery, but stormy weather drifted his vessel to the N of the inlet. First officer Robert Duffin of Captain John Meares' crew, while exploring the S shore of Vancouver Island in 1788, may have seen Mt. Baker, for he continued to where the width of the inlet was noted to increase. In 1789 Captain Robert Gray (American) penetrated the strait a distance of 50 mi., noting it turned northward, but he did not mention the mountain. Kendrick and the Spanish navigators Elisa (1791), Galiano and Valdez (1792) were also in a position to see the volcano.

[33] In 1790, when Spain exerted its greatest power in the Western Hemisphere, Ensign Quimper was dispatched by Spanish officials to investigate the Strait of Juan de Fuca. The first to positively examine the inlet beyond its entrance, Quimper was engaged in this exploration when his pilot sighted the volcano, probably during the last few days of June or the first in July (Majors, p. 3; see note 45).

[34] Maps prepared by Quimper's pilot, López de Haro, show both Mt. Baker and the Cascade Range in artistic depiction. One chart with a pictorial diagram clearly defines the moun-

tain as "La gran Montaña del Carmelo," although the Quimper narrative does not mention it (see Henry R. Wagner, ed., *Spanish Explorations in the Strait of Juan de Fuca,"* Santa Ana, 1933, p. 17, map p. 82). In the middle ages an order of monks, whose abode was Mt. Carmel in Palestine, was known as the Carmelites. Quimper's maps were not published until 1872, much later than those of Vancouver.

[35] George Vancouver, "A Voyage of Discovery to the North Pacific Ocean . . . under the command of Captain George Vancouver," vol. 1, London, 1798, pp. 221-22. Mt. Baker was shown and named on the chart prepared by Lt. Baker. This was the first published map in reference to Mt. Baker. Vancouver likely did not wish to admit that the inlet and sea he was exploring were the same as discovered by De Fuca and the Spanish navigators, for this would have been an admission he was in foreign territory (Easton, p. 9; see note 31).

[36] Theodore Winthrop states in *The Canoe and The Saddle* (Boston, 1862, p. 47) that he learned of the name Kulshan from the Lummi tribe at a salmon feast in 1853. "Kulshan," named Mount Baker by the vulgar, is their northernmost buttress up to 49 degrees and Fraser River. Kulshan is an irregular, massive, round-shaped peak, worthy to stand a white emblem of perpetual peace between us and our brother Britons." Easton (note 31) made the interpretation that the name was common tribal usage, "Koma" meaning White and Shining and "Kulshan" Precipitous, or "White, Steep Mountain." The Lummi Indians did not venture near the volcano, for this was the abode of the Nootsac (Nooksack) tribe.

[37] Hall J. Kelley in his geographical sketch of Oregon. The mountain was described as "huge piles of rocks, which seem to rise, in naked deformity, one above another" (*Hall J. Kelley on Oregon,* Princeton, 1832, p. 17).

[38] Report of George Gibbs to Captain George B. McClellan.

[39] "Report of George Gibbs on a reconnaissance of the country lying upon Shoalwater bay and Puget's sound," Olympia, W.T., March 1, 1954. House Ex. Doc. 129, 33rd cong., 1st sess., serial 736. The 1843 eruption was the first known, according to both Indians and Hudson's Bay officers.

[40] George Davidson, "Recent volcanic activity in the United States: Eruption of Mount Baker," *Science* 6, no. 138 (1885): 362. Davidson cites 1854 as a surveying date when he saw dense smoke clouds above Mt. Baker. The eruption of 21 March 1950 sent forth "volumes of smoke," according to the *Oregon Spectator*. It is conjectured that the 1870 eruption may have been a forest fire.

[41] Coleman was an original member of The Alpine Club (London) and the first to use an ice axe in the Western Hemisphere; he may have also been the first to use crampons. An artist who exhibited at the Royal Academy, Coleman ascended Mont Blanc twice and made alpine expeditions 1855-58.

[42] *Oregonian,* 9 August 1866; *Daily British Colonist,* 6 Sep-

tember 1866; *Mazama* 6 (1920): 38.

[43]On August 15 the Indians brought in two marmots "which they demolished at supper." The party camped twice in fir clumps near timberline on Marmot Ridge, and when fog cleared on the 16th the summit was seen for the first time.

[44]When in the middle of the vast firn tract (Coleman Glacier), Coleman noted there were 37 great intersecting crevasses. In his published account (1872) he relates: "We were in considerable anxiety concerning Stratton. Divested of rope and without a pack, he had made rapid progress. At one time we saw him crossing a spot exposed to avalanches of ice, and shortly afterward were greatly alarmed to see him take a jump, and then suddenly disappear . . . . It appears that he had fortunately fallen in with the tracks of a grizzly bear, and wisely concluded that what would bear its weight would sustain his also, he had followed it without hesitation across snow bridges over the chasms." Details of the successful ascent are given in the *Colonist* (Victoria) 22 and 25 August 1868. Each party member had alpenstocks and ice creepers, putting the creepers on when reaching frozen snow. There was one 150-ft rope, and each man carried a blanket at the saddle.

[45]E.T. Coleman, "Mountaineering on the Pacific," *Harper's New Monthly Magazine* 39 (Nov. 1869): 793-817. Also *Alpine Journal* V, no. 36 (1872): 357-367; vol. 8, no. 57 (1877): 233-242. See also Easton, note 31, pp. 31-37 and *Off Belay*, August 1976, pp. 2-5. A newly discovered account of the ascent by Stratton gives a valuable perspective (see Harry M. Majors, *Mount Baker, a Chronicle of its Historic Eruptions and First Ascent*, Seattle, 1978). Stratton found the staff from the previous attempt about 800 ft below the summit. With their one ice axe, some 350 steps were cut. Commenting on the Black Buttes, Stratton said, "The two dark peaks . . . run up like church spires" (p. 182) and from the summit he commented that "The east side of the mountain is perpendicular for hundreds of feet" (p. 184). Coleman's barometric estimate of 10,613 ft is quite close to the mark.

[46]*The West Shore* 10 (August 1884), p. 237. Early ascent chroniclers, such as the Mazama historians and Easton did not count this ascent.

[47]*Whatcom Reveille*, 8 July 1891. In addition to Lowe, the party was composed of W.A. Amsden, Hobert Clark, Henry Lowe, Percival J. Parris, Thomas Scatbo, G.W. Smith, and Ed Whitstruck (seven made the summit). This 1891 party travelled via the Middle Fork Nooksack River and Clearwater Creek, then descended by Glacier Creek.

[48]*Off Belay*, August 1976, pp. 6-10. Morovits told A.J. Craven, the first president of the Mt. Baker Club, about his 1892 climb: "I was packing my rifle, the Lord only knows why. We were all green as grass when it came to climb a real mountain." Morovits located in the area of Baker Lake in October 1891 and built a cabin. In 1894 Morovits pioneered a variation of the Boulder Glacier route. When he took a

party to the summit via that route in 1900, a large crevasse just below the summit nearly stopped them. To all appearances it would be impossible to pass. Morovits finally, however, found a place where the party could cross (Easton, p. 60, note 31). A member of this party, John A. Lee, later wrote: "Joe Morovits could not be excelled as a guide. He is a hardy, experienced mountaineer, persevering and willing to assume even more than his share of burdens." Prof. R.B. Vaile, also on the ascent, commented, "He knows the woods thoroughly and has a physique enabling him to carry a hundred-pound pack anywhere over the hills." Morovits made the first climb of Sherman Peak in 1907. By the next year he had made his seventh ascent of Mt. Baker.

[49]The party approached the 1500-ft ice precipice by traveling inside a crevasse on the Park Glacier slope, then tunnelled through a snow wall, later cutting 400 ft up blue ice. Here Kiser led along (with spikes on his boots), dragging a 400-ft rope, later used as an anchor with iron spikes. The climb took 18 hours r.t. from camp. A later appraisal of this adventure was that they accomplished "what is perhaps the most brilliant feat in the history of mountaineering in the northwest."

During this time Rodney L. Glisan and John A. Lee traversed from Camp Kiser to Boulder Ridge, an approach variation which required a bivouac just below the summit (reached August 9). This lengthy route took the Park-Boulder moraine, then the final SE slope, ultimately using five consecutive days because base camp had been moved. The same summer, J.R. Glascock, Jr. made the ascent of Baker alone (via Coleman Glacier, July 6).

[50]*Off Belay*, February, 1973. One route was by trail from Glacier Creek to Coleman Glacier and the summit saddle; the other was the Deming route via the Nooksack Middle Fork to Mazama Park and Deming Glacier. The 1911 race was won over the latter route because a train wreck slowed the pace of Harvey Haggard (who won in 1912, taking under 10 hours from Bellingham to the summit). A bull on the tracks was struck, derailing the train (Easton, pp. 117-20; see note 31).

[51]Frank, p. 86; see note 29. See also *Off Belay*, June, 1975, pp. 5, 6, 49 and *Summit*, April, 1975, pp. 4-7. Avalanches have occurred at fairly regular intervals since 1958. In April 1975 a heat increase created an elliptical crater lake 250 ft long, with collapse and melting of snow and ice on the crater's rim. The warm lake flowed through natural drains under the glacier to Boulder Creek until it closed up late in 1978.

A large debris avalanche descended Boulder Glacier from the crater rim on August 21, 1973, involving about 46,000 cu. yards of material and stripping bare the steep slope of Sherman crater; on the upper Boulder Glacier debris consisted of firn blocks as much as several meters across. This avalanche is not considered an isolated incident, but one episode of mass wastage related to heat emission in the crater rim (Frank, p. 83). Past mudflows have come as low down as the present Baker Lake area. The first known description of large avalanche deposits from Sherman Peak was given by Charles F. Easton (*Mazama* 5, no. 4 (1919): 341).

[52] The party had a crevasse problem 100 ft from the summit. "Robert Woods, resolving to make one more effort . . . . After an hour's persistent work with his ax he succeeded in getting up the other side of the crevasse . . . soon the air was rent with his triumphant whoops, which assured us that he had reached the summit" (*Hamilton Telegraph*, September 1, 1891).

[53] Coleman named Lincoln Peak for Abraham Lincoln and Colfax Peak for Schuyler Colfax, an Indiana congressman.

[54] Erratics transported by the Puget Sound Lobe occur at this level, an indication of the thickness of the ice sheet (Don J. Easterbrook and David A. Rahm, *Landforms of Washington*, Bellingham, 1970, p. 29).

[55] Donal M. Ragan, "Emplacement of the Twin Sisters Dunite, Washington," *Amer. Jour. of Science* 261 (June 1963): 549-565. The 10-mi. long and 4-mi. wide dunite body is located along a NW-trending fault. See also Bates McKee, *Cascadia*, p. 98. The rock of the range owes its roughness to differential weathering (the dunite weathers away while pyroxene and chromite crystals remain). The mineral olivine in dunite turns reddish-brown when exposed and weathered.

[56] Easton, p. 50; see note 31. Near the summit they climbed through a rock basin, and here noted, "Every sound in this basin is answered by surprising echoes twice repeated." This is likely the basin SW of the summit; here they reported that the perpendicular cliff "was surmounted with much difficulty and danger, tearing clothing and lacerating the fingers." The party erected a staff and cairn on the summit and commented that the "Sisters Range, with its needle-like pinnacles projecting above the snow, stretches away in the haze."

[57] Both Twin Sisters were climbed. A party composed of Mrs. Nellie Allen Gwyther, Tony Aronson, John Gwyther, Lillian Johnson, Mr. and Mrs. Mahely, Aubry Sinness, Grace and Jack Weller made the ascent from Whatcom in three days. Mrs. Gwyther later wrote: "The four women of us wore full length skirts and long puffed sleeves instead of the nifty outing garments and climbing togs of the present day" (Easton, p. 58). On the trek out Miss Johnson stumbled over a tent rope, breaking a leg; it took one week to get her out on a stretcher. In 1905 a party from the U.S. Geological Survey under Edward C. Barnard climbed South Twin and built a 7-ft cairn for triangulation (*Joint Report*, 1937, p. 336; see Section II, note 64).

[58] *Mountaineer*, 1916, pp. 59-62. The party traveled the wooded ridge between Sister and Green creeks, over "Panoram Knob," eventually reaching the Sisters Glacier. The account mentions covering a mile of snow to the peak, but does not describe the rock climbing necessary to reach the summit.

[59] Peter Misch, in *Geol. Soc. Amer.* Bull. 71, no. 12, pt. 2, p. 2069.

[60] The Gibbs description and Geographic Board notations strongly support this location for "Put-lush-go-hap." Custer's notation for the summit was 7687 ft, but his coordinates of 48°59.7' latitude and 121°38.8' longitude would place the summit E of Tomyhoi Lake. However his longitudes tend to be too far E; this would give weight to the Tomyhoi location. The Forest Service map of 1913 gives the name "Put hishgo hap" at the position of Tomyhoi Lake.

[61] Smith and Calkins, p. 86 and plate 4; see note 1.

[62] H.B. Ayres, *19th Annual Report, U.S. Geol. Survey*, pt. 5 (1899), plate 82. A plat map in the Easton Mt. Baker book, drawn by Banning Austin, shows "Baby Ruth Mountain" at the Mt. Sefrit location. The Forest Service map of 1913 shows the name Ruth here, as does the U.S. Geological Survey map of 1915, and the map of Jeffcott followed. The Mazama map of 1907 shows Ruth Mountain at its present location (Easton, p. 68, photo) and "Ruth Mountain Range."

[63] Such steep glaciers tend to build up accumulation to a critical level, discharge a sudden flow of ice, then return to a quiescent stage while accumulation again resumes; Austin Post and Edward R. LaChapelle, *Glacier Ice* (Seattle: The Mountaineers, 1971) p. 35.

[64] The Price Glacier originates above 8240 ft on the E flank of the summit pyramid and breaks steeply in a highly jumbled flow to 3895-ft Price Lake. Beginning in 1946 the glacier increased in volume, and by 1954 earlier exposed bedrock had been completely buried by advancing ice (William A. Long, in *Summit*, January-February 1963, pp. 19-25); the glacier segment beneath Nooksack Tower almost completely filled its cirque and was much thickened. The central lobe of the Price thickened and had coalesced with the other one, to move the terminus beyond the 1946 position. Up glacier, 0.7 km from the bare, narrow ice tongue at its terminus, is a 100-m icefall separating the lower glacier from its principal accumulation basin.

[65] *Mountaineer*, 1916, p. 11.

[66] While successive fresh end moraines occurring in three sets lie on the upper valley floor, with the innermost horseshoe-shaped complexes being sharp-crested arcuate loops, old ground moraine and alluvial drift outwash occur through a distance of 3 mi. downvalley. Vertical ice downwasting is apparent by the elevated trimlines as developed by earlier Neoglacial ice fronts. Despite the general long-term recession, between 1946 and 1958 there was an increase in ice volume, with the main glacier surface more heavily crevassed and the ice front extended (Long, see note 64).

[67] Custer described the mountain: "An immense rocky perpendicular wall, many thousands feet elevated above, the massive pyramidal base." His observations led to the conclusion that both Shuksan and Baker do not belong in the "main

body or Ridge of the Cascade Mountains." The survey's manuscript map lettered the mountain "T-Shuksan," while Baker was "Baker" or "Te-ko-meh." When the U.S. Geological Survey's triangulation party of 1899 located Shuksan, their records spelled it in the present form, which subsequently appears on maps.

[68] Curtis and Price appear to have made an effort to learn of a possible previous ascent. C.E. Rusk wrote the editor of *Mazama,* "The first ascent of Mt. Shuksan was made in 1897 by Joe Morovits . . . . I can secure affidavits to substantiate this ascent."Rusk stated that he would have tried Shuksan if he had not been satisfied that Morovits had made the ascent. Certainly Morovits was capable of unusual endurance feats, and he certainly had opportunity to make the climb during his many years of nearby residence. Perhaps the best solution is to state that about 1900 Morovits may have climbed Mt. Shuksan, and that in 1906 Curtis and Price definitely succeeded. Dolly Connelly argues with considerable authority that Morovits did reach the summit (*Sports Illustrated,* January 7, 1963).

Curtis and Price first attempted to climb along the crags of Shuksan Arm, spending 14 hours there. After a rest period they took to the SW slope, first working S along the mountain foot, then making a bivouac fire near 7000 ft. To avoid steep frozen snow they followed a rock spur as much as possible to gain the Sulphide Glacier. On the summit pyramid they took a narrow edge, dragging along their alpenstocks. Here they observed moss campion "which splashed the dark rocks a beautiful pink with its flowers" (*Overland Monthly,* August 1907, and Easton, p. 70; see note 31). Later Curtis wrote: "There was no trace of a previous ascent; no rocks had been disturbed and no cairn built. Nearly every rock on top was scarred by lightning, some being fused to glass"; *Mazama,* 3, no. 1 (1907): 29.

[69] As described in written communication, the Thompson-guided party began the North Face climb by keeping close to the profile as seen from Heather Meadows; at some distance to the ice shoulder they made a gradual upward contour across the upper face, taking about the same line now used; rockfall was experienced.

[70] Staatz, M.H., et al. "Geology and Mineral Resources of the northern part of the North Cascades National Park, Washington," *U.S. Geol. Survey,* Bull. 1359 (1973): 30-31.

[71] The Challenger Glacier, a broad cascading ice flow on the northern slopes of Mt. Challenger, has a width of 2.7 km and terminates at 1460 m. Part of the width of the glacier ends in an ice cliff; here a long ice tongue descends through a narrow rock defile at the western glacier margin. The upper region of the glacier increased in size in the late 1940s and in the 1950s (William A. Long, *Summit,* January-February 1963). Ice thickened above the Little Beaver cirque threshold.

[72] D.F. Crowder and R.W. Tabor, *Routes and Rocks: Hiker's Guide to the North Cascades from Glacier Peak to Lake Chelan* (Seattle: The Mountaineers, 1965) p. 33.

[73] When the 1931 party climbed the peak the nomenclature was not firmly established. The party assumed they had climbed the Mt. Terror massif, but then reconsidered and in the following year climbed the highest peak in the group and termed this Mt. Terror. The 1938 climb was by Ralph and Ray Clough, Charles Kirschner, and Charles Metzger, who on August 23 completed the climb via the SW ridge, possibly traversing all The Barrier pinnacles. Not knowing of the 1931 ascent they found "Mt. Terror" in the register and assumed this was the correct nomenclature.

The party used logging boots with tricounis and Swiss edge nails during their six-day trip (two days to Terror Creek basin). They climbed to the knife edge ridge of The Barrier and then generally kept on the E side, describing the ridge as ½ mi. long. At one 8-ft narrow step-face they had to hold the rock together while one man climbed. After this step climbing on tilted slabs became safer. From the summit they concluded that their position was higher than other peaks of the group.

[74] Peter Misch, "Geology of the Northern Cascades of Washington," *Mountaineer* 45 (1952): 11.

[75] The journal of Henry Custer (National Archives) describes the large glacier at the head of "Glacier Creek." He called the mountain "Wailagonahoist," estimating its height at 9000 ft. George Gibbs wrote that the glacier was said to have an extent of some 3 mi., with slopes up to 70 degrees in angle. On some of his sketches Custer labelled the summit "Glacier Mtn."

[76] The central part of the broad glacier ends in an ice cliff above a rock wall. The narrow bare ice tongue beneath this cliff extends roughly 2 km to a terminus that ends in a rock canyon, the final cirque of Little Beaver Creek; bedrock here contains a small lake. Elsewhere the glacier cascades in broken ice above the lower rock rim. Up-glacier several hundred meters from the ice-firn edge (which has a mean altitude of about 6000 ft) is a 300-400-m central icefall area on a moderately sloping angle. But both the E and W extremities of the glacier are smooth, low-angle, and but little crevassed.

[77] A taped interview with Berry (University of Washington Library-Manuscripts) confirms an ascent. The original Mt. Challenger party found initials corresponding to these names in a register.

[78] William A. Long, *Summit,* January-February 1963, pp. 18-20. Positions of large moraines several hundred ft thick beyond the glacier fronts indicate that the separate ice masses at an early time were one, a single large mass which filled the entire upper cirque. Moraines are fresh and apparently record a recent ice advance. Throughout part of its width, the terminus of Redoubt Glacier forms an ice cliff perched at the edge of the cirque. Here a small lake has appeared as a result of recent recession of the ice tongue. The two ice masses of Depot Glacier and the Redoubt Glacier are all separated by low rock divides.

[79] Baker, p. 47; see Section II, note 63.

[80] Bauerman, *Report of Progress,* p. 12B; see Section II, note 2. Bauerman went to the foot of the mountain's slope. In his report, he termed this "Chilukweyuk Mountain."

[81] The peak was improperly called Tamihi by the Boundary Survey, but its real name Slesse was given on the International Boundary Survey map of 1913. The name Tamihy Mountain has been used (Annual Report Minister of Mines, British Columbia, 1904, p. G-32), Canadian Tomahi or Tomyhoi, Silesia, and King George (American maps). Slesse was called "Tomahai" by E.C. Barnard of the American survey party in 1901. In 1935 survey station marks "Pierce," "Needle," and "Canadian Tamihi Peak" were located on the Slesse-Nesakwatch Creek divide.

"We had been two hours making the final climb. The plateau on which we stood was about a quarter of a mile in diameter, and embraced an extent of about eighty acres. The scene was grand in the nakedness of its desolation. The white surface of snow was unrelieved by a single rock . . . . We felt cut off from the world we had left."

EDMUND T. COLEMAN, 1869
First ascent of Mt. Baker

SECTION II

Northeastern Cascade Range

HARTS PASS, WASHINGTON, TO NICOLA RIVER, BRITISH COLUMBIA

(Slate Creek, Canyon Creek, Ross Lake, Skagit River, Klesilkwa River, Silverhope Creek, Fraser River, Nicola River, Coldwater River, Tulameen River, Similkameen River, Okanogan River, Columbia River, Methow River)

GEOGRAPHY

The North Cascades in this section include the mountainous terrain from E of the Methow River in Washington to the Nicola River in British Columbia and from Ross Lake to the Okanogan River. The range forms a N-S trend with broad summit crests averaging 7000 ft to 8500 ft in altitude, but the NW trend of such streams as the Methow, upper Skagit, and Skagit tributaries are anomalous to the structural crest and predate the Plio-Pleistocene Cascade uplift.[1] The configuration of the lower Fraser River in Canada is such that it divides the broad western portion of the Cascade Range from the Coast Mountains, then in its upstream course provides the western limit of the now narrowing northeastern Cascades.

Early geologists and topographers fundamentally agreed on certain division for North Cascade subranges, a system of nomenclature that has not always been carried forward with complete acceptance: (1) Skagit Range (or mountains): in British Columbia from Skagit River NW to Fraser River; (2) Hozomeen (Hozameen) Range: from Skagit River E to Pasayten River (E of Skagit-Sumallo River and Coquihalla River in Canada); (3) Okanogan Mountains or Range: from Pasayten River E to Mt. Chopaka.[2]

The Cascade Mountains in Canada form a triangular area between the Fraser River, Thompson River, Interior (Thompson) Plateau, and the 49th degree parallel of latitude,[3] extending a prong northward, where they diminish on the upland. There are two diverse topographical provinces here — the Cascade Mountains and the Interior Plateau.[5]

The Skagit Range is the most mountainous of the three North Cascade divisions in Canada and, using several local names, continues to the Fraser River. The Cheam and Hope Mountains and "Anderson River Group" and "Coquihalla Range" are essentially similar in their larger features but are separated by distinct natural boundaries.[6] The Silvertip Mountain portion of the Hope Mountains and Anderson River Group

provide the most startling topographic contrasts in the Canadian portion of this section. Valley glaciation scoured deep troughs, giving great local relief on steep-walled alpine peaks; ice sheet glaciation rounded high ridges and in many cases covered all but the highest peaks, and cirque glaciers carved wide basins and exposed extensive smooth rock slabs.

The Coquihalla River, which divides two portions of the Cascade Mountains, deeply incises a rugged landscape in British Columbia. In 33 mi. the river falls 3400 ft in a narrow valley and its tumultous course makes an incessant roar. Its opposite, the Coldwater, flows N to the Nicola River at Merritt, nearly parallel to Otter Creek, a Similkameen tributary.

Although these ranges are effective divides, several individual river systems transect them and generally flow through the highest terrain in opposition to their sources. There are some drainage reversals which probably result from the extreme effect of glaciation during the Pleistocene Epoch (Sumallo River-Nicolum Creek, Skagit and Skaist River-Similkameen River). The Klesilkwa River fork of Skagit River and Silverhope Creek are remarkable in that they slice deeply across the heart of the range, and like the trough valley occupied by Nepopekum Creek, probably predate the Cascade uplift.[7] The anomalous low, broad Klesilkwa-Silverhope pass was apparently shaped by a S-flowing tributary of the ice sheet which coalesced in the Skagit-Ross Lake Trough and occupied the North Cascades briefly.[8]

The Hozameen Range forms the divide between W-flowing streams which empty into Fraser River and those that drain by longer routes via the Nicola, Thompson, and Similkameen tributaries into the Fraser or Okanagan Rivers. The range consists of diverse terrain features but has a distinct continuity and geologic thread to separate it from the Skagit Range and Interior Plateau.[9] N and E of Manning Park the terrain is more subdued than in Washington

State[10] and gradually decreases in altitude:[11] at an elevation of about 6500 ft the range appears as a broad low-relief plateau with only a few widely scattered peaks and one prominent ridge.

Early nomenclature designated the Hozomeen Range as a geologic and topographic entity beginning S of the International Boundary, and including the Hozomeen Peaks; resistant volcanic greenstones formed peaks with bold relief, but river and glacier sculpturing of the softer strata along faults has given rise to certain open valleys of softened contour. The southern part of the range consists of complex, narrow rock ridges, some of them level-topped transverse spurs. Not really a part of this range is the great hulk of Jack Mountain, which culminates at 4 mi. from Ruby Creek, and rising sharply 7300 ft above Ross Lake. Numerous abrupt and deep V-shaped gorges and steep-walled canyons with local relief up to 5000 ft show thick beds of sandstone and conglomerate. A typical tributary entering the upper Skagit Valley from the E has a broad, gently arcuate, U-shaped headward segment that passes downvalley into a narrow, crooked, V-shaped canyon carved into a broad, steep escarpment.[12]

When the first of the great Pleistocene ice ages began about 3 m.y. ago one of the principal avenues of the ice invasion was the broad Skagit Valley, whose bedrock was more erodible than the surrounding terrain, and whose floor is now over 1 mi. wide at the International Boundary. In the upper Skagit, upper Methow, West and Middle Fork Pasayten valleys Pleistocene ice gouged out deep U-shaped cross-profiles.[13] Erratics and striations reveal that Cordilleran ice during late Pleistocene time flowed generally southward into the main Skagit Trough and through the uplands E of Ross Lake to override previously unglaciated divides.[14] The thick ice sheet also advanced into upper Chelan drainage basin and flowed over high passes into the Methow drainage.

On such peaks as Jack, Hozomeen, Castle, Robinson, Carru, and Lago, ice accumulated high on the northern and eastern flanks, etching out capacious cirques.[15] No mountain in this region is now draped with ice, as is common W of the Skagit River, but three glaciers on Jack Mountain and one on Crater Mountain are significant (the largest is 0.6 mi. wide and 1 mi. long). In Canada, small glaciers are virtually limited to those on Silvertip, Outram, and Anderson River Mountain, an effect of the topographic barrier of the higher Coast Mountains, which lessens the maritime effect on the Cascades and produces a drier interior in this northernmost portion of the range. Usually a short distance beyond the margins of small modern glaciers (reborn during Neoglaciation), are fresh unstable bouldery moraines, a product of the latest glacial pulse.

The major portion of the Pasayten Wilderness consists of terrain the early geographers termed the Okanogan Range. This grouping, which forms a divide between streams flowing N into the Similkameen and those draining S into the Methow River, extends in a span of about 20 mi. at the 49th parallel, and joins the main Cascade divide at Harts Pass. Near the Boundary the summits are formed dominantly by Tertiary-age granitics flanked farther N and S by lower summits and ridges of Mesozoic rocks. In the central and northern mountainous area summit altitudes average over 7000 ft, but the highest peaks — Robinson, Monument, Osceola, Carru, Lago, Ptarmigan, Windy, Remmel, Cathedral, Grimface, Lakeview, Snowy — have a nearly uniform summit accordance.

Ancestral glaciers shaped and scoured the highland to configure cirque walls, sometimes converging to nearly divide parts into small summit tables with precipitous walls; Apex, Amphitheatre, and Lakeview mountains are associated with a high summit accordance and are the most prominent examples of such topography.[16] Many high ridges and pyramidal summits in the Pasayten Wilderness are cut by steep cirques on their N and E flanks, sharply contrasting with smoother and more gentle S and W slopes.[17]

Above the upper ice limit, surfaces are greatly disintegrated, and widespread felsenmeer is usually present. The vast cirques of Amphitheatre Mountain are a fine example of the alpine evolutionary sequence from old upland surface and glacier barrens to alpine meadows and Hudsonian forest. Rapid weathering along joints loosens angular blocks, which in thinly forested areas stream downslope, in many places composing broad talus canyons. Small cone-shaped avalanche deposits frequently occur at major gully mouths or small stream valleys, sometimes with vegetative cover. On gently inclined slopes or level areas blocks are embedded in the soil and covered with grass and moss.

Between the Methow and Okanogan drainage the highland was covered by a more continuous icecap than the mountains W of the Pasayten River. The efficiency of the icecap as an erosive agent is remarkable in view of the fact the average depth of the ice was little more than 1000 ft. Erratics of northern provenance, striations and gently rounded saddles modified by ice flow indicate that the ice sheet postdated the most recent alpine advance.[18] This ice embellished the rolling uplands of Horseshoe Basin, Cathedral Park, and Spanish Creek, areas of subdued topography that underlay the former local icecap, and its scouring left a myriad of rock basins, many of which now contain lakes.[19] Barren moraine debris fills cirque floors, testifying to the recency of the latest ice retreat.

The Pasayten and Ashnola rivers are the principal N-flowing drainage systems of the Pasayten Wilderness, and the Chewack River, Lost River, and Andrews Creek are the comparable systems that drain the southern flanks. The major river valleys E of the Cascade divide, the Similkameen, Methow, and Okanogan, have gone through several stages since rivers formed their approximate present courses roughly 16 m.y. ago by eroding geologically young folded and faulted uplands. Most valleys in the eastern North Cascades include a canyonlike segment downvalley from the glacier-scoured headward reaches. A classic example is the wilderness gorge of Lost River, which slices deeply through some of the highest and most rugged terrain of this region. Below the junction of the Pasayten, and again lower in its course, the Similkameen has carved a particularly deep, narrow canyon.[20] Cordilleran ice during Pleistocene time first broadened the deeply incised trough, then upon retreating, deposited thick alluvium and glacial drift. Glacial choking and great gravel deposition of the trench caused the river, at about 5 mi. S of the International Boundary, to be deflected eastward to join the Okanogan River near Oroville. Possibly a glacier discharged here, producing a broad gap for the new river channel, and in later stages left the river gorge dammed with drift.[21]

During the latter part of the Pleistocene Epoch the Okanogan Lobe of the ice sheet pushed S and blocked the Columbia River's flow around the northern margin of the Columbia Plateau. The river was forced to flow southward across the basalt lava plateau and cut new channels; later ice withdrawal restored the river to its former channel. Catastrophic emptying of lakes dammed by ice in Montana and Idaho produced repeated floods of enormous magnitude, which swept across the lava field and cut a system of great coulees in the plateau.[22]

This region's characteristics include a predominantly short, dry summer season with large daily temperature ranges and infrequent severe storms. Radiation of heat into space occurs easily from both the ground and air, and frosts occur frequently as a result of surface cooling; the cause of cold nights is the drier air at higher altitudes. Most of the high terrain is snow-covered until June or later. The perennial streams nearly always rise in high, well watered mountain areas where snowmelt and the heaviest precipitation can sustain their flow.

There is a great climatic diversity caused by elevation differences, ranging from a semi-arid sagebrush desert on the far eastern slope to cool alpine forests in the highest mountains. The Ross Lake-Skagit Trough, which has been described as an ecotone by biologists because of its location in transition between wet and dry climates, receives 75-80 inches of annual precipitation, while the comparable amount on the eastern mountain margin is only 16 inches. In the higher regions most moisture falls as snow.[23] Autumn snowfall generally begins in late October, when the first savage storms may assault the mountains with devastating force. Winter is the dominant season in the northeastern Cascades; during this season continental polar air may bring very cold weather, sometimes with dry spells over a week in length.

Distance from the sea affects climate and therefore its topography and biological character. The influence of maritime climate diminishes in the Okanogan Range, lessening snow cover and affecting ecosystem components. There is an upward migration of timberline and alp slopes. There are elements of geomorphic features and vegetation to enhance the impression of similarity with leeward areas of the Canadian Interior Ranges (with similar temperature and moisture regimes).

The forests on this inland region of the North Cascades reflect the effect of diminished moisture: while sometimes dense on the shadow slopes there is a sparse cover on most sunny slopes. Windfall areas are typical near valley floors.

In the western portion of Manning Provincial Park, and in the upper Skagit, Sumallo, Klesilkwa, and Silverhope valleys, the familiar conifers — western hemlock, western red cedar, and Douglas fir — are the dominant species and sometimes are seen in truly magnificent stands, while ponderosa pine is characteristic on dry Skagit Valley slopes N of Lightning Creek. The open forests are dominated by ponderosa pine (up to 3000 ft), white pine, and lodgepole pine. In the Hozameen and Okanogan ranges subalpine fir is found above 3500 ft in conspicuous stands, and is joined by Englemann spruce — usually above 3800 ft, as aridity decreases with altitude.[24] Whitebark pine begins to appear above 5000 ft, and is widespread. In the world of wind-stress, these trees develop growth characteristics of "wind timber" (krummholz) and become bent, gnarled, and stunted from stress.[25] Alpine larch, which also grows at the highest elevations near timberline, has a craggy windswept form, adding its special golden color.[26] Eastward of the Pasayten River the ground flora decreases in density with mainly a grass cover at higher altitudes between widely spaced groves of larch and pine.

On both sides of the International Boundary, the meadow regions form heather carpets and are lush with floral variety. Such widespread species as the lupine, golden fleabane, Indian paintbrush, mountain valerian, Indian hellebore (up to 5 ft high), anemone, penstemon, and columbine are seen almost everywhere. Tiny delicate flowers and mosses such as stonecrop, white pussytoes, alpine and Tolmie saxifrage, phlox, mountain sorrel, moss campion, and rose crown pinch themselves into sheltered niches among the boulders above timberline during the brief summer, well adapted to withstand the extreme cold and dryness of the arctic-alpine environment.

The range of landforms, from desert foothills to alpine rock crags, also provides a wide range of wildlife habitat. The California desert bighorn is commonly seen in the Similkameen Valley and tributary slopes, and since they were introduced from British Columbia in 1957, are plentiful on Mt. Aeneas (near Loomis). Conspicuous mammals include white-tailed and mule deer, black bear, elk, goat, coyote, hoary marmot, and beaver (who pond many streams). There are also wolverine, muskrat, fisher, mink, otter, weasel, and the seldom-seen cougar. A few grizzly bears find range here, with more sightings in Canada than Washington State. The Columbian ground squirrel, red squirrel, and Golden-mantled ground squirrel are in much evidence in the forest zone. In Manning Provincial Park 164 bird species have been identified, including five resident grouse species.

In much of the Pasayten Wilderness and adjoining areas in British Columbia topography, snow conditions and climate tend to be excellent for ski touring. Here is extensive high altitude terrain with generally dry snow and weather superior to the W slope of the Cascades. Vast sections of rolling upland, such as Horseshoe Basin, Wolframite Mountain-Apex Pass, Tiffany Mountain, the Tulameen River country and surrounding uplands, Pasayten River country, and parts of both Manning and Cathedral Lakes Provincial Parks are safe from avalanches, a situation unique in the mountainous parts of the Cascade Range.

GEOLOGY

The distribution of bedrock formations in the northeastern North Cascades is largely controlled by major steep-dipping faults that divide the range into a series of geologically distinct blocks. Rocks within each of these blocks may have formed in widely separated areas and it is only within relatively recent geologic time (within the last 200 m.y.) that these blocks have been juxtaposed. These blocks slid past one another on great tears (faults) in the earth's crust into their present positions. The major blocks are, from E to W:

1. E of the Methow-Pasayten Fault is an area dominated by granitic and volcanic igneous rocks.
2. Between the Methow-Pasayten Fault on the E and the Hozomeen-Jack Mountain and Ross Lake faults on the W is a belt of predominantly sedimentary and volcanic rocks, called the Methow Graben.
3. Between the Hozomeen-Jack Mountain Fault and the Fraser River-Straight Creek Fault is an area underlain largely by gneiss and metamorphosed sedimentary and volcanic rocks.

Eastern block: In Canada, most of this area is underlain by Late Triassic (about 215 m.y.) volcanic rocks (Nicola Group), largely basalt and andesite, that may represent a chain of ancient oceanic volcanic islands. These rocks have been invaded and intruded at various times between about 50 and 200 m.y. ago by large bodies of granitic rocks. These granitic rocks, like those elsewhere in the North Cascades, formed by partial melting of material in the lower crust or upper mantle.

In Washington, the eastern block is largely made up of granodiorite, quartz monzonite, and gneiss is called by many geologists the Remmel Batholith. Late in the history of this block, from about 90 to 45 m.y. ago, thick piles of volcanic rocks were extruded onto the surface; these volcanics (and all older rocks) were deformed in the Tertiary by faulting and folding.

Near Princeton along the banks of Tulameen River are examples of explosive volcanism: highly viscous rhyolitic lavas erupted, so hot and plastic that they fused to form colorful welded tuffs.

Methow Graben (central zone): This area is composed largely of clastic (fragmented) sedimentary and volcanic rocks. These rocks were deposited between the Jurassic and mid-Cretaceous (a time span of about 100 m.y.) in a NW-trending marine trough that extended from S of Methow well into Canada. The oldest rocks in this trough are Early Jurassic (about 200 m.y.

old) volcanics called the Ladner Group which form a belt extending along the W side of the trough from Jack Mountain to Boston Bar, B.C. These are overlain by sandstone, siltstone, and shale (Dewdney Creek Group) and by the Early Cretaceous Jackass Mountain Group. Due to uplift about 100 m.y. ago the seas began to recede, and sediments deposited in the Late Cretaceous were nonmarine (e.g., the Winthrop Sandstone around Mazama).

In the Tertiary (3 to 70 m.y. ago) minor amounts of volcanic rocks were deposited, and a number of granitic plutons invaded the Cretaceous rocks of the Methow-Pasayten area.[27] The largest of these is the Golden Horn Batholith which forms the superb climbing at Liberty Bell Mountain. The most spectacular is the Needle Peak Pluton in the Anderson River area. Sparse jointing, massive rock, and glaciation have combined to produce a Yosemite-like topography.

On the lower parts of Jack Mountain the rocks are phyllite, a somewhat fissile (easily split) rock derived from Early Cretaceous rocks of the Methow Graben. The splitting is due to low-grade metamorphism and deformation. The Methow Graben is bounded by faults and there are many faults and folds within it.

Western block: This unit is bounded on the W by a complex fault zone that extends from near the S end of Ross Lake to Hope, B.C. and then a few km E of the Fraser River. W of this zone are the high grade Skagit and Custer gneisses that form the geological core of the North Cascades.

The Fraser Valley N of Hope is eroded along a great fault zone; geological terranes across this zone have been displaced as much as 200 km, on movements that took place about 80 m.y. ago (J.W.H. Monger, 1978).

Most of this western belt is underlain by rocks of the Hozameen Group. These rocks consist largely of argillite, basalt, chert, and minor limestone that probably formed the floor of the ancestral Pacific Ocean about 210 m.y. ago. Faulted into these rocks are bodies of serpentine and other ultramafic rocks that probably form the earth's mantle at a depth of 20 km or more. The western block was faulted against the Methow Graben in Late Cretaceous time (thrust eastward over the younger rocks of the graben). Small intrusions were emplaced along some of the many faults in Late Cretaceous and Early Tertiary time.

Mineralization is widespread in this section, and geologically favorable for occurrence of ore deposits. In the Pasayten Wilderness alone over 605 claims have been recorded since the 1870s.[28] The great concentration of metallic mineral deposits is on the Bonita Creek drainage. The historic Barron gold mine is adjacent to a granitic intrusion (Lower Cretaceous sedimentary rocks within the Methow Graben). Placers in the Ruby Creek-Canyon Creek drainage produced much gold before 1910.

Prospects on the slopes of the glaciated valley of Tungsten Creek have wolframite-bearing quartz veins, but the difficult terrain and scattered ore hindered development of these industrial minerals.[29]

Regional geology contributions were first made by British geologist Hilary Bauerman, who in association with the North West Boundary Survey traversed the sector near the 49th parallel in the summers 1859-1861. In 1901 George Otis Smith and Frank C. Calkins made a geologic reconnaissance from the eastern perimeter of the region to Pasayten River, then to Barron. Reginald A. Daly mapped the Boundary zone and made extensive studies 1901-1906, then interpreted the mountain structure of the broader region in a masterful report for the Canadian Government.

HISTORY

Various early accounts discuss the Okanogan Indian nation, which according to fur trader Alexander Ross had 12 well scattered peaceful tribes. The principal family bore the name *Conconulps,* of which Chief Red Fox was head. The Ross narrative states the chief traveled over the mountains to the Great Salt Lake (the Pacific Ocean) to trade with coastal tribes, using a western course that took about 15 days.[30]

The word Okanogan means "rendezvous" and in various forms was long used by trappers and traders. The Indians of what is now Washington State and British Columbia gathered at various Okanogan locations during potlatches to bring in supplies of fish and game.[31] The important streams of the region all had Indian names, some of which were altered but preserved. The Ross map of 1821 shows the "Sa-milk-a-meigh" River.[32] Some of the first prospectors found certain Indians hostile: one chief, Ashnola John, had scalps hanging in his cabin in the early 1900s.

In an effort by the United States to conciliate with regional tribes, Chief Moses was granted a large reservation W of Okanogan River; under various pressures the reservation was restored to public domain in 1886 and the Indians moved.

The great rivers of the Pacific Northwest guided the pioneer explorers to the fringe of the mountains. It was Lewis and Clark who determined that the Columbia broke through the Cascade Range.

The Fraser was first navigated by heroic men from the North West Company. In 1805 the company assigned Simon Fraser the task of extending operations into the territory explored by Alexander Mackenzie in 1793, and in 1808, Fraser, who still thought the river was the Columbia, undertook his historic mission to explore the river to tidewater in order to prove out a water route to the Pacific Coast and establish British rights to the entire Columbia region. His epic adventure into the unknown Fraser Canyon, and later return up the river, was filled with danger. When canoe travel became impossible, Fraser's party inched their way over narrow ledges and crossed some by means of Indian ladders. Fraser later admitted, "I have been for a long period in the Rocky Mountains, but have never seen anything like this country. It is so wild that I cannot find words . . . "[33]

David Thompson, surveyor and astronomer for the North West Company in 1810 led the expedition that was the first to traverse the upper Columbia regions; on his 1812 map wrote the name of an important river he passed, "Ookenaw-kane."[34]

Fort Okinakane, set up by David Stuart of the Astorians in 1811 at the Columbia-Okanogan junction, became the chief interior post of the Pacific Fur Company and later the North West Company and Hudson's Bay Company.

The history of the region at first was mainly concerned with the fur trade, which began after 1763 in Canada.[35] Fur traders were always seeking new post sites and better routes; for most of the early period the superior organization of the Hudson's Bay Company largely excluded American traders. The traditional annual brigade route from interior forts descended the Okanogan, then the lower Columbia Valley to Fort Vancouver for shipment to England.

But in the early 1840s American immigration over the Oregon Trail rapidly expanded, and after the first emigrant train of covered wagons arrived, the economic and political control the British had enjoyed was seen to be seriously threatened. "To most Americans Oregon, by the 1840's was manifestly destined to become a possession of the United States."[36] Because the fur trade was more lucrative to the N, and because of the pressure of American settlers, the Hudson's Bay Company in 1845 withdrew its headquarters northward 250 mi. to more secure Fort Victoria.

In 1846 locating a brigade route wholly within British territory from the lower Fraser to the southern interior of British Columbia became a dire necessity because of the agreement which established the 49th parallel as a political division. Alexander C. Anderson acted on the order of Chief Factor James Douglas of Vancouver Island to explore routes from the interior to Fort Langley. This scholarly officer was the prime initiator of overland exploration E and S of Hope, through the Cascades, in search of a route to the Thompson River to avoid the difficult Fraser Canyon.[37] The next company explorer to search for a suitable route was Henry Peers, who located a more direct but harder route than Anderson's; in 1849 work began in clearing the new trail.[38] But these were not very practical routes for brigades with their hundreds of heavily laden horses.[39]

In 1847 Anderson made another attempt to find a usable British route over the mountains, partially using an Indian horse trail from Nicola Lake to reach the Fraser below the worst of the canyon.[40] In June 1848 three brigades amalgamated under Chief Trader Donald Manson to follow this rough route to Fort Yale, with disastrous results.[41] By winter Fort Hope was erected as a step to abandon the rough Fraser route and adopt a new path to the interior. Brigades were then sent through the Cascades via the "Fort Hope Trail" to the mouth of the Fraser.

The discovery of placer gold in the early 1850s culminated in the great stampede of 1858, when some 20,000 gold miners poured into the Fraser Valley. In the course of trade with Hudson's Bay factors, 800 oz. collected by Indians was sent to the San Francisco mint on the steamship *Otter* in February 1858.[42] The dramatic news spread like wildfire, and shortly every available ship put out from San Francisco to head N.[43] The first Californians to arrive were immediately rewarded by the discovery of a rich bar (Hill's Bar) just below Fort Yale. By April the rush of thousands was on.[44] Between Hope and Lytton there were over 100 bars where gold was taken out.

During this boom Hope became important, and for all practical purposes was the capital of the country. Until 1858 the greater region had simply been British territory (called New Caledonia), but an Act of Parliament created the Colony of British Columbia and soon James Douglas was appointed governor.[45] As an added accommodation to the entering miners Douglas ordered a trail constructed from the head of Harrison Lake to the interior, to avoid the perilous Fraser Canyon,[46] and the British government in 1860-1861 completed the Dewdney Trail across the Hope Mountains to largely follow Anderson's route into the Similkameen district.[47]

In 1861 Governor Douglas realized that unless immense help was provided to the thousands of gold-seekers along the Fraser Canyon, with supply shortages and winter arriving, a great tragedy could occur. So he ordered his Royal Engineers to build a route to the interior; the result was the spectacular and dangerous 385-mi. Cariboo Road, much of it ledges in the steep escarpment.[48]

The Similkameen River was first found to be gold-bearing in 1853, but did not reach importance until rich placers were discovered in 1859. Hundreds of miners stampeded to the area and caused Okanogan City to mushroom to 3000 persons in its first months.[49] Most of the other attention along the Similkameen was from Princeton to Whipsaw Creek, where both gold and platinum occurred in some quantity. Later, the Tulameen was found to be placer-rich, and Granite Creek became the object of a small stampede.[50] Old towns such as Tulameen, Coalmont, and Granite City are reminders of this era.

Copper ores, carrying gold and silver, were discovered about 1887 near the mouth of Friday Creek. At Copper Mountain, 9 mi. S of Princeton, stocks of plutonic rock contain copper deposits.[51] In this district gold ore was mined at Hedley, bornite and chalcopyrite deposits are mined at Copper Mountain, and there are Tertiary coal measures at Princeton and Coalmont.

Although gold was discovered in the Skagit Valley in 1859, the greater Fraser and Cariboo discoveries quickly captured the attention of most miners. Two pioneers, Jack Rowley and John Sutter, found garnets ("rubies") at the mouth of Ruby Creek in 1872 and logically named the stream. Many miners worked the area, and in 5 years placers had produced an estimated $100,000 in gold.[52] A second rush to the area only prospered one year.[53]

Between 1887 and 1893 the Ruby Creek and Conconully districts were the most active mining centers in Washington. Ruby Creek still had intense activity in the 1890s, but the silver market depression of 1893 and the Klondike Rush of 1897 lured away miners. The most active time was 1894, the year after Alex Barron found the Eureka lode.[54] The mining camp of Barron was established in Eureka Gulch; by 1898 most of the gulch was staked.[55]

A great stimulus to activity came when Col. W.T. Hart built a trail over Slate Pass (later Harts Pass) in 1894-1895, and a wagon road in 1900-1902 from the junction of Methow and Lost rivers to the Bonita Mine. But by the time the road was completed the boom had ended, and Barron was deserted.

Mines in Allen Basin, principally the New Light and Mammoth, produced over $1.5 million in gold and silver from 1900-1942.[56] The New Light Mine, which still has some activity, part of Barron's original Eureka group, has had an estimated $1.2 million in total production since 1896. Although the Ruby boom collapsed in 1907, and even Barron was abandoned, some optimism continued, with new stamp mills being built and extensive workings at the old Anacortes gold mine, on Cascade Creek NW of Chancellor.[57] In summary, the area was heavily prospected for gold, silver, and copper.[58]

The Oregon problem arose from setting northern limits of the imprecisely defined Louisiana Territory. The region between the 42nd parallel and latitude 54°40', extending from the Pacific Ocean to the Rocky Mountains, was originally claimed by Great Britain, Spain, United States, and Russia on the grounds of various explorations and settlement. While Spain and Russia ceded rights to territory and renounced claims, the United States and Great Britain were unwilling to make concessions and each claimed the entire little-known and jointly occupied region in concern.

In the 1840s the British claim to all lands N of the Columbia River was being strongly contested. In an emotional atmosphere James Polk's Democratic presidential campaign platform of 1844 was enlivened by the assertion that the U.S. claim to 54°40' was "clear and unquestionable." The imperative final settlement of the boundary question was finally accomplished by the treaty concluded June 15, 1846 by which both governments agreed to the extension of the boundary line along the 49th parallel from the eastern slope of the Rocky Mountains to the middle of the channel separating the continent from Vancouver Island.[59] The terrain along the line in the Cascades was completely unknown, and even Indian information on drainages proved erroneous.

Even after Lewis and Clark made their historic exploration, various maps presented the Cascade Range and its major rivers with misconception.[60] In Clark's 1809 manuscript the Columbia loses itself in mystery northward, although the legend in this direction is "Okanakan." Until the Pacific Railroad Survey, most of the region had little resemblance to reality on maps, and even afterward, some showed "gold found" on blank spaces near the 49th parallel.

But after this treaty adopted the 410.2-mi. boundary W of the Rocky Mountains, almost 10 years elapsed before any steps were taken to survey and mark the line upon the ground.[61] In the meantime the Territory of Oregon was organized by an Act of Congress in 1848 and the Territory of Washington was organized from its northern portion in 1853. In 1849 Vancouver Island was constituted a British Colony. Gold discoveries increased jurisdictional problems near the 49th parallel.[62]

Such factors and pressures finally combined to implement the ground survey. In 1858 Queen Victoria appointed Captain John S. Hawkins of the Royal Engineers to establish the line boundary with the U.S. Commissioner, Archibald Campbell. John G. Parke, a major in the Corps of Engineers, took charge of the survey for the United States and Captain Robert W. Haig headed the British fieldwork. Hawkins and Haig met with the Americans at Semiahmoo Bay August 18, 1858 and because of the very difficult terrain and resultant great costs agreed to determine points only at convenient and necessary intervals on the boundary.[63] It was agreed that the line should be marked only through settled areas and at prominent stream crossings.[64] The boundary was first determined and marked upon the ground in 1857-1862 by parties selected by the Commissioners representing both governments.[65]

The reconnaissance work of the North West Boundary Survey parties from both nations was based on a system of triangulation points "for which numerous sharply defined peaks gave an excellent opportunity."[66] By the end of the 1858 field season the American survey party had conducted a reconnaissance and made barometric and astronomical observations 90 mi. eastward to the Skagit River,[67] and in 1859 surveying and marking were carried on to the Columbia River. During these first seasons the difficult, unknown, mysterious forested and alpine terrain of the North Cascades presented a most formidable problem. George Gibbs, a special observer attached to the Americans, gives a fair indication of the best contemporary knowledge of the range: from a summit near the upper Skagit River he noted that a "Sea of mountains stretched in every direction as far as the eye could reach . . . . To the south and southwest was the great mass of the Cascade range, Mount Baker being distinct among the rest."[68] During this period, Henry Custer proved to be the most dynamic explorer and interpreter of the mountain landscape, both W and E of the Skagit River.[69]

When the British party arrived from England in 1858, operations unfortunately coincided with the Fraser gold excitement. This event caused immense labor and supply problems, with consequent delays in the survey eastward to Chilliwack Lake. In 1859 Captain Haig and a proportion of Royal Engineers and other men spent months working eastward to the Similkameen, and work in the Pasayten and Ashnola valleys was completed.[70]

The field work of U.S. parties was completed in the 1861 season and that of British parties in 1862, but the computations and map drafting continued until 1866. The cost of surveys and boundary marking had been about $600,000, or $1,463 per mi.[71] The tables of longitudes for monuments and boundary topographic maps were jointly signed at Washington in 1869 by Hawkins and Campbell. But there has never been a complete recovery of all findings of the two commissions, partly because of economy and poor archival custody.[72]

Pioneer surveyors and scientific explorers reported the location and condition of some Indian trails. A.C. Anderson used various Thompson Indian trails in his brigade route explorations, and commented on the fact of a good horse trail from the Fraser Canyon near Anderson River to the Similkameen. The eminent geologist George M. Dawson mentioned some of the routes, including that from Nicola River to Vermilion Forks (Princeton).[73] The old Fort Hope Indian trail followed the E side of Skagit River, but was sometimes abandoned, becoming windfall-littered, when used by prospectors. Jack Rowley, a miner active at Canyon Creek from 1884 to 1902, used "Hidden Hand" camp on this route — now named for him. One of the established trails to be shown on the first government maps was the one along Chewack River.

Many trails were built and improved by miners and surveyors, and in Canada the Dominion Government kept up the Hope Mountains trail, the work of British troops engaged in the Boundary Survey.

Railroad exploration in the Methow Valley began when in 1853 Captain George B. McClellan made an ineffective attempt to find a cross-Cascade route. But James Tilton believed that a good route existed from the head of the Skagit River in British Columbia to Pend O'Reille, although he was uncertain about the mountain crossing.[74] In 1872 Tilton Sheets of the Northern Pacific Railroad ascended the Skagit and tributaries to Harts Pass, and in 1907 the Holman brothers were surveying along the divide northward.

In 1874 Henry Cambie and Joseph Trutch of the Canadian Pacific Railway survey examined branches of the Skagit River for a line, and in this exploration crossed to the South Similkameen via Allison Pass.[75] Under the railway administration of Sir Charles Tupper, the decision was made to build the line through the treacherous Fraser Canyon, despite the fact that the 60-mi. stretch between the canyon's mouth and Thompson River was considered to be the most difficult in the country. Engineer Cambie plotted the line's location in the canyon, which when constructed required 13 tunnels in the first 17 mi. above Yale, and some 600 trestles and bridges in the 127-mi. section Yale to Savona's Ferry near Kamloops. The first government contract was signed with contractor Andrew Onderdonk in 1880, and the project was completed July 1885.[76]

The Kettle Valley Railroad along the Coquihalla River, which had been traversed by Sir Edgar Dewdney to the Tulameen River for the Canadian Pacific Railroad, was not completed until 1916.[77]

Considerable ecological damage was done by various early mountain visitors. Early gold rushers, settlers, prospectors, and herders caused fire devastation, as noted by Martin Gorman in an 1897 timber study, but some of this destruction pre-dated the arrival of white men. In the Chewack River high country, the bighorns of the early 1900s vanished when introduced domestic sheep spread disease.

When the Forest Service began to administer lands designated under the Washington Forest Reserve, the entire mountain region was largely unknown and the only development was by ambitious miners. When the first Forest Service maps were issued in 1913, the only important named peaks W of the Chewack River were Jack, Hozomeen, Castle, Frosty, Robinson, and Monument. The Service inherited the network of prospector-built trails, and in the 1920s and 1930s improved and extended these, and built numerous fire lookouts on peaks and high ridges. The Service had its own corps of surveyors and map-makers, headed in the mid-1920s by the resolute Lage Wernstedt.[78]

The wilderness nature of the greater Pasayten region was protected by the North Cascade Primitive Area (established 1934), and new legislation now has made it the largest roadless area in the Cascade Range. Despite the invasion of some inappropriate roads and the subsequent tourism and continual threat of subdivision development of privately held lands in the mountain forefront, most of the villages in the Methow and adjacent valleys have kept their rustic charm, and a visitation is still an experience in anachronism. One should hope that county and other governmental planners will not permit this to change.

One of the threats to the integrity of the wilderness character of the region is inappropriate development of additional roads or highway access which would detrimentally affect visitor experiences on public lands. It can be anticipated that such an outstanding area will be subject to land development pressures and activities which do not complement the protection of the landscape.

LAND MANAGEMENT
Pasayten Wilderness
The Pasayten Wilderness and eastern portion of Ross Lake National Recreation Area of approximately 900 square mi. extends 54½ mi. along the International Boundary, from Ross Lake to Goodenough Peak. The Wilderness was established by Congress in October 1968, and is administered by Okanogan National Forest. Some mining and grazing is allowed because of prior practices; the Tungsten and Anacortes mines are the only significant mining operations remaining.

Passage of the North Cascades Act establishing North Cascades National Park, the National Recreation Areas, and the Pasayten Wilderness directs that the administrative units be further developed on a coordinated basis.

Manning Provincial Park
The park, wholly in British Columbia, is located 140 mi. E of Vancouver. Highway No. 3 bisects the park, providing motor access. The park was established in 1941 with 176,000 acres and has an administrative center, resort lodge, and a Nature House in the Pine-woods area, several miles E of Allison Pass. About 200 campsites are provided with road access.

Both the Skagit and Similkameen rivers begin within the park. See the Approaches/Trails for specific hiking routes.

Cathedral Provincial Park
This 18,217-acre mountain peak is located in British Columbia between the International Boundary and Highway No. 3, E of Ashnola River.

A 9-mi. jeep road (private) leads to trailheads and a resort at Quiniscoe Lake, where trails lead to a series of picturesque alpine lakes, meadows, and granitic rock formations. The Fish and Wildlife branch of the government manages a band of California bighorn sheep in the Ewart Creek drainage. Ashnola Mountain is noted for game, including mountain sheep. Archduke Francis Ferdinand of Austria and his suite of servants once made a lavish hunting trip here. Resort: Cathedral Lakes Resort, 1333 Balfour St., Penticton. Radiophone: Cathedral Lakes, Hedley Channel — Kamloops radio operator.

Ranger Stations:

Early Winters Visitor Information Center
Highway 20 near Methow Valley Highway
(509) 996-2534

Okanogan National Forest Headquarters
P.O. Box 950
Okanogan, WA 98840
(509) 422-2704

Twisp Ranger Station
Twisp, WA 98856
(509) 997-2131

Winthrop Ranger Station
Winthrop, WA 98862
(509) 996-2266

Tonasket Ranger Station
Tonasket, WA 98855
(509) 486-2186

Conconully Ranger Station
Okanogan, WA 98840
(509) 422-3811

Princeton Ranger Station
Princeton, B.C.
(604) 295-6998

Penticton Ranger Station
Penticton, B.C.
(604) 492-4285

Hope Ranger Station
Hope, B.C.
(604) 869-9961

Boston Bar Ranger Station
Boston Bar, B.C.
(604) 867-9313

Lytton Ranger Station
Lytton, B.C.
(604) 455-2325

Merritt Ranger Station
Merritt, B.C.
(604) 378-4265

Manning Provincial Park
Administrative Building — Highway 3
Write: Parks Branch, 1019 Wharf St.
   Victoria, B.C. V8W 2Y9

NOTE: In Okanogan National Forest, during the summer season, most Ranger Stations issuing Wilderness Permits are open weekends. Permits can be obtained by mail or by telephone for pickup outside station before or after business hours.

MAPS

Washington State Maps

U.S. Geological Survey (topographic)

Concrete (1955)	1:250,000
Doe Mountain (1963)	1:62,500
Horseshoe Basin (1956)	1:62,500
Mazama (1962)	1:62,500
Loomis (1956)	1:62,500
Ashnola Mountain (1969)	1:24,000
Ashnola Pass (1969)	1:24,000
Azurite Peak (1963)	1:24,000
Bauerman Ridge (1969)	1:24,000
Billy Goat Mountain (1969)	1:24,000
Coleman Peak (1969)	1:24,000
Crater Mountain (1963)	1:24,000
Castle Peak (1969)	1:24,000
Frosty Creek (1969)	1:24,000
Hozomeen Mountain (1969)	1:24,000
Lost Peak (1969)	1:24,000
Mt. Barney (1969)	1:24,000
Mt. Lago (1969)	1:24,000
Jack Mountain (1969)	1:24,000
Pumpkin Mountain (1969)	1:24,000
Pasayten Creek (1969)	1:24,000
Remmel Mountain (1969)	1:24,000
Robinson Mountain (1963)	1:24,000
Ross Dam (1963)	1:24,000
Shull Mountain (1969)	1:24,000
Skagit Peak (1969)	1:24,000
Slate Peak (1969)	1:24,000
Tatoosh Buttes (1969)	1:24,000
Robinson Mountain (1976)	1:100,000 metric
North Cascades National Park (1974)	1:100,000 metric
Okanogan National Forest — U.S. Forest Service	(planimetric)
Pasayten Wilderness Area (1978)	1:100,000 metric

(available from all Okanogan National Forest offices for small fee)

Province of British Columbia Maps

Federal topographic maps use the National Topographic System, a series designed to cover Canada in a regular manner using lines of latitude and longitude for the borders. All maps for areas peripheral to Washington State are on Index 2. These maps are printed in color, at varying scales: 1:25,000, 1:50,000, 1:250,000, 1:500,000 and 1:1,000,000.

Maps may be ordered by mail from: Geological Survey of Canada, Information Services, 6th floor, 100 West Pender St., Vancouver, B.C. V6B 1R8 (phone — 604/666-1271). Orders should state area (refer to Index 2 for scale and corresponding N.T.S. number). Correct payment must be made in advance; checks or money orders made payable to the Receiver General of Canada in Canadian funds. Price: $1.50 per sheet. Office open to public Monday to Friday, 9:00 AM to 4:15 PM.

Note: In the area covered by this guidebook, the Manning Park, Keremeos, and Ashnola maps are still produced in E and W halves of 15 minutes longitude each. They will be replaced by larger single sheets covering 30 minutes of longitude.

Provincial topographic maps, also based on the N.T.S., cover the province, but on scales of 1:125,000 and 1:126,720; maps are being phased to metric. Maps may be ordered by mail: Map and Air Photo Sales, Surveys and Mapping Branch, Ministry of the Environment, Parliament Buildings, Victoria, B.C. V8V 1X4 phone: 604/387-3174, or 387-3175. Enclose price of maps with order, adding 5% sales tax for orders within British Columbia (no tax if ordered from U.S.). Make payment to: Minister of Finance. Price: $2.00 per copy (add $1.00 total for maps sent in roll). Provincial maps may be purchased directly in Vancouver (800 Hornby St.), New Westminster (403-6th St.), Chilliwack, and Princeton.

Vertical air photos of terrain are available from the Victoria office. Index maps show flight lines, scales, and photo numbering. Prints can be purchased.

In British Columbia forestry maps are not available at ranger (field) stations.

British Columbia — Federal maps
Victoria-Vancouver 92 SE (1973)   1:500,000
Hope 92-H (1970)   1:250,000
 (120°00' to 122°00' and
 49°00' to 50°00')   (approx. 1"=4 mi.)
Penticton 82-E (1967)   1:250,000
 (Okanagan River west to
 120°00' and 49°00' to 50°00')
Ashcroft 92-I (1962)   1:250,000
 (120°00' to 122°00' and
 50°00' to 51°00')

Keremeos 82 E/4 West (1968)   1:50,000
 (119°45' to 120°00' and
 49°00' to 49°15')
Ashnola River 92 H/1 (1979)   1:50,000
 (120°00' to 120°30' and
 49°00' to 49°15')
Hedley 92 H/8 (1968)   1:50,000
 (120°00' to 120°30' and
 49°15' to 49°30')
Princeton 92 H/7 (1968)   1:50,000
 (120°30' to 121°00' and
 49°15' to 49°30')
Manning Park 92 H/2 East (1960)   1:50,000
 (120°30' to 120°45' and
 49°00' to 49°15')
Manning Park 92 H/2 West (1960)   1:50,000
 (120°45' to 121°00' and
 49°00' to 49°15')
Skagit River 92 H/3 (1975)   1:50,000
 (121°00' to 121°30' and
 49°00' to 49°15')   (approx. 1"=1 mi.)
Hope 92 H/6 (1976)   1:50,000
 (121°00' to 121°30' and
 49°15' to 49°30')
Spuzzum 92 H/11 (1976)   1:50,000
 (121°00' to 121°30' and
 49°30' to 49°45')
Boston Bar 92 H/14 (1976)   1:50,000
 (121°00' to 121°30' and
 49°45' to 50°00')
Prospect Creek 92 I/3 (1976)   1:50,000
 (121°00' to 121°30' and
 50°00' to 50°15')
Tulameen 92 H/10 (1968)   1:50,000
 (120°30' to 121°00' and
 49°30' to 49°45')

British Columbia — Provincial maps
Penticton 82 E/SW (1973)   1:125,000
 (119°00' to 120°00' and
 49°00' to 49°30')   (approx. 1"=2 mi.)
Princeton 92 H/SE (1969)   1:126,720
 (120°00' to 121°00' and
 49°00' to 49°30')
Tulameen 92 H/NE (1969)   1:126,720
 (120°00' to 121°00' and
 49°30' to 50°00')
Yale 92 H/NW (1976)   1:125,000 metric
 (121°00' to 122°00' and
 49°30' to 50°00')

Lytton 92 I/SW (1968)   1:126,720
    (121°00′ to 122°00′ and
    50°00′ to 50°30′)

Chilliwack Lake 92 H/SW (1972)   1:126,720
    (121°00′ to 122°00′ and
    49°00′ to 49°30′)

Selected References:

Baker, Marcus. "Survey of the Northwestern Boundary of the United States, 1857-61." *U.S. Geol. Survey, Bull. 174* (Washington, 1900), 78 pp.

Beautiful British Columbia, Winter 1975, pp. 11-17 (Manning Provincial Park).

Beautiful British Columbia, Fall 1969 (Cathedral Provincial Park).

Coates, J.A., "Geology of the Manning Park Area, British Columbia," *Canada Geol. Survey, Bull. 238* (1974).

Culbert, Dick. *Alpine Guide to Southwestern British Columbia,* Vancouver, 1974.

Daly, R.A. "Geology of the North American Cordillera at the Forty-ninth Parallel." *Canada Geol. Survey, Memoir 38,* pt. 2 (Ottawa, 1912), pp. 547-857.

Duffell, S., and K.C. McTaggart, "Ashcroft Map Area, British Columbia," *Geol. Survey Canada, Memoir 262* (1951).

Harcombe, Andrew, and Robert Cyca, *Exploring Manning Park,* Seattle and Vancouver, 1979.

Huntting, M.T. "Gold in Washington." *Wash. Div. Mines and Geology, Bull. 42* (1956), 158 pp.

Hessey, Charles D. "Across the North Cascade Primitive Area." *Living Wilderness* 25, no. 74 (1960-61): 5-9.

Holland, Stuart S. "Landforms of British Columbia." B.C. Department Mines and Petroleum Resources, 1976.

International Boundary Commission, "Joint Report upon the Survey and Demarcation of the Boundary between the United States and Canada from the Gulf of Georgia to the Northwesternmost Point of Lake of the Woods," Washington, 1937.

McTaggert, K.C., and R.M. Thompson. "Geology of part of the northern Cascades in southern British Columbia." *Canadian Jour. Earth Sci.* 4 (1967): 1199-1228.

Misch, Peter. "Geology of the Northern Cascades of Washington." *Mountaineer* 45 (1952): 4-22.

Smith, G.O., and F.C. Calkins. "A geological reconnaissance across the Cascade Range near the forty-ninth parallel." *U.S. Geol. Survey, Bull. 235* (1904), 103 pp.

Spring, Ira, and Harvey Manning. *101 Hikes in the North Cascades,* Seattle, 1979.

Staatz, M.H., et al. "Mineral Resources of the Pasayten Wilderness Area, Washington." *U.S. Geol. Survey, Bull. 1325* (Washington, 1971), 255 pp.

Tabor, R.W., J.C. Engels, and M.H. Staatz. "Quartz diorite-quartz monzonite and granite plutons of the Pasayten River area, Washington — Petrology, Age, and Emplacement." *U.S. Geol. Survey Prof. Paper 600-C* (Washington, 1968): c45-C52).

CRATER MOUNTAIN   8128 ft/2477 m

Crater is a craggy rock peak with an extensive slope glacier, about 3 mi. SE of Jack Mountain and on the rim of the long slope N of Canyon Creek. Crater's W peak is by far the higher of two summits; the E peak (7555 ft/2302 m) is ½ mi. distant. The exposed rocks on Crater are volcanics. The Jerry Glacier (7400 ft-6400 ft) nearly fills the high cirque NE of the true summit, and Jerry Lakes (near 5900 ft) are quite hidden from view in the basin N of the glacier.

The highest fire lookout in the area was sheltered in a tent on the true summit in 1929, then in a house built 1931-32; a tramway with wooden supports was used to hoist materials from the end of the horse trail. The lower lookout was built in 1938. The new lookout is on a 7054-ft spur 1 mi. E of the true summit.
ROUTE: Use McMillan Park-Jackita Ridge Trail◆. From Crater Lake take the subalpine meadow spur leading to the final southern rock spur of the summit. Several hundred ft of moderately steep rock complete the ascent (7½ mi. total). The E peak is best hiked and scrambled on its SE side.

JACK MOUNTAIN   9066 ft/2763 m

Jack is the dominant summit in this section, a massive uplift located N of Ruby Arm and E of Ross Lake. One of the 10 non-volcanic peaks in Washington State over 9000 ft, its expansive bulk highlights the eastern portion of the North Cascades, rising 7450 ft in 3 mi. on the Ross Lake flank. The true summit is on the NE portion of the massif (the SW summit is 8905 ft). The mountain's entire northern flank is engulfed in cirque glaciers: the Nohokomeen Glacier on the May Creek (NW) flank extends from 8600 ft to 5480 ft, is ¾ mi. in width at its apex and 1.3 mi. in length; a short steep rock wall stands above the wide final bergschrund and continues to the E-W summit ridge. Another important glacier, quite narrow and dramatic, extends on the flank of the mountain from about 8850 ft to 5400

to trail

JERRY GLACIER

Jerry Lakes →

CRATER MOUNTAIN from northwest
AUSTIN POST, U.S. GEOLOGICAL SURVEY

ft, draining to a NE branch of Devils Creek. But for the fact Jack is in the rain shadow of the Picket Range, glaciers would be even larger. Conspicuous, sharp moraine and hummocky cover of ground moraine extends below glaciers into partly tree-covered talus and heather slopes.

The mountain and its surroundings consist largely of a thick sequence of highly sheared and fractured Paleozoic greenstones (the same volcanic rocks of Hozomeen Mountain). Some geologists believe these rocks were thrust eastward over younger Cretaceous sedimentary rocks, exposed beneath the greenstone in Canyon Creek to the S. The Ross Lake fault zone borders Jack Mountain on the W.

The Indians called the mountain "Hokomokeen." The first description is that of topographer Henry Custer on August 2, 1859: "Hokomokeen rises its broad and bulky summit far up in the air." Custer also

called it "High Skagit Mountain." The Smith and Calkins reconnaissance map, which showed the mountain's glaciers, marked the feature as "Mt. Nokomokeen." The geologists estimated this mountain (and Hozomeen) "probably reach an elevation of 9000 feet, command attention from whatever side they are seen." The North West Boundary Map (1866) shows the mountain as "Skome-kah" (possibly meant to be "Skó-me-kan" or "Skonte-kan."

Indians once followed a trail high on the S slope to hunt goats and pick berries, and in 1916 cattle grazed on the mountain's lower slopes. The name Jack honors Jack Rowley, a leading gold prospector of the Ruby Creek district from 1884 to 1902. The first ascent was made by Edward C. Barnard and party in 1904; Barnard was a U.S. Geological Survey topographer assigned to the North West Boundary Survey (see Hozomeen Mountain for party name listing). The

JACK MOUNTAIN from northwest
AUSTIN POST, U.S. GEOLOGICAL SURVEY

notch

North Ridge

Southwest Ridge

NOHOKOMEEN GLACIER

surveyors placed a wooden triangulation station on the summit. Likely W.A. Reaburn was a party member (he told Glee Davis that Jack Mountain was the hardest of his climbs). Forest Farr and William Degenhardt made the ascent in July 1930. References: *Mountaineer,* 1931, pp. 33-35; 1952, p. 9.

ROUTE: Jack Mountain Trail♦ ends at about 6000 ft on the ridge W of Crater Creek. Hike to Little Jack Mountain (camping) and traverse the ridge to a notch 1.8 mi. SW of the summit (6080 ft+; camping). Ascend a short ridge step, then bear downhill (NE) along the cliff base. Continue to bear right, where a descent around a buttress is made. Pass the waterfalls above Crater Creek by skirting a cliff. Con-

tinue the traverse to a major gully that is directly beneath the summit (it is narrow at first, then broadens). Reach the summit ridge just W or E of the true summit; the E route is class 4 for one pitch and the W finish is scrambling. Time: 6 hours from Little Jack. Take ice axes and prepare for steep snow in early season.

Variations: Many variations have been done along the ridge, but these are longer, with much scrambling and loss of altitude. Some parties have begun the ascent sooner and kept rightward up steep heather to near the summit area.

NORTH RIDGE: This feature of the mountain begins as a lower northwestern shoulder between Devils and May creeks, then trends S to flank the Nohokomeen Glacier on its

JACK MOUNTAIN from east
AUSTIN POST, U.S. GEOLOGICAL SURVEY

W. While the climb has been reported as an attractive route with splendid scenery, the initial cross-country ascent is long and arduous. First ascent by Joe Vance and Bill Weitkamp on August 1, 1971.

From Devils Creek (see Ross Lake◆) climb wooded rocky slopes and light brush to the crest of the long NW shoulder. A black pinnacle (6937 ft) NE of the glacier snout is passed on the S by ascending a subsidiary point; descend 200 ft and climb sloping talus ledges past a natural arch. At the 7100-ft level leave the ridge briefly to avoid a notch; the ridge sharpens at 8200 ft but involves only easy scrambling to near the base of the 150-ft summit tower. Make an exposed, steep snow traverse above the upper NE face to the craggy E corner of the rock summit block. Class 4 moves and some scrambling soon lead to the summit; this section can begin on a broken crest, and some parties have climbed an 80-ft gully. Grade II; class 4. Time: 6 hours from ponds at 5700 ft on the shoulder. Reference: *Mountaineer*, 1972, p. 87.

Variation: By Mike Bialos, Bette Felton, Dick Kegel, and Russ Kroeker on Memorial Day weekend, 1976. Leave Ross Lake East Bank Trail◆ at May Creek, then ascend, keeping S of a seasonal May Creek tributary. Ascend through

or around occasional cliff bands, to reach the NW shoulder at about 5000 ft. Make a gradually rising traverse to the glacier's terminal moraine, then ascend the glacier to 8000 ft. Climb the moderately steep snow slope of the ridge headwall to the obvious notch (8200 ft) on the true N ridge. Early summer is the recommended season to do this climb. Time: 12 hours r.t. from 5000-ft camp. Reference: *Mountaineer*, 1977, p. 73.

NORTHEAST GLACIER: This glacier has narrow chaotic portions, and probably is only feasible in early summer. Beware of windslab danger (a large section of surface had broken beneath the summit prior to original ascent). First ascent by Fred Beckey, Dallas Kloke, and Reed Tindall on July 19, 1978.

From upper basin of Crater Creek (see South Face route) ascend moraine and snow slopes to the serrated rock col E of the mountain's Southeast Ridge. The only suitable crossing is somewhat W of the low portion of the col. Descend steep broken rock and snow gullies about 250 ft onto the glacier. Traverse to the narrow N portion and hope there is a route through. The original party later left the ice and ascended snow and rock of the right-flanking buttress, then traversed

ILLOCK
UNTAIN   WHITWORTH   MT. RIDEOUT   SILVERTIP   MT. OUTRAM   HOZOMEEN MOUNTAIN
             PEAK   MOUNTAIN
T.   North Peak   South Peak
BURN

Little Jackass Mountain

                                                                                   DESOLATION PEAK

Little Beaver Creek

        Ross Lake   Lightning Creek

ROSS LAKE from south
U.S. FOREST SERVICE

back on the ice to cross to the final SE summit notch.
Complete as per North Ridge. Time: 6 hours. Reference:
A.A.J., 1979, p. 184.

SOUTHEAST RIDGE: First ascent by John Anderson and
Alan Kearney in August 1977. Approach as for South Face
route. Climb obvious class 3 and 4 rock on crest to a rotten
headwall. Traverse left and up a broad gully for one and a half

leads to gain the crest again. A pitch through loose flakes
gets one over the difficulties. Several more pitches on the
crest lead to the false summit. Beyond a notch at the head of
the NE glacier two final short pitches lead to the summit.
Grade III; class 5.6. Time: 4-5 hours of rock climbing with
considerable class 3 and 4. Recommend hard hats.

SOUTH FACE: This is a good summit route. The final

portion may coincide with one of the earlier routes from the SW. Approach via Crater Mountain Trail and Jerry Lakes, then cross the intervening divide into upper Crater Creek basin. See McMillan Park-Jackita Ridge Trail♦. Note: From Jerry Glacier one can save altitude loss by finding a ramp beyond the first series of cliffs; this and a scramble lead to the N ridge of Crater. Follow and descend to the lower area of the ridge above Jerry Lakes; camping at the lakes or in upper Crater Creek.

Ascend the spur of Jack below the Southeast Ridge, then traverse scree and snow W to beyond a cliff band. Take moderately steep gullies (snow until late summer) to the summit ridge just W of the summit. Time: 6 hours from lakes.

JACKITA PEAK   7350 ft/2240 m

A small pyramidal rock summit 1.2 mi. SW of Anacortes Crossing, this peak is the highest on Jackita Ridge and the high point of the N-S divide between upper Devils and Canyon creeks. The ridge also has lesser S and NE summits. An ascent was made by the U.S. Coast and Geodetic Survey in 1926.

ROUTE: Use McMillan Park-Jackita Ridge Trail♦, which reaches to W of the summit; the completion is not difficult.

POINT 7270 is just SE of Devils Pass, the highest of small peaklets NW of Anacortes Crossing; the W slope is gentle.

SKAGIT PEAK   6800 ft+/2073 m+

This is more of an E-W ridge form than a peak, located E of Lightning Creek opposite Desolation Peak; the highest point is near the center of the ridge.

ROUTE: Hike the long W slope from Lightning Creek Trail♦ or the S slope from Three Fools Creek.

DESOLATION PEAK   6102 ft/1860 m

Located 2.5 mi. N of the mouth of Lightning Creek, E of Ross Lake. Desolation is a long N-S ridge, with long slopes on the Ross and Lightning flanks.

ROUTE: See Desolation Peak Trail♦. Distance from Lightning Creek to the summit is 5.1 mi. (all uphill). Desolation can also be reached on a long trek from Jackass Pass Trail♦. Ascend SW onto the divide and follow it S.

HOZOMEEN MOUNTAIN
8066 ft/2459 m

The remarkable double summit of Hozomeen, closely E of upper Ross Lake and S of the International Boundary, is one of the classic landmarks of the North Cascades. Though not of regionally outstanding height, the solitary location, vast local relief, and steeply pitched walls of the massive and spectacular summits, make the mountain unforgettable. Early scientists and surveyors all were awed by the mountain's mystique: Reginald A. Daly commented on "the nearly or quite inaccessible horn" of the South Peak. George Gibbs wrote "Hozumeen," which he saw from near the head of the Maselpanik. Gibbs' sketches of 1859 artistically depict Hozomeen, Jack, and other peaks to the S. Hilary Bauerman beheld the mountain at a distance. In his Report of Progress, he noted the remarkable peaks rise "to a height of about 1800 feet above the watershed. They are called by the Indians 'Hozameen'." Henry Custer, on the first Boundary Survey in 1859, had hoped to make the ascent, but was frustrated by clouds and smoke, as the "long and maybe dangerous ascent . . . would be useless." The official spelling of the survey was Hó-zo-meen.

The massive greenstone (metamorphosed basalt) of Hozomeen's summits rises with startling abruptness above the deep, tree-clad glacial canyons. These Paleozoic rocks extend from the major fault on the eastern flank of Hozomeen to the alluvium of Ross Lake (Skagit River.)[79] Hozomeen Ridge is composed of a sequence of greenstone with minor quartzite, argillite, and marble. Differences in composition and texture of the lava layers are emphasized in the weathering of the dark green cliffs.

The North Peak (the highest summit) has very long, precipitous walls on its S and W; its NE flank shelters several small ice patches in high cirques (the ice descends to 6200 ft). The col between the North and South Peaks is a ragged high gap (6497 ft). Near here the sheer walls of the South Peak rise in a spectacular manner to its over-8000-ft summit, and drop to 2800 ft to Lightning Creek in an abrupt mi. The adjoining Southwest Peak (7471 ft) and numerous crags and complex spur ridges adjoin the main peaks.

A station mark of the International Boundary Survey was set in a drill hole in solid rock by the Barnard party in 1904 "on the highest of the high rocky peaks of the Hozomeen Range" (North Peak). The field party included Edward C. Barnard, J.P. Breckenridge, J.G. Hefty, D.L. Reaburn, W.B. Reaburn, Thomas Riggs Jr., Sledge Tatum, and G.H. Wheeler. The ascent may have been done three times (per Glee Davis interview). References: Bauerman, note 2; Daly, pt. 1, p. 501; note 13.

NORTH PEAK   8066 ft/2459 m

NORTHEAST ROUTE: From the Silver-Skagit Road♦ one can ascend the border swath clearing, then bear right into forest to cross the divide into the basin NE of the summit. The swath is becoming overgrown, and most of the path here is left or right of the actual swath; keep to its right above 4000 ft to be in a position to follow the stream that

NORTH PEAK South Ridge

SOUTHWEST PEAK

SOUTH PEAK

Southwest Face

Southeast Route

West Ridge

from Hozomeen Lake

HOZOMEEN MOUNTAIN from southwest
DICK CULBERT

descends from the 6350-ft col N of the North Peak (a variation would be to leave the road about 1 mi. N of the Boundary, then ascend indistinct forested ridges to the open terrain and ridge trending NW of the objective). Traverse S into snow basins and cross some small snow/ice patches on the NE face. A steep snow slope provides access to 800-900 ft of class 4 rock below summit. Time: 7 hours. Reference: *B.C.M.,* July 1957.

Variation (Northeast Buttress): This climb is possibly slightly more difficult, but the rock is sounder. To reach the buttress from the basin turn E below the last northern slope and gain easy access; keep on the N side of the ridge to a level area. Then ascend easier scree and grass to within 500 ft of the summit. Here the climbing becomes steeper; turn right and ascend easy rock back to the ridge crest.

Approach Variation: The prominent timbered ridge visible from the road at 1½-2 mi. N of the border gives direct

access to the high bare summit N of the peak. First cross a long flat and travel the S bank of the stream which drains the basin "behind" the ridge. Near its foot cross to the N bank and find good travel. Re-cross the stream at 3500 ft and gain heavy timber of the "correct" ridge. At timberline a knoll is reached, then some ridge humps. Bear S across the head of a small snow basin to reach the main N-S ridge.

Approach Variation: From Camp Mowich on Skyline Trail♦ hike W to the first divide. Turn S toward Hozomeen; at 2 mi. is an open shoulder (camping, but water scarce in late season). Take a path over a steep knoll to Monument 74 (or traverse on E). On the northern edge of the Hozomeen basin, just below the crest, bear to the NE face. Time: 6 hours from Camp Mowich.

SOUTH RIDGE: Traverse N and ascend directly from Hozomeen Lake (Jackass Pass Trail♦). Ascend the gully immediately NW of the Southwest Peak, and at timberline

HOZOMEEN MOUNTAIN from east
M.H. STAATZ, U.S. GEOLOGICAL SURVEY

or in the basin higher, cross left to a gully leading to the high col between the main North Peak and the ragged crags on its South Ridge. When snow melts on this approach to the ridge, some loose rock is exposed. Then ascend the upper South Ridge; keep left of pinnacles. Class 4. Time: long day.

SOUTHWEST FACE: First ascent by Dick Culbert and Alice Purdey Culbert in August 1968. The ascent begins beyond Hozomeen Lake and climbs to the base of the walls at about 5000 ft (3 hours). One can turn the first cliffs on the divide of the NW nose and avoid difficulties to the 5500-ft level. Climb left into a chimney; in a steep area which has bulges above, a final cave pitch takes three placements for aid. The original party bivouacked on a big ledge above, which cuts under the largest of cliff bands at about 6000 ft (band about 800 ft in height and yellow-green in hue). The major wall is turned by five leads of climbing: climb a gully, then the right fork (much class 5). On top reach the great nose which displays the "Untouchable Towers." Traverse easy slabs to right around this group, then up the gully against the face to the gap behind the highest (now 600 ft below summit). After two class 4 leads up the nose traverse left into a gully which leads to the South Ridge one pitch beneath the summit. Grade IV; class 5.6 and A2. References: *B.C.M.*, January 1969; *C.A.J.*, 1969, p. 81.

SOUTH PEAK   8003 ft/2439 m

First ascent by Fred Beckey, Jerry O'Neil, Ken Prestrud, Herb Staley, and Charles Welsh on May 30, 1947. The ascent was not done again until ten years later by a B.C. Mountaineering Club group.

ROUTE: Original route. Take Jackass Pass Trail♦ and branch to Hozomeen Lake. Bypass the lake, then traverse NE, and turn E up the main gully between the North and South peaks. The ascent is somewhat loose and tedious but not difficult. Near the top of the gully climb a face via snow or ledge series to the central col between the S and Southwest peaks (5 hours). Climb E to the top of a steep rock buttress, descend to the gully on the E, and make a long gradually descending ledge traverse beneath the S wall of South Peak. At a snow basin ascend along its edge.

Note: Because of the length of the climb, it may be well to camp at about 6400 ft below the col between the South and Southwest peaks. The climb should be done in early season to assure running water.

Moderate scrambling up scree-plastered slabs leads to the main ridge of the South Peak (a sloping ledge is part of route). The continuing route is near the crest, where the opposite W wall overhangs. There is one brief tricky move (5.6). Time: 14 hours r.t. *Descent:* from fixed piton. References: *Mountaineer,* 1947, p. 51; *C.A.J.,* 1944, pp. 160-61; 1948, pp. 105-9; *A.A.J.,* 1948, pp. 15-18; *B.C.M.,* October 1957, December 1965, April 1975.

Approach Variation: From Willow Lake climb to the left (W) of the gully which descends from the col between the South and Southwest peaks. Later move E into gully. This approach route is bushy, but avoids the loose class 4 pitch on the Southwest Peak (however it is less recommended than the Hozomeen Lake approach). Meet the original South Peak route in the col (6920 ft+). Some parties have ascended the ridge from Hozomeen Lake to near the summit of the Southwest Peak, and here met the rock pitch; one can then traverse easily around or over the Southwest Peak's summit to the col. Time: 5-6 hours to col.

Scramble E from the col over a minor knot and descend a steep slabby gully. Traverse under the buttress of a lesser South Peak crag (may need to descend some until feasible to traverse onto main S face). Drop beside gully until able to cross.

NORTH RIDGE: This route is a long, exposed rock climb (some loose rock) done on a 3-day traverse by Fred Douglas and Paul Starr on Labor Day weekend, 1974. The original party crossed the central Hozomeen col from Hozomeen Lake and made a bivouac about 500 ft down the eastern basin. One brushy pitch traverses onto the long ridge, which provides variable climbing (5.4 maximum, but hard to protect). Grade IV. Time: 6-8 hours on rock (ascent).

SOUTHWEST PEAK 7471 ft/2277 m

This peak has not much relief above the saddle adjacent to the South Peak and is most easily reached from there. First ascent by John Dudra and Howard Rode in 1951.

SOUTHEAST ROUTE: This is the original route (not technical). Reach the col due N of Willow Lake per description for South Peak.

SOUTH RIDGE: By Dick Culbert, Gary Johncox, and Bill Sharpe in 1958. Ascend the ridge adjacent to Hozomeen Lake camp to the summit. This is a long climb with considerable scrambling, and includes one lead of class 4-5 on loose rock.

WEST RIDGE: By Juergen Oswald, Gernot Walter, and Edmund Zenger on July 26, 1969. This is the ridge-buttress which one sees from Hozomeen Lake (it descends the left flank of the Southwest Peak). From near the lake ascend a creek gorge toward objective, and pass well beyond the buttress toe. Above the first steep portion bear onto its crest by a ramp on the N face; this is the prominent ledge which rises above the first steep portion of the West Ridge (class 3). The first lead above is hardest, then follow the ridge to the

peak. Rock is fairly sound (class 4 to 5.5). Time: 2 hours lake to ledge, then 5 hours to summit.

NEPOPEKUM MOUNTAIN (B.C.)
6357 ft/1938 m

This is a small peak on the Skagit River divide near the western boundary of Manning Park. Sketches by George Gibbs made in 1859 on the Boundary Survey were done from the divide just S of the summit; members of this first survey certainly ascended to the summit. Station "Lightning" here was occupied by the 1905 U.S. survey, which described the mountain as round and nearly bald. Map: Skagit River 92 H/3.
ROUTE: Reach from Skyline Trail♦ (on divide S of summit). Hike NW to the summit — a fine viewpoint. Reference: *C.A.J.,* 1979, pp. 29-30 (winter).

SHAWATUM MOUNTAIN (B.C.)
7081 ft/2158 m

A prominent, gently sloped mountain with a double summit, on the Skagit River slope at the western border of Manning Park; relief from the valley is about 5400 ft. The West Peak is higher; the East Peak is a narrow crest circling NE, with a N-facing cirque between the summits.

Because the summit was used by the first Boundary Survey for extensive triangulation, Shawatum is of historical interest. While on a reconnaissance Henry Custer apparently made the first climb on either September 1, or earlier, 1859. A sketch made by George Gibbs dated August 8 from "Gardner's Station" gives the legend regarding Custer's occupation. The other station appears to be from the minor 6100-ft summit on the ridge to the NE.

Shawatum was shown on George M. Dawson's 1887 map, but has also been known as Steamboat and Lost Musket. In 1910 there was an ill-advised report of rich gold ores on the mountain, resulting in a brief stampede. Some 1200 mineral locations were made by spring and the townsite Steamboat was built, with stores and a hotel.[80] References: *B.C.M.,* September 1965; *C.A.J.,* 1970, p. 29 (winter). Map: Skagit River 92 H/3.
ROUTES: One can hike the spur road from Silver-Skagit Road♦ into upper Shawatum Creek; cross to the S side of the valley and ascend the forested NW ridge. One could also complete the climb from the NE from farther up valley. An approach from Manning Park is merely a hike, but quite long.

East Peak. First ascent of route, Keith Keats and Howard Rode April 19, 1951. Via the col between the summits (class 3-4); one can descend directly from the higher summit, then climb upwards or traverse around the S side.

MT. BRICE (B.C.)   7099 ft/2164 m

Brice is a middle-altitude summit 3 mi. N of Shawatum Mountain, between Twentysix and Twentyeight Mile creeks, and SE of Skagit River. The mountain is steep on the N but moderate on the S slope; the area is generally meadowy and pleasant. Map: Skagit River 92 H/3.

ROUTE: This is an easy trip via Shawatum Creek Road (see Shawatum Mountain).

HATCHETHEAD MOUNTAIN (B.C.)   6391 ft/1947 m

This is a lesser summit E of Skagit River, NNE of Mt. Brice. The mountain is of no climbing interest, but the Twin Moles, a striking rock crag, can be seen from the highway. The W slopes of the mountain were once hit by a major fire. Map: Skagit River 92 H/3.

ROUTE: Ascend from spur road up S ridge of Silverdaisy Mountain. Another spur leads S to col at 5500 ft in next divide. Then another spur leads into the head of Silverdaisy Creek. Gain Hatchethead from here; the SE ridge is a hike.

Twin Moles (est. 5500 ft/1676 m and 5700 ft/1737 m) is a double rock pinnacle on the W ridge of Hatchethead; the E pinnacle is higher. First ascent by John Dudra and Howard Rode in August 1965.

Hike via spur road and Skagit River Trail from the highway almost to Twentysix Mile Creek (est. 2½ mi.). Ascend E through bluffs and steep timber on the snout of Hatchethead's W ridge; one party approached by a central gully.

The E Mole is one class-4 lead on either the S face or W rib; a rappel bolt is atop. The W Mole is harder: make a short traverse from between the pinnacles to the S face gully; 40 ft of loose rock to the top. The gullies SW to Twentysix Mile Creek are scree and offer a good descent (old mine path here). Reference: *B.C.M., August 1965.*

SILVERDAISY MOUNTAIN (B.C.)   6700 ft+/2042 m+

Located 3 mi. SE of the Skagit-Sumallo River junction and S of the Hope-Princeton Hwy. Map: Skagit River 92 H/3.

ROUTE: Leave Trans-Canada Hwy 3♦ 28 mi. from Hope, just before Skaist River bridge. Hike the Giant Mascot Mine roadway (gated), SW to the col at the head of Silverdaisy Creek (5700 ft+). A spur leads to the mountain's S ridge to 6300 ft for an easy completion. Total distance: 3½ mi. An alternative route to the col is Silverdaisy Creek Trail♦.

FROSTY MOUNTAIN (B.C.)   est. 7950 ft/2423 m

Frosty is a dominant summit in the area N of the International Boundary, 1¼ mi. NE of Monument 77, and 5 mi. SW of Manning Park Lodge (on Castle-Lightning Creek divide). The SW peak is highest, with the E peak and the N peak shown as 7900 ft+. Frosty is in the Dewdney Creek group of volcanics and sediments, at the edge of the Castle Peak stock intrusion. The highest peak was visited by E.C. Barnard's 1904 survey party. Reference: *B.C.M.,* December 1960. Map: Manning Park 92 H/2 West.

ROUTES: About 5 mi. along Frosty Trail (see Windy Joe Mountain Trail♦) reach the meadowed area of Frosty's NE ridge. Continue upridge to the E peak, then scramble to the higher summit; long day r.t.

A new trail has been built to the mountain from Lightning Lakes. Begin at the dam and take Frosty Mountain Loop, which leads up the NNE ridge (this is a shorter route; one can make a circle tour).

CASTLE PEAK   8306 ft/2352 m

Castle is a regionally prominent peak located on the Castle-Freezout Creek divide 1½ mi. S of the International Boundary. The peak is within the largest intrusive mass exposed in its region.[81] The Castle massif was one of the centers of ice dispersal during heavy glaciation of the Hozomeen Range, and here valley glaciers moved out from a central icecap.

The broad North Face begins to steepen at 7000 ft. This impressive granitic face is made prominent by the presence of three buttresses, numerous ribs, and five crevassed ice remnants, one of which nearly extends to the W summit ridge as a glacier arm. There are prominent 18th century moraines below the ice (which ends at 6400 ft) and this till nearly extends to the larch groves at the saddle separating the basins N of the summit. Below the glacier sections are concentric fresh sections of terminal moraine which show the most recent advances and older successive stands of the glaciers. Recent glaciation of the basins has hindered tree growth, which is seen much higher on flanking ridges. Along the edge of the E-W Castle Peak ridge the contrast between the precipitous, recently glaciated North Face and the gentle, even-sloped S side is particularly conspicuous. If the southern slope was ever glaciated at a high level, the processes of weathering and rock and soil creep have long since erased identifying marks, but the U-shape of Castle Creek indicates a former movement of valley ice.

The rocky summit locale is a haven for miniature alpine plants, including cinquefoil, golden fleabane, phlox, moss campion, and shrubby penstemon.

On the map of the North West Boundary (1866) a high peak is indicated near the Boundary, W of Pasayten River; the title "Skwai-kwi-cht" is perhaps

FREEZOUT MOUNTAIN

JOKER MOUNTAIN

CASTLE PEAK

Pass Creek

1973

1979

North Face

Castle Creek

CASTLE PEAK from northwest
AUSTIN POST, UNIVERSITY OF WASHINGTON

meant for Castle Peak. The first ascent of Castle was made by the U.S. Geological Survey in 1904, under Edward C. Barnard. That year a triangulation station (Turret) was made on the crest of the high point 1 mi. S of Monument 77. References: *Appalachia* 24 (June 1943): 50; *Harvard Mountaineering,* 1943, p. 40; *Joint Report,* p. 418; Daly, pt. I, pp. 492-99; see note 13.

SOUTH ROUTE: Approach via the Crest Trail♦ (Castle Creek) to the gentle S slope, which is largely scree above the scattered timberline. Leave the trail in Castle Creek valley E of the peak and follow old valley path, then light bush to the S slope. There is considerable route latitude. The E ridge and SW slope are other apparent possibilities, but details not known. One can also approach Castle from Freezout Creek (see Joker Mountain).

NORTH FACE, WEST SIDE: First ascent by Fred Beckey, Philip Leatherman, and Greg Markov on September 1, 1973. An approach was made via Crow Creek branch of Castle Creek. The route is via the broad blocky buttress on the W of the main face (just W of the main glacier arm). There are several class 5 sections with much class 4. The final portion is the W ridge. Grade II. Reference: *A.A.J.,* 1974, p. 144.

NORTH FACE: First ascent by Fred Beckey, Rick Nolting, and Reed Tindall on August 1, 1979. From the pass at the head of Crow Creek, hike the moraine divide and slab to the lowest rock toe of the central buttress (est. 6800 ft). Clamber up blocks adjacent to the ice on the right, then begin climbing a white right-leaning inside corner with an easy jam crack. At its termination, find good protection, then make more difficult moves upward and left, eventually reaching a small alcove where two points of aid are used to gain access to a belay block. The route then follows the crest of an obvious continuing rib (some scrambling), or closely on either side, keeping right of a snow-filled slanting gully. At one area a short friction slab is climbed rightward. The rock is generally sound, with a variety of interesting moves on cracks, blocks and slabs, mixed with faster portions. When the rib pinches off, traverse right to the continuing rock couloir (two steep snow sections) which breaks at a northwestern rib of the final summit. Climb and scramble about two more pitches to the top. The descent was made via the E ridge to a deep notch, where snow and a small glacier section provide an easy descent northward. Grade III; class 5.8 and A1. Time: 15 hours r.t. from camp in upper basin of Crow Creek.

FREEZOUT MOUNTAIN
7744 ft/2360 m

Freezout displays very visible sedimentary rock beds on all flanks. The mountain is located 2.3 mi. S of the International Boundary and 1.5 mi. SW of Castle Peak. The W flank is indented by a cirque; the southern slopes are moderate. At 1.5 mi. N of the summit is a sub-peak (7647 ft).

ROUTES: The apparent way is from upper Freezout Creek (see Lightning Creek Trail♦). From Castle Pass the Elbow Basin-Three Fools Creek Trail provides a route over Two Buttes; one can reach Freezout from high open ridges. The final ascent is not difficult.

JOKER MOUNTAIN   7603 ft/2317 m

Joker is a minor summit at the terminus of a ridge 2½ mi. SW of Castle Peak, between upper Freezout and Three Fools creeks. The NE face is distinctive with steeply inclined sedimentary beds. Lage Wernstedt, who made the first climb in 1925 or 1926, named the peak for his dog.

ROUTE: Ascend the W ridge from Freezout Creek. Approach via Jackass Pass Trail♦ to Lightning Creek, then up into Freezout Creek. The trail extends to 5100 ft in the N fork.

MT. WINTHROP   7850 ft/2393 m

Winthrop is a pointed and isolated summit with a long eastern summit ridge, and a high extended NW ridge leading to a bald rocky summit. It is 1 mi. NE of Castle Pass, close to the International Boundary. The NE flank is moderately steep, but the S and W slopes are gentle. A known early ascent was by Everett Darr and H.L. Frewing in 1940. References: *Appalachia* 24 (June 1942): 50-51; *B.C.M.,* August 1970.

ROUTE: From Frosty Pass (see Crest Trail♦) hike the S ridge (1 hour).

BLIZZARD PEAK   7622 ft/2323 m

Flanks are gentle on this small but distinctive peak 1 mi. SE of Frosty Pass and 0.9 mi. NE of Hopkins Pass. An ascent was made by Lage Wernstedt in 1925.

ROUTES: One could ascend NE from Hopkins Pass or from the trail beneath the W slope S of Castle Pass at 6000 ft. See Crest Trail♦. Another route is from Frosty Pass via steep snow slopes on the N flank.

SMOKY MOUNTAIN   7580 ft/2310 m

Located 5½ mi. S of the International Boundary and 4 mi. W of Pasayten River; this is a minor peak which was ascended by Barnard's survey group in 1904.

ROUTE: The apparent routes to the summit are from Chuchuwanteen Creek (Frosty Creek Trail♦) or using Soda Creek Trail♦ and Soda Creek to reach the S slope; no apparent difficulties.

SODA PEAK   7762 ft/2366 m

Soda Peak is 2 mi. NE of Three Fools Peak, between Rock Creek and Chuchuwanteen Creek. It is the highest point on the long ridge connecting Three Fools and Smoky Mountain.

ROUTE: See route for Smoky. The ascent appears to be easy from the S slope; begin from Brown Bear Camp on Rock Creek Trail♦.

THREE FOOLS PEAK
7920 ft+/2414 m+

Despite its moderate altitude, Three Fools is an important summit, for it is the highest in the span between Jack Mountain and Castle Peak. The peak is located on the Cascade divide 1 mi. NNE of Woody Pass at the head of Three Fools Creek. The N summit is the highest point; there is a small rock pointer just S of the true summit. The entire massif has a broad, steep eastern facade, but the SW flank is of moderate gradient. The sedimentary rock (argillite is interbedded with sandstone and conglomerate) tends to reflect a reddish hue. Possibly Three Fools, Blizzard, or Smoky was the Skwa-kwi-eht summit listed by the North West Boundary Survey 1857-1860. The first climb may have been made by Lage Wernstedt on his 1925 surveying season.

ROUTE: Ascend the easy SW slope from the Crest Trail♦ just N of Woody Pass. One can reach the pass from Rock Creek Trail♦ or from Barron via Windy and Holman passes.

POWDER MOUNTAIN   7714 ft/2351 m
Located ½ mi. S of Woody Pass on the Cascade divide, this is a small peak of hiking interest. It has a steep E flank.

ROUTES: The easiest way is the S slope from the Rock Pass area (Crest Trail♦). One can also traverse W from Woody Pass and turn the cliffs to bear uphill NW.

HOLMAN PEAK   7550 ft/2301 m
Holman is a craggy peak of massive, thick conglomerate made up of very steeply W-dipping bedrock. This structural feature and glacial carving of the N flank create an asymmetrical shape to the upland ridge surface. Holman's eastern face displays steep joints and the jagged exposure of broken-off beds. There is an ice remnant beneath the steep N face. The Cascade divide meets the SW peak of Holman (7480 ft+), but the high point is the NE peak, which is .025 mi. distant. The name was given for the two Holman brothers, engaged in railroad surveying of the area in 1907. Possibly the first climb of the peak was by Lage Wernstedt in 1925.

ROUTE: Take the Crest Trail♦ to the W flank, where the route begins by traversing grass slopes among small trees to the ridge crest. The ascent is quite easy, although the terrain is rock. At the final summit there is about 150 ft of nice climbing: a 100-ft-wide block with large holds is climbed; use the hands easily (class 3).

SHULL MOUNTAIN   7830 ft/2387 m
This is a small but rugged mountain ridge about 2 mi. in length, trending N-S between upper Canyon and Shull creeks, 2 mi. WNW of Holman Pass. The N peak is higher, with the S peak at 7791 ft. Shull Lake is just NW of the mountain. On the ridge W of Shull Creek there are some rugged pinnacles; the highest — at 1.8 mi. NE of Devils Pass — is 7514 ft. There is a possibility Henry Custer climbed Shull on September 2, 1859. His notations for the following day remarked on the loveliness of fine meadows and a basin with "Three beautiful little lakes." Part of the scenario fits, but considering the estimated latitude, the basin of Frosty Lakes might be more logical.

ROUTE: One can make the approach to Shull from the Center Mountain Trail♦. From Sky Pilot Pass one can probably reach the peak by a ridge traverse near or below the crest. Rock Pass on the Crest Trail♦ may offer an eastern approach. Follow the summit ridge, and generally stay to the right of the crest.

EAST ROUTE: From the Crest Trail♦ N of Holman Pass, cross Canyon Creek and ascend the lower forest slopes of Shull. Contour across the head of a gully to reach the middle of the face S of the main summit. Easy talus and snow continue to the top; not difficult. Time: 2 hours.

JIM PEAK   7033 ft/2144 m
Made up of plagioclase arkose interbedded with black argillite, this small peak is in the area of Oregon Basin, an area of numerous claims and adits. Reference: *U.S. Geological Survey, Bull.* 1325, pp. 143-58.

ROUTE: See Crest Trail♦ (this passes on the E). The peak is very easy on the S and E.

Devils Backbone (7056 ft/2151 m) is the ridge just E of Jim, off the crest, but higher. Peak 7062 is closely N and also higher than Jim.

PASAYTEN PEAK   7850 ft/2393 m
This is a pyramidal-shaped peak located between the Middle and West Pasayten forks, about 3.75 mi. N of Slate Peak. The summit is quartz diorite of the Pasayten dike, which has intruded arkose and argillite. The most notable topographic feature is the short but rugged rock face on the E flank; Silver Lake (6256 ft) lies in the basin 0.9 mi. SE of the summit. Lage Wernstedt likely made the first climb in 1925 or 1926.

ROUTE: Reach via the West Fork Pasayten River Trail♦. Hike directly from where the trail crosses the stream (5050 ft); the ascent is long but easy.

BUCKSKIN POINT   7815 ft/2382 m
A high ridge, over 3 mi. in length, located between the West and Middle forks of Pasayten River, and E of

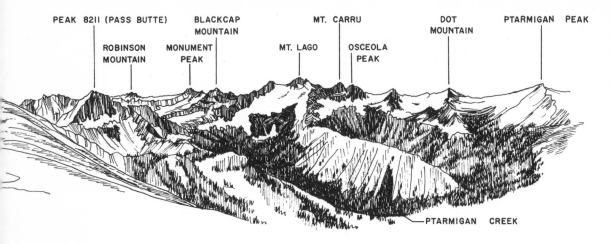

PEAK 8211 (PASS BUTTE)   BLACKCAP   MT. CARRU   DOT   PTARMIGAN   PEAK
                          MOUNTAIN   MOUNTAIN
ROBINSON   MONUMENT   MT. LAGO   OSCEOLA
MOUNTAIN   PEAK   PEAK

PTARMIGAN   CREEK

PASAYTEN WILDERNESS AREA from Many Trails Peak

Holman Peak. The high point is 0.9 mi. NE of Silver Pass. A southern high point is 7632 ft.
ROUTE: See West Fork Pasayten River Trail♦ to reach the W slope.

SLATE PEAK   7440 ft/2268 m
See Slate Peak Trail♦.

HAYSTACK MOUNTAIN (7303 ft/2226 m) is a rocky crag of rounded shape on the spur ridge 0.6 mi. NE of Slate's summit. There is a small cliff on its NE side. The West Fork Pasayten Trail♦ crosses W of the summit.

LAST CHANCE POINT
7046 ft/2148 m
The topographic culmination of the ridge separating Rattlesnake Creek and the Methow River, only 2 mi. from their junction. The summit is 2 mi. S of Robinson Mountain.
ROUTE: The route is an easy scramble up sandstone and over quartz porphyry dikes from the Harts Pass Road♦ above Dead Horse Point.

BEAUTY PEAK   7935 ft/2419 m
This summit is located in the shadow of Robinson Mountain (1.3 mi. ENE of latter) on a NW-SE trending ridge between Eureka and Beauty creeks. The area is rugged, with considerable local relief, and relatively inaccessible.
ROUTE: Perhaps the best — though difficult — approach

is to hike up Beauty Creek to 5800 ft, then ascend the long S slope; the NW ridge certainly can be done without technical problems, but again is difficult of access.

ROBINSON MOUNTAIN
8726 ft/2660 m
One of the highest and bulkiest summits in the northeastern Cascades, Robinson is visible from many distant viewpoints. The mountain is N of the Robinson Creek fork of Methow River, which flows some 4000 ft below the summit. Robinson's summit is 0.5 mi. from the NW-trending Pasayten dike. Most of the summit and W and SE ridges are interbedded andesite flows and purplish argillite, with minor arkose and volcanic sandstone (Rowland Tabor, written commun.); there are many quartz porphyry and diorite dikes and copper mineralization is present on the mountain. Robinson has a steep, broad NW face; high on the Beauty (NE) Creek flank there are three small ice patches. A sub-peak (Point 8410) is 0.6 mi. NE of the summit, and farther N is another prominent subpeak (Point 8440 ft+).

The name is given for brothers James and Thomas Robinson, early settlers who spent the winter of 1887 trapping in the area and had a cabin at Robinson Creek. The summit was first reached by Edward C. Barnard's 1904 U.S. Geological Survey party.
SOUTHWEST ROUTE: One can leave the Robinson Creek-Middle Fork Pasayten Trail♦ at about 5 mi. In June a long snow gully reaches to the summit (suggest ice axes); in

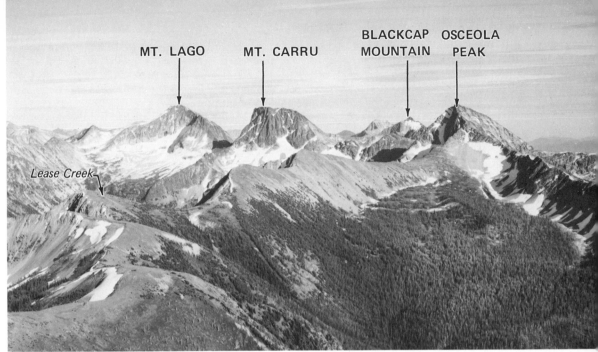

MT. CARRU *from northwest*
U.S. FOREST SERVICE

later summer the S and SW slopes are long, dry talus exposures.

SOUTHEAST RIDGE: From the top of switchbacks on the Beauty Creek branch trail a good summit route is reported (some scrambling, but not technical).

DEVILS PEAK   8081 ft/2463 m

Devils is 1.9 mi. NW of dominating Robinson Mountain. The peak is small but has rugged aspects and some steep flanks; a cirque on the NE may contain a rock glacier.

ROUTE: Reach the W side from Robinson Creek-Middle Fork Pasayten Trail◆. The ascent does not appear to offer technical problems, but will include talus and broken rock slopes.

WILDCAT MOUNTAIN
                              7958 ft/2426 m

Between Middle Fork of Pasayten River and the South Fork of Eureka Creek.

ROUTE: Reach from Ferguson Lake, which is on the peak's NW (at 6631 ft), or the pass S of Wildcat. The W slope is particularly easy. See Eureka Creek Trail◆.

MT. ROLO   8096 ft/2468 m

This mountain is a moderate summit located about 1 mi. E of Pasayten River Middle Fork and 4 mi. N of Robinson Pass. The name was applied by Lage Wernstedt for his assistant, Roland Burgess, when he made the ascent in 1925 or 1926.

ROUTE: The logical approach is to hike S from Freds Lake Pass (see Eureka Creek Trail◆). Bypass a hump en route to the summit (not technical).

OSCEOLA PEAK   8587 ft/2617 m

Osceola, one of the most significant summits of this region, is between Lease and Eureka creeks, and the Pasayten River Middle Fork. The mountain is a high rugged massif of folded Cretaceous arkose and argillite. Wide ridge arms border Pleasant Valley NW of the summit. There is a great contrast between the gradual, dry NW-facing scree slopes and the shaded, recently glaciated steep slope of a ridge on this flank. Here snow nivation hollows and extensive protalus ramparts have hindered tree growth.

First ascent by Richard Alt and Hermann F. Ulrichs in June 1933; there is a report that Lage Wernstedt made an ascent about 1925, but the later party reported no evidence of such on the summit.

ROUTES: Leave Eureka Creek Trail◆ (Freds Lake alternative) at the pass (est. 7100 ft) above Freds Lake. Hike past

Lake Doris and ascend the SW slope. The final portion is a rounded ridge.

The climb could also be made directly from upper Eureka Creek, taking the SW scree slopes.

MT. CARRU   8595 ft/2620 m

Carru, one of the most significant mountain formations of this region, is located between Mt. Lago and Osceola Peak on the Lease-Eureka Creek divide. Lease Creek valley has a broad upper sector, where there are well defined cirques and much evidence of glacial motion, including exhibits of 18th century lateral and terminal moraines. Carru has a short steep N and NE wall, beneath which is a cirque containing small ice remnants. The first ascent was made by Richard Alt and Hermann F. Ulrichs in June 1933.

ROUTE: See Eureka Creek Trail◆ for the way to upper Eureka Creek. The W spur (facing Osceola) is scree and appears the easiest. There are some gullies on the S flank that appear to offer no climbing problem, although the original party here reported some scrambling.

MT. LAGO   8745 ft/2666 m

Lago is one of the two highest peaks in this section of the Cascade Range, and has the additional distinction of having the easternmost glacier in the range. The mountain is located at the head of Eureka Creek with slope drainage to Ptarmigan, Dot, and Lease creeks. Rock is a granitic intrusive, cut by many dikes. The structure of the mountain is such that erosion has formed short, steep rock walls on the N and E flanks. Several high-level cirques contain small sections of glacier ice.

The mountain was named for Lage Wernstedt by one of his surveying companions. It is possible that Wernstedt made an ascent in 1926, but Dick Alt and Hermann F. Ulrichs, ascending from Eureka Creek, found no summit evidence of visitation and claimed the first ascent in July 1933.

SOUTH ROUTE: Approach as for Mt. Carru. There are three broad scree gullies on the S flank; all appear to be easy of ascent, as does the SW scree slope. Early summer snow cover might make the ascent more pleasant.

A route from the E (Ptarmigan Creek) would appear easy, but at the upper portion bear to the N ridge. Some snow climbing and rock scrambling should be anticipated.

BLACKCAP MOUNTAIN
8397 ft/2559 m

This is an interesting peak of locally important stature just 0.7 mi. N of the larger mass of Monument Peak on the Eureka-Monument Creek divide. The dark summit portion of the mountain is a composition of black hornfels atop pinkish granite porphyry. Residual patches of ice remain in Ice Age cirques N of the summit. The first ascent of Blackcap appears to have been made by Lage Wernstedt in 1925 or 1926.

ROUTE: Begin from Shellrock Pass (see Monument Creek Trail◆ and Eureka Creek Trail◆). From the spur ridge passed by the trail just E of the pass, the proven route is to traverse rock and snow basins southward, then to scramble directly up the E side (moderate rock climbing). Time: 2 hours.

It is speculated that the ascent could be made directly from upper Eureka Creek by traversing a cirque containing a small lake and ascending a broad couloir.

MONUMENT PEAK   8592 ft/2619 m

Monument is in the center of a rugged wilderness area E of Eureka Creek and S of the Mt. Lago-Carru group. The peak has a long scarp on the W, a steep N face, a broad cliff-band face on the E, and a long protruding S ridge; there is a broad glacier-scooped basin between Lake and Monument peaks. The peak is a large rock massif of mostly pink granite porphyry. The contact between granite and arkose passes just E and N of the summit. The western of two small summit points is higher. Climbing history is uncertain. No cairn was found on the summit during an ascent by Fred Beckey and John Roper on September 26, 1978.

ROUTES: The 1978 climb was done from Pistol Pass (Monument Creek Trail◆) via a long sidehill traverse into the Lake-Monument basin, then via the E rock ridge (class 3-4), and descent via the S ridge (time: pass to summit, 5 hours). As far as is known the easiest route is the S ridge or the SW scree slopes (latter from Eureka Creek Trail◆). An approach from Shellrock Pass to the SE basin is certainly feasible: climbing the last 200 ft of granite to gain the basin rim may prove the hardest problem on the ascent.

LAKE MOUNTAIN   8371 ft/2552 m

Lake is a high, important summit 1.6 mi. SE of Monument Peak and W of Lost River. The mountain is near the center of the Monument Peak granite, a circular stock 7 mi. in diameter exposed between Lost River and Eureka Creek. The N face of Lake is precipitous. Peak 8165 (just SE of Lake) has ice on its N flank. Lage Wernstedt was on the S shoulder of Lake, but it is not known if he made the ascent.

ROUTE: The W flank is the easiest, largely steep scree slopes with one obvious scree gully. One could also climb the NW ridge (appears to offer nothing more than easy scrambling); the easiest approach is Shellrock Pass (see Monument Creek Trail◆ and Eureka Creek Trail◆). Traverse S to the divide between Monument Peak and Lake.

MONUMENT PEAK *from southeast*
ROWLAND TABOR. U.S. GEOLOGICAL SURVEY

PISTOL PEAKS   7802 ft/2378 m

These are two rugged peaks, about ½ mi. apart, located between Monument and Eureka creeks and about 2 mi. SE of Lake Mountain. The SE Peak, about 0.8 mi. from Pistol Pass, is the higher. The lower peak is 7749 ft (2362 m). The entire flank on the N and NE of the peaks is quite steep rock.

ROUTE: Approach via Monument Creek Trail♦. When under the W flank (9½-10 mi.) it appears simple to ascend bushy rock and scree slopes to either summit; this approach seems the most direct, but does not look very attractive.

THREE PINNACLES   8124 ft/2476 m

This somewhat desolate appearing formation is composed of arkose and argillite with resistant beds of conglomerate. Located between Lost River and Monument Creek, there are three summits in an 0.6-mi. span; the northern is highest, the middle summit is 8123 ft (2476 m) and the S summit is 8082 ft (2463 m). The eastern flank, above the rough Lost River gorge, is the steepest. The first ascent was made by Lage Wernstedt in 1925 or 1926.

ROUTES: There appears to be no problem associated with an ascent from the W slope, except that it is long and tedious (begins at the 4600-ft level). There may be minor sections of scrambling near the summits and at notch crossings. It will be necessary to work out the routes in the upper area. The shortest approach is by Monument Creek Trail♦.

LOST PEAK   8464 ft/2580 m

Lost is near the southern end of the Lost Peak stock (granodiorite), between Lost River, Monument Creek, and Johnny Creek. The peak is high and rounded,

mostly covered with scree and blocks, but is steep on the N flank; there are small cliffs on the southern slopes. On the NE flank are a small ice gully and ice remnant. Lost has an 8327-ft NE summit. Apparently the first climb was by Lage Wernstedt in 1925 or 1926.
ROUTES: See Monument Creek Trail♦. It appears simplest to ascend from Monument Creek on the W or SW flank (from trail at 5200 ft) and enter the basin between Lost and Pass Butte. The NW summit ridge and W slope are also gentle.
    RAMPART RIDGE (7941 ft/2420 m) is to the NE of Lost, just N of Rampart Lake.

PASS BUTTE   8140 ft/2481 m
This is a moderately sloped summit 1.1 mi. WNW of Lost Peak, and connected by a ridge to a more impressive, unnamed 8211-ft summit to the NW.
ROUTE: Use Monument Creek Trail♦ to the SW spur of Pass Butte (at 6100 ft), then merely hike upslope through meadows and scree.

PEAK 8211   8211 ft/2503 m
This unnamed summit is ½ mi. NW of Pass Butte, and generally more impressive than the latter. The N flank (Ptarmigan Creek) is precipitous rock, but the W and E slopes are moderate.
ROUTE: The connecting ridge from Pass Butte is the apparent, and easy summit route. A more direct ascent can certainly be made from the trail.

MANY TRAILS PEAK   8241 ft/2512 m
An extensive N-S upland ridge, with the true summit at the N end (between Johnny Creek and Ptarmigan Creek). An excellent viewpoint, it is very obvious from Hidden Lakes. Rock is sandstone and argillite intruded by scores of andesite dikes (the dikes make it difficult to find the contact between granodiorite and the arkose-argillite sequence on the W flank). A known early ascent is that of Lage Wernstedt in 1926.
ROUTES: From Ptarmigan Creek (trail) opposite Dot Creek one can ascend from the 5200-ft level (see Monument Creek Trail♦). The long upsweep of the S ridge is a mere hike; the W slope is gentle.

DOT MOUNTAIN   8220 ft/2505 m
Dot is a gentle summit, easy on all flanks, 1 mi. SW of Ptarmigan Peak. A high ridge connects Dot with Mt. Lago (to SSE). Dot Lake (7076 ft) is at the head of Dot Creek, and ½ mi. SE of the mountain.
ROUTE: One could just hike upslope from Lease Lake (see Lease Creek Trail, branch of Tatoosh Buttes Trail♦); an eastern approach is via Ptarmigan and Dot creeks (see Monument Creek Trail♦).

PTARMIGAN PEAK   8614 ft/2626 m
Ptarmigan is a large massif, one of the most important summits of the region (located on the Lease-Ptarmigan Creek divide). It is very asymmetrical, with the S and W slopes gradual and the entire wide NE cirque steep and rugged. There are numerous cirques here, with two ice patches (8300 ft-7200 ft). Ptarmigan Lake (6702 ft) is NE of the summit.
ROUTES: Begin as for Tamarack Ridge, then hike across its W slope and bypass Point 7748. Then easily hike SE along the ridge crest to the summit.
    One could also reach the peak's SE slope from Ptarmigan Creek Trail, and then following Dot Creek for 2 mi. The western base offers a route from Lease Creek trail (long but simple route).

TAMARACK RIDGE   7748 ft/2362 m
A high, open ridge 0.9 mi. NW of Ptarmigan Peak, and S of Tatoosh Buttes (between Hidden Lakes and Lease Creek). Point 7748, which may not actually be part of the ridge, is west of Ptarmigan Lake; Point 7583, at the head of Little Willy Creek, is easy on the S and W.
ROUTE: Reach from Tatoosh Buttes Trail♦; from the high area merely hike southward.
    TATOOSH BUTTES (7245 ft/2208 m and 7200 ft+/2195 m) are minor summits, largely of hiking interest, in a vast floral parkland; the trail passes over the E butte, and nearly touches the W summit.

SETTING SUN MOUNTAIN
                                7255 ft/2311 m
Located W of McLeod Mountain and E of lower Lost River, Setting Sun is a moderate frontal peak of more interest to viewfinders than climbers.
ROUTE: One can reach the mountain via the route to Goat Peak Trail♦, keeping on road no. 3729. At 14 mi. reach a 5000-ft saddle; here is a simple cross-country hike N to the lower summit, from which the trek continues NW to the highest point.

McLEOD MOUNTAIN   8099 ft/2469 m
This is a pyramidal peak of strategic location on the S edge of the Pasayten Wilderness between Lost River and Goat Creek. There are interesting dry cirques on the peak's E flank. The NW sub-peak (8041 ft/2451 m) bears toward Sunrise Peak. McLeod has been a triangulation station for the U.S. Geological Survey since its ascent by Edward C. Barnard and party in 1904. Formerly known as Goat Mountain, the name was chosen in 1929 for Angus McLeod, an early Methow Valley pioneer.

ROUTE: Take Goat Creek Road No. 375 to the S flank (see Goat Peak Trail♦), then Long Creek branch no. 3735 to about 5200 ft. Gentle open-forested terrain with talus basins and gentle rock slopes bear to the summit.

SUNRISE PEAK   8144 ft/2482 m
Sunrise is between Lost River and Goat Creek at 8¼ mi. from the Early Winters Creek-Methow River junction, and is a prominent peak because of a lack of competitive topography. The S and SE flanks are gentle and open, with talus slopes extending beyond the sparse timber.
ROUTE: The simplest route appears to be via Goat Creek Road (see Goat Peak Trail♦) and its spur (logging spurs extend to about 4500 ft in Goat Creek valley), then hiking up-valley to the E slope of Sunrise.

BURGETT PEAK   7365 ft/2245 m
Located 1½ mi. SE of Sherman Peak, Burgett is a small peak, but is rocky on the N and E flanks. The earliest ascent was probably by Lage Wernstedt in 1925 or 1926.
ROUTE: Take Eightmile Creek Road (see Chewack River Road No. 392♦) and Deer Creek branch (W) to Ortell Creek (road no. 3713); this extends to within 1½ mi. of the peak. The S slope is easy.

SHERMAN PEAK   8204 ft/2501 m
Sherman is a rugged and important summit of this section, located on the divide W of Eightmile Creek at the head of Goat Creek. The peak is the climax of 2½-mi. Isabella Ridge, which everywhere has a precipitous, craggy rock facade on the NE; Sherman's opposite SW flank is gradual. The NW peak (8138 ft/2480 m) is equally rugged. Sherman was climbed by Lage Wernstedt in 1925, possibly the first ascent.
ROUTES: The most sensible approach is from the upper portion of road no. 375 (Goat Creek): from the elbow where the road crosses Goat Creek (4000 ft) follow a logging road N, then continue cross-country up the valley to the easy SW slopes of Sherman. Some common sense is necessary in route finding (the route is not difficult, but fairly long).

Another possible approach is from Copper Glance Creek Trail No. 519♦. From near the lake ascend to the ridge near Point 8011 (NW end of Isabella Ridge). From here it is over 1 mi. to the summit, with some certain scrambling and minor summits; one party reported an ascent of the NW peak, but halted at gendarmes trying to reach the main summit.

BIG CRAGGY PEAK   8470 ft/2582 m
The Craggys are a complex of high, rocky, and rugged peaks between Lost River and Eightmile Creek. Big Craggy, the highest of the peaks has a convoluted NW

to NE flank that is a mix of cliffs and steep rock gullies, but the S flank is a 30-degree scree slope; the ridge N of the peak extends to Point 8205. At 0.8 mi. W of Big Craggy is *West Craggy* (8366 ft/2550 m), equally rugged; from here a long high ridge extends N to *Eightmile Peak* (7756 ft/2364 m) — termed by maps as part of Isabella Ridge. The complex includes a ridge W to Point 8123 and a ridge S to Point 8112 (South Craggy).
ROUTE: Take Copper Glance Creek Trail♦ to 6100 ft. This route passes an abandoned mine and leads to the base of Big Craggy's S slope.

WEST CRAGGY
Lage Wernstedt climbed West and South Craggy in about 1925, and he may have reached other summits. The summit route seems best on the SW, but the approach is not simple. Another way is to cross the divide from Copper Glance Creek (circuitous but easy): leave the trail at 6200 ft and hike NW to the S ridge at 8000 ft, then keep on its W side.
NORTHEAST BUTTRESS: This prominent buttress is located on the E side of the ridge between West Craggy and Eightmile Peak; the feature is almost a small separate peak ½ mi. S of the latter (the buttress faces ENE, rising from 6800 ft to about 7500 ft, and can be seen from Eightmile Pass when focusing into the basin between the Craggys. The first ascent was by Steve Barnett and Pete Doorish in August 1974. The nine-pitch route follows the prominent ridge on the right side of the face; the first pitch is loose, but the remainder is sound. On the upper portion ascend the prominent dihedral. Grade III; class 5.8.

BURCH MOUNTAIN   7782 ft/2372 m
Burch is a relatively unimportant summit 1½ mi. SE of Billy Goat Pass.
ROUTE: Use Billy Goat-Larch Creek Trail♦.

BILLY GOAT MOUNTAIN
7639 ft/2328 m
This mountain, located between Drake Creek and Eightmile Pass, has several nearly level summits, all located in the area of Billy Goat Mountain andesite breccia. Numerous copper properties have been explored in the area of Billy Goat and Eightmile passes (see Staatz, pp. 22, 104-15; see note 15).
ROUTE: The ascent from Eightmile Pass is not difficult (see Eightmile Pass-Hidden Lake Trail♦). The central of the three high points is nearly due N of the pass.

NANNY GOAT MOUNTAIN
7700 ft/2347 m
A minor summit, but locally prominent (between upper Lost River and Three Fools Pass). The most

gentle slopes are on the W and the S ridge.
ROUTE: One could make the summit hike from Hoot Owl Camp (5480 ft) on the W. Use Eightmile Pass-Hidden Lake Trail◆.

DOLLAR WATCH MOUNTAIN
7679 ft/2341 m

It is known that Lage Wernstedt made the ascent of this minor summit near the head of the Pasayten River East Fork, and W of Dollar Watch Pass in 1926, but an earlier ascent is quite probable.
ROUTE: See Eightmile Pass-Hidden Lake Trail◆. Hike either Deception Creek or Stub Creek branch routes; the trail nearly reaches the summit.

TWO POINT MOUNTAIN
7955 ft/2425 m

The W peak of this moderate summit 0.8 mi. NE of Dollar Watch Pass is higher; the E peak is 7759 ft (2365 m). The N flank of the mountain is steep.
ROUTE: The long ridge on the SW leading to Point 7855 appears to be the best route; one could make the approach from Dollar Watch Pass. Another approach is from Larch Pass; the trail reaches to 7600 ft S of the E peak (see Billy Goat-Larch Creek Trail◆).

ASHNOLA MOUNTAIN
7780 ft/2371 m

Ashnola a minor summit 5.5 mi. S of the Canada Boundary between the upper Ashnola River and head of the East Fork Pasayten River. The first climb was made by the E.C. Barnard party during topographic surveying in 1904; they reached the summit by following the divide S from Park Pass.
ROUTES: The easiest method is to stroll W from Whistler Pass branch trail from the Billy Goat-Larch Creek Trail◆. Another route would be to ascend the mountain's SW flank from the East Fork Pasayten River Trail.

PEAK 7821   7821 ft/2384 m

This unnamed summit is located ½ mi. N of Corral Lake, W of Ashnola River, and about 2 mi. E of Ashnola Mountain. The peak is gentle except on the N.
ROUTE: Approach from Ashnola River to Corral Lake; the trail reaches to 7600 ft on the W slope (see Billy Goat-Larch Creek Trail◆).

QUARTZ MOUNTAIN
7539 ft/2298 m

Quartz is a minor summit about 2 mi. SW of Sheep Mountain. Sand Ridge (7567 ft), S of Peeve Pass, is an adjacent and similar uplift SE of Quartz. It is known

that Lage Wernstedt made an ascent in 1926, but as was the case with many gentle summits, an earlier ascent may have been made by herders, prospectors, and certainly game.
ROUTE: The Boundary Trail◆ between Bunker Hill and Peeve Pass reaches high on the S slope.

SHEEP MOUNTAIN   8274 ft/2522 m

Sheep is about 1.7 mi. S of the International Boundary on the Peeve-Martina Creek divide W of Ashnola River. The mountain is high and isolated, with rocky, moderately inclined felsenmeer-type upper slopes: both the N and S slopes are uniquely moderate. The rock is primarily a granodiorite-gneiss complex. Gneisses, cut by many dikes, underlie the boundary area here. Sheep Lake (7040 ft) lies in a narrow cirque closely E of the summit; on this flank of Sheep are two empty cirques. The mountain was climbed by the U.S. Coast and Geodetic Survey in 1925, but an earlier ascent was probably made by one of the Boundary Survey parties of 1904-1905. Reginald A. Daly, who called the mountain "Park," and estimated that the ice sheet extended to 7800 ft, may also have made an early ascent.
ROUTES: The shortest approach is by the steep 5-mi. trail to a position about 1½ mi. SE of the summit (see Ashnola River Trail◆). The final ascent is hiking.

Another route is to take Pasayten River Trail◆ (B.C.). At 2 mi. N of the Boundary ascend Peeve Creek Trail about 9½ mi. to a pass 1½ mi. N of Sheep (near Monument 90), then ascend a long ridge to the summit. The W slope of Sheep from the trail to Park Pass provides an easy route (see Billy Goat-Larch Creek Trail◆).

PEAK 7718 (Border Lake Peak) (B.C.)
7718 ft/2352 m

This is a small summit 0.4 mi. N of the Boundary at Monument 90 and 3.3 mi. W of Ashnola River. Smith and Calkins describe a peak with cirques containing rock rimmed tarns upon its NE flank, possibly this summit (Bull. 235, p. 92). Map: Ashnola River 92 H/1.
ROUTE: The ascent appears easy (see Border Lake, Pasayten River Area Trails◆).

BALD MOUNTAIN   7931 ft/2417 m

Bald is a gently contoured summit 3½ mi. S of the International Boundary, N of Spanish Creek fork of Ashnola River, and W of Spanish Camp. The summit offers a nice hike and a good viewpoint, certainly used by the first Boundary Survey.
ROUTE: See Ashnola River Trail◆, Andrews Creek Trail◆,

and Boundary Trail◆. Trail no. 533 passes high to the N of Bald; the NE slope is an easy completion.

FREDS MOUNTAIN   8080 ft+/2463 m+

This is a long ridge trending NW, NE of Ashnola Pass. There are some steep cirques on the E flank; the high point is near the ridge's northwestern end, and a 7960-ft+ point is 0.5 mi. to the SE. *Van Peak* (7665 ft/ 2336 m) is NW of Freds Mountain, and on the same ridge continuation.

ROUTES: Approach via Spanish Creek branch of Lake Creek-Ashnola River Trail◆. The SW slopes of the ridge appear to be hiking routes.

ANDREW PEAK (Andrews Peak)
8301 ft/2530 m

Quite gently sloped on the W and S, this peak is located 1½ mi. WSW of Remmel Mountain and 0.6 mi. SW of Andrews Pass. Maps that spell the name in the singular should be corrected.

ROUTES: See Andrews Creek Trail◆. From about 1 mi. S of Andrews Pass hike westward (partly on path) into the open basin S of the summit; from about 7300 ft near Rock Lake, hike NE upslope.

One can reach the peak from Andrews Pass, but bear around to the NW side of the summit. The W slope of the peak is an easy route from Glory Creek fork of Spanish Creek.

MT. REMMEL   8685 ft/2647 m

Remmel is one of the most massive and outstanding mountains in the Okanogan Range. Located 5.3 mi. S of the International Boundary between Andrews Creek and Remmel Fork of Chewack River, this rugged mountain has seven distinct cirques on the NE and SE vectors, some of which contain lakes. Cornwall Lake (6995 ft) is 0.8 mi. N of the summit, a lake is in the cirque E of the mountain, and Four Point Lake is 1 mi. E of the latter. George Otis Smith called the mountain "Methow Peak" during his 1901 reconnaissance. In 1904, when the summit was climbed by Edward C. Barnard's survey group, a notation was made that appeared in a later U.S. Geological Survey report: "station is on the high, bald, rocky summit of Mt. Remmel." The Forest Service later erected a summit lookout because of the scope of the vantage point.

SOUTHWEST ROUTE: From Andrews Pass (see Andrews Creek Trail◆) hike E, then bear S until under the main summit. Minor sections of rock scrambling lead to the summit.

SOUTHEAST ROUTE: Take Four Point Creek Trail (branch of Chewack River Trail◆) to the SE slopes of the mountain. Hike W up Four Point Creek to the saddle in the S ridge, then to the summit (no difficulties).

Other Routes: To reach the N side of the mountain, take the Remmel Creek Trail to about 2 mi. N of the summit. The NE ridge is reported to be a pleasant scramble. The NW ridge appears sensible as a route, but no reports ATP.

PEEPSIGHT MOUNTAIN
8146 ft/2483 m

Peepsight has a rounded, pyramidal shape. It is located on the Ashnola River-Andrews Creek divide about 7 mi. S of the International Boundary.

ROUTE: From Andrews Creek Trail◆ and the Peepsight branch, hike to 7300 ft on the E flank of the summit, then just walk upslope. One could also ascend from Peepsight Lake (7059 ft); see Lake Creek-Ashnola River Trail◆.

BLACK LAKE RIDGE   7828 ft/2386 m

This ridge is located W of Andrews Creek, between Lake Creek and Peepsight Creek. The highest summit is at the N end; other altitudes are 7730 ft, 7483 ft, and 7572 ft. The entire ridge is very graded on the SW, above Black Lake. There are a short cliff on the N and steep cirques on the N and E.

ROUTE: It appears simple to ascend from near Black Lake (Lake Creek-Ashnola River Trail◆).

PRESTON RIDGE (7845 ft/2391 m) is a NW continuation of Black Lake Ridge, and could be considered a SE outlier of Peepsight Mountain.

POINT 8025   8025 ft/2446 m

This summit is the highest on the ridge NW of Diamond Point (1.2 mi. NW of the latter), and 1¼ mi. from Ashnola Pass. The ridge remains at a high level for about 5 mi., with numerous small points above 7900 ft.

ROUTE: Use Lake Creek-Ashnola River Trail◆. From the area of Ashnola Pass one could traverse the basin of Spotted Creek (W) and hike NW to the summit. Another option is to travel from the S side of Diamond Point, then bear W and NW on the same ridge.

PEAK 7949   7949 ft/2423 m

Located 1.7 mi. W of Diamond Point between upper Diamond and upper Larch Creek. The ascent was made by Lage Wernstedt in 1926.

ROUTE: One can reach the peak from Billy Goat-Larch Creek Trail◆, then hike the W slope.

DIAMOND POINT   7916 ft/2413 m

Diamond Point and its ridge are located just S of Ashnola Pass. The southern flanks of the point are gentle, but the northern exposure has a short, steep area.

ROUTE: Hike from the trail on the S (use Lake Creek-Ashnola River Trail♦ and Diamond Point branch).

OBSTRUCTION PEAK

7940 ft/2420 m

This summit is about 3 mi. E of Billy Goat Pass; a subsidiary summit on the NE is Peak 7734, closely W of Kidney Lake. The slopes are quite moderate on the W. An ascent was apparently done by Lage Wernstedt in 1926.
ROUTE: The E side of the peak can be reached from Farewell-Disaster Creek Trail♦ and the W slope is encountered from Three Prong Creek Trail (see Lake Creek- Ashnola River Trail♦). The ascent should offer no problem.

MT. BARNEY   7828 ft/2386 m

This summit is in the frontal, or southern portion of the mountains of this section, W of Chewack River and about 4 mi. SE of Billy Goat Pass. The mountain has rocky exposures on its N flank, but is gently contoured elsewhere. When Lage Wernstedt made the ascent in 1925, he named the mountain for a cherished horse killed in a fall.
ROUTE: Reach via Farewell-Disaster Creek Trail♦. The logical route would be to hike westward from where the trail crosses the ridge.

FAREWELL PEAK   7430 ft/2265 m

Located between Chewack River and Falls Creek, 3 mi. SE of Mt. Barney.
ROUTE: The apparent route is to hike W from near Ike Mountain. Another possibility is ascend the N flank from Farewell Creek (see Farewell-Disaster Creek Trail♦).

DOE MOUNTAIN   7154 ft/2181 m

This is a gradual summit SE of Farewell Peak.
ROUTE: There is a summit trail from road no. 3728 (leaves Chewack River Road♦ about 2 mi. past Falls Creek campground). Distance is about 4 mi. One can continue N to *Ike Mountain* (7186 ft/2190 m).

CAL PEAK   7489 ft/2283 m

Located between upper Chewack River and Fire Creek, at 3.2 mi. ESE of Remmel Mountain. Slopes of the peak are of moderate gradient, but there is considerable local relief from the valley.
ROUTE: Hike NW toward the summit area from Fire Creek Trail (see Chewack River Trail♦).
   COLEMAN RIDGE (7621 ft/2323 m to 7645 ft/2330 m) is 1½ mi. W of Cal Peak, and slightly higher.

COLEMAN PEAK   7690 ft/2344 m

Located between Chewack River and Andrews Creek.

Flanks of the peak are of gentle gradient. It is known that Lage Wernstedt made the ascent in 1925.
ROUTE: Meadow Lake Trail (see Andrews Creek Trail♦) extends to above 7100 ft on the S slope of the peak (take southern trail branch).

NORTH TWENTYMILE PEAK

7437 ft/2067 m

Located 3 mi. E of Chewack River Road, SE of the Andrews Creek junction. The peak is just a large dome formation, rising above the low-relief upland surface, but is prominent in the local area. There is a lookout station on the summit.
ROUTE: Summit trail no. 560 leads from E branch of Chewack River Road♦ just N of Twentymile Creek. The opposite end of the trail can also be reached from Salmon Meadows Road♦ near Thunder Mountain.

SOUTH TWENTYMILE PEAK

6670 ft/2033 m

This small peak is S of Twentymile Creek branch of Chewack River and N of Boulder Creek.
ROUTE: South Twentymile Trail No. 372 extends to the summit in about 4 mi. from Bromas Creek branch (no. 3742) of Boulder Creek Road♦.

PEARRYGIN PEAK   6644 ft/2025 m

This lesser summit 8 mi. NE of Winthrop is prominent because of its nearness to the Chewack River. The summit was used for triangulation by Lage Wernstedt in the mid-1920s, but like other non-technical summits of the region, was probably ascended previously by sheepherders or prospectors.
ROUTE: Begin from Winthrop; take Bear Creek Road No. 3502 to Pearrygin Creek, then hike E on trail no. 526.

OLD BALDY   7844 ft/2391 m

This gradual summit is prominent because of isolation between the S and middle forks of Boulder Creek, 13 mi. NE of Winthrop.
ROUTES: A former route used the Golden Stairway Trail to the S of the summit, then took a spur to high on this slope. Now a faster route is from road 364 (see Middle Salmon-Boulder Creek Road♦) at 1.5 mi. SE of Boulder Junction. Trail no. 369 bears high on the W slope.

CLARK PEAK   7920 ft+/2414 m+

Clark Peak is a moderate summit 1½ mi. SSE of Tiffany Mountain, a monadnock similar to Tiffany.
ROUTE: The Clark Ridge Trail reaches to the saddle (est. 7300 ft) S of the summit (reach from Salmon Meadows G.S., then road no. 3714 and the trail). Another way to the peak is

via Roger Lake Camp on Boulder Creek Road♦; use trail no.
367 (Bernhardt Mine).

TIFFANY MOUNTAIN
8242 ft/2512 m
Physiographically, the Tiffany Mountain chain is a
line of monadnocks that rise 800 ft to 1400 ft above
the low-relief upland surface at the head of Boulder
Creek, in the eastern portion of the main range
between the Okanogan and Methow rivers. Its physical height makes it a dominating one: a survey report
from 1900 described Tiffany as a "round, double, bare
topped mountain." A survey station was then placed
on the higher and more southerly summit, and an 8-ft
rock cairn was built (*U.S. Geological Survey, 21st Annual Report,* pt. I (1899-1900), p. 357).

Most of the highland here slopes from 6800 ft near
North Twentymile Peak to 6000 ft near Starvation
Mountain. The upper slopes of Tiffany, Little Tiffany
(7988 ft), Middle Tiffany, and Rock Mountain (7980
ft) are characterized by block fields of locally derived
angular rock debris showing no evidence of having
been glaciated (Waitt, 1972, p. 96). These peaks have
well defined cirques directed N and E. Apparently the
first climb was made by the 1900 survey party.
ROUTE: Reach the mountain from Boulder Creek Road♦
and Tiffany Mountain Trail♦.

THUNDER MOUNTAIN
7073 ft/2156 m
This is a small summit located 2½ mi. SE of Thirty
Mile Meadows.
ROUTE: The summit is only 0.3 mi. from Salmon
Meadows Road♦ (at 6560 ft+); walk up from Thunder
Camp, just SW of the mountain.

WINDY PEAK   8334 ft/2540 m
Windy is an isolated, high, open-sloped peak rising
above the upland of the eastern part of the Pasayten
Wilderness. Its massive, gently sloped form can be
seen from considerable distances. Its granodiorite has
intruded gneisses and other rocks of the Horseshoe
Basin area. Windy, which is about 3 mi. S of the basin
and 3 mi. W of Iron Gate camp, was climbed by the
Boundary Survey in 1904, and possibly also by Smith
and Calkins in 1901.
ROUTE: See Windy Peak Trail♦, which ascends to the
summit.

CHOPAKA MOUNTAIN
7882 ft/2402 m
Chopaka, with its great 7000-ft fault-related northeastern scarp rising unbroken from the marshes
bordering the lower Similkameen River and Palmer
Lake (the remains of an apparently old glacier
drainage), forms an abrupt ending to the Okanogan
Range. Chopaka is carved from a complex of Permian
and Triassic metamorphosed basaltic lavas, breccias,
and mafic intrusive rocks which have been intruded by
granitic plutons, probably during Mesozoic time
(Rowland Tabor, written commun.). During the
Pleistocene the Canadian ice sheet completed erosion
that had removed much of the metamorphosed rock
and exposed parts of the underlying batholiths,
including the Similkameen on the N and the Loomis
on the S. Reginald A. Daly noted the exposures of
Similkameen Batholith on the mountain and that the
ice sheet extended to an altitude of 7200 ft (Daly, Pt.
2, p. 589; see note 13). There are two lesser summits
on the massif: *Hurley Peak* (7820 ft/2384 m) is to the
N, and *Joe Mills Mountain* (7716 ft/2352 m) is NW of
the true summit (the great scarp is most impressive
from Hurley).

During the first Boundary Surveys George Gibbs
noted the mountain's name as "Tschopahk," and on
the British map of Col. Hawkins the identification is
"Mount XLIX." One of the first discoveries of lode
gold in the area was in 1871 at the foot of the
mountain. Numerous claims have been made on the
mountain since that time, when it was discovered that
ore carried gold and silver. Gold Hill, across Toats
Coulee, later became known for its mining activity. In
the nearby Palmer district, minerals were first discovered about 1870 by "Okanogan" Smith; the
mountains were then included in the Chief Moses
Indian Reservation.

The first climb of Chopaka was probably made by
George Otis Smith and Frank Calkins on July 31,
1901.[82] As proof of the mountain as a great viewpoint,
Smith later wrote: "one sees the white dome of Mt.
Baker in the far distance." Barnard's survey group in
1904 also ascended Chopaka.
ROUTE: See Chopaka Mountain Trail♦.

SNOWY MOUNTAIN (B.C.)
8507 ft/2593 m
Snowy is a broad high summit in the Similkameen
Batholith, a bold massif 3½ mi. N of the International
Boundary and W of lower Similkameen River. The
mountain is covered with a felsenmeer surface and
contains at least one rock glacier. The northern
drainage is Susap Creek and the southern flanks slope
toward Snehumption Creek. Visitor interest focuses

on scenic vistas and bighorn sheep resident in the local area. The first ascent was probably made by the U.S. Boundary Survey party of 1904. It should be noted that the British survey party of 1860 was in this area and may have climbed such mountains as Snowy and Lakeview. Map: Keremeos 82 E/4 West.

ROUTES: From Trans-Canada Hwy 3♦ about 12 mi. S of Keremeos take a bridge across Similkameen River (4 mi. N of Osoyoos-Chopaka junction). Drive W to a fork (main road bears S) and climb slopes on a mining road S of Susap Creek. The southern branch climbs the shoulder S of Roberts Creek to near a 4600-ft saddle: shortly before this a spur traverses SW to about 5700 ft; above its end a trail begins. Follow this on a S bearing above Snehumption Creek, then ascend directly W to the summit of Snowy (5 hours).

The northern road branch climbs to 5000 ft on the divide N of Susap Creek; at the stream crossing it is feasible to follow the ridge directly SW to Snowy or take the Susap Creek Trail♦ to Joe Lake (7100 ft+), 4 mi. from Snowy. Continue on the trail to Harry Lake; take the left fork near the lake and follow a track up a small rocky valley between hummocks. Bear downslope to the low saddle on World's Ridge, then bear S uphill using the ridge path. From a farther saddle follow a game trail steeply up the mountain's slope, then bear to the final SW side of the summit.

PEAK 7970 and PEAK 8000

7970 ft+/8000 ft+; 2429 m+/2438 m+
Both peaks are NNW of Snowy Mountain, and are gently sloped except for the long western scarp flanking lower Ashnola River. Peak 7970 is 6 mi. SW of Keremeos, between Gillanders, Susap, and Hunter creeks; Peak 8000 is nearby S. Both peaks are hiking treks (see Susap Creek Trail♦).

SNOWSHOE MOUNTAIN
7823 ft/2384 m
Snowshoe is 3.7 mi. NW of Chopaka Mountain, and 0.8 mi. S of the Boundary. Most slopes on the mountain are moderate, with rounded contours.

ROUTES: Hike E from Horseshoe Basin♦ via Long Draw Trail; distance from the basin to the W side of the mountain is about 3½ mi. The ascent is not difficult.

One could also begin from the road end as per Chopaka Mountain Trail♦, but take the trail W to Olallie Creek, then NW to the W slopes of the mountain.

ARMSTRONG PEAK   8106 ft/2471 m
Unnamed on maps, this peak is located 4.8 mi. SW of Snowy Mountain, on the International Boundary N of Horseshoe Basin. There are two summit points on the boundary, one at Monument 103 (triangulated as 8106 ft) and one at Monument 104 (contoured as 8100 ft). It would appear that the highest point is just S of

Monument 103. There is a high point (8000 ft+) W of Newby Lake (½ mi. N of the summits). Snehumption Creek drains E from the peak. Map: Keremeos 82 E/4 West.

ROUTE: Approach from Horseshoe Basin♦. The S slope is merely a hike.

ARNOLD PEAK   8076 ft/2462 m
Located about ½ mi. S of the International Boundary above the NE portion of Horeshoe Basin.

ROUTE: The ascent is merely a hike from Horseshoe Basin♦.

ROCK MOUNTAIN   7617 ft/2322 m
This minor summit, located at the northwestern edge of Horseshoe Basin, was ascended by the Boundary Survey about 1860. It should be noted that nearby Peak 7845 (1.3 mi. NW) is higher, yet unnamed.

ROUTE: Just hike upslope from Horseshoe Basin♦.

TEAPOT DOME   7608 ft/2319 m
This rock summit is at the head of Haig Creek, N of Horseshoe Creek. There is a cliffy area above 7000 ft on the NE slope.

ROUTE: From Horseshoe Basin♦ (Boundary Trail♦) hike W to make the ascent via either the SW or SE slope; there may be some scrambling.

BAUERMAN RIDGE   8044 ft/2452 m
This high ridge of historic importance was named for Hilary Bauerman, British geologist who helped explore this region during the first Boundary Survey. The ridge is W of Horseshoe Basin, about 7½ mi. NE of Mt. Remmel; the highest point is just S of Scheelite Lake, where there is a short, but very sheer granitic face. A dikelike phase of the Cathedral quartz monzonite 3½ mi. long strikes NW from Bauerman Ridge to Wall Creek across the Boundary. There is much evidence of glacial drift on the ridge: a historic photograph shows the cirque wall of "massive" Cathedral granite (Daly, Pt. I, opp. p. 462).

HAIG MOUNTAIN (7865 ft/2397 m) is 2.7 mi. E of the high point of the ridge and 1.2 mi. S of the Boundary.

ROUTE: Hike the S slope anywhere from the Boundary Trail♦. This is an easily reached viewpoint from which to scan much of the Okanogan Range both in the United States and Canada.

WOLFRAMITE MOUNTAIN
8137 ft/2480 m
A gently sloped summit 1 mi. S of the International

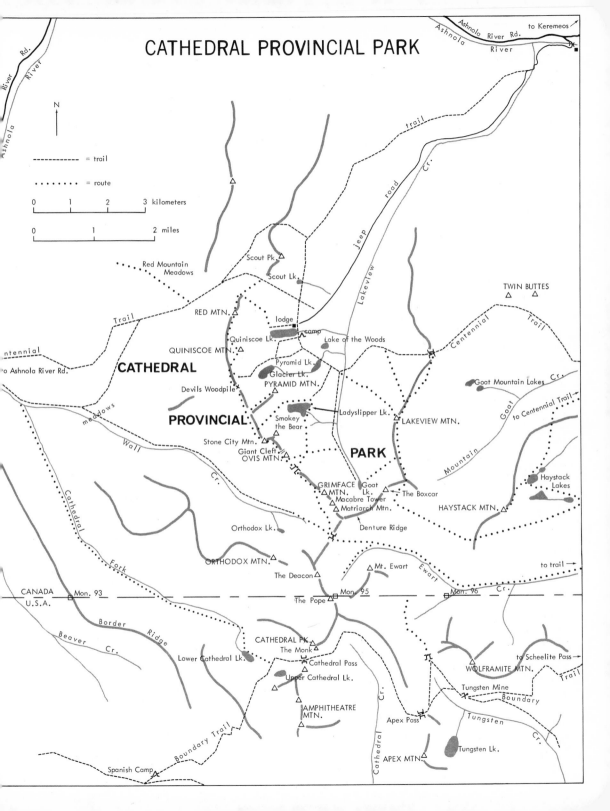

CATHEDRAL PROVINCIAL PARK

N

------- = trail

.... = route

0   1   2   3 kilometers

0   1   2 miles

to Keremeos

Ashnola River Rd.

Ashnola River

Ashnola River

Rd.

River Rd.

River

trail

Jeep road

Cr.

Lakeview

Red Mountain Meadows

Scout Pk.

Scout Lk.

RED MTN.

lodge

camp

Lake of the Woods

Centennial Trail

TWIN BUTTES

Quiniscoe Lk.

QUINISCOE MTN.

Trail

Centennial

Pyramid Lk.

Glacier Lk.

PYRAMID MTN.

Goat Mountain Lakes

Cr.

CATHEDRAL

to Ashnola River Rd.

Devils Woodpile

meadows

Ladyslipper Lk.

LAKEVIEW MTN.

Goat

to Centennial Trail

PROVINCIAL

Smokey the Bear

Mountain

Wall

Stone City Mtn.

Giant Cleft

OVIS MTN.

PARK

Haystack Lakes

Cr.

GRIMFACE MTN.

Goat Lk.

The Boxcar

HAYSTACK MTN.

Cathedral

Macabre Tower

Matriarch Mtn.

Orthodox Lk.

Denture Ridge

Fork

ORTHODOX MTN.

to trail →

The Deacon

Mt. Ewart

Ewart

Cr.

CANADA

U.S.A.

Mon. 93

The Pope

Mon. 95

Mon. 96

Beaver

Cr.

Border

Ridge

Lower Cathedral Lk.

CATHEDRAL PK.

The Monk

Cathedral Pass

to Scheelite Pass

WOLFRAMITE MTN.

Trail

Upper Cathedral Lk.

Tungsten Mine

Boundary

Cathedral

Cr.

Tungsten

Cr.

AMPHITHEATRE MTN.

Apex Pass

Boundary Trail

Spanish Camp

APEX MTN.

Tungsten Lk.

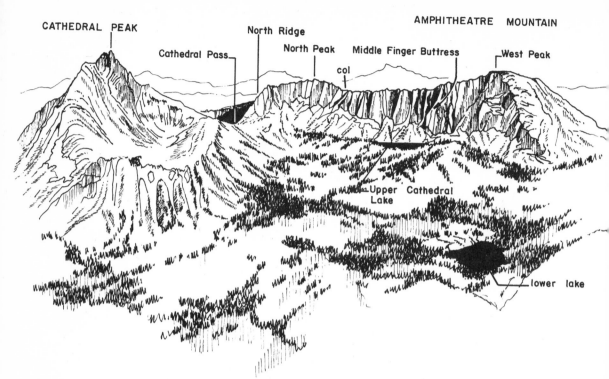

CATHEDRAL PEAK

North Ridge

Cathedral Pass

North Peak   Middle Finger Buttress

AMPHITHEATRE MOUNTAIN

West Peak

col

Upper Cathedral
Lake

lower lake

CATHEDRAL PEAK and AMPITHEATRE MOUNTAIN

Boundary, just N of Tungsten Mine. Tungsten-bearing veins, which contain ore of wolframite, crop out principally on the E and S slopes of the mountain and to a lesser extent on the E slope of Apex Mountain. Vein deposits of tungsten invariably occur in close association with granitoid rocks, and here were heavily explored by early prospectors.
ROUTE: Leave the trail ½ mi. W of Tungsten Mine, then hike the mountain's SW slope. See Boundary Trail◆ and Chewack River Trail◆ (Tungsten Creek branch).

APEX MOUNTAIN   8297 ft/2529 m
Apex is 2½ mi. S of the International Boundary and SW of Tungsten Mine. Slopes are steep above Tungsten Lake, with rock walls, but the mountain is gently sloped on the S and W (structural features of the granite are extensive joint systems on the NE face).
ROUTES: Reach the SW flank via Chewack River Trail◆. The summit is merely a hike from the 5600-ft level.

One can also make an easy ascent from Tungsten Lake (see

Chewack River Trail◆). Hike 0.3 mi. E of the lake to meet the easy E ridge, or hike ESE for 0.8 mi. from Apex Pass.
APEX BUTTRESS: This is the most prominent buttress on the left side of the lake cirque (about ¼ mi. from the NW spur). First ascent by Don Leonard and Pete Doorish in July 1975. There are seven pitches: all can be well protected by chocks. From the rockslide above the lake do two short pitches (5.7-5.8); keep left of rock scar. The third pitch (5.9) is face climbing to a roof, then jam over). Grade II; class 5.9. Time: 4 hours.

AMPHITHEATRE MOUNTAIN
                                   8358 ft/2548 m
An important, massive, sprawling formation S of Cathedral Pass, SW of the more pointed and dominating Cathedral Peak, Amphitheatre was so named because of impressive glacial sculpturing: there are great cirques on the E and W, and beneath the NW flank the Cathedral Lakes nest in timberline basins. On the mountain's E flank, long spurs protrude between cirques. In their report of the 1901 recon-

naissance, Smith and Calkins described the mountain as sculptured with "four or five cirques, so that there is only a remnant of the originally dome-shaped mountain mass."[83] The approximate uniformity of summit heights and flat upper surfaces are suggestive of an older topography. The vertical jointing of the granite has materially assisted the work of ice in the cirques, where the amphitheater cutting plainly began its work on a much less rugged topography.

The central peak (0.7 mi. S of Cathedral Pass) is the highest, the N peak (8200 ft+/2499 m) is 0.3 mi. S of the pass, and the S peak is 8269 ft (2520m). The W peak of the W arm (just SW of Upper Cathedral Lake) is 8252 ft (2515 m). The attractive buttresses of the northern faces are located between the W peak and Cathedral Pass. Beneath the N flank of the mountain is a broad talus slope, then meadowed parkland which leads to the Cathedral Lakes, nesting in ice scours. Some of the parkland earlier contained lakes, now a zone being replaced by Hudsonian forest.

The first ascent was probably done by Smith and Calkins in the summer of 1901, and certainly repeated by Barnard's 1904 survey party.

SOUTHWEST ROUTE: The best approach to the mountain is from the trail to Cathedral Pass, but there are many route connections (see Horseshoe Basin♦, Chewack River Trail♦, Boundary Trail♦, Ashnola River Trail♦). The ascent is easily done from the Remmel Lake area directly from the SW; one can cross the W spur ridge from Upper Cathedral Lake to reach this basin (easy); it is also feasible to ascend the W peak directly and follow the summit area to the main peak.

Other routes on Amphitheatre include a deep snow gully on the N side of the E ridge, and the scree gully and easy col SW of Cathedral Pass in the break on northern rock walls.

NORTH BUTTRESS (Middle Finger Buttress): The wide face above Upper Cathedral Lake has three major buttresses: this is the largest and westernmost (deep gullies outline it as a finger). First ascent by Dave Anderson, Don Harder, and Donn Heller in August 1971. The entry chimney is behind the finger (right side of large detached block about 50 ft high). Ascend the deep chimney (5.6) to block ledge, then aid (A1) up the dihedral to a hanging belay; continue the dihedral to its end, then work left 10-15 ft and follow cracks with poor protection to a ledge. Bear left again and ascend a dihedral (5.7+). Finish with three leads of pleasant 4th class climbing. See topo. Grade III; class 5.7 and A1. Selection: Stopper sizes to 2½" (most cracks are ¾" to 1½"). Time: 4 hours. Reference: *Mountaineer,* 1971, pp. 88-89.

Descent: Hike E to the small col SW of Cathedral Pass (class 3 from here).

MIDDLE FINGER BUTTRESS, RIGHT SIDE: This route takes the prominent cracks on the NW side of the

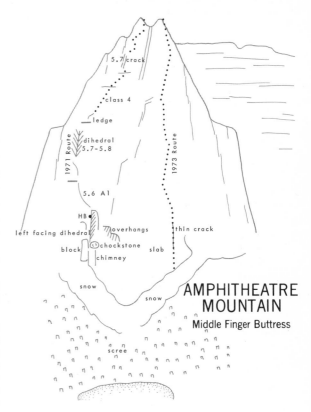

AMPHITHEATRE MOUNTAIN
Middle Finger Buttress

buttress starting about 200 ft from the 1971 route and meets it near the top. There are seven pitches (all free); first ascent by Ellie Brown, Pete Doorish, and Glen Wilson about July 15, 1973. Begin on a steep slab with thin finger crack part way up right side of buttress; second pitch takes a layback, then traverses left to an inside corner. Third pitch has a short 5.9 section; continue generally upward. Grade III; class 5.9.

NORTH RIDGE: This is the Cathedral Pass ridge which leads to the N peak. There are two notches that have scree gullies on their W sides. First ascent by Ellie Brown and Pete Doorish on August 29, 1973.

The rock is solid, with short pitches and scrambling between. The first step is rated 5.4, then above the first notch is 5.3; descend into the second notch (5.5) and then climb out again (5.3). Grade II; class 5.5. Time: 2-3 hours. Reference: *Mountaineer,* 1977, p. 108.

CATHEDRAL PEAK   8601 ft/2622 m

Cathedral is perhaps the most astonishing summit in the Similkameen subrange (Okanogan Range), not only for its esthetic qualities but for its dramatic contrast to the generally green, rolling parkland. Geologist Reginald A. Daly called the rock Cathedral batholith "after the fine monolithic mountain occurring within the limits of the granite."[84] Deep fractures which occur in parallel sets, with a narrow interval make the peak susceptible to erosion. Ice age glaciers quarried harshly, and they probably left behind the peak's S face, with its sharply defined joint planes: Cathedral is unique in that the S face is steeper and begins lower than the N face.

In their report Smith and Calkins describe observations "from the summit of Cathedral Peak" which they referred to as "conspicuous." The first ascent was made by Carl William Smith and George Otis Smith on August 3, 1901. The latter stated he chose the name because of its resemblance to a church.[85] In 1904 Cathedral was used as a triangulation station by Edward C. Barnard's Geological Survey topographic party, who reported they were on the extreme E end of a "bald castellated crag," estimated at 8600 ft altitude. Another rocky crag near Cathedral was used by triangulation parties during the placing of a boundary monument in 1905.[86] Subsequent climbing history is blank until the 1942 ascent by Everett and Ida Darr. References: U.S. Geol. Survey, *Bull. 235,* photo p. 88; *Joint Report,* p. 419; *Mountaineer,* 1964, pp. 88-89.

WEST RIDGE: One can approach by Boundary Trail♦ to upper Cathedral Lake (see also Ashnola River Trail♦, Chewack River Trail♦, and Andrews Creek Trail♦ and Wall Creek Route♦-B.C.). From Cathedral Pass climb directly up heather, scree, and a talus zone toward the prominent U-shaped gap (8400 ft+) in the skyline to the N. About 100 ft below the gap, angle right to stay below cliffs to the end of soil, then scramble over the first rock ridge at a small notch where the second (parallel) rock ridge is capped by a poised overhanging block. Drop a few ft into narrow canyonway between the ridges and follow it E about 40 ft. Exit up on left where a stone cairn gives a high foothold; scramble to the crest of second rock ridge. Follow E to the highest point, drop into little notch S and here one move requiring hands takes one onto the crest (walk to summit cross). Time: 1½ hours.

Alternative: From the N easy open slopes and a snow gully can be taken to the gap on the West Ridge.

NORTHEAST RIDGE: The route follows the prominent, winding ridge of Cathedral. By Ellie Brown and Pete Doorish in August 1973. First circle from the SE foot of the peak; the ridge begins broadly, to offer variety. About 400 ft from the finish is a fracture zone or dike to form a break in the continuity; Grade II; class 5.3.

SOUTHEAST BUTTRESS: This route offers nine to ten pitches of enjoyable crack climbing on good granite. It is an exceptional and challenging climb with good protection.

The route follows the ridge/buttress that lies behind The Monk as seen from the SE. There are four obvious steps, intersected by large grassy terraces. First ascent by Pete Doorish and Glen Wilson in July 1973; the route was done twice again in the next month, including an ascent by a Canadian party whose account erroneously identified it as the SW ridge.

Begin at the lowest part of the ridge, where the first step is left of The Monk and its intervening gully, well below the notch; one should begin at the low front of the step and traverse left, then up to the big ledge (easy class 5); one party bypassed via the gully, then did the face to the crest. Climb the second step from the ledge: begin in the chimney and then traverse right to obvious crack system (some 5.7 and 5.8 moves); later easier class 5 continues for several leads, generally following the crest of the buttress-ridge. The eighth pitch leads to a prominent headwall near the summit. The original party climbed this problem by face cracks in two pitches: the first one begins with a finger crack; the second is off size (5.9 if done directly). Note: The first pitch can also be done by a 5.8 crack just left. The step has been bypassed to the right, slightly on the E face (5.7). One ends at a table-top ledge; beyond the headwall is a last step (5.7) which is broken into two short portions. Grade III; class 5.9 (or class 5.8 if headwall is avoided); the route needs only chocks — include no. 9 and 10 hex.

Variation: By Clark Gerhardt and Elaine Meaker on September 6, 1974. This variation at the headwall makes a leftward bypass: first climb a pitch on the edge of the buttress (5.8); then drop down and traverse left 100 ft on ledge behind a flake; ascend a chimney system (large chimney) to easier climbing.

SOUTH FACE: This is a quite elegant 1000-ft face, perhaps the most esthetic in the area. Close jointing of the solid granitic rock has produced an excellent system of cracks and ledges. The route has much to recommend it. First ascent by Fred Beckey, John Brottem, Doug Leen, and Dave Wagner on September 28, 1968.

When hiking toward Cathedral Pass from the E, pass the lowest rock buttress and walk up the heather finger which slants left into the face. Pass a slabby groove at its head and continue up class 3 rock rightward toward midface. The first pitch bears left up a slabby ramp (5.5 start), and later works back up right to a small ledge below the obvious "Y" on the main white vertical face.

(2): Go up first crack right of "Y", off the left side of same small ledge (class 5.8); the last part works left easily to the invisible "Confession Box" (100 ft).

(3): Do 25 ft of aid (A1) on left, then free to right of a block; then climb a 40-ft chimney and cross right to a ledge (120 ft). An alternative is to step right into a jam crack (free but awkward start) at the beginning of the pitch.

(4): Ascend 170 ft up broken ramp and diagonal up left to a minor rib.

(5): Up a corner to its right, keeping right of the open "keyhole" blocks; end of lead is "Pulpit Ledge" (120 ft).

(6): Start at right edge of ledge: ascend crack with right-

CATHEDRAL PEAK from south
CHARLES HESSEY, JR.

CATHEDRAL PEAK
The Monk

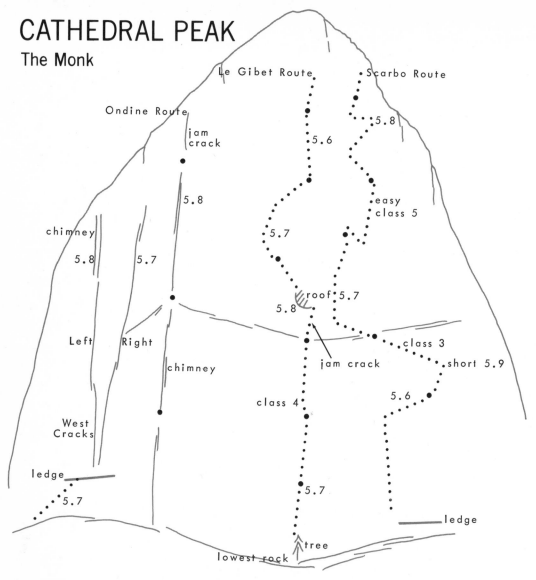

Le Gibet Route

Scarbo Route

Ondine Route

jam crack

5.8

5.6

5.8

easy class 5

chimney

5.7

5.8   5.7

roof 5.7

5.8

Left   Right

jam crack

class 3

chimney

short 5.9

class 4

5.6

West Cracks

ledge

5.7

5.7

ledge

tree

lowest rock

facing open book (some aid near start) which turns into right-curving chimney in 20 ft; here see large ceilings about 80 ft higher. A variation is to bear right on a 5.6 traverse, then up to meet chimney. The pitch continues up flakes, then traverses 5 ft right to a jam crack leading to base of prominent overhang. At its level is "Belfry Ledge" (on right).

(7): Up squeeze crack and blocks veering left, then broken rock to summit. Grade III or IV; class 5.8 and A1 (variations make route free); original climb used 35 pitons, but done

since all chocks (stoppers to 2½"); pitches 3 and 6 use most protection. References: *Mountaineer,* 1970, pp. 100-101; *A.A.J.,* 1969, p. 390.

THE MONK

This is the massive monolithic block on Cathedral's lower SE face that abuts the Southeast Buttress; the top of The Monk is about 80 ft higher than the connecting notch. There are a number of attractive routes on its outer S face (four-five pitches). Three of the routes were given names from Maurice Ravel's *Gaspard de la nuit* (Aloysius Bertand's French romantic prose poems set to music): *Ondine* (song of a water nymph, for purity of crack); *Scarbo* (creature of night — portrays a devilish dwarf); *Le Gibet* (a corpse hanging from gallows).

The routes, from W to E are:

WEST CRACKS: Left Crack: By Don Leonard and Pete Doorish in September 1977; class 5.8. Right Crack, same party July 1975; class 5.7.

ONDINE: By Pete Doorish and Bob Odum, September 1974. Follows single prominent crack; first pitch is chimney, then a jam crack; class 5.8.

LE GIBET: By Pete Doorish and Glen Wilson, July 1973. Start at low point of face; the crux goes around left side of prominent roof; class 5.8.

SCARBO: By Pete Doorish and Keith Hanson, August 1973. This is a winding route starting near the side of lowest area, off a large ledge; on third lead touches Le Gibet; class 5.9. All routes can be well protected by chocks. See topo. Descent: via NE gully (three 75 ft rappels).

THE POPE (Monument 95 Peak)
8264 ft/2519 m

This is the complex of crags and aiguilles in the locale of Monument 95, the highest point being 0.2 mi. S of the Boundary (the altitude at the border is given as 8000 ft+). The crags are at the western head of Ewart Creek, with Cathedral Fork to the S. Granite is solid for climbing, with numerous aiguilles, some with short faces, mostly facing NE. The complex has experienced some unrecorded rock climbing in the past decade.

In the summer of 1905 two United States monumenting parties began their work from Horseshoe Pass. Monument 95 on the N shoulder of Cathedral Peak was the only one difficult or dangerous to set. "It stands on a knife-like rock ridge so narrow that a place had to be blasted out to make room for the monument. At the upper end of the climb, monument and material had to be lifted up by ropes from shelf to shelf on the cliffs. In making the ascent one man lost his footing and fell 30 feet to a rock shelf below, but miraculously sustained only severe body bruises" (*Joint Report,* p. 77; see note 64). Party members were Edward C. Barnard, J.G. Hefty, W.B. Reaburn, Thomas Riggs, Jr., George Neuner, and W.W. Wineland. Map: Ashnola River 92 H/1.

ROUTES: One can approach via Wall Creek Route♦. An alternative is to hike cross-country from 1 mi. E of Cathedral Pass (Boundary Trail♦); from 7600 ft hike N of Cathedral Peak, then bear N on the Cathedral Fork slope. Some climbing has been done on the crags, but details are unknown.

MT. EWART (Sentinel) (B.C.)
8000 ft+/2438 m+

Distinguished only by a N-facing wall, Ewart is otherwise of minor importance; it is near the head of Ewart Creek, SE of the pass connecting to Wall Creek. Map: Ashnola River 92 H/1.

NORTH FACE: The eight-pitch route is mainly aid climbing. First ascent by Dave Anderson and Steve Barnett in August 1974. Make approach via Wall Creek Route♦. The line ascends midface: the first five pitches include interesting aid, then the final ones offer free climbing. Grade IV; class 5.9 and A3. The descent is on the S.

THE DEACON (B.C.)
8400 ft+/2560 m+

This summit is on the Wall-Ewart Creek divide, less than 1 mi. N of the Boundary, and SE of the pass (7600 ft+) between the two streams. The slopes are gentle on the S, but there is a steep E face.

ORTHODOX MOUNTAIN (B.C.)
8224 ft/2507 m

The high point 1 km W of The Deacon, between Wall Creek and its Cathedral Fork. The summit is steep on the N but low-gradient on the S; rock appears to be solid granitic. As triangulation station "Bosek" (estimated 8200 ft and 1.1 mi. from Monument 94, it was climbed by Jesse Hill of the Boundary Survey in 1935 (*Joint Report,* p. 419).

MT. GRIMFACE (B.C.)
8600 ft+/2621m+

This summit, E of Ashnola River in Cathedral Provincial Park, is perhaps the highest in the Similkameen subrange. The altitude 8701 ft was triangulated by early Boundary Survey parties, but some maps show it at near 8620 ft. Its precise locale is about 1¼ mi. N of Monument 95, on the divide between Wall and Lakeview creeks. The name was applied by Neal Carter, who with his wife Peggy made the first ascent (July 18, 1932 via the NW ridge), for the profile outline of a subsidiary crag resembling a human face from the W. They noted that the rock is "peculiarly eroded into immense semi-spheroidal masses which have the external appearance of stucco" (*C.A.J.,* 1932, p. 191). The Grimface-Stone City-Cathedral Ridge area has many unique terraces produced by quarrying. Surficial features exposed to the elements show soft-

Matriarch Mountain   Macabre Tower

MT. GRIMFACE from northeast
KARL RICKER

ened outlines caused by weathering.

Rock is granodiorite and quartz monzonite of the Similkameen Batholith; this intrusive has been called the Ewart Creek body (Rice, p. 36). It is coarse grained, light colored, and on the S is in contact with the red Cathedral body. Grimface is in a locale of high treeline: a scrub alpine fir has been noted about 200 ft below the summit.

The crest of Grimface trends SE-NW, but the various faces are complex, being somewhat divided by buttresses, crags, and chimney systems. The longest face is on the N, but the most attractive climbing has proven to be from both ridge notches and on the Wall Creek (S and SW) faces, where good jointing patterns have provided numerous crack and chimney systems, some of them not yet exploited. A high, S-jutting arete on this flank of the summit gives the mountain a

box-like shape when seen from the E or W. The arete extends to a steep S face, with a sharp SE corner; the total result of this and other features is to provide more quality rock climbing area on the mountain than one would expect from a frontal view.

It has been difficult to determine the complete climbing history of the area; some important routes on Grimface and on nearby crags may therefore not appear; various other short climbs are not included here because of the difficulty of locating them and lack of precise information. References: *C.A.J.,* 1932, p. 191 and photo p. 189; 1975, p. 66; 1976, pp. 57-58; 1977, p. 45; 1978, pp. 59-60. Map: Ashnola River 92 H/1.

NORTHWEST RIDGE: From Quiniscoe Lake (see Cathedral Provincial Park♦) hike to either Glacier or Ladyslipper Lake. Gain the divide beyond by scree gullies at the head of

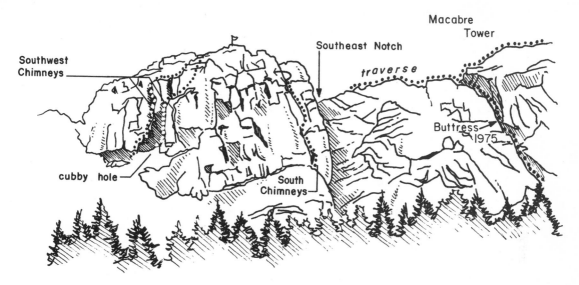

MT. GRIMFACE from Wall Creek

one of these basins. An alternative is to scramble up the ridge between the lakes to Pyramid Mountain. Once on the divide hike N of the easy Quiniscoe Mountain, or S on the W side of the ridge just past Ovis Mountain. Farther S a summit with a prominent W-facing chimney may be seen (Grimface). A "goat path" on the S flank of the main ridge can be taken toward the route. Scrambling begins at the last western notch: follow mainly on the N edge and in several hundred ft take the large gully/chimney that incises the ridge/buttress (class 3), then continue on to the summit. Rock is quite sound.

The ridge can be done in either direction (short pitches, short rappels, pleasant scrambling).

NORTHEAST FACE: The face as climbed is the final portion above a NE rock spur, to begin at about 8100 ft (UTM coordinates 705900m E and 5434000m N). First ascent by Steve Barnett, Fred Beckey, and Doug McCarty on August 12, 1973. Begin about 200 ft N of the mountain's Southeast Notch, and in two pitches climb to a small fir scrub. Two more pitches reach the eastern sub-summit rock knob. Class 5.7. Time: 2 hours.

SOUTHEAST NOTCH ROUTE: This was probably done first as part of a ridge traverse from the Wall Creek-Ewart Creek pass, by the Outward Bound staff in 1972 or 1973. The report stated the first pitch was fairly easy but exposed. The route was considered to be enjoyable with a variety of climbing to ridge walking (up to 5.7).

Note: The entire ridgetop traverse from the SE takes about one day; the Outward Bound party appears to have bypassed the summit of Macabre en route.

By scanning the area near the notch, two possibilities

seem apparent (one likely the above route). One is to climb a short chimney with a chockstone at its head, then continue up a right-bearing scree slope, then steep blocks. This is followed by a chimney of about 80 ft (with chockstones) and a walk right behind a big block; climb left and up to sandy ledges. Another route appears to begin about 100 ft N of the notch. This is a chimney and rock gully; then bear right on a ledge around a white wall, then left up blocks and cracks to the sub-summit knob.

SOUTH CHIMNEYS: This is a chimney system on the left side of the gully dividing the main and more frontal SE summit crag. The rock is good. There is a total of 400 ft of chimneys on this 600-700 ft route. First ascent by Bob Cuthbert, Robin Mounsey, and David Nichol in September 1973. From Wall Creek Route♦ scramble up a gully to the SE side of Grimface (or make a downhill traverse from Cathedral Ridge). At the bottom of the gully traverse left to gain the foot of the chimney that splits the S face. One begins at a small cave quite heavy with goat droppings. Climb the chimney to a rubble pocket where the gully widens, then up twin cracks on the left-hand wall to gain a deep cleft (three pitches of chimneys and gullies to twin cracks). Climb a sloping chimney, then go under an enormous chockstone at the top of the pitch to reach a terraced area. Walk through a granite corridor to the crux; this is a crooked squeeze chimney (slightly overhanging, with a small chockstone near the top); finish near the top of the W shoulder. Grade II or III; class 5.8. Time: ½ day. Reference: *C.A.J.,* 1974, p. 62.

SOUTHWEST FACE: This is a relatively short face on Grimface, about 400 to 500 ft in height, beginning with a large and obvious "cubby hole" (squared inside cleft) beneath the upper W ridge. The known routes are described below, and while the descriptions are believed to be accurate, the order may not be correct (or two of the routes may nearly coincide). The tentative order from left to right:

(1) A four-pitch chimney route, first done by Robin Mounsey and party in September 1973; the route begins on the far left corner of the cubby hole. Class 5.8.

(2) A route on the left side of the cubby hole was done by Steve Barnett, Fred Beckey, and Doug McCarty on August 15, 1973. The route aids a dihedral crack to a large ledge, then works right and up to an obvious crack in a groove. Aid was done here; scramble to a belay and then climb over a giant block (toward left) and then climb a steep crack system. Finally climb over blocks and stem a chimney to a ledge; a final strenuous jam crack (5.8) leads to the upper W ridge. Grade II; class 5.8 and A2.

(3) A route featuring a right-facing corner (four pitches) was done by Dave Anderson, Julie Brugger, and Cal Folsom in July 1973. The climb begins by jam-crack climbing; a series of cracks continues to about 100 ft W of the summit. Class 5.8.

(4) A five-pitch chimney route begins at the far right corner of the cubby hole, done by Outward Bound staff in September 1975. Class 5.7-5.8.

OVIS MOUNTAIN and "SMOKEY THE BEAR"

Note that these summits have an abrupt separating notch (Giant's Cleft) formed by the erosion of a basalt dike; the former is an easy scramble from the top of cleft. For location of Ovis, Smokey the Bear, and Stone City see Cathedral Provincial Park♦ and special map.

STONE CITY MOUNTAIN   8570 ft/2612 m

EAST FACE: This is an 800-ft face of solid rock (six leads). By John Halliday and Philip Kubik, July 1st weekend, 1975. Climb the broken face N of the prominent gully (northernmost gully of the Stone City-Smokey the Bear massif); from near the middle of the broken region up and slightly left, following cracks and ledges (three leads) to near the edge of face. The fourth lead continues up a left-facing flake; then traverse right into a narrow chimney and ascend to its end. The final lead traverses right and onto a ledge; then climb a 45-degree snow gully. Grade III; class 5.7 and A2 (aid at two places); take 12 hexes from no. 4-10 and a few pitons including KB. Time: 8 hours.

MACABRE TOWER   est. 8500 ft/2591 m

This formation is a rock blade SE of Mt. Grimface, which could be considered the middle peak of the latter. Ice attack in cirques has exploited the vertical joints and left a nearly perpendicular face of rock on the N. A route was done by Frank Baumann, Peter Macek, Murray McPhail, and Karl Ricker on July 1st weekend, 1975. In the Wall Creek Valley, the second major gully SE of Grimface (between rock buttresses)

leads to the ridge crest. A chimney on the N side leads to a minor point; then continue on slabs and ledges (class 3-4); downclimb or rappel a rounded slab to a vertical notch (piton rappel). Then climb to a horizontal crack, then to a shelf (5.2). Continue to a flake above a sloping shelf, then a short chimney. Class 5 (used several large hexes). Descent: To Macabre-Matriarch notch via rappels (30-ft vertical wall), then into gully on W side.

BUTTRESS ROUTE: A four-pitch route on the crest of the first major buttress SE of Grimface was done by the Outward Bound staff in September 1975; the buttress can be identified as left of a deep and important gully. Begin from the Wall Creek slope (see Wall Creek Route♦). Class 5.7.

MATRIARCH MOUNTAIN

This is the peak adjacent to and E of Macabre Tower, and adjacent to Denture Ridge on the Wall Creek-Lakeview Creek divide; there is a long rock face on the latter flank. First ascent by Outward Bound party in 1972 or 1973 via traverse from Wall-Ewart Creek pass. A path from Stone City Mountain on Cathedral Ridge can be taken along the Wall Creek slope; from the pass at the valley head it appears that a scrambling talus ascent of the SW ridge would lead to the crest, with minor notches to negotiate. A potential route appears to begin on the SW face from the third major gully SE of Grimface Mountain: scramble on rock (possibly also steep snow) to near the Macabre-Matriarch notch. Then it appears a route (class 4-5) ascends to the NW ridge of Macabre, which leads to the notch.

Denture Ridge appears to have interesting climbing opportunities, especially on the N face.

LAKEVIEW MOUNTAIN (B.C.)
8622 ft/2628 m

Lakeview is the quite massive, high summit 1.7 mi. NE of Grimface, between Ashnola River and Ewart Creek in Cathedral Provincial Park, entirely within the granitic intrusion. Most of the mountain's slopes are of gentle gradient, the upper surface consisting of bald, rocky (felsenmeer) terrain.[87] The double summit 1.3 mi. S of Lakeview (S of Point 8477) is known as *The Boxcar* (8500 ft+/2591 m+). The first summit visitation was made by the U.S. Boundary Survey party of 1904, under Edward C. Barnard. Map: Ashnola River 92 H/1.

ROUTES: The best route is via Goat Lake: ascend the larch-spruce hillside, then scree in a NE direction to the Boxcar-Lakeview saddle. Pathways among grass patches and boulders lead to both summits, but Boxcar is more the scramble of the two.

Another route is from where the Centennial Trail♦ crosses the divide N of the summit (see Cathedral Provincial Park♦). A cairned route leads to the bouldery summit area. Most flanks of Lakeview offer summit hiking routes. Time: 3 hours from Quiniscoe Lake.

HAYSTACK MOUNTAIN (B.C.)
8541 ft/2603 m
This broad massif with gentle flanks is 2.4 mi. SE of Lakeview Mountain and N of upper Ewart Creek; the three Haystack Lakes are on the NE flank of the mountain. Triangulation station "Walls" was placed here in 1935 (about 1¼ mi. NE of Monument 96, on the S end of "a rocky mountain with domes" — *Joint Report,* p. 419). Map: Ashnola River 92 H/1.
ROUTE: See Ewart Creek Trail♦. From the trail on the N valley flank in Mountain Goat Creek (est. 3 mi.) a path leads to the 7100-ft lakes — a long day from the road. The mountain offers an easy ascent here via its northern shoulder. One can also reach the summit from The Boxcar by traversing about the rim of Mountain Goat valley and along the divide over the W summit.

CRATER MOUNTAIN (B.C.)
7522 ft/2293 m
A summit of minor importance located 3½ mi. N of the lower Ashnola River and SW of the Ashnola-Similkameen junction. The slopes are gentle, with considerable meadow; there are some interesting columnar basalt cliffs. Map: Ashnola River 92 H/1.
ROUTE: From Ashnola River Road♦ just beyond where it first crosses to the W side of the river a rough road extends to the summit via the NE flank. Another road begins at Crater Creek (11 mi.) and leads to 6500 ft. An easy open hike continues.

CHUWANTEN MOUNTAIN (B.C.)
7048 ft/2148 m
A bald knob at 2.7 mi. N of Monument 83, this is the highest summit on the Castle Peak-Pasayten River divide. The ascent was probably done 1859-1860 by the Boundary Survey; it was definitely done in 1904 by Barnard's party, who called it "Station Roche." Map: Manning Park 92 H/2 East.
ROUTE: The ascent is a hike from the Monument 83 Trail♦ (about 8 mi. total from the highway). Leave at about 5000 ft and ascend easily through pines.

THREE BROTHERS (B.C.)
7453 ft/2272 m
This is a series of summits on a high ridge located on the divide E of the upper Similkameen River, in the Hozameen Range 5.5 mi. NE of Allison Pass. The area is one of vast floral meadows and open ridges. The highest summit is the E peak; the W peak is 7382 ft, and the NW peak is 7367 ft. Rock is part of the Cretaceous Pasayten Group. The vast ice sheets of the Pleistocene overrode the mountain. Map: Manning Park 92 H/2 West.
ROUTE: See Manning Provincial Park♦ (Heather Trail♦). Open meadows and ridges lead from the trail, which traverses high on the SW summit slopes. *Big Buck Mountain* (7031 ft/2143 m) is almost crossed by the route. The trek is an all day r.t., but easy, and it is a fine ski tour. References: *B.C.M.,* September 1963, June 1972.

SNASS MOUNTAIN (B.C.)
7580 ft/2310 m
Snass is a prominent regional mountain, the highest summit on the Snass-Skaist divide (located W of Skaist River). It was ascended by members of the Boundary Survey in 1859. Map: Princeton 92 H/7.
ROUTE: From about 6 mi. up Snass Creek Trail♦ double back to the SE through a divide to Paradise Valley at about 4900 ft, then follow blazes S to Punchbowl Lake (5400 ft+; camping). Ascend S to the prominent gap about 400 ft S above the lake and follow the W ridge of the mountain. Allow a full day r.t. from lake and back to highway.
Variation: From the lake hike SE via a small valley to a subsidiary col, then cross a snow basin beyond; climb steep snow to the base of the final peak (a good spring route).
SNAZZY PEAK (est. 7300 ft/2225 m) is a minor rock summit closely SE of Snass. First ascent by Donald Cowie and Howard Rode in 1955. From the summit of Snass descend, then follow the W ridge of objective (class 3 scrambling, or detour via scree).

MT. DEWDNEY (B.C.)   7368 ft/2246 m
Named for the Canadian trail pioneer, Dewdney is W of Snass Creek at 4 mi. N of the Trans-Canada Hwy and 4 mi. W of Snass Mountain (highest summit on the Snass-Sowaqua Creek divide); slopes are mainly gentle. Reference: *B.C.M.,* February 1958. Map: Hope 92 H/6.
NORTHEAST RIDGE: Follow the Snass Creek Trail♦ about 1½ mi. to the gully descending N of Mt. Ford (beyond heavy timber). Ascend the gully to the ridge, then follow this NE to the base of Dewdney's summit area. Climb directly by a rock scramble (or first traverse W if desired). The gully is bushy after snow melts. Time: 6 hours from road.
WEST RIDGE: Follow Eighteenmile Creek Trail♦ to near its end at Ghost Pass. Hike up the W ridge of the mountain to the high shoulder, then to the summit (easy, pleasant

route but longer than the NE).

MT. FORD (6900 ft+/2103 m+) may be reached easily by taking the Northeast Ridge of Dewdney S from the gully head; Ford's summit is 1.9 mi. SSW of Dewdney. References: *B.C.M.*, April 1958, February 1972.

MT. OUTRAM (B.C.)

8000 ft+/2438 m+

This is the dominant barren peak on Manson Ridge, NE of the western Manning Park entrance, at the head of Seventeenmile Creek (9 mi. NE of Silvertip Mountain). Outram rises in a long relief from 2100 ft at 2.8 mi. from the Sumallo River. Much of the mountain above the 6000-ft level is open slope, with the finest assortment of arctic flora in the northern Cascades (a great variety of lupines, saxifrage, gentians). There is a small glacier on its steeper NE flank, much shrunken judging from early historic reports. During early visitation, much of the lower area was burnt over by prospectors, the mountain then being known as "Seventeenmile hill" (Cairnes, 1922, map). The name is for Sir James Outram, English general and a hero of the Indian mutiny at Lucknow 1857-1858. First ascent by Leslie C. Ford, Fred Perry, Herbert Selwood, and T.L. Thacker on August 12, 1924. References: *B.C.M.*, January 1941, November and December 1941, January 1942, October 1947, December 1958, October 1969. Map: Hope 92 H/6.

SOUTHEAST ROUTE: Begin from Trans-Canada Hwy 3♦. The Mt. Outram Trail (see Eighteenmile Creek Trail♦) follows up the ridge S of Seventeenmile Creek; cross the stream at 5500 ft and keep left to a tiny lake (6200 ft+). Then follow the broad meadowy ridge, which is simple and pleasant. Time: 6 hours from road. This is also a nice ski tour.

Other routes: The ascent has also been done from the gravel pit at Mile 14 using the steep SW ridge (also high meadows and easy); also the valley W of the mountain and its N fork (hanging valley) to NW of the summit, then taking an easy ridge scramble; also from due E or NE (original route).

MacLEOD PEAK (B.C.)

7100 ft+/2164 m+

This is a rocky, high peak located 3.7 mi. NW of Mt. Outram, between Eight Mile and Eleven Mile creeks. Maps show the summit at the E peak; the W peak is nearly as high, ½ mi. distant. The southern slopes are the most moderate. This is probably the Manson Mountain shown on early maps at 7115 ft and plainly

visible from Hope (mentioned in the Cairnes geologic report). References: *B.C.M.*, October 1955 and 1961. Map: Hope 92 H/6.

ROUTES: See Trans-Canada Hwy 3♦. From N of Eleven Mile Creek climb to the main W ridge via bush, rockslide, and timber (not pleasant). The ridge between the highway and Eleven Mile Creek is taken over the W peak; continue by the sharp connecting ridge (class 3). Time: allow all day r.t. Descent: Can use a steep gully.

Another route is to begin via the Eight Mile Creek Road, which becomes hiking in 1 mi. Ascend the fork which zigzags to the ridge at about 3200 ft (timber and some cliffs); about 5 hours for first peak.

PEAK 7200 + (2195 m+) is located 1.4 mi. E of MacLeod (3 mi. NW of Outram). First ascent by Joe Hutton and Roy Mason in 1956. The ascent can be done via Eleven Mile Creek but is brushy; it is better to follow the N side of the stream via an old logging spur, then rise to the lowest ridge point connecting the peaks; a scrambling heather ledge route completes the route.

TULAMEEN MOUNTAIN (B.C.)

7499 ft/2286 m

A significant summit in the Hope Mountains portion of the Hozameen Range, 7 mi. NNE of Mt. Outram on the Coquihalla-Tulameen River divide. The mountain is steep on the N and NW, but otherwise of moderate gradient. The E summit is slightly higher than the W (latter is 7200 ft+). Possibly Tulameen is Ee-shal-lul-luk Mountain of an early Boundary Survey manuscript map. Map: Hope 92 H/6.

NORTHEAST ROUTE: See Tulameen River Road♦. Drive old Vuich Creek mining road to about 5000 ft on its tributary Amberty Creek. From Treasure Mountain Mine area hike ridges SW. An alternative is to use the Vuich Creek trail, the E slope of the mountain. The trip is largely open ridges; easy and pleasant — one long day r.t.

DEWDNEY CREEK ROUTE: From the end of the road (see Coquihalla River Road♦) a trail leads E. On the valley's E flank bear to the divide N of the mountain. This is a longer route than the one from the NE.

MT. SNIDER (B.C.)   6700 ft/2042 m

Between Sowaqua Creek and Dewdney Creek at 4½ mi. from Coquihalla River (3½ mi. NW of Tulameen Mountain). Map: Hope 92 H/6.

ROUTES: One can reach the NW side of the mountain from logging roads. The Dewdney Creek Road has branches to over 4000 ft (condition uncertain). The SW slope can be reached from Sowaqua Creek (logging tracks extend to 3700 ft).

COQUIHALLA MOUNTAIN (B.C.)
7088 ft/2160 m

This is an important peak regionally, located SE of Coquihalla River about 10 mi. S of Coquihalla summit. Its locale is the Bedded Range, a dioritic plug surrounded by basalt and rhyolite flows of the Coquihalla Series (Cairnes, Memoir 139, p. 77; see note 5). Map: Hope 92 H/11.

ROUTE: See Coquihalla River Road◆. The objective is to first reach the Hidden Creek-Unknown Creek ridge. From the Needle-Hidden Creek crossing several hundred meters N of large iron railroad bridge, ascend forested slopes along the N edge of a prominent landslide. At its head bear E to reach the N ridge of Unknown Ridge (keep on landslide until 4000 ft). Hike S on the crest to the upper meadows of Hidden Creek basin; from the saddle of Hidden and Jim Kelly Creek ascend the W ridge of the mountain or the easy SW slopes (no difficulty). Time: 8 hours r.t.

MT. COULTER (B.C.)   6563 ft/2000 m

Located between Outram (Slide) and Wray Creek branches of Nicolum Creek and W of the latter (in the Silvertip-Hope subrange). Map: Hope 92 H/6.

ROUTE: Make the easy ascent from Outram Creek — see Mt. Potter. The ascent is short and the forest open.

MT. POTTER (B.C.)   6200 ft+/1890 m+

A rather minor summit located between upper Sumallo River and Outram Creek, S of the Sumallo bend. Map: Hope 92 H/6.

ROUTE: From Outram Creek Road (Trans-Canada Hwy 3◆) take the road to near the valley head. Ascend a cat road through forest to the shoulder W of the summit; continue on meadows.

MARMOT MOUNTAIN (B.C.)
6800 ft+/2073 m+

Located 2¼ mi. SW of the Skagit-Sumallo River junction in the Silvertip-Hope Mountain subrange. The mountain is of minor interest in the regional scale, but is moderately rough and forested. Map: Skagit River 92 H/3.

ROUTE: The most apparent route is the S slope, but this may be difficult to reach (the Skagit trail is on the opposite side of the river); wading the river may be feasible (or logs?). Expect some bushy travel on lower slopes.

SILVERTIP MOUNTAIN (B.C.)
8500 ft+/2591 m+

Silvertip is the dominating summit in the Hope Mountains of the Skagit Range, N of the International Boundary. It is located just 4 mi. NW of the Skagit-Klesilkwa River junction, with long steep slopes above these low valley bottoms; local relief is up to 6700 ft. Rock is of the Paleozoic Hozameen Group — mostly andesite flows and pyroclastics (greenstones); the area also has some Custer Gneiss, chert, and limestone. There is a small glacier on the upper eastern slope, draining to Silvertipped Creek. Indians used the term "Kleh-kwun-num" for the Hope subrange; Henry Custer's 1859 sketch titles Silvertip "East Skagit Mountain," but the series 68 manuscript map of the Boundary Survey shows "Nuk-a-lah-woom Mountain." Silvertip can be seen from many distant viewpoints, including from Washington State on the Lynden Hwy just S of Alderbrook. The first ascent was made by Norman Kellas on September 1, 1940 via the SE ridge. References: *B.C.M.*, November 1940, January 1967, June 1967. Map: Skagit River 92 H/3.

NORTH ROUTE: The North Route from the Sumallo River Road◆ has three possible beginnings: the gully (on left), the spur, and the direct way to the Silvertip-Rideout col (only good when snow-filled, but danger from cornices and avalanches).

NORTHEAST RIDGE: This is a rather long, but usable route concluding with some rock climbing near the summit; the route is preferable when snow is gone because of spring avalanche danger. First ascent by Alan Melville and party of 12 on July 2, 1950 (via Silvertipped Creek). The best beginning now is from the Sumallo River road fork at the ski area. Ascend to the ridge: from the ridge col (5400 ft+) the distance to the summit is 2½ mi. Class 3. Time: long day r.t.

Variation: From Silver-Skagit Road◆ at Skagit River crossing ascend logging spur on W side of river (or via Silvertipped Creek); bear to the ridge N of Silvertipped Creek, then follow this to the NE ridge. There is some bush travel on the route; one party ascended a snow gully for several thousand ft. Reference: *Avalanche Echoes*, August-September 1950.

SOUTHEAST ROUTE: The original ascent used this flank of the mountain, beginning near the Klesilkwa-Skagit River junction, then taking the "snout" of the dry SE ridge to where the slope flattens at 7500 ft (7 hours); the final portion was done on the S, where rock is loose but not difficult. A version of this route was used by Howard Fraser and Howard Rode on April 4, 1950, following a ridge nose and up a creek bed, then a snow gully and a ridge to the 7250-ft bump on the SE ridge (a long route). Reference: *B.C.M.*, July 1955.

Drive and hike the road to just before its end at final W fork (est. 3900 ft). Here one can study the broad spur bearing S toward the upper W ridge, where it joins at about 7600 ft. Find an old mining track switchbacking sharply uphill leftward in the alder and follow it 15 minutes, then ascend to a prominent snow tongue extending into the alder and scree. The route ascends scree on its NW side, then up the first gully seen from below (may be snow in gully). Exit gully and cross a snowfield, then climb above the spur (steep snow) to the W ridge. Follow this ridge, keeping S of a prominent bump. Note: Avalanche danger exists on this flank of the mountain in spring and early summer; later the route will have brushy sections. On the descent there are some glissading opportunities. Class 3. Time: 6-8 hours.

Variation: The steep snow gully left of the spur leads into an avalanche basin at 5500 ft, then bears up and left over loose moraine. There is some scrambling up rocky flanks to the W ridge. This variation can be dangerous if conditions are not optimum; a good descent route if snow is in glissade condition.

Variation: Follow the old road track to about 4300 ft. Beyond its end (hike right at final fork) ascend directly, or along old track to a mining cabin still visible at the base of a cliff; lower slopes here are scree and alder. Take gully to right above cabin and follow a rope to another cabin on the cliff's ridge nose. Ascend through basin headwall (couloir?) to the Silvertip-Rideout col (6700 ft+), then follow the W ridge. The route is best early when brush is covered.

SOUTHWEST ROUTE: This ascent involves some 6500 ft of altitude gain, and is best when snow covers brush slopes (late spring). Use the gully system S and W of the summit (gully crosses Silver-Skagit Road♦) near gravel pit 3½ mi. W of Skagit River crossing. Climb slopes E of the gully for about 1500 ft, then traverse into it above a gorge; keep right at first fork and left at second. Leave the gully at 6500 ft and ascend to the mountain's W ridge. Long day r.t. Reference: *B.C.M.,* June 1955.

Variation: Approach the W ridge as per Rideout Mountain.

MT. RIDEOUT (B.C.)   8029 ft/2447 m

Rideout is a high, craggy peak 1.7 mi. W of Silvertip Mountain; the northern flank is especially steep and alpine. First ascent by Jack Bussell, Herman Genschorek, Ian Kay, Alan Melville, and Walter Sparling on June 11, 1950 (from Silverhope Creek). Reference: *C.A.J.,* 1951, p. 165. Map: Skagit River 92 H/3.

EAST ROUTE: Ascend to the NW shoulder of Silvertip, then descend the ridge to the connecting col (6700 ft+). The continuing ridge is class 3. A more direct ascent is only suited for early season.

Note: The SW route is very long and a poor choice; if used, begin from the gravel pit, ascend ridge to left of nearby creek, then bear right around cliffs above timberline (see Silvertip Mountain-Southwest Route). The route would be best when gullies are snow-filled.

NORTH FACE: This is a 3000-ft face of poor rock quality. First ascent by Dick Culbert and Fred Douglas in 1970. Reach the base via an ascending traverse over rockslides from the end of Sumallo River Road♦. Start on the left side of the face, bearing rightward to the left side of a small shoulder in

midface. Continue up an indistinct buttress; avoid problems first on the right, then to left. There is much class 4 and 5, with scree on some ledges. Grade III; time: long day. Reference: *B.C.M.,* February-March 1970.

MT. PAYNE (B.C.)   8100 ft+/2469 m+

This is the prominent pyramidal-shaped peak on the rugged Silvertip-Hope subrange at 1.2 mi. WNW of Mt. Rideout (on the Klesilkwa-Sumallo River divide and slightly higher than the latter); there is a similar 6000-ft relief on the S flank. The name is for Father Damasus Payne, hiker and climber from the Jesuit monastery at Mission. First ascent by Jack Bussell, Herman Genschorek, Ian Kay, Alan Melville, and Walter Sparling in 1950. Map: Skagit River 92 H/3.

ROUTES: The best way now is via the final W fork of Sumallo River (see Mt. Rideout); expect some bush and cliffs. No details ATP.

A long route has been done from the SE, leaving the Silver-Skagit Road♦ 6 mi. W of the Skagit crossing. Ascend a N-S ridge to the col (7200 ft+) SE of the summit, then the ridge (bypass a pinnacle on its S); class 3.

A SW ridge has been done directly to the summit (John Holmes and Roy Mason, 1956). From Mile 19 on the road cross ¼ mi. of slash to the foot of a steep narrow ridge. There are some cliffs and bush before steep meadows and easy rock leading to the summit. Time: 7 hours. Reference: *B.C.M.,* November 1956.

MT. FORDDRED (B.C.)
7100 ft+/2164 m+

On the main divide of the Hope-Silvertip Mountain subrange (at 4.2 mi. NE of the latter); there is much pleasant meadowland below the summit area, but lower slopes are wooded and brushy. The N side of the summit area holds perennial snow. The mountain is within the exposed granitic intrusive, and displays a craggy summit. First ascent by Dick Culbert and Paul Plummer in 1964. Map: Skagit River 92 H/3.

SOUTHEAST ROUTE: From near the end of Sumallo River Road♦ in the W fork at 4500 ft ascend to meadows and the col S of the summit (6600 ft+); the completion is easy. Time: 3 hours.

WEST ROUTE: From the Silver-Skagit Road♦ at the mouth of Hicks Creek ascend E up the open stream valley, then forest to finish by the easy S or SW slopes.

PEAK 7100 + (2164 m+) (unnamed) ¾ mi. S of Forddred is slightly higher; reach from the separating col (reported an easy scramble).

EATON PEAK (B.C.)
6900 ft+/2103 m+

This summit is in the granitic intrusive (Chilliwack

Batholith) on the Silverhope-Sumallo River divide at 7.8 mi. NW of Silvertip Mountain. Eaton Lake is to its NW. First ascent by Jock Butcher, Ernest Jenkins, and Fred Rogers on October 15, 1950. References: *B.C.M.,* September 1956, April 1958, December 1958, October 1970. Map: Skagit River 92 H/3.

ROUTES: From the W end of Eaton Lake (Eaton Lake Trail♦) climb S up steep timber and brush, then subalpine terrain and open bouldery slopes. At 5000 ft traverse E and cross a spur, then traverse below the SE face of objective. Gain the summit ridge at the low point E of the summit (6300 ft+), then ascend the easy final SE spur. Class 3. Time: 4 hours from lake.

Note: Original party climbed around N wall of summit ridge to take a route near its W end; a solid rock pitch led to a long exposed summit ridge. A descent variation to the N is not recommended.

The E face was climbed by Paul Hinkley and Jerry Schmiesing on October 12, 1969 — possibly a new route.

PEAK 7126 (Crescent Lake Peak)
(Mt. Grant) (B.C.)   7126 ft/2172 m
A significant, rugged peak with some steep portions; it is in the granitic intrusive. This is the most northerly of the summits above 7000 ft on the main divide of the subrange between Silvertip and Hope mountains, located just N of the W end of Eaton Lake (4 mi. from Silver Lake). The peak has a steep N face but is gently sloped on the S. There was no record of a previous visit when a party on June 16, 1951 reached the summit, but it is uncertain if this was the first ascent (Paul Binkert, John Booth, Dick Chambers, Jim Irving, Don Montgomery, Jim Teevan). The proposed name (Grant) is for Captain John M. Grant of the Royal Engineers, who rebuilt a portion of the old Dewdney Trail. Map: Hope 92 H/6 West and Skagit River 92 H/3. References: *B.C.M.,* July 1951 and September 1956.

ROUTE: See Eaton Lake Trail♦. From the lake find a trapline path up through timber NW. An obvious ridge to open meadows leads to the broad summit. Steep meadows and scree patches are the total difficulties. Note: An ascent from Wray Creek Road (see Trans-Canada Hwy 3♦) is probably feasible.

WELLS PEAK (B.C.) 6000 ft+/1829 m+
A small peak located 1¼ mi. E of Silver Lake on the Silverhope-Nicolum Creek divide (Silvertip-Hope subrange). Similar to other summits of this group, the peak has rocky, rough slopes with brush and subalpine forest at the lower altitudes. Map: Hope 92 H/6.

Take the Four Mile Creek Road (see Trans-Canada Hwy 3♦) which now extends to 3700 ft in the valley N of the summit, to permit a hiking ascent from here (barely over 1 mi.).

SILVER BLUFFS. A rock climb on the W face above Silver Lake (about 2500 ft to 4000 ft) was done by Dick Culbert and Alice Purdey in 1966. From near the N end of the lake take a creek bed to the buttress; the route is class 4 and 5 on granite.

HOPE MOUNTAIN (B.C.)
6026 ft/1837 m
Hope is a large hulk of the Chilliwack Batholith only 2¼ mi. SSE of Hope townsite, and quite dominant from this locale. It is the northwestern end of the extensive Hope-Silvertip Mountain subrange (see Cairnes, Memoir 139, p. 83). A manuscript map of the early Boundary Survey shows the mountain as Ste-teh-mia. References: *B.C.M.,* June 1956, July 1961. Map: Hope 92 H/6.

ROUTE: From just beyond the S bend and bridge on Trans-Canada Hwy 3♦ 2.6 mi. from Hope there is a slow lane pullout. Climb right above the gravel cut, then bear left to overgrown roadway; a blazed route then curves right to a mossy rockslide. Cross this to blaze and find route, keeping E of a stream until in hanging valley. From about 3500 ft altitude bear to right across valley with large timber, then gain the divide at its low-area (4600 ft+) about ¾ mi. SE of the summit; follow the broad ridge NW to the top. The trek is easy, but allow 10 hours r.t. By 1981 the best route should be to use the Four-Mile Creek Road (see Trans-Canada Hwy 3♦) and branch (Two Mile) into the hanging valley.

OGILVIE PEAK (B.C.)
5900 ft+/1798 m+
A locally important peak just 3.5 mi. N of Hope. Map: Hope 92 H/6.

ROUTES: Take Squeah Road♦ to beyond a hill crossing; 2.5 mi. from Hope a logging road (uncertain condition) bears E steeply to about 3000 ft on the flank NW of the peak; the S branch leads to about 4000 ft on the main W ridge. Hike the N side of the ridge and take meadows to the summit.

The N branch of the road crosses the valley at about 4200 ft on the N side of a farther ridge spur. Hike S to its crest and follow the easy ridge.

JORGENSON PEAK (6000 ft+/1829 m+) is to the N of Ogilvie; reach by the N spur road. Hike E to the lowest point on the divide, then follow this 1.3 mi. N.

SQUEAH MOUNTAIN (5900 ft+/1798 m+) is NNE of Jorgenson (only 3.7 mi. E of Fraser River). The best approach is probably from Suka Creek (see Squeah Road♦).

SPIDER MOUNTAIN (5200 ft+/1585 m+) is at the head of Suka and Qualark creeks; the S slopes are gentle. Map: Spuzzum 92 H/11. It is best to reach the mountain from West Ladner Creek Road (see Coquihalla Road◆) or the Qualark Creek Road (see Squeah Road◆). A summit to the NE (6009 ft) is best reached from the road into upper Siwash Creek; hike the easy W ridge.

NEEDLE PEAK (B.C.)

6900 ft+/2103 m+

This is an impressive granitic formation near the Anderson River Group, located between Boston Bar Creek and Coquihalla River. The peak has distinctive SW and NE ridges and an eastern buttress. Reference: *B.C.M.*, March 1975. Map: Spuzzum 92 H/11.
SOUTHWEST RIDGE: From Coquihalla River Road◆ hike up the S side of Needle Creek, then avoid brush by contouring into the valley, crossing the stream at 4000 ft. Best in early season due to higher snow cover on long hillside. Can camp in basin. Bear high right into the N valley flank and make a rising traverse to the col SW of the summit; the ridge is narrow but not difficult. Time: easy day r.t.
EAST BUTTRESS: First ascent by Fred Douglas and Paul Starr June 1974. This is reported as a good rock route; two pitches of 5.6-5.7 (remainder easier).
NORTHEAST RIDGE: This appears to be a gymnastic scramble; no details.

ANDERSON RIVER GROUP (B.C.)

The name "Anderson River Group" has evolved for the spectacular granitic topography in the Cascades (Needle Peak Pluton) centering 20 mi. (32 km) NE of Hope and 18 mi. (29 km) SE of Boston Bar. The setting is uniquely rugged, with dramatic cliffs, polished domes and slabs, and glacier-carved valleys where small cirques often hold perennial snow. In some aspects, the peaks resemble those in Arctic locations or Tuolomne Meadows (Yosemite). Because the summits are of moderate altitude (6000-7000 ft) some slopes have unpleasant brush. The exposed rock tends to have few fractures, but instead features enormous slabs covered with crescent-shaped exfoliations. Geologist George M. Dawson was one of the first to take notice of the impressive rock formations: "Looking up the valley of the Anderson, in a bearing of S 6° E, a great block of higher mountains at a distance of about thirteen miles, can be seen. On the west of the group is an irregular conical peak, nearly vertical on one side. These summits must reach an altitude of 7,000 to 8,000 ft" (Dawson, p. 37B; see note 73). With the planned improved road access, the entire Anderson River and related Coquihalla-drainage peaks are destined to become an important rock climbing center, with many new routes still to be pioneered.

The various summits have been named for alpine ruminants of Europe, Peru, and the Himalaya. Anderson River Mountain, Chamois, Ibek and Steinbok peaks form the impressive western grouping. Alpaca, Guanoco, and Llama peaks and Zopkios Ridge are to the immediate E, on the divide with Coldwater River, and merging with the peaks on the rim of Falls Lake cirque; on Zopkios Ridge various names refer to strange crossbreeds with the Himalayan yak.

The approach for the western peaks is the Anderson River Road (Fraser River Hwy◆), via the logging camp at the main and N forks; the North Main Road is the central entry for climbing and hiking. The eastern peaks are reached from Coquihalla River Road◆ and the gas pipeline roadway, and a logging spur into the upper Coldwater River. Alpine hiking and ski touring possibilities increase toward the E side of the area. A pleasant ridge traverse is the rim of Falls Lake cirque: begin via the pipeline roadway SW of Falls Lake Creek (see Nak Peak), then hike along Zopkios Ridge, then continue around the rim over Zoe Peak. References: *B.C.M.*, October 1970; *C.A.J.*, 1975, p. 66; 1976, pp. 54-56. Map: Spuzzum 92 H/11.

ANDERSON RIVER MOUNTAIN (B.C.)

6485 ft/1977 m

This summit, formerly called the North Peak, is the northwestern outlier of the impressive western cluster of the range. There is a small glacier beneath the steep eastern granite wall. The first ascent was made by the 1961 party (see Ibex Peak), who ascended SE from Anderson River forks.

CHAMOIS PEAK (B.C.)

6600 ft+/2012 m+

One of the four stalwarts in the western grouping of the range, this impressive peak is the first SE of Anderson River Mountain. The E face and its flanks are impressive apron-walls. The striking feature here is a pyramidal rampart termed "Les Cornes" (E corner). The first ascent was made by the 1962 party (see Ibex Peak) during their traverse. The route began at Anderson River forks.

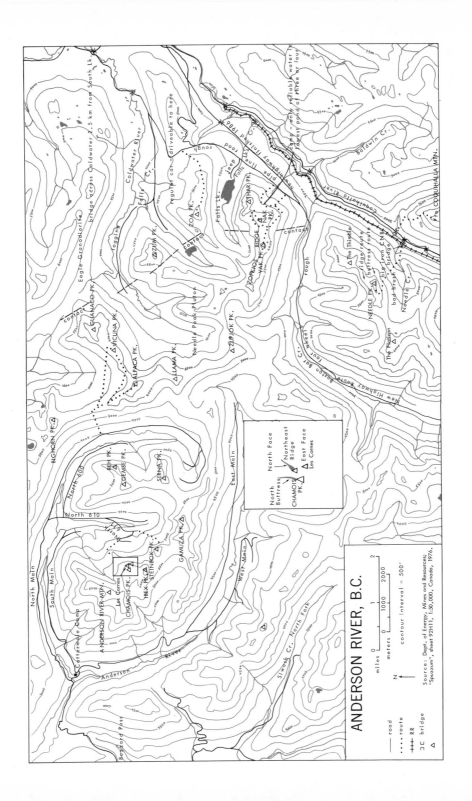

ANDERSON RIVER, B.C.

road ——
route ·······
RR +++
bridge ⊐⊏
△

miles 0   1   2
meters 0   1000   2000

contour interval = 500'

N ←

Source: Dept. of Energy, Mines and Resources;
"Spuzzum", sheet 92H11, 1:50,000, Canada, 1976.

North Buttress
North Face
Northeast Ridge
East Face
CHAMOIS PK. △
△ Les Cornes

CHAMOIS PEAK – North Buttress
ED ZENGER

NORTH BUTTRESS: This 700-ft buttress is a nice rock climb of about 12 pitches, very solid and clean. First ascent by Peter Stange and Ed Zenger on July 26, 1975. Approach the col between Anderson River Mountain and Chamois Peak, then over a small ridge (can camp under N buttress of Chamois). On the buttress a 40-ft lead goes to the base of a lieback (5.4); this widens into a grassy gully, then a chimney. A gully is taken for three leads to a narrow exposed ledge; here bear right to a low-angle slab. Two leads go up cracks and chimneys (5.2); traverse across a slab under a large overhang, then a scramble and a 5.4 lead takes one to another slab. Easy cracks and slabs are taken up and left to the ridge crest. Grade II; class 5.4 maximum; two-thirds of climb is class 4 or 3. Time: 4 hours. Reference: *C.A.J.*, 1976 (photo) pp. 55-56.

LES CORNES

NORTHEAST RIDGE: This route, listed in *C.A.J.*, 1976, p. 56, under the heading "Chamois Peak," actually leads to the first pinnacle of Les Cornes. The first party was B.

Casselman, Dick Culbert, and Neil Humphreys. The route is somewhat dirty.

NORTH FACE: The route leading to the second of Les Cornes (pinnacles) is "behind" the Northeast Ridge, in the cirque between the N buttress of Chamois and the Northeast Ridge of Les Cornes. First ascent by John Bates and Ed Zenger in 1975. This route is somewhat rotten and unrewarding. Mainly class 3-4 with four pitches of class 5 near the top. Grade II; 5.7. Time: 3 hours.

The route is erroneously listed in *C.A.J.,* 1976, as East Face of Chamois Peak.

EAST FACE: This route begins in the center of the face on the opposite side of Les Cornes from the Bates-Zenger route. First ascent by Paul Berntsen and Steve Woodhouse, June 1978. First follow a class 4 ramp leading up and left to a point midway up the face. Here turn directly up for about six leads of sustained and exposed 5.6 to 5.7. Excellent belay ledges.

Original descent by same route because of poor visibility (chock rappel anchors).

IBEX PEAK (B.C.) 6600 ft+/2011 m+

This rugged granitic dome is the third from Anderson River Mountain (0.9 mi. distant), and was once referred to as North Anderson River Peak. It is the highest summit in this knot of peaks (higher than Chamois, to which it is connected as a massif); there are some spectacular walls and slabs on its E face, with numerous climbing opportunities. First ascent by Asger Bentzen, Hamish Mutch, Bob Woodsworth, and Glenn Woodsworth on August 31, 1962.

ROUTE: Ascend SE from Anderson River forks up open wooded ridge to near the summit of Anderson River Mountain, then make a descent SE across a gorge between Anderson River Mountain and Chamois Peak (loose, class 3). Hike over or around Chamois Peak (easy) to the base of Ibex. The final dome is best climbed on excellent but slabby rock just to the right of the N ridge (class 3). Time: 6 hours.

STEINBOK PEAK (B.C.)
                              6500 ft+/1981 m+

Originally known as South Anderson River Mountain, this peak is slightly lower than Ibex Peak, and 0.3 mi. distant. The distinctive feature of Steinbok is the long Northeast Buttress and its flanking walls. First ascent by Dick Culbert in 1961.

ROUTE: Bypass Ibex to the W to gain the W ridge of the summit horn; one can cross slabs to reduce the distance. Time: 2½ hours from Ibex. One could also reach Steinbok via North 610 Road E of the peak and climbing to N of the summit.

NORTHEAST BUTTRESS: This is the striking buttress on Steinbok, and the 19-pitch climb, which took 2½ days to complete, is the most difficult done to date in the area. First ascent by John Howe and Scott Flavelle in July 1979.

Approach by North 610 Road (see Fraser River Hwy♦). Begin by climbing the forest and talus left of the buttress to the slab wall left of its base. Climb class 3 slabs rightward to small ledges left of the buttress (where it drops off). Make a right traverse (class 5) to the prominent brush line. Climb the brush cracks until possible to traverse out right onto slabs. Thin climbing (to 5.9) continues for four pitches on slabs (good belay ledges). From the highest ledge on the right follow face cracks and thin corners above, staying as close to the buttress as possible. Two pitches below the end of the difficulties a ledge leads right to below a prominent roof (Mosquito Roof). Nail face crack to the roof, then free overhang and corners above to class 4 rock that leads to the summit. Grade V; class 5.9 and A3. Bring a full rack of stoppers and the larger hexes, a full rack of pitons with emphasis on lost arrows and blades, and plenty of mosquito repellent. Two bolts used for belays. Most pitches are mixed free and aid. Descent: To slabs S, then traverse right to the notch W of the peak. Reference: *C.A.J.,* 1980.

SOUTH RIDGE: This is the left skyline as seen from the valley on the E. First ascent by John Bates and Ed Zenger in September 1975. The route has three class 5 leads, but most of the climbing is scrambling (the class 5 can be bypassed on the W). Class 5.6; time: 2 hours.

GAMUZA PEAK (6300 ft+/1920 m+) is 0.8 mi. SE of Steinbok. The best approach is North 610 Road (see Fraser River Hwy♦). The col on the E appears to be the best way of reaching the summit ridge; no details ATP.

GEMSE PEAK (B.C.) 6100 ft+/1859 m+

Gemse is E of the western peak grouping, about 2½ mi. E of Anderson River Mountain. The S ridge appears to be the easiest route and can be done as a hike-scramble ridge traverse over Serna Peak; use North 610 Road (see Fraser River Hwy♦).

EAST RIDGE: First ascent by Philip Kubik and Ed Zenger on October 11, 1974. Ascend to the Gemse-Reh col (class 3-4 from the NW). The crux on the ridge is a 125-ft slab (5.5 near the top); rock is crumbly with some bush. Most of the route is class 3-4. Time: 1½ hours. Reference: *C.A.J.,* 1975, p. 66.

NORTHWEST BUTTRESS: First ascent by Sara Golling, Neil Humphries, and Chris McNeil in 1975. The first several pitches are class 4; there is some class 5 higher, with one aid move (slabs are difficult to protect). Class 5.8.

SERNA PEAK (5800 ft+/1768 m+) is a lesser summit between Gemse and Gamuza peaks. Reach from North 610 Road (see Fraser River Hwy♦).

REH PEAK (5800 ft+/1768 m+) is the NE peak of Gemse. Reach from North Main Road (see Fraser River Hwy♦). The SW ridge is reported as not difficult, but the beginning from the SE is brushy class 3 and 4 to reach the ridge. The N ridge is a pleasant

Northeast Buttress

STEINBOK PEAK – Northeast Buttress
ROBIN BARLEY

YAK PEAK

ZOPKIOS RIDGE

Falls Lake Cirque

YAK PEAK from east

climb of three to four pitches along a knife-edge ridge (5.2); first climbed by Philip Kubik and Ed Zenger in October 1974.

VICUNA PEAK (B.C.)
6900 ft+/2103 m+

Vicuna is 5.2 mi. from Anderson River Mountain, a nice summit E of the main Anderson River Group.
WEST RIDGE: First ascent by Philip Kubik and Ed Zenger on October 13, 1974. Begin near the W end of North Main Road (Anderson River forks road; see Fraser River Hwy♦). The climb begins at the left side of a prominent white ledge; follow dirty cracks and ledges up and left for two leads (5.5) out onto the NW face. Return to the ridge by one 5.6 lead and one class-4 pitch to easier climbing on the ridge. Descent: By the NE ridge (class 2-3 except for a 30-ft rappel), then 1000 ft of bushy ledges from col to valley (can rappel some). Reference: *C.A.J.*, 1975, p. 66.

Other summits in this portion of the group are Llama, Alpaca (6700 ft+/2042 m+), and Guanaco (6900 ft+/2103 m+) peaks and those on Zupjok Ridge (6000 ft+/1829 m+); connecting ridge routes generally appear to be the best method of attaining summits here.

YAK PEAK (B.C.)   6600 ft+/2012 m+

Both Yak and Nak peaks are on Zopkios Ridge, between the Coquihalla and upper Coldwater rivers, closely SW of Falls Lake (about 3 mi. NNE of Needle

Peak). Yak Peak, which is in the Needle Peak Pluton, has an impressive N face, overhanging at the top and facing the lake basin (Cairnes, Memoir 139, photo); the contact between the pluton and Eagle granodiorite runs approximately between Yak and Nak peaks. Note: The new Yale 92 H/NW map has the names reversed and has spelled Zopkios Ridge incorrectly; the Federal map is correct. See special map for Anderson River Group.
ROUTES: See Coquihalla River Road♦. One can drive the rough dirt road to Falls Creek, but the continuation to the lake is four-wheel. From the gas pipeline roadway SW of Falls Lake Creek hike upslope to the NW; 1 hour to basin between Thar and Nak peaks (the only reliable water is lowest of several ponds — camping). Hike W around a ridge spur, then upslope toward Nak Peak; to reach Yak continue on a NW traversing rise.

An alternative way from the Thar-Nak basin is to hike to the col: either traverse over Nak via the NE ridge, or traverse around the N side of Nak (talus) to the col between Nak and the lesser peak on the W side (Baby Yak) and then to the E slopes of the final summit (not technical).

One can find good climbing on the adjacent E face slabs. Here a S spur provides numerous crack and apron problems. The first climb of the central crack system on this face was done by Roman Babicki and Alfred Meninga in September 1979 (three hard free pitches).

There are lesser summits to the W and NW on Zopkios

Ridge, some of which have interesting rock faces on the Falls Lake cirque.

NAK PEAK (B.C.)   6700 ft+/2042 m+

Nak is located closely E of Yak Peak on the Zopkios Ridge portion of the Anderson River Group (see Yak Peak). (For those confused by the nomenclature, a nak is a female yak.)

ROUTES: See route for Yak Peak; continue upslope after the ridge spur; not difficult.

The N ridge is a scramble from the pond basin between Nak and Thar, and a pleasant view-route.

The E face has short routes (two-pitch); class 4 routes were done here by Jack Bryan, Dick Culbert, Philip Kubik, Wayne Saunders, and Ed Zenger in 1974.

JULY MOUNTAIN (B.C.)
6973 ft/2125 m

Located 3½ mi. W of Coldwater River and S of Juliet Creek fork, N of the Anderson River Range. The peak is generally of moderate slopes, with excellent hiking opportunities in the area. Map: Spuzzum 92 H/11.

ROUTE: Reach from Coldwater River Road◆ about 4 mi. N of Coquihalla Lakes, then hike upslope westward; route appears easy. The gas pipeline road is actually closer, if driveable; possibly logging roads extend W in this locale.

STOYOMA MOUNTAIN (B.C.)
7486 ft/2282 m

This mountain is of no mountaineering interest, but is a high formation near the northern extremity of the Skagit Range, located only 1 mi. from the 50th parallel, 3 mi. E of the main divide, and 13½ mi. NE of Boston Bar on the Fraser River between Spius and Prospect creeks. First ascent by E. Machalette in 1911. Map: Boston Bar 92 H/14.

ROUTE: Begin just W of Canford on Hwy 8 (see Spius Creek Road◆). Ascend the lower Spius Road on the W side of the valley; this eventually descends to Prospect Creek, then ascends S across the E flank of Stoyoma at about 4500 ft. At U.T.M. coordinates 5538000 N by 630000 E search for old road leading W uphill: this goes to the 6000-ft lake at 1½ mi. SSW of the summit (not possible to drive final portion ATP); cabin at lake. Hike N to the summit (1 hour).

PEAK 7400 ft (Stoyoma's Widow)
7400 ft+/2256 m+

This summit is 3 mi. WSW of Stoyoma, between Ainslee Creek and northern branches of upper Spius Creek. From the lake take the trail which traverses W; keep S of the crest until near minor humps (easy route). One could also descend into the cirque basin N of the cabin, then hike W past the lake chain directly to the summit.

MT. HEWITT BOSTOCK (B.C.)
7100 ft+/2164 m+

This is an important summit located on the main Cascade divide 4 mi. WNW of Stoyoma Mountain, 12 mi. NE of Boston Bar. The massif (in the Mt. Lytton batholith) is large, with a northwestern outlier that continues high over the 7000-ft level. There are some moderately large high lakes NW of the summit which drain to Prospect Creek. The mountain is named for a Speaker of the Canadian Senate. Map: Prospect Creek 92 I/3.

ROUTES: Use Prospect Creek logging road (see Spius Creek Road◆) until almost due N of objective, then take branches to reach a flat plateau at about 5100 ft. Find an obvious cattle trail at the edge of logging slash, leading SW above unnamed tributary of Prospect Creek which drains the N side of the main summit. The trail eventually leads to the nest of lakes due N or NW of the summit.

Another approach is by the trail to Peak 7400 (see Stoyoma Mountain). Hewitt Bostock is 3 mi. NNW of the latter; continue NW along or near the divide. One long day r.t. from lake at end of road.

JACKASS MOUNTAIN (B.C.)
6588 ft/2008 m

About 4 mi. E of Fraser River and 10 mi. SE of Lytton, between Siska and Mowhokam Creek branches and the Fraser. Map: Prospect Creek 92 I/3.

ROUTE: Reach via Mowhokam Creek Road (see Fraser River Hwy◆). There seems to be no simple way up: leave about 2500 ft, due E of Jackass, then hike slopes and ridges. There is no road up Siska Creek from the Fraser, but trails may exist.

KANAKA MOUNTAIN (6200 ft+/1890 m) is located 1.8 mi. NNW of Jackass. Hike up Siska Creek, then the long N ridge of Kanaka; one could traverse SE to Jackass Mountain.

MT. LYTTON (B.C.)   6706 ft/2044 m

The mountain, about 8 mi. SE of Lytton, is quite broad and rounded (Mt. Lytton batholith), with numerous small high lakes in the plateau area of the summit. The name is for Sir Edward Bulwar Lytton, Colonial Secretary to Governor James Douglas. Reference: *Canada Geol. Survey, Memoir 262*, p. 151, and Ashcroft Map Area, p. 8 (Duffel and McTaggart). Map: Prospect Creek 92 I/3.

ROUTES: The best way currently is to use logging roads S from Thompson (see Fraser River Hwy◆-Nicoamen River) to NE of the mountain. There is a trail along the divide W of the road, above the head of Gladwin Creek and N of the summit.

A jeep road from 4 mi. S of Lytton bearing to about 6400 ft W of the summit is reported to be in disfavor now.

MT. ZAKWASKI (B.C.)   6703 ft/2043 m
This is a gently sloped, largely forested mountain located 6.2 mi. E of Mt. Lytton, at the southwestern head of Nicoamen River. Much of the surrounding area is a plateau of about 6000 ft altitude. Map: Prospect Creek 92 I/3.
ROUTE: The apparent road approach is via logging routes in the Nicoamen drainage. Roads also lead W from the Nicola River to S of the summit. See Mt. Lytton.

NOTES — SECTION II

[1]J. Hoover Mackin and Allen S. Cary, "Origin of Cascade Landscapes," *Wash. State Div. Mines and Geol.*, No. 41 (1965): 13. The NW structural trend was established during Eocene folding, then consequent raising of the mountains changed drainage alignments. This pattern, established in the Oligocene, still persists in the Cascades.

[2]This pattern of division was established by Bauerman, geologist to the British Boundary Survey (Hilary Bauerman, "Report on the Geology of the Country near the Forty-Ninth Parallel of North Latitude, and West of the Rocky Mountains," *Geol. Survey Canada, Report of Progress*, 1882-83-84, pp. 8B-9B). Bauerman considered the Skagit River to divide the Cascade Range, with the western portion (Chilukweyuk chain) to have the highest peaks and the eastern portion distinguished as the Hozameen chain. See also Smith and Calkins, p. 14, and Daly, pt. 1, pp. 41-42 (note 13). Along the 49th parallel of latitude from the Gulf of Georgia to the Rocky Mountains the whole phalanx of closely set mountain groups are difficult to decipher in comparison to most of the western United States, where the structural treatment, enforced by relatively clear-cut separation of the component ranges, is a fact.

Although various maps have not always agreed, the more recent authoritative Canadian maps show the Skagit Range W of the Sumallo-Nicolum valley, with the Hozameen Range to its E, and continuing northward on the E flank of the Coquihalla River. The Okanogan Highlands in early usage were designated as E of the Okanogan River and N of the recent lavas of the Columbia Plateau, but the low-relief upland surface between the Methow and Okanogan rivers could be considered part of this same highland.

[3]Rather than Cascade Range, Canadian maps use the term "Mountains" when applied to the region N of the 49th parallel. R.A. Daly pointed out the difficulty in describing the mountains along the International Boundary, for the same range may bear different names with authorities. According to early usage, the Cascade range, or Cascade chain or Cascade mountain chain (a) extends from Mt. Shasta into Yukon Territory, (b) extends from Mt. Shasta to the British Columbia boundary, (c) extends from Mt. Shasta to the Fraser River, and E of it to the Thompson River — Reginald

A. Daly, "The Nomenclature of the North American Cordillera between the 47th and 53rd Parallels of Latitude," *Geog. Jour.* 27 (1906): 586-606. See also Daly, Memoir 38, pt. I, p. 22,40-41; note 13. Daly's map on p. 24 shows the Cascade Range limits at the Fraser-Thompson junction. The continuity of crestline across the Fraser River caused some early observers to consider the Cascades and Coast Mountains in Canada as the same range.

Late 19th and early 20th century maps frequently lettered "Cascade Range" (or Mountains) inland from the sinuous Northwest Coast, a usage which apparently began with the Map of British Columbia — Joseph Trutch, Victoria, 1871; this is continued in New Map of British Columbia — R. T. Williams, Victoria, 1884 and in *Stanford's Compendium of Geography and Travel, North America*, London, 1883 (Prof. F. V. Hayden section). In this decade Prof. Israel C. Russell affected this usage, for he was inclined to consider the Cascade Mountains as continuing into Canada.

From road builder Alfred Waddington we find "The Cascade range forms the Coast line of the Colony, which it follows, from near the mouth of the Fraser into the Russian [now American] Territory." "Its crest, starting from Mount Baker, a few miles south of the Boundary line, passes . . . a little north of the head of Bute Inlet . . ." (Alfred Waddington, *Overland Route through British North America*, London, 1868, pp. 31-32). In Europe, Stieler's Handatlas continued the "Cascaden Kette" across the Fraser River.

[4]H.S. Bostock, "Physiography of the Canadian Cordillera, with Special Reference to the Area North of the Fifty-Fifth Parallel," *Canada Geol. Survey, Memoir 247* (1948): 79-80. The Geographic Board of Canada has long recognized the master trench of the Fraser as the dividing line in British Columbia between the Cascade Mountains and the Coast Mountains. The highest mountains in the northernmost Cascade Mountains include Silvertip, Outram, Frosty, Lakeview, Grimface, Tulameen, Dewdney, and Stoyoma. The eastern margin of the Cascades here is transitional, into a zone through which summit altitude progressively diminishes and dissection decreases to the Thompson Plateau. The boundary between the Cascades and the Plateau follows the Nicoamen River, thence near the 5000-ft contour W of Prospect Creek to the heads of the Tulameen and Skagit rivers, and then down Copper Creek across to the Ashnola and NE to the Similkameen Valley. The plateau surface is near 7000 ft around the borders of the Okanogan Mountains, but is lower to the W. In the Okanogan Highlands in Washington, an isolated outlier is Mt. Bonaparte (7280 ft), SE of Oroville. See also *British Columbia Dept. Mines and Petrol Res. Bull. No. 48.*

[5]Clive E. Cairnes, "Coquihalla Area, British Columbia," *Canada Geol. Survey, Memoir 139* (1924):3.

[6]From N of the Klesilkwa River to the Coquihalla River the nomenclature is Hope Mountains, and W of Coquihalla and Coldwater rivers it becomes the Anderson River Group (beyond which Stoyoma and Lytton mountains maintain the general character of the range). See Cairnes, p. 11; see note 5.

Earlier usage had termed the "Hope Mountains" from the Klesilkwa River northward and eastward, and continuing E of the Coquihalla River. In the early part of the century the Klesilkwa was considered the dividing line between the Skagit and Hozameen ranges (Charles Camsell, *Canada Geol. Survey, Summary Report,* Dept. of Mines, 1911). The natural limits of the NW-SE-trending Hope subrange is a 9-by 21-mi. unit deeply separated from other mountain groups by the upper Skagit River on the SE, the Sumallo-Nicolum trench on the NE, and the Klesilkwa-Silverhope depression on the SW flank. The subrange begins at the Fraser River where Hope Mountain rises steeply from near sea level to 6000 ft. A high, erratic crest with rocky, rugged, and brushy flanks, partially intruded by granite, continues to 8500-ft Silvertip Mountain. Cordilleran ice, entering from the NW gouged deep through-valleys which are now the main water drainages. Cairnes suggested that Silver (Silverhope) Creek above Silver Lake was at one time tributary to Skagit River because of the increasing width of the valley between the lake and Boundary area — Clive E. Cairnes, "Reconnaissance of Silver Creek, Skagit and Similkameen Rivers, Yale District, B. C.," *Canada Geol. Survey, Summary Report*, Part A (1923): 50A.

The Hozameen Range and Interior Plateau are modified partly because of the bedded and less resistant rock lithology. But the mountains W of Coquihalla River are in part quite different because of their harder granitic composition. The topography of the Cascades here has been greatly modified by glacial processes; the major ice movements came from the NE. Summits bear the rounded surfaces and deep scars of heavy glaciation, but when by reason of height they escaped such action in the Anderson River Group they are sharply pointed. Cairnes mentions two "needles" on either side of the headwaters of Boston Bar Creek which are of massive granite (p. 14).

[7]Cairnes, 1923, p. 49A; see note 6.

[8]Waitt, 1977, pp. 188, 190-91; see note 12.

[9]Canadians, from Bauerman to Bostock, spelled Hozomeen with an "a". Smith and Calkins's maps affirmed the use of the "o", which was the official spelling of the American party of the North West Boundary Survey; this was adopted from the Indian tongue as Hó-zo-meen (signature of Lt. John G. Parke, Chief Astronomer and Surveyor, George Clinton Gardner Notebook, vol. 1 (1859), Bancroft Library).

[10]Where the Hozameen Range is separated from the waters of the Skagit and Similkameen, the lowest portion of the divide is Gibson Pass. The portion in Manning Park, and also E of Coquihalla River was once covered by great ice sheets, but now there exist only a few small pocket glaciers. Deeply cut valleys have produced a relief of 6000 ft or more in many localities (Bostock, p. 79; see note 4). One example is Tulameen Mountain, which rises 6200 ft above Dewdney Creek valley. The tributaries to the Coquihalla River lie in valleys which tend to be extremely precipitous.

[11]Bauerman, Section and Page 8B; see note 2. See also Map of the Province of British Columbia, compiled by J. H.

Brownlee, Lands and Works, Victoria, 1893. Also Map of British Columbia to the 56th Parallel north latitude, compiled and drawn under direction of Hon. J.W. Trutch, Victoria, 1871.

[12]Richard B. Waitt, Jr., "Evolution of Glaciated Topography of Upper Skagit Drainage Basin, Washington," *Arctic and Alpine Research* 9, no. 2 (1977): 185.

[13]Waitt, 1972, p. 41; see Section III, note 3. The Hozameen and Skagit ranges were possibly not covered by such continuous icecaps as was the area farther E because of their deeper preglacial channels. Aided by steeper valley gradients, the outflow of ice toward the lowlands and sea was faster in western ranges (Reginald Aldworth Daly, "Geology of the North American Cordillera at the Forty-Ninth Parallel of Latitude," *Canada Geol. Soc.*, Memoir 38, pt. 2, 1912, p. 594).

[14]Waitt, 1977, p. 187; see note 12. This was the Cordilleran Ice Sheet, which exceeded the altitudes of most of the early Fraser alpine glaciers. Far-traveled erratics in deeply ice-scoured cols between adjacent cirques, as well as on divides far above the presumed limits of local cirque and valley glaciers indicate that the ice sheet invaded the region, burying all but the highest peaks. Drift throughout the region demonstrates a brief southward excursion of the ice sheet (p. 183) and granite erratics in the cirque at the head of the Pasayten West Fork show that the most recent ice ascended the valley (Waitt, 1972, p. 3; see Section III, note 3). High relief ice-contact topography indicates that the tongue of Cordilleran ice in Pasayten Valley disappeared largely by downwasting — Richard B. Waitt, Jr., "Rockslide-Avalanche Across Distributary of Cordilleran Ice in Pasayten Valley, Northern Washington, *Arctic and Alpine Research* 11, no. 1 (1979):40. In Pasayten West Fork Valley the dispersal of major avalanche debris and erratics from downvalley sources to walls and cirque floors at the valley head indicate that the last ice occupation was by the ice sheet, whose distributary tongues, emanating from the interior of British Columbia, ascended N-sloping valleys (p.34). Ice in upper Pasayten drainages crossed divides to contribute to glaciers occupying such valleys as Slate Creek, Robinson Creek, Ruby Creek, and Rattlesnake Creek (see also Staatz, p. 40; note 15). During his pioneering reconnaissance in 1901, Smith noted "The Pasayten glacier . . . left evidence of its extent in the character of the Pasayten valley and the boulders found along the upper slopes. Granite blocks too are found thousands of feet above the present streams, on the tops of V ridges bounding both forks . . . . Such blocks of granite may be regarded as evidence of an ice sheet, possibly with a south movement" (Smith, Notebook, p. 98; note 16).

[15]M.H. Staatz, et al., "Mineral Resources of the Pasayten Wilderness Area, Washington," *U.S. Geol. Survey, Bull. 1325* (Washington, 1971): 39. Conclusions here state that W of Lost River there were no continuous icecaps, but studies by Waitt (1977) disclose a wide range of erosional evidence.

[16]George Otis Smith (Notebook 1232, 1901) observed "the peaks forming the divide and near the divide between the

Methow and Ashnola waters are characterized by the cirques on the north faces . . . . Every peak has at least one such amphitheatre with the flat debris covered bottom often containing small ponds . . . . cutting back of these cirques rarely produces anything like a 'matterhorn'." Median altitudes of both today's empty cirques, modern glaciers and reconstructed early Fraser alpine glaciers of the Skagit drainage basin rise systematically eastward, away from the source of Pacific moisture (Porter, 1964; Waitt, 1977). The regional trend of altitudinal variation is shown by cirques near Tiffany Mountain, which have a mean altitude of 7060 ft, 860 ft higher than the mean for Tower Mountain (Porter, p. 41).

[17] Smith and Calkins compared the asymmetrical summit forms as "a characteristic profile like that of a breaking wave" (Smith and Calkins, p. 91; see Section I, note 1). Reginald Daly noted some 25 cirques where the Okanogan Mountains cross the Boundary. While topography plays a modifying role in cirque orientation, the prevailing direction is N to E. These cirques are sunk in granitic rocks in which natural joint planes render plucking easy. The glaciers which headed in these cirques followed the same drainages that were occupied by the earlier thicker ice sheet. Daly observed that in general, the upper ice limit here followed the 7800-ft contour (Daly, pt. 2, p. 592; see note 13). The later glaciers formed numerous end moraines (example: Chewack River valley near Thirty Mile camp).

[18] Waitt, 1972, p. 34; see Section III, note 3. Parts of the Okanogan Mountains are unusual in having a high-relief alpine-glacial landscape overprinted by ice-sheet erosion. In the northern Methow landscape surface drift is ubiquitously of northern provenance, and mantles high ridge crests, as well as valley floors (p. 1). N-derived erratics testify to southward invasion of Cordilleran ice. Judging from Puget Lowland chronology, the ice sheet arrived in the Methow region by 16,000 years B.P. and was largely diminished by 13,500 years ago. It is believed the Okanogan Lobe started to retreat before 13,000 years ago when floodwaters of Lake Missoula last poured across the channelled scabland and canyon of the Columbia River. Soon after merging with Cordilleran ice delivered to the lowlands via the Okanogan and Fraser valleys, the ice sheet must have rapidly disappeared from the North Cascades, apparently largely by downwasting (Waitt, 1977, p. 190).

[19] Lake basins scoured by ice include Remmel and Cathedral; Peepsight, Kidney, and Glory are among lakes formed by Neoglacial dam blockades.

[20] Bauerman (p. 6B; see note 2) considered the South Similkameen originated in three small lakes "fed by the melting of the snow on the Hozamen Mountains." This junction is Vermilion Forks, where the old Brigade Trail reached the Similkameen Valley.

[21] Bailey Willis, "Changes in River Courses in Washington Territory due to Glaciation," *U.S. Geol. Survey, Bull.* 40 (1887): 479. See also p. 9. A deep drift-filled abandoned channel extends S from Miner's Bend. After a study in the late 1880s Willis suggested the pre-glacial course of Similkameen River flowed S through a well defined valley to join the Columbia S of Conconully, citing also evidence of continuous terraces. Damming along the trench floor has created Palmer and other glacial lakes. In the southern Okanogan area many constructional drift terraces were built in streams and lakes between masses of residual ice; they occur through a great vertical range (Richard Foster Flint, "Glacial Features of the Southern Okanogan Region," *Geol. Soc. Amer., Bull 46*, No. 2 (1935): 184). Terraces built up when ice in the Okanogan Trench and Columbia Canyon had wasted enough to permit water to drain from one tributary around spurs to the next down-valley tributary, thus building thick sediment along the valley sides (Flint, p. 185). Wasting of the Okanogan Lobe of the last ice invasion gave rise to vast quantities of stratified drift, the distribution of which shows that the ice wasted rapidly off the highlands while it remained in the more protected main valleys (p. 192). Channels cut by streams along former ice margins increase in proximity to Okanogan River; some channels lead across minor divides and some are a series where escaping water must have flowed across ice. George Gibbs noted the striking change in scenery when descending the Similkameen Valley, which had scattered pines alone appearing upon the terraces, but otherwise was almost destitute of timber. He observed that the valley of the Okanogan was nearly 400 ft lower on the 49th parallel than the Columbia (George Gibbs, "Physical Geography of the North-Western Boundary of the United States," *Jour. Amer. Geog. Soc.,* IV: 356).

[22] Bailey Willis (1887) first called attention to the former existence of glaciers in northern Washington, and Israel C. Russell (1898) published vivid accounts of the impressive traces left by the Okanogan Lobe on the lava plateau embraced by the Great Bend of the Columbia. Daly (1912) commented that at the 49th parallel the Cascades were buried to an altitude of 8000 ft during Fraser glaciation and that the Ashnola River valley carried a load of ice 3000 ft thick. "Below the 7,800 foot contour the peaks and ridges to the east of Cathedral Peak were covered by the ice" (Daly, pt. 2, p. 592; see note 13). High summits such as Remmel and Cathedral are sharp-crested and contrast markedly with the ice-scoured lower surfaces. Bostock noted that the Pleistocene ice overrode peaks to 8500 ft in nearby British Columbia and that alpine ice was directed northward in opposition to that of the main ice sheet. Smith and Calkins found evidence of glaciated walls of granite and schist; "An interesting topographic detail is the remarkably level tops of these E W ridges. Shoulders of this character with elev. approx. 6000' extend outward both to E & W from the craggy peaks on the divide" (George Otis Smith, Notebook No. 1232, U.S. Geol. Survey, Denver, p. 81).

[23] The site and duration of precipitation is determined largely by atmospheric processes over a large area; however, local factors are important in modifying the intensity and amount of precipitation. Although the passage of air over the mountains results in cooling, adiabatic warming occurs as air descends (5.5° F per 1000 ft).

[24]Subalpine fir reaches to 7000 ft near Slate and Windy passes; a specimen has been noted at 8400 ft on Mt. Grimface. Another factor which transcends the basic distribution by climate is the geographic range of individual species. The Englemann spruce does not grow into the maritime climate in the North Cascades.

[25]Stephen F. Arno and Ramona P. Hammerly, *Northwest Trees*, Seattle, 1977, p. 25.

[26]*Ibid*, pp. 47-52. The western larch (*Larix occidentalis*) is a much larger tree and grows at lower altitudes.

[27]The Eocene Monument Peak stock is a granitic body that intruded the older sequence near Lake Mountain, and is exposed between Lost River and Eureka Creek (Staatz, p. 61; see note 15). Younger than any surrounding stocks, it underlies an area of about 50 mi² (its most dramatic exposure is the 5100 vertical ft from the gorge of Lost River). Typically, beyond its margins many granite sills and dikes intrude sedimentary rocks. The Monument Peak stock intruded the southern margin of the Lost Peak stock, an oval-shaped body of granodiorite and quartz monzonite (R. W. Tabor, J. C. Engels, and M. H. Staatz, "Quartz diorite-quartz monzonite and granite plutons of the Pasayten River area, Washington — Petrology, Age, and Emplacement." *U.S. Geol. Survey Prof. Paper 600-C* (Washington, 1968): C48). The Castle Peak stock, in spectacular exposure on the peak of this name, was emplaced at 49.5 m.y. (Tabor, p. C-45).

[28]Lode deposits are vein deposits in sulfide-mineral zones. Mineral production from lode mines has been small, with only a few carloads of tungsten ore shipped. Quartz veins and mineralized shears related to intrusive bodies are common.

[29]Tungsten minerals were discovered in 1898 by the staff of the International Boundary Commission, but claims were not located until 1908, when a tunnel was driven on Wolframite Mountain. Coarse biotite-granite is the predominant rock type and it alone contains tungsten veins (the important ore minerals of the element tungsten are scheelite and wolframite). Claims are on the slopes of Wolframite and Apex Mountains up to 8000 ft in altitude. Most development was done 1915-1918, including the sawmill and concentrator. A total of six cars of tungsten ore was shipped before 1920, and some 30 tons in 1936 (p. 89). This "Boundary Group" and other prospects nearby are reached by an 18-mi. jeep trail; no production has been done since 1938 (pp. 89-97). The property has an old 10-ton mill and several buildings. See also Daly, pp. 459-64 (see note 13), and Harold E. Culver and W.A. Broughton, "Tungsten Resources of Washington," *Wash. State Div. of Geology, Bull. 34* (1945): 36-41.

[30]Alexander Ross, *Adventures of the First Settlers on the Oregon or Columbia River,* ed. Milo M. Moore, London, 1849, pp. 290-91. He also mentions a tributary called Battle-le-mule-emauch or Meat-who (p. 289). Governor George Simpson of the Hudson's Bay Company referred to tribes as Meatuho, Okinagan, and Samilkumoigh.

[31]The Okanogan River is one of the great branches of the Columbia, coming S from Canada nearly to 48° N latitude to join the main stream at the site of old Fort Okanogan. No two writers seem to agree on the name, and many have not even confined themselves to a single spelling. Ross (*First Settlers*, p. 41) writes Fort Oakinacken. Brown (p.31) states that Ross was the first authority on the name; the derivation is lost, but he said the Indians pronounce it "Oak-kay-nock-kin." Alexander Henry's copyist's perversion of the name was "Chanauegon." The map of Henry S. Tanner (1829) "United States" shows "Otchenankane River." Coues notes (p. 786) that the latest G.L.O. map of Washington Territory (prior to 1897) has "Okinakane," which is the spelling used by the Pacific Railroad Exploration. The old post of Fort Okanogan, on the NE side of the river, seems to have been the first site to acquire the river's name.

[32]Map of a Part of Washington Territory, September 1, 1859, by James Tilton. Public Document, Ser. No. 1026. Its branch, the Pasayten, may have meant something in Indian, or in French as translated. Lt. Charles W. Wilson of the British Boundary Commission noted the river in his diary as "Pesayton" but the United States survey in 1859 used "Pay-say-ten." Henry Custer wrote that the Similkameen-Pasayten junction had an Indian encampment with tents and horses, and was known as "Yak-to-lo-meen." Spellings officially adopted by the United States Boundary Survey in 1857 were Náis-nu-lah River, Tcho-pahk Mountain, Waî-haist Mountain, Sháh-wa-tum Mountain, Skwai-kwi-ĉht Mountain, Chu-chu-wán-ten Creek, Kwee-kwe-ahula (Nicolum Creek), Kleh-la-woon (Sumallo River), and Ne-pó-pe-eh-kum Creek. The upper W fork of the Skagit was called Kle-śil-kwu (Baker, p. 60; see note 63), but the official map of British Columbia (1895) spelled it Klesilkwa, which remains today. Names that were ignored by prospectors were Slukl-te-koi-kai (Ruby Creek) and Skweh-kwai-eet (Three Fools Creek).

[33]J.H. Stewart Reid, *Mountains, Men, and Rivers*, New York, 1954, p. 63. Fraser's intrepedity came to a failure, for the river proved to be neither the Columbia nor a navigable substitute. It was for David Thompson to trace the Columbia to the ocean in a series of journeys 1807-1811. The Aaron Arrowsmith Map of America (London, 1793) indicates Mackenzie thought the Fraser and Columbia (his Tacoutche Tess) the same. The 1802 revision still continued the error, compounded by the fact Vancouver missed the Fraser mouth and therefore did not show on his chart published in *Voyage of Discovery,* 1798. Although the entire region is largely devoid of detail, the Albert Gallatin map of 1836 correctly shows both the Fraser and Columbia as separate streams. The Arrowsmith maps are shown in Carl I. Wheat, *Mapping the Transmississippi West 1540-1861,* vol. 1, San Francisco, 1957, pp. 175, 178, 180.

[34]David Thompson was the first white man to voyage on the upper reaches and the main upper tributaries of the Columbia River. On July 6 he saw "high woody mountains of the Oachenawawga River" (Judge William C. Brown, "Old Fort

Okanogan and the Okanogan Trail," *Oregon Hist. Soc. Quart.*, 15, no. 1 (1914): 1-38). Thompson was a great pathfinder and his efforts in crossing the Canadian continental divide made him the greatest geographer of his time. Thompson's 1814 map of the Northwest Territory based on his surveys 1792-1812 was the best map in British America.

35 The fur traders ranged over an immense area of over a million square mi. of plains and mountains, where no whites had fixed a permanent home. The North West Company opened the inland Oregon country to trade and settlement, but did not explore the mountains, and in 1821 ceased to exist in name by merging with the Hudson's Bay Company. Its charter gave governmental powers such as civil jurisdiction for the domain W of the Rocky Mountains and from the Columbia River to Russian Alaska. The Hudson's Bay Company had fallen heir to a country of unsuspected wealth, yet costs in distant realms were exorbitant, and political tensions were a concern. In 1824 after 3 years' control Gov. George Simpson observed "our Council know little about that Country" (Frederick Merk, ed., *Fur Trade and Empire: George Simpson's Journal, 1824-1825*, Cambridge, Mass. 1931, pp. 243-44).

36 Oscar Osburn Winther, *The Old Oregon Country* , Stanford, 1950, p. 7. President Polk, angered by a British rebuff in 1845 that the boundary question be settled on the basis of the 49th parallel, determined to force the issue and in a public message implied either the British would have to surrender the entire region to 54°40' or force would be used to displace them. The American faith in expansionist destiny was well expressed by *Hunt's Merchant's Magazine*, which in 1846 wrote "No power on earth, nor all the powers of the earth, can check the swelling tide of the American population . . ."

37 Anderson spent several years exploring various routes and opened trails through the Hope Mountains. After pursuing a route from Kamloops via the Fraser, Lillooet River, and Harrison Lake to Fort Langley in May, 1846 he took a return route (beginning May 28). See Alexander Caulfield Anderson, "History of the North West Coast," Victoria, 1878, Ms. journal, Bancroft Library. He ascended the Fraser by canoe as far as the Que-que-alla (Coquihalla) and then "struck out across the Cascade Mountains to the heads of the Similkameen." For guides he had a chief of the Chilwhoe (Chilliwack) and assistants. On May 31 his course was ESE via the Simal-â-oueh (p. 144); Anderson could not identify the river, but was inclined to set it down as the Skatchet (Skagit), although the Indians told him this was the Noosakh, which discharged near Bellingham Bay. He crossed Sk-hâest Mountain Pass and on June 3 reached a marvellous small lake (p. 149) with a resemblance to the Committee's Punch Bowl at the summit of Athabasca Pass in the Canadian Rocky Mountains (see Hubert Howe Bancroft, *History of British Columbia,* San Francisco, 1887, p. 163). His actual route was Snass Creek and its E fork to the pass and lake, 32 mi. N of the Boundary, then through Paradise Valley to

Tulameen village and N past Otter Lake to Kamloops. When Anderson met the Similkameen chief Old Blackeye at his lodge near Otter Lake he learned the route was in the outline of a great arc, and that an old Indian horse route led directly from the height of land (p. 149). Anderson termed this "Blackeye's Portage" and later marked it on a map made for Governor Douglas. Subsequently this more northern version of Anderson's basic route was cleared for brigade transport by Henry Peers to Vermilion Forks (now Princeton). The Peers route via Manson Mountain served as the main trail until 1860, when the government road was constructed more closely along Anderson's route (see also R.L. Reid, "Whatcom Trails to Fraser River Mines," *Wash. Hist. Quart.* 18: 273-74.

38 After the terrible episode with the New Caledonia brigade on the Fraser route, Anderson urged Governor George Simpson of the Hudson's Bay Company to find alternatives near his 1846 Similkameen route, which had been suggested by Old Blackeye and others (Akrigg, p. 13; see note 39). He recommended one of the company clerks, Henry Peers, who set out to locate a feasible route. By fall Peers reported a usable way via the Coquihalla River, Peers Creek, Manson Mountain, Sowaqua Creek and later over a high pass and down Podunk Creek. Here the trail utilized part of Blackeye's, which took it over Lodestone Mountain and down to Tulameen River (see Brigade Trail◆). Late in 1848 the company trusted that the Peers route would be practical, and constructed a new post (Fort Hope) at the Fraser-Coquihalla junction. In 1849 work proceeded on the trail; windfalls were chopped and a path cleared (p. 26). But not enough was done for the route to replace the heartbreaking Anderson River-Spuzzum-Fort Yale route for the brigade of that year. On their return E the men became a work force on Peers's route, which then became practicable. While this route was more direct than Anderson's, it proved more difficult: the company lost 60 to 70 horses in the October snows of 1857 or 1858 ("Old Pack Trails in the proposed Manning Park Extension," Similkameen Parks Society (1977), p. 11, and 36th Annual Report, Okanogan Historical Society (1972), p. 18).

39 G.P.V. Akrigg and Helen B. Akrigg, *British Columbia Chronicle 1847-1871,* Vancouver, 1977, p. 7. See also Bancroft (note 37) for a summary of the Anderson explorations.

40 Setting out from Kamloops, he descended the Nicola and with Indian guides followed a route southward to the mouth of Anderson River (Akrigg, p. 8; see note 39). He realized the route into the canyon was impassable with horses, so followed an Indian horse trail SE via Spius and Uztlius creeks, then struck S up Anderson River and crossed a pass to meet the Fraser at the Indian village of Kequeloose, below the worst of the canyon. He then worked his way downstream to Yale for the canoe journey to Fort Langley. When Governor Douglas looked at the ferry-point near Spuzzum he ordered a horse trail built to detour W of the river (the "Douglas Portage").

41 The three brigades were the New Caledonia, Fort Kamloops, and Fort Colville, under Manson, but guided by Anderson. The journey became a nightmare, with 50 men laboring to get 400 horses and loads across the surging Fraser current near Spuzzum. Many horses and loads were lost, both on the way out and returning; it has been said 70 horses were lost; Akrigg, pp. 12-13 (note 39) and Ormsby, p. 91 (note 44).

[42] Akrigg, p. 105; see note 39.

[43] War between the United States and Indians in Washington Territory made it dangerous for prospectors to use the Okanogan route to the Thompson and Fraser rivers, so the only safe route was by sea to Victoria or Bellingham Bay, then by small boats and canoes into the Fraser.

[44] Estimates for the number of miners in the Fraser Valley in 1858 vary from 10,000 to 30,000. In the latter half of the year the total yield from diggings was valued at $550,000 (Bancroft, note p. 470; see note 37); see also Margaret A. Ormsby, *British Columbia: A History*, Vancouver, 1958, p. 165, and Frederic W. Howay, *The Early History of the Fraser River Mines*, Victoria, 1926. Miners ruled by vigilante committee and late in 1858 Governor Douglas asked a force of Royal Engineers to help control lawlessness. A sort of comic opera war then arose near Yale, called Ned McGowan's war. Early in January 1859 an outbreak occurred at Hill's Bar, near Yale. Prominent was Edward McGowan, a notorious character who had been in the 1849 California gold rush and was still wanted in San Francisco. He was reported to have conspired to overthrow British authority. Col. Moody with 25 engineers under Capt. Grant set out from Fort Langley. Douglas got aid from 100 marines as reinforcement, but at Yale the problems proved trivial, merely a petty squabble (F. W. Howay, *British Columbia from the Earliest Times to the Present*, Vol. II, Vancouver, 1914, pp. 61-65). See also Don Waite, *Tales of the Fraser Canyon Illustrated*, New Westminster, 1974, pp. 28-29. Judge Matthew Begbie virtually alone brought law and order to Fraser River mining camps.

[45] Because of the gold rush and fear of American annexation of the Fraser area, the British realized a properly constituted government would have to be provided immediately. Douglas, with his customary enterprise, had already extended his authority from Vancouver Island to the mainland, but the peculiar problems of the area were very different. So the British government decided to establish the mainland as a separate Crown Colony with a government of its own. Queen Victoria chose the name British Columbia instead of New Caledonia used by the British House of Commons (Akrigg, p. 137; see note 39). On August 2, 1858 royal assent was given to the Act.

[46] Douglas put miners to work constructing a mule trail along portages of the Harrison-Lillooet route, under A.C. Anderson's supervision. By October 1858 the new route was hastily completed (Akrigg, p. 118; see note 39). Much work was done on this route in 1860, but Douglas was equally interested in improving the Fraser Canyon route, so had a new pack trail built there. Money was appropriated to eliminate the "Douglas Portage." The Royal Engineers blasted the way around rocky bluffs, but building contracts were let to civilians.

[47] The route, built to keep resources from flowing to the United States, and to make the whole economy of the colony converge on the Fraser River, was about 4 ft in width. The Dewdney Trail was completed in 1860 (Akrigg, p. 197; see note 39), and later extended to the Rocky Mountains. The route went via Nicolum Creek, Sumallo River, Skagit River, Snass Creek, and Whipsaw Creek to Princeton — much better than the old brigade route over Manson Mountain. Sgt. William McColl and Cpl. Charles Sinnatt of the Royal Engineers in 1860 explored the way to Punch Bowl Lake using the same route as the 1858 Whatcom Trail (the latter went from Chilliwack Lake to Paradise Valley to meet Blackeye's Trail, but was abandoned in 2 months), but decided to return and use the N fork of Snass Creek to Paradise Valley. Governor Douglas met Dewdney at Hope to discuss building this into a wagon road; in 1861 Douglas promised miners that a road would be built to the Similkameen, then on to Rock Creek. Capt. John M. Grant with 80 sappers and 90 civilians relocated the route beyond Skagit Bluffs (via Skaist River, crossing at Hope Pass), finishing it in 1862; other parties of the engineers widened the Dewdney Trail between Hope and Skagit Bluffs (p. 211). But work on this 25-mi. section was abandoned when the news of the rich Cariboo discoveries came. For some 25 years the Dewdney route served as a vital way to the coast, where pack trains could transport goods without the expense of custom houses. Points of contact on the route included the Hudson's Bay post at Keremeos and Allison's Ranch at the forks of the Similkameen. An interesting reference is the British Columbia-Hope to Similkameen and Rock Creek map, by Col. Hawkins, R.E. The map "Gold Regions of Fraser River, B.C." by Hon. John Begbie (1861) shows "new trail to Shemilkakeen." The Trutch map (1871) shows the trail up Skaist River to Hope Pass E of Skaist Mountain, then to Whipsaw Creek. The Cairnes report of 1920 mentioned the "old Dewdney trail" was well preserved, in contradiction to the report of the U.S. Army Engineers, who in 1883 found the trail overgrown and impossible.

[48] After the cutting of a 25-mi. mule trail from Yale to Boston Bar, the Royal Engineers in 1861 began to survey the entire route to Cook's Ferry (now Spences Bridge); by May 1862 much of the wagon road was completed with cribbing support. At first Governor Douglas ordered Captain John M. Grant to begin construction of the hardest stretch of the Cariboo Road. This began the first 6 mi. (to Pike's Riffle), with contracts let out to private contractors to build the remainder under military supervision (Akrigg, pp. 249-50; see note 39). In May 1862 a force of 53 sappers under Grant were dispatched to Yale to begin the great wagon road (F. W. Howay, *The Work of the Royal Engineers in British Columbia 1858 to 1863*, Victoria, 1910, p. 8). After the engineers selected the site, Joseph Trutch supervised the

construction of a bridge crossing the Fraser at Spuzzum. Miles of wire were used and then suspended from towers built on rocky banks. This was the first crossing of the river span (1863), and the structure stood until the flood of 1894. Truch and his associates agreed to build in return for a 5-year charter on tolls. By the beginning of 1863 the road was well on the way to completion, with the Yale-Spuzzum portion in usage, and the Boston Bar-Lytton section ready. The difficulties of Jackass Mountain are discussed in Howay, *Early History*, pp. 101-2. Eventually stage coaches and freight wagons were put into service to haul passengers and supplies to the gold fields.

[49]Sheldon L. Glover, "One Hundred Years of Mining," *Wash. Div. of Mines and Geology, Biennial Report No. 5* (1954), p. 12. A Sgt. Compton, with the U.S. Boundary Survey party, discovered gold on the Similkameen near the border in 1859. With other soldiers, he panned gold secretly, but news soon leaked (Akrigg, p. 164; see note 39).

[50]In 1885 John Chance discovered Granite Creek, the premier placer stream of the district. Chance and his partners were taking animals W along the Dewdney Trail and discovered gold on July 5, and soon Granite City evolved (36th Annual Report, Okanogan Historical Society (1972): 131-34. There was a discovery in 1884, but the party was driven out by high water (4th report, 1930, pp. 10-11). Soon miners streamed to get here, many of them tramping the Dewdney Trail. The search for gold and platinum of the Tulameen placers led to the discovery of silver-lead ores in Tertiary rocks of Summit Camp in 1895 on the Tulameen-Coquihalla divide.

This mining camp, on Treasure Mountain, has numerous properties. Fred Sutter's original discoveries led to much excitement and staking, but no real work was done until 1910. Claims were also staked near the head of Whipsaw Creek in 1908-1909. A 24-mi. pack trail led from Tulameen to Summit Camp and continued W via Dewdney Creek. To the NW of this locale the entire Coquihalla Valley is in a mineral province of variety and wealth, but of quite difficult access. Some silver-lead deposits have been located and some gold has been mined in this drainage (the chief properties are situated near the mouth of Dewdney Creek). There are also a few claims near the junction of the Skagit and Sumallo rivers, all underlain by rocks of the Hozameen Group; mineralization was discovered in 1911, with some drilling begun in 1955 at Mammoth Mines.

[51]Copper Mountain is a nearly flat-topped spur between the main Similkameen River valley and the more shallow valley of Wolf Creek on the E. High-grade copper ore was discovered in 1884, but the site was not staked until 1892; a company was formed to develop claims eight years later. See V. Dolmage, "Geology and Ore Deposits of Copper Mountain, British Columbia," *Canada Geol. Survey, Memoir 171* (1934).

[52]L.K. Hodges, *Mining in the Pacific Northwest*, Seattle, 1897, p. 56. Hodges states that placers were first operated by miners returning from the Cariboo, and he estimated

2500 men were there the first season.

[53]Discovery of placer gold in the Slate Creek District is credited to Jack Rowley, who in 1879 is said to have dreamt of a "hidden hand" pointing to riches in Canyon Creek, a faith that became fulfilled by the end of summer when his Discovery Mine produced an estimated $1,000. That year Albert Bacon started his Nip and Tuck Mine above Ruby Creek, which was sold to George Holmes (who eventually took out $7,000 in gold). Bacon and Rowley returned to Skagit Flats, and so began the 1879-1880 boom. Commercial enterprise largely met failure: the Ruby Creek Mining Company spent over $300,000 building their camp, sawmill, flume, and hydraulic plant on the gravel bar where Ruby Creek entered the Skagit, but only $3,000 was retrieved and the buildings were abandoned about 1900 and sold to the operator of Ruby Creek Inn. In 1906 a flume was built for 6 mi. at the mouth of Ruby Creek in a major placer effort, but gravel washing largely proved a failure (see Skagit County Historical Society, *Chechacos All: The Pioneering of the Skagit*, Mt. Vernon, 1973, p. 89).

Volumes of material have been written and recited about the excitement, discoveries, and schemes of prospecting. One of the most unusual is that of Tommy Rowland (now remembered by Roland Point on Ross Lake), who once promoted a greenhorn into staking him to full diving gear for the exploration of 18-inch-deep cracks in streambeds to search for gold (Forest Service history files, Mt. Baker National Forest). A story is also told of the feat of Dirty Dan Harris's cattle drives up the Skagit Gorge to Hope, then via the Fraser Indian trail to feed starving miners.

[54]The Eureka lode was discovered by Alexander M. Barron in September 1893. After free-milling gold was found in the soil prospectors rushed to the Slate Creek District. A stamp mill was erected on the bank of Bonita Creek, and in 2 years some $120,000 was produced. The New Light Gold Mining Company built a new mill on Bonita Creek at 5500 ft to treat the ore from the lode. The upper mine workings are at Slate Hill (6626 ft).

[55]There were 2812 claims staked in the Slate Creek District between 1894 and 1937, and since the 1870s over 600 lode and placer claims have been recorded. The Azurite and Eureka Mines were the major gold producers. Barron was established about 1900 just below the Eureka mill and later the townsite relocated to near the Slate and Bonita Creek junction. At this time stamp mills were apparently operating at the Azurite, Gold Hill, Bonita, Mammoth, Chancellor, Barron and Anacortes sites. John Siegfried of North American Mining Company built a mill camp at Mill Creek and a narrow wagon road to Barron in 1895.

[56]M.T. Huntting, "Gold in Washington," *Wash. Div. Mines and Geology, Bull. 42* (1956).

[57]The oldest claim dates to 1892. The prospects and mine here center on quartz veins. There was extensive development in 1901 (Hodges, p. 57; see note 52) and in 1936 a 50-ton mill was erected. The main adit was at 5700 ft, with

workings up to 6730 ft. Prospects include those near the top of Jackita Peak, in the cirque at the head of Friday Creek, and along the Friday-Cascade Creek ridge. Anacortes Gold Mining Co. stated the prospects had 3000 ft of underground workings. Now only mill ruins and several collapsed buildings are to be seen on the Anacortes Crossing Trail (Bull. 1325 pp. 160-62). Various other nearby prospects include those in Devils Park, on slopes of Jack Mountain, Devils Dome, Devils Pass trail, near Nickol Creek, and along Canyon Creek. The adits N of Slate Peak (Gold Ridge claims) were recorded prior to 1900. Heavy prospecting has been done near Windy Pass, Oregon Basin, Jim Peak, and N along the Three Fools watershed. Sulfide mineralization was noted by early prospectors near upper Lightning Creek, with many claims staked 1910-1911. Robinson Creek was the scene of considerable gold and copper prospecting along mineralized shear zones.

[58]Staatz, pp. 104-15; note 15. Most claims are between 4500-5300 ft altitude, but several prospects are near Eight-mile Pass near 6500 ft. The New Hope prospect in this vicinity is near Billy Goat Pass, all in the area of volcanics W of the Eightmile Creek Fault.

[59]Such an artificial boundary division was created in haste and with little consideration of potential problems. "The line of demarcation . . . was an absurdity in a land where natural boundaries such as rivers and mountain ridges were to be found in all directions" (Akrigg, pp. 2-3; see note 39).

[60]The 1806 map of Nicholas King, drawn for the War Department from the notes of Meriwether Lewis, runs the Columbia River N to the trunks of the Mackenzie. Drawing heavily on the 1802 Aaron Arrowsmith map, it shows the northern branch of the Columbia as Tacoutche River (the Tacoutche Tesse of Mackenzie). In the 1804 Arrowsmith and Lewis map, "British Possessions in America" the Tacoutche Tesse merges into the River Oregon, and the completed 1814 Lewis and Clark map still confused the Fraser and Columbia as one. Before the 1850s the fragmentary information contained errors which often were perpetrated through cartographic copying. One misconception was the double-crest of the Cascades, similar to the misconception of the Sierra Nevada as extending unbroken into Oregon along the present eastern border of California.

[61]In 1856 Congress passed an Act to provide for the demarcation of the boundary between Washington Territory and possessions of Great Britain in accordance with the provisions of Article I of the 1846 treaty. The U.S. Commission was organized in 1857 and Archibald Campbell was appointed commissioner, and together with Captain James C. Prevost of Great Britain was instructed to lay down the boundary line from the western shore of Georgia Strait to the Pacific Ocean. They disagreed as to its location, a dispute that was settled by arbitration in 1871 by Emperor William of Germany.

[62]Angus McDonald, "A Few Items of the West," ed. F. W. Howay et al, *Wash. Hist. Quart.* 8 (1917): 201.

[63]Marcus Baker, "Survey of the Northwestern Boundary of the United States 1857-1861," *Bull. No. 174, U.S. Geol. Survey* (Washington, 1900), pp. 15-16. See also *Foreign Office Correspondence,* in Herman J. Deutsch, "A Contemporary Report on the 49° Boundary Survey," *Pacific NW Quart* 53, no. 1 (1962): 15, 16. The heads of the two commissions disagreed on various matters. Hawkins wanted more detailed demarcations and stable iron boundary markers, but Campbell considered stone cairns adequate.

[64]International Boundary Commission, "Joint Report upon the Survey and Demarcation of the Boundary between the United States and Canada from the Gulf of Georgia to the Northwesternmost point of Lake of the Woods," Washington, 1937, xiii-xv.

[65]Hawkins and Archibald Campbell were Commissioners from 1857 to 1869. Most of Campbell's staff were new to the Pacific Coast. Clinton Gardner was assistant surveyor and astronomer to Lt. Parke.

[66]The 49th parallel was determined by astronomic observations at certain stations and then connected when possible by survey lines. Short pieces of the line were run E and W from astronomic stations. Successive stations were connected by survey lines when possible from astronomic observation, and intermediate monuments were placed by computed offsets up the parallel. During the 1858-1862 period 32 astronomic stations and 161 monuments were set W of the summit of the Rocky Mountains. The topographic effort was comprised of geodetic work, by mathematic instruments, and description or artistic field reproduction of natural features using preliminary sketches. The result was to produce quite correct maps over the whole extent of the boundary line. Latitudes were determined with zenith telescopes, azimuth and time with transit, and longitude by chronometer and by moon culminations (Baker, p. 27; see note 63). Prominent, yet accessible summits were sought for triangulation. In the section of the range between the Skagit and Similkameen rivers, Shawatum Peak was selected for one of the topographic points.

Although surveyors used sextants to determine positions, one of the problems they had in determining accurate locations was in the vertical measurement for balancing (the effect of geographic mass caused gravity deviations). Astronomic observations were fortunate to be accurate within 300 ft (an error of 1 second in sighting equals 1 ft error in 40 mi.; the surveyors were probably off at least 30 seconds). Because of rough terrain and errors in reckoning procedures boundary positions were sometimes off 200 ft or more. Station errors of this amount were found in less mountainous country. After this first boundary survey was completed topographer Arthur O. Wheeler wrote, "it is expected that very large discrepancies will be found when the stations in the mountainous regions of the Cascade Range or the Rocky Mountains are connected" (A.O. Wheeler, *The Selkirk Range,* Vol. I, Ottawa, 1905, p. 186).

[67]Baker, p. 16; see note 63. See also *Joint Report,* note 64.

[68]"Physical Geography of the North-western Boundary of the United States," *Jour. of Amer. Geog. Soc.*, IV, p. 352. Gibbs made many geographic observations, including those of biotic zone changes and the size of timber. On August 25, 1859 he made a topographic sketch that shows Hozomeen and the Skagit Range beyond. Because of his ability to manage men in the field, Gibbs had been entrusted with much of the reconnaissance of the final third of the survey to the Rockies. In 1860 Gibbs estimated that he had supervised the cutting of 275 mi. of trail and had completed his geologic reconnaissance. In November 1860 the American and British commissioners met at Fort Colville to discuss the completion of the survey. Lt. Parke, Gardner, Custer, Major, Kennerly, and several others wintered near Colville, while Campbell and Gibbs left for Washington.

[69]Custer's complete reconnaissance was made from Puget Sound to the plains of Saskatchewan, and his report to the U.S. Boundary Commission is dated May 1866 at Washington. Custer, a Swiss, was with Clarence King on the Geological and Geographical Exploration of the 40th parallel in 1867-1868. This resolute adventurer explored the Skagit River both N and S of the 49th parallel by canoe, and nearly reached Ruby Creek canyon. He ascended Three Fools Creek and climbed the "Kakoit" peaks (perhaps Devils Dome or the ridge to the NE), then ascended a higher summit for the view (perhaps Shull or a peak at the head of 'Chu-chu-wán-ten' Creek and called 'Skwai-kwi-cht' by Lt. Parke). Custer had envisioned an ascent of Hozomeen, but clouds and smoke prevailed to make the "long and maybe dangerous ascent . . . would be useless and labor thrown away" (Records relating to the United States-Canadian border, R.G. 76, National Archives). Custer visited the Sk'haist Mountain Range (Manning Park) on September 10, 1859 to study the topography, and eventually reached the Brigade Trail. Waí haist Mountain, shown on some manuscript maps, may have been climbed by Custer or others from the Boundary Survey. Its selection is curious, for tables of location related to the survey place it at the same longitude as Hozomeen and Shawatum (Baker, p. 61; see note 63). Lt. Parke, Peabody, and Gardner ascended Nepopekum Creek on August 1, and traversed the divide bordering Similkameen sources, including a "knife edge" above Lightning Lakes (Gardner, journal, p. 104).

[70]Deutsch, p. 23; note 63 citing from *Foreign Office Correspondence*, pp. 39-40. In addition to Hawkins and Haig, the British party included Lt. Charles Wilson (secretary and adjutant to Hawkins), Dr. David Lyall, John Keast Lord (naturalist), and Hilary Bauerman (geologist). Captain Haig and Darrah were astronomers. The party was greatly delayed because the Royal Engineers were kept busy with gold rush assignments by Governor Douglas. Haig reported that Lt. Anderson had undertaken a re-survey between Chilliwack Lake and Skagit River. This span had been surveyed the previous year by Duncan McDonald, a worthless surveyor (Hawkins' dispatches, Lt. Col. Hawkins to Sec. of State,

Dalles, Oregon, 29 May 1860).

[71]Baker, p. 18; see note 63. A total of 190 mi. of the boundary project had been marked and surveyed, but there were still gaps totaling 220 mi. Eventually separate reports were made to both governments, but official treaty maps of the survey represented mostly a joint effort.

[72]Deutsch, p. 32; note 63. See also Joint Report, note 64. See also Otto Klotz, "The History of the Forty Ninth Parallel Survey West of the Rocky Mountains," *Geog. Review* 3, no. 5 (1917): 382-87. A bizarre fate befell the reports. The American reports became lost and the British report was not located until 1898; after a long search in Victoria, Ottawa, and London failed, Klotz discovered the report in the Royal Observatory at Greenwich.

Later, urgent questions arose regarding the adequacy of the markings. For a distance of 108 mi. through the Cascade Range to Similkameen River the boundary had originally been marked by 21 cairns and one benchmark (*Joint Report*, p. 29; see note 64). A joint examination of the boundary between Georgia Strait and the summit of the Rocky Mountains was made in 1901 and 1902. By concurrent action of both governments the commissioners were designated to act jointly to renew lost or damaged monuments and to place additional ones. Later, during renewed field operations carried on until 1907, the boundary line was retraced, with closer markings by stone and iron monuments.

It was not until the completion of re-surveying in 1908 that vistas were cut through all the forested portions of the boundary. By the treaty of that year the official maps showed the entire course of the North West Boundary and locations of marks and monuments.

[73]Dawson, Report of Canadian Pacific Railway, 1877, Appendix E, pp. 36B-41B. Dawson followed the Royal Engineers' trail up Nicolum Valley to Beaver Lake and then the Sumallo River. He noted that about 13 mi. S of the Nicola-Coldwater junction an Indian trail crossed to Boston Bar. Much used by Indians, the route was via Spi-oos Creek and led to Anderson River. A government trail was built via the Coldwater and Coquihalla rivers to Hope, a route that was used to export cattle from the interior.

[74]James Tilton to Thomas A. Canfield, General Agent N.P.R.R., Olympia, W.T., 12 September 1867, Northern Pacific Railroad, Secretary Series, Lake Superior and Puget Sound Company, Minnesota Historical Society.

[75]Dawson, Canadian Pacific Railway, p. 478; see note 73.

[76]Pierre Berton, *The Last Spike*, Toronto, 1971, pp. 182-93. Onderdonk was a well-financed American engineer and contractor with a reputation for efficiency and performance. He made it clear to the government that he would have the entire 127-mi. section for Emory's Bar (Yale) to Savona's Ferry, or none. Although his bid was higher than others, he was awarded the contract because of his backing and reputation. Construction began at Yale May 14, 1880, and when completed the average cost of 1 mile of track proved to be $80,000. The completed project was a wonder of its time,

but in the final analysis the task would have been impossible without the importation of a great Chinese work force from both San Francisco and China, a move much resented by local labor. In spring, 1881 Onderdonk imported two shiploads of coolies, each of 1000 men (Ormsby, p. 281; note 44). See also Waite, pp. 54-89; note 44.

[77] In 1901 Dewdney made surveys through the rugged Hope Mountains and established three possible routes from Hope to Princeton. Eventually the Coquihalla, Coldwater, Otter, and Tulameen route was chosen and the construction was directed by engineer Andrew McCulloch. In 1913 grading was begun Hope to Coquihalla Summit and on July 31, 1916 the line was officially declared completed (Barrie Sanford, *McCulloch's Wonder — the Story of the Kettle Valley Railway*, Cloverdale, 1977, p. 196).

[78] Wernstedt made many hundreds of panoramic photographs from summits of peaks and high ridges. He surveyed most of the geographic features of the area, and named many of them for purposes of identification. The maps produced as a result of his field work were the standard of the area between 1925 and 1965. With his horse "Little Willy" and an assistant (usually Frank Burge or Roland Burgess), Wernstedt spent entire summers in the high country with his surveying equipment and pack outfit. Some of the work led to mountaineering, and many of his climbs were first ascents. The full story of his achievements will never be known, but various documentation indicates that he ascended Blizzard, Three Fools, Lago, Pasayten, Three Pinnacles, Castle, Jack, Farewell, Diamond Point, Quartz, Rolo, Sheep, Blackcap, Shull, Many Trails, Buckskin, Osceola, Holman, Lost, Crag, Joker, Tamarack, Ptarmigan, Saddle, Smoky, Barney, Sherman, Balk, Coleman, Ashnola, South and West Craggy, Old Baldy, North Twentymile, Dollarwatch, North Tiffany, Windy, Nanny Goat, Eightmile Ridge, Peepsight, McCall Butte, Setting Sun, Remmel, Rock, Pistol, Goat, Pearrygin, Peak 8168, and possibly Monument and Carru. It is impossible to trace all the alpine visitations of Forest Service pioneers. Possibly some ascents were made by Nels Bruseth, who is known to have been high in the Freezout Peak area in 1935.

[79] Layering of weathered outcrops and dark-green cliffs is produced by differences in texture and composition. Between the two main peaks a small quartz diorite intrusive cuts the greenstone. Daly, who studied the "remarkable double summit of Mt. Hozomeen" (p. 500) identified the age of the rocks and termed the "Hozomeen series" (p. 479). He commented on the unusually well defined nature of the mountain group's topographic and structural relations.

Steep faults bound the flanks of the Hozomeen Group (Staatz, p. 45; note 15). Ancient greenstones and cherts float on a substratum of Cretaceous rocks forming part of a huge thrust sheet. This eastward-directed Jack Mountain overthrust (from Hozomeen to Jack), which carried Late Paleozoic strata over Cretaceous rocks in the Methow Graben, has possibly issued from the Ross Lake fault zone — a horizontal displacement of differently aged rocks.

[80] Geol. Survey Canada, *Summary Report*, Department of Mines, 1911, pp. 115-24. In August 1910 announcements were made in Vancouver newspapers of gold discoveries by two prospectors, Greenwalt and Stevens (p. 116). A geologic reconnaissance made in 1911 by Charles Camsell showed there was no legitimate reason for the excitement.

[81] The granodiorite is a Tertiary stock which cuts the tilted Cretaceous sandstones and argillites of the Pasayten Series. From the N the plunging contact surface between the units is readily seen for 1500 vertical ft. Reginald Daly estimated the small stock at 10 mi^2 (Daly, pt. 1; pp. 492-99; see note 13).

[82] Frank C. Calkins notebook, No. 1235, North West Boundary, p. 30 (photo of summit area, perhaps Windy Peak). In Smith's journal (p. 45) dated July 20, at the altitude of 8730 ft he noted a flat-topped peak higher than Chopaka but lower than the peak to the NW.

[83] Smith and Calkins, p. 91; see Section I, note 1.

[84] This is a NW-trending dikelike body of quartz monzonite that intruded older granitic rocks, and lies across the Canadian boundary NE of Cathedral Peak. The dike is about 1400 ft wide and 3½ mi. in length.

[85] In his letter of 4 August 1901 (G.O. Smith to "Little Chum"): "we climbed to the very top of the sharpest peak that we've seen yet — one to which I've given the name of Cathedral Peak." Smith used the name Cathedral "because it looks something like a big church" (George Otis Smith Letters, University of Wyoming Library). This collection includes Smith's sketch of the peak. When near the summit the party witnessed two mountain sheep scampering off. More bighorns awakened from a nap and stared at them, while five sheep were standing on rocks below.

[86] *Joint Report,* p. 77; see note 64. "Monument No. 95 on the north shoulder of Cathedral Peak was the only one difficult or dangerous to set." Barnard's 1905 album contains photography including that of a man climbing with a transit, and being belayed with a sitting belay (File 46, Box 14, Inventory 287, Cartographic Archives, Washington). The monument is 0.8 mi. N and a bit E of Cathedral Peak. The map was surveyed in 1904, with triangulation by Sledge Tatum and topography by J.G. Hefty. The 1913 International Boundary map shows the summit of Cathedral listed at 8530 ft.

[87] Holland (1964) states that the high peaks of the Okanogan Range, including Lakeview, represent remnants of a now-elevated and dissected Tertiary surface. The rounded forms of Lakeview and Boxcar are not likely a result of glacial action, but more likely reflect a position as remnants of a low-relief surface. Ice flowed between Lakeview and the Ewart Creek valley to leave U-shaped gaps between Lakeview and Boxcar and between Boxcar and Denture Ridge. The upper ice level is judged to be about 8200 ft (Paul Z. Melcon, "Tors and Weathering on McKeen Ridge, Cathedral Provincial Park, British Columbia," Ms. Thesis, Simon Fraser University, 1975, p. 40).

SECTION III

Northeastern Cascade Range

LAKE CHELAN AND RAINY PASS TO METHOW RIVER AND HARTS PASS

(*Lake Chelan, Stehekin River, Bridge Creek, Granite Creek, Canyon Creek, Slate Creek, Methow River*)

GEOGRAPHY

Methow region topography varies from gently sloping glacial valley floors to sheer cirque walls and sharp ridges punctuated with occasional dramatic granitic rock peaks, some of the most spectacular and unusual geologic landmarks in the Cascades. A visual fantasy unfolds as the transition is made from gentle valley flood plains and evergreen-covered foothills to the raw, heavily glaciated valleys and floral meadows with arctic vegetation.[1] The relatively dry Methow uplands make a dramatic transformation in relatively few miles from the moisture-rich, green W-side forests, yet provide an equal contrast to the great basalt desert of Eastern Washington which was created during Miocene and Pliocene volcanism.

Distant and sheltered from Pacific moisture, the Methow is a distinct subregion of the Cascades with respect to alpine climate, and often comes under the influence of continental air masses. Regional precipitation is 50 to 80 inches annually, most of it falling as snow in winter and spring to produce drainage runoff peaks in May or June.[2]

At one favored break midway between Lake Chelan and the Okanogan River the Methow Valley enters the Columbia. The Methow drainage system incises a widespread low-relief erosion surface sloping southward from 7000 to 4000 ft. The main valley, which is both a structural and topographic depression, and located midway between facing fault-related scarps, is excavated in Mesozoic sedimentary and volcanic rocks that have been downfaulted between crystalline blocks.[3] The deeply gravel-filled Methow trends in a SE course generally parallel to rock structures and along the sedimentary block axis. A necessary consequence is the tendency of its tributaries to head in one of the crystalline rock blocks and to descend to the Methow generally across structural trends.[4]

While the Methow is the most important regional drainage system, the deepest trough is that occupied by Lake Chelan. No other large lake in the contiguous United States is so entrenched into a great mountain chain, or has such a diversity of vegetation and climate.[5] Lake Chelan's basin drains an estimated 1080 mi² with a very regular high local relief from the normal water level (1098 ft) to the over-8000-ft summits of the Methow Mountains.

Early naturalists termed the mountains of this region, which divides Lake Chelan from the drainage basin of the Twisp, as both the *Methow Mountains* (Bailey Willis) and *Methow Range* (Willis, Martin Gorman).[6] These mountains extend from Twisp Pass 41 mi. SE to Cooper Mountain; the northwestern portion is a sharp divide and the remaining span forms a broadly rounded ridge.[7] The crestline of the Methow Mountains (averaging 5300-8000 ft) has hindered the cutting back of cirques to produce "Matterhorn" types. Many of the high peaks are rounded crests of coarse bedrock blocks, above a semi-barren zone higher than timberline.

Most of the glaciated valleys of the region head in cirques devoid of ice, usually directed N to E. In this terrain there are many rock-rimmed lakes set in picturesque parklands. Cirques are sometimes deep, well formed and open into glacial troughs that are U-shaped downvalley to a confluence with trunks.[8] This indicates that alpine glaciation, not ice-sheet glaciation, was the primary sculptor of the landscape. S of North Navarre Peak cirques are poorly developed. Between Star and North Navarre the NE-facing cirques feed into V-shaped stream erosional valleys.[9]

In the northern portion of the Methow region, the crest between Washington Pass and Mebee Pass is characterized by enticing and rugged, high granitic peaks, broadly rounded ridge crests and low trough-shaped passes generally strewn with boulders stranded from southward Cordilleran ice movement; numerous peaks rise high enough to have escaped the heavy glaciation of the Ice Ages.

Rocks of the Methow uplift consist of ancient schists, together with intruded granitics. The Harts

Pass-Methow Pass area consists mainly of slates and other marine deposits, uplifted and strongly folded. Quartz diorite to granite plutons dated from Middle Cretaceous to Late Eocene intrude both the Methow sedimentary block and adjacent crystalline blocks. The Golden Horn batholith is the youngest (Early Tertiary) of granitic bodies in the Cascades. Well jointed, and with uniform magmatic texture, it is now outlined by extensive spires on ridges, notably on Kangaroo Ridge, Snagtooth Ridge, Silver Star Mountain, The Needles, Mt. Hardy, Cutthroat Peak, Golden Horn, Tower Mountain, and the Liberty Bell group.[10] Other plutonic rocks include the Oval Peak and Cooper Mountain stocks.[11]

The Methow region has been greatly affected by both alpine glaciers and the Pleistocene Ice Sheet, which arrived about 16,000 years B.P. The Late Wisconsin Ice Sheet from Canada entered the region mainly from the NW to spill over Harts Pass and travel the entire Methow Valley. Unlike alpine glaciers, the ice sheet selectively deepened valleys aligned NW-SE, thereby enhancing the topographic grain that was originally etched out by stream erosion, and it beveled off ridge crests and excavated anomalous U-shaped troughs across divides.[12]

The upper limit of glacial evidence, a surface sloping from 8000 ft in the northern Methow region to 3000 ft in the Columbia Valley, indicates that the ice sheet over the northern areas was almost continuous, and broken only by a few scattered nunataks. High peaks such as Gardner and Silver Star were nunataks and caused a split of the ice sheet S of Early Winters valley to form a continuous nunatak here.[13] The lower end of Lake Chelan was covered by ice during the maximum advance of the ice sheet glaciation of Chelan Trough, but the Okanogan Lobe invaded lower Chelan Valley from the opposite direction, building the 400-ft morainal embankment that impounds the lake.

One of the most interesting effects of past glacier action appears in Early Winters valley, where hanging tributaries are separated by arete-like ridges. Glacier ice estimated 1 m.y. ago cut a valley trench from upper Early Winters basin around in an arc to State Creek (Chelan drainage), but this erosional feature was altered by headward advance of the glacier in Early Winters valley.[14]

An apparent abrupt amelioration of the climate which struck the 40- to 50-degree latitudes in the Western Hemisphere about 14,000 years ago caused glaciers to fluctuate in response. The thick ice sheet in the northeastern Cascades disappeared largely by downwasting and regional stagnation rather than backwasting as a mode of retreat.[15] The numerous deep, locally constructed coulee systems of lower Methow Valley all relate to ice-sheet deglaciation and not to the alpine phase.[16]

Snow blown off ridge crests by prevailing SW winds help feed the small reborn glaciers. Strong winds cause drifting to the lee of crests and peaks,[17] and consequently the existing glaciers and perennial snowfields lie within the confines of sheltering cirques having a northerly or easterly orientation. A few recent glacier sites have been occupied by rock glaciers. These have been identified in the lee of several of the highest peaks, including Silver Star, Star, and Oval.[18] Deep frost due to refrigeration of subsoil beneath felsenmeer is more likely to occur in this continental-type climate.

A dry coniferous forest habitat is characteristic of eastern Cascade slopes. At lower levels there is a thin timber density on sunny montane slopes, and the dominant tree species is the ponderosa pine. At medium altitudes Pacific silver fir and western larch, and at higher levels subalpine fir and Englemann spruce are added. Of special interest is the subalpine larch (Lyall's) which remains erect while its associates in this belt are wind-cripples (this larch is abundant along the Methow Mountains, and is very notable at such locales as War Creek Pass and Washington Pass). The windswept, often-treeless ridges support an extensive arctic-alpine vegetation with many rare species.

The overpowering immensity of Lake Chelan has inspired humanity since the first visitors. The rugged lake canyon remains virtually as Professor William D. Lyman found it in the late 1890s, when he described the terrain about midway along the lake as "a stupendous line of bluffs, four or five thousand feet high, tops streaked with snow . . ."[19] "Here is the home of that rare and beautiful animal known to the Spanish as the *mazama,* often called the Rocky Mountain goat. It is the game *par excellence* of Chelan . . . . On the rugged crags of Goat Mountain, secure in their inaccessible fortresses, these beautiful creatures can be seen leaping about like lambs at play."[20] The mountain goat has long coarse white hair and smooth black pointed horns (both sexes). Soft convex pads on their hooves enable goats to cling to rock in an amazing fashion.[21]

It is estimated that 150 species of birds make visitations in this region. The larger ones seen are the blue, ruffled, and Franklin's grouse. Most of the high lakes were barren until man stocked them with trout.

In this region are marvelous winter ski or snowshoe touring possibilities; conditions are often similar to those prevalent in the Rocky Mountain states. Much of the region from the S end of the Methow Mountains to Harts Pass has great potential for winter touring. The best access is from the Methow frontage or the North Cascades Highway. Certainly the basins and ridges in the proximity to the highway provide unique touring resources.

The winter traveler must be acutely aware of avalanche gullies, wind-slab, and local conditions on exposed, unprotected slopes. Bowls and gullies form a large proportion of the active avalanche starting zones. Travel on ridges is generally safer than on open slopes, but small bands of timber, common in this region, usually only give a false sense of security. It is recommended that probes, avalanche cord, and electronic transceivers be taken on mountain tours. Generally the best time to tour is spring, when avalanche activity is the most predictable.

Recent studies indicate that a higher incidence of avalanches occurs in the Cascades than in any other mountain range in the western United States. Some 70 avalanche paths have been identified along the North Cascades Highway.[22] Progression of avalanche occurrences throughout the Cascade Range can be correlated with frontal system movement. Intense systems with open warm sectors which produce rain, following a large quantity of snowfall, create the clearest avalanche pattern. Study has shown that as long as significant precipitation is continued at warm temperatures in slide zones, the possibility of avalanche release is high. Rain following newly deposited snow always presents additional loading and possible lubricating effects.

Invasions of cold dry arctic air can produce easterly winds that form wind slab conditions. Release of avalanches in these situations may be independent of any frontal activity. Slopes with weak layers can remain unstable for long periods; new snow or a warming trend may produce release danger. The most dangerous slabs tend to form on slopes above 30 degrees, where there is substantial variation in density between the snow surface and bed.

In early winter there can be deep slab instability due to TGM (temperature gradient metamorphism), most serious when long periods of cold, clear weather have persisted after an early storm has produced a thin, unconsolidated snowpack. The probability is greater on slopes that have depth hoar. TG layers are commonly found just above the ground surface. Avoid suspected areas of wind deposition and TGM. Shaded N and E slopes are the most dangerous in early season unconsolidated snowpack situations (in deep and shaded gullies the snow surface remains at relatively low temperatures).

In springtime melting and freezing have important implications in avalanche instability. Lubrication of sliding surface is the result of free water percolation to a hard layer. Compaction of the snowpack increases stability. During the mid-season transition the snowpack consolidates and deep slab instability is seldom a danger beyond a few days after a storm.

Reference: *Avalanche Handbook;* Ronald I. Perla and M. Martinelli, Jr., U.S.D.A. Forest Service, Fort Collins, CO (1976).

HISTORY

Recorded history of the Methow Mountains began when David Thompson discovered the Methow River on July 6, 1811. Here he encountered an Indian tribe and their village — his term "Smeethowe" refers to the salmon catch traditionally conducted there.[23] Guided by local Indians, Alexander Ross in the summer of 1814 was probably the first European to penetrate the uncharted mountains, but his account is marred by vagueness and his route pattern is conjectural.[24] One can surmise that Indians made their way up the main valleys in search of beaver, and it is known that Okanogans and neighboring tribes visited the coast in the vicinity of the Fraser's mouth, traveling there by both the Methow and Similkameen routes.[25]

Men involved in the Pacific Railroad survey in 1853 commented on the rough mountain country. Captain George B. McClellan wrote about the N fork of Twisp River rising on a high, bare ridge of granitic mountains. Lt. Johnson K. Duncan, who simultaneously explored to beyond Mazama on the Methow, did not find Harts Pass because the canyon became too difficult for horses, but correctly interpreted the drainage patterns for his mapping.

Perhaps the first white men to voyage up Lake Chelan were D.C. Linsley and John A. Tennant, on July 14, 1870, to make railroad surveys in the drainages beyond the head of the lake.[26] Ten years later Lt. Thomas Symons and Lt.-Col. Henry C. Merriam traveled the lake for 24 mi. with three Indians, and "found it to increase in rugged grandeur and beauty at every paddle-stroke."[27] Merriam later explored the lake to its head.

After leading an Army exploration via Twisp River in 1882, Lt. Henry H. Pierce claimed the discovery of Lake Chelan's second head and a new river entering, which he charted as "Pierce's River."[28] He described the valley of the Stehekin beyond Rainbow Falls: "The canyon walls, between which Pierce River finds its way, are of gray granite, exceedingly rugged and forbidding, rising to a height of 4,000 feet above the stream . . . . Mountain goats find pasture among the cliffs . . ."[29] Others rejected Pierce's geographic beliefs regarding the lake and river; the puzzle resolved when Lt. Samuel Rodman canoed to the lake head.[30]

In 1883 Lt. George B. Backus led a small detachment to find a pass described to Pierce by Indians — one of several of his efforts to cross the range to the Skagit River. With a small group he went up the "Twitsp" and reached a pass; he decided it was too rough for a railroad but possible for a wagon route.[31] In September Backus found the old Indian trail, probably over Mebee Pass, to be best suited.

After discoveries in 1884 there was hectic prospecting activity near the head of Twisp River,[32] where the "State Trail" was being built from Twisp. In 1892 many claims were staked around Gilbert's Camp on North Creek, and soon many cabins were built (on Gilbert Mountain the pioneer claim was the aptly titled "Mountain Goat"), but by 1921 Gilbert was a deserted camp of 12 dilapidated buildings and a ranger station.

Cady Pass was named for mine promoter James Cady, who in 1902 built a wagon road from Slate Creek across the pass to his mines in Mill Creek, where the predominant rocks are argillite, quartzite, and conglomerate of the Pasayten Formation. H.J. and C.R. Ballard were among those that located the Azurite group of claims near the head of Mill Creek. In 1930 a narrow road was built to these claims and during mine development a vast sum was invested by Eastern interests. Azurite Mill — operating from 1932-1939 — produced $972,000 in gold.

During the mining era various government surveyors, geologists, naturalists, and railroad surveyors also trekked the high ridges, drainage valleys, and climbed some summits. About 1890 John F. Stevens explored the Methow Mountains to an unknown extent for a railroad pass. Professor Israel C. Russell's geologic reconnaissance took him into Early Winters valley, possibly far enough to see Liberty Bell.[33]

U.S. Geological Survey parties (1897-1899) under W.T. Griswold and R.A. Farmer surveyed Lake Chelan's shoreline and the entire span of the Methow Mountains.[34]

The earliest trails were built in Twisp, Bridge, and Early Winters Creek valleys (the Forest Service built the trail over Rainy Pass in 1906 but the Granite Creek trail was not completed until 1927). Now the entire Methow-Chelan region is served by an extensive trail network, many of which follow the routes of adventurous prospectors and shepherds. The North Cascades Highway through Washington and Rainy passes follows old routes and now provides tourist access to some of the most spectacular and once remote alpine areas.

Various early explorers and pioneers must be given credit for bestowing many colorful names to the region (but a diligent search of Forest Service and other records fails to disclose precisely how such names as Silver Star, Kangaroo Ridge, and Liberty Bell originated).

Early settlers (including miners and sheep herders) and hunters often began fires.[35] Settlers found a favorable climate and broad picturesque valley for their lives as trappers, miners, and livestock owners. Those settling near Winthrop arrived in 1886-1887. Guy Waring of Massachusetts arrived in 1891 and novelist Owen Wister visited him the following year (Waring had opened a store and saloon). For decades Winthrop was a small townsite, favored by the horseback culture, little altered until the completion of the $24 million highway in 1972. Stehekin, near the head of Lake Chelan, became settled in 1885, and in 1890 J. Robert Moore settled on his point, then built his picturesque hotel. An outgrowth of the steamboats which plied the Columbia River in the early 1850s were the boats on Lake Chelan. The first private trip was made in 1889 by the original *Belle of Chelan.*

Little is known about early mountaineering except that U.S. Geological Survey teams ascended summits such as the Navarre Peaks, Star, Reynolds, Tower, and Gardner for triangulation purposes. Forest Service surveyor Lage Wernstedt scrambled some summits in 1925 and 1926, and did extensive explorations and cartographic work. The climbing done by Hermann Ulrichs in the 1930s was the first by someone of a recognized mountaineering background. A four-man party from the Sierra Club "discovered" the rock climbing potential here in

1937, and proceeded to make the first climbs of Cutthroat Peak and South Early Winter Spire. The Beckey-Varney ascents on Kangaroo Ridge ushered in a new era; now the climbs on Liberty Bell are among the most famous in the Cascades and the normal route is still regarded as one of some character. The concentration of routes has produced a tradition, where a decade ago, there was none. The longest routes are over 1000 ft high, often combining difficult artificial pitches with nearly vertical free climbing. Certainly nowhere in the Cascades is there so much concentrated emphasis on routes of superlative quality and difficulty.

Administration of a portion of this region is by the National Park Service (Lake Chelan National Recreation Area). The remainder of the mountainous terrain is managed by the U.S. Forest Service, much of it as "backcountry" status.

References to the region include: Hermann F. Ulrichs, "The Cascade Range in Northern Washington," *Sierra Club* Bull. 22, no. 1 (1937): 69-79 (also in *A.A.J.*, 1936, pp. 462-74); and Fred Beckey, *Challenge of the North Cascades,* Seattle, 1969, pp. 17-58, 202-15.

LAND MANAGEMENT

Ranger Stations:

Chelan (National Park Service)
206 Manson Road
Chelan, WA 98816
(509) 682-2549

Chelan (Forest Service)
428 W. Woodin Ave.
Chelan, WA 98816
(509) 682-2576

Stehekin (National Park Service)
Stehekin - head of Lake Chelan

Twisp (Forest Service)
Twisp, WA 98856
(509) 997-2131

Winthrop (Forest Service)
Winthrop, WA 98862
(509) 996-2226

Early Winters Information Center (Forest Service). On North Cascades Hwy (No. 20) at 1.6 mi. W of Mazama junction and 15 mi. from Winthrop. (509) 996-2534

Okanogan National Forest Headquarters
219 Second Ave. South
Okanogan, WA 98840

Campgrounds

There are many campgrounds in the region covered by this section: most forest access roads have at least one, and there are several on the North Cascades Highway. For locations, use fees, and capacities see Okanogan National Forest Map or National Forest Campground Directory.

MAPS

Topographic (U.S. Geological Survey)

North Cascades (1972)	1:250,000
North Cascades National Park (1976)	
	1:100,000 (metric)
Methow (1899)	1:125,000
Stehekin (1904)	1:125,000
Twisp (1969)	1:62,500
Mazama (1962)	1:62,500
Robinson Mountain (1963)	1:24,000
Thompson Ridge (1969)	1:24,000
Twisp West (1969)	1:24,000
Cooper Mountain (1968)	1:24,000
Big Goat Mountain (1968)	1:24,000
McAlester Mountain (1969)	1:24,000
Gilbert (1969)	1:24,000
Sun Mountain (1969)	1:24,000
Prince Creek (1969)	1:24,000
Oss Peak (1968)	1:24,000
Stehekin (1969)	1:24,000
Mt. Arriva (1963)	1:24,000
McGregor Mountain (1963)	1:24,000
Azurite Peak (1963)	1:24,000
Slate Peak (1963)	1:24,000
Silver Star Mountain (1963)	1:24,000
Washington Pass (1963)	1:24,000
Midnight Mountain (1969)	1:24,000
South Navarre Peak (1968)	1:24,000
Martin Peak (1969)	1:24,000
Hungry Mountain (1968)	1:24,000
Hoodoo Peak (1969)	1:24,000
Oval Peak (1969)	1:24,000

Planimetric (U.S. Forest Service)

Wenatchee National Forest Map
Okanogan National Forest Map

SOUTH NAVARRE PEAK
7870 ft/2399 m

The two Navarre Peaks, the southernmost high massif on the Methow Mountains, are located on the Foggy Dew-Safety Harbor Creek divide. Martin Gorman believed them to be the most prominent in these mountains (Gorman, p. 311; see note 6), and the noted geologist Bailey Willis wrote, "The Navarre Peaks are the southeastern representatives of a large number of points which closely approach or slightly exceed 8,000 feet in elevation, and which are linked together by high ridges branching out from and on a general level with the central divide."[36] Early maps indicate they were used for triangulation, so the peaks were definitely climbed between 1897-1899. The name honors Ignatius A. Navarre, early Chelan resident, judge, and government surveyor.

ROUTES: Approach via Grade Creek Road♦. Take the trail 1 mi. E of South Navarre Camp (Navarre Trail from Summer Blossom); follow it to the central Navarre saddle (7640 ft+), then ascend the easy summit slopes. Another route is to hike up the easy S ridge from the area of the camp.

NORTH NAVARRE PEAK
7963 ft/2427 m

Linked with South Navarre, this is the first high massif on the crestline east of Lake Chelan. A triangulation station mark was built here, 6 ft in height.[37]*Bryan Butte* (7855 ft/2394 m) is a high spur ¾ mi. E of the summit.

ROUTE: The ascent is best done via the S ridge from the central saddle; the trail reaches to above 7840 ft on the S spur (see South Navarre Peak).

SUNRISE PEAK   8002 ft/2439 m

Sunrise is a low-gradient pyramidal summit located about 2 mi. NW of North Navarre Peak.

ROUTE: The easy ascent can be made from Horsethief Basin, using either Summit Trail♦ or the higher Navarre Trail. Sunrise Lake and the pass just W (see Foggy Dew Creek Trail♦) offer an eastern approach to the peak.

UNO PEAK   7640 ft+/2329 m+

A small summit located between Lake Chelan and Safety Harbor Creek at about 2½ mi. W of South Navarre Peak.

ROUTE: Uno Peak Trail between Safety Harbor Creek and East Fork of Prince Creek (no. 1260) reaches to 7000 ft on the NW. Unfortunately the trail is open to ORV use (see Safety Harbor Creek area♦).

OLD MAID MOUNTAIN
7882 ft/2403 m

This is a gentle but protruding mass about 2 mi. W of the Chelan Crest, between the East and Middle Forks of Prince Creek. The formation is a high E-W ridge; a point ¾ mi. E is 7820 ft.

ROUTE: The ascent can readily be made from the trail in either valley (see Prince Creek Trail♦).

SWITCHBACK PEAK   8321 ft/2536 m

About 1 mi. S of Martin Peak and 2/3 mi. SW of Cooney Lake.

ROUTE: Make the easy ascent from the connecting trail at the divide crossing to the S of the summit (see Summit Trail♦ and Foggy Dew Creek Trail♦).

MARTIN PEAK   8375 ft/2553 m

Located on the Chelan crest about 4 mi. N of North Navarre Peak, this is a distinctive although moderate peak. There is a slightly lower but perhaps more outstanding peak at 1 mi. NNE of Martin: this peak of 8270 ft (2521 m) has been called *Cheops* by one source; it has an 8112-ft peak closely NE and still farther E is an 8033-ft (2449 m) summit with a steep E face.

ROUTES: From Summit Trail♦ at the head of Middle Fork Prince Creek hike to the crest pass just N of Martin Peak (or approach the pass from Martin Lakes — see Eagle Lake Trail♦). The easy ascent is then made from the N spur. Martin Lakes is the best approach for the other summits described. Other slopes on Martin appear to offer hike-scramble type routes, with no apparent problems.

MT. BIGELOW   8440 ft+/2573 m+

Closely NW of Upper Eagle Lake and 1½ mi. E of Hoodoo Pass, Mt. Bigelow is one of the more important summits in the Methow Mountains. Its northern cirque, which is over ½ mi. wide, has a sloping rock wall, two ice remnants, some perennial snow, as well as a rock glacier formation at a lower level; just S of the summit is an E-facing rock wall. There is a small peak (8202 ft/2501 m) 0.6 mi. SSE of Bigelow, and a peak (7890 ft/2405 m) with a steep N face on the divide at 1½ mi. E. The entire locality takes on a craggy, desolate, rock-dominated scene by midsummer.

ROUTE: From the head of the cirque beyond Upper Eagle Lake the route is an all-talus hike (see Eagle Creek Trail♦). The summit could also be reached from the head of Middle Fork Prince Creek.

HOODOO PEAK   8464 ft/2580 m

Hoodoo is a rocky crest with a hump-shape E of the

FINNEY PEAK

7985

Lake Chelan

Prince Creek

Surprise Lake

FINNEY PEAK from north
U.S. FOREST SERVICE

Chelan crest, located E of the head of East Fork of Buttermilk Creek. It has a very long, gradual NW gradient, and on the NE flank there is a rock glacier (7500-7200 ft).
ROUTE: Use Libby Lake approach (see Libby Creek Road) for an ascent of the gradual and easy S slope.

RAVEN RIDGE 8580 ft+/2615 m+
This ridge is a high E-W outlier spur SE of Hoodoo Peak (N of Crater Creek) which surpasses it in height. Raven Ridge is a rock-dominated eminence, much of it a craggy nature with small faces and a considerable

area of bedrock blocks on gentle gradients. E of the highest point is a peak at 8572 ft (2613 m) with a steep northern face. Farther E is an 8208-ft (2502 m) point with another steep N face (on Crater Creek-South Fork Libby Creek divide).
ROUTES: Approaches can be made from Libby Lake or Crater Creek Trail♦.

FINNEY PEAK 8110 ft/2472 m
Finney is the high point on the W side of Prince Creek, only about 4 mi. from the waters of Lake Chelan. The rocky summit is small but distinguished,

FINNEY PEAK   STAR PEAK   CARDINAL PEAK

Lake Chelan

Fish Creek Pass

rock glacier

West Fork Buttermilk Creek

STAR PEAK from northeast
AUSTIN POST, U.S. GEOLOGICAL SURVEY

and with open forest and a basin above Surprise Lake. There is a NW summit at 7985 ft (2434 m). *Skookum Puss Mountain* (7240 ft+/2207 m+) is about 1 mi. nearer the lake, and here is considerable local relief. Another nearby peak is *Baldy Mountain* (7810 ft/2381 m), at 1.2 mi. NW of Surprise Lake. These summits are mostly gentle shapes.

ROUTE: Approach from Prince Creek Trail♦ (long uphill walk from boat stop on Lake Chelan). A hike to the saddle between Finney's summits is a reasonable route. Baldy can be done via the easy S ridge, from the trail NW of Surprise Lake.

STAR PEAK   8690 ft/2649 m

Gently sloping Star Peak, one of the highest summits on Chelan crest, has been described as "A pointed rocky peak lying on the main divide between Lake Chelan and the Methow River."[38] From the W Star presents a uniquely light-colored tone. The steepest flank is the E, where two small ice patches remain below the upper rocks; here is also an inactive rock glacier. There is some ice on the moderately steep N flank. The ridge crest to the SE of Star remains high, with an 8155-ft point about 1 mi. distant. A spur SW of Star separates easy talus slopes on the W and S. The first climb was made by the U.S. Geological Survey in 1898 or 1899 (party included A.H. Sylvester).

ROUTE: From Summit Trail♦ at the head of North Fork Prince Creek or from Fish Creek Pass (see West Fork Buttermilk Creek Trail♦).

OVAL PEAK   8795 ft/2681 m

Oval's broad, rounded form is the highest on the Chelan crest. A gentle divide on the S leads into Buttermilk Ridge, but on the NE the peak is steep. Here there is an ice remnant. The nearly continental climate has resulted in geomorphic features, including a rock glacier (7500 ft to 7200 ft). A high ridge S of Oval reaches Point 8267, just E of Middle Oval Lake. Oval and Star probably were the "Wonder Mountains" as described by Lt. Henry H. Pierce from the Twisp Valley in August 1882; their appearances resembled the point of an egg and a pyramid — both snow-capped.

ROUTES: To hike the gradual S slope approach from West Fork Buttermilk Trail♦. An unverified northern route appears feasible. Take the Eagle Creek♦ and Oval Creek♦ trails about 4½ mi., then follow the exit stream 1 mi. to Duffy Lake.

PEAK 8392   8392 ft/2558 m

This summit is just S of Middle Oval Lake and 1 mi.

NW of Star Peak. This unnamed peak's N face is the steepest in the area (there is a small rock glacier).

GRAY PEAK   8082 ft/2463 m

Gray is a gentle peak located on the Chelan crest between Eagle Pass and Fish Creek Pass.

ROUTE: A mere hike to the summit from Summit Trail♦ SE of the peak; near the head of East Fork Fish Creek is a high trail saddle. Gray can also be approached from Oval Lakes (see Eagle Creek Trail♦). There is a 7925-ft point at 0.7 mi. N of Gray, W of West Oval Lake.

BATTLE MOUNTAIN   7710 ft/2350 m

A high ridge point on the Chelan crest at 0.8 mi. NW of Eagle Pass, the peak is of only local significance, and offers a summit hike along the ridge from Eagle Pass, or by ascending the SW slope from Summit Trail♦.

A higher unnamed peak at 1.3 mi. NW of Battle, triangulated at 7816 ft (2383 m), is located between the South Fork of War Creek and Eagle Creek. The most gradual profile is on the SE (Eagle Creek drainage).

SPLAWN MOUNTAIN   7450 ft/2271 m

This small summit is located 2 mi. W of Sun Mountain.

ROUTE: Simply hike up from 6700 ft on Summit Trail♦.

SUN MOUNTAIN   7492 ft/2284 m

Sun is a cluster of small summits on the Chelan crest where it corners to the N, then W, between War Creek and the North Fork Fish Creek drainages. Slopes are gradual except on the N. The map-marked Sun is at the N end of two ridge legs; there are two SE summits and one western that are slightly higher.

ROUTE: Reach Sun Mountain from the Summit Trail♦ by ascending N in the upper valley of North Fork Fish Creek.

BLACK RIDGE extends N and NE between Mack Creek fork of War Creek and the latter's S fork. Its highest point (7582 ft/2311 m) is 1½ mi. N of Sun.

TWIN PEAKS   7686 ft/2343 m

Mapped also as Moore Mountain, this double summit is located about 5 mi. SE of Stehekin, and only 3 mi. directly from Lake Chelan. The peak's position near the lake provides high relief here, from the flanking valleys of Fourmile and North Fork Fish Creek. The NE summit is higher; the SW is mapped at 7641 ft (2330 m).

ROUTE: The logical approach is from the North Fork of Fish Creek Trail♦. There is no apparent difficulty aside from the long altitude gain from the trail at about the 4800-ft level.

PURPLE MOUNTAIN   7161 ft/2183 m
NW of Boulder Butte and War Creek Pass, near the end of a NW-trending ridge. Purple has a long S slope.

BOULDER BUTTE (7350 ft/2240 m) is less than ½ mi. from War Creek Pass.
ROUTE: See War Creek Trail♦. Merely hike W from the pass to the summit; the ridge can be followed readily to Purple Mountain.

CAMELS HUMP   8015 ft/2443 m
A lesser summit on the Chelan crest, about 1 mi. S of Reynolds Peak, this peak is distinctive because it is the highest point between the crest and War Creek Pass. Camels Hump varies in gradient from gentle on the southern slopes to moderately steep on the N.
ROUTES: One can readily reach the peak via the War Creek Trail♦, then its branching ridge trail. An alternative would be to leave the trail at about the 5000-ft level and ascend NW. The SE slope or the NE ridge appear to be largely a hike with considerable talus. One could also make the ascent from the W, at the head of Boulder Creek (see Boulder Creek Trail♦).

REYNOLDS PEAK   8512 ft/2594 m
Reynolds is the most impressive peak between the southern extremity of the Methow Mountains and Mt. Silver Star. There are two quite separate summits, with a sharp dividing col and perennial snow and glacier ice in the high bowl E of the summits. The higher S peak is a large rock pyramid, with three ridges; the N peak (8384 ft/2556 m) — 0.3 mi. NNW of the main peak — is gentle on the SE, but has a long, steep 2300-ft sloping N rock face above Reynolds Creek. A survey party, including Albert H. Sylvester, made the apparent first climb in 1898 or 1899. Reynolds is the "Cathedral Mountain" which inspired Lt. Henry H. Pierce, for in his account (August 17, 1882) he described its gables, dark ribbed central dome, and snow-covered roof, "the form of some quaint temple of worship."[39]
SOUTH ROUTE: The southern fork of Reynolds Creek bounds the E and S slopes of the peak. One could reach this locale from Reynolds Creek Trail♦, from Camels Hump, or from War Creek Trail♦ at about 4700 ft, then cross War Creek Ridge at above 6800 ft. Ascend a shallow, open basin (talus) on the SE flank of the higher S summit. At its head a gully leads to the ridge SE of the summit. The final peak is a sloping rock horn: there is about 300 ft of scrambling (class 3 — firm rock).

EAST ROUTE: Use Reynolds Creek Trail♦ for 4 mi.; cross to the creek, then continue upward to the right of vine maple slopes via an old slide path (minor brush). Once above timberline the route to the N peak is apparent: continue up the basin on a snowfield. From a scree slope turn right to more stable rock and the summit. Time: 5 hours from road.

To climb the S peak from the snowfield, traverse into the depression (talus and snow and ice) between the summits, then find a gully leading to the E (skyline) spur. Here a distinct rounded rib leads to the summit (class 3 or 4). Steeper climbing routes beneath the summit on the N may be feasible but have not been verified.

RENNIE PEAK   7742 ft/2360 m
Although lower in altitude than nearby Reynolds Peak (which is 1.2 mi. SE), Rennie also has a steep N face. The rock wall here is quite broad, and extends above the valley of Louis Creek branch of Twisp River South Fork.

An ascent of the SE flank appears most feasible, with an approach from the Reynolds Creek Trail♦. One could also take the trail to its end at about 6900 ft on the ridge SE of Rennie and then hike 0.6 mi. to the summit.

PEAK 8142 (Mt. Gibbs)   8142 ft/2482 m
This unnamed peak, on the main crest between Rennie Peak and McAlester Mountain, is the highest in this link (and higher than these flanking peaks). It is located 2.7 mi. NW of Reynolds Peak. There is a broad interesting N face, showing steep rock with banding and some small snowfields and ice remnants above the talus (South Creek, Bugger Lake drainage). The SW slope is the most gradual. The name Mt. Gibbs is suggested for George Gibbs, early explorer, geologist, and ethnologist of Washington Territory.
ROUTE: From South Creek Trail♦ take branch no. 428 to Louis Lake (est. 5400 ft), then hike from the valley head to the peak's gentle upper S slope; this appears to present the most favorable route to the summit.

McALESTER MOUNTAIN
7928 ft/2416 m
McAlester is an important summit on the Chelan crest, located where the main ridge breaks N, at about 6 mi. N of Stehekin. The mountain is located between Rennie, South, and Rainbow creeks. The summit form is broad and rounded, but the mountain is steep and rocky on the N and E, where there are perennial snowfields and small glaciers. There is a high spur ridge to the E, with a summit (7880 ft+/2402 m) about 900 ft distant from the true summit. Five small cirques on the N flank contain ice patches; the largest

of these drains to a small lake (6303 ft) at the head of Rainbow Creek.

ROUTES: The SE and NW flanks offer simple routes to the summit. One can approach via Boulder Creek Trail♦ and Rennie Creek, or via Rainbow Creek Trail♦. One could leave the latter at 4200 ft on the mountain's W slope for a relatively easy route.

McGREGOR MOUNTAIN
8122 ft/2476 m

McGregor is an important regional mountain, a large individual massif trending E-W in the bend between Bridge Creek and the Stehekin River. The long S slope above the latter has an unbroken slope of 6600-ft relief. The extensive ice sections of the Sandalee Glacier are on the northern flank of the mountain; six separate ice segments total 1.1 km² on the South Fork Bridge Creek drainage. Rock glaciers have also been noted on the N slope of the McGregor crest. The mountain has a high point just W of the true summit (8000 ft+/2439 m+) and a high point at ⅞ mi. E of the summit (7865 ft/2398 m). The mountain has a rocky S spur and to the W is the craggy area of the summit lookout. The name is for Billy McGregor, a resident of the Stehekin Valley in the 1890s.

ROUTE: Take McGregor Mountain Trail♦ to the talus area beneath the summit (5 hours). Then an easy rock and boulder scramble is made on the final SW slope.

BOWAN MOUNTAIN   7895 ft/2406 m

This is a quite rocky mountain 3½ mi. E of McGregor Mountain, on the Stehekin-Bridge Creek divide. Rainbow Ridge, which has some high points between 7200 ft and 7500 ft, trends ENE from Bowan.

ROUTE: No specific information has been acquired. A suggestion is to ascend from the W, from the pass at head of Rainbow Lake Trail♦.

STILETTO PEAK   7660 ft/2335 m

Stiletto, while of modest altitude, is a prominent peak between Twisp Pass and upper Bridge Creek; the N flank is steep and rocky, but the S is relatively gentle. There is an unnamed higher peak (7805 ft/2380 m) located 0.6 mi. to the E. There is a high lake (6795 ft) at ⅜ mi. E of the peak. A trail once led from the Croker Mine on Bridge Creek to a former fire lookout cabin on a 7400-ft E crag near the summit. Reference: *Mountaineer*, 1935, p. 10.

ROUTES: The old trail route still offers a logical way, less than 2 mi. from Fireweed Camp to the peak; scrambling completes the climb to the summit, which provides a marvelous panoramic viewpoint.

Another approach is to locate a path beginning on the N side of Twisp Pass (2 mi. to summit); a variation is to begin at Dagger Lake.

HOCK MOUNTAIN   7750 ft/2362 m

This summit is on the Chelan crest at 1½ mi. SW of Twisp Pass, at the head of the Twisp River's South Fork. The N face is steep granitic rock.

ROUTE: From McAlester Creek Trail♦ the W slope is apparently a straightforward route.

PEAK 7905   7905 ft/2409 m

This unnamed summit is about ¾ mi. W of Crescent Mountain, and linked to it by the same ridge S of South Fork Twisp River. Peak 7905 is actually a more significant, higher summit. There is a very steep 1000-ft N face, with steep flanking ridges on the NW and NE. There is a lake (6768 ft) in the basin SW of the peak.

CRESCENT MOUNTAIN
7816 ft/2382 m

Crescent is located within the Twisp River drainage basin in the rugged locale between South Creek and Twisp Pass. The mountain has very steep, although short granitic N faces, which actually extend laterally for over 3 mi. to McAlester Mountain, and include the wall beneath Peak 7905. The distinctive feature of the face on the NNE just beneath the summit is a very steep triangular-shaped rock wall. On Crescent's lower slopes a wagon road led to the Crescent Mine (4800 ft) during the mining boom before the turn of the century.

ROUTES: One could make the apparently easy ascent from South Creek Trail♦ or via the Twisp River's South Fork (begin from Twisp Pass Trail♦ No. 432). The S slope of Crescent is not difficult, and the W slope provides easy scrambling; there appears to be no climbing history on the N faces.

SOUTH CREEK BUTTE (7670 ft/2338 m) is a high point SW of Crescent Mountain.

GILBERT MOUNTAIN   8023 ft/2445 m

The large massif of Gilbert is N of the terminus of Twisp River Road, with the summit located ½ mi. SE of North Lake. The slightly lower N peak (7917 ft/2414 m) is ¾ mi. W of the lake. Gilbert Mountain forms an enclosure around the head of North Creek, then makes a high connection with the S terminus of Kangaroo Ridge. There is a small amount of ice on the NE flank of the main peak. A miner-built trail once reached claims high on this peak.

ROUTES: Any flank of the mountain provides a route.

NORTH GARDNER   GARDNER MOUNTAIN
MOUNTAIN

NORTH GARDNER and GARDNER MOUNTAINS from southwest

From North Lake (see North Creek Trail♦) one can ascend SW to the ridge at 7240 ft (1 mi. W of summit), then follow the easy ridge.

An abandoned mine trail begins about ½ mi. on Twisp Pass Trail No. 432♦. From about 5900 ft climb a gully or a rock slope to the ridge just W of the summit. One could also make the ascent from the W slope from about 2 mi. along Copper Pass Trail. Time: 4-6 hours for any of the routes.

The N peak can be ascended easily via its S ridge. Begin from the saddle (7160 ft+) W of the claims above North Lake.

ABERNATHY PEAK   8321 ft/2536 m

Abernathy is an important regional peak, moderately rugged in shape, between Cedar Creek, Wolf Creek, and the Twisp River's N fork. Abernathy's flanks tend to be rocky, gully-dissected, with extensive scree slopes above timberline. This is particularly evident on the Wolf Creek (eastern) flank. Abernathy Ridge, which extends some 6 mi. SE, has a 7855-ft point S of Gardner Meadows. The peak's name was shown on 1913 maps and its flanks were well explored during the heyday of the Gilbert and North Lake mining boom; there is a mine near the N ridge at about 7400

ft and a cabin was once located at the saddle (est. 7680 ft) at 0.6 mi. N of the summit.

ROUTES: The mine trail branch of North Creek Trail♦ extends to the saddle described above. The final ascent is via the NW ridge, at most an easy rock scramble beyond a small notch. Time: 5 hours from road.

Variation: Leave from about 2 mi. up the trail (4300 ft) and ascend a long gully-basin to the N ridge.

The route from Scatter Lake is a satisfactory ascent (see Scatter Creek Trail♦). Hike upslope to the NW without apparent difficulty.

MIDNIGHT MOUNTAIN
7595 ft/2315 m

Midnight is a high eminence with much local relief, located only 2½ mi. from Twisp River. The mountain is without obstruction from Methow Valley, so is quite prominent from this vantage. The true summit is 0.4 mi. from the triangulation station point (7480 ft) to the SE. The ridge continues SE to *Three AM Mountain* (7180 ft/2188 m), an extension of Canyon Creek Ridge.

ROUTES: Routes to Midnight are summit hikes from trail origins. A route to the N side would use trail no. 403 from

Twisp River Road♦ to Slate Lake, or the branch road into Little Bridge Creek (no. 3401). Perhaps the most logical route is from Three AM Mountain (see Canyon Creek Ridge♦), which has a trail start at about 4000 ft.

STOREY PEAK   7821 ft/2384 m

This moderate summit is located 2 mi. E of much higher Gardner Mountain, between Huckleberry Creek and Wolf Creek's N fork. The S slope is quite gradual.

ROUTE: The apparent way is via the North Fork of Wolf Creek (see Wolf Creek Trail♦). Then take North Fork Trail No. 528. The E slope offers a potential cross-country route to the summit.

GARDNER MOUNTAIN
8897 ft/2712 m

The combined Gardner-North Gardner massif, located 19 mi. NW of Twisp, is the highest in the Methow Mountains. Gardner is an extremely sprawling and high NW-SE trending massif, with two distinct summit points (the northern is higher). Gardner has a more desolate appearance than most of the surrounding peaks because of its sedimentary and volcanic rocks, and is more valuable as a high viewpoint and for ski touring than mountaineering. The mountain is well above the timberline zone on all flanks. The NE face, which holds two glaciers, is the steepest slope (Huckleberry Creek basin). A U.S. Geological Survey party in 1898 or 1899 visited the summit and built a 7-ft cairn on "the higher and more northerly of two peaks on a high mountain lying on the west side of the Methow River, between the headwaters of Early Winters and Wolf creeks; there is a sharp rocky peak about a mile to the north, a little higher than the station."[40] Albert H. Sylvester was in this surveying party.

ROUTE: The easiest summit route to Gardner is via the long SE ridge leaving Wolf Creek Trail♦ before reaching Gardner Meadows. It is suggested to generally stay S of the ridge crest (or ascend the S slope). If a western approach is used, the scrambling ascent from the central saddle (8160 ft+) adjacent to North Gardner offers no technical problem if one keeps W of the crest.

NORTH GARDNER MOUNTAIN
8956 ft/2730 m

Physically connected to Gardner, which is 0.8 mi. SE, this slightly higher peak of the large mountain massif is the highest point in the range NE of Lake Chelan. Like its companion summit, North Gardner is not in the granodiorite complex, and although it has a rough, craggy shape, the softer, more erodible rock

does not result in the spectacular, distinctive appearance of nearby Mt. Silver Star and Kangaroo Ridge. North Gardner is broad when seen from the NW or SE, but appears as a narrow pyramid from the NE and SW. The NW face is long and moderately steep; the gullied SE flank has three high snow couloirs beneath the summit. Locally, the position of the mountain is between Wolf, Cedar, and Huckleberry creeks.

Both Gardner and North Gardner have numerous high scree basins under their summits and spur ridges; some of these hold snow until midsummer. Frost riving has produced numerous gullies and open cirques. There are high subsidiary points on ridges S, WSW, and NE of the true summit. The logical time for the ascent is late spring or early summer.

ROUTES: From Cedar Creek Trail♦ a log crossing at about 3 mi. may be found across the creek (at about 0.1 mi. past a campground; est. 3950 ft). Ascend the slope opposite directly to about 5400 ft, then slant to the 6000-ft level on the prominent N ridge. This crest is mostly level for about 2 mi. until a large snowfield is reached. Ascend a moderately steep gully to the right skyline of the peak to reach the ridge at about 7800 ft. Its continuation is taken to the summit. Time: 7 hours from trail.

The W slope appears as a suitable route. One could travel S via the stream entering Cedar Creek from the W flank of the Gardner massif, then make the ascent from Shelokum Lake (route not verified).

From Wolf Creek (see Gardner Mountain) one could apparently easily ascend the slope SW of Gardner to Point 8487 (the S peak of North Gardner); then continue along the ridge about ½ mi. to the summit. The final S ridge is a scramble-hike; one could also follow the connecting ridge from Gardner.

SNAGTOOTH RIDGE

This ridge of ragged reddish-toned towers extends 1 mi. S of Silver Star Mountain as the Willow-Cedar Creek divide — a mini-Chamonix without the glaciers. While the individual shape and height of the crags and towers presents a random appearance, the overall plan is a uniform, masterful emplacement. The pinnacled aspect is due to widely spaced joints where notches are etched out by the difference in resistance to weathering. The granitic rock of these startling towers is more weathered and friable than on neighboring crests, possibly a consequence of differential cooling at depth which affected the texture in comparison to other rock of the area.

Altitudes of the various summits decrease pro-

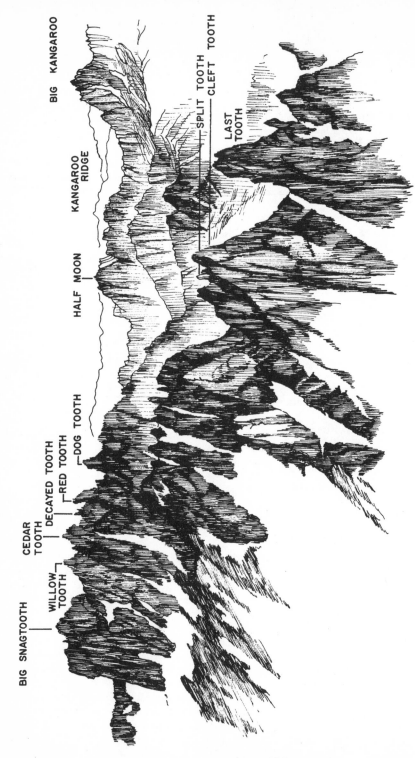

BIG KANGAROO

KANGAROO RIDGE

HALF MOON

DOG TOOTH

RED TOOTH

DECAYED TOOTH

CEDAR TOOTH

WILLOW TOOTH

BIG SNAGTOOTH

SPLIT TOOTH

CLEFT TOOTH

LAST TOOTH

SNAGTOOTH RIDGE *from northeast*

gressively from the southern extremity of the ridge for a distance toward Silver Star, then increase in height. The lowest notch (7720 ft+) is near the ridge midpoint. Climbs are short, but tend to be interesting rock climbing problems: usually several towers can be done in a few hours. Most climbing can be protected by runners with very little use of hardware.

The usual approach is the Willow Creek Route♦. A good campsite is in one of two basins below timberline, where water runs all summer. The long W slope leading to the ridge provides a simple ascent; once on the S half of the ridge all travel between towers is done on the WSW slope. The other approach is Cedar Creek and its NW branch (Cedar Creek Trail♦) to reach the E flank of Snagtooth Ridge.

BIG SNAGTOOTH   est. 8350 ft/2545 m
This is the southernmost and highest point on Snagtooth Ridge, a blocky crag with extensive scree slopes below its S face. The rock portion of the formation is not large, but is steep on all flanks, with a vertical SE nose. In about 1925 Lage Wernstedt was on the promontory SE of the summit, from which he photographed and surveyed. First ascent by Fred Beckey, Jerry O'Neil, and Charles Welsh on September 29, 1946.
SOUTHWEST FACE: The best approach is from Willow Creek: cross the SE basin head over the ridge at about 8000 ft, close to Snagtooth Ridge, and contour briefly on the West Fork Cedar Creek slope. The climb is on the eroded rock of the SW face, beginning in a gully and then climbing along the S crest (over two lesser points). A shoulder was used on the original climb on an airy spot on the summit block's NW corner, but can possibly be avoided. The leader may need to stand on the belayer's outstretched hand; class 4.

Another way to reach the final pitch is from the col (est. 8200 ft) adjacent to Willow Tooth; climb to a ledge and traverse on the W side.

WILLOW TOOTH   8330 ft/2539 m
A small tower across the col (often snow-filled) from Big Snagtooth. First ascent by same party, same date.
ROUTE: Climb the short S face of SE corner; about 40 ft of steep rock (good holds; class 4). See Big Snagtooth approach.

CEDAR TOOTH   8280 ft+/2524 m+
Located just N of Willow Tooth. First ascent by same party, same date.
ROUTE: Via short S side (class 3-4). Another method is to take the chimney, then ledge system on the N side (a short class 3-4 lead).

DECAYED TOOTH   est. 8150 ft/2484 m
This is a pointed crag N of Cedar Tooth; probable first ascent by Les Davenport and Martin West on July 12, 1970.
ROUTE: Ascend the broad gully between Cedar and Decayed Tooth (class 2), then scramble on the SE corner to a large ledge extending around to the E and N. The 40-ft summit block is done on the NE corner (class 5). An apparently easier route on the W edge of the N face is so weathered that protection is not available.

RED TOOTH   8240 ft+/2512 m+
Red Tooth is a weathered reddish tower, very sheer on all faces, the most imposing on Snagtooth Ridge; the summit point is on its southern corner. First ascent by Fred Beckey, Jerry O'Neil, and Charles Welsh on September 29, 1946.
ROUTE: Via the NW face, using a 120-ft crack to a notch just N of the summit (class 5 and one aid piton on original). A shoulder stand was used to work onto summit pitch, which bears rightward from notch. Class 5.7 and A1 (one move).

DOG TOOTH   8200 ft+/2499 m+
This pyramidal tower, which resembles a grey-hued tooth, is located just N of Red Tooth; its W face is steep, with vertical-trending flakes. First ascent by Helmy Beckey and Larry Strathdee in September 1944.
ROUTE: Via the N face (about 150 ft of class 4, with some loose rock). The final 80 ft are along the right side of narrow N crest then bear left to the summit; class 4, but chock or piton protection may be desirable.

GREY TOOTH   est. 8000 ft/2438 m
Grey, Split, Cleft, and Last Tooth are small towers on the nearly level crest between Dog Tooth and the lowest Snagtooth notch. The crest here has a wide but short E-facing wall cut by several ramps and gullies (master joints). Grey, Split and Cleft Tooth stand closely together. First ascent by Fred Beckey and Art Maki in June 1953.
ROUTE: Approach from the S. The climb is easily done on the W face (class 3 and 4).

SPLIT TOOTH (est. 8000 ft/2438 m) first ascent by same party. The route is on the NW — one class 4 lead.

CLEFT TOOTH (est. 8000 ft/2438 m) first ascent by same party. The route is on the S side — class 4.

LAST TOOTH   8000 ft+/2438 m+
This is the northernmost tower of climbing interest; it

is somewhat isolated from the others. First ascent by Ed Coulter and William Fix on May 17, 1953.

ROUTE: From the E flank ascend the snow gully to the gap on the N. Then follow the exposed skyline ridge (class 4).

SILVER STAR MOUNTAIN
8876 ft/2705 m

Silver Star, the alpine climax of the Methow Mountains, is a grand mountain fortress of magnificent diversity. Its large granodiorite bedrock mass, split complexly along erosion joints, occupies the Cedar-Early Winters Creek divide 4 mi. NE of Washington Pass. Despite a chaotic appearance, Silver Star has a finished design — on an immense scale. Gables of rock strike and dip in seemingly planned directions, each in some manner imitating the others in a repetitive scheme. Differential weathering occurs at varying rates and scales and contributes to the breathtaking scenery. The jointing bedrock pattern has a strong influence on the landform shapes. Vertical joints commonly arise due to lateral extension of the rock mass during uplift. Coarse-grained granitic rocks, such as these on Silver Star, most commonly give rise to weathering residuals; metamorphic rocks are more easily decomposed than igneous rocks due to internal structuring, so their weathering less frequently results in residual landforms.

The highest summit (East Peak) is separated from the slightly lower West Peak, some 200 yards distant, by a col (8600 ft+) which is at the apex of the Silver Star Glacier. A northern spur of the West Peak extends prominently at a high level toward its connection with the "Wine Spires" (Chablis to Burgundy Spire). While the glacier on Silver Star's N slope (0.6 km²) is now divided into three sections, it surpasses in size any other at its eastern longitude in the Cascades.[41] There is an active rock glacier on the mountain's northern flank, well E of the summit (see Silver Horn), a phenomenon made possible by a periglacial climate, the correct altitude, and the presence of talus blocks. Professor Israel C. Russell, who made an early study of geology and glaciers in the region, and who traveled part of the Early Winters Creek valley in 1898, was not aware of this existing ice, for he wrote there are "no glaciers on the east side of the Cascade divide."[42] The summit of this dramatic mountain provides an engaging panorama of the complex, spectacular ridges and formations nearby.

The first ascent, previously attributed to Hermann Ulrichs in 1932, was made by Lage Wernstedt in about 1926, probably via the S gully, according to photographic evidence.[43] First winter ascent by Fred Beckey and Michael Borghoff in March 1965. References: *A.A.J.,* 1936, pp. 468-69; *Sierra Club. Bull.* 22, no. 1 (1937): 75-77; *Mountaineer,* 1953, pp. 25-26; *Mazama* 50, no. 13 (1968): 20.

SOUTH ROUTE: From the upper basin of Willow Creek (see Willow Creek Route◆) climb a long scree slope to the lowest saddle (7720 ft+) between Snagtooth Ridge and the Southwest Buttress of Silver Star. Contour around the E slope of the ridge for about 100 yards; a long talus gully leads to the col separating the two main summits of Silver Star. Snow should be expected in early season. From the col scramble broken granite to the summit (class 3-4). Time: 5-7 hours.

Variation: At about 8000 ft in the talus gully (where it veers left) climb a long narrow couloir directly toward the main summit. In several hundred ft reach a chimney system trending rightward, toward the summit. Climb a chimney and ledge system direct to the summit rockpile (class 4); rock is solid granite here, where in lower gullies it is reddish and with scaly surface.

Approach Variation: From the head of the NW branch of Cedar Creek (see Snagtooth Ridge) ascend the valley directly to the long talus gully.

SOUTHWEST BUTTRESS: This buttress first trends E, then NE, terminating at the West Peak. First ascent by Chris Kopczynski and John Roskelley in August 1967. Ascend scree on the W side of the mountain to the 8000-ft level, where entrance to the buttress can be made via a 60-ft chute. Rock climbing (class 4) begins here, with exceptionally weathered (loose) rock. Follow the buttress to the W Peak (climbing becomes easier). Time: 3 hours from scree.

WEST FACE: First ascent by Carla Firey, Brad Fowler, and Earl Hamilton on July 3, 1973. This route follows the crest of an arete that slants from right to left, and ends on a prominent tower slightly below the ridge crest. Climb the arete (class 3 for 400 ft) beginning near left of large gully which descends the center of W face. Continue up an abrasive squeeze chimney (class 4 and 5) to a good ledge, then a larger chimney (30-40 ft) opening to the left. Climb to another ledge, below an overhang. Take the ledge left around a corner and up a short dihedral. Climb up-left to a small notch; cross this and ascend a system of parallel ramps until possible to work back left onto a sloping ledge below overhanging flakes. Climb up and rightward, around and over the overhang (pulling on flakes) onto a sloping ledge (5.7 or 5.8). From a cheval belay on the easy pitch ends at an apparent impasse below a 90-ft block. Move left (piton protection) around an exposed corner (use aid sling on nubbin). Traverse, crossing a 5-ft gap, then take a squeeze chimney to the West Peak. Downclimb the same

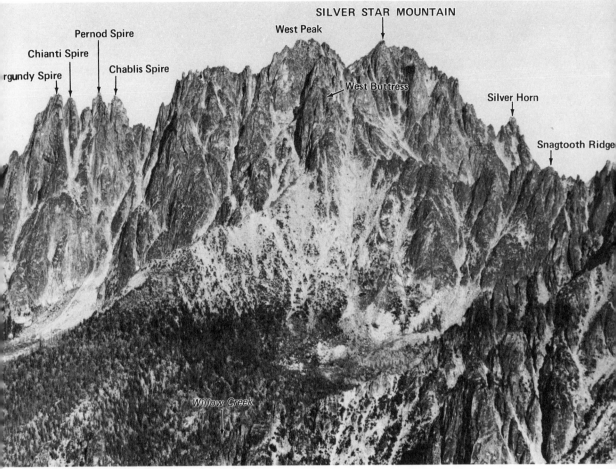

SILVER STAR MOUNTAIN

West Peak

Burgundy Spire

Chianti Spire

Pernod Spire

Chablis Spire

West Buttress

Silver Horn

Snagtooth Ridge

Willow Creek

SILVER STAR MOUNTAIN from west
AGRIS MORUSS

pitch and traverse to a rotten ledge connecting with the main peak col. Grade III; class 5.7-5.8 and A1 (all chocks and one piton).

SILVER STAR GLACIER: First ascent by Fred Beckey, Joe Hieb, Herb Staley, and Don Wilde on May 31, 1952. One can approach via Silver Star Creek♦ to the glacier, but it is shorter to ascend to Burgundy Col (see Willow Creek Route♦), then descend 100 ft (snow) on the E slope, then traverse E across segments of the glacier (stay closely beneath Burgundy Spire). Once past the sharp buttressed rock toe of Point 8640 ascend the glacier to the summit col (possible schrund several hundred ft below col). Make the final broken-rock ascent to the East Peak. Time: 5-7 hours from road. Class 3. Crampons advisable in late summer.

SOUTHEAST FACE AND UPPER EAST RIDGE: First ascent by Oscar Pennington and Hermann F. Ulrichs on September 8, 1932. The face is nearly 2000 ft in height, solid and steep, yet with some broken areas; expect some snow on the face in early summer. The final part of the route is an impressive, towered, jagged crest.[44]

Make the approach via the NW branch of Cedar Creek (see Snagtooth Ridge). Climb the S face to a junction of a rib on its SW; a ledge trends diagonally across the face above (toward the rib descending from the East Peak). Slabs and broken rock lead to the crest of the knifed, long upper East Ridge. At a deep notch, the original party slid down a slab (steep 20-ft slab on N face). Various gymnastic problems arise on the exposed ridge, which leads to the summit (class 4).

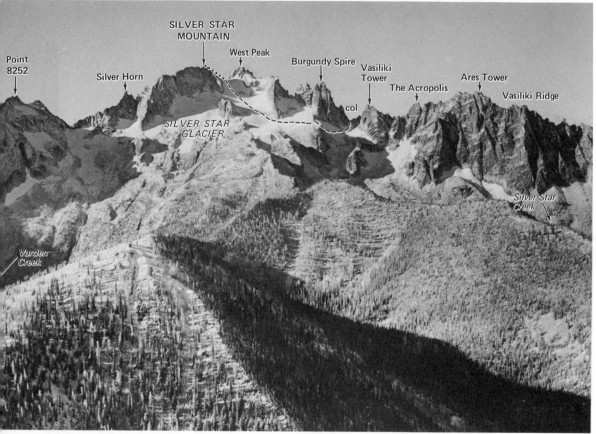

Point 8252
Silver Horn
SILVER STAR MOUNTAIN
West Peak
Burgundy Spire
Vasiliki Tower
The Acropolis
Ares Tower
Vasiliki Ridge
SILVER STAR GLACIER
col
Silver Star Creek
Varden Creek

SILVER STAR MOUNTAIN from northeast
U.S. FOREST SERVICE

WEST PEAK   8840 ft+/2694 m+

First ascent by Fred Beckey, Joe Hieb, Herb Staley, and Don Wilde on May 31, 1952. From the summit col climb a snow finger on the NE face to broken rock just E of the top. The summit is a leaning block (class 4). An alternative route is from the S gully; a broken gully leads close to the summit of the West Peak. Some parties have found the rock traverse to the central col awkward. The S gully can be approached from Willow Creek and the notch near Last Tooth, or from Cedar Creek. References: *A.A.J.*, 1953, pp. 541-42; *Mountaineer,* 1953, p. 25.

The West Face and Southwest Buttress routes (Silver Star) actually finish on this West Peak.

SILVER HORN   8351 ft/2545 m

This very prominent granitic tower is located on Silver Star's E ridge at about 3/8 mile from the summit. Silver

Horn Col (7680 ft+) is the sharp ridge gap on its E. A section of the Silver Star Glacier lies N of the col and Silver Horn. About 1 mi. E of the col, in the N-facing rock cirque E of the main glacier body, an active rock glacier is advancing into larch trees and spilling reddish boulders over live vegetation.[45] The highest rocky point on the ridge E of the col (8252 ft) has been given the fatuous name "Left Thigh"; its ascent appears simplest from the S with an eastern completion. First ascent (Silver Horn) by Fred Beckey, Joe Hieb, Art Maki, and John Parrott in July 1953. References: *Mountaineer,* 1953, p. 67; *A.A.J.,* 1954, p. 172.

ROUTE: Approach by Cedar Creek Trail♦. Hike the NW branch of Cedar Creek into the hanging valley, then ascend scree gullies to the Silver Horn Col. Cross the glacier on the

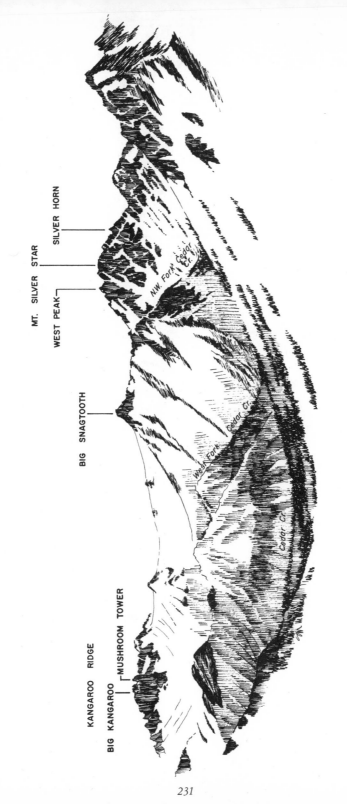

SILVER HORN

MT. SILVER STAR

WEST PEAK

SILVER HORN

BIG SNAGTOOTH

KANGAROO RIDGE

BIG KANGAROO

MUSHROOM TOWER

N.W. Fork Cedar Cr.

West Fork

Cedar Cr.

Cedar Cr.

KANGAROO RIDGE and SILVER STAR MOUNTAIN from southeast

231

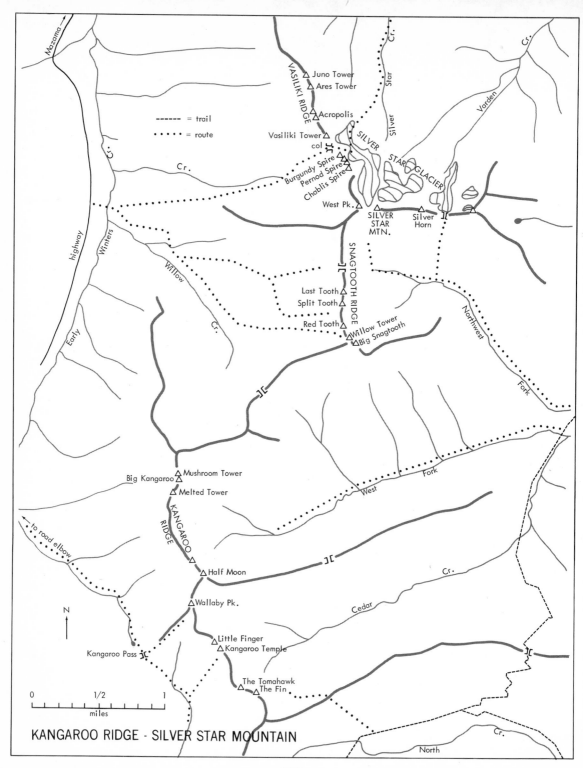

= trail
= route

Mazama

VASILIKI RIDGE

△ Juno Tower
△ Ares Tower

△ Acropolis

Vasiliki Tower △
col

Burgundy Spire △
Pernod Spire △
Chablis Spire △

SILVER STAR GLACIER

Star Cr.

Silver

Varden

West Pk. △
SILVER STAR MTN.
Silver Horn △

Cr.

highway

Winters

Cr.

Willow

Early

Cr.

SNAGTOOTH RIDGE

Last Tooth △
Split Tooth △

Red Tooth △
Willow Tower △
Big Snagtooth △

Northwest Fork

Big Kangaroo △ Mushroom Tower
△

△ Melted Tower

KANGAROO RIDGE

West Fork

to road elbow

△

△ Half Moon

△ Wallaby Pk.

Cedar Cr.

N

Little Finger △
△ Kangaroo Temple

Kangaroo Pass

The Tomahawk △
△ The Fin

0   1/2   1
miles

North Cr.

KANGAROO RIDGE - SILVER STAR MOUNTAIN

N and traverse W about 400 yards. Ascend a steep and corniced snow gully which reaches to the narrow gap W of Silver Horn's summit. Climb eastward: at one point a shoulder stand was used to gain a slab/block (with large perched rock) on the summit ridge. A mantle completes the ascent of the rectangular summit block. Class 4.

A potential alternative approach to the gap W of the summit is from the edge of timber in the hanging valley. Ascend a long gully (snow in early summer) on the SW flank of Silver Horn.

CHABLIS SPIRE   est. 8350 ft/2545 m

This is the southern of the four very striking Silver Star (Wine) Spires, located on the jagged rock crest N of Silver Star's West Peak, between Willow Creek and the Silver Star Glacier. Dimensionally these spires are among the largest such formations in the area. While they could be considered a single massif, the summits are individually separate and distinctive. Chablis Spire culminates in a curious "rabbit ear" appearance, the granitic rock being very light-toned and solid. Long slabs and crack patterns make for delightful rock climbing here.

First ascent by Fred Beckey, Richard Berge, and Wesley Grande on June 17, 1952. References: *A.A.J.*, 1953, pp. 541-42; *Mountaineer*, 1953, p. 26.
ROUTE: Reach the E flank of Chablis as per Silver Star Glacier route. Leave the glacier about 50 ft right of the rotten gully which leads to the notch S of the spire. This point is a few ft S of a huge, loose white flake attached to the wall. From a small ledge a short overhanging flake can be overcome (shoulder used on original). Follow a small line of cracks to the top of a large slab, where a good anchor (pitons) can be set. Climb 25 ft on delicate holds and then take a steep pitch to a ledge belay (class 5). Traverse left 50 ft, then diagonal right on slabs and ledges to a point slightly N of the summit (level with Chablis-Pernod notch). The final lead bypasses a false summit block by ledges to its left. Grade I or II; class 5.5-5.6. Time: 2 hours from glacier (7 hours from road).

Approach Variation: One can climb the W gully from the Willow Creek basin. A steep gully leads to the notch S of Chablis; take an ice axe for possible steep snow in gully, and plan on some rock climbing.

PERNOD SPIRE   8441 ft/2573 m

This sharp rock formation rises immediately N of its lower companion, Chablis Spire, and has a distinctive northward tilt. The upper part of the Spire is very solid. Pernod is the highest of the "Wine Spires," and one of the first difficult summits to be climbed in the area. First ascent by Fred Beckey, Richard McGowan, and Donald Wilde on September 14, 1952. References: *A.A.J.*, 1953, pp. 541-42; *Mountaineer*, 1953,

pp. 26-27; *Appalachia* 29 (June 1953): 402.
ROUTE: From the end of the first lead on Chablis Spire, traverse right on ledges for two to three leads, then up one lead (steep gully — poor rock here) to the N notch of the spire (class 4). Ascend the NE corner, to gain a slab-ledge (class 5); safety bolt here. A 20-ft section leads to another narrow ledge (large angle used for aid on original). From the skyline corner at a platform one party climbed a 6-ft wall, then took ramps left, then back right to the ledge where the pendulum is made. A bolt is used to anchor a 10-ft pendulum swing around the right corner to an open gully. Climb a crack 20 ft on high angle slabs to a platform on the N face (covered here with tilted blocks). From its far end ascend a 40-ft crack (class 5 with one aid move) to the W edge of the final summit block; this is done with aid of two bolts (hangers in). Grade II; class 5 and aid. Time: 3 hours.
Note: When climbing Chablis Spire first, make two rappels, then traverse.

CHIANTI SPIRE   est. 8400 ft/2560 m

The third of the Silver Star Spires from Chablis, Chianti Spire is separated from Burgundy by a narrow gap with sheer flanking walls. The E face beneath the gap is fractured by a long, deep chimney with an unpleasant appearance. First ascent by Joe Hieb and Art Maki on September 14, 1952. References: *A.A.J.*, 1953, pp. 541- 42; *Mountaineer*, 1953, p. 27.
ROUTE: From the notch N of Pernod Spire (use Pernod route, then descend) rappel the W couloir some 250 ft to its fork with a gully beneath Chianti. Ascend the latter to the Burgundy notch. A lead on friable rock (class 5) is followed by one on steep, sound rock. The final summit block can be scaled by a shoulder stand and by flipping the rope over a flake (can be done free). Class 5.6; selection should include angle sizes.

BURGUNDY SPIRE

8400 ft+/2560 m+

The northernmost of the four Silver Star "Wine Spires," and also the most challenging and impressive of the dramatic quartet. The valley and glacier-facing walls are truly spectacular, and compare to the Liberty Bell massif in size. The ascent of Burgundy is becoming a classic, just for the sake of attaining the elusive summit, one of the most difficult in the Cascade Range. By 1965 the ascent had been done three times (using three aid pitons then), but now three routes are done free. It is hoped that climbers will take precaution not to mar the routes, and will use chocks only.

First ascent by Fred Beckey, Michael Hane, and John Parrott on August 17, 1953 (via N face). References: *A.A.J.*, 1954, p. 172; *Mountaineer*, 1953, pp. 27-28; *Appalachia* 29 (December 1953): 571.
NORTH FACE: From the glacier edge climb a narrow

BURGUNDY SPIRE from northeast
FRED BECKEY

300-ft snow couloir (the first E of Burgundy Col — see Silver Star Mountain). Climb the obvious left-bearing rock trough (class 3) to where it steepens and broadens below a 200-ft lichen-streaked wall. From ledges above the trough take a leftward zigzag climbing line, upward through flakes and ramps and cracks; the harder climbing begins above a large detached leaning block. Pass a lichen-clean triangular patch about 20 ft on its left, while ascending the broken crack (left of deep open book). A rightward step-around to reach a ramp (5.5) and higher another rightward step-around are the hardest points. The last portion of the gap atop the wall is a narrow face adjacent to a dihedral. See topo. From the terrace atop the wall climb easily leftward to the corner ridge crest (class 4), ending at a large level step (on left corner).

Now climb near the left extremity of a 70-ft wall-slab beneath the final summit arete (exposed, partly overhanging). The crux of this pitch is near a small horn: several face holds are used up and left (bolt nearby for protection); lean left for exposed 5.8 hand jam (can place large hex). Swing up on jam and find good hold, then up low angle slab to belay.

Follow the thin arete, bypassing the first tower on the left. There are two ways to complete the ascent: the original party threw a rope over the steep second tower for prusik, then climbed a very thin, flawless edge to an overhanging gap, then placed an aid bolt on the far wall. The popular completion of the route now is to take one of the alternatives on the last part of the Corkscrew Route to cross to the W side of the arete, then traverse to the area of the flaring chimney (see topo). Grade III; class 5.8. Time: allow a full day. Descent: Four or five rappels with some downclimbing.

CORKSCREW ROUTE: First ascent by Carla Firey, Brad Fowler, and Jim McCarthy on July 1, 1973 (also first free ascent of Burgundy). Begin at the lowest part of the West Face and very near a long left-trending gully that separates

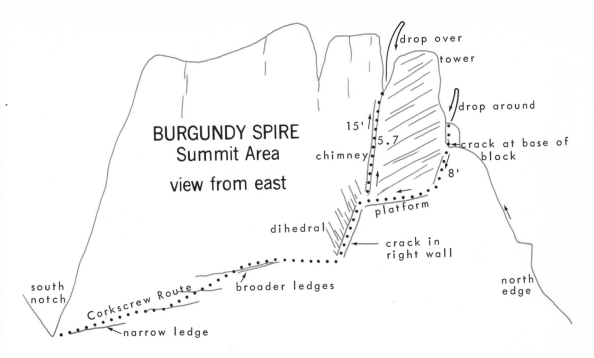

BURGUNDY SPIRE
Summit Area
view from east

drop over
tower

drop around

crack at base of
block

8'

crack in
right wall

15'

5.7

chimney

platform

dihedral

south
notch

Corkscrew Route

broader ledges

narrow ledge

north
edge

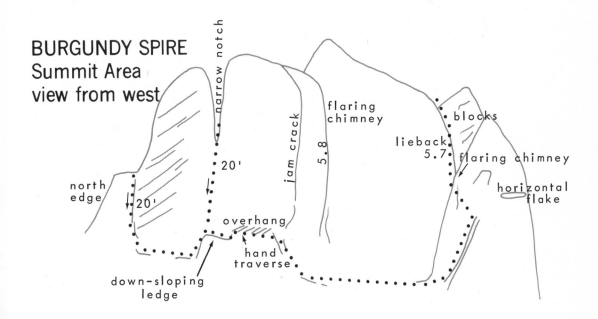

BURGUNDY SPIRE
Summit Area
view from west

narrow notch

flaring
chimney

blocks

lieback
5.7

flaring chimney

jam crack

5.8

horizontal
flake

north
edge

20'

20'

overhang

hand
traverse

down-sloping
ledge

Burgundy from Paisano Pinnacle. The route ascends five-six pitches, then traverses the large sandy bench rightward to the sandy bowl at the base of the hanging Burgundy-Chianti couloir (eight pitches — class 4 to 5.6; many scrub trees at first). Ascend the couloir to the notch (loose and unpleasant). Traverse an improbable ledge E, then around a corner N onto a series of upward-sloping ledges. These lead to a dihedral with a large crack in the corner and another in the right wall. At the top of the crack is a platform below a narrow 15-ft chimney splitting the ridge N of the summit (one pitch). From the crest descend same chimney on opposite (NW) for about 25 ft, where it is feasible to traverse a down-sloping ledge. Then hand-traverse under an overhang and around a small rib to an uneven ledge (same as final belay of the Northwest Face route). The 1973 party ascended the deep off-width crack (5.8) directly to the summit; the alternative is to traverse S, where the final pitch begins right of a flaring chimney. Traverse left into the crack (wide corner lieback or jam to the top — 5.7); this appears to be the same as original Northwest Face route completion. Grade III; class 5.7 (all chocks).

WEST FACE (Annie Green Springs Route): First ascent by Chris Greyell and David Jay on October 15, 1978. The West and continuing SW face on the Willow Creek flank of Burgundy Spire begins at about the 7000-ft level; the sharp edge where the Spire corners is on the SW. This route begins from the large chockstone several hundred ft up the gully that divides Burgundy from Pisano Pinnacle. Traverse ledges right 100 ft, then up some class 3 to a large ledge. Angling left, follow interesting jam cracks (5.8) for three pitches to the SW corner gully and great sandy ledge. Traverse up and left for several class-4 pitches to just below the large obvious roof about midface. From its right side climb a 5.8-ramp to gain ledges above, then traverse over to the crack system above the center of the roof. Climb these cracks for 1½ pitches (5.7) to just below an 8-ft square roof on the left skyline. This crux pitch follows the crack to the roof and then left around it to gain the WNW "ridge" (5.9); follow this feature for three pitches to the summit (probably same or nearly same as 1958 route). Grade III; class 5.9. Take chocks to 3-inch and many runners. Time: 8 hours from base. Reference: *A.A.J.*, 1979, p. 183.

NORTHWEST FACE: First ascent by Donald N. Anderson and Jim Richardson in June 1958 (second ascent).

From Burgundy Col scramble lower pitches to the right-tilting sandy bench area on the NW corner of the summit formation. From the upper right-hand end of this bench climb a medium-long pitch up and slightly left (moderately difficult); at the end of the pitch one gets behind a large flake for belay. Traverse sharply right on steep rock around a whitish corner about 15 ft from the belay (good protection cracks). Climb up and right (minor aid), then ascend a face to a ledge which ends the short pitch. Now climb down and right, then up into a groove (minor aid); climb around some flakes to a belay in a superb "postal box." One short pitch continues on the West Face, then climb open grooves and

cracks toward the summit. A final chimney ends in an airy step onto the S false summit (5.7 chimney and crack). Route errors will force the climb to be more difficult. Grade II or III; class 5.6 and A2 (original). Time: 9 hours from col.

Note: Original party made rappel to Chianti notch, then descended the rock gully, then a wall (West Face) in two rappels.

PAISANO PINNACLE
est. 7900 ft/2408 m

This is a pinnacle or frontal pillar adjacent to the lower Northwest Face of Burgundy. A technical route exists on the W face, following a very narrow, obvious ridge; first ascent by Carla Firey and Jim McCarthy in September 1971. Approach by the Paisano-Vasiliki Tower gully. Begin rock climbing on the left side of the face, from a small notch which is behind a rock knob (on right) above the ridge base. The cracks on the route are first indistinct, but later become very apparent; the hardest area is about two-thirds of the distance up the route. Pitches are rated 5.7, 5.5, 5.6, 5.7, 5.7, and 5.6. To descend: downclimb (class 4) to the notch, then rappel. Grade III; class 5.7.

VASILIKI RIDGE

The ridge spur trending NNW for about 3 mi. from Burgundy Spire and Col, between Silver Star and Early Winters Creek is marked by sharp crags and towers with steep rock faces on the E; the W slope of the ridge has a moderate gradient. Good camping can be found in the basin SW of the ridge (about 6400 ft) — see Willow Creek Route♦. From here a snow gully leads to Burgundy Col. The wanderings of climbers in the 1950s blessed the area with imaginative names, sometimes in abuse of such privilege, but adding character to the ridge. The only exploratory information prior to specific first ascents is that Lage Wernstedt was on the ridge crest in about 1926.

VASILIKI TOWER   7920 ft+/2414 m+

This formation is the southern tower of the ridge; it has a moderate N flank, but is steep on the S and E. First ascent by Joe Hieb and Donald Wilde on May 31, 1952. References: *Mountaineer*, 1953, p. 25; *A.A.J.*, 1953, pp. 541-42; *Appalachia* 29, no. 116 (1953): 401.

NORTH RIDGE: This, the original route, is a rock scramble (class 3).

SOUTH FACE: First ascent by Ed Cooper and Al Murdoch in June 1959. The route follows a direct line from Burgundy

Col to the summit. There is about 300 ft of climbing (class 4); the last lead is a high-angle slab capped by an overhang (class 5). References: *Mountaineer*, 1960, pp. 89-90; *A.A.J.*, 1960, pp. 120-21.

NORTHWEST DIHEDRAL: First ascent by James D. Price and James A. Wilson on June 13, 1967. About 100 ft below Burgundy Col traverse upward-left; cross a large gully on a broad ledge, then climb a rib and bear left into the next gully (the last obstacle is a smooth slab — one piton). Now climb the obvious dihedral, jamming several parallel cracks (5.4). From a belay platform traverse left to the North Ridge (about two leads).

THE ACROPOLIS 8040 ft+/2450 m+

This castle-shaped formation is located N of Vasiliki Tower. First ascent by Joe Hieb and Donald Wilde on May 31, 1952 (Southwest Corner).

SOUTHWEST CORNER: Climb a sloping wall between two cracks on the corner. Follow a narrow, rotten edge; the summit is the far end. Class 4. Time: 1½ hours.

SOUTH FACE: First ascent by Don Dooley, Marilyn Jensen, and Stan Jensen on July 22, 1972. The route consists of three leads — decomposed rock reported. Class 5.5. Reference: *Mountaineer*, 1972, p. 87.

CHARON TOWER 8000 ft+/2438 m+

A symmetrical grey-toned pyramid S of The Acropolis. First ascent by Joe Hieb and Donald Wilde on May 31, 1952. The short route is via the N side (class 3).

ARES TOWER 8190 ft/2496 m

The highest point on Vasiliki Ridge, features four points of nearly equal height (the northern is highest). First ascent by Fred Beckey and Herb Staley on May 31, 1952.

ROUTE: Climb a steep 50-ft face on the W side of the tower to within 75 ft N of the summit. Traverse under a block, then ascend the ridge. Time: ½ hour.

JUNO-JUPITER TOWER
7920 ft+/2414 m+

This is the twin tower with nearly converging summits; Juno is the northern and Jupiter the southern. First ascent by Fred Beckey and Herb Staley on May 31, 1952.

ROUTES: Climb Juno on the NW (class 3). Climb Jupiter from the S (class 2). One can reach the central notch by rappel from either summit.

APHRODITE TOWER
7720 ft+/2353 m+

A sharp, dark-colored tower some 200 ft above the ridge crest. First ascent by Fred Beckey and Herb Staley on May 31, 1952.

ROUTE: Climb to the ridge notch S of the tower, then to the right edge of the lower of two narrow, offset horizontal ledges (S face). Climb a 12-ft crack to the upper ledge (can place protection at left edge of lower ledge and an angle on upper). Then traverse left to upper W face, where a 20-ft lieback leads to the top. Time: 1 hour.

BACCHUS TOWER
7600 ft+/2317 m+

This is the northern of the significant ridge towers. First ascent as above. The short route is on the S face (class 3).

SUNSET BUTTRESS

This feature is a large NW-facing slabby rock buttress at the far N end of Vasiliki Ridge. It is best approached from the highway from its N end; scramble up long slide paths leading directly to the base (3 hours).

UP, UP AND AWAY: First climbed by Eric Sanford and Gil Webber in August 1978. From the very lowest place on the face ascend a corner system with trees. Follow this, occasionally stepping out onto the face until it steepens. On the third lead pass over a small roof and continue up the crack system gradually heading right. The route ends on the NW corner of the rock after five pitches. A 500-ft scramble leads to the summit. Grade II; class 5.8.

DAVID AND GOLIATH: By Eric Sanford and David Spaulding in July 1978. Starting several hundred ft uphill from the lowest area (right of above route) climb broken rock for four leads to a large terrace beneath a steep wall. Climb off-width cracks and chimneys for two leads to the summit. Grade II; class 5.5.

KANGAROO RIDGE

The spectacular 3-mi. ridge of crags, massive fins, and spires collectively termed Kangaroo Ridge is an excellent example of the Golden Horn granodiorite. The N-trending ridge is characterized by a reddish tone, jagged skyline, deep couloir dissection, and long talus slopes beneath distinctive summit formations. Despite uniformly inclined W slopes, these pink monoliths stand exposed with often sheer N and E flanks. The ridge was never wholly topped by ice of the glacial epoch.

Kangaroo Ridge is a bizarre museum of breathtaking rock sculpture, and abounds with unique curiosities of form, such as giant ceilings in the midst of smooth walls, strangely formed knife-edges, and summits which cap in overhangs. The casting off of

Big Kangaroo

slab

Mushroom Tower

BIG KANGAROO from southwest
ERIC SANFORD

successive shells gives the domes roundness; the sparsely jointed granite tends to exfoliate in curved shells. Sometimes differential weathering along cracks has developed circular pits; lichen cover is less extensive than on rock farther W in the range, but can be heavy on some slabs.

The NW portion of Kangaroo Ridge forms a jagged crown between Willow and Early Winters creeks, a section of unnamed crags and buttresses. Kangaroo Pass divides the stream draining to the North Fork of Twisp River from the headwaters of Early Winters Creek (ice-flow striations exist to 7250 ft above the pass). Cedar Creek and its W fork drain the ridge's E flank, each with long, deep basins. The southern portion of the ridge becomes connected to Gilbert Mountain, at a lower section where individual crags lose their identity. The name Kangaroo Ridge was first shown on 1926 Forest Service maps.

Rock climbing was initially slow to develop, but now has achieved a certain popularity. To reach the summits S of Kangaroo Pass, best approach via the cross-country route from Copper Pass Trail (see Twisp Pass Trail◆) or from North Creek◆. For the northern summits, hike along the W side of Early Winters Creek from the oxbow bend on North Cascades Hwy◆. All upper valleys of the ridge provide good camp spots, and there is a pleasant small lake on the N side of Kangaroo Pass. References: *Mountaineer*, 1943, pp. 12-14; *Mazama* 50, no. 13 (1968): 15-20.

MUSHROOM TOWER
8180 ft+/2493 m+

The precipitous tower with a bulge-like summit block is some 200 yards N of Big Kangaroo. First ascent by Fred Beckey, Helmy Beckey, and Walt Varney on June 21, 1942. Reference: *Mountaineer*, 1943, p. 13.
ROUTE: From the gully on the W flank of Big Kangaroo (est. 7800 ft) traverse N under the upper ridge cliffs to talus beneath Mushroom Tower. Climb steep cracks and ledges on the face just right of the narrow 200-ft 70-degree N arete. A

steep sloping ledge leads to the narrow crest at the foot of the mushroom. A wide ledge on the E crosses the face about 40 ft beneath the summit: here a 10-ft overhang (shoulder stand) and a 10-ft high-angle slab (very difficult friction) are taken on the summit runout. Grade I; class 5.9 or 5.10. A rappel bolt is at the summit.

Variation: By Lloyd Anderson, Maury Muzzy, Philip Sharpe, and Roe (Duke) Watson on May 27, 1961. Continue on the final ledge beneath the overhang. At the far end step across and down briefly across a gap; climb left a few ft and then up a small groove (est. 5.5) to the summit.

POINT 8183   8183 ft/2494 m

The northern culmination of the ridge is ⅜ mi. N of Big Kangaroo. It can be visited by hiking and scrambling from near the crest, or from W slopes.

BIG KANGAROO   8280 ft+/2524 m+

The needle-like block perched atop a narrow rock fin on the Big Kangaroo massif is the ridge's high point; the 50-ft block partially overhangs on the E. The formation has both a high E and a S spur, only about 100 ft lower than the summit. On the W fork Cedar Creek drainage there are a large South Face, E face, and spur, and on the NE face there is a distinctive long left-curving snow finger extending toward the E spur. First ascent by Fred Beckey, Helmy Beckey, and Walt Varney on June 21, 1942.

WEST ROUTE: The long reddish W-facing scarp of the ridge beneath Big Kangaroo is marked by a series of parallel gullies, usually snow-filled into July. From the last large meadow in the upper basin of Early Winters Creek ascend the gully (or adjacent slope) which descends from the crest just S of the true summit. At about 7500 ft bear left via a connecting ramp to another gully, and follow to the western base of the summit rock area. Reach the ridge crest N of the summit needle by a 45-degree gully and some steep rock ribs. Follow the crest S, then make an exposed traverse on the W face of the block (tiny footholds) to a 3-ft ledge on its SW corner. Friction and small holds lead to a final straddle on the S edge. Class 5.4. Time: 5 hours from valley. Reference: *Mountaineer,* 1943, p. 13.

SOUTH FACE: This is a major wall in the area, some 900 ft in height; it terminates on the high spur SE of the summit needle. The established route takes the obvious chimney system that veers left and splits the massive granite. First ascent by Fred Beckey and Dan Tate on May 29, 1967.

From a western approach cross Kangaroo Ridge between Half Moon and Big Kangaroo at a notch — est. 7500 ft. Descend a couloir (snow in early summer) and then traverse N. The route follows the chimney system. The next to final lead is the hardest — a lieback. Reach the flat promontory E of the summit. One tricky pitch on more eroded rock follows a sharp edge to the S side of the summit needle. Grade III; class 5.7 or 5.8 (25 pitons used on original). References:

A.A.J., 1967, p. 351; *Mountaineer,* 1967, p. 131.

Approach Variation: Via Willow Creek and then a traverse of the slope in the basin of Cedar Creek's W fork.

MELTED TOWER   7920 ft+/2414 m+

The outline of the short but prominent tower about 200 yards S of Big Kangaroo is a curved horn with a squarish summit. First ascent by Fred Beckey, Helmy Beckey, and Walt Varney on June 21, 1942. Reference: *Mountaineer,* 1943, p. 13.

NORTH FACE: Make the approach from the W, from upper Early Winters Creek basin, or traverse below the ridge line from near Big Kangaroo. A chimney and scree lead to the foot of the final 120-ft face (75 degrees in angle to nearly vertical at the top). The first section is fairly solid, but rock becomes more friable on the steep upper section. Class 5.6 or 5.7.

SOUTH FACE: First ascent by George Mustoe and Ron Sheats on May 30, 1975. Climb a long gully from the meadows to a notch immediately S of the tower. From here a very difficult 75-ft wall is climbed to a vertical crack system, followed by 100 ft of scrambling; class 5.7.

The unnamed spire just S of Melted Tower can be climbed from the notch via two pitches of pleasant climbing along the knife-edged granite arete. Class 4.

HALF MOON   7960 ft+/2426 m+

This striking free-standing rock formation is perhaps the most artistically formed on Kangaroo Ridge: from one perspective it appears as half of a moon (curving to the SW) and from another, as an upright book. There are no easy summit routes — several of its walls are smooth and precipitous. Two blocky rock horns are perched on the hostile SW ridge. To the SE of Half Moon, on the Cedar Creek flank, is a curious S-facing rock dome with a sheer face below its 7600-ft summit. First ascent by Fred Beckey, Helmy Beckey, and Walt Varney on June 17, 1942 (via North Route). References: *Mountaineer,* 1943, p. 12; *Mazama* 50, no. 13 (1968): 16-18.

NORTH ROUTE: The popular approach is over the top of Wallaby Peak. Descend the N ridge, first rock then snow, and glissade a snowfield on the E flank. Traverse slopes (snow) under the S face of Half Moon to an eastern rock spur (to the right is a sheer white dome which produces a sequence of multiple echoes). Make a short steep descent (usually snow), then a long exposed traverse of the E face on loose ledges to the W edge of the N face. Climb 200-300 ft of mediocre rock to reach a minor level shoulder on the N arete (last 20 ft difficult due to crumbly rock); this shoulder bears up a narrow crest to the final N ridge (this last 200 ft is sound rock). Climb along the crest (or face) to a sloping ledge below a short slab face. Mantle moves (class 5) climb to the crest of a thin rib; continue by straddling or careful walking to the final easy crest. Class 4-5. Time: 4-6 hours.

HALF MOON

Big Kangaroo

South Face

Dome 7600 feet

HALF MOON from south
TOM MILLER

Descent: Bolts may be in place for rappels; some parties rappel the NW face from the shoulder.

Approach Variation: Take North Lake Trail♦ (cross-country) to the S end of Kangaroo Ridge. A rising traverse under the upper cliffs will lead to the talus (or snow) beneath the S face (one can use this approach from summits at the S end of Kangaroo Ridge).

SOUTH FACE: This sheer 500-ft face rises from the snowfield usually at its base; the face is jointed into deep cracks from base to summit. The face can immediately be seen to have technical climbing potential. First ascent by Fred Beckey, David Collins, and John Rupley on October 20, 1957. Use the Wallaby Peak traverse or North Lake cross-country route (see North Creek Trail♦) as an approach. A scramble of 75 ft leads to a 100-ft section of crack which is mixed free and aid. Liebacks and jam cracks follow for 200 ft (class 5). Grade III; class 5 and aid. References: *A.A.J.*, 1958, p. 83; *Mountaineer*, 1958, p. 105.

NORTHWEST FACE: This slabby face rises some 900 ft on the valley wall of upper Early Winters Creek basin. First ascent by Fred Beckey and Tom Stewart on September 11, 1966. The route follows the central open book. The two hardest moves are at rightward traverses: one is above the overhanging chimney, poorly protected; the other is a long, exposed crack. Most of the rock is solid, but some cracks, flakes, and holds tend to be friable and eroded. Grade III; class 5 and aid (the original party used 33 pitons — all free but two moves). References: *A.A.J.,* 1966, p. 134; *Mountaineer,* 1966, p. 201.

CHOI OI and HAI TOWERS (est. 7850 ft/2393 m) are the two prominent horns W of Half Moon's summit. First ascents by Christine Devin, David Devin, William D. Devin, and David Upham in September 1967. From Half Moon's summit descend 25 ft W, then descend the long sloping ridge to tower base (exposed lieback). Climb the E face for 60 ft (steep friction ledge) to under an overhang (safety piton). An exposed leftward traverse, then the skyline ridge (class 4) leads to the split summit (75 ft above start). A rappel on the W face will reach Hai Tower.

Another way to the platform at Choi Oi's base is via the ledge from zigzag ridges (see below) formed by huge slabs, then up 35 ft to base of two summit blocks (exposed class 4). The original party climbed Hai Tower from the E base of Half Moon to a corridor-like chimney formed by a large flake. Stem chimney, then two bolts on wall (aid), then scrambling to ledge. Ascend a series of zigzag ridges.

WALLABY PEAK   7995 ft/2437 m

This hump-shaped rock formation is about ½ mi. E of Kangaroo Pass (it was formerly termed Point 8000). The peak is steep and slabby on the E and NW. As a climb it is sensible to combine with the ascent of Half Moon. First ascent by Fred Beckey, Helmy Beckey and Walt Varney on June 17, 1942. Reference: *Mazama* 50, no. 13 (1968): 16.

ROUTES: From Kangaroo Pass (6671 ft) the ascent is merely a hiking-scramble, with final reach on the SW ridge. The traverse onward via the N ridge is easy, but prepare for snow in early summer. The N ridge can be approached directly from Cedar Creek; another approach is from the notch N of Kangaroo Temple for a traverse beneath the E face.

THE TOMB   est. 7800 ft/2377 m
A crag located about ½ mi. N of Kangaroo Temple, and S of Wallaby. The SW face was first climbed by Greg Markov and Mark Weigelt on July 4, 1972 (three pitches). Begin at right corner of the face and climb a right-curving dihedral to a belay just above a pine bush. Then make a difficult move down and traverse left to a second dihedral (5.7). Ascend this to a sloping ledge, then bear right around a corner and make a sharp left move to avoid a rotten bulge. One pitch (loose)

completes the route. Class 5.8 (selection of six-eight pitons, and chocks). Time: 2½ hours on rock. Reference: *Mountaineer,* 1972, p. 87.

KANGAROO TEMPLE (The Temple)
7572 ft/2308 m

This massif, of a block-shape with a truncated summit, is one of the largest on Kangaroo Ridge. Long appreciated for its esthetic qualities, the formation more recently has gained renown for its quality climbing. While diminutive in relation to the Liberty Bell group, this rock mass has sufficient bulk to offer more climbing opportunities and sustained climbs than other formations in the ridge. Formerly referred to simply as "The Temple," the prefix eliminates confusion with Mt. Temple in the Cashmere Crags. The granitic rock is generally quite compact, but yellowed areas tend to be crumbly; the large crystals are caused by hydrothermal alteration of the magma after intrusion. Sometimes localized weathering has formed surface pits. Exfoliation is apparent on this massif — old shells can be noted decomposing into sand. First ascent by Fred Beckey and Helmy Beckey on June 20, 1942 (via Northwest Face). The North Face route was subsequently found to be more direct and feasible. Reference: *Mountaineer,* 1943, pp. 13-14.

NORTH FACE: First ascent by Dick Crain, Donald (Claunch) Gordon, Dick McGowan, and Tom Miller on Memorial Day weekend, 1954. From Kangaroo Basin ascend to the notch immediately N of the summit. Begin via a minor spur, then climb steep but broken rock, first left, then bearing right of a minor nose (class 4). In 200 ft reach a good belay ledge with scrub trees. Traverse W past a huge block and continue to a sharp corner (60 ft from belay — class 4); the belay spot is a 5-ft tree around the corner. Traverse S for 35 ft (easy ledge) to the first crack system (has small shrub). Lieback and jam this right-slanting crack (class 5). Edge around a scrub tree patch 65 ft higher, then make a sandy scramble to the summit. Grade I; class 5.6. Time: 2 hours from notch. Reference: *Mountaineer,* 1954, p. 64.

Descent: The fastest descent from the summit is a scramble W down the sand-slab to the thick tree patch above the dropoff. From a tree at its N edge make a 65-ft rappel, then pendulum N to the obvious ledge with a 5-ft tree at its opposite end. Work to the tree, then turn the sharp NW corner. From footholds 6 ft lower, traverse the North Face (class 4) to the scrub trees on a ledge; these provide a rappel anchor.

NORTHEAST FACE: First ascent by Fred Beckey and Dan Tate in May 1967. From the N notch ascend leftward on broken, moderately steep slabs. A trough (possibly slippery) leads into the final exit chimney, which forms part of a large right-facing open book with a smooth right wall. Grade II;

KANGAROO TEMPLE from northwest
TOM MILLER

class 5.6 (seven pitons used). References: *Mountaineer*, 1967, p. 131; *A.A.J.*, 1967, p. 352.

EAST FACE: This seven-pitch route begins about 200 ft above the lowest rock toe, where the first grassy ledge enters the face on the N. The best approach is via North Creek Trail♦. First ascent by Fred Beckey and Thom Nephew on October 7, 1971.

Ascend a full lead up the face to the right of the prominent gully/chimney to a tree (5.3). Work into the gully and climb the eroded left wall (safety bolt); move left of the bolt and finish the wall to a minor rib (5.6). Ascend one pitch on broken rock (class 4), then an easier one to the notch where the S spur meets the face. The next two pitches are the same as the initial ones for the Southeast Buttress Route (face

pitch, steep groove). Ascend a right-slanting ramp with short walls (jams, mantles — 5.7). Then step around a corner atop the ramp and ascend the summit gully. Grade III; class 5.8. Original selection: one 2½-inch, one 2-inch, one 1¼-inch, one 1-inch, one ¾-inch, one Leeper, two horizontals, one ¼-inch hanger, many runners. Time: 5 hours on rock. Reference: *Mountaineer*, 1971, p. 88.

SOUTHEAST BUTTRESS: This buttress forms the skyline profile of Kangaroo Temple viewed from the basin. First ascent by Fred Beckey, John Parrott, Louis Pottschmidt, and Herb Staley on June 12, 1955.

From the lower SW flank of the peak ascend the wide gully (keep W of rocky S spur) to a notch at the upper SE face (walking and scrambling to here). The first short pitch leads

KANGAROO TEMPLE

Southwest Face

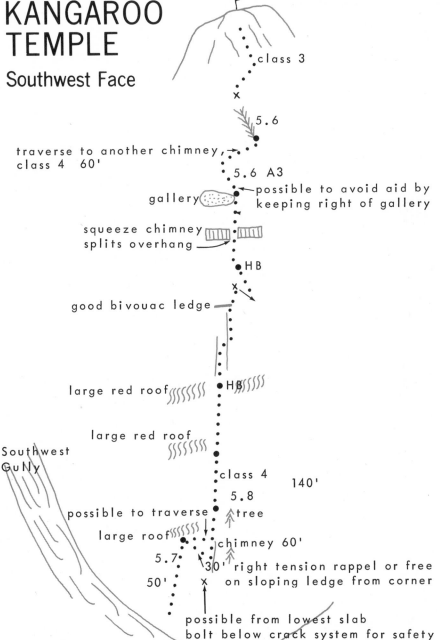

class 3

5.6

traverse to another chimney,
class 4 60'

5.6 A3

possible to avoid aid by
keeping right of gallery

gallery

squeeze chimney
splits overhang

HB

good bivouac ledge

large red roof

HB

large red roof

Southwest
Gully

class 4   140'

5.8

possible to traverse   tree

large roof

chimney 60'

5.7   30' right tension rappel or free
          on sloping ledge from corner

50'

possible from lowest slab
bolt below crack system for safety

to a belay pine on a large ledge (5.0). The next pitch climbs a steep face (first left, then right) to a ledge with pine scrubs. Continue up a smooth-walled groove; this was done with an aid piton on the original climb, but done free on East Face route (5.8). A section of mossy rock progresses to a ledge, then a slab leads to a large belay pine on ledges. Climb a crack leftward above the belay (20 ft), then friction left 15 ft to a N-facing chimney which divides a white wall. This 2-ft chimney flares at the start (5.7), then handles easier; once atop, bear left to broken rock. Grade II; class 5.8 (take small selection including 2-inch). References: *A.A.J.*, 1956, p. 122; *Mountaineer*, 1955, p. 55.

Descent: Can rappel from pine atop chimney; next anchor at belay pines.

SOUTH FACE: This face has a deep W-facing chimney; the route climbs to its right, then works into its upper portion. First ascent by Fred Beckey and Donald (Claunch) Gordon on October 8, 1956.

From the ridge which connects with the East Face, traverse W along the principal wide ledge to the corner of the South and East Faces. Ascend a smooth difficult pitch on this corner (class 5). Make a leftward slab traverse into the chimney, which is steep and loose here. Above is a formidable appearing corner at the intersection of wall planes. The key to the pitch is a hidden chimney; once through, moderately difficult climbing continues to the scrambling at the top area. Grade II or III; class 5. References: *A.A.J.*, 1957, pp. 145-46; *Mountaineer*, 1958, p. 107.

SOUTHWEST FACE — 1965 ROUTE: This route intersects, and possibly merges for a distance with the 1964 route; the two certainly meet at "The Gallery." The climb has a variety of interesting face and crack problems; while there tends to be some loose rock, most of the climbing is secure. First ascent by Bill Marts, Steve Marts and Don McPherson in either June or August 1965. This ascent used about 50 pitons (some for aid), and spent 2½ days on the route. Subsequent parties have begun left and higher than the original start, and reported that the route was six leads of class 5 and one of class 4 (perhaps later climbs kept farther right on the final three leads).

The original party began at a slab right of the SW gully, then bore toward a crack leading to the large roof (50 ft, 5.7). They traversed right 30 ft to a tree in the principal crack system (tension rappel done). The 1972 report indicates two pitches on slab prior to the long principal crack (same 30-ft traverse). The end of second pitch is a short shallow chimney which is hard to protect (5.6-5.7); tree belay (?). The next pitch has some loose material below the hardest free move of the climb (a jam over a bulge where it is hard to use feet); 140 ft — 5.8. On the fifth pitch (1965) work from left crack to right; the pitch is a hard layback, curving right, with very continuous 5.7 (good ledge at lead's end). Climb right around a corner and 15 ft up to a bolt. The 1965 party apparently made a 25-ft rappel to a ledge in a chimney, then climbed a squeeze that splits an overhang and ends at the right side of "The Gallery" cave (end of sixth

pitch — 130 ft). Note: Subsequent parties have reported cracks (some liebacks) here, but no rappel; one member of the original party recalls that their rappel was after the cave, to reach a new crack system. The original party also reported that beyond the cave is a pitch rated 5.6 and A3, and possibly a 60-ft traverse to another chimney (perhaps joining the South Face route).

More recent parties have dropped slightly after the cave and traversed right to reach an obvious short dihedral, then ascended directly, past small caves, to reach the summit area. A final pitch is blocky and slightly loose. Grade III; class 5.8 (original party used pitons KB to 3-inch; a chock selection is adequate, but include large hexcentrics. Time: allow all day.

SOUTHWEST FACE — 1964 ROUTE: This route begins at the base slabs on the SW side of the peak, near the two flanking gullies (these are snow-filled in early summer). The climb is about 700 ft in height (eight pitches). First ascent by David Hiser and Norman Weber on July 8, 1964.

First lead is slabs (mixed free and aid), upward. Traverse left (N) to some trees; possibly this involved a left tension traverse into a series of dihedrals and chimneys to a tree-filled alcove below a prominent chimney. Then climb two leads directly upward, over small overhangs, in a chimney system; one ends here below a large overhang near the buttress nose (at this height the face has rounded into a buttress). Climb around to the right (S) and up two more leads of vertical cracks and dihedrals to trees on a sloping ledge (the final part is a 5.6 jam crack). This reaches "The Gallery" — a deep long cave with a window to the W (enter on S and exit via window to reach W side of the buttress). Two more pitches lead to the summit: the report indicates that class 4 climbing led to buttress nose, then work left on small pedestal (and up on rurp), then 5.5 face climbing to an easy slab; this leads to a belay tree on the nose. Climb left 20 ft and up onto a sloping ledge bearing upward-right. Then about 200 ft of class 3 to the top. Grade III (used 14 pitons — 6 of these for aid on original). Time: 8 hours. Reference: *A.A.J.*, 1967, p. 351.

NORTHWEST FACE: This is the first ascent route, one with the merit to become popular, but is seldom climbed. The route is located just right of a rock tongue of 5 ft width; the climb actually begins left of this feature, but traverses right above it, to essentially ascend a 400-ft intermittent crack system — the NW chimney — which becomes well defined at about the 150-ft level. Rock is reasonably solid, but tends to slope down. The first two of three continuous pitches are the hardest.

Begin on the right side of the gully leading to the N notch (about 200 ft below notch) at a flat, table-sized rock. The first pitch is steep but sound: the crux is a 10-ft overhanging section with possible poor protection. Make a short left traverse, then climb the wall below the chimney (vertical and difficult). Here one is a short distance below the chimney, which is branched like an inverted Y. A side-chimney on the left affords entrance to the main crack: to reach it

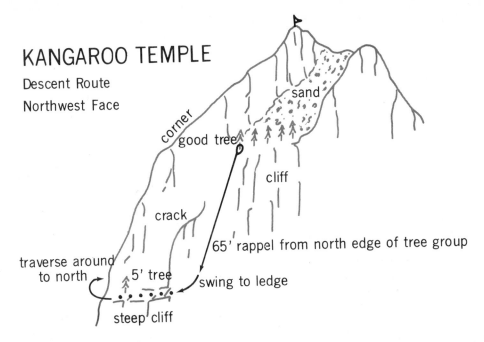

KANGAROO TEMPLE

Descent Route

Northwest Face

corner

good tree

sand

cliff

crack

65' rappel from north edge of tree group

traverse around
to north

5' tree

swing to ledge

steep cliff

requires climbing a difficult 20-ft section, partly overhanging, on small holds. A steep wall is traversed leftward to the left chimney. Stem to a belay position in the chimney. Wedging and stemming for about one-half lead brings one to a projection on a rib between the chimney branches, and here the angle decreases. Two short pitches lead to the "Dance Floor" — a 30-degree slab. Traverse left to bypass a wall, and meet the narrowing shallow chimney of the normal route; jam and lieback to the easy summit slabs. Grade II; class 5.7 (14 pitons used on original; has been done all chocks). Time: 3 hours. Reference: *Mountaineer,* 1943, pp. 12-13.

LITTLE FINGER   7400 ft+/2256 m+

The 200-ft rock tower immediately N of Kangaroo Temple was first ascended by Fred Beckey and Helmy Beckey on June 17, 1942 (via S face).

ROUTES: From the notch the steep S face offers solid class 4 climbing (good runner protection). Begin on the W side of the notch; after 50 ft reach a ledge with a pine bush, then climb left across the face to a crack system, and then up to a ledge with a bush. Finally scramble up, keeping right of a dark slab.

The N face offers a similar route (class 4).

THE PLATYPUS   est. 7200 ft/2195 m

This is a squat crag that abuts the ridge near the S face of Kangaroo Temple. A route on the W face follows the obvious left-hand chimney system; first ascent by Greg Markov and Mark Weigelt on July 3, 1972. The route is three and one-half pitches (class 5.7 — 2 hours); take chocks including a few large hexcentics. Reference: *Mountaineer,* 1972, p. 87.

THE TOMAHAWK   7320 ft+/2231 m+

This red-toned tower, with a white crown, resembles the Indian weapon which inspired the name. It is near the S end of Kangaroo Ridge, immediately N of The Fin. First ascent by Fred Beckey and Helmy Beckey on June 16, 1942 (via Southeast Route). Reference: *Mountaineer,* 1943, p. 12.

SOUTHEAST ROUTE: From Kangaroo Basin on the W flank of the ridge climb open forest and talus to a break on the S face. Ascend here, then climb left on the 200-ft SE face (a slab-face with scrub evergreens near the top). Class 4. Alternatively, one can begin the climb from the notch adjacent to The Fin. Time: 1 hour on the rock.

SOUTHWEST FACE: First ascent by Greg Markov and Mark Weigelt on July 3, 1972. Begin via the gully on the N side of the W face. When able, traverse on a ledge beneath a low angle slab. From a tree climb slab to alcove on lower right corner of a large flake/chimney (class 4). Climb inside the flake (stemming, jamming, lieback) to a belay (crux is 5.9). The next pitch climbs to a large chimney, which reaches to the final platform. The final pitch ascends the obvious chimney on the N side of the summit block (5.7). Grade I; class 5.9. Time: 3 hours. Reference: *Mountaineer*, 1972, pp. 86-87.

THE FIN   7360 ft+/2243 m+

At the S end of Kangaroo Ridge, where the crest curves E of The Tomahawk, there is a wedge-shaped crag. The steepest flank is on the E, where the broad basin of Cedar Creek provides a scenic contrast to the dramatic rock forms of the ridge crest. First ascent by Fred Beckey and Helmy Beckey on June 16, 1942 (Southeast Route). Reference: *Mountaineer*, 1943, p. 12.

SOUTHEAST ROUTE: From Kangaroo Basin on the W flank one can hike to the Fin-Tomahawk notch in about 1 hour. Climb along the right side of the E ridge, a pleasant short rock climb (class 4).

NORTH FACE: First ascent by Dallas Kloke and Bryce Simon on June 23, 1976. From the Fin-Tomahawk notch descend a snow gully to the base of this 700-ft face. Begin at the lower left portion: climb two leads to a bench with several trees (poor rock). Ascend diagonally right (unroped) on ledges to center face. Climb 40-50 ft and then traverse left and up to an 8-ft tree which leans against a short overhanging wall. Use the tree for footing to ascend this short pitch. From a good belay above continue diagonally right one lead, then directly up for three more leads to the summit. The upper half of the face is solid rock (can use nuts and slings for protection). Grade II; class 5.7. Time: 6 hours on face. Reference: *Mountaineer*, 1977, pp. 107-8.

POINT 7002   7002 ft/2134 m

Located 0.6 mi. W of Abernathy Pass, between North and Cedar creeks.

NORTH FACE: Route done by Geoffrey Childs (solo), June 1980. The route is on the right (W) side of the 1200-ft N-facing wall. Locate a straight dike in the center of the lower slabs. Climb two pitches of class 4-5 to a bush and ledges. Traverse up and right to friction, cracks, and a chimney leading to a tree ledge. Continue up and right to reach the left-facing dihedral system; difficult face, crack, and at the top, chimney climbing with some aid leads to a second tree-system and sandy ledges. Scramble right, then up into a low-angle corner which is taken for four pitches to the top slabs. Walk off via Abernathy Pass. Class 5.9 and A3.

COPPER POINT   7840 ft/2390 m

Copper Point, a rocky peak ½ mi. ENE of Copper Pass, was used for a triangulation station during surveying. The northern of two summits is higher; the entire E flank (Kangaroo Basin) of the formation is steep and rocky, but much less conspicuous than nearby Kangaroo Ridge. A minor point (7565 ft/2306 m) 0.7 mi. WNW of Copper Point on the Early Winters Valley rim has been referred to as *"Pica Peak."* It is difficult to assess early climbing history, since a number of prospectors, surveyors, and mountaineers have been active in this locale. A climb on Point 7565 (SE ridge) was reported as a new route in 1973.

PEAK 7800+ (Blue Lake Peak, Wamihaspi Peak)   7800 ft+/2377 m+

An unnamed summit, 0.6 mi. due E of Blue Lake, is the high point between the Early Winter Spires, Copper Creek, and Blue Lake. On its E (Early Winters) flank there is an extensive rocky face above talus slopes; here a long rocky ridge leads SE toward Copper Point to form the basin rim. The peak has short rock faces on the W and the N. From the northern vantage the peak shows a double summit, with the higher point a rocky knob on the W and a shoulder point immediately E. The saddle dividing these two summits (7600 ft) has a perennial snowfield on its N flank; this is the old hiking route from Copper Pass Trail to the Liberty Bell area. Three slightly lower summits (7651 ft, 7400 ft+, 7509 ft) crown a western ridge that curls a tight horseshoe about Blue Lake.

The first ascent of Peak 7800+ was probably made by Fred Beckey, Jerry O'Neil, and Charles Welsh on September 28, 1946. The summits about Blue Lake were climbed on a traverse in 1964 by Donald N. Anderson and Larry Scott, who reported their names as "Philadelphia, Kings, and Saratoga."

SOUTH EARLY WINTER SPIRE   7807 ft/2380 m

Located just over a mi. S of Washington Pass, the two Early Winter Spires are virtually one granitic massif split by a deep cleft formed as a consequence of a master joint. Both the sheer E and W faces of the spires are made prominent by the presence of this gigantic fracture, which divides them. Early Winter Spires, Liberty Bell Mountain, and associated towers are a tribute to the power of ice wedging. When the granodiorite cooled about 48 m.y. ago, it contracted along master joints (widespread vertical cracks). After erosion stripped away overlying rock and debris from the granodiorite, soil acids borne by percolating water attacked the rock along joints, cleaving it deeply into

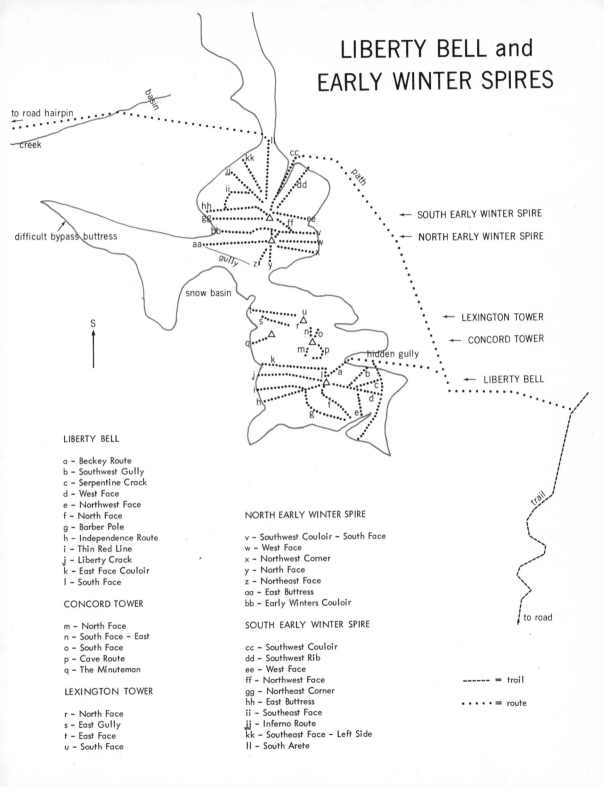

LIBERTY BELL and EARLY WINTER SPIRES

to road hairpin

creek

basin

difficult bypass buttress

snow basin

gully

path

← SOUTH EARLY WINTER SPIRE

← NORTH EARLY WINTER SPIRE

← LEXINGTON TOWER

← CONCORD TOWER

hidden gully

← LIBERTY BELL

trail

to road

LIBERTY BELL

a – Beckey Route
b – Southwest Gully
c – Serpentine Crack
d – West Face
e – Northwest Face
f – North Face
g – Barber Pole
h – Independence Route
i – Thin Red Line
j – Liberty Crack
k – East Face Couloir
l – South Face

CONCORD TOWER

m – North Face
n – South Face – East
o – South Face
p – Cave Route
q – The Minuteman

LEXINGTON TOWER

r – North Face
s – East Gully
t – East Face
u – South Face

NORTH EARLY WINTER SPIRE

v – Southwest Couloir – South Face
w – West Face
x – Northwest Corner
y – North Face
z – Northeast Face
aa – East Buttress
bb – Early Winters Couloir

SOUTH EARLY WINTER SPIRE

cc – Southwest Couloir
dd – Southwest Rib
ee – West Face
ff – Northwest Face
gg – Northeast Corner
hh – East Buttress
ii – Southeast Face
jj – Inferno Route
kk – Southeast Face – Left Side
ll – South Arete

------ = trail

• • • • • = route

domes and towers which would exfoliate independently. The water that seeped behind flakes and through cracks often froze and thawed (expanding with a force of 1000 lbs. per square inch), thus peeling the surfaces to smooth formations. Countless storms and thaws flushed shattered rock from terraces and ledges to reveal today's spectacular shapes.

Loosely placed lettering on Forest Service maps prior to and current at the time of the first ascent made it difficult to discern which of several summits was intended to be "Liberty Bell." Using the logic that it should be the summit of the greater massif with the highest altitude, the party applied this name to their account ("our first choice was Mount Liberty Bell, which appeared difficult on all sides"). In a later evaluation of nomenclature, which needed more singular identity because of an increased interest in summits and new routes, it was decided that originators of the name "Liberty Bell" had intended it for the dome-shaped massif nearer Washington Pass,[46] and the term "Early Winter Spires" was applied to the higher southern summits. (Although other features in the area are called Early Winters, the singular form seemed less clumsy applied to the Spires, and this usage is now reinforced by time.)

In their report of the first ascent, made using the Southwest Couloir on July 20, 1937, the party of Kenneth Adam, Raffi Bedayn, and W. Kenneth Davis was credited; however, only the names Bedayn and Neil Ruge appeared in the summit register. References: *Sierra Club Bull.* 23, no. 2 (1938), p. 46; *Mazama* 50, no. 13 (1968), pp. 15-16, 18; *Mountaineer,* 1943, p. 13.

SOUTHWEST COULOIR: This is the deep gully between the prominent South Arete and Southwest Rib. The couloir is the quickest way to or from the summit, but has little appeal as a climb (the South Arete is much more pleasant). Watch for party-inflicted rockfall.

Approach its base from Washington Pass by ascending SW of Liberty Bell through open forest and scrub-tree basins. A more direct but steeper approach is a 2000-ft ascent from the highway hairpin turn E of Washington Pass. Ascend the talus fan at the S end of the loop, through a bottleneck and then up gullies and talus (or snow) to the level ridge (7320 ft+) S of the spire. A final narrow gully or broken rock to its right can be taken to the ridge crest, then traverse several hundred yards on the W slope to the couloir's base, about 100 ft below ridge crest.

Shortly above its base is a giant chockstone; friction and stem 15 ft easily via the right wall border. Then walk up the loose couloir; in 200 ft, where it splits, keep right. The route narrows, then ends at a little notch just E of the true summit. Scramble left to the top. Time: 4 hours from road. Reference: *Mazama* 50, no. 13 (1968): 16.

SOUTHWEST RIB: This is the prominent crest bordering the Southwest Couloir on the W. First ascent by Donald N. Anderson and Larry Scott on August 20, 1964.

From the top of the giant chockstone in the couloir traverse left across ledges some 200 ft to the obvious 80-ft jam crack; it is difficult (5.8) at one spot near base (bongs). Top of crack is an area of scrub pines (original party traversed in from couloir at this point). A slab leads to a yellow band. Take a slightly overhanging 15-ft crack (A1, small angles) that becomes a left-facing dihedral; ascend this free to a broken overhang, just right of the crest. Climb this direct; all free except one large chock for aid. Then ascend a 70-degree black slab (max. 5.4); the last 50 ft are up small grooves with good protection. To the left are parallel jam cracks 3 ft apart; climb these with a foot in each. A class 4 ledge crosses the face and around a corner right. A short chimney leads to the top of the "dolphin" formation (giant boulder rests here).

Face climb left of a crescent-shaped crack to soon reach a bolt on the edge of the rib. Work slightly left at a little step, then continue up clean rock about one and one-half leads to broken rock W of the summit. Grade II; class 5.8 and A1 (can be 5.6 and A1 by shorter original route); bring several bongs, including a 4-inch and a 3-inch, and a selection of 12 pitons and chocks. Time: 5 hours. Reference: *A.A.J.,* 1966, p. 133.

WEST FACE: This route leads from base of WNW face to the upper portion of the Southwest Rib. First ascent by Fred Beckey and Jim Madsen on July 10, 1967.

Begin from grass slopes via an open book system that veers left. In several pitches reach the base of the "dolphin" rock, under its mouth. Then climb up and left on slabs into the deep chimney. Follow through the top into deep open book to the crest of the rib at top of "dolphin"; follow rib to summit. Grade III; class 5 and aid (48 pitons used). References: *A.A.J.,* 1967, pp. 350-51; *Mountaineer,* 1967, p. 131.

NORTHWEST FACE: This route takes a slightly rightward bearing at the left (E) of the large white overhangs near the middle of the face. First ascent by Paul Boving and Steve Pollock on October 9, 1976; first free ascent by Boving and Matt Kerns in July 1977. The route begins with a shallow left-facing corner, then up past the left side of a small roof (5.10 and A1 or 5.11 — 3 hours on original); step right and follow a short steep crack to a small tree belay. Jam and lieback up and right to a ledge with a tree (5.9), then scramble to the base of the large left-facing dihedral. From a belay surmount a huge double-roof (right of a large obvious chimney) with jams and liebacking (5.10) and up the off-width flake to good ledges above. A few easier pitches lead to the summit: the fifth pitch is identified by twin cracks. Class 5.11.

LOWER EAST FACE AND NORTHEAST CORNER: A long and interesting climb, one of the first in the area

South Arete

East Buttress

The Midnight Ride

Early Winters
Creek

SOUTH EARLY WINTER SPIRE from south
DOUG LEEN

249

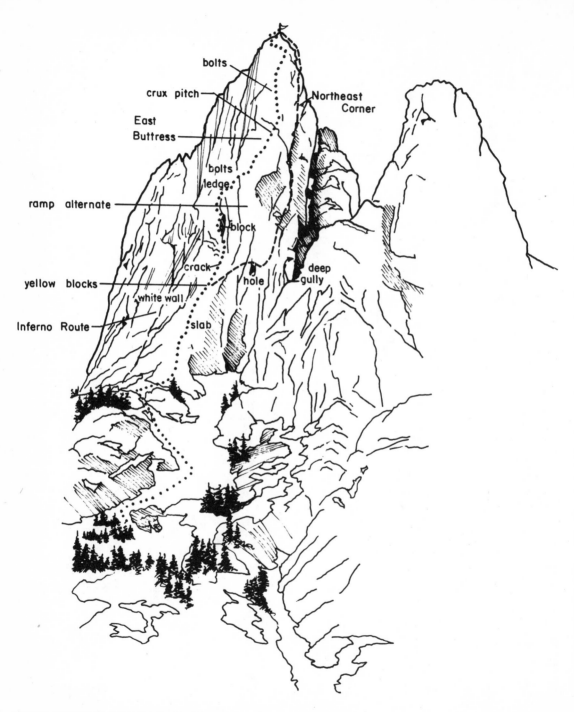

bolts

crux pitch

Northeast
Corner

East
Buttress

bolts
ledge

ramp alternate

block

crack

yellow blocks

hole

deep
gully

white wall

Inferno Route

slab

SOUTH EARLY WINTER SPIRE – East Buttress

involving a bivouac. The lower portion of the route is near the N corner of the E face, then the line follows around the corner to the summit area. Approach as per East Buttress route. First ascent by Don McPherson, Steve Marts, and Fred Stanley in July, 1965.

Begin near N corner of the East Face, then continue directly to trees above (class 4). Traverse right to an open book (chimney), then climb about 35 ft (here a piton can be placed to the right for aid to a ledge). Traverse right from above a small tree, out of a groove, then ascend a crack to a flaky ledge; this is taken to a small tree. At this point one is about 300 ft up the face. Now rappel 25 ft to a cave on the NE corner, then climb right a short distance and climb a loose chimney to a ledge; this long pitch has poor rock and poor protection — 5.7. Now climb a series of easy ledges for about 200 ft (class 4). Climb the large chimney about 50 ft down from the end of the ledge system — 5.8 and A1 (this is the same ledge met on the direct). Keep right of the narrow E buttress, and take a chimney to ledges bearing to the N face. A wide and somewhat rotten steep gully leads to the summit (easy class 5).

Another report states: after the 200-ft ledge series, climb a slanting groove cutting up the face to a small belay ledge (free and aid). Continue up a short crack system to a flake just right of a prominent ledge. A long lead ascends the chimney above to an extensive ledge; from its end 200 ft of climbing ends at the summit.

Grade III; class 5.8 and A1. Selection of 25 items should include one 2-inch, two 1½-inch, two 1-inch, three ¾-inch, four baby angles, four horizontal sizes (not known if chocks will suffice). Reference: *A.A.J.*, 1966, p. 133.

EAST BUTTRESS DIRECT: This spectacular route, first done July 29, 1968 on a 2½-day ascent by Fred Beckey and Doug Leen, is becoming a classic. The climb may take more than one day, but bivouac sites can be found without a need for a hammock. The climb involves considerable aid, but the majority is free. Pitch number 4 is more than 150 ft, and the belayer will have a problem in leader communication, and hauling can be a problem here if there is more than one load. Pitch number 5 probably should be divided at the bivouac ledge, but for speed one could belay at the two bolts where there is a footing; the end of number 6 can easily be reached from here.

The approach begins at the upper end of the road hairpin: hike up a dirt and rock couloir in the direction of the spire's base, then ascend an easy route through talus blocks and gullies to the major gully descending from between the Spires; ascend the latter (snow until late season) past the first cliff band on the left. Traverse left on ledges with small trees to the rock toe of the East Buttress.

(1) Begin with free climbing, using bushes and tie-off loops for protection, then climb on aid to a hanging belay at a tree.
(2) Begin with awkward placements (per original), then a good bong crack in a dihedral facing left is unmistakably the route. Continue up about 100 ft, bypassing a small overhang to a large tree ledge (angle and bong sizes used); A2.

(3) Continue up in a similar crack (three bongs) and then move left onto a bolt placed to avoid an apparently large loose block. Pendulum left into a low-angle dihedral and continue with free and aid to the base of "triangle ledge." A bivouac can be made here.
(4) Start on 5.8 move up and right, and then use a 14-bolt ladder on the left edge of the triangle to the ridgeline. Continue on bolts around the corner to a small flake (small angles), then continue on three bolts and one bathook placement to a vertical crack on the buttress. Aid this crack to where it becomes hard free (past a hole) and then fork right on aid again to a small ledge; 5.7 and A2.
(5) From primitive ledge continue up and right (some aid) on a deteriorating crack, then poorly protected free climbing (5.8) followed by two hook moves lead to a spacious sloping ledge (possible bivouac spot).
(6) A bolt ladder begins at extreme left edge, and meets an arcing (rotten) crack; A3 angles and a bolt allow mantling to an awkward ledge. Two more bolts and another mantle bring one to free climbing up and left (this pitch has some difficult moves and poor placements).
(7) Continue free for 60 ft to a sandy ledge; 5.6.
(8) From ledge climb right and upward for 150 ft to a ledge at 60 ft beneath the summit; 5.4.
(9) Begin on right edge of ledge. The pitch has a 30 ft leftward section to an exposed step-around, then 40 ft to the summit; 5.4. Grade IV; class 5.8 and A3. Original selection: two 4-inch, four 3-inch, four 2½-inch, two 2-inch, three 1½-inch, four 1-inch, five ¾-inch, eight baby angles, six LA, four KB, two Leepers, two bathooks. Will go on chocks (take large hexes). References: *A.A.J.*, 1969, pp. 387-88; *Mountaineer*, 1970, pp. 103-4; *Summit*, 1969, pp. 16-21.

LOWER EAST BUTTRESS AND SOUTHEAST FACE: This indirect route ascends a system on the lower East Buttress just N of the direct route (near gully that separates the Spires), then traverses left to the upper E portion of the Southeast Face; the original climb used about 50 pitons and required 2 days. First ascent by Donald N. Anderson, Paul Myhre, Jim Richardson, and Margaret Young in June 1965.

Begin at the right corner of the lower East Face (see East Buttress Direct), and climb the same two moderate introductory pitches. From a large bushy pine follow the left crack along a series of yellow blocks to a bush (routes diverge near here). Continue an upward-right pattern, following the crack to a belay point. Above a small crumbling flake 25 ft of aid leads to a good belay. The next pitch has two bolts to protect a classic jam crack. From the ledges above take the second crack series to the left, and climb about 150 ft (about 35 ft of this is aid). From a ledge pendulum left, piton a few ft on the farthest crack, and continue the pendulum to reach the bivouac ledge (original party). Walk to the S end of the ledge and rappel to a lower ledge (now on the SE face). Climb up from its left end via a jam crack behind a tree. A steep gully (mostly class 4) provides access to the South Arete just above a short horizontal stretch. Grade III or IV. Reference: *A.A.J.*, 1966, p. 133.

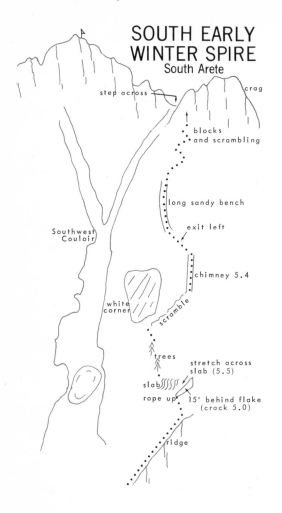

SOUTH EARLY
WINTER SPIRE
South Arete

step across

crag

blocks
and scrambling

long sandy bench

exit left

chimney 5.4

Southwest
Couloir

scramble

white
corner

trees

stretch across
slab (5.5)

slab

rope up   15' behind flake
(crack 5.0)

ridge

move onto a 2-inch ledge and make a long step into the now wider crack. Subsequent climbing becomes class 4 and 3. Grade III; class 5.8 and A4. Original selection: one 3-inch, two 2½-inch, two 2-inch, two 1½-inch, two 1-inch, three ¾-inch, two baby angles, three horizontals, four rurps.

SOUTHEAST FACE — 1977 ROUTE: This route begins just right of the center of the broad face; first ascent by Duane Constantino and David Whitlaw in July 1977. Reach the route from the level ridge S of the Spire by traversing along the base of the wall to where the white rock on the left meets the darker-toned rock. For four leads follow a shallow corner (with a tower on left) dividing dark lichened rock on the left from steeper white rock. The fifth pitch climbs from a bolt belay below a prominent yellow overhanging block through a 5.8 corner. Move right around the base of the block (5.9 and up); the last portion of the block is flaring off-width and overhanging (A2). Then climb two pitches (5.6) in a steep gully, leading into a dirty gully just below the ridge crest (class 4). Grade III or IV; class 5.9 and A2; the aid pitch was 45 ft — take 4-inch to 5½-inch tube chocks (route goes clean). Reference: *A.A.J.*, 1979, pp. 183-84.

SOUTHEAST FACE — THE MIDNIGHT RIDE: This is a steep wall of about 600 ft with numerous flaring and arching cracks and corners; some cracks are discontinuous. The original party spent two days on the climb (much of it aid), and made one tension traverse. First ascent by Henry Coultrip and Eric Sanford in October 1977. From the ridge at the S end of the Spire descend 100 ft and then follow a flaring, bottoming gritty crack which leans left until under a small overhang (where it fades). Climb up and right over this feature to another system, which also leads and leans up and left. Continue until it is possible to make a series of hook and piton moves (scary) to the right where a good crack is followed to more broken rock above. From here is scramble to the summit. Grade III or IV; class 5.9 and A4. One needs pitons for this climb, especially 1-inch and 2-inch, plus hooks and some special pitons and bongs. A new route was done on the Southeast Face by Bob Christianson and John Roskelley, about 1968; details are not known.

SOUTH ARETE: This well defined, sharp and blocky arete rises some 600 ft to the summit in a distinctive fashion from the ridge S of the Spire. This is an enjoyable and moderate route for almost any climbers, and a good introduction to the area. First ascent by Fred Beckey and Helmy Beckey on June 19, 1942.

Approach as for Southwest Couloir, then continue to where scrub conifers meet the arete. The first pitch climbs a 15-ft crack behind (left) a flake, then stretch across a slab (5.5) left to a small tree. Scramble broken rock 60 ft to a belay below the whitish S corner that splits the arete. Ascend an easy gully, then a chimney with a chockstone for 100 ft (5.4). Exit left and ascend a long sandy bench, climbing out on the broader section of the true arete. Slabs and a narrow crest lead to the eastern summit outcrop. Class 4 with some easy class 5. Time: 2 hours. Reference: *Mountaineer*, 1943, p. 13.

SOUTHEAST FACE — INFERNO ROUTE: This route uses a chimney crack system near the N edge of the steep Southeast Face; this is reputed loose except for the last hard lead, a challenging crack problem. At some point above here the route crosses the 1965 line of ascent. The route name is derived from the hot spell during the ascent. First ascent by Steve Marts and Don McPherson in August 1966.

Make the basic approach as per East Buttress Direct but continue up to the tiny rock bowl left of the buttress. Begin the roof climb up and right, then traverse back into the chimney in about 50 ft (5.6). The rock in the chimney becomes more reliable on the pitch to a belay to below small trees (120 ft—5.8). The next lead reaches a ledge at the base of a jam crack (130 ft—5.6). A difficult 60-ft lead climbs a crack which turns into a squeeze chimney. Three consecutive rurps were placed to bypass a 6-10-inch vertical crack: then

NORTH EARLY WINTER SPIRE
7760 ft+/2366 m+

Nearly identical in appearance to the larger South Spire, its greatest face is on the E, above Early Winters Creek; from the W its outline appears remarkably symmetrical. At one time this spire was referred to as the Middle Peak of Liberty Bell. The Lower Southwest Face Variation has become the most popular start for the climb. The first ascent was made by Wesley Grande, Pete Schoening, and Dick Widrig on May 28, 1950. References: *Mountaineer*, 1950, p. 41; *A.A.J.*, 1951, pp. 171-72; *Mazama* 50, no. 13 (1968), p. 18.

SOUTHWEST COULOIR AND SOUTH FACE: From the W slopes ascend into the gully between the South and North Spires. The original route, helped by high snow level and a shoulder stand, climbed the lip of the overhanging chockstone above the gully cave's right wall. A down-slanting ledge leads to another chimney (possible verglas) with very smooth walls. Climb to the snow/scree gully, then ascend it some 200 ft to the spire notch. Here a series of chimneys (class 4) on the South Face lead to the summit (two pitches). It is possible to use one of several cracks here; the best is to work left on the face, then up. About midway from the notch to the summit there is an off-width jam crack about 25 ft high (5.6). Grade II; class 5.8 (aid climbing may be normally included; the lip of the cave overhang was only 40 ft above the snow on the original). Time: 3 hours.

Descent: From the summit downclimb to the S and W until it is possible to rappel into a chimney on the S side of the summit block. A second rappel leads to the spire notch, then downclimb W. There is a bolt atop the chockstone for the final 50-ft free rappel.

Variation (Lower Southwest Face): First ascent by Richard McGowan and Tim Kelley on July 4, 1954. Begin at a crack system on the West Face, and ascend good rock. Climb steep slabs, bearing rightward, and traverse right on an obvious ledge across the lower face to join the couloir route above the chockstone. The original climb used six pitons and three bolts for safety. Reference: *Mountaineer*, 1954, p. 64.

A different beginning to this variation now seems to be the most popular route: from the left side of the cave friction left 10 ft (5.1), then climb a jam crack and face friction (5.3) to a slab left and above the chockstone. The crux crossing involves delicate friction (5.6) — probably the bolt-protected original crossing.

Variation: By Eric Sanford and David Spaulding in July 1978. This variation began at the Northwest Corner, climbing a crack from the left for two pitches. Then climb right on slabs until a prominent ledge is reached. Traverse right on the easy but exposed ledge and gain the notch between the Spires.

Variation: Two rappels from the top of the South Spire to the central notch.

WEST FACE: The main feature of this classic and pleasant

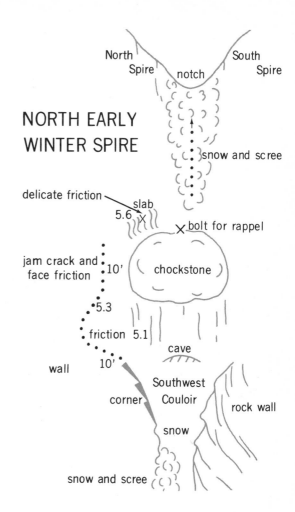

NORTH EARLY WINTER SPIRE

climb is a long right-slanting crack which is difficult to distinguish from beneath; it is the system right of the left-facing dihedral near the N corner. First ascent by Fred Beckey and Dave Beckstead on June 17, 1965.

The climb begins from a patch of matted evergreens about 100 ft above the base of the lower left corner of the West Face. Climb a short rotten wall (facing NW) to a ledge with shrubs, then climb a steep 70 ft dihedral to a large grassy platform. Continue above its left edge, climb a chimney (5.0), then climb to the top of a broken dihedral of very white rock (small ledge belay). Climb about 15 ft up a wall, then around a blind corner (flake) right on aid to the solitary mid-face crack. Climb this crack (aid and free) to a hanging belay at a small tree (140 ft). Continue up the crack until it fades; a bolt allows a rightward pendulum across the slab to a more receptive crack. Interesting face climbing leads to

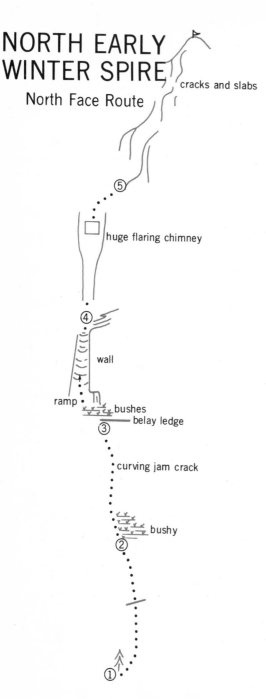

NORTH EARLY WINTER SPIRE
North Face Route

cracks and slabs

⑤

huge flaring chimney

④

wall

ramp

bushes

belay ledge

③

curving jam crack

bushy

②

①

easier summit slabs. Grade III; class 5.7 and A1 (original climb used 38 pitons and three bolts). Time: 5-6 hours. References: *Mountaineer*, 1966, p. 201; *A.A.J.*, 1966, p. 133.

Variation: By Donald N. Anderson, Donald Cramer, Bruce Schuler, and Fred Stanley in July 1965. Begin just to the right of the lowest portion of the face. One pitch (5.6) leads to the grassy platform (pitch described as a short difficult crack followed by a narrow chimney).

NORTHWEST CORNER: First ascent by Paul Boving and Steve Pollock on September 25, 1976. From the base of the Northwest Corner of the spire, lead up various cracks (per West Face route) and small dihedrals to a tree belay in a dihedral: a small tree here grows at the base of a block below the thin left-leaning white flakes. The second lead climbs a thin dihedral crack to the obvious zigzag lieback flakes; follow these to the base of a large outside corner on the far left side of the West Face. Make a belay at a small ledge at the base of the large left-facing dihedral here: one long lead completes the dihedral at a belay in a small alcove-cave (5.9). Climb left and up a difficult steep corner (overhangs the slab face) to easier ledges and a scramble to the summit (100-200 ft). Grade II; class 5.9 (all chocks).

NORTH FACE: This route is about midway between the 1958 and 1976 routes, and features an obvious large flaring chimney (recess). First ascent by Greg Markov and Doug Martin in July 1976. Begin at the W side of the North Face and first scramble to a belay at bushy scrub pines, then climb past a short bulge. Continue up easy steps, then up a left-curving crack (fist jam size) for a short distance; step out of the crack to a bushy ledge (belay). Go left to a ramp, then follow it beneath a wall to the chimney (belay near its base). Climb the latter (chockstones at top) to a belay spot higher, from where cracks and slabs lead to the summit. Grade II; class 5.7. Time: 4 hours.

NORTHEAST FACE: This is a 400-ft climb on the N edge of the upper E face; the rock is solid, but tends to be lichen-covered. First ascent by Fred Beckey and Joe Hieb on August 31, 1958.

From W slopes hike to the level ridge on the N of the spire. Round the corner E and traverse 100 ft. Now ascend up and left to a leaning pedestal (class 5). Above it there is occasional aid on thin, steep face cracks; a bolt can be used for a belay anchor at the top of the pitch. Then an easy gully ends in a chimney leading to just N of the highest portion of the summit. Grade II; class 5 and aid. References: *A.A.J.*, 1959, p. 304; *Mountaineer*, 1959, p. 108.

EAST BUTTRESS: This route is one of the longest in the area, and has numerous class 5 and mixed aid leads. One should plan on a possible bivouac at the base or top of the route. First ascent by Steve Marts, Don McPherson, and King McPherson in July 1965.

Approach from road below.

(1) Begin the climb about 200 ft above a large dead tree, via a diagonal ledge which bears right onto the ridge crest.

(2) Climb 40 ft, move right, and climb up to a stance about 25 ft below a small pine in a vertical crack (5.7).

EARLY WINTER SPIRES

South Spire North Spire

East Buttress

Northeast Face

East Buttress

Northeast Corner

gully

East Face

The Minuteman

Lexington Tower

Concord Tower

roofs

slab

M&M ledge

Liberty Crack

Barbar Pole

North Face

Independence Route

Thin Red Line

lip

Liberty Crack

LIBERTY BELL and EARLY WINTER SPIRES
STEVE MARTS

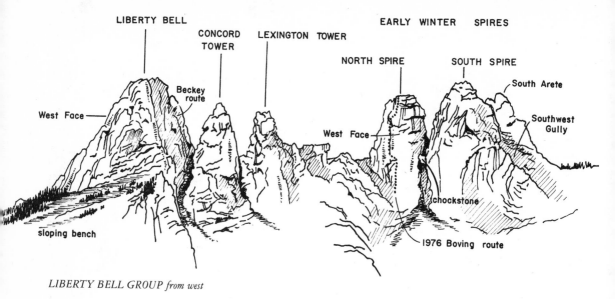

LIBERTY BELL

CONCORD
TOWER

LEXINGTON TOWER

EARLY WINTER SPIRES

NORTH SPIRE

SOUTH SPIRE

South Arete

Southwest
Gully

West Face

Beckey
route

West Face

chockstone

sloping bench

1976 Boving route

LIBERTY BELL GROUP from west

(3) Ascend the crack (A2) to a hidden overhang. Surmount the overhang on the right; this leads to easier climbing.

(4) Climb class 3 to the first of three large benches on the buttress.

(5) The original party went right off the bench (sloping ledge with 5.6 climbing). Second party went left of this ledge 4th class to a pine tree (good bivouac ledge).

(6) Climb a 4th class pitch onto the second bench.

(7) Traverse left and climb a chimney toward a small overhang (A1), which is passed on the right, to the buttress crest.

(8) Third class leads to third bench.

(9) Traverse left 40 ft. The last two pitches are a distinct joy:

(10) Climb straight up a chimney with several trees, to regain the buttress crest.

(11) A 25-ft sloping lieback on the N side of the crest leads to the summit (easy class 5). Grade IV; class 5.7 and A1. Original selection: one 2-inch, one 1½-inch, two 1-inch, three ¾-inch, four baby angles, four horizontals, two KB.

EARLY WINTERS COULOIR: First ascent by Gary Brill and Lowell Skoog on May 6, 1978. The route climbs to the notch between the South and North Spires (from E). The upper couloir is five pitches in length (40-50 degrees); the sixth pitch used stemming between rock and snow, and some aid to pass a large cornice on the left. From the notch one class 5 pitch completes the summit portion.

Variation: By same party, May 15, 1977. This route climbs just beneath the N wall of the North Spire to the ridgeline. The angle is 40-50 degrees with occasional steeper rock sections (used safety pitons).

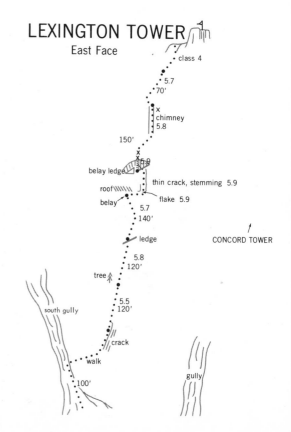

LEXINGTON TOWER
East Face

class 4

5.7
70'

x
chimney
5.8

150'

x
5.9
belay ledge

thin crack, stemming 5.9

roof

flake 5.9

belay

5.7

140'

ledge

CONCORD TOWER

5.8
120'

tree

5.5
120'

south gully

crack

walk

gully

100'

LEXINGTON TOWER
7560 ft+/2304 m+

The southern of the two similar towers closely flanking Liberty Bell on its S, Lexington is thinly shaped when viewed from the E or W, and on the E the long and steep facade reflects the character of all the faces of this area on the Early Winters flank. Broken rock reaches high on the S to beneath the summit section. First ascent by Tim Kelley and Richard McGowan on July 5, 1954 (via North Face). Reference: *Mountaineer*, 1954, p. 64.

NORTH FACE: This 200-ft route begins in the Concord-Lexington notch, where the hardest section is just 20 ft from the start (5.6). Then continue on broken rock to a sloping terrace; belay and then do one lead up to the break between the summits. The highest point is to the W (climb around its S side). Time: 2 hours.

EAST GULLY: This route leads to the Concord-Lexington Tower notch. First ascent by Sandy Bill, Cindy Wade Burgner, and Frank Tarver in June 1966. There is some snow climbing involved. The ascent includes climbing some chockstones (easy class 5), but is mostly gully climbing and not highly recommended. Time: ½ day.

EAST FACE: This route, which almost faces SE to end on the rock armchair SE of the summit, offers much sustained and exhausting free climbing. The climb was originally done with some aid, but has been pushed free; can be well protected. In early summer water in cracks and roofs can hinder climbing. First ascent by Steve Marts and Don McPherson in June 1966.

Ascend the S gully of Lexington (probably snow at base) for about 100 ft, until possible to walk right to a crack and chimney system in midface (class 4). The first lead goes to a tree (5.5); continue with some good jamming to a ledge (120 ft — 5.8). The third lead is jamming and lieback climbing to a roof (belay at right side of corner). Traverse right to below a solid flake and jam this until crack narrows (5.9). Jam and stem about 30 ft (5.9) to a belay ledge beneath another roof (roof on left). An exhausting fifth lead begins in a flaky 5-inch offsize crack which becomes solid (5.9); reach two bolts. The lead ends at a belay bolt in the chimney's right wall. A 70-ft lead (5.7) ends with a bit of friction, then fourth class climbing completes the route. Grade IV (short); class 5.9 (originally 5.9 and A3). Selection: one 3-inch, one 2½-inch, four 2-inch, four 1½-inch, three 1-inch, four ¾-inch, four baby angles, five horizontals, one KB. Time: one long day.

SOUTH FACE: This is a one-pitch climb from the notch on the S. First ascent by Donald N. Anderson and Larry Scott in 1964. Class 5 and a small amount of A1.

CONCORD TOWER 7560 ft+/2304 m+

Immediately S of Liberty Bell, and similar to Lexington Tower, this is the wedge-shaped tower with

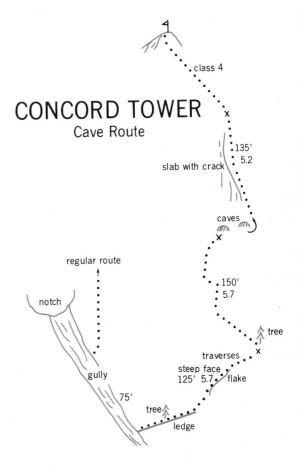

CONCORD TOWER
Cave Route

class 4

.135'
5.2

slab with crack

caves

.150'
5.7

tree

traverses
steep face
125' 5.7 flake

regular route

notch

gully

75'

tree

ledge

a long sheer E face. First ascent by Fred Beckey and John Parrott on June 12, 1956 (via North Face). References: *Mountaineer*, 1955, pp. 55-56; *A.A.J.*, 1956, p. 122.

NORTH FACE: From 20 ft below the notch adjacent to Liberty Bell climb a crack system 50 ft to a rock bench with a belay bush (low class 5); begin the second pitch at a small ledge with a small tree some 30 ft right. This pitch works directly up cracks some 60 ft before traversing up and left 30 ft on slabby rock (tricky balance on traverse — 5.6); early in summer this pitch might be wet. Here continue up leftward more easily, crossing in front of a large vertical block; one can belay 20 ft left of its top (full 150-ft lead). A friction ramp continues up and left to a ledge in the notch just E of the summit. Here climb a deceptive steep crack 12 ft to the summit (5.6). Time: 1½ hours.

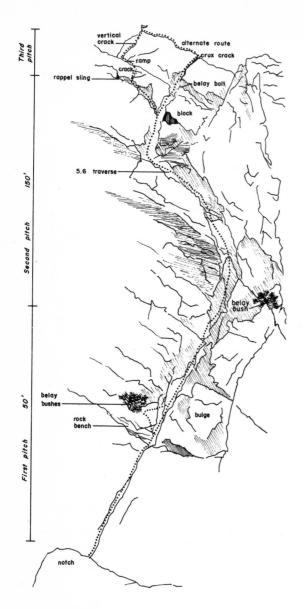

CONCORD TOWER – north face

SOUTH FACE, EAST SIDE: First ascent by Donald N. Anderson, Donald Cramer, Bruce Schuler, and Fred Stanley in 1965. This route is actually the easiest on Concord, but has not become popular. From the notch adjacent to Lexington Tower traverse 30 ft E to where a crack system leads to a position E of the summit (1½ pitches — 5.2 to 5.4). Ascend the ridge and then the summit block per North Face.

Variation: By Eric Sanford and Dick Sundstrom in June 1978. From the notch drop 50 ft E and climb onto the face (terraces and large holds; a few awkward moves). Climb directly up large cracks from the end of the ledge and belay at a small tree. Continue up and left through small bushes (good protection) to final pitch; class 5.8.

SOUTH FACE, CENTER: This route is about 100 ft W of the 1965 line. First ascent by Mark Fielding and Frank Tarver on May 29, 1966. From the notch adjacent to Lexington Tower climb up and then diagonal left toward the right edge of the summit block. The first pitch takes some aid in large cracks to a hanging belay (A3); the second pitch is mostly free, then finish as per North Face route. Class 5.7 and A3; selection should include numerous angle sizes and four 2-inch sizes. Time: 3 hours.

NORTH FACE, CAVE ROUTE: This route begins about 75 ft W and down from the Liberty Bell notch, then ends on the slabby upper W face. First ascent by Ron Burgner and Don McPherson in 1968. First ascend a narrow ledge (with tree) rightward. A hard move off the ledge leads up to a solid flake which offers some enjoyable jamming (125-ft lead — 5.7). Climb left out on a sloping ledge where another short tricky move leads to a cave (150 ft). Climb out its W entrance via knobs to the sloping W face; here is a long crack (5.2) — 135-ft pitch. Continue on the slab to the summit (class 4). Overall class 5.7 maximum.

MINUTEMAN TOWER   est. 7000 ft/2134 m

Actually a separate tower, this rock abutment forms the lower SE face of Concord Tower; its ascent is actually a partial route on this face of Concord. The route is considered a highly enjoyable one-day program.

EAST FACE: First ascent by Scott Davis and Bill Lingley on July 30, 1967. Begin at the rock apron's left base (above rockslide) and climb three leads on the left corner. Traverse below a 20-ft evergreen, then climb to the right corner of tower via a long crack. The final three leads climb the central crack of the rock shield of tower: climb cracks from right to a bush, then continue through a prominent overhang and jam a 2-inch crack to the top. The climb involves six class 5 pitches (one included the use of four placements for aid). Grade III; class 5.8 and A1. Selection: a stock of 15 pitons/chocks should include four 2-inch bong sizes. References: *A.A.J.,* 1968, p. 136; *Mountaineer,* 1968, p. 203.

Descent: Rappel N side until possible to cross gully adjacent to Liberty Bell. Downclimb to a bush which anchors a final 150-ft rappel.

Descent: Rappel 150 ft from a flake near the notch to the rock bench, then do a short rappel.

Variation: By Donald N. Anderson and Larry Scott in 1964. Via the large block (belay bolt at top). A 15-ft diagonal crack leads up and right (5.7) to just W of the summit point.

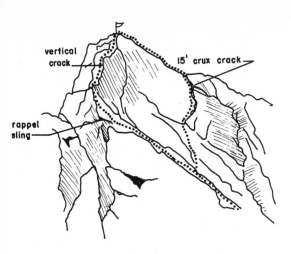

vertical crack

15' crux crack

rappel sling

CONCORD TOWER from north – summit detail

LIBERTY BELL   7720 ft/2353 m

Rising almost directly from the alpine fir and Englemann spruce forest immediately S of Washington Pass, this appropriately named domelike mass has come to embody the spirit of rock climbing in this region. Until recently Liberty Bell had not captured the imagination of anyone outside the climbing sphere, but it has become classic in our sense because of an elegance from both near and afar. The granitic formation is steep on all faces, especially on the E, where there is a sheer wall over 1000 ft in height. Differential erosion has created a pattern of chimneys, gullies, crack systems, and ribs, and a generally uneven surface is a result of variations in composition. The footings of the steep North Face begin at 6600 ft, and on the complex W facade a large bench at about 7000 ft angles from N to S; at its southern height the terrace narrows and is cleaved by a deep gully. The massif has a protruding western point, perhaps only 50 ft lower but several hundred ft distant from the true summit.

When seen from Washington Pass, the origin of the name is most apparent. The structure of the mass resembles the classic definition of a bell more than its southern counterpart, now called the Early Winter Spires. Liberty Bell is not as monolithic as Yosemite rock, yet exhibits smooth sweeping rock planes. The rock is generally sound except where differential weathering has formed along cracks.

Despite a generally formidable appearance, Liberty Bell has yielded some eleven routes, including three on the E face. Most routes are interesting, safe, yet demand technique; generally they are most enjoyable when a rope of two can lead through. A number of near-rivalries for the completion of some of the technical routes provides further evidence of Liberty Bell's stimulating influence.

Naturalist Martin Gorman, who visited the valley of Early Winters Creek in 1897, probably referred to Liberty Bell and Early Winter Spires when commenting that among the most prominent summits of the region "are a pair of remarkable, round, dome-like peaks, known as "The Towers," with a height of probably 7000 to 7500 ft."[47]

The first ascent was made by Fred Beckey, Jerry O'Neil, and Charles Welsh on September 27, 1946. First winter ascent by Fred Dunham and Gene Prater on March 29, 1972. References: *Mountaineer*, 1947, p. 49; *A.A.J.*, 1948, p. 101; *Appalachia* 29 (1953): 402-3.

SOUTHWEST FACE (BECKEY ROUTE): This, the original and still most popular route, involves about 400 ft of distinctly sporting climbing, consistently interesting, but nothing severe, on quite sound rock. The normal approach now is from the W, taking the Blue Lake Trail at about 1.5 mi. W of the Washington Pass Overlook turnoff (small pulloff); the trail parallels the road (E) for about 300 yards, N and at about 1.5 mi. crosses the second meadow (polished granite slabs on left). Here where the main trail makes a sharp right, take the uphill path through talus and light bush and open slab to the final steep principal scree gully between Liberty Bell and Concord Tower. Ascend to its head immediately S of objective summit.

(1) From 30 ft below the notch at the gully head traverse the obvious ledge (with bushes) left and around the corner to a belay bush (40 ft — class 3). Climb either the minor rib on the right or the chimney directly ahead over the chockstone system to the ledge and tree (class 4 — 5.2).

(2) From the belay ledge climb directly into a long narrow chimney with two rock obstructions either by climbing a narrow crack directly up from the tree (5.4) or by climbing a chimney (5.3) behind a flake on the right. The remainder of the 120-ft chimney is mixed class 4 and 5. Once at its top diagonal 30 ft slightly up and rightward on the slabby nose to a good belay tree and ledge.

(3) Climb straight up 40-degree slabs to where a thin vertical crack (in dihedral) divides a 20-ft-long slightly overhanging slab (5.2). Find the old piton (solid) in this crack and tie in with a long runner. From here there are two possible variations on the crux move: (a) Make a 4-ft leftward finger traverse across a vertical slab (strenuous but easy), then climb a 5-ft crack to an easy ledge; make an ascending rightward traverse along a friction ramp under a short wall,

LIBERTY BELL

North Early Winter Spire

Northwest Face

bench

North Face

Barber Pole

red gully

The Bong

East Face

LIBERTY BELL from north

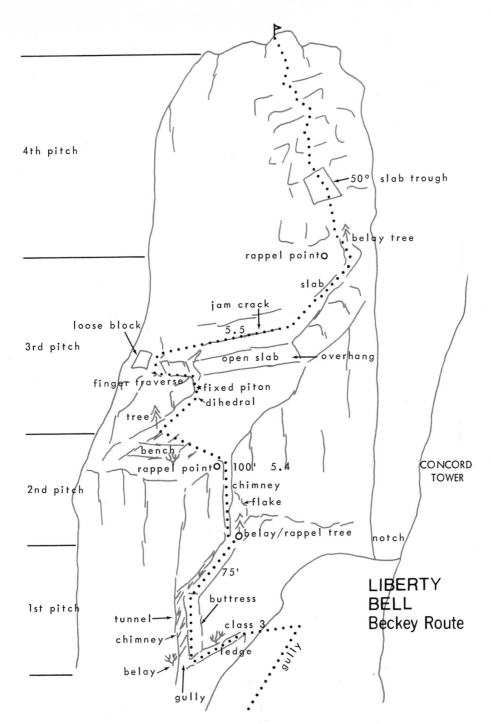

4th pitch

50° slab trough

belay tree

rappel point O

slab

jam crack

5.5

loose block

3rd pitch

open slab ← overhang

finger traverse

★ fixed piton

dihedral

tree

bench

rappel point O 100' 5.4

2nd pitch

chimney

← flake

O belay/rappel tree

notch

CONCORD
TOWER

75'

buttress

1st pitch

tunnel →

class 3

chimney →

ledge

gully

belay →

LIBERTY
BELL
Beckey Route

gully

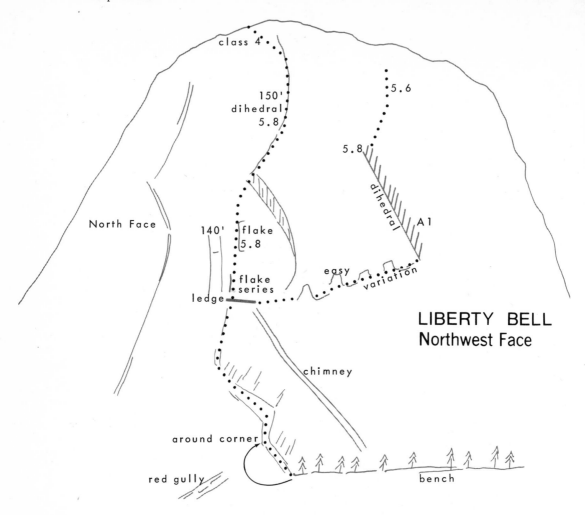

class 4

150'
dihedral
5.8

5.6

5.8

dihedral

A1

North Face

140'   flake
5.8

flake
series

ledge

easy   variation

LIBERTY BELL
Northwest Face

chimney

around corner

red gully

bench

using a combination of friction and lieback moves in a jam crack on the left, then move around the corner in an open book and steep slab 30 ft to the belay spot (a crack leads to a tree and ledge — 130-ft pitch — 5.5). (b) Climb rightward under the wall on a long upward slanting fingertip traverse, then move around to the corner and upward to a belay spot by a tree (5.6) or up on easy ledges.

(4) Scramble across narrow shelves, ledges, and blocks on the right side of the ridge crest to a 12-ft 50-degree slab; climb this (5.0 to 5.5 depending on one's height) and scramble 100 ft to the summit, keeping right. There is one 10-ft easy bouldering move above a platform. Grade I-II; class 5.5. Time: 2 hours from notch.

Descent: Head SW toward notch from summit; after doing a bit of careful downclimbing above a spacious ledge, continue easy downclimbing left of rib, away from normal

route. Descend as feasible, then rappel from a tree (end of third lead). Swing hard to W on full 150-ft rappel (two ropes), then find another pine bush on wall for a final 50-ft rappel into the gully (rope tends to jam on this rappel; advise slings on pine); by using a different anchor one rope is sufficient for two rappels.

Variation: By Mike Bialos and Frank Tarver on May 29, 1965. Below the fingertip traverse, left of the nose at the end of the second pitch, climb leftward to a jam crack, then friction a slab back to the right (two-pitch variation; 5.7 — take chocks to 2-inch).

Variation: On second pitch instead of finishing by the chimney climb left on the face, then up to the slabby nose (5.6).

SOUTHWEST GULLY: First ascent by Donald N. Anderson and Fred Dunham on June 5, 1962. Leave the principal gully S of Liberty Bell at about 400 ft below the notch. Ascend a steep gully with a massive left wall which veers up and left. This has a large cave in a short distance, then becomes chimney-like, with several chockstones. The first pitch has a bulge (protection advised); second pitch is scrambling; third pitch has some aid to pass cave (in early season a snow base provides an easier start; original ascent used aid to bypass a frozen waterfall). Reach the summit crest just W of the summit. Class 5 and A1 (original ascent used five aid pitons because of snow and ice on rock). Reference: *A.A.J.*, 1963, p. 474.

SERPENTINE CRACK: This twisting crack slices through overhangs on the West Face about 300 ft S of the original West Face route. It is an elegant route on solid rock. The start is identified as just right of the large white arch. First ascent by Fred Beckey, Doug Leen, and David Wagner on July 6, 1967.

First climb slab to chimney system leading to Serpentine Crack. Climb the chimney, sometimes working on the rib left. On the second pitch a wide overhanging crack needs protection to 4 inches. The next pitch begins from a hanging belay, and takes the long awkward left-arching crack across a blank face in an exposed maneuver; this section takes much use of small and medium angle or chock sizes, mostly aid. Near the end of the fourth pitch a hidden keyhole (to right) allows a squeeze move to pass a bulge. Work right, then do a pitch of friction and face climbing to the crest of the easier western summit spur. Scramble on to the top. Grade III on original 35 pitons used). Original selection: one 4-inch, two 3-inch, two 2½-inch, five 2-inch, four 1½-inch, one 1¼-inch, two 1-inch, two ¾-inch, two Leepers, three LA. References: *Mountaineer*, 1968, p. 202; *A.A.J.*, 1968, p. 134.

WEST FACE: First ascent by Fred Beckey and John Rupley on June 15, 1958. The route begins via slabs below and left of big white arch of the West Face. First pitch (trends left) has some spurious nailing (poor cracks); three bolts. Turn a corner on a rib and enter a long V-crack; this is mostly routine aid. Then a smooth wall is climbed (bypass a roof; knife blades used on original). A rotten gully with overhanging bushes leads to a secure stance. Climb left to top of a chimney, then left-traverse across a smooth slab to a hidden chimney. The last serious lead is a vertical rotten wall (several pitons and one bolt for aid). The route leads to W summit spur, then scramble onward. Grade III (used about 30 pitons on original). Time: 6 hours. References: *A.A.J.*, 1959, pp. 302-3; *Mountaineer*, 1959, pp. 107-8.

Variation: By Fred Beckey and Roger Johnson, June 1967. An open book to N of route beginning is done (mixed free and aid — no bolts) to join the route at beginning of V-crack.

NORTHWEST FACE: One of the earliest technical efforts in the area, a fine climb of some 700 ft. First ascent by Hans Kraus and John Rupley in August 1956; first free ascent by Sandy Bill, Ron Burgner, Ian Martin, and Frank Tarver on August 23, 1966.

The route begins near the N end of the large sloping bench that foots the Northwest and West Faces of Liberty Bell. The approach with least effort is via the S gully (per normal route), then climbing broken, steep rock to the opposite end of the bench. It is also feasible to begin at the depression at the head of snow/talus below and N of the mountain, then ascend about 400 ft of easy rock (rightward trend), climbing into the red gully; the climbing here is class 3-4, with possibly some easy class 5 (rock sometimes friable). The bench can also be reached from its NW (outside) corner (more difficult).

The route can take an obvious right-facing chimney (5.6 at its narrowest area) for one and one-half pitches or more to a large belay ledge; much of the chimney is from 2 ft to 4 ft — squeezes and stems. Face climb a series of little flakes immediately right of two obvious shallow cracks (on smooth face) — these are the thin left-leaning broken flake edges which lead to the left side of a lieback flake (about 80 ft up) which is the crux and strenuous (5.8 and hard to protect; original did 20 ft of aid). The last part of the 140-ft pitch goes right on a ledge belay recess to begin a low-angle dihedral with slabby flanks (thin crack; 5.7-5.8). This pitch is 150 ft (eight aid pitons used on original). An easy ledge bears left (class 4) and traverses to the summit area. Grade II or III; class 5.8 (can be done on chocks — take sizes to 2½ inches). Time: 4 hours.

Variation: The large belay ledge can be gained on the N side of the lower-corner buttress (two pitches). Start at N end of the bench and turn the corner, possibly dropping slightly. Climb left, and enter a broken chimney on lower portion. Climb ledgy rock with ramps and cracks; 5.6.

Variation: From the large ledge traverse right (class 4), then climb three pitches. First do 40 ft of aid (A1), then climb 40 ft up a deep, large (left-facing) chimney — 5.4. Continue the chimney 100 ft to a left exit (belay ledge), then climb a flake to an overhanging bulge (5.8 or aid); continue on a dihedral system and face climbing.

NORTH FACE: First ascent by Fred Beckey and Ed Cooper on July 4, 1959. First free ascent by Ron Burgner and Don McPherson on August 21, 1966. The face features two E-trending diagonal ramps. The route begins on the lower Northwest Face, then takes a long leftward diagonal to the upper NE corner of the North Face. The trickiest part is a friable trough above a little snag on about the fourth or fifth pitch.

From the large platform at the NW corner of the W bench, walk, then downclimb and rappel once (total about 200-ft descent) into the prominent red gully (or enter from below — see Northwest Face route). It is important to connect with the long ramp system (appears as a left-facing open book) which immediately diagonals left and upward; see cairn on ledge leading left (some parties have erred and ended on Barber Pole Route, which is on a parallel ramp lower). Traverse E on the ramp system for about nine leads (some long runouts) and then bear right to complete the ascent on broken rock area: this final section is a series of gullies and chimneys — the hardest part is a step-right from

Concord Tower

normal route

The Minuteman

shield

overhang

dihedral

Hercan Roofs

slab

crack-ramp

M&M Ledge

Barber Pole

long crack

Liberty Crack

roof

Cascade Ceiling

Thin Red Line

Independence Route

Baer Ceiling

lip

a chimney to a crack to get around a roof. Grade II; class 5.7–5.8. Original selection: one 2-inch, one 1½-inch, two 1-inch, three ¾-inch, three baby angles, four LA (can be done all chocks). Time: 5 hours from base. References: *A.A.J.*, 1960, p. 116; *Mountaineer*, 1960, p. 81.

Variation: By Ron Burgner and Don McPherson on August 23, 1966. Leave the system at end of third pitch. Ascend directly up the left-facing open book. The first pitch of 80 ft passes a small pine and ascends a groove (5.9 or 5.7 and A3). The next pitch is 135 ft (5.7), followed by another of this length (5.6) which has a large pillar with a chimney behind. Third class beyond.

BARBER POLE ROUTE: The name for this route arises from the twisting pattern from the lower North Face to the upper E face. The route was originally done by error; the party intended to climb the North Face. First ascent by Sandy Bill, Cindy Wade Burgner, and Frank Tarver on June 16, 1966. From the highway at the pass summit, hike to the base of the North Face. Starting at right-center of the lower face, climb up and slightly left, eventually reaching sandy ledges which can be walked left to the "Bong," a large rock projection with a few scrub trees (exposed class 3 to here). Climb up and left to a long slanting ramp-ledge which leads toward the NE corner of the peak. The ramp thins out just short of the corner. Here one can continue on what is remaining of ramp (hard lieback friction — maybe 5.8), or friction climb up 10 ft (mid-5) to easy ramp above (two or three leads to here).

From a bouldery-blocky ledge here continue leftward: climb a series of intermittent finger cracks (5.7) and face holds near the ledge, traversing to and over a series of small terraces and eventually crossing the Independence Route (dihedral and hidden crack) to the right side of a large sloping ledge (M & M Ledge).

Turn a quick corner (right) onto a hidden crack (a leftward sloping dihedral or lieback-ramp) and continue upward via a series of cracks (5.7) to the base of what appears at this point to be a pedestal. Here by climbing either completely on or left (face) of a chimney crack formed by the pedestal (flaring off-width — 5.8) a large chockstone is reached and surmounted by squeezing behind it. From here on finger cracks and small face holds (5.8) the top of the pedestal is finally gained (one lead from M & M — belay in recess).

The next pitch climbs directly up the blocky crack system (slightly loose) (5.7) to an area of relatively low-angle slab beneath large white roofs (Hercan Roofs), here meeting Independence again (belay at left side of slab — 150 ft — 5.7). It is best to complete per the latter, traversing right to the corner.

Note: The original party climbed through the roofs, bearing right above them (A2 — about six placements), to reach big blocks (meet Independence). Grade III; class 5.8 and A1, or 5.9. Original selection: one 2-inch, two 1½-inch, three 1-inch, three ¾-inch, four baby angles, eight LA. Time: 6 hours.

Variation: From the bouldery ledge climb a 50-ft right-facing dihedral (5.7) to a large low-angled slab. Climb left and up over several steps, eventually moving left across face

to minor ledges and top of pedestal of original route.

INDEPENDENCE ROUTE: This was the second of the multi-day routes on Liberty Bell's E face which were done in the mid-1960s. It is the right-hand of three long climbing lines, and keeps close to the right side of the face, following a fairly direct line through various ceilings; some belays are hanging or quite primitive. The first ascent, which took 3½ days, was made by Alex Bertulis and Don McPherson finishing on May 26, 1966. An earlier attempt, in 1965 by Hans Baer, Tom Quinn, and Frank Tarver went as far as the Baer Ceiling, to help establish the route. The second ascent was made by Sandy Bill and Frank Tarver in 1967.

(1) Begin climbing at the lowest area on the face, following a series of small handholds that lead to a large platform above a bush; one can also begin farther right and take a ledge leftward.

(2) Above the platform use two bolts to overcome a vertical, crackless slab and continue up and toward the right side of a prominent ceiling (5.7). Traverse left under the ceiling (A2) to a horizontal crack. Pendulum down and left to a 4-inch ledge system leading up to an open book with a vertical crack (5.8): a better alternative eliminates the pendulum by traversing above the bolts, using friction, small holds and long reaches (5.9); the pitch ends in a sling belay in open book.

(3) Aid up the open book (A2) toward a tree (runner), then continue on a crack diagonalling right, ending in a flake (A2). Above is a belay ledge with a large horn (5.6).

(4) Traverse left and step into a large chimney (5.8) and continue stemming to the "Baer Ceiling" (5.7); sling belay. Original party made hammock bivouac under ceiling.

(5) Place a horizontal piton in a vertical crack right of the ceiling. Aid out, and nail straight up, using mostly knife blades and then angle sizes ½-inch to 2-inch (A4); make belay from under the square ceiling.

(6) Aid straight over the ceiling, over a slight overhang; then rightward and up the next three ceilings ("Cascade Ceilings"). Two good 3/16-inch bolts lead up and right over a blank wall; from second bolt reach far right and place a 1½-inch size into the large flake. Aid down and under the "Pine Tree Ceiling" (sling belay here); this is a long lead (35 placements on original, A3) with rope friction problem.

(7) Aid straight up from the ceiling (A1) to where a small roof is encountered (original hammock bivouac). Continue aid up a crack just left of the roof, but keep rightward bearing (A4); the lead ends on the right side and under the "Well Hung Ceiling" where bolts are fixed for sling belay and protected bivouac.

(8) Aid rightward over the ceiling (to its right corner) and continue the open book crack. A series of three more small ceilings are encountered on this pitch before a large bouldery ledge (just above a tree) is reached (5.7, A2); Barber Pole Route joins from right.

(9) Climb a lieback crack leftward to terraces (5.6 — A2 original, but can be done 5.7).

(10) Traverse left on a diagonal catwalk (5.5) to M & M Ledge

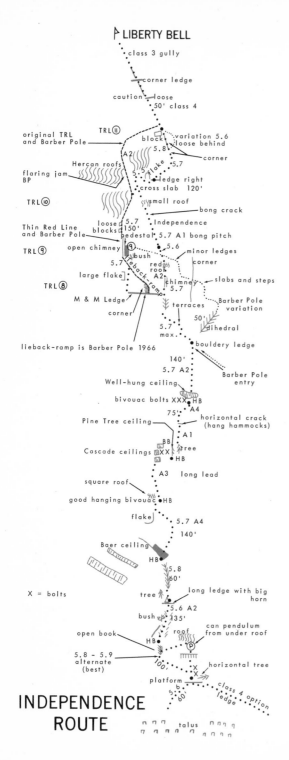

(the large sloping ledge); original party bivouac.

(11) To the right of ledge climb a crack-chimney system (5.7) to a small reddish roof; aid over its left edge, then take the right—hidden—crack until it is feasible to climb free to a belay ledge above (5.6).

(12) From a dead tree stem up a chimney (5.7), then jam the right side of a large flake (left of chimney — 5.7). Continue over the top of a red horn, where a prominent bong-size crack begins (need numerous sizes 2 to 3 inches); the crack ends in a small roof where a good sling belay is made (A1).

(13) Climb the slabs to the large Hercan Roofs on the left, then traverse right under roofs about 30 ft (5.6) and down-climb a right-facing open book to a flake belay on a 2-ft ledge leading right.

(14) Continue to a dihedral and a series of finger cracks (5.8) on the exposed but solid NE corner; one can make a short right traverse on the North Face (5.6-5.7), then climb straight up to rejoin the corner at a large ledge (this variant, taking a gully-groove, is less exposed but looser). From just left of the corner climb one short 5.0 pitch, then take ramps and slabs easily to the summit (about three class-4 leads). Grade V; class 5.8 and A4. On original 180 pitons and five bolts used. Original selection: one 4-inch, two 3½-inch, one 3-inch, two 2½-inch, three 2-inch, four 1½-inch, four 1-inch, six ¾-inch, six baby angles, three Leepers, seven LA, five KB; chocks are useful; may possibly need hammock. Reference: *A.A.J.,* 1967, pp. 291-93.

Variation: (Second ascent party) leads 11 and 12 can be avoided by using Barber Pole variation of the left to reach the slabs right of the roofs.

THIN RED LINE: This route, probably the most technically difficult in the area, required only 2½ days on the first ascent. This was accomplished by Jim Madsen and Kim Schmitz July 29, 1967 (next ascent by Al Givler and Jim Langdon on July 13, 1969).

Starting right of Liberty Crack (at est. 6800 ft) climb up a discontinuous crack, then a shallow right-facing open book; use several bathooks to bypass blanks. Reach a belay stance on a ledge near a flake below a small roof (5.7 and A3 or 5.8). Free climb left and onto a loose block (5.8) to the start of another crack. Aid this over a small (A3) roof and up until the dihedral starting a series of left-arching overhangs is reached. Climb up dihedral (first free, then aid) to two bolts (A3—sling belay). Then aid up and left 50 ft to another hanging stance (bolts). Aid and free up and right over last part of arches (bad blocks, A3 and 5.8), then up a 5.6 jam; then aid a short A2 arch right to a three-bolt belay. Pendulum right across a blank face, make a difficult 5.9 mantle and more free climbing to a bolt (which is 15 ft from belay) — 5.9. Then aid (A2) a large roof in midface. Aid the roof lip (A4) to a small tree belay. Aid and free climb a series of vertical cracks up and right to a stance on a prominent block (A3 but mostly free). Step left to ramp and continue into a dihedral (5.8). Aid this to a hanging belay below a small roof on left; a short rightward pitch (A1 around roof) leads to a mantle onto large sloping M & M Ledge.

The original party aided the crack off the left edge of the ledge, then later climbed free. It is simpler to follow the Barber Pole Route line here, which leaves the ledge near its far right side behind a non-obvious corner, climbing the lieback-ramp.

Here the original party followed the 1966 Barber Pole finish through the right side of the roofs. A more efficient completion is per the Independence Route — crossing the slab to its right corner. Grade V; class 5.9 and A4. About 250 pitons, 15 chocks, two bathooks, and four bolts were placed on original. Current selection: 12 LA, two KB, hooks, two baby angles, one std. angle, one 1-inch, 20-25 wired stoppers, 10-12 nuts to no. 9 hex, three-five nuts 2-inch to 3-inch, 50 free biners. Reference: *A.A.J.*, 1968, pp. 134-35.

Variation (first pitch): To left of original start (reported dangerous; 5.9 and A4); done by Hargis and Langdon.

Variation (Liberty Loop): By Chris Chandler, Pete Doorish, and Jim Langdon in August 1975. This large variation, beginning right of the Thin Red Line, took four days to complete six leads; 26 bolts were placed, all with hangers.

Begin at lowest slab of the face. There are several leads with A4 placements, and cliff hangers are needed. The third lead used 10 KB, two copperheads, two cliff hangers, two rurps and six bolts. The fifth lead of 60 ft took 5 hours and numerous bolts (then meets main route). Selection: 12 KB, 15 wired stoppers, six LA, six angles to 1¼-inch, 10 miscellaneous chocks to 2-inch, two cliff hangers, two rurps, two bashies, and hammocks.

LIBERTY CRACK: This route on the 1200-ft E face has now achieved the reputation of a classic climb. It follows a prominent crack system near the S fringe of the wall; at about 500 ft below the summit there is a left-bearing system of ledges and ramps which lead to a broken summit area. The system does not become continuous until three initial aid pitches past roofs are completed; then the route takes the crack system into the right-facing dihedral topped by an obvious block. Not until the eighth and ninth pitch are there comfortable ledges. It is best to do the climb in one long day, perhaps fixing two or three pitches, because the final pitches are difficult for a haul bag. First ascent by Steve Marts, Don McPherson, and Fred Stanley on July 16-19, 1965. A five-day winter ascent was made in 1977 by Jamie and Matt Christenson, Dale Farnham, and John Znamierowski. First clean ascent by Mark Gallison, Dave Seman, and Steve Swenson in July, 1974.

(1) Enter from left to a class-5 ramp, then up a solitary crack to a semi-hanging belay stance 30 ft below the "Lithuanian Lip" roof; A1 — 120 ft.

(2) Aid the single crack over the 10-ft roof (fixed), then continue past three bolts at 20 ft to a bolt belay. A2.

(3) Place a blade high and directly above the last bolt, then continue past two more bolts to a small ledge. Continue on difficult aid (A3) past one more bolt to a small overhang. Bypass this feature on left by a good crack and soon establish

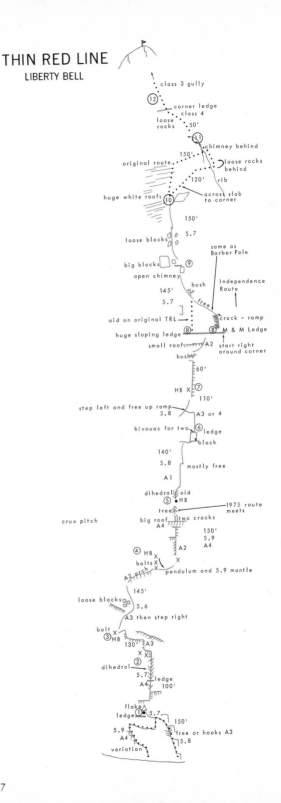

THIN RED LINE
LIBERTY BELL

class 3 gully
corner ledge
class 4
loose rocks   50'
chimney behind
150'
original route   loose rocks behind
120'   rib
huge white roofs   across slab to corner
150'
5.7
loose blocks
same as Barber Pole
big blocks
open chimney   bush   Independence Route
145'   free
5.7   crack - ramp
aid on original TRL   M & M Ledge
huge sloping ledge   start right around corner
small roof   A2
bush
60'
HB
110'
step left and free up ramp
5.8   A3 or 4
bivouac for two   ledge
block
140'
5.8   mostly free
A1
dihedral   aid
HB
tree   1975 route meets
crux pitch   big roof   two cracks
A4   150'
5.9
A2   A4
HB
bolts
A2 arch   pendulum and 5.9 mantle
145'
loose blocks
5.6
A3 then step right
bolt
HB   130'   A3
dihedral
5.7
A4   ledge
100'
flake
ledge   5.7
150'
5.9   free or hooks A3
A4   5.8
variation

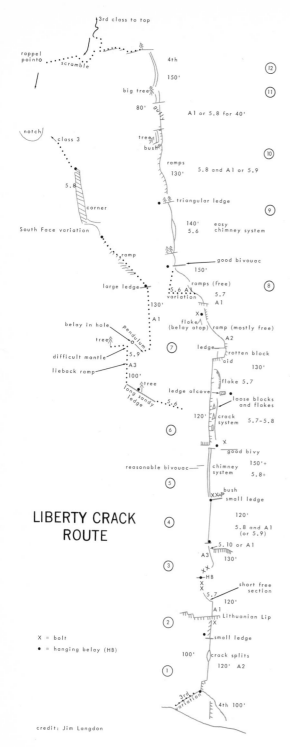

LIBERTY CRACK
ROUTE

credit: Jim Langdon

a sling belay; this is the crux pitch.

(4) Continue up the hand-size crack to a small ledge system with a bolt anchor (120 ft — 5.8 and A1); this is a hammock bivouac spot.

(5) Continue up a narrow chimney (a crack-dihedral system with some loose blocks and flakes) to a small but good ledge 75 ft higher (total pitch is 150 ft+); 5.8.

(6) Continue up same system to a small belay nook in dihedral above loose flakes, 30 ft above a small tree; 5.8.

(7) Lieback around right of a large flake, then aid (A1 or 2) the crack left of large rotten block (can be done either side) which overhangs the dihedral. The pitch continues up a loose crack to a left-sloping ramp (5.9 or A1) which is taken about 30 ft (ramp traverse ends at exposed corner); bolt belay anchor atop flake, or belay on ledge higher. Note: A bivouac ledge: from end seventh pitch rappel from bolt 100 ft to ledge on SE face.

(8) Climb free 20 ft to another left-sloping ramp, after which an airy traverse leads to the continuous tree-dotted ramp system (lead reaches large bushy pine) 5.7 and A1 or 5.8.

The remaining pitches are not noteworthy, consisting largely of class 4 except some possible aid on ramps: at first bear left easily past a white gnarled stump, then up an easy chimney system to a triple ledge (here on SE corner). On tenth pitch climb ramps 130 ft (difficult free last 10 ft; possibly aid). The eleventh pitch is hard free or possibly short aid on the first 40 ft, then an easy leftward ramp and a short dihedral are followed to a sandy ledge behind a pine. Climb 120 ft leftward along easy ramps (one 5.7 move). A final pitch bears rightward easily to the summit (150 ft — class 3). Alternatively, a long ledge (class 2) leads S directly to rappel point (to S notch). Grade V; class 5.9 — A3.

The original climb used 150 pitons and 10 bolts (2½ days); eight (?) bolts are now established. Original selection: one 3-inch, two 2½-inch, three 2-inch, two 1¼-inch, three 1½-inch, four 1-inch, five ¾-inch, eight baby angles, 12 horizontals, four Leepers, four KB. Now take two each stoppers, no. 2-8 including half sizes, two each hexes no. 7-10, two baby angles, two LA, and 20 tie off loops, runners. Estimated time now: 1½ days. References: *A.A.J.*, 1966, pp. 132-33; 1967, plate 41; *Climbing*, May-June 1977, pp. 6-8; Steve Roper and Allen Steck, *Fifty Classic Climbs in North America*, Sierra Club, 1979, pp. 133-37.

Variation: By Hans Baer, Alex Bertulis, Mark Fielding, and Jim Madsen in June 1966. On the upper third of the face, this variation continues more directly, following a line through a deep chimney and ceiling. The route and variation used 125 pitons on the original.

(9) (Variation begins) Climb directly up toward the prominent dihedral and huge ceiling ("Medusa's Roof"). Continue up a ledge system to just below a large snag and across the face, diagonalling right and up to an obvious crack. Climb the crack into the dihedral (5.5 — A1).

(10) Continue up the dihedral to a stance just below the ceiling (5.8 — A1).

(11) Climb into the ceiling and stem across to a small porthole looking out from the face. Throw an extra climbing rope through the hole for pendulum to a large ledge on the S side of the chimney (A1).

(12) From the ledge use a 2-inch angle (aid) to overcome the vertical, then step across to the right side of the chimney. Continue free to a bushy tree some 30 ft up and follow the crack system left and just above the tree. A large belay platform exists at the end of the lead (5.8 — A1).

(13) Continue up the large crack above the belay ledge and traverse some 70 ft to the N along a wide terrace (5.5 — A1); the scramble to the summit is class 3. Reference: *A.A.J.*, 1967, pp. 293-94.

Variation (South Face): By Al Givler and Mark Weigelt in 1968. This five-pitch variation starts at the beginning of the seventh pitch. First traverse left (5.6) to a long sandy ramp with a tree. Left and up is a hard lieback ramp (hard to protect, finish with difficult mantle to belay in a hole) 100 ft; 5.9 and A3. Pendulum right and nail steep A1 pitch, partly overhanging to large ledge (130-ft). Bear left on a ramp. The last pitch is a corner (?); 5.8 (?). Beyond, is class 3.

EAST FACE COULOIR: This route climbs the single couloir system S of the E face routes, emerging at the S notch of Liberty Bell. The climb is enjoyable. The first ascent was made by Cary Kopczynski, Chris Kopczynski, and John Roskelley on June 29, 1968.

Start at left side of gully at the dihedral in a chimney. Climb chimney to slabs (belay at a stance). Traverse right for 25 ft (5.7) and continue straight up slabs to snow in gully (ice in August). Total above chimney about 150-175 ft. Continue up snow and ice of the gully for several hundred ft, climbing over one small chockstone and reaching large chockstone that blocks the gully. Climb rock face (vertical) on left side (40-ft lead; two aid pitons this lead). Then 200 ft to notch (can complete via normal route or South Face). Grade II; class 5.7 and A1 (bring crampons). Time: 4 hours.

SOUTH FACE (Overexposure): This is the shortest route on Liberty Bell, approximately the rappel route, since it climbs directly from the S notch. First ascent by Ron Burgner and Don McPherson on August 25, 1966.

Climb as far up the notch as possible, then out on a ledge which immediately drops off for several hundred ft. Work out as far as feasible, then climb directly up to the tree on the rappel route (60 ft from ledge; 5.7). A lieback (5.6) leads to another tree belay in 60 ft. Climbing then becomes class 4 to the first rappel tree, where difficulties are over. Class 5.7; a small selection is sufficient, as trees can anchor runners. Time: 2 hours.

WHISTLER MOUNTAIN
7790 ft/2374 m

Whistler is a small pointed outlier peak with long ribs and gullies on its S and E, located about 1 mi. E of Rainy Pass.

ROUTES: The W flank is the simplest: hike up from Rainy Pass, first in open forest, then meadows. A scree (or snow) depression leads to the summit.

The N ridge is an enjoyable short climb (from connecting notch to Cutthroat Peak); mostly class 3 with short sections of class 4. Rock is good.

The SE rib, first climbed by Alan Kearney and Barry Nelson September 1, 1977, takes a lieback and face pitch on good rock (5.7), then scrambling on unstable rock.

A winter climb via the E couloir to the N ridge, then seven pitches on the ridge, was done by Steve Costie, Richard Filley, and Dave Lord in February 1977.

PORCUPINE PEAK   7762 ft/2366 m

This is the unofficial name for the multi-spiked peak between Porcupine and Swamp creeks. The main summit has a steep, broad granitic face overlooking Swamp Creek. About ¼ mi. to its SW is a 7600-ft+ summit, whose rock scarp extends to about 5200 ft above Granite Creek. The first ascent is unknown.

ROUTES: A route was done by way of Porcupine Creek and the basin SE of the main summit to the 7480 ft+ pass between the summits by John Roper on June 19, 1976; a ridge scramble completes the ascent.

Either the SE couloir (from Porcupine Creek) or the W ridge provides a route to the flat area near the SW summit; the ridge can be taken to the main summit.

CUTTHROAT PEAK   8050 ft/2454 m

Cutthroat is the prominent rocky peak on the high point of the divide between Rainy and Washington passes, the culmination of several granitic ridges that form a "starfish" ground outline; principal ridges trend W, N, and S. Jointing plays an important role in the evolution of weathering residual shapes. This rugged peak has no really easy summit route, but a bypass has been found from the original climb. There is a lesser North Peak (7865 ft/2398 m) which the topographic map erroneously infers is the summit. At 0.3 mi. SW of the true summit there is a 7720-ft (2354 m) rock point.

It would seem only chance prevented a successful first ascent when Hermann Ulrichs approached the summit in 1934 and time problems and the appearance of inaccessibility frustrated him some 300 ft from the top; the first successful party later found his cairn.[48] First ascent by Kenneth Adam, Raffi Bedayn, and W. Kenneth Davis on July 22, 1937. First winter ascent by Paul Ekman and Joe Weis on January 1, 1977 (via South Buttress). Initially, Cutthroat was seldom ascended, but now well over 50 ascents have been recorded, and its popularity increases because of proximity with the North Cascades Hwy. References:

CUTTHROAT PEAK
WHISTLER MOUNTAIN
North Peak
Molar Tooth
Cutthroat Pass

CUTTHROAT PEAK from north
U.S. FOREST SERVICE

A.A.J., 1936, p. 472; *Sierra Club Bull.* 23, no. 2 (1938): 46-47; *Mazama* 50, no. 13 (1968): 19-20.
WEST RIDGE: This is approximately the original route, and is the one still normally climbed. However, some parties use the Southwest Gully to approach the ridge, and there are at least two important variations on the summit tower. In general, the climb is enjoyable, not severe, and on occasionally sound rock near the summit; however, there is considerable unpleasant loose rock in the gully sections.

From North Cascades Hwy♦ at 1.8 mi. W of the Washington Pass scenic turnout, cross State Creek and ascend hillslope and meadows through light brush into the basin

SW of Cutthroat's summit area. From the cirque bowl, take a dirt gully, which has considerable loose rock in it. Ascend the most westerly gully on the S flank of the West Ridge (narrow and scree or snow; rock loose on gully flanks). Scramble (class 3) to a small notch on the ridge above a step. A 50-ft class 4 pitch leads to easy scrambling along the ridge for about 400 ft; one spot is weathered and exposed. A notch and flat shelf (holds snow much of year) mark the beginning of the main summit block. Two routes can be used to complete the ascent: (1) the direct W finish (about 200 ft) used by the original party; this is solid but more difficult than (2) the NW ledge and North Ridge completion (class 4); this option is easier, but less aesthetic than the direct finish.

(1) Scramble about 20 ft, then work leftward (more difficult) to behind a block. Climb right onto the exposed SW face, taking the obvious ledge to a platform and into a narrowing 15-ft chimney (chockstone near top — 5.5). From its top climb easily rightward (around the corner) on a short slab, then scramble leftward to the summit. Grade I; class 5.5 or 5.6. Time: 4-5 hours from Washington Pass. *Descent:* Fixed rappel ring to reach shoulder atop Southwest Gully.

(2) Possibly first done by David Collins and Stuart Wilson on July 4, 1965. From the NW corner of the shelf follow the very prominent heathery 300-ft ledge across the NW face (class 3; reminiscent of the E-side ledges on Forbidden Peak). Then work back right toward the summit: one lead of 130 ft on sound rock (class 4), then 100 ft of unroped scrambling. This is also a good descent route.

Variation (Southwest Gully): This gully parallels the S side of the West Ridge, meeting it at the notch near the large shelf (where ridge joins final summit tower). The gully is in places quite deep and narrow, and tends to be eroded and downsloping. Ascend this feature about 300 ft to a narrow shoulder beneath the summit block (class 4; falling rock danger). For descent: pitons in place for rappel (test them). References: *Mountaineer*, 1973, p. 83; *A.A.J.*, 1974, p. 143.

NORTH RIDGE: This route — a pleasant rock climb on solid granite — was taken on the second ascent of Cutthroat. First ascent by Fred Beckey, Jim Crooks, and Ed Kennedy on August 19, 1940. From Crest Trail◆ N of Rainy Pass climb open forest slopes into the NW basin of the peak. Ascend the NW face for 300 ft onto the North Ridge (keep well S of the 7520-ft+ notch between the main and North Peaks). Follow the ridge to the final pitch: here bear left into a broken chimney which angles rightward (one can recognize the chimney by a series of overhanging blocks on the profile of nose to left). From a belay platform the summit is reached in about 50 ft (class 4 and 5).

Variation: By Scott Davis and Peter Davis in August 1973. From Washington Pass make a rising traverse to 7400 ft (possible snowfield) beneath the prominent notch of the North Ridge. Once on the ridge, follow superb rock to the false summit, and continue to the true summit; on this portion, the route may be somewhat E of the 1940 climb.

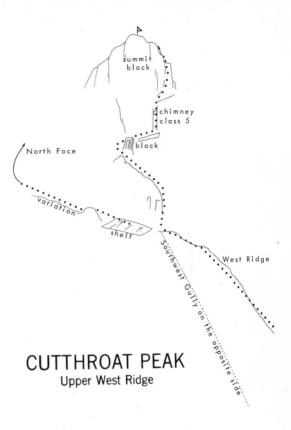

CUTTHROAT PEAK
Upper West Ridge

The route is mostly class 3 and 4, with a few class 5 moves (2 hours from notch).

EAST FACE: This six-pitch climb ascends near the center of the face, using the only apparent free route; about 100 ft to the right is a possibly much easier gully and 100 ft left is a possible aid route. First ascent by Dale Bard, Yvon Chouinard, and John Cunningham in July 1976. Make the approach from Washington Pass (2 hours). Begin at the 7200-ft base on a difficult slab, which leads to a ledge. The second pitch is in a corner (5.7 or 5.8). Third pitch is the crux (5.10). The route ends on the false summit. Grade III; class 5.10 (two pitches).

SOUTH BUTTRESS: This prominent feature of Cutthroat is a broad buttress, nearly a face, with numerous climbing possibilities on well jointed rock. Most portions of the climb have route latitude and are not very serious, but there are some distinctly interesting pitches. The route has variability, but is generally forced leftward on the buttress, finally emerging at the notch between the two "rock humps" which appear as the summit as seen from the highway when directly beneath the peak (the actual summit is not visible until this notch is gained).

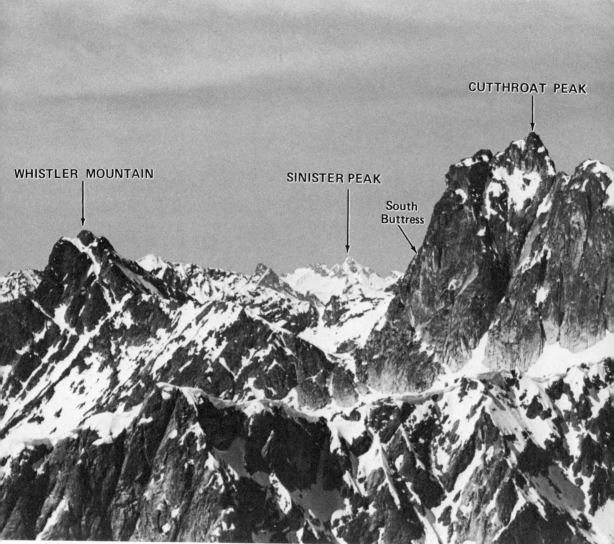

CUTTHROAT PEAK from east
ERIC SANFORD

First ascent by Fred Beckey and Donald (Claunch) Gordon on September 28, 1958 (on a marathon from end of Twisp River Road). The original party climbed five leads (class 4), then traversed about 25 ft left into a rotten awkward chimney (using bongs in latter); a sand slope was taken to a rampart, then a slab, short wall, and a vertical jam crack to a sharp, deep notch. Some parties avoid the final chimney and keep closer to the right side of the buttress. The following description is one version of the ascent.

Begin the climb where the grassy SE spur merges from a rounded alp to the lower broken-rock section of the buttress. Hike and scramble along the crags of the spur, possibly making a short rappel into a notch, or approach from the highest gully on the W, climbing to the notch. Once on the buttress follow easy scrambling for four pitches (many variations possible). Then the route steepens: a short steep face (5.5-5.6) with cracks leads to more broken but still steep climbing; here one is close to the ridge crest, but still

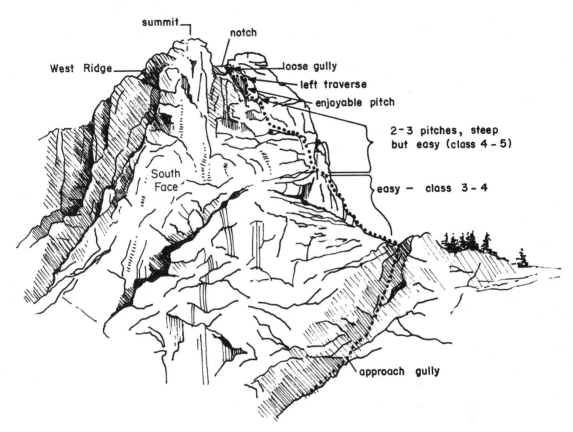

summit

notch

West Ridge

loose gully

left traverse

enjoyable pitch

2-3 pitches, steep
but easy (class 4 - 5)

South
Face

easy - class 3 - 4

approach gully

CUTTHROAT PEAK – South Buttress

slightly W. This area runs to about two pitches. The next pitch is a very enjoyable short (10-ft) right traverse. Just above, a large ledge system leads to the base of a major crack system which extends for a full 120-140 ft (5.6-5.7) — solid and airy. The next pitch traverses left almost full rope, with a short but awkward section, which puts one at the base of a gully/chimney with an ugly appearance: either the left or right side can be climbed. The right side is reported to be the more enjoyable — fairly steep and solid 5.6. This system takes one and one-half pitches and the final move back left into its very top is either a Tarzan jump for a bush or a delicate down-traverse (5.7-5.8). Hike a sand gully to the notch between the "humps," then descend to the first of three dike notches (behind). Traverse easily right around the E; here easy scrambling on this flank leads to the true summit. Grade III; class 5.7. Time: 5-6 hours from road. References: *Mountaineer,* 1959, pp. 108-9; *A.A.J.,* 1959, p. 304.

Variation: After the final notch descend 100 ft to the W. Circle back right and take the normal West Ridge completion.

SOUTH FACE OF SOUTH BUTTRESS: This narrow smooth face rises from a grassy basin W of the South Buttress. Rock is generally good and the route unfolds with the climb, but is not apparent from beneath. The upper portion of the face is divided by a loose-appearing gully. First ascent by Steve Marts, Don McPherson, and Fred Stanley on July 3, 1965. Above and left of a perennial snowfield climb from the right into an obvious chimney at left side of face. Stem this 300 ft to a huge ledge system (unroped) about one-third up face. Several leads reach a small tree below a minor roof; the last pitch is 5.6. Pass the roof to the left on aid (poor aid) to avoid an awkward mantle. A left traverse leads to a steep ledge and an obvious chimney that ends (80 ft; 5.7 and A4). From the end of the ledge climb around and up a rotten corner to reach another chimney (130 ft; 5.6). The next lead passes a tree; end at a ledge in 120 ft (5.7). A 60-ft pitch (including a 5.5 chimney) and a 140-ft pitch (5.7) lead to third class at the top of the buttress. Grade III; class 5.7 and A4 (one piton); used 19 pitons on original (no bong sizes needed). Time: 7 hours. Reference: *A.A.J.*, 1966, p. 134.

NORTH PEAK
Use the North Ridge approach, then continue to the 7520-ft+ saddle. Climb the S ridge of the peak (moderate rock, unknown rating).

MOLAR TOOTH   7547 ft/2300 m
This feature is a sharp, narrow rock fang situated on the Cutthroat-Porcupine Creek divide 0.9 mi. N of Cutthroat Peak and 1.2 mi. W of Cutthroat Lake.
NORTHEAST ARETE: A six-lead route to the N of the deep gully which cleaves the East Face. First ascent by Alex Bertulis, Charles Raymond, and Patricia Raymond on September 19, 1971. Begin via the chimney left of the detached pillar (to right of a large overhang); easy class 5 (170 ft). Ascend a class-4 lead, then traverse left one lead. From a belay ledge, ascend upward, generally following an arete on the face. Grade II; class 5.6. References: *Mountaineer*, 1971, p. 88; *A.A.J.*, 1972, p. 115.

STATE CRAG   7560 ft+/2304 m+
This formation is a gently sloping asymmetrical peak whose northern crest is a group of four towers dubbed "Index" (the highest point), "Fickle," "Ring," and "Pinky," with a generic name *Towers of the Throat Gripper*. The highest point was reached by Lage Wernstedt in 1925 or 1926.
ROUTES: The direct approach to the high point is from Washington Pass; one can downclimb along the crest of the towers. One can also approach via Cutthroat Creek Trail♦. Before reaching the lake, cross the stream and follow semi-open slopes to the NE end of the towers.
  "Fickle" was climbed by a Mazama club group via the S side in 1968. The other towers were climbed by John Bousman and Earl Hamilton on June 17, 1970 on a traverse; rock was reported as sound. The route done was considered Grade II; class 5.6. Reference: *Mountaineer*, 1971, p. 88.

M AND M WALL
This is the steep wall which appears above the highway about 1 mi. NE of the highway hairpin below Washington Pass. The orange-toned wall can briefly be seen up a gully; a large cave can be noted just beneath the top. The route has about 600 ft of difficult climbing (allow full day for fast party). After midsummer the creek in the gully tends to be dry. First ascent by Mead Hargis and Jim Langdon in September 1969.
  Ascend left of gully until sidewalls become steep. Move into gully and follow easy slabs until a tree ledge is taken to the right below the main part of the wall. The route follows a complicated dihedral system on the lower slabs. Key points

higher are a mangled tree and the super cave. Grade IV; class 5.8 and A4 (about 80 pitons and one bolt used). Original selection: 3-inch to rurp sizes; chocks useful. Reference: *Mountaineer*, 1970, pp. 110-11.
  Descent: Via next gully N.

THE SNOUT (Golden Ramp Route)
This formation is a rock buttress S of Cutthroat Creek, about ½ mi. from the horse camp. First ascent of route by Jay Ossiander and Mark Weigelt in 1970.
  Hike S, keeping on W side of a gully until above a cliff band, then traverse to the climb's base. Begin in a dihedral with a small roof; after one pitch, ascend left and walk to a pine. Continue up a dihedral to a roof, then use a ramp to a ledge. Make a hard (5.9) traverse right off the ledge and then go up to a short dihedral. The next pitch is a short 2-inch crack, then right on a ledge. The next pitch has some hard face climbing (5.9) and ends in a chimney. Ascend a dihedral (2-inch jam which is 5.10 at first). The final pitch is a chimney (5.7). Grade III; class 5.9 or 5.10 and A1. A small selection of pitons was found sufficient on the original climb. Reference: *A.A.J.*, 1971, p. 349.

THE NEEDLES   8140 ft/2481 m
The Needles are a small cluster of distinctive granitic towers cresting a high-standing ridge NW of Early Winters Creek and N of Pine Creek branch (about 5 mi. N of Washington Pass and 2.5 mi. ENE of Tower Mountain). The summit tower is a 250-ft monolith at the western end of the main E-W row of summits, which is over 1 mi. long. This tower is the fifth from the E end; the third point has a slab and pinnacle for climbing; small pinnacles also trend N of the highest summit. Ages of frost weathering along bedrock joint planes created the shapes of The Needles after erosion of overlying material had been completed. First ascent by Helmy Beckey and Larry Strathdee in September 1944. Reference: *Mazama* 50, no. 13 (1968): 18.
EAST FACE: From North Cascades Hwy♦ near Pine Creek (est. 4600 ft) ascend the long valley slope to the summit cluster: the first 2000 ft are slightly brushy. Keep well below the ridge level on an open, high slope and traverse left (NW) to beneath the summit tower. From the final notch (7800 ft+) on the ridge climb the SE face. Here is some 200 ft of solid rock (class 4 with one class 5 portion); the crux is a 20-ft lieback pitch in an open book (above a ledge at 80 ft under the summit). The final 50 ft become easier. Grade I; class 5.5. Time: 6-8 hours from road.
  Descent: Two rappels to notch.

TOWER MOUNTAIN   8444 ft/2574 m
Although Tower lacks a classic form in the sense of elegance, it is one of the outstanding, distinctive peaks in the Methow Mountains. Its location is on the

Southeast Face

from Pine Creek

THE NEEDLES

main Cascade divide between Swamp, Pine, and Cataract creeks 5 mi. NE of Rainy Pass. There is an impressive, sheer face on the NE, where rock appears to be shattered, and probably unpleasant for steep climbing. Two vestigial glaciers exist under the N and E rock walls. The summit shows a triangulation mark on 1913 Forest Service maps, but it is uncertain which surveyors made the first ascent, and when it was done (a 7-ft cairn was built). The ascent may have been done by a U.S. Geological Survey party.[49]

SOUTHWEST GULLY: Approach from either the Crest Trail♦ or the W side of Tower about midway between Methow and Granite passes, or by Pine Creek♦ 4 mi. cross-country along the creek to the E side of the summit where camp can be made in heather meadows. From here cross the divide just S of the summit massif and traverse NW on steep snow or rock hillside to the SW face.

Ascend large snowfield or talus slope to the bottom of the left-bearing gully below the main SW face cliffs. Enter and ascend gully to its top at the point where the W ridge connects with the summit cliffs. Note: Entering is easy when snowfield covers first cliff, but could be more difficult later; the gully is climbed either on the bottom or on the left wall to avoid loose rock and scree. Then cross the notch and continue out onto the W face. Climb upward (right) to the summit ridge which is followed S to the summit. Class 3. Time: 2 hours from gully base. Advise taking rope for rappel, hard hat, and in early season take ice axe. Large parties not recommended because on loose rock.

Another route report is to approach from Snowy Lakes, using an easy rise to a steep scree notch W of the summit. Scrambling, then class-4 rock leads to a broad gully S of the summit. Incomplete details for remaining ascent. Note: It is an error to try the ascent from the SE, along the divide, for an effective summit route.

GOLDEN HORN   8366 ft/2550 m

Golden Horn, located E of the curve of the upper Methow River's W fork, not only has a compelling name but striking appearance. From the S and W the peak appears as a small rock horn with long scree slopes, but its N and E faces are sheer. It is in an area of lovely larch groves; Nugget and Snowy lakes are nearby. First ascent by Fred Beckey, Keith Rankin, and Charles Welsh on September 18, 1946. References: *Mountaineer*, 1946, p. 30; *A.A.J.*, 1947, p. 436.

SOUTHWEST ROUTE: From the Crest Trail♦ there is a path from campsite 1 mi. E of Methow Pass to Snowy Lakes (easy cross-country route); or from upper Methow River Trail♦ about ½ mi. N of the pass. Climb a gully and talus to within 70 ft of the summit, then ascend the final block from either the S or N (class 3). Time: 6 hours from Horseheaven Camp.

NORTH FACE: First ascent by Fred Beckey and Roe (Duke) Watson on July 27, 1958. This route climbs the deep couloir

MT. BALLARD

*South Fork
Slate Creek*

MT. BALLARD from east
U.S. FOREST SERVICE

leading just W of the summit. The nearly vertical pillar on the NE corner is just left of the route. From Golden Horn Lakes hike on to the head of the NW amphitheater of the peak. From the ridge on its N, climb gullies and loose rock walls alongside the great couloir which bisects the N face. The route is finally forced left over a great chockstone in the couloir (class 5). Above, easy scrambling leads to the summit block. Grade II. References: *A.A.J.,* 1959, pp. 304-5; *Mountaineer,* 1959, p. 108.

NORTHEAST ARETE: This steep arete distinctly separates the North Face from the E face. First ascent by Gordon Skoog and Jim Walseth on August 8, 1979. An approach was made from Snowy Lakes by descending one of the scree couloirs which exist on the Tower Mountain-Golden Horn barrier (easier in early season with snow). Using a gully/chimney system (5.5) the base of the NE arete is gained. The route follows the obvious line of the edge, either on or just right of its crest, which makes for exhilarating, rather dangerous and continuous steep rock climbing. The crux is encountered on the first pitch: mantle a detached block, then climb a dihedral (5.8). Grade III; class 5.8. Reference: *A.A.J.,* 1980. Time: 6 hours on rock.

Note: Recent appraisal has given most of the route a shaky rating, despite the classic appearance. There are numerous fragile flakes of dubious stability; protection is sometimes insecure on leadouts.

HOLLIWAY MOUNTAIN
8000 ft+/2438 m+

Somewhat overshadowed by neighbors, this peak is about 1 mi. N of Golden Horn. Its N face is steep, with a succession of ribs and couloirs, but on the E and W sectors the peak is gentle.

Ascent history is unknown. Reach Holliway via Golden Horn Lakes, SW of the summit (use Crest Trail♦ or Methow River Trail♦).

MT. HARDY   8080 ft+/2463 m+

Hardy is a significant pointed-shaped peak with a steep NE face, which rises from the valley of the Methow River's W fork. The granitic summit is located on the Granite Creek-upper Methow divide, but is incorrectly located on the Mt. Arriva topographic map (name lettered at a 7197-ft point 0.7 mi NW of Hardy). First ascent by Sidney Schmerling and Hermann F. Ulrichs in August, 1933. Reference: *A.A.J.*, 1936, p. 473.

ROUTES: Use Crest Trail♦ or Methow River Trail♦ to reach Methow Pass. Make a traverse 1½ mi. W along the divide, then climb the moderate SW slope to the summit.

Variation: One could reach the rocky NW flank by climbing out of the valley opposite Golden Horn, to reach the divide just N of the summit; there is a sub-peak on the ridge NW of the summit, but an apparent rocky route along the ridge should be feasible. Another approach would be to ascend the featureless W slope from the North Cascades Hwy♦ at Granite Creek.

METHOW PINNACLES
7564 ft/2306 m

This is the provisional name for the long sprawling massif culminating in three pyramidal summits between Mt. Hardy and Mebee Pass near the headwaters of the Methow River. The N peak (main summit) is broad and craggy, and together with the pointed middle summit (7520 ft+) forms a steep and broad 1400-ft-high gullied (E-facing) "Chinese rock wall." The surface of this wall, which at the 7000-ft level spans nearly 1½ mi., has been modified by parallel gully erosion at fracture zones subsequent to glaciation; the deepest incision is the couloir between the N and middle summits, which contains some snow and ice. The more detached, pointed S peak marks the end of the Pinnacles formation. Massive Golden Horn granodiorite, the youngest granitic rock in the area, intruded Cretaceous sediments here as liquid magma, then crystallized (Misch, 1952, p. 21).

First ascent by Sidney Schmerling and Hermann F. Ulrichs in August 1933; the N and middle peaks were climbed during a N-S traverse.

ROUTE: From Mebee Pass Trail (see Methow River Trail♦) near the pass the distance to the N summit is ½ mi. The original route took the N slope from the trail, with some serious scrambling at times (see ridge traverse described below).

NORTHEAST FACE: First ascent by Peter Misch and Dee Molenaar on August 8, 1950. The route ascends a gully system on the long rock wall to reach the summit ridge at about 200 yards N of the main summit (est. 7400 ft). The route began by a wide snow gully. The large chockstone is passed on the left by a delicate slab traverse (class 5) to reach a face on the right (to avoid an overhang higher). Climb slabs, ribs, and shallow couloirs right of the main gully, which is later re-entered; crampons were used to the main notch. The route briefly followed the S side of the ridge around a buttress, then over slabs back to the ridge, which was taken to the main summit. The route makes an exposed descent to a notch, then climbs two chimneys and easy rock to the middle summit. The return was made by traversing scree slopes on the W slope to the N end of the massif, crossing a notch, then taking a ravine down to Mebee Pass. Grade II. Time: all day.

AZURITE PEAK   8400 ft+/2560 m+

This major regional summit is located just NE of Azurite Pass. Maps indicate the same altitude for the two small summit points (N and S), but the latter is slightly higher. The intrusive contact of the underlying Golden Horn granodiorite is well exposed on the S and SW flanks where the sediments of Cretaceous strata have been thermally metamorphosed. Azurite is steep on the E, where there is some glacier ice (7600 to 6300 ft); here an alpine spur from the summit extends nearly due E. First ascent by Sydney Schmerling and Hermann F. Ulrichs in August 1933, possibly from the N. A photo taken by Lage Wernstedt in 1925 indicates his altitude high on the peak, but there is no proof that he reached the summit; the 1933 party found no cairn.

ROUTES: From Azurite Pass (see Methow River Trail♦) climb talus NE to the upper rocks (moderate scrambling here). Expect some scrambling and exposed but not technical rock climbing. Time: 4 hours from pass.

The N ridge, leading toward Mt. Ballard, appears a reasonable route from the Glacier Pass approach.

MT. BALLARD   8280 ft+/2524 m+

This massive peak on the long ridge between Mill and South Fork of Slate Creek has two summits: maps give an elevation of 8301 ft (2530 m) for the N summit; the southern summit is just slightly higher, but not over 8320 ft (2537 m). Ballard has rugged N and NW slopes; there is a steep wall on the upper E face N of the summit. The entire eastern facade is rocky, beset with couloirs and slanting ledges; snow remains in and on these for much of the summer, especially on the N peak. The mountain was named for H.I. Ballard of Barron, early packer and hotel operator.

ROUTES: Via the long mountain slope above the Azurite Mine (see Mill Creek Trail♦). There is some 4000 ft of ascent, but the slope is moderate. Ascend a small stream on the SE slope, then scree or snow leads to a position on the S ridge, or the saddle S of the summit. This route is probably the easiest.

Via the N ridge, summit rocks involve a short scramble (unknown difficulty). Keep to W of N crest to avoid rock climbing.

McKAY RIDGE   7000 ft+/2134 m+

A secondary, yet prominent ridge, with the highest point some 4 mi. W of Mt. Ballard. The N flank has a steep 3000-ft relief. East Creek Trail♦ crosses the SE end of the ridge.

MAJESTIC MOUNTAIN
7510 ft/2289 m

This is a long ridge bordering the W valley wall of Mill Creek; the highest point is at the N end. Point 7450 is the central one and Point 7400 is near the S end; the entire span is about 3 mi. One could traverse the ridge or approach from Mill Creek Trail♦. No technical difficulties.

The claims of the Azurite and Gold Hill mines are on Majestic's slopes. The claims of Gold Hill mines, made by H.I. Ballard and others in 1930, are on the SW slope, and can be reached in 4 mi. by trail via East Creek.

NOTES — SECTION III

[1] A striking landform of the region is the dry valley that leads across a spur between Methow tributaries or along the side of a trunk valley (largest of these anomalies is Alta Coulee). Major coulee networks descend along both the E and W sides of Methow Valley.

[2] An 11-year study of Methow River hydrology (drainage area 1772 mi^2) showed one of these months as highest runoff. Discharge records for the Stehekin River (344 mi^2) show June generally highest, with May following.

[3] Richard B. Waitt, Jr., "Geomorphology and Glacial Geology of the Methow Drainage Basin, Eastern North Cascade Range, Washington," Ph. D. Dissert., University of Washington, 1972, p. 1.

[4] *Ibid.*, p. 22. The upper Twisp and Eightmile valleys probably originated as subsequent streams along erosionally weak faults — a headward development by the successive capture of small tributaries. The NW trend of the Methow is distinctly anomalous to the N-S trend of the Cascade Range, and the river predates the Plio-Pleistocene uplift. The Columbia Basalt (Late Miocene) spread over older volcanic rocks and drowned the lower end of the Methow. As the Columbia incised this basalt, the Methow concurrently incised the graded Okanogan surface (p. 24).

[5] The large variation in annual precipitation is shown by measurements taken along Lake Chelan, where the range is from 277 mm. at Chelan to 864 mm. at Stehekin (Austin Post, et al, "Inventory of Glaciers in the North Cascades, Washington," *U.S. Geol. Survey Prof. Paper 705-A* (Washington, 1971), p. A5.

[6] Bailey Willis, who intensively explored the area in 1897, in *U.S. Geological Survey Prof. Paper No. 19* (1903) uses the legend "Methow Mountains" (pl. 8 and on pp. 66-67), but he also uses "Range" (p. 75) and map (pl. 18). In describing the mountains Willis wrote, "a portion of it, known as Sawtooth Ridge, extends with serrate and glacier-bearing peaks into the heart of the high Cascades" (p. 66). Martin Gorman used "Methow Range" (Martin W. Gorman, "Eastern Part of Washington Forest Reserve," *19th Annual Report U.S. Geological Survey, 1897-1898*, pt. 5 (Washington, 1899), p. 316. The Kroll map of 1899, which shows mining claims, terms the terrain SE of Twisp Pass "Summit of Methow Range." The first map produced as a result of the wagon road survey of 1895 used the legend "Range" near Twisp Pass.

[7] Willis considered the limits of the Methow Mountains to be Lake Chelan on the SW and the Twisp-Methow drainage on the NE. "They have a very definite watershed from which all streams flow by the shortest routes to Chelan, Twisp, or Methow rivers. West of a line drawn north and south about 3 miles east of Navarre Peaks the crest is narrow and often rugged, but high spurs extend out on either side to distances of 3 or 4 miles, maintaining . . . the general altitude of the watershed" (Willis, p. 67; see note 6).

[8] The cirques are a result of ice action and intense weathering into broad, cliff-walled basins. The gradational process has eventually reduced them to basins on lower and mid altitudes. There is often a volume and depth of talus in these cirques.

[9] S of the great elbow of the Twisp valley the lower end of Twisp and Methow tributaries are V-shaped stream valleys. The heads of these streams (such as Libby and Buttermilk Creek) are cirques established by alpine glaciation (not ice sheet); Waitt, p. 47; see note 3.

[10] Folds of Cretaceous sediments have been displaced by this

intrusive body, which on its E lies against older rocks of the Methow Graben. This pluton has extensive outcrops, ranging from N of Twisp River to the edge of Azurite Peak. On the W and SW the Golden Horn granodiorite is in contact with quite different and older (Late Cretaceous) Black Peak granodiorite and quartz diorite (the contact can be seen W of Liberty Bell and Cutthroat Peak). See Peter Misch, "Geology of the Northern Cascades of Washington," *Mountaineer,* 1952, p. 17. The mechanical weathering of granite that produces the exfoliating domes, and the streams, all erode the same foundation. The pinkish color is due to domination of potassium feldspar (phenocrysts in granites are usually pink potassium feldspar).

[11] Waitt, pp. 12-13; see note 3.

[12] *Ibid.,* p. 24.

[13] Continental ice flowed SE over Delancy Ridge into Early Winters valley; only The Needles could have protruded above maximum ice-sheet surfaces (*ibid.,* p. 86). In the trunk Methow Valley, the downvalley limit of confluent tributary glaciers is Early Winters Valley. The change from glacial to non-glacial profiles in Methow Valley is at Carleton (*Ibid.,* pp. 53-54).

[14] Washington Pass is the "hanging" intersection of State Creek valley, through which ice once descended from the upper Early Winters cirque. At a later date, the lower valley glacier broke down the rock barrier between Kangaroo Ridge and Washington Pass to capture the ice of State Creek Glacier. This capture resulted from competition between former alpine glaciers which were powerful erosive agents in coarsely jointed granite (Richard B. Waitt, Jr., "Late Pleistocene Alpine Glaciers and the Cordilleran Ice Sheet at Washington Pass, North Cascade Range, Washington," *Arctic and Alpine Research* 7, no. 1 (1975), Univ. of Colorado, p. 27). This cirque capture is indicated as a Late Wisconsin event, estimated at 18,000 years B.P. (p. 30).

[15] Waitt's investigation of the glacial record preserved in the Methow River drainage has led to some re-interpretation of the history of the last glaciation in northern Washington, and the extent and nature of the massive Cordilleran Ice Sheet that entered from British Columbia some 20,000 years ago. Deglaciation of the Methow region did not produce end moraines; instead kame terraces, eskers, and associated ice marginal channels indicate deglaciation by downwasting. In the lower Methow Valley ice-dammed lakes as high as 2000 ft above modern valley floors in tributaries were a characteristic of the deglaciation, and ice-marginal channels were cut then (pp. 30, 110). The Methow region is unique in the environmental history of the Cascades, for valleys S of Chelan Trough are nearly free of stagnant ice deposits.

[16] Waitt, p. 111; see note 3. The great numbers of smaller coulees occur across almost every upland pass below 6000 ft as well as on most spurs downvalley from Winthrop. The size and density of coulees increases with increasing distance from headwaters (large volumes of ice drainage was associated with deglaciation).

[17] This can be seen from the accumulation forms of existing summer snow and from aerial photography. Accumulation is largely in cirques. If the peak or nunatak is in the form of a ridge following the wind direction, then a wind channel is formed on one or both sides, with less accumulation.

[18] The phenomena of rock glacier movement implies the presence of permafrost in the stony, silty alpine soil that makes up much of the glacier-like detritus mass. Soil frost tends to intensify when the surface is continuously in the shadow of the mountain mass several months each winter. Coarse boulders on the N slope of Mt. Silver Star are subject to mass wasting by creep of felsenmeer and also by rock glacier flow (Will F. Thompson, "Cascade Alp Slopes and Gipfelfluren as Clima-Geomorphic Phenomena," January 1963, Natick, Mass., p. 7).

[19] W.D. Lyman, "Lake Chelan, the Leman of the West," *Overland Monthly* 33 (1899): 198.

[20] *Ibid.*

[21] Shallow soils combined with cold temperatures above 7000 ft result in conditions that are inhospitable to plant life other than lichen and mosses. This lack of vegetation coupled with the rigorous climate and the extensive rock outcrops and talus discourages most large animals from occupying the higher terrain. Smaller animals such as marmots, squirrels, mice and pica, as well as hawks and some other birds, find adequate protection and food to survive the austere habitat.

[22] Edward R. LaChapelle and Terence Fox, "A Real-Time Data Network for Avalanche Forecasting in the Cascade Mountains of Washington State," Nat. Acad. of Science, *Advanced Concepts and Techniques in the Study of Snow and Ice Resources* (Washington, 1974), p. 339.

[23] Judge William C. Brown, "Old Fort Okanogan and the Okanogan Trail," *Oregon Hist. Soc. Quart.* 15 (March 1914): 11.

David Thompson built a canoe near the site of Kettle Falls and between July 3 and 15, 1811, voyaged to Fort Astoria. He noted "high woody mountains of the Oachenawawgan R" and at the mouth of the Methow River was the salmon fishery of the "Smeethowe" Indians (see also J.B. Tyrrell, ed., *David Thompson's Narrative of his Explorations in Western America 1784-1812,* Toronto, 1916, p. 480). Alexander Ross (*Oregon Settlers,* p. 50) states the Indian name for the river was "Buttle-mule-emauch"; it was also known as the "Meathow" or Salmon Fall River, and apparently Indians also referred to it as the "Mooyie." The Wilkes Expedition of 1841 gives us "Nachinchin" and also Barrier River (the latter usage is corroborated by George Gibbs and was shown on numerous maps (*Reports of explorations and surveys to ascertain the most practicable and economic route for a railroad from the Mississippi River to the Pacific Ocean, Sen. Ex. Doc. No. 78,* 33rd Cong., 2nd sess. (Washington, 1855), vol. 1, p. 412); the citation is popularly known as *Pacific Railroad Reports.* This term does not imply any natural obstruction to navigation, but in those times a fish-weir was set across the stream. Although names vary, all maps of the period correctly agree that the Methow River trends NW.

On David Thompson's adventurous trip he disembarked once or twice; in the process he chased a sheep and killed rattlesnakes. Although his map outlines Lake Chelan his narrative does not mention it (he may have received a description of the lake from Indians). See T.C. Elliott, "Journal of David Thompson," *Oregon Hist. Soc. Quart.* 15 (March 1914): 52. Thompson states, "we saw mountains before us whose tops have much snow in places" (pp. 52-53).

[24] Paramount in the Ross enigma is that he does not mention Lake Chelan, although he was told by Indians that the stream they passed drained the lake (Alexander Ross, *Adventures of the First Settlers on the Oregon or Columbia River,* Lakeside ed., Chicago, 1923, p. 151). This first recorded reference to the lake is on August 27, 1811 when David Stuart of the Pacific Fur Company (which included Ross) passed a stream Indians called Tsill-ane that they informed the traders came from a nearby lake. See also Bruce Mitchell, "By River, Trail, and Rail," *Wenatchee Daily World,* Supplement, 1968, p. 3. Since Ross mentions the lake as a consequence of his 1811 trip up the Columbia, yet makes no reference in *Fur Hunters* it is reasonable to assume he did not meet or near the lake during his Cascade Range exploration. The adventure of Ross in July and August, 1814, is described in *The Fur Hunters of the Far West, A Narrative of Adventures in the Oregon and Rocky Mountains,* which did not appear in London until 1855 with a crude map (drawn in 1821 with additions to 1825; later the manuscript map was acquired by the British Museum). Ross was one of the founders of Fort Okanogan, erected in 1811, and which belonged to the Pacific Fur Company, North West Company, and later Hudson's Bay Company. The 1821 map, a relic of great interest, is shown in Wheat, *Mapping* Vol. II (1958), p. 106, with text pp. 107-11. On this still virtually unknown map the main Columbia is shown extending N from N of the confluence of Lewis' R (Snake River) and many western branches are shown (but no sign of Lake Chelan). Well W of the Okanogan drainage is the legend "Alexander Ross on his route across land to reach the Pacific in 1815." The map clearly labels the "Sa milk a meigh" and dots his route up the E bank of the "Meat-who," then later NW and W. The vague turn-about point is shown as far W from the Okanogan River as the Snake is from the 49° parallel.

Much conjecture has been expressed regarding the Ross route. My speculation is that he followed the coulee network of ice drainage channels and glacially scoured troughs that roughly parallel the Methow River on the W (between modern Carleton and Winthrop), then up either the Twisp or Early Winters valleys to cross the main divide at Rainy Pass or a pass farther N (see Waitt, Fig. 10 and 27 regarding ice marginal channels; see note 3). Several early railroad explorers mentioned they were told Indians took horses via Twisp Creek and also used Bridge Creek and "Pierce River" (Albert B. Rogers Diary, 1887, p. 62). Although Ross began with two Indian guides on July 25, his help failed him. If he

traveled 66 mi. in three days after crossing the height of land it would seem doubtful that he was on Cascade River. The Ross account suffers the lack of identifiable detail characteristic of most explorers' journals. Some writers have broadly accepted that Ross crossed Cascade Pass, but this view should not become orthodox, for the case is far from certain.

[25] Brown, p. 12; see note 23. Indians on the E slope of the Cascades acquired horses from the Southwest in the 18th century, and this revolutionized their mobility. These Indians were members of the Salishan linguistic family. The Okanogans lived along the Okanogan and Similkameen rivers; the Methows and Chelans were a smaller group. The Thompsons (in British Columbia), whose population was estimated at 5000, came to the North Cascades in the summer season (James Tait, "The Thompson Indians of British Columbia," in *Memoirs of the Amer. Museum of Natural History* 2 (1900): 168, 268, 270, 390). In September 1853 Captain George B. McClellan learned of an Indian trail from the Methow Valley to Puget Sound (Philip Henry Overmeyer, "George B. McClellan and the Pacific Northwest," *Pac. Northwest Quart.* 32, no. 1 (1941): 41). On his most advanced probe, into the S fork of the Twisp (War Creek) on September 30, the report concluded "The trail is said to pass . . . over a very difficult country, to the stream emptying into the head of Lake Chelan" before crossing onward to the Skagit River (General report of Capt. George B. McClellan, Corps of Engineers, U.S.A., in Command of the Western Division, *Pacific Railroad Reports,* House Doc. 129, 33rd Cong. — 1st sess., serial 736, p. 149). On the Columbia, near Chelan, Quiltanese — the Spokane chief who had joined them — told McClellan that after paddling to the end of the lake the Indians used a "steep and bad foot-trail to the summit," before reaching the "Scatchet River" (McClellan Journal, Library of Congress, p. 107).

The McClellan route is clearly seen on I.I. Stevens' Preliminary Sketch Map of Northern Pacific Railroad Exploration and Survey (1855) in Wheat (Carl I. Wheat, *Mapping the Transmississippi West 1540-1861,* IV; San Francisco, 1959, p. 12). The mystique of Indian routes in this region is given additional background by ancient paintings on rocks above Lake Chelan. An early historian, Prof. William D. Lyman, who went up the lake probably in 1898, commented that "About halfway up the lake . . . the first of a remarkable series of painted rocks. These consist of rude pictures, in some sort of red pigment, on the smooth white walls which project here and there into the water. The pictures portray men, tents, goats, bears, and other animals . . . . The Indians know nothing of their origin. They seem to have been there from immemorial time."

[26] An account which appeared in 1891 related that a Mr. McKee, an old pioneer who had prospected the Chelan district for 16 years, had made the trip uplake long before any white men were in the country (*Chelan Falls Leader,* 1 October 1891, p. 5; see also 29 December 1892). Apparently the first white men to voyage the lake without native support

were Henry Dumpke and William Sanders, who had come overland from the Methow River in summer, 1886, then built a canoe at Canoe Creek.

27 Report of Lt. Thomas W. Symons, Corps of Engineers, *Report of the Chief of Engineers, U.S. Army* (1879-1880). Annual Report of Secretary of War, 1880. *Hs. Ex. Doc.,* 46th Cong., 3d sess., vol. 2, pt. 3. Merriam in spring 1880 thoroughly explored the lake to its head on a boat survey and obtained data from the Indians. [*Report of the Chief of Engineers, U.S. Army. Hs. Ex. Docs.,* 48th Cong., 1st sess. (Washington, 1883-84), p. 2312.] See also Report of Thomas W. Symons, 1st Lt.-Corps of Engineers, "Report of examination of upper Columbia River and territory in its vicinity in Sept. and Oct. 1881," *Sen. Ex. Doc. No. 186 and 188,* 47th Cong., 1st sess. (Washington, 1882), serial 1991, p. 123. The map on p. 14 shows existing trails and wagon roads.

28 1st Lt. Henry H. Pierce, "Report of an Expedition from Fort Colville to Puget Sound, Washington Territory by way of Lake Chelan and Skagit River during the months of August and September, 1882," Report of Chief of Engineers, U.S. Army, Annual Report of Secretary of War, 1883-1884 (Washington, 1883). Records of the Office of the Adjutant General. Record Group 94, National Archives. After two miners suggested the second head of the lake, Pierce seems to have been convinced Merriam's description did not fit the lakehead, and that the Sta-he-kin was 20 miles S. The expedition is well documented in the Downing book (Tacoma) and on a microfilm at the University of Washington Library. Downing was a civilian artist and topographic assistant on this and other Army expeditions.

29 *Ibid.,* p. 17.

30 Samuel Rodman, Jr., "Explorations in the Upper Columbia Country," *Overland Monthly,* 2d series, vol. 7, London, 1886, pp. 255-66. Rodman refers to the lofty peak "Loochoo-pan" of the Indians (Broken-stone Mountain) above Methow Valley, which he believed was volcanic rock (p. 260). He found no signs of previous visitation in the canyon near the source of a Methow tributary (Ne-quam-tum) and did not find a good pass (p. 262). Rodman then went up the Twisp valley to a pass ("region of eternal snow" — p. 263). He came upon two miners who had taken 2½ months to hike 70 miles along the divide to the head of Lake Chelan. Rodman could see the lake (perhaps near War Creek Pass) "Nestled away down below me, its waters were a perfect emerald green, and as smooth as glass" (*ibid.*). Because of the question about the form of the lakehead, Rodman decided to take the trail down the Methow, and on to the foot of the lake. After undertaking a boat trip he found the pole the Indians had placed, to settle the question (p. 265). He mentioned that Indians at the foot of the lake traded with those W of the Cascades, and that they journeyed via the lake.

31 The description of a "high conical peak" (Silver Peak) W of their camp may have been Crescent Mountain; they reached to about 5600 ft according to Griffin (Walter R. Griffin, "George W. Goethals, Explorer of the Pacific Northwest, 1882-84," *Pacific Northwest Quart.* 62, no. 4, 1971, p. 138). The "zigzag peaks" whose "outline resembled sawteeth" could reasonably be the Twisp Pass and upper South Fork locale. Erroneously the party thought that the W-flowing stream at the pass was a Skagit branch. They believed that the route had potential for a wagon road, but dense smoke obscured the view W. Backus and Arthur J. Chapman went farthest up the "Papoose Methow" (either Early Winters Creek or the Methow's W fork) but estimated they were still a day's hike from the divide.

32 Miners came early to the Methow Mountains (by 1875 according to what Lt. Henry H. Pierce learned). The lettering "Gold Mines" appeared NE of Lake Chelan on the 1865 Surveyor General Map of Washington Territory.

33 I.C. Russell, "A Preliminary Paper on the Geology of the Cascade Mountains in Northern Washington," *20th Annual Report U.S. Geological Survey, 1898-99,* pt. 2 (Washington, 1900), map opp. p. 192.

34 Copper bolts were set in rock for station marks along the lake at such places as Safety Harbor, near Graham Harbor, near Prince Creek, Canoe Creek, and near Twin Harbors. At Twisp Pass an iron post was placed, marked "6066." The Methow quadrangle was triangulated in 1897 and 1899 (Bailey Willis conducted surveying and physiography, and A.H. Sylvester did triangulation); the Chelan quadrangle in 1897 and 1902; the Stehekin quadrangle in 1901 and 1902.

35 Gorman (see note 6) noted that the Methow trail to Slate Creek was burnt over by trail builders in 1895. His forest study showed an alarming rejuvenation problem because of the mountainous, dry climate, and he noted the importance of the forest for water conservation.

36 Bailey Willis, "Physiography and Deformation of the Wenatchee-Chelan District, Cascade Range," *U.S. Geological Survey Prof. Paper No. 19* (Washington, 1903), p. 67. Willis believed that the peaks and spurs are clearly derivates from a plateau.

37 *21st Annual Report U.S. Geological Survey, 1899-1900,* pt. 1 (Washington, 1900), p. 359.

38 *Ibid.,* p. 360. A station mark with an aluminum bolt was set in solid rock; a 5-ft cairn was constructed on the summit.

39 Pierce, p. 14; see note 28.

40 21st Annual Report, p. 361; see note 37.

41 On the N flank Neoglacial moraines were produced during advance and retreat of small cirque glaciers developed during intervals of colder climate, following the last Pleistocene deglaciation.

42 Russell, p. 192; see note 33.

43 Photography by Lage Wernstedt showing the summit rocks is unmistakable; this was first identified by Beckey among photography stored at the Winthrop Ranger Station in 1969 and field checked by William Fix May 23, 1976.

Wernstedt's pictures clearly show Liberty Bell and Kangaroo Ridge, and looking E, a downward azimuth depicts the rock formation "Two carrots and a cat," similar to the pictures taken by Ulrichs in 1932.

[44] Because they had never seen the mountain's facade previously, and had entered the final valley in the dark, they did not know what to anticipate. There was no loose rock at the base. "We stepped from heather onto the wall. Silver Star rises with nearly perpendicular walls right out of the vegetation" (Hermann Ulrichs, interview 17 December 1972). The beginning proved slow and awkward. One problem was the time factor: they had only one afternoon to make the climb. The descent was made to the col on the W, then down the loose S couloir. See *Sierra Club. Bull.* 22, no. 1 (1937): 75-77.

[45] Active rock glaciers occur below snowline, formed under the influence of a periglacial climate in an area lacking the net snow accumulation required for a conventional glacier to form. A permafrost environment must be present (mean annual temperature less than 0° C) to enable the snow and water which trickles down to interstices between rocks to remain as ice. An abundant supply of blocky debris is necessary for formation of rock glaciers; intense frost action is ideal for frost riving of fractured bedrock cliffs. For a classic study of these slow-moving surficial deposits, see Clyde Wahrhaftig and Allan Cox, "Rock Glaciers in the Alaska Range," *Bull. Geol. Soc. Amer.* 70 (1959): 383-436.

[46] In early accounts and maps, the name given for the several summits was "The Towers." Evidence of the name "Liberty Bell" for the summit nearest the pass is given by this lettering on a photograph taken by Lage Wernstedt while surveying for the Forest Service in the mid-1920s.

[47] Gorman, p. 317; see note 6. This name is shown on a map surveying Cascade wagon roads during 1895 (Cascade Wagon Road Correspondence, Record Group No. 53, Department of Highways, PSH No. 17; Washington State Archives, Olympia, Washington).

[48] On July 17, 1934 Ulrichs made a "dizzy traverse" under the W arete, reaching the same couloir used by the 1937 party. O'Brien was on the N side and they later met. Because they were only planning a reconnaissance, they had no rope (O'Brien had ruined his boots and only had basketball shoes), so did not dare continue; lateness was another factor. Ulrichs reported finding a sheep camp beneath Cutthroat.

[49] A report of an incomplete ascent was made in 1925 by the U.S. Coast and Geodetic Survey (*Joint Report,* p. 362; see Section II, note 64): "The mountain is difficult to scale and was covered with snow in June 1925, when the station was marked. The summit could not be reached at that time." A 5-ft cairn was built on a point of ridge about 185 m SE of and 90 m below the highest point.

APPROACHES

ROADS

The forestry road situation in *British Columbia* is difficult to determine on a long-term basis, as roads may be gated during logging operations to prevent theft and minimize fire risk, or closed off after cutting is completed and simply allowed to deteriorate with washouts, slides, and windfalls (the heavy rainstorms during the winter of 1979-80 washed out road sections and weakened bridges not noted in this text; conditions are impossible to determine ATP). Conversely, when the forestry cycle turns to logging, roads with a recent record of impassability may provide good access, although there is always a possibility of fire closure in summer. Steep spurs shown on maps may be impossible to drive, even by jeep. In general, forest roads are built for pickup truck standards, not for cars. It is wise to allow time to walk the final portions of steep spurs, even if you expect them to be open. Ranger stations and timber companies can often provide current information on washouts, and can advise on gate and fire closures.

Watch for logging trucks! *Use your headlights at all times on logging roads.* Obey all warning signs and give industrial traffic the right-of-way. On active logging roads, it is best to follow a truck. When parking do not block road; leave room for others to pass. To inquire about gated roads in Liumchen Creek, Foley Creek, Nesakwatch Creek, and Centre Creek, phone Cattermole Timber Company: (604) 823-6525.

In *Washington State* the U.S. Forest Service is in the process of renumbering roads. In due time this changeover will affect the numbering system given here.

Anderson River Road (B.C.). See Fraser River Hwy♦.
Ashnola River Road (B.C.) leaves Trans-Canada Hwy 3♦ at 2 mi. (3.2 km) W of Keremeos, and extends to within about 2 mi. of the International Boundary; the road end is at 33 mi. (about 2 mi. past Wall Creek).

A bridge crosses the Ashnola River at 9.8 mi. and leads to Ewart Creek Trail♦. An exit at 14.7 mi. (22 km) leads ½ mi. to the bridge and Cathedral Lakes Resort private jeep road (and public trail). See Cathedral Provincial Park♦ (Trails).
Bacon Creek Road No. 3717 leaves North Cascades Hwy♦ 5.0 mi. NE of Marblemount and extends 6.1 mi. to an end in the low valley bottom (est. 1200 ft). At about 1.5 mi. branch no. 3708 (East Fork) steeply extends onto the S and W slopes of Oakes Peak (to est. 4000 ft).
Baker Lake Hwy (Forest Hwy No. 25) begins 17.5 mi. E of Sedro Woolley (near Birdsview, 21.0 mi. from I-5; see North Cascades Hwy♦) and reaches the Forest boundary in 12.6 mi. and Baker Lake (672 ft) in 16 mi. (boat ramp at Shannon Creek Campground). The main road passes W and N of the lake and extends into Baker River valley (800 ft; 28 mi. at end; road no. 382). A logging road may continue around the end of the lake to Scott Paper Company lands, bridging the river. Camps are at Boulder Creek (17 mi.), Park Creek, Morovits, Shannon Creek. Branches of the main road leading toward areas of alpine interest are:
Loomis-Nooksack Road No. 3725 leaves (W) at 13.2 mi. (just beyond Rocky Creek bridge) and ends in about 13 mi. (at 2900 ft) closely S of Bell Pass. Branch no. 372 at 3 mi. (right) reaches to Schriebers Meadows at 3400 ft (meets Baker Pass Trail at 5.1 mi.).
Baker Dam Road No. 3720 leaves (E) at 14.1 mi. and crosses Upper Baker Dam; reach Anderson Creek Road No. 3721 in 1.8 mi.; this is the first road left after crossing Upper Baker Dam. Proceed left on no. 3721 for 9.5 mi. to Anderson Lakes trailhead (4200 ft; the road ends about 0.5 mi. farther).
Marten Lake Road No. 385 leaves (N) at 19.5 mi. and reaches Baker Hot Springs in 4.2 mi. The road then switchbacks W to about 3500 ft on the Park-Rainbow Creek divide. Branch A (Boulder Ridge) leaves uphill at 1.7 mi. and meets the Boulder Creek trailhead in 2.5 mi. (2600 ft).
Morovits Creek Road No. 3816 leaves at 20.5 mi. (W) and reaches the hot springs in 3.7 mi. (connects with no. 385).
Shuksan Lake Road No. 394 leaves at 24.0 mi. (N), near Shannon Creek camp, and continues W and N for 9.5 mi. to Section 16. Branch D leaves at 4 mi. and is 3.0 mi. long (to Sections 22 and 14; currently washed out at 2 mi.).
East Shannon Creek Road No. 3817 leaves at 24.5 mi., just beyond Shannon Creek Campground road and extends N to an end (est. 2800 ft; 4 mi.) in the direction of Shuksan Lake. Here is access to Shuksan Lake Trail.
Upper Baker Road No. 382 leaves at 26.0 mi. (on left).
Boulder Creek Road No. 370. From Chewack River Road♦ at 7.0 mi. the road extends about 10 mi. to join Middle Salmon-Boulder Creek Road No. 364 (22 mi. NW of Conconully). From this junction the road meets Salmon Meadows Road No. 391 at 12.5 mi., then continues N to Long Swamp (Toats Coulee Road♦), then E to Loomis. The eastern connection is from Tonasket on U.S. Hwy No. 97.
Britton Creek Road. (B.C.) See Tulameen River Roads♦.
Buttermilk Creek Road No. 3301 leaves the Twisp River Road♦ at 10.8 mi. (first take road no. 3324 for 1.1 mi.). West Fork Road No. 3322 branches at 4.5 mi.; Buttermilk Butte Road No. 3235 branches at 7 mi., then extends about 2½ mi. to meet East Fork Buttermilk Creek Trail in 2½ mi.
Cathedral Provincial Park. (B.C.) See Trails.
Chewack River Road No. 392. The road extends from Winthrop (Methow Valley Hwy♦) to Thirty Mile

Campground (3100 ft) in 29 mi.

Eightmile Creek branch (no. 383) extends 16.4 mi. N of Eightmile G.S. (at 9 mi.) to Billy Goat Corral.

Chilliwack River Road. (B.C.) Most of this road is now hard-surfaced. Leave Trans-Canada Hwy♦ at Chilliwack-Sardis sign (Vedder Road), then drive S to Vedder Crossing. Turn sharply E at near side of Chilliwack River bridge (mileages begin here). At 6.8 mi. (11 km) the main road crosses a bridge to the S side of the river. Reach Chilliwack Lake (N end) at 25.5 mi; new Provincial Park — camping and boat launching site. The road continues around E side of lake to lakehead (Sapper Park; campsite); public boat launching site near Paleface Creek.

Tamihi Creek Road. Make a reverse turn (W) after first bridge crossing; in a short distance the Tamihi road veers S; one can drive about 8 mi (est. 2500 ft), within about 1 mi. of the International Boundary.

Borden Creek Road leaves main road just before its crossing of Slesse Creek (at about 13 mi.; 21 km) and ascends to logging network on flank of McGuire Mountain (roads go to 4000 ft) E but one may have to hike above 3300 ft.

Slesse Creek Road. Begin at 13.2 mi. (21.3 km) on E side of main Slesse Creek bridge. At 3.5 mi. keep left, then in about 0.8 mi. cross to the W side. At 6.2 mi. cross the last bridge to the E side (here about 1.2 mi. from the Boundary and near the end of driving).

At about 3.5 mi. a fork crosses Slesse Creek to a steep logging spur bearing SW, climbing to about 3200 ft on the flank of Canadian Border Peak (can only drive to about 1500-ft level ATP).

Just before the final bridge a cat-road continues along the W bank, then climbs SW to cross the Boundary on a ridge of The Pleiades and extends to Red Mountain Mine (4000 ft); hiking only.

Chipmunk Creek Road. Use Rico bridge (16.6 mi.; 31.2 km) across Chilliwack River and then keep left; in a short distance take the branch climbing to the head of Chipmunk Creek valley (est. 9 mi., 3800 ft). The main road generally takes the low branches.

Mt. Thurston Road is currently not passable by car. Continue W on Chilliwack Bench Road (on N side of river — per Rico bridge turn) and keep right at a major fork (est. 2 mi.). The roadway extends to the 5000-ft level SW of Mt. Thurston's summit, then crosses the Mercer-Thurston saddle (est. 7 mi.; 4900 ft+) toward Chipmunk Creek drainage.

Foley Creek Road. A good logging road leaves at 17.3 mi. (27.8 km) northward. This road reaches Foley Lake at 4 mi., then continues on the S and E side of the valley (est. 8.5 mi. to end; 3100 ft). Currently there is a gate at 5 mi.

Airplane Creek Road turns uphill from the Foley Road about 1 mi. before the lake; this road is quite steep and may be gated.

Nesakwatch Creek Road (Middle Creek) leaves at 17.2 mi. (27.7 km) just before the main road crossing of Chilliwack River. Continue along the S side of the Chilliwack valley and after crossing Nesakwatch Creek ascend the E side of its valley; there is a gate at about 4 mi. and a SW fork (toward Mt. Slesse) at 5 mi. The road continues to within 700 ft of the Boundary (est. 9 mi.; 3300 ft). There are various spurs in the valley, some not in condition for auto usage.

The Mt. Rexford Route♦ begins at 5.7 mi. on the main road.

Centre (Center) Creek Road leaves at 21.7 mi. (34.9 km); one can drive 6.5 mi. (to 4100 ft) up the valley; there is an uphill spur at 6.0 mi. (3900 ft).

Radium Creek Road leaves at 24.4 mi (39.3 km) just W of Post Creek. The road crosses a subdivision at 0.7 mi. and crosses the river to a parking area; one can jeep another 0.5 mi. Extensive logging is planned, with roads into the valley, by 1982.

Chilliwack Lake (N end). At 25.6 mi. (41 km) reach turnoff spur which leads 0.7 mi. to the lake and boat launching area.

Paleface Creek Road leaves at 30.6 mi. (49.2 km), about 5 mi. from Chilliwack Lake junction. The main fork goes 3.5 mi. to about 4200 ft (very rough); this leads to open cross-country travel (the N fork is washed out).

Depot Creek Road from near the SE end of Chilliwack Lake (32.6 mi.; 52.5 km) has permitted devastating logging impact and unsightly clearcuts up to the International Boundary and on the periphery of North Cascades National Park; it has provided foot access of questionable virtue; the road is currently gated at the Cattermole Timber buildings (be prepared to walk beyond here). The roadway extends over 2 mi. on the N side of Depot Creek. At the prominent Y the uphill fork leads to a log loading area (est. 2700 ft); parts of the road and extension spurs are in rough shape ATP.

Extension of the road along the lake beyond Depot Creek was carried out by the Canadian Army Engineers in 1970. Construction was continued to the end of the lake (est. 34 mi.), now the site of Sapper Park, a fragile, swampy estuary area. The unconsolidated, deep alluvium here will ultimately settle the issue of unwise planning. The beautiful site is better for boats and shorebirds than motorized tourism. The work began as an employment project for men experiencing problems securing gainful employment. Such alternatives as planting new trees would have been a wiser project.

Coldwater River Road. (B.C.) This is the continuation of Coquihalla River Road♦ from the summit, bearing N to Brookmere and Hwy No. 8 at Merritt, and is to be part of the new through highway. Distance Merritt to Brookmere is 27.4 mi.

A branch road at about 10 mi. N of Coquihalla Lakes extends NW to Murray Lake and Maka Creek. At about 4 mi. NW of Murray Lake a branch extends SW into upper Maka Creek (possibly rough). Various forks and trails lead N to the divide at about 5500 ft. At about 14 mi. NW of Murray Lake there is a connection to Spius Creek Road♦. Britton Creek Road♦ now connects Coquihalla Lakes directly with Tulameen. See Tulameen River Roads♦.

New logging roads are being pushed 4 mi. W into upper Coldwater River from N of the watershed summit.

Cooper Mountain – South Fork Gold Creek Road No. 3107 extends from near Chelan to Cooper Mountain (5869 ft) in 19 mi. Begin by Hwy No. 150 W of Chelan; in 2 mi. turn uphill and continue past Echo Valley ski area. On the watershed divide near Ski Peak there is a junction with Grade Creek Road♦ and an E turn to the Methow Valley Hwy♦ (reaches at 5 mi. S of Carlton).

Coquihalla River Road. (B.C.) The present roadway begins at Hope and Kawkawa Lake (see Squeah Road♦ — but continue ahead at the bridge). Follow the road to Coquihalla Lakes (41 mi./66 km); the road is not currently open in winter, and is subject to delays because of logging and construction. There is a branch E (Britton Creek Road♦) to Tulameen at about 1 mi. beyond the lakes. From this junction the main road continues 42 mi. (67.6 km) to Merritt (see Coldwater River Road♦). The gas pipeline roadway (jeep) is routed via Boston Bar Creek, the route of the new four-lane through highway (1986).

Ladner Creek Road branches W to beyond the forks of Ladner Creek. The West Ladner Road goes to Carolin Mines (est. 5.5 mi.) and exits at about 15½ mi; the East Ladner Road exits at about 18 mi. (atop a sand hill) and extends 8-9 mi. to near the head of the E fork.

Boston Bar Creek branches W at about 20 mi. and parallels the Coquihalla-Coldwater road system (all jeep road). To reach the Falls Lake area (jeep to about 4300 ft) begin on the gas pipeline roadway 2.5 km N of Coquihalla Lakes (cars have managed to within 2 mi. of Falls Lake Creek).

Peers Creek Road extends SE at 8 mi. and is open about 3 mi. One can hike the left fork to reach the valley head. See Brigade Trail♦.

Sowaqua Creek Road extends SE at 13 mi. (now impassable). It is hoped the remainder of this virgin-timber valley will be protected by inclusion in Manning Park.

Dewdney Creek Road extends SE at 15 mi. to beyond the last forks (est. 8 mi. — 3500 ft), but is currently only passable for 6 mi. There is a fork into Cedarflat Creek (at est. 5 mi., jeep only).

Dailey Prairie Road. Take Mt. Baker Hwy for 16.8 mi. (from Bellingham at I-5 to Welcome Store). Then turn right on Mosquito Lake Road. Drive S on latter about 4.6 mi. to Porter Creek bridge; at S end of bridge turn left on Forest Road No. 3807 (in 0.5 mi. an entry on right is alternative access from Hwy No. 9) and follow about 4 mi. Cross Clearwater Creek on a curved concrete bridge and in 0.3 mi. turn down (right) on the first road, which is gated during summer periods; at 0.4 mi. cross Middle Fork Nooksack River (log bridge), take the main logging road upward and then cross Galbraith Creek in 1.7 mi., then at 2.4 mi. take the right fork. Follow the road holding left past spurs for about 2 mi., then bear straight ahead. Travel on this road past one junction for 0.7 mi. to a road junction on the SE corner of Dailey Prairie. Here turn left (E) and drive about 0.4 mi. to another fork (right branch crosses Orsino Creek to spurs southward). One can currently climb E another 0.2 to 0.4 mi. to end of passable road in the basin between Twin Sisters.

An alternative ending is to take the uphill fork NE of Dailey Prairie (0.7 mi. before the SE corner), then follow it toward the West Ridge of North Twin Sister. Allow 2 hours from Bellingham.

South Approach: From I-5 at Burlington drive E beyond Sedro Woolley, then N on Hwy No. 9 to just past Acme. Turn right on Mosquito Lake Road: follow about 7.5 mi. to the Nooksack River Middle Fork bridge, and in 0.5 mi. take the first right to join road no. 3807.

Note: The route to the Twin Sisters Range is across timber company lands (Georgia-Pacific, Publishers Paper, and Scott Paper Co.). During fire season or at special times the gate on the N side of the Middle Fork is locked. This route, which is the best access for avoiding logging truck traffic, travels through forest land that is under intensive management. The gate is usually open from mid-September to late June, and may even be open during portions of the summer season, depending on management activities. For information call Georgia-Pacific Corporation (Timber Department) for road status (206/733-4410 during business hours).

Diobsud Creek Road No. 3603 is a timber access road which leaves North Cascades Hwy♦ 3 mi. NE of Marblemount. The road extends to about 3500 ft on the W valley slope of Bacon Creek (7 mi.). The Diobsud Creek Trail leaves the road at 1.5 mi.

Fraser River Hwy (Trans-Canada Hwy No. 1). (B.C.) Between Hope and Hwy No. 8 (Nicola River) there are numerous branches that lead to alpine areas. See also Trans-Canada Hwy 3♦, Squeah Road♦, Coquihalla River Road♦, and Coldwater River Road♦. Hwy no. 8 branches from the Fraser at Spences Bridge and extends through Merritt.

Siwash Creek Road. On the E side of the Alexandra Bridge at Spuzzum (40 km from Hope) follow the logging road S; keep left at 3.6 mi. and right at 7.3 mi. The S road branch extends past the forks of Siwash Creek, and will be extended to the SE.

Anderson River Road (Cattermole Road). See special map. The road may be gated during hazardous weather: for information call Cattermole Timber Company: 823-6525. Begin as per Siwash Creek Road. Keep left at 7.3 mi. and climb steep switchbacks to the divide at Buzzard Pass, then descend to the forks of Anderson River and cross the bridge just N of the Cattermole logging camp (11.7 mi.; est. 2200 ft). The left fork here (North Main) goes into the North Fork to the valley head (est. 9 mi.); reach fork North 610 at 3.7 mi. (3400 ft) from the bridge (this fork enters the valley to the S, with several forks (up to 4200-ft level) that give approaches to climbing). From the logging camp the E road is being built to the valley head (about 10 mi.) from camp to an end at 4500 ft+.

East Anderson River Road begins where the Fraser Hwy crosses Anderson River (62 km from Hope or 1.6 km S of

Boston Bar). At 9.5 mi. from Boston Bar a S fork leads to Gilt Creek and a connection to Siwash Creek Road (may not be drivable). At 11 mi. a fork extends SE along East Anderson River and continues about 11 mi. into this valley. From this same junction a road extends to Utzlius Creek, then climbs NE to cross the divide (30 mi.) to Spius Creek (currently rough).

Another fork at 5 mi. from the main highway turns N along the powerline and then in 0.5 mi. turns right; a jeep road connects with the Spius Creek roads.

Mowhokam Creek Road. This road turns from the main highway at about 10 mi. N of Boston Bar (at Fishblue Lake sign). In about 10 mi. there is a branch into the E fork which extends about 6 mi. The main fork continues across the divide (at 18 mi. — 3800 ft) to Nicoamen River Road.

Nicoamen River Road begins from the Fraser Hwy at Thompson, and extends S (W of Nicoamen River) to the area NE of Mt. Lytton (3500 ft+). The road now continues over the divide to join Mowhokam Creek Road.

Gold Creek Road No. 3201 leaves Methow Valley Hwy◆ about 5 mi. S of Carlton and extends to a connection with Libby Creek Road. Foggy Dew Road No. 3110 branches at 5.2 mi., then extends about 4 mi. up-valley. Crater Creek Road No. 3109 departs at 6.9 mi., and extends 4.8 mi. to its end.

Grade Creek Road No. 3001. From Chelan (on U.S. Hwy No. 97) take Hwy No. 150 to within 2 mi. of Manson, make a right turn, drive via Rose Lake and upper Joe Creek Road to Grade Creek Road, which reaches nearly to the Navarre Peaks (South Navarre Camp at 6500 ft is 34 mi. from Chelan), then loops back to become Cooper Mountain-South Fork Gold Creek Road◆ near Ski Peak.

Harts Pass Road No. 374 crosses 6197-ft Harts Pass (usually open July to September only). The road is narrow and steep in portions (no trailers allowed). From Mazama junction (13.5 mi. from Winthrop on Methow Valley Hwy◆ and 2 mi. E of Early Winters Visitor Center on North Cascades Hwy◆) the road leads 18.5 mi. NW to Harts Pass, generally following the route over historic Slate Pass, renamed for Col. W.T. Hart, who built a wagon road to the mines in 1900. The road descends NW from the pass to Barron and Chancellor (12 mi.). In 1935 the Forest Service rebuilt the narrow-gauge road to Barron to be suitable for auto traffic. The Windy Pass spur (via Barron) is an uphill fork 2.8 mi. beyond Harts Pass; presently gated and locked (see Windy Pass Trail◆).

There is a parking area at the pass for trail hikes. Here a steep 2-mi. spur road leads to the Crest Trail◆ N and Slate Peak observation point (see Slate Peak Trail◆). There are campgrounds at Methow River (Ballard), Harts Pass, and Chancellor.

Hunter Creek Road. (B.C.) See Trans-Canada Hwy◆. The road extends to about 4000 ft in the W fork; the final portion is reported to be rough.

Jones Lake Road (B.C.) leaves Trans-Canada Hwy◆ at Laidlaw Road exit; the frontage road meets Jones Lake Road in

0.5 mi. Climb steeply, keeping ahead at the 3 mi. fork, and reach Wahleach (Jones) Lake at 5.8 mi. (store, boats — 2105 ft). At 7.9 mi. keep uphill on the Flat Creek continuaton and at 8.9 mi. bear uphill. The road now ends at 9.7 mi. (15.6 km) at a large washout; closures may appear lower unless the road is repaired. Branch spurs extend to about 3500 ft on the N side of Mt. Barr and to 5000 ft near the ridge crest E of the lake. The system of roads bearing right at the 3 mi. fork extend W of the lake toward Mt. Cheam.

Libby Creek Road No. 3203. Leave Methow Valley Hwy◆ 1½ mi. S of Carleton; a branch at 7.6 mi. via road no. 3201 and Mission Peak Road No. 3234 leads to North Fork Libby Creek trailhead.

Liumchen Creek Road. (B.C.) Begin from Cultus Lake at Sleepy Hollow Road (2.9 mi. from Vedder Crossing); turn right (Frost Road) in 0.2 mi., then right at the next main fork (about 2 mi.), which leads toward Liumchen Creek valley. The road into the main fork (southward, to near the Boundary) is to be expanded, and will likely be gated. The SW fork of the road extends toward International Ridge; the E fork, which continues low at the 2-mi. fork, bears N of Church Mountain to connect with Tamihi Creek roads, and forks climb SE toward Liumchen Ridge.

Manning Provincial Park (B.C.) (see Trans-Canada Hwy 3◆). This picturesque wilderness park of 174,080 acres is 139 mi. (224 km) E of Vancouver in an area giving rise to the headwaters of both the Skagit and Similkameen rivers. There are a variety of attractive vantage points, gentle peaks, lakes, streams and meadows in the park (see Trails). Much of Manning Park is excellent ski touring terrain.

Park Headquarters is shortly E of Allison Pass (1079 m altitude), the watershed divide 43 mi. (69.2 km) from Hope and 42 mi. (67.6 km) from Princeton, just E of the Nature House and Manning Park Lodge. Park phone is (604) 840-8836; headquarters are open during business hours. No wilderness permits are needed in the park, but U.S. permits may be obtained at the Ranger Station.

The park's car campgrounds are: Skagit River, 16 km W of headquarters; Coldspring, 2 km W of headquarters; Hampton, 3.2 km E of headquarters; Mule Deer, 9.6 km E of headquarters; and Lightning Lake, 1.6 km S of headquarters.

For added information, write to: Provincial Parks Branch, 1019 Wharf St., Victoria, B.C. V8W 2Y9. For road reports call (604) 929-2358.

Gibson Pass Road begins from the highway at Nature House and extends to the area of the pass (10.4 km S of headquarters), where there is a downhill and cross-country ski area; there is a winter camping area at Strawberry Flats along the road (firewood provided). From the road a marked trail branches left to Lightning Lake and an 8.1 km fire spur (locked) bears right to Poland Lake.

Blackwall Peak Road bears N opposite Nature House and in 8 km reaches The Lookout. The road continues to Alpine Meadows (13.3 km) where there are scenic vistas, floral meadows, and hiking trails.

Methow Valley Hwy No. 153 begins at Pateros on U.S. Hwy No. 97. Reach Twisp in 33 mi., Winthrop 41 mi., bridge across Methow (W) in 49 mi., Mazama junction (North Cascades Hwy♦) in 54.5 mi., and Harts Pass in 73 mi. Marblemount to Winthrop via North Cascades Hwy♦ is 87 mi.

Distance from Twisp to Conconully is 24 mi. (Loup Loup Road is 10 mi., then the road bears NE to Conconully.)

Middle Fork Nooksack River Road No. 3807. Normal access is via Mosquito Lake Road, beginning 16.8 mi. E of Bellingham (see Dailey Prairie Road♦); an alternative is from Hwy No. 9 at Acme. At 12.5 mi. (about 3 mi. inside the Forest boundary) the road leaves the Middle Fork valley (shortly past Rankin Creek; 2500 ft elevation) and switchbacks very rough 1700 ft toward the SW flank of Mt. Baker. The whole system is subject to fire closures.

Middle Salmon-Boulder Creek Road No. 364 extends 22 mi. from Conconully to join Boulder Creek Road♦ at 1.5 mi. S of Roger Lake.

Mt. Baker Hwy No. 542 begins at Bellingham (I-5 exit no. 255) and reaches Hwy 9 junction (N) at 10.0 mi., Hwy 9 (S) at 14.7 mi., Sumas-Kendall Road at 23.2 mi., Glacier at 33.4 mi., Glacier R.S. at 33.8 mi., and Austin Pass in 57.3 mi. Part of the Mt. Baker Recreation Area, the scenic pond-dotted Heather Meadows (4000-4400 ft) are underlain by columnar andesite, which can be seen exposed on Table Mountain and other nearby outcrops. Mt. Baker Lodge, built on the site of the historic first lodge, completed in 1927 but razed by fire in 1931, is near the center of the area. There is also a public warming hut. The paved road climbs 1.3 mi. to Austin Pass (4742 ft), once called Wild Goose Pass, but renamed for Banning Austin, who led a road survey for the State to Beaver Creek in 1893. This portion of the road has a seasonal snow closure, and the 1.3-mi. continuation to Artist Point (est. 5050 ft) may not be open until August.

Forest camps near the highway (all mileages read E from Glacier) include: Douglas Fir (2.4 mi.), Nooksack (4.4 mi.), Bridge (5.7 mi.; on Deadhorse Road), Excelsior (7.4 mi.), and Silver Fir (13.4 mi.).

Glacier Creek Road No. 3904 begins 1 mi. E of Glacier and extends S, then W to Grouse Butte and Grouse Ridge. The road reaches Mt. Baker Trail (parking area) in 8.0 mi. (3600 ft+). The viewpoint is at 9.2 mi.

Deadhorse Road No. 3907 begins at about 100 yards on Glacier Creek Road and reaches Skyline Trail at 13 mi. (est. 4400 ft).

Canyon Creek Road No. 400 begins 2.5 mi. E of Glacier and extends 15.2 mi. to an altitude of 4110 ft. (Canyon Creek Campground is 7.2 mi. on the road.) Excelsior Pass Trail♦ (Damfino Lakes Trail♦) begins at 14.8 mi., near 4100 ft.

Canyon Ridge Road No. 408 departs at 7.2 mi. and extends 8 mi.; one can reach Canyon Ridge Trail near the 4500-ft level (logged area).

East Church Road No. 4015 begins 5.5 mi. E of Glacier and is 3.0 mi. long. Church Mountain Trail begins here at the 2600-ft level.

Wells Creek Road No. 403 leaves the highway 8 mi. E of Glacier and continues onto Cougar Divide at 12.4 mi. (est. 4600 ft).

Twin Lakes Road No. 401 leaves the highway at Shuksan 13.1 mi. E of Glacier). The steep roadway extends 7 mi. to Twin Lakes (5120 ft+), but the final miles are four-wheel. It is best to park at the stream crossing beyond the Tomyhoi Lake Trail (4.6 mi.). Campground at Twin Lakes.

Hannegan Road No. 402 (Ruth Creek Road) leaves the highway at the bridge beyond Shuksan (13.3 mi. E of Glacier). In 1.3 mi. take left fork and continue 4 mi. to road's end (3040 ft) in Ruth Creek. Hannegan Camp and shelter here. Last miles may be boggy during spring snow melt. Branch No. 404 (Nooksack North Fork) is the right fork. Follow about 2.8 mi. to end at 2550 ft (now blocked where fork goes to river).

White Salmon Road No. 3920 leaves the highway 4 mi. beyond Hannegan Road and switchbacks E and downhill to near White Salmon Creek (2930 ft; 1.9 mi.).

North Cascades Hwy No. 20 connects Methow Valley Hwy♦ and I-5 near Burlington in the Skagit Valley. This controversial cross-mountain highway crosses the range via Rainy and Washington Passes, once the sole domain of hiker and horseman. On the E slope are a rest area and information center at Early Winters and campgrounds at Early Winters, Klipchuck, and Lone Fir. A road spur extends 1 mi. W at Cutthroat Creek (11.4 mi. from information center); there is an overlook with picnic area at a short spur just E of Washington Pass. The highway is generally open between April and June for the summer season, and closed by November. Watch for parking bans.

Cedar Creek branch no. 3630 is ¾ mi. long; it leaves the highway at 2.7 mi. W of the information center.

Points of interest and junctions related to mountain approaches on the W slope are (mileages from Burlington): Baker Lake Hwy exit, 22.5 mi.; Baker Lake R.S., 24.5 mi.; Sauk Mountain Road, 36.8 mi.; Rockport (road from Darrington), 39 mi.; Marblemount, 47 mi.; Newhalem, 61 mi.; Diablo townsite exit, 66.5 mi., Diablo Lake Resort exit, 67.9 mi.; Ross Dam Trail, 74.7 mi., Happy Flat parking area, 134 mi. Highway campgrounds are at Rockport West (State Park), Bacon Creek (5 mi. NE of Marblemount), Goodell Creek (15 mi. NE of Marblemount), and Colonial Creek (23 mi. NE of Marblemount).

Pasayten River Road. (B.C.) See Trans-Canada Hwy 3♦. Drive through millyard at Pasayten Forest Products. Ask *permission* to continue. Close all gates properly. A bridge crosses Similkameen River and the road winds uphill (keep right fork 1.5 mi. from bridge). At 12 mi. (19.3 km) a washout has given problems (closed ATP) in the past. One more mi. leads to Pasayten River bridge, about 2 mi. from the Boundary.

Rainy Pass marks one of the few places in the North Cascades where one can park a car in the subalpine area and yet easily ramble in several directions across gently rugged ridges and explore delightful meadow terrain. New tourist facilities and trail parking. On the W side of the pass is a picnic area with parking; on the E side is the trailhead for the Crest Trail♦ (N).

Ross Lake, now the heart of a National Recreation Area, is heavily used for boating, fishing, and shoreline camping. The lake's waters can get very rough with little warning: Federal boating regulations apply (life jackets are required). The fishing season is mid-June to end of October; State fishing licenses are required.

There are 15 boat campsites on Ross Lake ATP (fires permitted, but all overnight camping requires backcountry permits): Roland Point (4 mi. by boat from Ross Dam), May Creek, Rainbow Point, Devils Camp (Devils Dome Landing), Ten Mile Island, Lightning Creek (12 mi. by boat), Cat Island, Boundary Bay, and Hozomeen (19 mi. by boat); the latter camp has only 72 sites, often filled on summer weekends (for information call Marblemount R.S.). See Ross Lake East Bank Trail♦ for hiker route connection.

Hozomeen, near the N end of the lake, has a boat launching ramp, dock, and gasoline; the road approach is Silver-Skagit Road♦ from British Columbia. It is possible to carry a canoe from the Happy Flat parking lot on North Cascades Hwy♦ (13.7 mi. from Newhalem) about 600 ft altitude down to the lake by trail (strenuous) for launching. Ross Lake Resort has boats and motors for rent at Ross Dam and Hozomeen. There is also a boat taxi service for hikers. Advance contact can be made by phone: 206/Newhalem 7-4735; reach the resort via the Diablo Lake boat or by trail from the highway.

To reach Diablo Lake Resort take a short road spur from the North Cascades Hwy♦ at 7 mi. from Newhalem. For taxi service on lake and boat rentals phone Newhalem 7-5578. There is a boat ramp at the Thunder Arm bridge on Diablo Lake. Seattle City Light operates a boat between Diablo and Ross Dam.

Salmon Meadows Road No. 391. From Conconully (16 mi. NW of Okanogan) the road passes Salmon Meadows (9 mi.) and Lone Frank Pass (15.3 mi.) to meet Boulder Creek Road♦. Continue northward about 18 mi. to Long Swamp (see Toats Coulee Road♦) and E to Loomis.

Sauk Mountain Road No. 3602 at entrance of Rockport State Park (7.4 mi. E of Concrete) extends 7 mi. to Sauk Mountain Trail♦.

Scott Paper (Hamilton) Road. Road approach to southern summits of Twin Sisters Range. Begin from Hamilton gate of Scott Paper Company. Continue N on road no. 200, crossing the South Fork Nooksack in 9 mi. At about 16 mi. take the diagonal rough road rightward that leads along the lower W slope of the range. At a standing tree grove below the road turn left through the logged area. A climbing traverse to the left leads to a heather outcrop (camping) below Shirley Peak.

Silver-Skagit Road (Ross Lake Road) (B.C.) provides a northern approach to Ross Lake Recreation Area in the United States and to the Skagit Range, the Hope subrange, and Hozameen Range bordering Silverhope Creek, Klesilkwa River, and Skagit River. Prior to flooding in 1950, timber logged in Skagit Valley was taken out by this road. The road leaves Trans-Canada Hwy♦ at 30.9 mi. E of Chilliwack-Sardis exit (1.8 mi. W of Hope) to reach Skagit River bridge at 29 mi., the International Boundary at 37.5 mi. (60 km) and Boundary G.S. at 38 mi. There is an upward fork to Hozomeen Forest Camp at 39.9 mi. and a fork to Ross Lake Resort (Hozomeen) at 40 mi. (boats and store). The boat launching area is at 40.7 mi. The Skagit River valley N of the lake is designated as Skagit Recreation Park Reserve, an area which is in jeopardy because of the threat of Seattle City Light's proposed flooding if High Ross Dam is constructed.

Eureka Creek Road (W) is currently in four-wheel (jeep) status, leaving at 4 mi. from the highway (6.4 km) on right, then hairpin right again in ½ mi.; keep left at about 2 mi. and continue steeply to the area of Eureka Mine (5500 ft) in about 4 mi.

Sowerby Creek Road (W) leaves SW at about 0.3 mi. beyond the Eureka turnoff; in about 1½ mi. the road crosses Sowerby Creek (bad bridge). Rough roads extend into both forks: in the main fork the road climbs W to over 4000 ft; from the S fork a jeep road climbs E to over 5000 ft on the ridge of Mt. Stoneman.

Yola Creek Road (W) leaves at 12.6 mi. (20.3 km) and extends to the valley head SE of Mt. Northgraves (est. 6 mi.; 4000 ft); there is a washout area shortly after the valley turns S at Cantelon Creek junction (may need to hike); the Cantelon branch road extends about 3 mi. to 3500 ft.

Hicks Creek Road (W) leaves at 14.6 mi. (23.5 km) and extends nearly to Greendrop Lake (4 mi.; 3500 ft); the Centennial Trail♦ continues to the lake and Chilliwack River valley.

Upper Silverhope Creek Road (W) leaves at 18 mi. (29 km) and extends about 7 mi. to 4500 ft, SW of Klesilkwa Mountain (good condition).

Upper Klesilkwa River Road (W) begins at 19 mi. (30.5 km) and extends about 3 mi. to 4500 ft NE of Klesilkwa Mountain.

Maselpanik Creek Road (W) leaves at 23 mi. (37 km) and forks in about 4 mi. with parallel roads along both sides of the creek (connecting again in 4 mi.). The E-side spurs extend to 5000 ft, about 1.2 mi. N of the Boundary (est. 10 mi. total; can drive to 4300 ft at present). The W fork extends to 5000 ft opposite the valley of Depot Creek. This road is likely to be gated until about 1983: inquire about gate key and access from Whonnock Lumber Company, 293 Fourth St., Hope (phone 869-5617). No access permitted during high fire danger.

Shawatum Creek Road (E) exits at 1.8 mi. S of the Skagit River bridge, but is only open about 1 mi. (one can hike onward to the valley head along the N side of the stream).

Spius Creek Road. (B.C.) The upper road begins on Coldwater River Road♦ 22 mi. (35.4 km) SW of Merritt (about 6 mi. N of Kingsvale) then bears SW to upper Spius Creek; one can also reach the road from Murray Lake at about 34 mi. (54.7 km) from Merritt. A rough road bears W across the divide to connect with roads leading to Boston Bar (see Fraser River Hwy♦). From near the fork of Spius and Maka Creek, rough roads lead W to high on Stoyoma Mountain's S flank. There is a logging truck warning on the Spius roads.

The lower Spius Creek Road begins from Hwy No. 8 near Canford and is reconstructed to the Prospect Creek area. An old road turns W into Prospect Creek (forks at est. 4100 ft), then S over 5000 ft in altitude. From the forks (near Pole Gulch) a side road extends S to a 4800-ft pass E of Stoyoma.

Squeah Road. (B.C.) Begin at Hope (Trans-Canada Hwy 3♦ — at 6th Ave.), make a left to the ball park and here right to crossing of Coquihalla River bridge; turn left on Union Bar Road and follow to Pretty Logging Co. road. Continue on the E side of Fraser River about 10 mi. (road becomes four-wheel after several miles). The continuing Suka Creek Road is currently nearly impassable after the Qualark Creek fork, but the latter road can be taken to about 4000 ft (old trail continues). The system may be expanded to join the West Fork Ladner Creek Road.

Stehekin River Road is an old road (1913 maps showed it extending to Bridge Creek), and one without access except by trail or boat. Bus service and taxis are available from Stehekin. Lake Chelan Boat Company operates daily boat service from Chelan and Twenty Five Mile Creek (except in winter season). Campgrounds are at Weaver Point (reach by boat), Purple Point (reach by boat), Harlequin, High Bridge (11 mi. from Stehekin), Tumwater, Dolly Varden, Shady, and Bridge Creek (16 mi. from Stehekin). Hikers arriving overland at the road should be able to meet transportation to Stehekin at least twice a day during the summer season.

Sumallo River Road. (B.C.) Leave Trans-Canada Hwy 3♦ at Sunshine Valley subdivision 13.5 mi. (21.7 km) from Hope. The road extends S for about 8 mi. into the main valley (est. 4400 ft) to beneath Silvertip Mountain; currently the road is quite rough (jeep) after 6 mi; the branch up the third W fork is currently not passable. The eastern (improved) road fork (about 4 mi.) leads to a ski development.

Thornton Creek Road No. 3745 (Sky Creek Road) leaves North Cascades Hwy♦ 11.7 mi. NE of Marblemount. Keep right at 3.5 mi. The road is closed to vehicles at 5 mi. (2700 ft). A western branch extends into Damnation Creek valley.

Toats Coulee Road No. 390. Begin at Tonasket or Oroville (U.S. Hwy No. 97), then drive to Loomis, continuing N and W to Toats Coulee Road. At 10 mi. from Loomis the road forks; the N fork and Ninemile Creek roads branch here). The middle fork (Iron Gate-no. 390A) branches at about 15 mi. from Loomis and continues 7 mi. (rough) to an end at 6000 ft near the Pasayten Wilderness boundary. The main road continues W to beyond Long Swamp camp (7.2 mi. from middle fork); from the camp Salmon Meadows Road♦ extends S.

Trans Canada Hwy. (B.C.) Distances from Chilliwack-Sardis junction to highway fork at Hope: Laidlaw Road — 21.8 mi. (35.1 km); Hunter Creek Road — 25.8 mi. (41.5 km); Silver-Skagit Road — 31.1 mi. (50 km); Hope junction — 33 mi. (53.1 km).

Trans-Canada Hwy 3 (Hope-Princeton Hwy). (B.C.) This major roadway branches from Hwy No. 1 at Hope, crossing the Cascade Mountains in Manning Provincial Park. Distance from Hope to Park headquarters is 43 mi. (69.2 km) and to Princeton is 88.5 mi. (134 km).

Four-Mile Creek Road (W) branches at 4 mi. (a new road) and extends into basin between Hope Mountain and Wells Peak.

Eightmile Creek Road (E) branches at 8.5 mi. (only open 1 mi.).

Wray Creek Road leaves at about 7 mi. and bears to the NW side of Wray Creek valley to about 4300 ft (condition unknown; possibly closed at 2 mi.). A fork leads NW into Berkey Creek for at least 4 mi.

Outram Creek Road (Slide Creek) leaves at 11.9 mi. at Hope Landslide and extends some 3 mi. W.

Sumallo River Road♦ exits at 13.5 mi.

Gibson Pass Road and *Blackwall Peak Road* exit at 43.1 mi. See Manning Provincial Park♦.

Pasayten River Road♦ exits S at 1.7 mi. E of the Park's E entrance 54.7 mi. (88 km) from Hope.

Whipsaw Creek Road exits W at 5.5 mi. S of Princeton. Poor roads via the N side of the valley extend to Hope Pass; a spur along the divide S of the pass leads to a trail connection with Nicomen Lake. A rough road connection from Hope Pass follows the old Blackeye's Trail route over open divides and crosses Granite Mountain and Lodestone Mountain on the way to Tulameen — all needless roadways that mark up the high upland.

Tulameen River Roads. (B.C.) A road of varying quality connects Trans-Canada Hwy 3♦ (at Princeton) via Tulameen, then N and eventually W to Brookmere (see Coldwater River Road♦); here is a connection S to Coquihalla Lakes. From Princeton (renamed from Vermilion Forks in 1860) the route follows the Tulameen Valley (Indian for red earth), then the Otter Valley with its string of lakes. Indians long traded here and fur brigades camped at Otter Lake en route from Hope to Nicola River.

Mileages: Princeton — 0; Coalmont — 11.8 (19 km); Tulameen — 16.7 (26.9 km); fork W — 40.0 (64.4 km); Coldwater Road — 49.9 (80.3 km); Brookmere — 50.6 (81.4 km). There is a connection from near Brookmere to the summit of Mt. Thynne (6630 ft/2021 m).

From Coalmont the Granite Creek Road connects to Whipsaw Creek Road. Near here is the locale of Granite City, which became rich on placer gold and once had a population of 2000 — with 13 saloons.

From Tulameen, Britton Creek Road now bears NW into Lawless Creek. The road passes above Murphy Lake into Britton Creek, then leads to its head, then northward down to near Coquihalla Lakes (est. 24 mi., 38.6 km total). A road bears SW from Tulameen along Vuich Creek to Treasure Mountain.

Twisp River Road No. 349 extends from Twisp on Methow Valley Hwy♦ to road's end at 3680 ft (25½ mi.). War Creek junction is reached in 15 mi., South Creek Trail at 21.8 mi. and North Creek Trail at 25 mi.

TRAILS AND ALPINE HIKING APPROACHES

"Ashes to ashes and dust to dust, if the horse flies don't get you, the mosquitoes must."

Dwight Watson

Note: Backcountry use permits are needed in North Cascades National Park and in the Pasayten Wilderness (obtain these at ranger stations). Maximum group size is 12 persons.

General hiking references to the region are: *101 Hikes*, Seattle, 1979 and *Mountaineer*, 1969, pp. 60-68.

Airplane Creek Trail. (B.C.) See Chilliwack River Road♦. Begin via Mt. Laughington logging road from Foley Lake Road after crossing to S side of creek, just below the mouth of Airplane Creek. Follow the logging road (now gated) N to the first switchback (2000 ft), where the old trail begins; may be hard to locate. One may be able to drive the road to 3500 ft and traverse rightward to the trail. Slash reported to be a problem in locating trail.

The trail traverses NW to Airplane Creek, crosses, then climbs steeply N to the high basin SE of Baby Munday Peak (6.5 km); there is a campsite at 5200 ft S of the peak.

Albert Camp Trail No. 375. See Horseshoe Basin♦.

Anderson Lakes Trail No. 611 leads to the four shallow Anderson Lakes, set in a meadowy area NW of Mt. Watson, and has a fork leading to the two Watson Lakes. This is a heavily used foot-trail (no horses or motorized vehicles); keep on the trail in meadow areas to prevent erosion. Both trails are usually snow-covered until July. The area has been extensively glaciated. Small glaciers and permanent snowfields remain on Mt. Watson and Bacon Peak.

Taking Baker Lake Hwy♦ and Baker Dam Road, follow road no. 3721 to the trailhead at 4300 ft. From the trail fork (2 mi.) it is less than 0.5 mi. to the first Anderson Lake (4400 ft+); the two smaller lakes of the group are on a ledge about 0.5 mi. E of the main lake.

Watson Lake Trail No. 611B. From the trail fork, switchback ¼ mi. through a timber stand to a saddle, then descend another 1.4 mi. to Watson Lakes. From Little Watson Lake (4400 ft+) hike around the N shore to the larger lake. These beautiful deep blue lakes, located in the depression between Mt. Watson and Anderson Butte, will mirror reflections in the correct lighting.

Anderson Butte. At the trail saddle (1 mi.) a left branch (A) climbs 0.8 mi. to the 5420-ft former lookout site. The summit of the Butte (5700 ft+/1737 m+) is a short hike to the E.

Andrews Creek Trail No. 504. This major trail leaves Chewack River Road♦ at 23.5 mi. from Winthrop (3050 ft). There is a junction with Meadow Lake Trail No. 505 at 5.5 mi. (E to Meadow Lake, Coleman Peak, Coleman Ridge, Fire Creek). Reach Andrew Pass (6680 ft+) at 12.4 mi. (good campsites at 9 and 12 mi.). Northward are trail connections to Spanish Creek, Boundary Trail♦, Cathedral Lakes, and Remmel Creek Trail. Distance to Spanish Camp is 15 mi., Boundary Trail♦ 15.6 mi., and Cathedral Lakes 18 mi.

Peepsight Creek Trail No. 525 bears W at 8.1 mi. to cross Crazy Man Pass (7440 ft+), pass Rock Lake, and loop back to Andrews Pass.

Ashnola River Trail No. 500 is an old trail with beginnings in Canada. The map of the International Boundary Commission dated 1913 shows a trail from Ashnola River over Cathedral Pass, and also marks trails up Pasayten River, Castle and Chuwanten creeks.

Begin from Ashnola River Road♦ in British Columbia and reach the Boundary in about 3 mi. At about 2.5 mi. farther meet Boundary Trail♦ (E and W) and Ashnola River shelter (5040 ft+). The trail E bears across the N flank of Bald Mountain to Spanish Camp, then to Horseshoe Basin. For the continuation S along Ashnola River see Lake Creek-Ashnola River Trail♦.

Sheep Mountain Trail No. 529 (using Boundary Trail♦ to Martina Creek) ascends NW to Ramon Lakes (7018 ft and 7150 ft) on the N flank of Sheep Mountain (est. 3-4 mi.) and continues to Park Pass (6886 ft) near the Boundary. A fork leads to Sheep Lake, located in a basin closely SE of Sheep Mountain. In 1901 geologists Smith and Calkins noted the "beautiful open character of the uplands" at Park Pass (Bull. No. 235, p. 19) where five valleys have been cut back to make a low saddle with radiating spurs. Ramon Lakes, which span the timberline zone here (alpine larch stands), are among the most lovely and fragile in the North Cascades; the highest tarns are flanked by tundra grass and talus blocks.

Baker Pass Trail No. 603. Follow Loomis-Nooksack Road and road no. 372 to the 3200-ft+ trailhead at the SE edge of Schriebers Meadows (see Baker Lake Hwy♦); shelter at 0.5 mi. from road. Reach the attractive terrain of Baker Pass (4962 ft) in 3 mi.; here one can cross to Mazama Park on the Middle Fork Nooksack River drainage (see Ridley Creek Trail♦). The entire area offers good open hiking and ski touring terrain above the meadow level.

A scenic high trek continues N, leaving the trail just E of Baker Pass, and along Railroad Grade (5000 to 6000 ft), an old lateral moraine of the Easton Glacier. The glacier, which terminates at 5500 ft, can be reached almost anywhere; a good spot to reach the ice is about 6100 ft from Railroad Grade. One can easily cross Mazama Park NW to Meadow Point, an overlook of the Deming Glacier.

About 1 mi. before reaching Baker Pass (4400 ft+) a left trail fork (A) leads to Park Butte (5471 ft) and its lookout house; this is a locale for scenic panoramas.

Baker River Trail. See Upper Baker River Trail♦.

Bastile Ridge Route. Bastile Ridge is a 2.5-mi. E-W-trending crest N of Roosevelt Glacier and S of Smith Creek. Begin as Mt. Baker Trail♦. A short distance beyond Grouse Creek find an unmarked path left, which leads to a view of Coleman Glacier snout in 1 mi. Blazes lead through alder to Heliotrope (Kulshan) Creek (est. 3800 ft), which is a difficult ford unless crossed by a log. A short thicket leads to Glacier Creek (2 mi.); cross here (footbridge gone ATP) or closer to glacier if water is high. Take an alder path and ascend NE to a small meadow (4 mi.) which leads above Chromatic Moraine to the crest of Bastile Ridge. Here is a long strip of medial moraines, in parallel, below Bastile Ridge. They are arranged in huge windows: one of grey rocks, one of red, and another of black, and once interspersed with gleaming white ice. Charles F. Easton (Whatcom Museum) wrote: "It is doubtful if the world can duplicate."

Follow the ridge to its climax (Point 7842), or traverse to the edge of Roosevelt Glacier. One can hike the glacier to the pass (7600 ft+) crossing to Mazama Glacier (see Skyline Divide♦).

Smith Basin, at the head of Smith Creek between Bastile and Chowder ridges, contains Bastile Glacier (0.7 mi. long), most of its mass being NW of Point 7842.

Bell Pass Trail No. 603. Begin from near the end of Loomis-Nooksack Road (see Baker Lake Hwy♦) (16 mi., 2900 ft). The trail extends about 2 mi. NE to Bell Pass (3964 ft), then continues about 2.5 additional mi. to Baker Pass♦.

Big Beaver Creek Trail. One can begin by hiking West Ross Lake Trail to the vicinity of Big Beaver Landing, or reach trailhead by boat. The lower Big Beaver Valley is a mosaic of aquatic and semi-aquatic communities, and the ancient red cedars are the best remaining example of valley-bottom forest in the Cascades. Beaver Pass (3620 ft) was smoothed over by glaciers during the ice ages.

Leave the North Cascades Hwy♦ at Mile 134 (Happy Flat). The trail first descends 0.7 mi. to Ross Dam, then reaches campsites at Pumpkin Mountain (7 mi.), Big Beaver (7 mi.), Thirtynine Mile (12.1 mi.), Luna (15.2 mi.), and Beaver Pass (22 mi.); deduct 7 mi. if starting from Big Beaver Landing. Fires are permitted at the established campsites listed above. Distance from Beaver Pass to Little Beaver Creek♦ is 3.5 miles.

Luna Lake High Route is a strenuous cross-country route which leads to the high saddle S of Luna Peak, and can be continued then to either Luna Creek cirque or McMillan Creek cirque. Rather than taking the steep forested spur between McMillan Creek and "Access Creek" (the unnamed tributary 2.5 mi. N which heads steeply on the E face of Luna Peak) recent experience has found a superior route avoids the subalpine part of this spur ridge. Hike away from the trail to cross Big Beaver Creek N of "Access Creek," and hike its N side in open forest to the cirque head; here a broad talus couloir (some snow) bears SW to near timberline on the ridge leading westward. Follow this, then ascend the high SE and S slopes of Luna Peak directly to the gentle saddle (7120 ft+) S of Luna Peak. To reach Luna Lake descend W on snow and glacier slopes and traverse rocky basins. Take ice axes. Time: 8 hours to lake. See Challenger Arm to Luna Lake and Picket Pass Route for continuation to head of McMillan Creek Cirque.

Challenger Arm Route. Leave the trail about 1/3 mi. S of Beaver Pass and just S of bushy slides. Ascend the ridge slope W through light forest undergrowth to timberline (moderately unpleasant). From the first high shoulder cross a short, steep rocky area just S of the ridgetop to gain easy meadow and talus slopes S of the broad crest. Follow benches to Wiley Lake (6640 ft+, 5 hours) at the eastern terminus of the first glacier on Challenger Arm. Along the ridge there is an interesting contact between the older gneiss and younger intrusive granite rock. Continue easily along the S margin of the glacier nearly to Point 7374, then descend to the northern edge of the Challenger Glacier. References: *B.C. Mountaineer*, July 1974; *Routes and Rocks*, pp. 39-40; see Section I, note 82.

Challenger Arm to Luna Lake and Picket Pass. Descend the gentle eastern glacier arm, then deglaciated rock barrens rightward to a broad rocky knoll with the highest vegetation (good camp; est. 5900 ft). Traverse sloping moraine barrens SW about 1 mi, keeping well above cliffs but below the glacier. Locate an easy route down slabs and debris to the central cirque of Luna Creek. Beneath the spectacular icefalls of the cirque glacier cross a nearly perfect arcuate moraine, then residual snow (4200 ft) to its far arm; the level ablation moraine behind the rock dam is underlain by stagnant glacier ice protected from melting by rock debris. It is best to descend as low as "Lousy Lake" and then diagonal up again where the moraine is not so steep. Will Thompson called the dead ice beyond the immense terminal moraine "a very pig of a glacier, rooting in boulders, stagnant and buried deep in its own debris."

Traverse on a gradual rise across sloping moraine to Luna Lake (4880 ft+); camp on the N side. One is likely to hear avalanches all night here. A snow gully and ledges eastward lead through gneissic cliffs; the reddish fin above the slabby basin edge is of a shattered gneiss breccia (this breccia lies closely above the quartz diorite of the Chilliwack Batholith exposed in the lower portion of the cirque). Ascend SE to the Luna-McMillan Creek ridge; once over the crest (7040 ft+) it is feasible to scramble W or keep on its S side (see Mt. Fury).

From the high slopes bearing toward Mt. Fury's East Peak make a gradually descending traverse. Either descend below a slab cliff and a rocky buttress to reach the lower middle section of the glacier on the SE side of the peak or climb a rocky face via heather ledges to intersect the Mt. Fury climbing route high on the glacier. Continue W to the 7280-ft+ col between the East Peak and Southeast Peak to take a route nearly over the latter en route to Picket Pass or (easier) cross the ridge at 7360 ft (slightly N) for a steep snow gully descent into upper Goodell Creek; one can then traverse easily to Picket Pass. Note: One can finish the route to Stetattle Ridge (see Easy Ridge Trail◆-Picket Pass Route). Do not descend McMillan Creek; a party is on record taking three days to reach Newhalem via Goodell Creek — a considerable amount of crawling on hands and knees was necessary. Reference: *Routes and Rocks*, pp. 32-34; see Section I, note 82.

Billy Goat-Larch Creek Trail No. 502A and 502. The trailhead for this important route is 25.5 mi. from Winthrop (see Chewack River Road◆ and Eightmile Road). The trail climbs from the corral at road's end (4400 ft) for 2.5 mi. to Billy Goat Pass (6600 ft+), then descends to Drake Creek trail junction (5 mi.) and ascends again to Three Fools Pass (6 mi. — 6000 ft+). At the crossing of Diamond Creek Trail No. 514 branches E to Diamond Point and Lake Creek-Ashnola River Trail◆.

The main trail continues via Larch Creek to Larch Pass (13 mi. — 7320 ft+). Corral Lake (7152 ft) can be reached about 2 mi. NE of Larch Pass via a branch path. Where the main trail crosses the basin at the head of Pasayten River East Fork, one can hike W to Whistler Pass (7480 ft+), which is 0.9 mi. E of Ashnola Mountain.

Boundary Trail◆ (18.2 mi.) is intersected at Peeve Pass (6840 ft+). Just W of this junction trail no. 506 extends N to Park Pass (6886 ft), only ½ mi. from the Boundary. Sheep Mountain is some 20 mi. distant via this route, but only about 5 mi. from British Columbia (Ashnola River Road◆).

Burch Mountain (7782 ft/2372 m), an old lookout site, is 2.6 mi. SE of Billy Goat Pass, and can be reached by a trail which circles S of the summit. From beyond Burch Mountain, trail no. 516 descends along Three Prong Creek to meet Lake Creek; a high route from this trail can be taken W to Fool Hen Lake (7301 ft).

East Fork Pasayten Trail No. 451 branches NW from Larch Creek to cross Dollar Watch Pass (6960 ft+) for a descent to Hidden Lakes (see Eightmile Pass-Hidden Lakes Trail◆).

Boulder Creek Trail No. 605 (Boulder Ridge). Reach the trail via Baker Lake Hwy◆ and Marten Lake Road. The trail uses a cat track through an old clearcut for 1000 ft (NW), then enters big timber; continue to a small meadow (2.1 mi., 3400 ft). Continue on trail remnants and through light bush in a NW direction, traversing to a draw (½ mi.), then ascend to Boulder Ridge. Open terrain here leads to Boulder Glacier higher and N of the snout (at about 6000 ft). The trail is usually snow-free by July.

Boulder Creek Trail No. 1245 begins 2½ mi. N of Stehekin. First use Rainbow Creek Trail◆ for 2 mi.; Rennie Camp (4400 ft) is 6 mi. from the road. In the high area near the head of Boulder Creek watch for cairn markers; the trail reaches War Creek Pass at 9.9 mi.

Boundary Red Mine Route. From Silesia Creek (see Slesse Creek Road-Chilliwack Lake Road◆) an old roadway and trail ascends to the historic mine, at about 4000 ft just S of the International Boundary on the rough NE flank of Larrabee (Red) Mountain. Some of the old claims have been staked high on the N flank of The Pleiades, in alpine terrain.

Boundary Trail No. 533 is a generic name for a combination of existing routes closely S of the International Boundary which begin as Iron Gate Trail (see Horseshoe Basin◆). The trail is routed along Teapot Dome and Bauerman Ridge to Scheelite Pass (15.6 mi.), Tungsten Pass (17.7 mi.), Apex Pass (18.8 mi.), Cathedral Pass (21 mi.), Upper Cathedral Lake (22.1 mi.), Spanish Camp (26 mi.), Ashnola River Trail◆ (33.3 mi.), Sheep Mountain Trail (36.6 mi.), Bunker Hill (46.2 mi.), East Fork Pasayten River (52.9 mi.), Chuchuwanteen Creek (60 mi.), and Castle Pass (69.3 mi.) on the Crest Trail◆. The route is planned westward to Lightning Creek and Ross Lake.

Boundary Trail has numerous N-S connections, including Tungsten Creek, Lower Cathedral Lake and Border Ridge, Wall Creek and Cathedral Park, Remmel Lake, Remmel Creek, Ashnola River, Sheep Mountain, Billy Goat-Larch Creek, East Fork Pasayten River, Pasayten River, and Monument 83. There are shelters at Tungsten Mine, Ashnola River, and Barker Brown cabin (3 mi. W of Ashnola River).

Bridge Creek Trail (also known as Pacific Crest Trail) extends 13.7 mi. from the Stehekin River Road◆ to Rainy Pass. Camps are at North Fork (2.8 mi.); Six Mile (6 mi.); South Fork (7 mi.) — at junction of Rainbow Lake Trail; Hideaway Camp (6 mi. from Rainy Pass); Fireweed Camp (5.3 mi. from Rainy Pass) — junction with Twisp Pass, McAlester Creek, and Stiletto Peak trails; Croker Cabin (2.7 mi. from Rainy Pass) — a former mining camp.

Brigade Trail (Peers Creek to Tulameen) (B.C.), used 1849-60, was laid out by Henry Peers. The route now begins on the W side from the head of Peers Creek logging road; old Manson Camp is 14 mi. from Hope (see Coquihalla River Road◆).

The trail climbs over a 4750-ft saddle on Manson Ridge into the Sowaqua Creek drainage and then crosses Fool's Pass. A long traverse leads to the Sowaqua, where the Ghostpass Trail comes down the W bank. A camp of historic interest is Campement du Chevreuil (Camp of the Deer) at 6100 ft on the N shoulder of Mt. Davis (19 mi. from Manson Camp — S of Tulameen Mountain). The route descends past Palmer Pond and then the N side of Podunk Creek to Horseguard Camp on the Tulameen River, then ascends E to Lodestone Mountain to meet Blackeye's Trail on the plateau.

Now one can reach the opposite end of the trail from Granite Mountain jeep road (see Trans-Canada Hwy 3◆) and Whipsaw Creek Road — and the Indian trail — at a sign "stock trail 452" about 4.5 mi. S of where the road to Badger Creek branches E. The route then drops to the Tulameen.

References: "Old Pack Trails in the proposed Manning Park Extension," Okanogan Similkameen Parks Society (1977), pp. 8-16; 36th Report of Okanogan Historical Society (1972): 14-48 and 37th Report (1973): 17-20; H.R. Hatfield, "Blazing Trails," *Western Living* 4, no. 2 (1974): 56-58 and map, p. 58.

Canyon Creek Ridge provides a feasible hiking route to Three AM Mountain (est. 8 mi.) and to Midnight Mountain, beyond. The route has excellent vistas. Leave Twisp River Road♦ via Little Bridge Creek Road No. 3401 (at est. 8 mi.), then follow road no. 3424 to trail no. 404, which extends to the ridge.

Canyon Creek Trail No. 754 connects Chancellor (Harts Pass Road♦) with North Cascades Hwy♦ at Granite Creek (9¼ mi.); there is a footlog below the highway at 3.5 mi. past Panther Creek and a bridge ½ mi. S.

From 3 mi. SW of Chancellor, *Mill Creek Trail No. 755* extends to Azurite Pass (6680 ft+). The Azurite Mine (now closed) is about 5 mi. up this trail on the W side of the valley; claims extend to 7400 ft. From Mill Creek a branch trail leads N to Cady Pass (5960 ft+) and a connection to South Fork Slate Creek; this is an 8½-mi. connection to the road at 5½ mi. W of Harts Pass, using the route of Cady's historic wagon road. The lookout on Cady Point (6542 ft) was established in 1935; reach by path along ridge for 0.9 mi. NW of Cady Pass.

Cathedral Provincial Park (B.C.). Protected status has been given a unique highland on the northern fringe of the Okanogan Range closely N of the International Boundary, in the transition zone between the plateaus of the British Columbia Interior and the North Cascades of Washington State. The topographic center of the Park is near Stone City Mountain, at 49°03′ N lat. and 120°12′ W long. Here are great contrasts in relief and topography, with scenic delights that include a series of lovely, high rock-bound lakes which drain into Lakeview Creek, just N of the batholith (the geologic contact with the older metamorphic rocks lies just N of Ladyslipper Lake). The highest summits within the Park are Mt. Grimface and Lakeview Mountain, both over 8600 ft in altitude. Here glacial action has scoured the exposed batholith to an altitude of about 7500 ft, although the ice may have gone higher — the ice sheet extended to 8000 ft on the southern Interior Plateau (Holland, Stuart S. "Landforms of British Columbia." B.C. Dept. of Mines and Petroleum Resources, 1976).

The principal streamflows are the Ashnola River and its forks: Lakeview, Ewart, and Wall creeks; a major portion of the Park lies within the basin drained by 13-mi. Lakeview Creek, a heavily glaciated hanging valley. The forest is generally not dense, featuring a variety of species from ponderosa and lodgepole pine, giving way higher to Englemann spruce, subalpine fir, and alpine larch. Meadows near timberline are especially colorful and lovely.

High ridges of the Park are very exposed to winds that remove snowfall, creating a moisture stress that is a significant factor in limiting vegetation. Keremeos, at an altitude of only 1410 ft and NE of the Park, receives only 10 inches of mean annual precipitation, but Cathedral Ridge, lying over 8300 ft and 1000 ft above the local timberline, has a mid-latitude alpine climate, with June being the month of maximum summer rainfall. This high area is characterized by a frost penetration to depths of over 40 inches, with a frost-free season of probably less than 20 days (Melcon, p. 150; see Section II, note 118).

The area abounds with periglacial forms, including two-stage rock glaciers in the Goat Lake basin. Surficial features include multiple spheroidal weathering forms on exposed ridgetops, tors, relict sorted stone polygons, stripes, stone nets, and festoons.

Spheroidal blocks and tors have survived in a line where both glacial erosion and slope processes were least effective. Neither ice or periglacial conditions could have displaced tor blocks on Cathedral Ridge.

Tors are a bedrock landform of distinctive appearance, upstanding "boulderized" bedrock blocks and superincumbent blocks characterized by etching at joint planes and rounding of corners. Both the bedrock and superincumbent blocks are delineated by rectangular horizontal and vertical planes. Tors were formed in a coarse-grained quartz monzonite pluton of Jurassic age. They were exposed to meteoric weathering during Eocene time, buried beneath volcanics and sediment, then re-exhumed during the major Pliocene orogeny (Melcon, p. 165). Tors seem to be isolated by subsurface chemical weathering. They probably formed in the outer portion of the pluton soon after the quartz monzonite unroofing in early Tertiary time. The sharp contact of the pluton and Triassic rock indicates a conduit for magmatic injection (Melcon, p. 130). Usually 15 to 30 ft high, these forms with the distinctive rectangular configuration are now restricted to the bedrock of Cathedral Ridge. The partial exhumation of the weathering front exposes the spheroidal bedrock at the surface as a tor.

Spheroidal boulders here are corestones detached from the bedrock. Some boulders have concentric indurated shells 1 inch thick; the weathering intensity increased radially outward. The spheroidal and ellipsoidal forms are caused by subsurface water penetrating dilated joints. Chemical weathering causes joint-bound blocks to be separated from bedrock and rounded. In deep weathering the chemical processes are not necessarily the same throughout a profile and rainwater may become acidified. Weathering pits are the result of differential weathering beneath partially detached indurated layers. Stone stripes may be seen on the ridge, composed of Princeton basalt. Jurassic plutons intruded the rocks of the Nicola Group here. (The Nicola Group is an andesite lava flow that covers much of the Princeton map area. Basalt, sediment, and andesite fill some joints in the quartz monzonite and exist on some surfaces.) The coarse quartz monzonite is of interest because of large crystals — some are up to ⅜ inch long.

Of added interest is the presence of a band of California bighorn sheep and numerous mountain goats in the area.

Although there is a private resort at Quiniscoe Lake, there has not been easy access to the public campground at the lake. The Park has fragile areas, particularly at the lakeshore, and certainly could become subject to overuse. New Park trails are well signed.

For approach to the Park, see Ashnola River Road♦. One can hike from the 2800-ft level to Quiniscoe Lake (6700 ft+) by the 9-mi. high trail near the jeep road, or make arrangements with the resort for transportation on the 10-mi. private road. Another approach is to take the Centennial Trail♦ from the road at Wall Creek (20 km to Quiniscoe Lake).

There is a cairned route from the Centennial Trail W of Scout Lake to Red Mountain; one can scramble over the summit and continue easily to Quiniscoe Mountain. The route continues S to Pyramid Mountain (an outlier E of the ridge which is a felsenmeer of broken basalt) and Stone City Mountain (0.7 mi. SW of Ladyslipper Lake), where huge flattened boulders (tors) are stacked atop each other. Just beyond is Giant Cleft, a basalt dike 10 ft wide that cuts through the granite; rapid weathering of the dike has resulted in a deep vertical chasm. Typically flanking spurs of Cathedral Ridge here are narrow debris chutes.

Local trails from Quiniscoe Lake extend to Pyramid, Glacier (7200 ft+), Ladyslipper (7200 ft+), and Goat Lake (6800 ft+, in the upper basin of Lakeview Creek). On the trail from Quiniscoe Lake to Red Mountain are marvelous floral exhibits and waterfalls. From Glacier and Ladyslipper lakes several hiker routes can be made crossing Cathedral Ridge to the Wall Creek slope and valley. There is a direct route from the W end of Glacier Lake to the ridge S of Quiniscoe Mountain. There is a route SW of Ladyslipper Lake taking a gully to the ridge between Ovis and Grimface.

Ladyslipper Lake nests in a large talus basin with fragile meadows at its open end, the entire scene a sharp contrast to the emerald-green waters. Here are the Nicola lavas from the Princeton area, and patterned ground is in evidence here. Polygons can be found on the flat-topped andesite ridge between Ladyslipper Lake and Lake of the Woods, giving way to stone stripes as the slope increases in angle just above timberline.

It should be noted that there is some area nomenclature confusion. The lodge operators and others have ignored the original Grimface Mountain name (now official) and applied "McKeen" to their maps; there are some other contradictions, including misnamed features on the Parks Branch folder (1977) and the Ashnola River topographic sheet (1979). The correct nomenclature for features includes Red Mountain (8100 ft), Quiniscoe Mountain (8369 ft, 0.5 mi. SW of Quiniscoe Lake), Pyramid Mountain (an E-W ridge extending N of Ladyslipper Lake), Devil's Woodpile (columnar basalt on ridge near Pyramid), Smokey the Bear (several hundred meters SE of Stone City Mountain), Ovis Mountain, Grimface Mountain, and Denture Ridge (trends E of Macabre Tower and Matriarch Mountain).

For other trails see Wall Creek Route♦ and Ewart Creek

Trail♦. See Grimface Mountain for area references. Map: Ashnola River 92 H/1 (note some nomenclature errors).

Cedar Creek Trail No. 476 extends from Cedar Creek road branch (North Cascades Hwy♦) to West Fork Cedar Creek (6½ mi.) and Abernathy Pass (9 mi.). There are good camp spots at 2.6, 4.1, and 6.5 mi.

The NW fork of the creek (est. 6¼ mi.) provides a good cross-country route to the hanging valley S of Mt. Silver Star. Follow the N side of the stream, where there is an old path littered with windfalls.

Centennial Trail (B.C.) basically follows the Monument 83 Trail♦ and Skyline Trail♦.

The route E from Manning Park♦ goes within 0.5 km of Monument 83, then branches downward (at 14.5 km); from here it is 1.7 hours to the ridge (1846 m) overlooking Pasayten Valley (campsite in burn on ridge). At Pasayten River (1169 m) the trail is within 0.8 km of the U.S. border (a loop goes to the border and the Parson Smith treesite near Monument 85 (277 m to monument). Once the main trail reaches the valley floor it is 2.4 km to the suspension bridge (camping at E end). Then angle up-valley 45 minutes to Pasayten burn (1692 m) — part of trail is up skidway. Now follow the border to Monuments 87 and 88; then the trail climbs out of Peeve Creek and bears N to Trapper Lake (from camp at Peeve Creek it is 4.5 hours to Trapper Lake (known both for mosquitos and fine views of Cathedral Park peaks). See also Pasayten River Area Trails♦.

From the S end of the lake (1969 m) cross Easygoing Creek and hike via the ridge overlooking Ashnola River. The route meets the valley (1323 m) at 31.6 mi. (51 km) on Ashnola River Road♦ (recommended to allow 2-3 days; 18 hiking hours).

Note: To reach trail directly from Pasayten River Road♦ (see route to Trapper Lake for hike to suspension bridge): distance from bridge is ⅜ mi. to trail junction that leads to Pasayten Road.

The section from Ashnola River Road♦ at Mile 31 to Quiniscoe Lake begins at the N side of Wall Creek (3800 ft+; see Wall Creek Route♦). Take the S trail fork, which climbs to 7500 ft on Cathedral Ridge to circle back S to Quiniscoe Lake (20 km). The trail then descends E to Lakeview Creek before climbing to the high northern shoulder of Lakeview Mountain, then continuing S of Twin Buttes; these are two small cinder cones (7486 ft/2282 m and 7664 ft/2337 m). The trail then descends into Mountain Goat Creek to reach Ewart Creek Trail♦. The distance from Monument 83 to Cathedral Park is about 32 km. It should be noted that between Lakeview Mountain and Twin Buttes there are many confusing cattle trails and wrong paths can lead to endless cowpies.

Centennial Trail (B.C.) is a project conceived by the Canadian Youth Hostels Association in 1964 and completed in co-operation with various other clubs and agencies as an E-W hiking route. The trail is routed along the lower Fraser and Chilliwack rivers, but only applies to mountain areas in this section from Chilliwack River Road♦ at Post Creek to the Silver-Skagit Road♦ at Hicks Creek (14.6 mi.). Parts of the Centennial Trail follow the old Whatcom and Brigade trails.

Center Mountain Trail No. 754 is an alternative route to Holman Pass on the Crest Trail♦ (9.8 mi.). Begin at Chancellor (see Harts Pass Road♦). The trail climbs steeply from 2850 ft to 6300 ft on the W side of Center Mountain, then bears N near the ridge to Sky Pilot Pass (6.6 mi. — 6280 ft+) and a junction with Devils Ridge Trail♦.

Chain Lakes Trail No. 682 begins at Artist Point (end of Mt. Baker Hwy♦). The trail makes a 6.7-mi. loop to Mt. Baker Lodge. See also Table Mountain-Ptarmigan Ridge♦.

Chewack River Trail No. 510. The Indian name "Chewack" was first shown on Boundary Survey manuscript maps of 1859. It can be noted that the NW branch of the river was termed "Kai sahl kan Creek" on the North West Boundary map of 1866. When continental ice came from the NW before about 13,500 years ago, the main ice stream cut down the main trench more efficiently than the smaller tributaries and upper glacial troughs.

From the confluence of Eightmile Creek valley and above, all western Chewack tributaries are U-shaped troughs whose bedrock floors hang 400 to 600 ft above the valley base. But major eastern tributaries (Thirtymile, Twentymile, Boulder Creek) are normal stream-erosional valleys. Only the northernmost tributary (Horseshoe Creek) contributed confluent ice to the E side of ancient Chewack Valley Glacier (Waitt, p. 51; see Section III, note 11). The northernmost Chewack tributaries (Horseshoe, Tungsten, Cathedral, and Andrews creeks) curiously do not head in cirques, but ascend gradually to a broad upland surface of low relief.

From the end of Chewack River Road♦ at Thirty Mile Campground reach Tungsten Creek Trail at 8.1 mi. (est. 4700 ft); the main trail follows Remmel Creek and reaches Remmel Lake (6871 ft) at 17.1 mi. The gentle divide is crossed to Spanish Camp (locked Forest Service cabin) and Boundary Trail♦ (18.1 mi.).

Fire Creek Trail No. 561 (at 5.2 mi.) extends W to connect with Coleman Ridge and Meadow Lake. Basin Creek Trail No. 360 (at 6.4 mi.) bears NE to Windy Peak Trail♦ N of the summit.

Tungsten Creek Trail No. 534 reaches Boundary Trail♦ at 14.3 mi. (from road), then Tungsten Mine (mining cabin; 6720 ft). Here a path leads about 1 mi. S to Tungsten Lake (7040 ft+).

As Boundary Trail the route ascends W over Apex Pass (7280 ft+) and reaches Cathedral Pass (7560 ft+) at 19 mi. The two Cathedral Lakes (7360 ft and 6800 ft+) are nested in magnificent glacial cirques about 1 mi. W of the pass. The lakes and pass area can also be reached via Wall Creek Route♦ from British Columbia.

Fourpoint Creek Trail No. 505 departs from the main Chewack trail at 12.1 mi. and leads W to Fourpoint Lake and S along Coleman Ridge to connect with Fire Creek, Meadow Lake and Andrews Creek.

Chilliwack River Trail. Note: Backpacking permits are needed for this trail and all branch routes. The trail extends along a densely wooded valley, a major drainage of this section. See Hannegan Pass Trail♦ for first section. Across the pass the trail forks at 5 mi. (from road); keep right and descend through Hells Gorge to reach U.S. Cabin (10.0 mi., 2480 ft+). The river ford at 11.0 mi. is now replaced with a cable car crossing, which leads to the trail division toward Whatcom Pass at 12.1 mi. The valley trail continues past Indian Creek at 15 mi. (shelter), Bear Creek at 18 mi. (shelter), Little Chilliwack shelter at 20 mi., and the International Boundary at 21 mi. In 1.5 additional mi. the S end of Chilliwack Lake is reached just E of the road bridge (see Chilliwack River Road♦). Camping with fires permitted at Copper Creek, U.S. Cabin, Indian Creek, Bear Creek, and Little Chilliwack. Also at Graybeal and Tapto on Brush Creek Trail.

Brush Creek Trail No. 674. From the Whatcom Pass junction the trail ascends 5.1 mi. to the narrow defile (5206 ft); no camping at the pass (Graybeal shelter is 2.2 mi. on the trail). For continuation see Little Beaver Creek Trail♦.

Whatcom Pass-Redoubt High Route. Ascend open forest toward Tapto Lakes for a few hundred ft, then bear rightward (NE) on the slope of upper Little Beaver Creek to Middle Lakes (5600 ft+), then continue the traverse beyond East Lakes onto the slope high above Pass Creek. Continue the long traverse NNE to the lake (with small glacier) and open basin at the head of Pass Creek. (*Routes and Rocks*, pp. 25-27 — see Section I, note 82 — advises ascending 200 ft above and beyond the lowest Pass-Indian Creek saddle (5680 ft+), then traversing down and across the cliff-like area toward the lake.) Bypass the lake on its E, then ascend NW across the high open ridge to the head of Indian Creek (see Indian Creek Trail♦).

Whatcom Pass-Challenger Glacier Route. The usual route from the subalpine ridge S of the pass is to make a southward traverse to the slabs near the terminus of the East Whatcom Glacier (possible broken ice here in late summer); the alternative is to cross the glacier higher (at 5600 ft), below the upper icefall. To avoid descending cliffs to the lower Challenger Glacier, keep high via snow, talus, and rock outcrops on the S flank of Whatcom Peak on a rising traverse toward Perfect Pass (6240 ft+). At a small rock knob below the final large snowfield on Whatcom, a break in the cliff edging the glacier permits a short snowband descent to the glacier. Reference: *Routes and Rocks*, pp. 27-32; see Section I, note 82. For continuation to Wiley Lake High Route and Luna Lake see Big Beaver Creek Trail♦; for continuation to Picket Pass see Easy Ridge Trail♦.

Indian Creek Trail. Begin at Indian Creek shelter (2320 ft+) and ascend 3 mi. to Packsack claim camp; the trail is evident for another ½ mi., to the first gravel side-streams. Continue on the N side of Indian Creek at about 4000-ft level, generally several hundred yards from the creek (at the major brushy area ascend and cross talus some 200-300 ft above the creek level). An open area over ¼ mi. long is brushy and strenuous (at about 4 mi.). This is followed by open forest. As the main creek climbs N, keep away from it (old trail tread visible). Follow cedar shrub slopes and open talus on rising rightward bearing several hundred ft above the creek. Once in the open upper basin ascend to the upper left side (talus and heather) to the Indian-Bear Creek saddle (6480 ft+). Do not cross the small U-shaped rocky gap on the basin's right side with a long talus slope beneath.

From the saddle hike rightward; where the slope steepens continue, then watch for a spot to begin a gradual 200-ft descent to bypass a rock toe, then traverse to Bear Lake. To reach the Bear-Redoubt Creek divide (6560 ft+), make a gradual rising traverse instead of descending. One can cross readily into Redoubt Creek basin; or hike N along the divide, then bear rightward to the edge of the Redoubt Glacier at about 7200 ft. Time: 8 hours Chilliwack Lake to head of Indian Creek. References: *Mountaineer*, 1945, pp. 5-10; *A.A.J.*, 1973, pp. 27-33.

From Indian Creek one can hike SE into the unique U-shaped tributary of Lake Reveille.

Bear Creek High Route. An old fire trail begins just E of Bear Creek shelter (2300 ft), but fades after a 1000-ft gain in altitude. One can then traverse into Bear Creek valley and hike cross-country to the valley head and ascend to Bear Lake (allow one day). A less brushy route is to continue above the trail to Ruta Lake (5040 ft+) on Bear Mountain's NW ridge (4 hours from shelter). Continue along the easy divide (but keep S of a knoll — Point 6824) to a level area at saddle (6480 ft+) above timberline (camping). Then descend steeply NE in a gully (snow or talus) to round great cliffs at about 5500 ft. Make an eastward traverse under the mountain's N face on snow, the glacier edge, or moraine to bypass the final rock face. Rise slightly (to about 6000 ft) to reach the higher eastern glacier segment. Traverse to the ridge top (est. 6700 ft — camping) or to Bear Lake (5760 ft+). Time: allow one day. One can cross the divide to Redoubt Creek basin at about 7000 ft and continue along its edge to the 7200-ft divide with Redoubt Glacier; a good alpine traverse route leads to Silver Lake (see Silver Lake Route♦); — allow 6-8 hours Bear Lake to Silver Lake.

Middle Peak High Route. Begin from Little Chilliwack River at about ½ mi. W of Little Chilliwack shelter (shortest approach is from Chilliwack Lake). Ascend the long forest slope, then ridgecrest westward toward Middle Peak. Near timberline goat trails lead to steep heather and the glacier on the Hanging Lake flank. Traverse NW on snow below the glacier, then bear left to make the ascent of Middle Peak (7464 ft/2276 m) via a gentle firn band on its N side. The summit of Middle Peak is capped by shale and conglomerate altered by the heat of intrusion of underlying batholith. To the SW there is a rugged alpine spur ridge that provides some scrambling and snow traversing. Begin by making a descending traverse high on the Little Chilliwack slope; keep below a rock wall on a route to the Ensawkwatch-Little Chilliwack divide. The route continues W to Rapid Peak (7059 ft/2152 m), then continues W along the Rapid-

Ensawkwatch Creek divide almost to Point 6521 before descending to Silesia Creek (see Silesia Creek Trail♦ and Chilliwack River Road♦-Slesse Creek Road). Reference: *Routes and Rocks,* pp. 9-11; see Section I, note 82.

Mineral Mountain High Route. From Hannegan Pass (see Hannegan Pass Trail♦) follow faint treads SE around a knob (5963 ft). Then make a long traverse across rough subalpine terrain to Chilliwack Pass (4160 ft+). Traverse talus N of the pass, then find a way through brush and cliffs to the N ridge of the knob (5694 ft). The route follows the ridge to the summit of Mineral Mountain. A continuation can be made down the crevassed glacier on the E slope, then followed to Easy Ridge. See *Routes and Rocks,* pp. 19-20; see Section I, note 82.

Redoubt High Route is a rugged, taxing route along a steep bare ridge high above the wooded valley of Bear Creek; it is scenic, but not the easiest way to Bear Lake or Redoubt Glacier. The best beginning ATP is to hike a steep road spur leading S from Depot Creek Road (see Chilliwack River Road♦) to about 5000 ft; the alternative is to ascend a timbered crest between Depot Creek and Chilliwack Lake. The complex lower ridge crest has brush and cliffs. A rocky notch just E of Point 6019 can be a problem (class 3 scrambling): keep high beneath Nodoubt Peak; some pinnacles and gullies at Point 6404 require scrambling (keep on ridge crest here), then traverse near 6000 ft on the Bear Creek slope. Time: one full day. References: *Mountaineer*, 1973, p. 32; *Routes and Rocks,* pp. 25-27; see Section I, note 82.

Chopaka Mountain Trail. Chopaka, located in an enclave of State land on the eastern fringe of the Okanogan Range, has a trail extending nearly to its plateau-like summit (see Chopaka Mountain). This is a good early season trek (May is good). From Toats Coulee Road♦ turn right (N) on Ninemile Creek Road, which extends about 8 mi. to 6200 ft. The shortest way to the summit is to begin hiking on the jeep track, then in ½ mi. (6600 ft) bear directly NE uphill toward the broad plateau summit area (2 mi.). The longer trail climbs N and E to the saddle (7280 ft; 4 mi.) between Joe Mills and Chopaka; from here merely hike S to the summit. Reference: *101 Hikes.*

Hurley Peak is an easy 1-mi. hike from Chopaka via the 7300-ft connecting saddle. There is a long escarpment from Chopaka and its flanks down to the Similkameen River valley, a slope over 10 mi. long related to thrust movement.

Note: The Chopaka area has been heavily overgrazed, and is subject to water contamination ATP (including Cold Spring camp).

Church Mountain Trail No. 671. Church Mountain is a prominent E-W-trending ridge between Canyon Creek and North Fork Nooksack River. It rises from an altitude of only 1000 ft above sea level in 1.5 mi. linear distance. The first climb of the mountain was made in late June 1891 by W.H. Garrett, John Lynch, W.H. Radcliffe, J.T. Shaw, Richard L. Smith, and E.T. Thomas — members of a Blaine prospecting party. The first winter ascent of Church was made by Heinz Arens and Hermann F. Ulrichs in March 1930.

Drive to the trail via East Church Road (see Mt. Baker Hwy♦). Reach the lookout site (6100 ft+) in 4 mi. A building was erected in 1928 just E of the true summit (6315 ft); the lookout, standing until 1966, was one of the most important in the Cascades. From here there is a small rock-and-heather summit (6200 ft+) to the NW, and the basin of Kidney Lakes, at about 6000 ft elevation to the N.

Copper Creek Trail No. 1276 extends from Bridge Creek Trail♦ to reach Copper Pass (6680 ft+) in 4½ mi. Maps of 1913 showed both Twisp and Copper Pass.

Copper Glance Creek Trail No. 519 begins at 12.5 mi. on Eightmile Creek Road (see Chewack River Road♦). Here is a 3.3-mi. trail to Copper Glance Lake (6080 ft+), located in a basin closely N of Sherman Peak.

Copper Ridge Trail (Copper Mountain Trail) begins on the Chilliwack River Trail♦ (4400 ft+; 5.0 mi. from the road) and follows scenic, alpine Copper Ridge, between upper Chilliwack River and upper Silesia Creek for 5 mi. to the 6260-ft lookout location. The trail continues to Copper Lake (5200 ft+) in 2 additional mi. (camping is restricted to Egg Lake and Copper Lake). An attractive easy ridge high route extends NW to Copper Mountain (7142 ft/2177 m) and can be continued to Silesia Creek (*Routes and Rocks*, pp. 11-12; see Section I, note 82).

The trail from Copper Lake continues NE along the ridge, then descends to Chilliwack River (5 mi. from the lake and 1 mi. N of Indian Creek, and meets the main trail (2300 ft).

Crater Creek Trail No. 416 leaves Eagle Lake Trail♦ at about ½ mi., then reaches Crater Lake in 3.2 mi. The upper lake (6969 ft) is ½ mi. SW.

Crater Mountain Trail. See McMillan Park-Jackita Ridge Trail♦.

Crest Trail. The section from Stehekin River Road♦ is identical to Bridge Creek Trail♦ (part of this portion may be re-routed higher).

From Harts Pass to Rainy Pass (30.2 mi.): the trail crosses Brown Bear Road No. 3739 (Meadows Campground; 6400 ft — 2.2 mi.). See Harts Pass Road♦. The first of a constant succession of fine panoramas is the high portion on the E shoulder of *Tatie Peak* (7386 ft/2251 m), a short walk from the trail, and at 7 mi. the extensive meadows of Grasshopper Pass (6720 ft+); camping. The pass is an especially broad segment of the crest which was deeply eroded by glacier ice. During the alpine phase Glacier Pass was probably a ragged col between competing cirques (Waitt, p. 74). Reach Glacier Pass (5520 ft+) at 8.2 mi. (campsite below pass at head of Brush Creek); the trail descends to the 4300-ft level in the valley of the upper Methow, then rises S to Methow Pass (19.7 mi. — 6560 ft+); camping near basin head N of pass. An easy route can be taken to Snowy Lakes Pass (6840 ft+) with its lovely high lakes. Methow and Snowy Lakes passes are strewn with perched boulders of Golden Horn granite and apparently were lowered many hundreds of ft as the Cordilleran Ice Sheet spilled from the Methow into Swamp Creek (Waitt, 1972, p. 75).

The trail continues 3 mi. to Granite Pass (6280 ft+), then 2.5 mi. to Cutthroat Pass (6800 ft+), a broad trough with perched boulders up to 15 ft in diameter. Striations add to the evidence indicating ice sheet passage from the Skagit drainage. Rainy Pass (4840 ft) is reached in 5 mi. at North Cascades Hwy♦.

Branch trails are West Fork Methow No. 480 (E) at 12.7 mi.; Mill Creek Trail No. 755 (N) at 13.7 mi.; East Creek No. 756 (N) at 14.7 mi.; Cutthroat Trail No. 483 (S) at 25.2 mi.

The Crest Trail from Harts Pass to Monument 78 on the Canadian border is 32.2 mi. (51.8 km). Monument 83 is the alternative terminus. Trail mileages are given from Harts Pass (see Harts Pass Road♦), although one can drive to the first elbow on the Slate Peak roadway (trailhead at 1.2 mi.). The trail passes Benson Basin (3.5 mi. — campsite), then passes just W and below Buffalo Pass (6520 ft) and reaches Windy Pass (6257 ft) at 4.9 mi. (camping). An alternative to Windy Pass is the old mine roadway from Barron (via the trail connection to West Fork of Pasayten River); from the pass a hike can be taken N to the summit of *Tamarack Peak* (7307 ft/2227 m).

The route descends into Windy Basin and continues to Foggy Pass (6160 ft) and Oregon Basin (6.9 mi. — campsite); *Jim Peak* 7033 ft/2144 m) is an easy short hike to the NW. The main trail crosses Jim Pass and Shaw Creek to Holman Pass (14.4 mi. — 5040 ft+); camping just W of pass. Here is junction with Devils Ridge Trail♦ (W) and Holman Creek Trail (E). Then the trail passes beneath Goat Lakes (15.4-15.7 mi.; meadow camping).

At 2.8 mi. N of Holman Pass the Crest Trail divides, the E fork crossing the ridge and contouring Rock Creek basin at about 5800 ft (under Powder Mountain); the other fork crosses the ridge at Rock Pass (6491 ft) and contours the basin at about 6200 ft. Note: Snow persists late in this basin; possible cornices and drifts. Under such conditions the lower trail is advised; a branch trail (Rock Creek) descends E to Pasayten River.

Reach Woody Pass (6624 ft) at 19.7 mi. (camping in tamaracks on minor ridge nearby). *Powder Mountain* (7714 ft/2351 m) is an easy hike along the crest 0.3 mi. S. The main trail reaches Hopkins Lake, a gem of greenish color with an escaping waterfall at 24.6 mi. (camping). At Hopkins Pass (24.9 mi. — 6122 ft) the main trail leads N and an old alternative bears NE (Chuchuwanteen Creek); camping at the pass or to E.

The route reaches Frosty Creek Trail♦ (Boundary Trail♦) E at 28.2 mi. and Castle Pass (5451 ft) at 28.4 mi. (campsite 0.5 mi. from pass).

Here Elbow Basin-Three Fools Creek branch trail no. 749 begins a route that leads to Ross Lake in 27 mi. The trail first leads to scenic Twin Buttes (6534 ft/1992 m), then drops to Big Face Creek (6.2 mi.), ascends to Elbow Basin (9.1 mi.), then descends S (see Three Fools Creek Trail♦).

The distance from Castle Pass to Monument 78 is 3.8 mi. (campsite W of monument). For continuation to Manning Provincial Park♦ see Windy Joe Mountain Trail♦ (B.C.).

Note customs requirements upon entering Canada.

Alternative route: (Frosty Pass to Monument 83) est. 10 mi. Use Frosty Creek Trail♦ (Boundary Trail♦). There is a ford at Chuchuwanteen Creek (6 mi.) and junction with Harrison Creek Trail (E) at 9 mi; campsite about 0.5 mi. N. For continuation see Monument 83 Trail♦ (B.C.).

Cutthroat Creek Trail No. 483 leaves North Cascades Hwy♦ at end of spur (4500 ft). Distance is 2 mi. to 4935-ft Cutthroat Lake (no camping) and 6 mi. to Cutthroat Pass and Crest Trail♦. In the broad trough of the pass there are perched boulders up to 15 ft diameter. Striations indicated ice sheet passage from the Skagit drainage into Cutthroat Creek. A map produced as a result of the 1895 wagon road survey called the stream Cedar Creek.

Damfino Lakes Trail No. 625. Take Canyon Creek Road (see Mt. Baker Hwy♦) 12.5 mi. to trailhead. Hike the trail 0.7 mi. to the junction with Canyon Ridge Trail. The nearby Damfino Lakes are at an elevation of 4400 ft+. One can continue E on High Divide Trail (see Excelsior Pass Trail♦).

Delancy Ridge is a cross-country route from North Cascades Hwy♦ offering scenic vistas of the Silver Star area; the highest point on the ridge is 7228 ft (long gain from valley).

Depot Creek Route (B.C.) is a possible route to the Redoubt Glacier, Silver Lake, upper Bear Creek, and Redoubt Creek basin. A clandestine trail was brushed out along Depot Creek in 1974 (with hundreds of marker tags — since removed); it crossed the Boundary illegally, bringing into focus the problem of over-impact of the fragile high country in North Cascades National Park.

The route will become less attractive with regeneration of undergrowth and possible disrepair of the Depot Creek logging road (see Chilliwack River Road♦). The trail parallels the N side of the creek through slash, then bears back to the creek; for 2 mi. the path keeps within 300 ft of the creek (there are some blowdowns and alder patches). The brushy headwall (near waterfalls) steepens at 3500 ft; rock may be slippery because of spray. Talus leads to the 4300-ft level at a small saddle; a descent leads into an open basin (camping). The route leads to the glacier at about 5700 ft. Time: 1 day or less to camp spots in basin or at ridge (about 7200 ft) on the divide with Redoubt Creek. The latter position involves the ascent of the main body of Redoubt Glacier in a SW direction; at the W end of the long ridge leading to Twin Spires are moraine-boulder areas where one can camp.

Lake fork: A route can be taken along the SW-forking stream which enters Depot Creek at 2.3 mi. from the Boundary (about 3300 ft). The lower stream course is barely incised, so not obvious at first, but at a higher level follows a narrow valley. Cross Depot Creek, then ascend the forest slope well right (NW) of the stream to avoid cliffs; when the gradient eases ascend talus; an easy talus draw leads to a lake (5280 ft+) nesting in a tight bouldery hollow. The valley continues W, mostly filled by a snowfield-glacier that extends to the divide with Bear Creek. Above the S slope of the

lake is another glacier extending to a col, also on the Bear Creek divide. A route eastward from the lake can be taken to the western edge of Depot Glacier and West Depot Glacier; the route crosses a small bench (an unmapped lake near 5500 ft), then turns across the crest of a sharp intervening ridge at timberline before traversing sharply S to the glaciers.

Desolation Peak Trail No. 746. Begin from Lightning Creek campground (see Ross Lake♦). Total distance is 6.5 mi. from Ross Lake to the 6985-ft lookout.

Desolation Peak is named for fire-swept slopes (fire of 1926). A tent lookout was built in 1929, prior to the structure of 1932.

Devils Ridge Trail No. 752. This upland trail begins at Devils Landing on Ross Lake♦ (9 mi. on lake) and in 5.5 mi. climbs to Dry Creek Pass (5840 ft+). Bear Skull shelter (6000 ft) is a short distance beyond. From here it is a 2-mi. stroll N along the Dry-Grizzly Creek ridge to the summit of *Spratt Mountain* (7258 ft/2212 m).

The high point of Devils Ridge (7330 ft) is 1 mi. NW of Devils Dome; merely hike upslope from the trail at 6300 ft when S of this summit.

At 7.8 mi. reach the site of the old *Devils Dome* lookout (6982 ft), built in the mid-1930s. The true summit is at 7400 ft (2256 m), a location that may have been the Kakoit Peak climbed by Henry Custer on September 1, 1859.

In 2 more mi. the trail reaches Skyline camp (6300 ft; water may be gone in late summer); at 11.5 mi. reach Devils Pass (6040 ft+). Here is a junction with McMillan Park-Jackita Ridge Trail♦. The continuing trail leads E to Deception Pass (5480 ft+), Sky Pilot Pass and Center Mountain Trail♦ (16.3 mi.) and Holman Pass on the Crest Trail♦.

Dewdney Trail. (B.C.) See Snass Creek Trail♦ and Skaist River Trail♦.

Dock Butte. This 5210-ft summit, about midway between Concrete on the Skagit River and Mt. Baker, is a superb viewpoint. Use road no. 3725 for 7 mi. (see Baker Lake Hwy♦) Blue Lake Road, then turn left onto no. 3770 for another 7 mi. to end (3900 ft+). Follow Blue Lake Trail No. 604 for ¼ mi., then take right fork (A) to Dock Butte; 1.5 mi. total. The final part is largely meadow (snow to midsummer here). The summit provides fine mountain panoramas and the basin between Dock Butte and Washington Monument is a refuge for elk.

Eagle Creek Trail No. 410 extends 7.3 mi. to Eagle Pass (7240 ft+) and a connection with Summit Trail♦ (6500 ft). To reach the trailhead follow Twisp River Road♦ about 15 mi., cross the bridge beyond War Creek camp and turn left on Eagle Creek Road No. 338 about 1.5 mi., then right about 1.5 mi.

Eagle Lake Trail No. 431 extends from road's end in Crater Creek (see Gold Creek Road♦) to Eagle Lake (6490 ft) in 5 mi. The trail reaches Horsehead Pass (7520 ft+) at 6.7 mi. and Summit Trail♦ in 1.6 mi. more. To reach upper Eagle Lakes (7050 ft and 7110 ft) take a ½-mi. spur trail, leaving at a junction (4.4 mi.).

East Creek Trail No. 756. From North Cascades Hwy♦ (25 mi. from Newhalem) the trail distance to Mebee Pass is 9.4 mi.

East Fork Bridge Creek Trail leaves Bridge Creek Trail♦ at Fireweed Camp and reaches Twisp Pass in 5 mi., following the route of an Indian path.

East Fork Buttermilk Creek Trail No. 420 extends from Buttermilk Butte Road (3920 ft+ — see Buttermilk Creek Road♦) to reach Hoodoo Pass (7440 ft+) in 6½ mi.

Easy Ridge Trail. Easy Ridge is a broad, mostly level-topped, steep-sided ridge that trends NW from Whatcom Peak to the Chilliwack River, a distance of about 5 mi. The broad meadowy ridge, an alpine park with small conifers, white granodiorite rock outcrops, decked with grass, heather, and ponds, provides one of the finest viewpoints in the North Cascades: the Picket Range and Chilliwack peaks are especially close. Henry Custer climbed onto Easy Ridge on August 10, 1859, during his reconnaissance mapping with the Boundary Survey, en route to Whatcom Pass. He mentioned the numerous small ponds on a "gently inclined plain of vivid green."

Begin at 9.5 mi. from road (see Chilliwack River Trail♦) (2560 ft+). Here ford the river (or use logs opposite U.S. cabin) and in 2.6 mi. ascend the trail to a saddle on Easy Ridge (5120 ft+). The old lookout site is on a knoll 1 mi. N (5640 ft).

Perfect Pass Route. Follow the ridge SE skirting almost over 6613-ft Easy Peak, then make a long descending traverse on the Baker River slope toward Perfect Pass. A bit of caution and route study are needed to cross the only obstacle on the traverse, on the SW slope of Whatcom Peak. This feature is an eroded gully (est. 5400 ft) along a volcanic dike which cuts the quartz diorite at 0.5 mi. E of Perfect Pass; make an upward traverse via ledges into the gully, then climb out on its SE side. It is recommended to rope up and belay here. Continue to traverse the long slope, then ascend easily to Perfect Pass (6240 ft+) at the W edge of the splendid Challenger Glacier. Time: 8 hours from Chilliwack River. Reference: *Routes and Rocks*, pp. 17-18; see Section I, note 82.

Mineral Mountain High Route is an alternative cross-country route to Easy Ridge. From Hannegan Pass traverse SE (keep below the glacier of Ruth Mountain) to Chilliwack Pass (4160 ft+). The slope E is brushy: traverse talus and ascend cliffy spur to round the N and E side of knob (5694 ft). Continue SE over Mineral Mountain (6781 ft/2067 m), then descend a small glacier on the E. Descend a series of benches and stairs carved by ice erosion into points; then continue to the broad saddle (4640 ft+) between Mineral and Easy Ridge. Reference: *Routes and Rocks*, pp. 19-20; see Section I, note 82. One can continue to Easy Ridge and the dike route to Perfect Pass.

Picket Pass Route is a taxing alpine traverse, one requiring competence and good equipment. Ascend Challenger Glacier to the notch (7520 ft+) between Challenger's West and Middle peaks. The opposite S side is moderately steep snow, but provides a good route downward; a little ridge trending left enables one to walk from the snow down into the basin SW of Challenger, where there is a nearly flat glacier. Note: An alternative is to cross a notch on the ridge W of the West Peak (est. 7450 ft): take a small glacier SW to near the lower end of the prominent lateral moraine S of the ice; cross the moraine and traverse a ledge eastward between cliffs to the snowfield beneath the 7520-ft+ notch.

Traverse the glacier and alp slopes below Crooked Thumb; one can descend another 800 ft to a series of slabs which lead to a campsite at about 5500 ft. The higher route traverses and descends alp slopes, talus, and snow NW of Phantom Peak. Several hours are needed to reach and climb over a small depression in a bald rock spur ridge (between two branches of Picket Creek) W of Phantom (est. 6080 ft); continue SE through a cirque on a long bouldery-snow sidehill to the Picket-Goodell Creek Pass (6000 ft+).

To descend into cliffy upper Goodell Creek, do not descend directly (or ascend if coming from the S) the cliffs beneath the pass. A better route is to ascend the divide about 300 ft vertically above and NE of the Pass (per Mt. Fury climbing route), then turn down broken ledges (right) where angle is least. Descend to snow and scree beneath the cliffs and traverse until beneath the pass. Continue down and rightward on a very steep (slippery) grass slope to the foot of the cliffy area. To reach Picket Pass, make a long traverse across talus below Mt. Fury's cliffs (at 4400 ft), then ascend the first large tree strip (500 ft higher are open slopes); bear SE toward Picket Pass (6400 ft+; good camping); then descend S across steep snow and talus of a small open bowl to a spur. Cross the spur (where it merges with steeper cliffs above) to a broad steep ramp descending S into the McMillan Creek cirque. Descend a small meadow on a ramp to a slab barrier. At the lowest meadow peninsula traverse E about 100 ft on ledges to a broad nose forming a ramp's edge; descend broken rock with cedar shrub to the lower-angle rock, rubble, snow. From below the upper glacier a broad ledge leads SE across a stream and around rocky corners to an exposed vertical walled slot; descend the slot and lower glacier remnant to a tarn (4260 ft+). Then ascend a small creek, keeping close to cliffs to minimize brush travel. Rock outcrops here are overhung by the glacier beneath Mt. Terror (serious danger). The ledge safest from falling ice debris begins just E of the creek issuing from the main rock gully to rubble slopes; the lower end of the diagonal ledge is narrow, steep, and has an alder thicket; the upper end is a good wide ramp. Make an upward traverse, then bypass gullies by climbing to snow and ice. Make a SE diagonal ascent to beneath McMillan Spire at 5600 ft, then to the pass (6320 ft+) W of Elephant Butte (see Stetattle Creek Route♦). Reference: *Routes and Rocks*, pp. 27-32; see Section I, note 82.

Eaton Lake Trail (B.C.) begins at a left spur of the Silver-Skagit Road♦ about 10.2 mi. (16.4 km) from the Trans-Canada Hwy. The trail begins on the S side of Eaton Creek. Time: 3 hours (2 mi., 3.5 km). The lake (4300 ft+) is surrounded by steep wooded slopes and slide alder on talus fans. A blazed trail continues NE to Outram Creek Road (see Trans-Canada Hwy 3◆).

Eighteenmile Creek Trail (Ghostpass Trail) (B.C.) now leaves Trans-Canada Hw 3◆ just inside the W Manning Park entrance (17 mi. from Hope) and follows the N side of the creek to Ghost Pass (5 mi. — 4600 ft+); Ghostpass Lake is closely across the divide to Sowaqua Creek (see Brigade Trail◆).

Mt. Outram Trail (Seventeenmile Creek) begins at the above start at the highway and extends to about 6500 ft on the SE slopes of Mt. Outram.

Eightmile Pass-Hidden Lake Trail No. 477. This important route into the Pasayten Wilderness begins from the end of Eightmile Creek Road (see Chewack River Road◆) and first crosses Eightmile Pass (1.6 mi.-5400 ft+) to Drake Creek (4 mi.-camping). The trail then climbs to Lucky Pass (5760 ft+) and takes a high slope traverse (old burn) above Lost River to cross to Cougar Lake (14.1 mi.) and continues to First, Middle, and Big Hidden Lakes (71-acre Big Hidden, at 17.5 mi., is 4316 ft); there is a shelter ½ mi. N of the lake. The trail continues NW from the junction with East Fork Pasayten River Trail No. 451 to Boundary Trail◆ (21.9 mi.) and on to Pasayten River Trail◆.

There is an interesting drainage derangement in Hidden Lakes valley. Ptarmigan and Johnny creeks flow NNE into the trough of the lakes, then bend abruptly SE to form Lost River, whose headwaters captured these source streams through intensive scouring by a SE-moving ice sheet (Waitt, 1972, p. 28).

Branch trails are at Drake Creek (E); Deception Creek (N) at 11 mi.; Ptarmigan Creek (S) at 15.3 mi. to Shellrock Pass; Stub Creek Trail No. 458 (E) from Middle Hidden Lake to Dollar Watch Pass (Stub Creek G.S. is an administrative site only); Tatoosh Buttes Trail No. 485 (W) to Tatoosh Buttes and Lease Creek; Middle Mountain Trail No. 462 (E) connects to Deception Creek Trail; East Fork Pasayten River Trail No. 451 (E) to Dollar Watch Pass and Larch Creek. A cross-country route to the three Johnny Lakes (est. 5 mi.) can be made from Johnny Creek (est. 12 mi. on main trail); the route is possibly brushy and difficult. Area reference: *Mountaineer*, 1977, pp. 9-10.

Elbow Lake-Lake Wiseman route. Take Loomis-Nooksack Road to near its end (see Mt. Baker Hwy◆), then Elbow Lake Trail No. 697.1 for ½ mi. To reach Lake Wiseman leave the trail and hike NW for 1.3 mi. on a moderately steep slope to the ridgetop (4900 ft+). A rocky descent leads to the lake (4100 ft+); 3 hours.

Elbow Lake (3384 ft) is reached by continuing on the trail (est. 1.5 mi.). Another route to Elbow Lake is from 10.8 mi. on the Middle Fork Nooksack Road◆ (Green Creek Trail — about 1 mi. beyond Wallace Creek). The trail crosses the river, takes Green Creek, then Hildebrand Creek (the area about the lake is very fragile); total 3 mi. Note: The valley floor of Green Creek is difficult cross-country travel. A better route to Twin Sisters Range is from Lake Wiseman: traverse

the slope of Green Creek to the "Green Creek Glacier" and Skookum Peak.

A crossing of Twin Sisters Range can be begun from near the end of Loomis-Nooksack Road; hike cross-country W along an upper W fork of the Nooksack South Fork and cross Boot Lake Pass (5600 ft+); connect with Scott Paper Road◆ at Hayden Creek.

Eureka Creek Trail No. 474 (Ferguson Lake Trail) is a connection between Middle Fork Pasayten River and Eureka Creek (see Robinson Creek-Middle Fork Pasayten Trail◆). The trail begins about 2.5 mi. N of Robinson Pass, then ascends to near Ferguson Lake and climbs over the high ridge pass SE to the S Fork of Eureka Creek. The trail descends to Eureka Creek (7 mi.) above where the river is cut into a deep gorge, then climbs N and E to the valley head and Shellrock Pass (7480 ft+); see Monument Creek Trail◆.

Freds Lake alternative route: This is more efficient in terms of altitude loss. Leave the Middle Fork at 6.8 mi. N of Robinson Pass (trail no. 471) to Freds Lake and Lake Doris, then continue directly E across the head of Eureka Creek to Shellrock Pass. Reference: *Mountaineer*, 1978, pp. 140-42.

Ewart Creek Trail (B.C.) begins at a left fork of Ashnola River Road◆; across the bridge take a narrow dirt road 2.2 mi.(cabin) and here ford Ewart Creek (find old roadway). Begin the trail along the W bank to opposite Flatiron Mountain, then at about 2.5 mi. cross E. Here is the junction with the trail to Joe Lake (see Susap Creek Trail◆).

At Mountain Goat Creek (est. 5 mi.) there is a connection with Centennial Trail◆. The valley trail continues SW in deteriorating condition (an extensive burn and many windfalls reported in upper valley). An old trail once crossed the Boundary at Scheelite Pass (probably not hard to follow). The Ewart Creek approach provides an easy approach to Lakeview Mountain, Haystack Lakes, and the western flank of Snowy Mountain. The old trail and its branches are of historic interest since they lead to old border survey campsites. It should be pointed out, perhaps for the benefit of the land administrators, that much of the high plateau country surrounding Ewart Creek is being heavily overgrazed and polluted during the summer season. The tundra grassland at the higher altitudes is extremely vulnerable to trampling and overuse. In some localities of Cathedral Provincial Park and adjacent forest lands both people and cattle are blighting the landscape in a manner that will be difficult to correct later.

Excelsior Pass Trail No. 670 (High Divide Trail). Begins on Mt. Baker Hwy◆ (1800 ft+) 8 mi. E of Glacier and extends steeply to Excelsior Pass (5300 ft+) in 4.5 mi. Here a way trail continues ¼ mi. E to Excelsior Mountain (5699 ft), then as High Divide Trail No. 630 continues E for 4.5 mi. to Welcome Pass. The High Divide Trail is planned to continue W to Church Mountain.

Damfino Lakes Trail◆ continues N from Excelsior Pass to the lakes (1 mi.), then descends to Canyon Creek Road.

Canyon Creek Trail No. 689 extends NW from Damfino Lakes and follows the ridge W to Canyon Ridge Road near the Forest boundary (at 7 mi. on the road).

Farewell-Disaster Creek Trail No. 517 leaves Chewack River Road♦ at Lake Creek (drive NW via short spur at 2800 ft). One can hike to Crystal Lake (7.2 mi.) and Kidney Lake (10 mi. — 7203 ft).

Fish Creek Trail No. 1248 extends from Moore's Point (make boat landing or hike 6½ mi. from Stehekin) to a branch at 3½ mi. The East Fork meets Summit Trail♦ in about 6 mi. and the North Fork bears NE to a similar junction in 4 mi. Fish Creek Pass (7480 ft+), above the head of the East Fork, leads to West Fork Buttermilk Creek.

Foggy Dew Creek Trail No. 417 extends from Foggy Dew Road end (see Gold Creek Road♦) to Summit Trail♦ in 8.4 mi. via Merchants Basin (6800-7200 ft) and Switchback Pass (8080 ft+) in 7½ mi. ORV's are currently allowed here.

At the 5-mi. point, Martin Creek Trail branches N and reaches Cooney Lake in 3.3 mi. At 6 mi., a short spur trail extends to Sunrise Lake (here a pass (7760 ft+) can be used to cross the divide SW of the lake).

Frosty Creek Trail No. 533 (Crest Trail♦ alternative) (Boundary Trail♦) extends W from Chuchuwanteen Creek at 1 mi. S of the Chuchuwanteen ford. See also Monument 83 Trail♦ (B.C.) and Soda Creek Trail♦.

Cross Frosty Creek on logs, then reach Frosty Lake (5343 ft) in 3.5 mi. (camping). The ridge above Frosty Pass (5.5. mi. — 6480 ft) is a nice viewpoint. Connection here with Castle Pass (0.2 mi. W).

From about 3 mi. along the trail a path leads NE to The Parks and Point 6613, a scenic high meadow area crossed by surveyors during the first Boundary Survey.

Frosty Mountain Trail. (B.C.) See Manning Provincial Park♦. The summit trail can be taken from the Lightning Lake parking lot (6 mi. to 7950-ft at summit). Also one can take the Windy Joe Mountain Trail♦, then branch W off Monument No. 78 Trail (total distance 8 mi. by this route).

Galene Lakes Trail. (B.C.) At 1.5 mi. N of the Boundary cross the Skagit River by bridge (unsafe for cars); hike N to the end of a road spur; ascend directly uphill to meet a trail at about 4000 ft on the ridge SE of Galene Creek. The lakes are between 5200 ft and 6100 ft+. Time: 4-5 hours.

Wright Peak (6700 ft+/2042 m+) is just N of the lakes; take gradual meadows and the S ridge to the top.

Gargett Mine Trail No. 676 (High Pass). Begin N on Winchester Mountain Trail♦ for 0.2 mi., then take the right fork to cross Low Pass (5600 ft+) at 1.5 mi. and reach High Pass (5920 ft+) at 2.2 mi. The trail continues 0.3 mi. to the base of The Pleiades; the Gargett Mine (5700 ft) is on Larrabee Mountain (downward to the NW). Take ice axes if the terrain is snow-covered. Note: The old trail from High Pass to Silesia Creek is abandoned.

Goat Mountain Trail No. 673 begins on Hannegan Road at 2.5 mi. (2400 ft+) — see Mt Baker Hwy♦ and leads to the old lookout area (4115 ft) using an eastern fork. The trail climbs a broad burnt slope to about 5700 ft (about 3 mi.) from where snowfields and open slopes lead to the 6721-ft western summit. See Goat Mountain.

Goat Peak Trail. From North Cascades Hwy♦ (see Methow Valley Hwy♦ and Harts Pass Road♦) turn E to Mazama, then S about 1.7 mi. on county road to Goat Creek Road No. 375. Follow the latter about 2 mi., then turn left on no. 3729 for 5 mi., then right branch no. 3735 for 3 mi. to end at a new trail on the N ridge of Goat Peak (5800 ft). The summit (7001 ft/2134 m) is about 2 mi. distant. There is a lookout station which provides an excellent vantage of the alpine peaks W of Methow River.

Goodell Creek Route (Terror Creek basin). The road leading from Newhalem (see North Cascades Hwy♦) along the E side of Goodell Creek extends about 2 mi. up the valley to a washout (800 ft); keep high and E at a gravel pit. Hike the old road tread about 3 mi., taking the obscure upper fork toward Terror Creek (the spar tree in large logging patch at 1700 ft is gone; look for cairns). Ascend the prominent, steep, forested NE-bearing spur which begins about ¼ mi. before Terror Creek (between a small creek and the gorge of Terror Creek). A blazed trail climbs steeply up the right side of this spur-ridge to a hump at est. 3000 ft, and another at 3200 ft. Continue up the steep and intermittently brushy ridge to a rockslide bench at est. 5000 ft. Contour bush left below cliffs est. ¼ mi. into a rather steep brush-talus gully which is wooded and broadens higher. Follow this gully, keeping below the cliffs on the right, to meadow benches and an obvious notch on the ridge (est. 5700 ft). Ascend a stream bed for another 200 ft, then contour on heather benches 1.5 mi. northward to the higher of two notches in the left-hand ridge (extending off a small peak to the right). From the notch (est. 6200 ft) drop 400 ft (snow) to a moraine flat, and 100 ft more to an alp campspot at large trees (huge boulder for weather protection). Time: 7-10 hours from road.

Make a long westward traverse across Terror Creek basin at about 6000 ft. From the western edge of Terror Glacier ascend W (from 6100 ft to 6400 ft) to cross The Barrier (serious scrambling). One way to cross is to take benches below the glacier to a diagonal sloping ledge which leads steeply S (a dirt gully with goat paths suggests belaying); the ledge ends at est. 6150 ft just beneath highest tree scrubs. From N of the lowest part of the divide (also N of The Chopping Block) traverse slabs westward across The Barrier, then make a short descent on a snow ramp into Crescent Creek basin (6000 ft). Note: The Barrier, which forms a long rock wall flanking the W end of Terror Glacier, is a formidable problem to cross, especially from the W because of limited visibility. One must do this crossing near the end of the glacier (as described) or by serious scrambling on the first notch below Mt. Degenhardt. Time: 12-14 hours to The Barrier.

The biotite gneiss of the Picket Range is cleanly exposed in both the cirques of Terror and Crescent creeks. This Skagit gneiss was formed by metamorphism of sedimentary and volcanic rocks about 200 m.y. ago. Many dikes of several ages and types criss-cross the gneiss. References: *Routes and Rocks*, pp. 44-45 (see Section I, note 82); *Mountaineer*, 1978, pp. 107-8.

During the first crossing here in 1931, from Mt. Degenhardt to Terror Glacier, the bergschrund at the base of the 300-ft rock cliff was a problem to cross.

The Barrier-Crescent Creek Route. Upon reaching the area of the spar tree, ascend the spur 200 ft E to above the old clearcut, then hike across the forest and brush slope to Terror Creek (cross this at about 2100 ft). Gain about 400 ft westward to reach steep forested cliffs that mark the base of The Barrier, then climb brushy cliffs (route finding needed) to where the ridgetop levels (est. 3500 ft). On the crest, travel is easy along the forest rib (The Barrier) to timberline; keep right of brush and waterfalls. When the forest thins traverse left through huckleberry bushes to a campsite (est. 5400 ft) in the small open basin beneath The Chopping Block (Pinnacle Peak). Time: 10-12 hours from road. Reference: *Mountaineer*, 1970, p. 102. Note: One can hike the open slabs of The Barrier beyond the cirque, toward Mt. Degenhardt.

To reach Crescent Creek basin make an easy climb of 1000 ft to the saddle right (N) of The Chopping Block; then descend a steep snow slope on a diagonal (300 ft) into the basin; small camp spots exist near the tree line or on benches.

After the traverse of the basin one can ascend the S side of the Himmelhorn-Ottohorn notch on steep snow and some loose rock. Descend 200 ft on the opposite N side, where the glacier firn is very steep and crevassed (crampons). Cross W onto rock to avoid a schrund, then descend the rock to where a rappel is made into a moat. Descend the glacier some distance, then traverse N to the base of Frenzelspitz. Descend the divide to its N (one rappel en route) to Picket Pass.

In 1970 an 11-day traverse was made by Carla Firey, Joan Firey, David Knudson, and Peter Renz, taking this route. The traverse continued via Picket-Goodell divide, Pioneer Ridge, Jasper Pass, Mt. Despair, Triumph Pass, and Thornton Lakes.

Hanging Lake Trail. (B.C.) From Sapper Park at the end of Chilliwack River Road♦ (S end of lake) the trail follows the river bank S, then steeply climbs to the lake (4480 ft+; 2.5 km); the trail is closely N of the Boundary. One can continue around Hanging Lake to the upper lake (some brush) and to the area of Middle Peak and Mt. Lindeman. The Canadian survey party in the season of 1908 called falls below the lake "Bridal Veil." Several earlier Boundary Survey parties had visited the lake during vista work and to place border monuments on the divide.

Hannegan Pass Trail No. 674 is a historic trail route, continuing on to Chilliwack River Trail♦. The pass was named for Tom Hannegan, the State Road Commissioner, by Banning Austin during a cross-Cascade road survey in 1896, although Henry Custer had visited it during the first Boundary Survey. Geologists Smith and Calkins visited the pass in 1901; their journals discuss the lava and breccias of the rock and their map suggests the large size of the glacier on Ruth Mountain. The trail crossing to Whatcom Pass and Boundary Ranger Station on Skagit River was built before 1913.

Begin at the end of Ruth Creek Road (see Mt. Baker Hwy♦ — Hannegan Road) and in 4 mi. reach Hannegan Pass (5066 ft) — no camping; one can camp at road's end at 3.5 mi. Note: The E side of upper Ruth Creek basin regularly receives avalanches in the spring season. There are fine ski touring opportunities near the pass and on Ruth Mountain, but one should be aware of possible avalanche dangers.

Hannegan Peak (6186 ft/1886 m) is a hike from the pass. Tertiary volcanics with intricate flow patterns and intrusions are very visible on the W side of the peak, which was apparently climbed by Banning Austin and R.M. Lyle in 1893.

Mamie Pass (5200 ft+) can be reached by a gully and rock scrambling route from the road end. A cross-country trek is moderately steep and rocky, but quite feasible. A mining trail which once crossed Mamie Pass from Lone Jack Mine to Silesia Creek was much used by 1897-99 prospectors.

Heart Lake Route. A possible approach to the southern end of Twin Sisters Range is via this scenic 15-acre lake located in a subalpine basin. Take Loomis-Nooksack Road (see Baker Lake Hwy♦) about 11 mi., and turn left on no. 3724 to its end in est. 3 mi. (2500 ft). Hike W through timber to the outlet stream (0.5 mi.), then follow the stream 1.7 mi. to Heart Lake (4100 ft). Cross-country travel is not difficult.

Heather Trail (Three Brothers Mountain) (Alpine Meadows Trail). (B.C.) See Manning Provincial Park♦.

Begin from parking lot at end Blackwell Peak Road. The trail passes closely W of the summit points of *Three Brothers Mountain* (7453 ft/2272 m) between 9 and 13 km. Camping at Buckhorn (4.6 km), Four Brother; shelter at 13.4 km. The trail continues over Nicomen Ridge and drops to meet Grainger Creek route at Nicomen Lake (lake and camp at 1.6 km below ridge) 14 mi. (23.6 km) from road.

Other trails: at 1.6 km N of hwy crossing at Sunday Creek a road climbs to 5000 ft on ridge and a trail leads up *Friday Mountain* (6400 ft/1951 m).

Near the E Park entrance a trail near Bonnevier Creek can be used to join Heather Trail near Big Buck Mountain (21.7 km).

Horseshoe Basin (Iron Gate Trail) (Boundary Trail No. 533♦). Horseshoe Basin is a roughly E-W elongated area of partly undissected upland without sharp alpine summits. This plateau upland, with more abrupt margins, has a subdued topography, occupied in the past by ice which has left lakes and moraines. In the basin are various pre-granitic metamorphosed rocks — such as schists, quartzites, and gneisses — well exposed to view; felsenmeer (rock seas) are much in evidence on ridges near the basin. Horseshoe Pass is about 7100 ft between Horseshoe Creek and Long Draw fork of Toats Coulee in the center of the basin.

From the end of middle fork of Toats Coulee Road♦ (Iron Gate Camp) reach Sunny Camp in 3.6 mi. and Sunny Pass (4.1 mi. — 7120 ft+) and the tundra meadowland of Horseshoe Basin (4.6 mi.). The old Tungsten Road drops left and the trail contours right to the basin; Cougar Camp (6960 ft+) at 5½ mi., is near the center. From here one can hike up

Pick Peak (7620 ft/2323 m), *Horseshoe Mountain* (8000 ft/ 2438 m), *Arnold Peak* (8076 ft/2462 m), and *Armstrong Peak* (8106 ft/2471 m).

The main trail continues W to Tungsten Mine and Cathedral Pass (as Boundary Trail♦).

Horseshoe Basin (Albert Camp Trail No. 375). From Loomis take Toats Coulee Road♦ 10 mi. to a N (right) fork, leading about 5 mi. to Fourteenmile Campground. From here the trail leads to Albert Camp (6960 ft+) and Sunny Pass (7120 ft+), and at 8.5 mi. joins Boundary Trail♦ at the edge of Horseshoe Basin.

Horton Butte Trail can be taken from Fish Creek to the 6834-ft (2083 m) summit of the butte (trail no. 1250) and connects to the Summit Trail♦. A branch trail leads E to Surprise Lake (6143 ft).

Jackass Pass Trail connects Hozomeen Campground (see Silver-Skagit Road♦) with Lightning Creek Trail♦. The initial rise is steep. After leveling at 2700 ft it reaches a junction (3 mi.): Hozomeen Lake is ¾ mi. N on a side trail (camping and fires); Willow Lake is on the main trail, reached in 2 mi. (shelter, camping, fires).

Jack Mountain Trail No. 737. This steep 3-mi. trail begins just beyond Ruby Creek barn on Ross Lake East Bank Trail♦. The route becomes a meadow path for another mi. to about 6000 ft on the SW slope of Jack Mountain; an old campsite is "Little Jack."

Keep Kool Trail No. 699 leaves Twin Lakes Road (see Mt. Baker Hwy♦) at 2.3 mi. (3050 ft). The trail climbs steeply to a heather-huckleberry meadow area. Continue on path NW uphill and through ponded benches and hilly meadow terrain to the broad saddle (5440 ft+) W of Yellow Aster Butte; est. 3 mi. The area of the saddle is pleasant meadow terrain with many small ponds and smoothed rock bosses, a wildflower mecca (camping). Many quartz veins form impressive outcrops on glaciated rock surfaces.

One can hike SW about 2 mi. to Welcome Pass, along a route for a possible (unnecessary) High Divide Trail.

Yellow Aster Butte (6145 ft/1873 m). From the meadows SSW of the Butte ascend heather slopes directly to the central saddle. From here both the highest (N) summit, and the grassy-knob S summit are hikes. The N summit is a minor rock horn with an overhang on the N. The Buttes are composed of a grey phyllite resting on a large slice of basement Yellow Aster Complex imbricated with rocks of the Chilliwack Group; the N summit is entirely the Y.A. rock. Reference: *Mountaineer,* 1916.

Lake Ann. From Austin Pass (see Mt. Baker Hwy♦) follow trail dropping E into basin of Swift Creek. From junction with Swift Creek Trail (2½ mi.) the way begins to climb 900 ft in 1½ mi. to the lake. Blueberries in season, and views any time.

Lake Creek-Ashnola River Trail No. 500. This through trail begins at the end of 2-mi. Lake Creek spur no. 3801 (3162 ft) from Chewack River Road♦. Reach Black Lake (3982 ft) at 4.2 mi. (this 66-acre lake is the largest in the Pasayten Wilderness). Reach junction (W) with Three

Prong Creek Trail No. 516 at 6.4 mi. and junction with Diamond Point Trail No. 514 at 9.6 mi. (one can hike up the stream to Fox Lakes — 6697 ft and 6785 ft).

The main trail reaches Ashnola Pass (6200 ft+) at 11.8 mi., Peepsight Lake Trail (E) at 13.7 mi., Spanish Creek Trail No. 503 (E) at 17.4 mi., and Boundary Trail♦ at 18.9 mi. Peepsight Lake (7059 ft) is at the head of Ashnola River. See also Ashnola River Trail♦.

Larch Creek Trail No. 502. See Billy Goat-Larch Creek Trail♦.

Libby Creek Trail No. 415 extends from Mission Peak Road at 3893 ft (see Libby Creek Road♦) to Libby Lake (7618 ft) in 5.3 mi.

Lightning Creek Trail No. 733. The deep canyon of Lightning Creek and its main branches have been carved by both glacial and stream action. The section of the upper valley between the trail and Lightning Lakes in British Columbia is very brushy and rough, and not advised for travel.

The route begins at the dock at Lightning Creek (see Ross Lake♦; hike or use boat). The trail rises 1000 ft, then levels above the creek; at 3.8 mi. make a footlog crossing (Deerlick Camp), then hike 2.8 mi. upstream to junction with Upper Freezout Trail (note: latter extends about 5 mi.). A bridge crosses to Nightmare Camp on the W bank; then Willow Lake (2853 ft) is reached in 2 mi. In 2 mi. W a ¾-mi. spur trail forks to Hozomeen Lake (2823 ft). From the fork the road end at Hozomeen Campground is reached in 3 mi. via Jackass Pass. See Silver-Skagit Road♦ for road approach.

Camping is permitted at Lightning, Deerlick, Nightmare, Willow Lake, Hozomeen Lake, Hozomeen camp.

Lightning Lakes Trail. (B.C.) See Manning Provincial Park♦. This is a unique chain of lakes, connected by a stream to the Similkameen drainage, and at the opposite direction nearly feeding to upper Lightning Creek (Washington State) through an almost level 3800-ft+ trough. It has been speculated that upper Lightning Creek probably drained E at one time, but extensive downcutting through a pass just W of Thunder Lake has reversed the drainage. Stream piracy probably was accelerated by Pleistocene meltwaters.

The hike begins at the parking lot 2.4 km from Nature House (Gibson Pass Road). Boats are permitted on the lakes (no motors). Reach Flash Lake (3.2 km), Strike Lake (6.4 km), and Thunder Lake (12.9 km). Travel beyond is not recommended. In boundary mapping days the lakes were more appropriately called Quartet Lakes.

Little Beaver Creek Trail. Little Beaver Creek, one of the largest streams of the region, meanders down a wide U-shaped, densely forested valley which was deeply ice-scoured to the level of the lower steep cliffs. When these taper back at the Pleistocene ice maximum occasional hanging tributaries (Perry, Redoubt, Pass creeks) enter from the N. The trail extends from a landing on Ross Lake to Whatcom Pass in 17.5 mi. Campsites where fires are permitted are Little Beaver, Perry Creek (shelter — 4.6 mi.), Stillwell — 11.4 mi. (shelter closed to camping to allow vegetation to recover; campsites have been relocated S across the creek along trail to Beaver Pass), and Twin Rocks — 13.9 mi.; no camping at Whatcom Pass. The final 3 mi. gains 2200 ft (56 switchbacks) to the 5206-ft pass. For trail continuation see Chilliwack River Trail♦. The junction with Big Beaver Creek Trail♦ is at Stillwell (12 mi.).

Perry Creek Route. There was a trail into this hanging valley in early Forest Service days, but it is now vanished. However, the route is mostly in open forest, with only huckleberry undergrowth. Begin the route at about 5 mi., on the W side of Perry Creek. Pass the waterfalls near the creek; continue high in timber where avalanches have created a windfall zone, then bear into the nearly level hanging valley. The best travel is in the forest near the W side of the stream; later use occasional talus toes which lead to the meadow at the valley head (about 4200 ft). To cross the high SW ridge of Mt. Spickard to Depot Creek cirque, ascend N via talus gullies and a cliff band, then a small glacier to a high ridge saddle (8000 ft+) 0.4 mi. SW of Mt. Spickard. There is a small glacier on the opposite W flank, easy of descent.

This crossing is not technically difficult, but does involve laborious talus, some easy scrambling, and glacier travel.

Pass Creek Route. Experience has shown this to be a possible, but not easy route to the high country. The best beginning from the trail is up a cedar grove 0.2 mi. E of Pass Creek; gravels and a stream channel lead to the first obvious gully E of the creek gorge. A continuing cliffy brush route leads to a spur crest (old burn); the route continues on a westward traverse below cliffs to a 5200-ft corner above the creek. The objective — gaining the open basin W of Peak 7732 — involves climbing and traversing through cedar and small cliffs to reach the basin. The snowy open upper basin, which has a small lake and glacier, permits an easy crossing to the head of Indian Creek. Note: The upper half of Pass Creek valley has also been done on the W side, but rough travel also reported. References: *Mountaineer*, 1973, p. 30; *Routes and Rocks*, pp. 37-38; see Section I, note 82.

Liumchen Ridge Trail. (B.C.) The best approach ATP is from Liumchen Creek Road♦, then take the East Fork which climbs onto Liumchen Ridge; the trail begins uphill at about 4100 ft, climbs to the ridge crest at Point 5556, then continues S (see Liumchen Mountain); branches bear SE to Church Mountain and SW to Liumchen Lake (4500 ft).

Because of possible road closures it is well to have another option. One can meet the trailhead by taking the road as per Tamihi Creek, then continuing W about 1.5 mi. to a logging road bending acutely SE. This climbs a series of "S" bends, generally bearing E (currently a washout at 3000 ft), then swinging W toward the far ridge.

Lost River Trail. See Monument Creek Trail♦.

Lucky Four Mine Trail. (B.C.) See Jones Lake Road♦, which is the standard approach to the peaks at the eastern end of the Cheam Range. Reference: Annual Report, Minister of Mines, 1953.

Hike blocked roadway (3300 ft) to end of last switchback (4100 ft), then find trail markers rightward through slash to the old trail (built about 1915), which makes a traversing climb to a campsite on a little spur near timberline under Conway Peak (5500 ft/1675 m). The trail continues rightward and up through boulders to "Timberline Ridge," then traverses the ridge to Lucky Four Mine, which is close to the glacier of Foley Peak (est. 6300 ft, 3.8 mi./6 km).

Manning Provincial Park. (B.C.) See Roads. Also Heather Trail♦, Lightning Lakes Trail♦, Skyline Trail♦. Reference: 40th Report, Okanagan Historical Society (1976), pp. 124-35.

Martin Creek Trail No. 429 leaves Eagle Lake Trail♦ at 2.3 mi. (5700 ft) and can be taken 8 mi. to Cooney Lake and the Foggy Dew Creek Trail♦. A branch trail can be taken 1 mi. to Martin Lakes, nested in the high basin NE of Martin Peak.

McAlester Creek Trail connects Bridge Creek Trail♦ at Fireweed Camp with McAlester Lake and Rainbow Creek Trail♦ (3½ mi.).

McGregor Mountain Trail No. 1238 leaves the Stehekin River Road♦ at High Bridge Ranger Station (1600 ft) and extends about 7½ mi. to the high basin fringed with western larch; then about ½ mi. of scramble-hiking leads to the rocky summit. Coon Lake, a shallow lake with a beaver lodge, is first reached; the trail then ascends through a dry ponderosa belt, then amid a wetter forest and timberline species (Heaton Camp is at 7200 ft).

McMillan Park-Jackita Ridge Trail No. 738. The usual start for this high route is Panther Creek bridge on North Cascades Hwy♦; take the 3.3 mi.-connection from Ruby Creek bridge. A shorter route to the trail beginning ATP depends on the existence of a log across Canyon Creek (cables also cross Ruby Creek W of here): leave the highway at an open area 3.4 mi. E of Panther Creek, where a log crossing of Granite Creek leads to a trail downstream (the Canyon Creek log may be just E of the old guard station).

From the Granite-Canyon Creek junction (mileages begin here) the trail climbs steeply to McMillan Park-Crater Mountain junction (3.7 mi. — 5280 ft). The trail continues to Devils Park at 7.1 mi. (shelter — 5840 ft+), then winds N along Jackita Ridge to reach Anacortes Crossing (13.2 mi.) and Devils Pass (15.2 mi. — 5800 ft+); there is a shelter 0.5 mi. E of the pass. Devils Ridge Trail♦ extends W to Ross Lake and E to Holman Pass.

Crater Mountain Trail bears left at the McMillan Park junction to reach Crater Lake in 0.7 mi. (5800 ft+); just before the lake a 1.5-mi. trail climbs E to an old lookout site. From the lake a 2.5-mi. path and scramble route leads W to the former lookout station on Crater's higher summit (see Crater Mountain). Jerry Lakes (5930 ft and 5900 ft+) are N of the mountain: one can hike from the trail beyond the lake to the 7160-ft+ pass between the two main summits of Crater Mountain, then make a leftward traversing descent of Jerry Glacier (ice axes and rope).

Methow River Trail No. 480 extends from end of Rattlesnake Campground Road (¾-mi. spur no. 3700 at 8.7 mi. from Mazama junction; see Harts Pass Road♦) to reach the Crest Trail♦ in 8 mi. Horseheaven Camp (4550 ft) is reached in ½ mi. from the junction. This valley has commonly been called West Fork of Methow River.

The Azurite Pass Trail begins at about 9 mi., and extends 2½ mi. to the pass (6680 ft+). This is an old trail, used long by miners.

The trail to Mebee Pass (6480 ft+) begins at about 9½ mi. and reaches the pass in 3½ mi.

Branch trails may be built up Cataract Creek and up Golden Creek to Golden Horn Lakes.

Mill Creek Trail. See Canyon Creek Trail♦.

Monument Creek Trail No. 484 (Lost River-Monument Creek-Ptarmigan Creek Trail). To the Indians Lost River was "Apiow" — a term that signified the river enters a canyon wall. The river gorge, with a 3400-ft base altitude, is a unique wilderness canyon without trail.

Begin the route off Harts Pass Road♦ at 6.7 mi. from Mazama junction. After following Lost River 3.6 mi. the trail crosses Eureka Creek, then sharply ascends the dry ridge and slopes SW of Pistol Peaks (no water along ridge in summer), then crosses Pistol Pass (10.7 mi. — est. 7100 ft). Lake of the Woods can be reached by path beyond the pass.

The trail then descends to Monument Creek; along its cascades are fine examples of flat jointing in granite. After the creek crossing (15.1 mi.) the trail rises to near Shellrock Pass (junction with trail no. 484A to the pass and Eureka Creek at 17.8 mi.), then continues over Butte Pass (18.3 mi.) and down Ptarmigan Creek to Hidden Lakes (25 mi.) to meet Eightmile Pass-Hidden Lakes Trail♦.

Monument 78 Trail. (B.C.) See Windy Joe Mountain Trail♦. The total distance from the highway in Manning Provincial Park♦ to the border monument is 6.5 mi. (10.5 km).

Monument 83 Trail (Chuwanten or Chuchuwanteen Trail) (B.C.) See Manning Provincial Park♦ (Roads). The route begins near Hampton Creek Campground, 43.3 mi. (69.7 km) from Hope (3.2 km E of Headquarters) as a gated jeep roadway and extends 16.1 km (about 10 mi.) to Monument 83 on the International Boundary, where there is a lookout tower (6520 ft+). A continuation E can be made via the Centennial Trail♦.

The Crest Trail♦ (Alternative) leads in 3½ mi. (5.6 km) to Chuchuwanteen Creek (called Chuwanten in Canada); the ford here can be difficult in high water. There is good camping ½ mi. S of the Boundary and there is a cabin at the Frosty Creek-Chuchuwanteen Trail junction (4600 ft).

Note: Every person crossing the Boundary must report directly to the nearest Customs House in the country entered.

Mt. Baker Trail No. 677 is a historic trail built from Glacier in 1911 to promote the Mt. Baker marathons, followed by the construction of Kulshan Cabin (4700 ft) by the Mt. Baker Club in 1925. The trail distance from Glacier Creek Road (see Mt. Baker Hwy♦) is now only 2 mi. The cabin sleeps 24. The continuing path to the Coleman Glacier, whose snout at 4100 ft is about 0.5 mi. NE, begins by crossing a small stream leftward; a left fork extends to

Survey Rock (glacier views) and the climbing path extends uphill via The Hogback to the glacier margin at 6000 ft (1.5 mi.). There are some level tent sites here.

Nearby Heliotrope Ridge offers hiking treks, viewpoints, and at the right time, wildflower exhibits including mountain heliotrope (valerian family), for which the ridge was named.

A minor trail from the main route forks left (Harrison's Trail) just after crossing Grouse Creek, and traverses to Kulshan (Heliotrope) Creek, and Glacier Creek (bridge gone ATP — 3700 ft); fording either stream can be dangerous, and discretion must be used. The best plan is to follow a path along Glacier Creek to near the Coleman Glacier snout, then cross where the stream is more braided.

Mt. Cheam Trail. (B.C.) Take Trans-Canada Hwy♦ to Bridal Falls exit (1 mi. E of Rosedale overpass). Drive 0.2 mi. E along Popkum frontage roadway; at 10500 Popkum Road (building sign) a dirt roadway turns uphill: the first section (to 4300 ft) is quite steep and may not be passable for standard cars. The roadway (orange markers) begins by climbing to cross Bridal Veil Creek at 1500 ft, then left at a fork, to re-cross the creek at 2500 ft. At the next intersection keep right and eventually reach into a broad bowl (Killarney Valley); find the steep trail at 10 km, near road's end.

In spring and early summer the upper trail slopes can have slide danger, and the exposed SW summit ridge may be corniced. The proximity of the summit height (6913 ft) to the Fraser Valley provides a truly spectacular vista. The total distance is 14.5 km (allow 12 hours r.t. from valley).

Mt. Elk-Mt. Thurston area. (B.C.) These are two minor subalpine summits at the western end of the Fraser-Chilliwack River divide.

Approach: Begin at the gravel pit by Elk View Road at 7.5 mi. S of Bailey Road. Reach this by Prest Road (Chilliwack) on Trans-Canada Hwy♦; turn S and in 2.5 mi. meet Bailey Road, then in 0.3 mi. turn E and S on Elk View Road; 7.5 mi. to gravel pit. Hike along a meadowy ridge to Elk (4700 ft/1433 m; 2½ hours) and Thurston (5335 ft/1626 m, 4 hours).

One can continue to Mt. Mercer (5 more km); see Mt. Mercer Trail♦. The area can offer fine ski touring opportunities. See also Mt. Thurston Road (Chilliwack River Road♦).

Mt. Ford Trail. (B.C.) Mt. Ford (4600 ft+/1402 m) is on the Foley Creek-Chilliwack River divide, and offers a nice viewpoint. From Chilliwack River Road♦ at 18.6 mi. on the road a jeep trail leads 4 km to the summit.

Mt. Laughington Trail. (B.C.) Logging has obliterated the old trail from the lower part of the road system ATP. Currently it is best to take the Airplane Creek Road (see Chilliwack River Road♦) to the third switchback, then follow it left to logging area (may need to hike). The old trail (marked) leads N to the 5800-ft+ (1768 m+) summit. The upper terrain is pleasant hiking. Time: 3 hours.

Mt. Mercer Trail. (B.C.) From Mt. Thurston fork of Chilliwack River Road♦ the trail extends to the summit (5500

ft+/1676 m). The upper slopes of the mountain are gentle, and provide good ski touring terrain. The summit is 0.5 mi. from the roadway, the trail leaving where the road reaches the ridge W of the summit.

Mt. Rexford Routes. (B.C.) Take Chilliwack River Road♦ and Nesakwatch Creek branch for 5.7 mi. (about 3.5 mi. beyond the main creek crossing) to where a spur turns sharply uphill (est. 2900 ft). The trail to the meadows NW of Mt. Rexford is designated by aluminum markers on right. A trail connection also leaves from the main road at 6.0 mi. (on uphill side). Follow trail markers steeply E to timberline (campsite near 5900 ft; 4 km); possible camp and water at "Y" gully en route. Also see Mt. Rexford.

The Rexford E-side approach via Centre Creek valley begins from a road spur, leaving the main road westward at 2600 ft. Take the spur to the hairpin at 3200 ft, then find a cross-country route S to a camp area at about 4000 ft.

The Illusion Peaks cross-country route begins off the same spur, but continue on the zigzags uphill, finally staying left to 4800-ft level. Here a climbing path bears SW upslope.

Mt. Stoneman Route. (B.C.) Take Silver-Skagit Road♦ and Sowerby Creek branch. Begin at high road spurs W of the mountain; probably can drive S fork of road to W of mountain. This is an easy but not especially rewarding trip to the 5600-ft+ (1706 m+) summit via the SW slopes. Hike road spurs E as necessary, and then take open ridge NE to top.

Noisy Creek Trail No. 609 begins on the S shore of Baker Lake (at the mouth of Noisy Creek); it is best to use one of the six boat launch sites on Baker Lake (see Baker Lake Hwy♦); or one can rent a boat at Tarr's Resort — 22.5 mi. on the road. One can also ford Baker River (26.5 mi. on road), then take a trail (poor ATP) about 2.5 mi. along the lake.

The entire route in the valley of Noisy Creek is in dense low-altitude forest. The trail along the creek crosses in 1 mi.; one can continue another 2 mi. (trail remnants, some brush), then take a taxing eastward climb up a long forested ridge that reaches the Bacon Creek divide closely SW of Green Lake. The lower portion of the route will have heavy timber and undergrowth, but the final mi. is moderately open subalpine terrain, with increasingly better travel. To reach Mt. Hagan and Berdeen Lake follow the divide northward; the high country near the lake, on the SE slope of Hagan, offers easy travel. Exposed rock formations here are both the Chilliwack Batholith and the phyllite of Mt. Shuksan. For details on the high route from Mt. Watson to Mt. Blum see *Mountaineer*, 1967, pp. 119-23, Bacon Peak and Mt. Blum.

Nooksack Trail No. 680 (Nooksack cirque). See Mt. Baker Hwy♦-Hannegan Road and branch no. 404. The trail ends at the river bank in about 1 mi. The Nooksack North Fork here has been eroded to base level and continues to be a large source of alluvium and glacial debris. The stream is braided and the valley floor deeply buried.

The hike continues about 3 mi. over cobblestones along the E side of the valley; sometimes paths can be taken into the bush from the gravel bars to avoid wading (usually some braids must be forded). A great boulder in the ground

moraine (est. 3500 ft, 4 hours) E of the main valley provides protected shelter for 12 persons.

The National Park Service should realize the wilderness value of such an unusual river-bar trek to a great glacial cirque in the North Cascades, and abandon continuing proposals to build a trail the entire distance, despite the fact that high meltwater may make some stream wading dangerous.

North Creek Trail No. 413 extends from Twisp River Road♦ (3662 ft) to North Lake (5760 ft+) in 4.6 mi. A path continues W to mines at the 6600-ft level. Some early mining maps showed the lake's name as Glacier Lake.

A branch trail at about 3¼ mi. crosses Abernathy Pass to Cedar Creek; the trail is faint, but the route is easy.

A good cross-country route exists to the southern portion of Kangaroo Ridge: leave the trail at the pond (est. 4 mi.), then hike uphill to the divide saddle (6720 ft+). An easy traverse on the Cedar Creek slope of about ¾ mi. leads to good campsites on the flank of the ridge.

Oakes Peak Route. See Bacon Creek Road♦. The trek is a rewarding summit viewpoint (5696 ft/1736 m), but not recommended as a continuation to Triumph Pass.

Oval Creek Trail No. 410A leaves Eagle Creek Trail♦ in 1½ mi., and can be followed to Fish Creek Pass and Oval Lakes. Distance to the high lakes varies from 7 to 9 mi. Reach Summit Trail♦ at 8.7 mi. (6800 ft).

Pacific Crest Trail: See Crest Trail♦.

Pasayten River Trail. (B.C.) See Pasayten River Road♦. On the roadway about 0.8 km from the Boundary meet Centennial Trail♦. Here a trail loop extends to the Boundary; an old brushy area is probably now cleared out with good trail connection to the U.S. side. Pasayten cabin (3900 ft) is just beyond the junction with the East Fork. See also West Fork Pasayten River Trail♦.

Trapper Lake Trail has a connection E at 1.8 km N of the Border (see Pasayten River Area Trails♦).

Pasayten River Trail. See West Fork Pasayten Trail♦ and Robinson Creek-Middle Fork Pasayten Trail♦. See also Pasayten River Trail♦ (B.C.).

Pasayten River Area Trails. (B.C.) Maps: Ashnola 92 H/1 West and Princeton 92 H/SE. Similkameen Falls-Trapper Lake Trail (15 mi./24 km) begins just S of the bridge at the falls. Reach by a S turn off Trans-Canada Hwy 3♦ (about 56.5 mi./95.5 km from Hope), then drive through the old resort (private property) and camp to the bridge; ask permission to park in campground. At 3 mi. on the trail cross old logging road and follow skid track; at 3½ mi. take right fork to avoid swamp and at 4½ mi. continue southward. There is a good camp at Calcite Creek (6½ mi.). The trail climbs through an old burn and lodgepole forest to 6800 ft (9.7 mi.) in alpine terrain (camping). Placer Lake (5400 ft+) is a detour 1 mi. N.

At 12½ mi. the trail reaches 7200 ft at the upper area of *Flattop Mountain* (7430 ft/2265 m, 1.7 mi. NNW of Trapper Lake), a good viewpoint. A downgrade to the S leads to Trapper Lake (6400 ft+) — camping. From the lake there are connecting trails to Ashnola River via Easygoing Creek, to Border Lake (S), Pasayten River (W) and Monument 83. There is a scenic hiking route SW to Bristleback Ridge.

The trail from Trapper Lake reaches Ashnola River Road◆ in 7½ mi. (see Centennial Trail◆). The trail to Border Lake (6900 ft+) is 6 mi. long; this lake is only 0.4 mi. from the border at Monument 90, and a path continues across to Park Pass. The trail from the S slope of Flattop Mountain goes N to Placer Mountain, where a jeep road crosses the divide from Ashnola River. In 1858-60 the entire area of these trails was explored by the Boundary Survey party, who occupied a number of high points for triangulation.

Pasayten River-Trapper Lake Trail (B.C.) (12 mi.): See Pasayten River Road◆ for route to Pasayten River bridge (the bridge crossing Peeve Creek is about ¼ mi. farther on the road). A junction is met in ¼ mi. from the latter bridge; various routes can be taken to meet this trail. Take right fork and follow logging side road to old log landing ¼ mi. from junction; shortly bear SW (cross-country) to meet the trail.

Note: Here a branch goes ⅜ mi. NW to the suspension bridge across the Pasayten (see Centennial Trail◆).

Bear S through balsam, spruce, and lodgepole forest into the "Bunkerhill" burn (crosses a logging road that is an alternative from the junction ¼ mi. from the Peeve Creek bridge). The trail winds upslope and continues to the U.S. Border, shortly reaching Monument 87. Cross Peeve Creek (est. 4½ mi.) and then reach Monument 88 (where the 1970 fire began). After leaving the border follow up a fork of Peeve Creek and generally bear NE and N to a major trail junction at 11 mi. (trail to Border Lake and a bypass of Trapper Lake). One mi. to camping at N end of Trapper Lake.

Pierce Lake Trail (B.C.) begins 1 mi. E of Slesse Creek bridge (1200 ft) just W of Pierce Creek (see Chilliwack River Road◆). Drive ½ mi. SE on rough road to steeper grade, where trail begins on left. Cross Pierce Creek at 3200 ft and pass E of Pierce Lake (4500 ft+, 8 km) to an old cabin 400 ft higher. To reach the upper lake climb SE toward cliff; an old mine trail traverses a ledge S to lake outlet (5800 ft+). Pioneer geologist Reginald A. Daly mentioned the three tandem cirques, two of them occupied by rock-basin lakes, en route to the gold property exploited by G.O. Pierce at the turn of the century.

Pine Creek offers a cross-country route from North Cascades Hwy◆ (3600 ft) at Lone Fir Camp to Granite Pass (a new trail may be built in the valley).

Price Lake Route. From the end of Nooksack North Fork Road (see Mt. Baker Hwy◆-Hannegan Road) descend to the old parking lot; walk 100 yards beyond the road, then cross the river on a log jam just downstream from Price Creek outlet. Stay on the right side of the creek for about ¼ mi. (to toe of hill) until a box-shaped canyon is reached. Cross a large log to the left (E) side of the creek, then climb a steep bank; follow steep game trails in open forest to the moraine above Price Lake (the route here generally keeps close to the creek gorge). The water of Price Lake (3895 ft) is heavily silted from glacial input; bypass the lake on its E.

An alternative start is to follow the trail nearly ¼ mi., then hike through forest to ford the river above Price Creek's outlet. The ascent is made left of the creek, first keeping in open forest, then farther away when the canyon forms (later hike about 200 ft above the stream and continue to the moraine).

Note: The best approach to Price Glacier is via the lake, rather than Nooksack Arm, once used via the long gully from the river valley.

Prince Creek Trail No. 1255 begins on Lake Chelan (boat stop), then branches E on the middle fork to pass Cub Lake (5200 ft); shelter. The trail intersects with Summit Trail◆ at 11 mi. (6600 ft), then continues past Boiling Lake (6920 ft+) to the divide at Horsehead Pass (7520 ft+). Branch routes can be taken to Star Lake, Surprise Lake, or Bernice Lake. Prince Creek's N fork has a 2.4-mi. connection trail (no. 1254) to the Summit Trail◆ (named for a horse named Prince who in 1886 fell descending to Lake Chelan). The trail is closed to ORV travel from Lake Chelan, but unfortunately open from Cub Lake to the Crest Trail and Horsehead Pass.

Post Creek Trail (B.C.) is part of the Centennial Trail◆. See Chilliwack River Road◆, Radium Creek Road. Just before reaching the lake (about 25 mi.) begin the trail up the E side of Post Creek. The trail soon crosses to the W side and continues to Lindeman Lake (2700 ft+, 2 mi.) and past Greendrop Lake (3300 ft+, 6 mi.). Time: 2½ hours. A cat track continues along the N side of Hicks Creek to Silver-Skagit Road◆ (11 mi.).

Purple Creek Trail No. 1246 extends from Stehekin to Purple Pass (7.4 mi., 6880 ft+, 57 switchbacks) and War Creek Pass (7.8 mi., 6760 ft+). The name is for W.F. Purple, an 1882 Stehekin settler. Camping at Lake Juanita, between the two passes; here is the junction with Summit Trail◆ and Boulder Creek Trail◆. A spur path leads N to Boulder Butte, a former fire lookout.

Radium Creek Trail. (B.C.) See Chilliwack Lake Road◆, Radium Creek Road. Continue the abandoned road to new trail markers. The path bears S from above the road to Radium Lake (cabin; 4800 ft+, 5.5 km). The trail continues to the col (6200 ft+) between Mt. Webb (Radium) and Macdonald Peak (6.5 km). Webb is an easy 1-hour hike from the col, and provides a marvelous vista of Chilliwack Lake. Note: By about 1982 logging will cause extensive changes in this area.

Rainbow Creek Trail No. 1235 begins 2½ mi. N of Stehekin; at 5½ mi. there is a fork (the N fork leads to Rainbow Lake). The main trail divides again in about 4 mi. The E fork crosses the divide (South Pass) to South Creek Trail◆; the N fork crosses the ridge to meet McAlester Creek Trail◆. McAlester Pass (est. 6000 ft) is at 10 mi. McAlester Lake (5507 ft) is ½ mi. W of the pass (camping and fires permitted); other camps are at Rainbow Creek bridge and Bench Creek (5½ mi.). From McAlester Pass an easy trek can be taken to the summit of Peak 7628 (2326 m).

Rainbow Lake Trail (South Fork Bridge Creek) extends to

the lake in 6 mi. from Bridge Creek Trail♦. See Rainbow Creek Trail♦. Camping and fires below lake.

Reynolds Creek Trail No. 402 reaches the Chelan-Methow divide in 6.6 mi. at 6874 ft and connects to Boulder Creek. Begin on Twisp River Road♦ at Mystery Camp (18.8 mi.), then take road no. 3423 for 1 mi.

Ridley Creek Trail No. 696. See Middle Fork Nooksack River Road♦. The trail begins off the short spur at the first switchback (est. 12½ mi. on road — 2400 ft), just N of Ridley Creek. Distance is about 3 mi. to the meadowland of Mazama Park; reach the Baker Pass Trail♦ at 4300 ft. Note: The river crossing at 0.2 mi. from the trailhead is dangerous if logs are washed out.

Robinson Creek-Middle Fork Pasayten Trail No. 478. Middle Fork Pasayten River valley is apparently eroded out along a fault, a break formed by movements of two blocks of rock in the earth's crust. The result is a long straight valley. The trail begins at Harts Pass Road♦ 8.1 mi. from Mazama junction and crosses Robinson Pass (6200 ft+) at 9.1 mi. N of the pass extensive meadows in the upper valley of the Middle Fork are periodically buried under snow avalanches from gullies on the Slate Peak ridge. The trail meets Eureka Creek Trail♦ (E) at 11.0 mi. and another route to upper Eureka Creek via Freds Lake and Lake Doris at 15.5 mi. A northern fork of the latter branch (no. 471) leads to Pleasant Valley and *Point Defiance* (7403 ft/2256 m), then connects with Three Forks.

The main trail reaches Three Forks (cabin) and West Fork Pasayten Trail♦ at 21 mi., Tatoosh Buttes Trail♦ (E) at 21.9 mi. near Pasayten G.S., Soda Creek Trail♦ at 22.9 mi., and Boundary Trail♦ (Harrison Creek Trail) at 27.2 mi. For continuation see Pasayten River Trail♦ (B.C.).

A fork of Tatoosh Buttes Trail (Lease Creek, No. 470) extends SE to Lease Lake in 5.4 mi. This attractive lake is set in a deep basin N of Osceola Peak and Mt. Carru.

Approach Variation: (Buckskin Ridge trail no. 498). At the second switchback on the Slate Peak spur road take a packer's trail northward along the Middle Fork slope. The trail first angles 100 yards over the ridge at Slate Pass (6960 ft+), then descends into the basin E of Slate Peak to traverse the slope to Silver Lake; at about 2.5 mi. a spur path descends sharply to the Middle Fork trail (eliminates the hike over Robinson Pass). The hillside trail continues N along Buckskin Ridge and eventually joins the Middle Fork trail S of Three Forks.

Rock Creek Trail No. 473 extends from near Three Forks on West Fork Pasayten Trail♦ to Woody Pass on the Crest Trail♦ (7.6 mi.); campsite at 6.5 mi. Above the trail one can see outcrops of the plagioclase arkose and argillite sequence. Lake of the Pines (5783 ft) is a cross-country trek opposite Rock Creek.

Ross Dam (Lake) Trail. From North Cascades Hwy♦ at Happy Flat a trail, becoming a dirt road, descends to the boat landing near the dam powerhouse; (600-ft descent in about ¾ mi.) one can hike across by suspension bridge here, then N along West Ross Lake Trail. See Big Beaver Creek Trail♦. There are morning and afternoon boat connections on

Diablo Lake. See Ross Lake♦.

Ross Lake East Bank Trail. The trailhead is on North Cascades Hwy♦ near Panther Creek bridge (18.5 mi. from Newhalem; at curve 200 yards W of creek). Hike down to Ruby Creek bridge, then 2.8 mi. to East Bank Trail. Take the upper fork in 0.1 mi. Initially the trail climbs 4.5 mi. to Hidden Hand Pass (2520 ft+) before descending to Roland Point. Distance from the beginning of the East Bank Trail to Devils Creek is 10 mi., Lightning Creek 14 mi., Three Fools Creek 18 mi., and Canadian border 31 mi.

Campsites where fires are permitted are at Ruby Pasture, Hidden Hand, Roland Creek, Roland Point, May Creek, Rainbow Point, Devils, Lightning, Deerlick, Nightmare, Willow Lake, and Hozomeen.

Safety Harbor Creek area. Trail No. 1261 and Uno Peak Trail No. 1260 can be taken from spur road no. 3007 at 4400 ft (see Grade Creek Road♦) to Crows Cabin and the saddle between Big Goat Mountain and Uno Peak (unfortunately open to ORV travel here); a branch trail leads atop *Big Goat* (7100 ft/2164 m), then N to *Ferry Peak* (7727 ft/2355 m) and a pass on its N. A spur trail leads to the summit of *Vie Mountain* (7777 ft/2370 m); the trail continues to East Fork Prince Creek Trail No. 1257 (at 7100 ft) then to Summit Trail♦ (at 6500 ft; total 9.2 mi.)

Sauk Mountain Trail No. 613. Begin from Sauk Mountain Road♦. The trail (begins at 3650 ft) to the 5537-ft summit is only 2 mi. long, but has 26 switchbacks on its steep course. The lookout, built in 1928 near the summit, offers a fine vista of the western slope of the North Cascades: in clear weather sights include Mt. Rainier, Mt. Baker, the Skagit peaks, and the Skagit River winding to Puget Sound. This is an especially rewarding winter or spring alpine trek. See Sauk Mountain.

Scatter Creek Trail No. 427 leaves Twisp River Road♦ at 22 mi. and extends 4.2 mi. to Scatter Lake (7047 ft).

Shuksan Arm Route. From Austin Pass (4732 ft) hike trail to Panorama Dome (5043 ft). Descend into the first notch, then ascend easily to Point 5538, a heathered rock knob 0.7 mi. from Austin Pass. Cross-country travel is straight-forward for 1¼ mi. to where ice begins on the N slope of the arm. From the 5600-ft level at this position it is an easy descent to Lake Ann.

Silesia Creek Trail No. 672. From Twin Lakes (see Mt. Baker Hwy♦) the trail crosses Skagway Pass (no altitude gain) and descends 4.7 mi. to Silesia Shelter (2560 ft+). Upper Silesia Creek Trail No. 690 continues, reaching Rapid Creek at 2½ mi. and ending at 4½ mi. (the final 2 mi. may be poor). From the shelter an old trail extends downvalley to connect with Slesse Creek road spur, but may be overgrown from disuse (see Chilliwack Lake Road♦); the portion to the Boundary (about 2 mi.) is in good condition ATP.

Lone Jack Mine: Once across Skagway Pass a right fork of the trail leads to historic Lone Jack Mine (4800 ft).

Silverdaisy Creek Trail (B.C.) begins from Skagit River Trail♦ about 1 mi. S of Trans-Canada Hwy 3♦. The trail ascends the E side of Silverdaisy Creek to the 5700-ft+ pass at its head.

Silver Lake Route. Silver Lake is in the heart of an unusually scenic, rugged, and remote area of the North Cascades, closely S of the International Boundary, with a 7100-ft local relief from Ross Lake. When Canadian geologist Reginald A. Daly mapped this area in 1901-1906 the hanging lake was not mapped and the glacier on Mt. Spickard (then Glacier Peak) was shown to cover the lake trough; the remaining glacier SW of the lake is now much reduced. Thomas Riggs, an American surveyor, in the summer of 1905 described the lake "of indigo, over a mile long." For much of the summer the lake has surface ice, and mini-bergs are common sights after this melts.

The best approach is via Ross Lake by boat to the trail closely N of Silver Creek (some location problem ATP); the longer option is via the Skagit bridge 1.5 mi. N of the border (see Silver-Skagit Road♦), then taking a connector trail (about 4 mi.). The trail ends just past an old mine cabin (est. 2.5 mi.; est. 2900 ft). The route then traverses slide patches and strips of fir/hemlock (some blazes) well above the creek on the N valley slope. Descend to the stream at the main creek forks (3200 ft+); the route usually taken keeps close to the main stream, ascending a course through forest and subalpine brush (keep away from cliffs and the central waterfalls). Higher, bear right (uphill) on talus sections to avoid steep cliffs, then stay high to find the most open route to the 6763-ft lake (the entire trek is taxing beyond the trail and requires good route finding judgement).

Silver Lake is situated in a pocket with a narrow notch for the water's escape. One can camp on a knoll 200 yards NW of the outlet or on the terminal moraine at the W end of the lake. Time: allow two days. The lake can be bypassed on both sides, but the N is preferable; ice on the S fringe may require steep traversing. A continuing easy pass (7360 ft+) leads to the basin of Depot Creek. This route first descends over large talus to get around a buttress, then traverses the basin onto Redoubt Glacier and up to the snow col SE of the crags leading to Mt. Redoubt; one can descend and traverse to the heather ridge S of Redoubt. See Depot Creek Route♦, Chilliwack River Trail♦-Bear Creek High Route and Indian Creek Trail. References: *B.C.M.*, July 1958; *Mountaineer*, 1978, pp. 149-51.

Silver Star Creek. Begin from North Cascades Hwy♦ (7.5 mi. W of Early Winters Information Center) on the E bank of the creek; climb open forest to where the valley levels, then cross to the W bank. Game paths continue to the lower basin (about 4800 ft); ascend, keeping to the W flank. The scattered timber ends near 6400 ft, a good area for camping. The route is quite open and provides good access to Silver Star Glacier.

Skagit River Trail (B.C.) connects Silver-Skagit Road♦ (at Skagit River 27 mi. from Trans-Canada Hwy — begin on E bank spur) with Trans-Canada Hwy 3♦ at 22.6 mi. from Hope. This section of the Skagit River, still virgin forest, was used by the Whatcom Trail route of 1858. This hike takes most of the day (est. 10 mi.-16 km).

Skaist River Trail (B.C.) is a portion of Captain John Grant's 1861 Hope Trail. At Mile 28.2 on Trans-Canada Hwy 3♦ (E of Skaist River bridge) follow the broad, U-shaped valley to 5970-ft Hope Pass (about 14 mi.). Here meet cattle roads that become jeep and logging routes in Whipsaw Creek drainage. Reference: Robert C. Harris, *Old Pack Trails*, Okanagan-Similkameen Parks Society, 1977; pp. 24-27.

Just E of Hope Pass an old trail intercepts and climbs over *Skaist Mountain* (6300 ft/1920 m) and then descends to cross the Dewdney Trail at the Hubbard-Granite Creek divide, then over Granite Mountain to the Tulameen Plateau. Note: The Nicomen Ridge trail S from Hope Pass may be in poor condition.

Grainger Creek Trail branches from the main trail at 3.5 mi. and extends to 5800-ft Nicomen Lake (see Heather Trail♦).

Skyline Divide. This is the N-S trending divide between Glacier and Deadhorse Creek. Trail no. 678 leaves from Deadhorse Road (Mt. Baker Hwy♦) and reaches 6000 ft on Skyline Divide (est. 3 mi.), then bears SW near the crest. Continue on the alpine divide SE, then follow the upper W side of Chowder Ridge (between Deadhorse-Dobbs Creek and Smith Creek). In early times one observer counted a herd of 42 goats on the divide, and the same number on the Sholes Glacier. Reference: *101 Hikes*, p. 22. Continue S easily around the E end of Bastile Ridge to the northern slopes of Mazama Glacier. One could continue NE to Camp Kiser (take ice axes and rope).

The high point of Bastile Ridge (7842 ft) is between the Bastile and Mazama glaciers. One can cross Bastile Ridge to the gentle Roosevelt-Mazama Col (7600 ft+). One could continue W on the Roosevelt and Coleman glaciers to reach Kulshan Cabin; take glacier travel equipment.

Skyline Trail (Centennial Trail♦) (B.C.). See Manning Provincial Park♦ for approach. Also Silver-Skagit Road♦. W approach: The trail extends from the old Whitworth Ranch onto the low divide between Lightning and Nepopekum creeks at Gibson Pass; leave the Silver-Skagit Road at 8 mi. S of Skagit River bridge (about 35 mi./56 km). The Skyline Trail reaches Skagit Ridge in 8 mi. where an easy hike can be made N to *Nepopekum Peak* (6357 ft/1938 m). E approach: Leave Gibson Pass Road on left at about 5.5 mi. at fire access spur; at Despair Pass (5600 ft+) 3.4 mi., take right branch to near summit of *Snow Camp Mountain* (6497 ft/1980 m) and the shoulder of *Lone Goat Mountain* (6575 ft/2004 m). The trail descends to Camp Mowich (7.5 mi.; 5600 ft — shelter), then rises to Skagit Ridge. *Red Mountain* (6633 ft/2022 m) to the N of the divide is easily reached from Mowich Creek. Reference: *B.C.M.*, March 1942, September 1942, August 1970, October 1970.

Lone Mountain (5900 ft+/1798 m), between the Boundary and Thunder Lake, was occupied by the Boundary Survey in 1935. Certainly most of the high points in this area were visited by earlier surveyors.

Slate Peak Trail leads to the summit of 7440-ft Slate Peak, a well known vantage point, in only ¼ mi. from the spur road off Harts Pass Road♦. From the road near the summit West Fork Pasayten Trail♦ descends NE and the trail along Buckskin Ridge bears N from Slate Pass.

The Forest Service built a lookout cabin on the summit in 1924 because the peak has a broad vista for fire spotting. For a justification that remains more obscure the Air Force in 1960 began an undertaking to lower the summit 70 ft for the construction of a radar station, later considered unnecessary and removed. The environmental damage of this project and the accompanying road scar still blight the area.

Slesse Mountain Trail (B.C.) begins at Mile 6 on Slesse Creek Road (see Chilliwack River Road♦); find trail markers atop a steep bank, just before a tributary stream, 200 m after the last (third) bridge. A work party in 1965 drove 2400 nails and placed 600 markers. The trail, which begins at the 2000-ft level, is steep; some suggest carrying an ice axe for slips. The trail roughly follows a ridge on the W side of the side stream coming from Slesse and is well marked to 4000 ft, where there are open meadows. Follow switchbacks up, eventually heading southward to gain a ridge. Turn left (N) again to a knoll; descend into a saddle marked by dead trees, where there is a campsite (5800 ft, 5 km; 4 hours; no water in late summer). Reach talus slopes at 6000 ft and alp slopes above. There is a high camp with snowmelt water and quite spectacular views at 6800 ft on the ridge 0.5 mi. NW of the summit of Slesse.

To reach the high camp: from the usual campsite ascend toward the ridge and scree bowl below the mountain, then cross the spur on the N to the main divide. Traverse N about ¼ mi. and look for meadow and snow.

Alternative descent: One can hike northward to Pierce Lake (trail). On the traverse around Crossover Peak one may need to descend to 5400 ft on its E ridge.

Snass Creek Trail (Dewdney Trail) (B.C.) is the old Dewdney Trail route of 1860, which used the dry N fork of the upper creek via the 4850-ft pass to the meadows of Paradise Valley. The historic route continues to the Hubbard-Granite Creek divide and intersects a jeep road, then goes E down Granite Creek and over a pass to below Hudson Bay Meadows, then on to 47 Mile Creek and Whipsaw Creek. Reference: *Old Pack Trails* (1977), pp. 20-24 (see Skaist River Trail♦).

The route taken by A.C. Anderson in 1846 and DeLacy (Whatcom Trail) in 1858 follows the E fork of Snass Creek through a pass to Punch Bowl Lake (5400 ft+); reference pp. 16-19. A meager trail here has six alder slides in the final 2 mi. before the pass. Note: The lake can also be reached from the main trail across the Tulameen divide and hiking SE. The two historic routes meet at 2.5 mi. below the lake (Tulameen side) and run together for 5 mi. The Whatcom Trail route meets Granite Mountain N-S jeep road just N of Wells Lake and continues to Lodestone Lake.

The hiking trail begins from Trans-Canada Hwy 3♦ at

24.4 mi. (39.3 km) from Hope and follows W side of Snass Creek.

Soda Creek Trail No. 453 extends from Robinson Creek-Middle Fork Pasayten Trail♦ at 2 mi. N of Three Forks to Boundary Trail♦ in 3.9 mi (at Chuchuwanteen Creek). See also Frosty Creek Trail♦.

Soda Peak route, an old sheepherder path, takes the N side of Soda Creek to the valley head, then bears E and S to lower Rock Creek.

Sourdough Mountain Trail No. 739. Sourdough Mountain (5985 ft/1824 m) is a superb viewpoint from which to obtain a perspective of the Picket Range, Jack Mountain, and the Pyramid-Snowfield Peak group. The original horse trail was built by Glee Davis in 1916; the next year he built the first summit lookout, using hand-split cedar; the structure was rebuilt in 1933. The name Sour Dough, shown on maps dated 1913, was applied during mining times to the 2382-ft summit just opposite the terminus of Ruby Creek (on the old Goat Trail) after a pail of sour dough had spilled from a falling horse.

The trail begins at Diablo townsite past the powerhouse (see North Cascades Hwy♦) and in a steep 5-mi. ascent rises from 900 ft to the summit. A continuing trail descends E below Pierce Mountain to meet West Ross Lake Trail at about 2100 ft (see Big Beaver Creek Trail♦). Point 6107, on the long ridge leading toward Elephant Butte, is 1 mi. NW of Sourdough Mountain (campsite at Sourdough Creek).

Sourdough Lake (4623 ft) which drains to Ross Lake, can be reached by hiking up Sourdough Creek from the trail crossing, then through the ridge saddle. Point 6607, a rounded hump 1 mi. NE of the lake, could be ascended readily by its SW spur.

South Creek Trail No. 401 extends from Twisp River Road♦ (est. 3200 ft) and reaches South Pass (6280 ft+) on the Chelan divide in 7.3 mi. A branch trail extends from near the 2-mi. point to Louis Lake (5351 ft).

Spanish Creek Trail No. 503. See Lake Creek-Ashnola River Trail♦. This trail connects with Andrews Creek Trail♦ (est. 4 mi.); a southern fork extends about 3 mi. along Glory Creek to Glory Lake.

Stetattle Creek Trail. Before prospectors arrived in the Skagit Valley it is said Indians would not camp where Stetattle Creek entered because of bad luck pertaining to a battle lost to northern Indians. On some early maps the name was given as Skeedadle Creek. Follow trail no. 761 into the valley (begins at 920 ft at Diablo townsite) about 4 mi. to beyond Torrent Creek fork (1840 ft); the trail may fade by 3.5 mi. Leave the valley and ascend the forested far slope, keeping on a leftward bearing to shortly reach high heather slopes. Keep S of the crest on a long traverse to the saddle (6320 ft+) E of McMillan Spires. A traverse on glacier and snow descends into McMillan Creek cirque. Time: allow 20 hours; despite the problems of this route, it has proven to be the best way to the McMillan cirque. See also Stetattle Ridge Route♦. A climbing route crosses the ledge series on McMillan Spire's E face: from the saddle N of Azure Lake, take a narrow ridge SW; ledges connect with gentle slopes S of the spire.

Azure Lake (4055 ft) can be reached by continuing up the forested valley. This is a rough trek. Massive, brushy cliffs ring the lake on all sides. It may be possible to reach Terror Creek basin from Azure Lake by crossing the lake outlet and climbing SW up a brushy cliff-rib, but the route is untested.

Stetattle (Sourdough) Ridge Route. This long ridge is of interest because of its scenic vistas, and a variety of rocky knolls, glaciated rock humps and meadowed alp slopes. There are clean outcrops of biotite gneiss along the route, and of further geologic interest is the deep notch at the head of Torrent Creek (E of Elephant Butte) weathered out of crushed rock along a fault. Sourdough Creek also flows on rocks pulverized by this fault.

Begin the route as per Sourdough Mountain Trail♦, but leave just before reaching Sourdough Creek (4960 ft). Diagonal W to a saddle on a spur ridge (5500 ft). Follow the spur northward to good traversing terrain, then follow the long SW slope of the ridge (keep below the crest). It is necessary to descend directly to the gap at the head of Torrent Creek (4920 ft+), then make a rising traverse SW to reach a small lake (5135 ft). Pass the cliff-like spur W of the lake by working S, then bearing N on a bushy traversing ledge. Ascend around a spur, then keep sidehilling above timberline westward below Elephant Butte to the pass on its W. Continue as per Stetattle Creek Route♦.

Point 6728, (2051 m) 2¼ mi. ESE of Elephant Butte, and *Point 6495* (1980 m; 1½ mi. SE of latter) can be reached easily from the long traverse.

Elephant Butte (7380 ft/2249 m) is merely an alpine hike from the saddle on the W. Two other summits westward are 6889 ft and 6914 ft; they could be climbed without technical difficulty by following the ridge, or traversing beneath them. Reference: *Route and Rocks*, pp. 42-43; see Section I, note 82.

Stiletto Peak Trail extends from Bridge Creek Trail♦ at Fireweed Camp and climbs to an old lookout site (est. 7400 ft); a route to this point can be taken also from Twisp Pass (2 mi.). The views of high peaks in a vista from Mt. Goode to Silver Star are superb.

Summit Trail No. 1259 (Chelan Crest Trail). Begin from Grade Creek Road♦ (South Navarre Camp) at 6400 ft. Along Safety Harbor Creek the trail climbs through meadows of Miners Basin (4 mi.) and across a ridge to upper Horsethief Basin and Sunset Pass (7360 ft+), which is the divide to East Fork Prince Creek. Because the route is open to ORV travel from the trailhead to Surprise Lake there is considerable conflict with hiker and horseback usage.

A more alpine variation is the higher Navarre Trail No. 424 which begins from Summer Blossom (6400 ft) on the road about 1 mi. E of the normal start. This route climbs over the high saddle between the Navarre Peaks, reaching to 7840 ft+ on the S spur of North Navarre, and then follows

the crestline or just W of it. The trail connects with Summit Trail♦ at Horsethief Basin (at Sunset Pass). A northern trail fork climbs the 7640-ft+ pass to Sunrise Lake and Merchant Basin, continuing to Cooney Lake and Foggy Dew Trail♦ (6.9 mi.).

Short spur trails off the main trail lead to Boiling Lake and Horsehead Pass (7520 ft+), E, and to Hoodoo Pass (7440 ft+) to the N. The main trail crosses Chipmunk Pass into Barren Basin and the North Fork of Prince Creek (14.5 mi.; 5600 ft), then to East Fork Fish Creek (18.5 mi.). The North Fork Fish Creek Trail is reached at 24.5 mi. and War Creek Pass in an additional 5.2 mi. A continuation via Purple Pass leads to Stehekin (38 mi.).

Numerous branch trails and cross-country routes can be followed. These include:

Horsethief Basin across the open divide to Sunrise Lake (7228 ft).

Trail from East Fork Prince Creek drainage to just S of Switchback Mountain and over divide to Cooney Lake (7241 ft).

Martin Lakes cross-country route via saddle N of Martin Peak.

Upper Middle Fork Prince Creek to S of Barren Mountain; a high cross-country route to the North Fork.

North Fork Prince Creek Trail and connection with Horton Butte Trail.

Bernice Creek branch of Prince Creek to Star Lake (7240 ft).

Branch trail from upper East Fork Fish Creek across Fish Creek Pass (7480 ft+) to Oval Lakes and W Fork Buttermilk Creek drainage.

Fish Creek Pass is 0.5 mi. NW of Star Lake (7173 ft) which rests in a high basin SW of the Pass.

North Fork Fish Creek branch trail to Eagle Pass (7240 ft+) and Eagle Creek.

Summit viewpoints of hiking access include *Sun Mountain* (7492 ft/2284 m), *Splawn Mountain* (7450 ft/2271 m), and *Boulder Butte* (7350 ft/2240 m).

Susap Creek Trail. (B.C.) See Snowy Mountain for road approach and trail to Joe Lake. The trail basically extends W near Susap Creek to the lake (7100 ft+), where there is camping, a cabin and reputedly excellent trout fishing. The trail then ascends NW to 7700 ft, then descends westerly, bearing around the N shoulder of Flatiron Mountain, then drops steeply to Ewart Creek at Juniper Creek fork (see Ewart Creek Trail♦).

From Joe Lake a S branch of the trail extends to Harry Lake (7200 ft+, camping) at 1.3 mi. NW of Snowy Mountain. The trail continues in a large loop, first descending SW to upper Juniper Creek, then rising to high lakes 2 mi. N of the International Boundary, then looping E to cross a pass to upper Snehumption Creek, then bearing NE to meet the southern road fork. Map: Keremeos 82 E/4 West.

Swamp Creek Route begins on North Cascades Hwy♦ at 34.4 mi. from Newhalem. This is an easy 3-mi. cross-country route to the Crest Trail♦ between Methow and Granite Pass.

Swanee Lake Route. (B.C.) From about 5.5 mi. past Silver Lake on the Silver-Skagit Road♦ (est. 1400 ft) hike first N on an old road, then cross Swanee Creek. Follow the N side of the stream steeply to the lake (4200 ft+, 4 km); there is no established trail ATP.

Swift Creek Trail No. 607. Begin from near Baker Hot Springs (Morovits Creek Road for 3.5 mi. — see Baker Lake Hwy♦). The trail begins at 1100 ft+ altitude and remains level for 2 mi. to Swift Creek, then ascends gradually N to a junction with Lake Ann Trail (8 mi. — 3920 ft+); shelter at 2 mi.

Table Mountain-Ptarmigan Ridge. Table Mountain is a picturesque feature W of Austin Pass underlain by massive andesite flows from Mt. Baker; these rest unconformably on greenstones of the Chilliwack Group.

Once an old stream valley filled by lava flows from Mt. Baker eroded away to become a high ridge (a topographic inversion). When local alpine glaciers here were overwhelmed by Pleistocene continental ice flowing southward, boulders of foreign rock were deposited by ice whose surface was still higher. From the road end on Kulshan Ridge (5040 ft+) — see Mt. Baker Hwy♦ — there are two ways of reaching the summit (5742 ft) by trail. The E side can be ascended directly by Table Mountain Trail No. 681 (by using a W-side descent, a 3.5-mi. loop hike is possible). The left branch of this trail (at ¼ mi. — no. 682) traverses the S flank of Table Mountain and in 1 mi. reaches to near the saddle (est. 5100 ft) adjacent to Ptarmigan Ridge. Here a continuing trail (no. 683) traverses along or near the ridge to the area of Camp Kiser (7 mi., 5840 ft), which is 0.3 mi. SW of Coleman Pinnacle; the camp area is 0.5 mi. of benches at timberline (good camping, plenty of marmots, no wood). When hiking it is best to first keep on the N side of Ptarmigan Ridge; the trail bears S of Point 5841, then E and S of Coleman Pinnacle. Snow crossings are frequent, depending on the season, and the path is not always visible; when visibility is poor, route finding may be difficult. An easy alpine trek continues W by staying along the N edge of Sholes Glacier and N of Landes Cleaver. References: *Mountaineer,* 1916; *Mazama* 12 (1930).

Chain Lakes are a complete hydrological system, a stream-connected lake system which begins NW of Table Mountain and SW of Mazama Dome; from Iceberg Lake (4720 ft+), the largest lake, the stream flows to tiny Mazama Lake to Wells Creek, eventually draining to North Fork Nooksack River. The lakes can easily be reached by trail from the W end of Table Mountain (the right-hand fork meets the first lake in ½ mi.). The trail continues E over Herman Saddle (5280 ft+), then descends to Bagley Lakes and Heather Meadows at the roadway (4200 ft). From the saddle an easy hike-scramble can be made in a NE direction to *Mt. Herman* (6285 ft/1916 m).

Tatoosh Buttes Trail No. 485 begins from Robinson Creek-Middle Fork Pasayten Trail♦ and in 1.4 mi. reaches a junction with Lease Creek Trail. Tatoosh Buttes, a high parkland, are reached at 6.5 mi. and Eightmile Pass-Hidden Lakes Trail♦ at 10.6 mi.

Thornton Lakes Trail. See Thornton Creek Road♦. Hike the roadbed about 2 mi., then beyond Thornton Creek (3000 ft) find the steep trail which climbs to a subalpine ridge (4880 ft+); the trail descends about 500 ft to the larger (SE) Thornton Lake (campsite; total 4.2 mi.). Cross the outlet stream and ascend a rocky, burnt spur S of the upper lakes. It is feasible to continue cross-country to a depression E of Point 6234 on the alpine ridge dividing the Thornton and Triumph Creek drainages. For continuation see Triumph Pass route♦.

Three Fools Creek Trail No. 749. Three Fools Creek was named about 1893 when three novice prospectors, discovering pyrite in its waters, thought it was gold. Placer claims in the Three Fools and Lightning Creek drainages show no evidence of mining. Early Boundary Survey personnel adopted the Indian name Skwa-kwi-eht for the creek. The Kakoit Mountain ascended by Henry Custer in 1859 may have been near the head of Three Fools, or on the divide between the latter and Devils Creek. The higher summit which he climbed to the E may have been Blizzard, Smoky, or Three Fools Peak.

The trail begins 3.8 mi. from Ross Lake (see Lightning Creek Trail♦) and reaches Little Fish shelter (4 mi.), then ascends W of Elbow Creek, through Elbow Basin, and via Big Face Creek to Castle Pass (see Crest Trail♦).

At Elbow Basin (est. 5500 ft) a path leads ¼ mi. down to a cabin. Freezout Lake (5680 ft+) is W of the basin, and N below the trail level.

Tiffany Mountain Trail. Follow Boulder Creek Road♦ to Freezout Pass (6500 ft) and the trailhead, about 2 mi. N of Roger Lake. Trail no. 345 leads 3 mi. E to the high summit (see Tiffany Mountain).

An alternative route is to continue 4 mi. N past the pass to Tiffany Spring and trail no. 373; follow the latter about 4 mi. to a junction, then turn W to Whistler Pass (7480 ft+) and the summit.

Tomyhoi Lake Trail No. 686. This is an old mining trail which begins on Twin Lakes Road at 4.6 mi. (3600 ft) — see Mt. Baker Hwy♦. The trail crosses Gold Run Pass (5360 ft+) at 2 mi., then descends 2 mi. to Tomyhoi Lake (3680 ft+). Steep snowfields on this descent can be dangerous; the route is not recommended as a continuation to Tamihi Creek Road in British Columbia due to thick brush and extensive windfalls in very mature forest.

Triumph Pass Route is a more direct route to the Triumph Creek-Thornton Lakes divide than Thornton Lakes Trail♦. Leave the road before Thornton Creek (est. 2800 ft) and ascend the forest slope NW to the long heathery ridge (5200 ft) extending toward Mt. Triumph (keep S of cliffs and brush on the valley slope of Thornton Creek). Follow the ridge until just beyond Thornton Lakes to a col (6000 ft+) which is the next to last one before rising toward Thornton Peak. Make a scrambling descent for 400-600 ft on the W slope to get below cliffs on the Triumph Creek slope, then make a traverse of about 1¼ mi. to the S edge of a steep rock rampart descending from Mt. Triumph (est. 5400 ft). Angle down leftward to a stream, then cross to the opposite side and enter steep and cliffy timber at the lower portion of the rampart. Bypass cliffs here at 5000 ft and ascend diagonally N to Triumph Pass (5440 ft+); there is a timber patch camp just S of the pass. Time: 6 hours.

A variation at the beginning is to use a northern road spur which extends to about 3300 ft.

Tungsten Creek Trail. See Chewack River Trail♦.

Twisp Pass Trail No. 432 extends from the end of Twisp River Road♦ (3527 ft) in 4.2 mi. to the 6064-ft pass. *Lincoln Butte* (7065 ft/2153 m), just E of the pass, offers an easy trek for a good vista.

A branch trail (no. 426) to Copper Pass departs at 1.7 mi. and extends 4 mi. to cross the pass to Bridge Creek.

Kangaroo Ridge cross-country route: leave Copper Pass Trail at 2 mi. (at first rockslide on left, about 400 yards past old cabin — possibly find "K" on tree); keep below windfalls and cross first creek, then follow old grazing path on left side of valley. Reach good camping sites in the basin in 1 to 1½ mi. (5800 ft-6000 ft). Kangaroo Pass, at the head of the basin, was designated "Rocky Pass" on 1926 maps, with a trail shown.

Twisp Pass Trail No. 1277 reaches the pass in 4.2 mi. from Fireweed Camp on Bridge Creek Trail♦. Dagger Lake (5508 ft) at 3 mi. is a campspot.

Upper Baker River Trail No. 606 originally extended about 8 mi. to Bald Eagle Creek, but constant channel changes made maintenance costly. The valleys of Picket and Bald Eagle creeks are two of the most primitive and jungly in the Cascades. See Baker Lake Hwy♦-Upper Baker Road: keep right at final fork (no. 382 — ½ mi.; left is Griner's shelter); proceed ¼ mi. to end on gravel bar (760 ft altitude). In 2.5 mi. of primeval fir and cedar forest reach Sulphide Creek (shelter) where the train vanishes; one can continue with difficulty 2 mi. to Crystal Creek. Note: In late summer or early fall during dry seasons one may be able to make good progress up the valley by taking to gravel bars and wading shallow channels.

Follow gravel bars and forest on the N side to opposite Bald Eagle Creek (2 mi.). Continue along the forest edge until difficult travel suggests wading, or taking to gravel bars and snow slides on the opposite bank (crossings difficult during high water). At Mineral Creek cross to the N side again and ascend the forest spur NE between Mineral and Picket creeks to est. 4800 ft, then traverse E on easy slopes with a few minor cliffs. A bench leads onto the glacier SW of Mt. Challenger (see Easy Ridge-Picket Pass Route♦). Time: allow 2 days for this strenuous route, and expect considerable bushy travel. Reference: *Routes and Rocks,* pp. 20-21; see Section I, note 82.

Mt. Blum Route. The subalpine portion of this trek is prospective. Cross the underbrush of the flat valley at the mouth of Bald Eagle Creek southeastward, then ascend the steep forest spur southward to open subalpine terrain; continue up to the Lonesome Creek-Baker River ridge E of Point 6700, the last part being a small glacier. Here an easy ridge route leads SW toward Mt. Blum (keep S of ridge points). Blum and Hidden creeks are not advised as routes.

Pioneer Ridge High Route is a strenuous trek, beginning in the brush of Baker River (est. 1120 ft) on the E side of Bald Eagle Creek, then ascending the steep rocky ridge NE to its first craggy high points. Follow the ridge generally E (scrambling and some bush) to a high barren saddle on Pioneer Ridge (light-colored quartz diorite); cross the ridge at the NE end of a small glacier between Points 6744 and 6719, then traverse and descend to get below a glacier on the E slope of the ridge. Make a SW traverse around the headwaters of Picket Creek; a steep couloir descent problem is reported at about ½ mi. NE of the lake draining to Goodell Creek. The route can be continued to the eastern headwaters of Picket Creek and the western flank of the Northern Pickets (campspot W of Phantom Peak). Time: allow 2 days from Baker River to Picket Range. Reference: *Routes and Rocks,* pp. 21-24; see Section I, note 82.

Varden Lake (6195 ft) is about 4 mi. (cross-country) from North Cascades Hwy♦; from 5 mi. W of Early Winters Information Center follow Varden Creek 2½ mi. to a fork, then ascend SE to the lake. The divide to Cedar Creek can readily be reached.

Wall Creek Route (B.C.) is a fairly strenuous but attractive hike of about 8 mi., partly along (wet) cattle trails, from a campspot on the Ashnola River Road♦ at 31.1 mi. (3900 ft), 1 mi. past a corral. First ford the river (beware when water high), then hike N to a log crossing of Wall Creek. The trail follows the N side of the creek to reach the Wall-Ewart Creek pass (7600 ft+); one can take a cross-country hike to Ewart Creek Trail♦ (note: upper Ewart Creek valley reported difficult because of windfalls).

Centennial Trail♦ follows the first part of the route; an alternative trail connection to Quiniscoe Lake climbs uphill (N) about 1 mi. past Cathedral Fork.

A cross-country route can be taken via Cathedral Fork SE to cross the Boundary and reach Spanish Meadows and Cathedral Lakes (6-8 mi.). This is probably the shortest route into this area, but still a long day (see also Chewack River Trail♦). A variation of this route is to take a high traverse on the S flank of the divide (under Orthodox Mountain) and later descend S under The Deacon into Cathedral Fork, then take the trail to Cathedral Lakes.

War Creek Trail No. 408 extends from end of War Creek spur road (no. 334) off Twisp River Road♦ (cross Twisp River bridge, turn right on road no. 3412, then left on no. 334). War Creek Pass (6760 ft+) is 9.3 mi. The trail here connects with Chelan Crest Trail♦ (SE) and also a connection to Stehekin. War Creek (once called the Twisp's S fork) was an old Indian route, and the trail itself was in existence before 1898.

Washington Pass. Various hiker and climbing-approach paths lead to the Liberty Bell massif. From about 1 mi. W of the pass a trail leads to Blue Lake (6254 ft) set in a rock-rimmed basin; no camping here. A well treaded hiker fork (left) leads upslope to the boulder slopes and meadows beneath Liberty Bell, and is the standard climbing approach to this flank. An attractive viewpoint-hill (7560 ft+) just N of Washington Pass is an easy stroll. All trails and paths in the area are closed to machine travel.

Welcome Pass Trail No. 698. Hike or drive (depending on vehicle and/or conditions) a rough logging road (no. 4021) which leaves Mt. Baker Hwy♦ at 12.5 mi. E of Glacier. After 1.5 mi. the steep trail continues 1.8 mi. to the 5120-ft+ pass. The area here is exceptional for scenic vistas and wildflowers, particularly lupine meadows. Here is a connection with High Divide Trail (see Excelsior Pass Trail♦).

West Fork Buttermilk Creek Trail No. 411 (see Buttermilk Creek Road♦) leaves from W fork road spur (no. 3222) and reaches Fish Creek Pass (7480 ft+) in 9.5 mi. Small lakes on the SE slope of Oval Peak (6700-6900 ft), on the W flank of the upper valley, can be reached cross-country.

West Fork Pasayten Trail No. 472. This through trail begins from the road near the summit of Slate Peak (see Slate Peak Trail♦). At 8 mi. Holman Creek Trail (no. 472A) extends as a 2.2-mi. connector to Holman Pass on Crest Trail♦ (camp 0.2 mi. N of trail junction). A hummocky moraine-like accumulation opposite Holman Pass comprises angular boulders of arkose derived from a rockslide avalanche from the eastern side of the valley. The debris displays topography of kettles and other ice-disintegration landforms and is anomalously dispersed upvalley, signifying that the avalanche spread across and was reformed by an upvalley-sloping distributory of the Cordilleran ice sheet (Waitt, 1979, p. 33).

At Three Forks (14 mi.; cabin) there is a junction with Rock Creek Trail♦ and Robinson Creek-Middle Fork Pasayten Trail♦ (see latter) for continuation to Boundary Trail♦, and Pasayten River Trail♦ (B.C.).

Williams Ridge Trail. (B.C.) Leave Chilliwack Lake Road♦ at 20.9 mi. (sign on left). The steep trail ends on the ridge between Mt. Ford lookout and Williams Peak (4 km, 4700 ft). It is another 1½ hours E to the base of Williams Peak (7 km, 6000 ft), but the trail fades at about 5500 ft.

Williamson Lake Trail. (B.C.) See Chilliwack Lake Road♦ -Foley Lake Road. Cross the log jam at the lake outlet (1800 ft+) and follow the trail around the W end of the lake, then climb steeply in a NW direction (markers). Near timberline a path bears rightward to Williamson Lake (5400 ft+), S of the Foley-Welch Peak col. This is a good campsite (former location of hut destroyed 1972 by avalanche).

For climbing routes to the W, instead of hiking to the lake, continue up the ridge, then traverse below cliffs into the cirque immediately SW of Welch Peak (5 km).

Willow Creek Route is a popular way to reach Mt. Silver Star, the "Wine Spires," and Vasiliki Ridge. Leave North Cascades Hwy♦ about opposite the valley entrance (12.3 mi. W of Early Winters Information Center; park at wide highway shoulder area with mountain sign) and descend about 200 ft to the creek (log crossing). The best route is to ascend along the N valley slope (a worn path ascends left of a dry gulch), then bear rightward into the upper basin; camping near head of Willow Creek at about 6000 ft (2 hours). By bearing toward Burgundy Col, locate campsites in a basin (est. 6400 ft) beneath the col; easy scree slopes lead to the col (7760 ft+) between Vasiliki and Burgundy Spires and an entry to the Silver Star Glacier.

Winchester Mountain Trail No. 685. The 6521-ft (1988 m) summit of Winchester is only 0.4 mi. NW of 5120-ft+ Twin Lakes (see Mt. Baker Hwy♦); the trail distance is 1.5 mi. The lookout building here has been on site since 1935. Jack Post, of mining note, may have been among the first to scramble to this summit. About 1895 he named Twin Lakes and then the mountain (for his rifle).

Windy Joe Mountain Trail (Pacific Crest Trail). (B.C.) See Manning Provincial Park♦. Begin 1.6 km E of Park Headquarters (44.1 mi./70.9 km from Hope) on the S side of the highway; turn right and park in lot. In a masterpiece of planning, the trail parallels the noisy pavement (0.4 km), then follows a fire road to Windy Joe junction (4.2 km). The 5989-ft summit is a fine viewpoint (5.6 km; 2 hours).

Frosty Mountain Trail branches S at 4.6 km (5200 ft) and makes a connection to Lightning Lakes at 8 mi. (13 km). At 500 m on this trail Pacific Crest Trail (Monument 78 Trail) bears left for a 7.2-km hike to the Boundary. Note: Anyone crossing the International Boundary into the U.S. needs a Wilderness Permit. Every person crossing should report directly to the nearest Customs House in the country entered.

Windy Pass Trail (Allen Basin) is a connector to the Crest Trail♦ from Barron (5280 ft) along Bonita Creek and through Indiana Basin to the 6257-ft pass. Reach Barron via New Lite Mine roadway (steep — may be closed to traffic) which begins 2.8 mi. from Harts Pass (see Harts Pass Road♦).

The old Mammoth Mine camp is only 0.8 mi. from the roadway beginning; a trail leads E up to mine levels. There are numerous historic mine sites and old trails in Allen Basin as elsewhere in the watershed.

Windy Peak Trail No. 342 leads to the summit of the 8334-ft peak, an excellent high viewpoint which is an old lookout site. One can begin at Long Swamp camp on Toats Coulee Road♦ and ascend northward via Hickey Hump (est. 9 mi.). The trail continues NE 6 mi. to Sunny Pass (see Horseshoe Basin♦). Clutch Trail No. 343 extending W from Iron Gate camp is a direct connection to the main trail at 5.4 mi.

Wolf Creek Trail No. 527. From Winthrop take the county road on the S river bank for 4 mi., then left on spur no. 351. Keep left at 4.9 and 5.0 mi. from Winthrop; find the trail at a gate (5.6 mi., 2400 ft). Gardner Meadows (5700 ft) are reached in 11 mi. Wolf Creek heads in cirques, and has a U-shaped upper valley, but its lower 10 mi. has the V-shaped cross-profile of a tributary that did not deliver alpine ice to the ancient Methow Valley glacier.

Index

Peak	Feet	Meters	Page
Abernathy Peak	8321	2536	224
The Acropolis	8040+	2450+	237
Alpaca Peak (B.C.)	6700+	2042+	201
American Border Peak	8026	2446	45
Amphitheatre Mountain	8358	2548	182
Anderson Butte	5700+	1737+	290
Anderson River Group (B.C.)			196
Anderson River Mountain (B.C.)	6485	1977	196
Andrew Peak	8301	2530	177
Apex Mountain	8297	2529	182
Aphrodite Tower	7720+	2353+	237
Ares Tower	8190	2496	237
Armstrong Peak	8106	2471	180
Arnold Peak	8076	2462	180
Arrowtip Tower	est. 6250	1905	42
Ashnola Mountain	7780	2371	176
Azurite Peak	8400+	2560+	277
Baby Munday Peak (B.C.)	7200+	2195+	120
Bacchus Tower	7600+	2317+	237
Bacon Peak	7066	2154	68
Mt. Baker	10,778	3285	25
Bald Mountain	7931	2417	176
Baldy Mountain	7810	2381	221
Mt. Ballard	8280+	2524+	277
Barbara Peak	5902	1799	43
Mt. Barney	7828	2386	178
Mt. Barr (B.C.)	6228	1898	118
Battle Mountain	7710	2350	221
Bauerman Ridge	8044	2452	180
Bear Mountain	7942	2421	103
Beauty Peak	7935	2419	170
Berdeen Peak	6484	1976	71
Big Bosom Buttes	6521	1988	49
Big Buck Mountain (B.C.)	7031	2143	191
Big Craggy Peak	8470	2582	175
Mt. Bigelow	8440+	2573+	218
Big Goat	7100	2164	308
Big Kangaroo	8280+	2524+	239
Big Snagtooth	est. 8350	2545	227
Billy Goat Mountain	7639	2328	175
Black Buttes	9443	2878	36
Blackcap Mountain	8397	2559	172
Black Lake Ridge	7828	2386	177
Black Ridge	7582	2311	221
Blizzard Peak	7622	2323	168
Block Tower	est. 6250	1905	42
Blue Lake Peak	7800+	2377+	246
Mt. Blum	7680	2341	71
Border Lake Peak (B.C.)	7718	2352	176
Boulder Butte	7350	2240	222
Bowan Mountain	7895	2406	223
The Boxcar (B.C.)	8500+	2591+	190
Mt. Brice (B.C.)	7099	2164	166
Bryan Butte	7855	2394	218
Buckskin Point	7815	2382	169
Burch Mountain	7782	2372	175
Burgett Peak	7365	2245	175
Burgundy Spire	8400+	2560+	233
Cal Peak	7489	2283	178
Camels Hump	8105	2443	222
Camp Peak	7700+	2347+	112
Canadian Border Peak (B.C.)	7400+	2256+	136
Mt. Carru	8595	2620	172
Castle Peak	8306	2352	166
Cathedral Peak	8601	2622	183
Cedar Tooth	8280+	2524+	227
Chablis Spire	est. 8350	2545	233
Mt. Challenger	8236	2510	101
Chamois Peak (B.C.)	6600+	2012+	196
Charon Tower	8000+	2438+	237
Cheam Peak (B.C.)	6913	2107	119
Cheam Range (B.C.)			118
Cheops	8270	2521	218
Chianti Spire	est. 8400	2560	233
Choi Oi	est. 7850	2393	241
Chopaka Mountain	7882	2402	179
The Chopping Block	6805	2074	87
Church Mountain	6315	1925	44
Church Mountain (B.C.)	5531	1686	138
Chuwanten Mountain (B.C.)	7048	2148	191
Cinderella Peak	6400+	1951+	43
Cirque Tower	est. 7700	2347	66
Clark Peak	7920+	2414+	178
Cleft Tooth	est. 8000	2438	227
Cloudcap Peak	7429	2264	66
Coleman Peak	7690	2344	178
Coleman Pinnacle	6414	1955	35
Coleman Ridge	7645	2330	178
Colfax Peak	9443	2878	36
Concord Tower	7560+	2304+	257

Peak	Elevation		Page
	Feet	Meters	
Copper Mountain	7142	2177	124
Copper Point	7840	2390	246
Coquihalla Mountain (B.C.)	7088	2160	193
Mt. Coulter (B.C.)	6563	2000	193
Crater Mountain	8128	2477	157
Crater Mountain (B.C.)	7522	2293	191
Crescent Creek Spires	7840+	2390+	91
Crescent Lake Peak (B.C.)	7126	2172	195
Crescent Mountain	7816	2382	223
Crooked Thumb	8120	2475	99
Crossover Peak (B.C.)	7142	2186	136
Mt. Crowder	7082	2159	72
Mt. Custer	8630	2630	112
Cutthroat Peak	8050	2454	269
Damnation Peak	5653	1718	76
Davis Peak	7051	2149	76
The Deacon (B.C.)	8400+	2560+	187
Decayed Tooth	est. 8150	2484	227
Mt. Degenhardt	8000+	2438+	86
Desolation Peak	6102	1860	162
Mt. Despair	7292	2223	73
Devils Backbone	7056	2151	169
Devils Dome	7400	2256	298
Devils Peak	8081	2463	171
Devils Tongue	8048	2453	111
Mt. Dewdney (B.C.)	7368	2246	191
Diamond Point	7916	2413	177
Diobsud Buttes	5893	1796	68
Doe Mountain	7154	2181	178
Dog Tooth	8200+	2499+	227
Dollar Watch Mountain	7679	2341	176
Dot Mountain	8220	2505	174
Early Winter Spires			246, 253
Eaton Peak (B.C.)	6900+	2103+	194
Mt. Edgar (B.C.)	6500+	1981+	116
Eightmile Peak	7756	2364	175
Elephant Butte	7380	2249	77
Mt. Elk	4700	1433	305
Eureka Peak (B.C.)	6400+	1951+	118
Mt. Ewart (B.C.)	8000+	2438+	187
Farewell Peak	7430	2265	178
Ferry Peak	7727	2355	308
The Fin	7360+	2243+	246
Finlayson Peak (B.C.)	7236	2206	116
Finney Peak	8110	2472	219
Flattop Mountain (B.C.)	7430	2265	306
Foley Peak (B.C.)	7500+	2286+	122

Peak	Elevation		Page
	Feet	Meters	
Mt. Ford (B.C.)	4600	1402	305
Mt. Ford (B.C.)	6900+	2103+	192
Mt. Forddred (B.C.)	7100+	2164+	194
Freds Mountain	8080+	2463+	177
Freezout Mountain	7744	2360	168
Frenzel Spitz	est. 7450	2271	92
Friday Mountain (B.C.)	6400	1951	302
Frosty Mountain (B.C.)	est. 7950	2423	166
Mt. Fury	8292	2527	93
Gamuza Peak (B.C.)	6300+	1920+	199
Gardner Mountain	8897	2712	225
Gemse Peak (B.C.)	6100+	1859+	199
Genesis Peak	7244	2208	77
Mt. Gibbs	8142	2482	222
Gilbert Mountain	8023	2445	223
Ghost Peak	7840+	2390+	100
Goat Mountain	6891	2100	49
Goetz Peak (B.C.)	6600+	2012+	122
Golden Horn	8366	2550	275
Granite Mountain	6124	1867	49
Mt. Grant (B.C.)	7126	2172	195
Gray Peak	8082	2463	221
Grey Tooth	est. 8000	2438	227
Mt. Grimface (B.C.)	8600+	2621+	187
Guanaco Peak (B.C.)	6900+	2103+	201
Hadley Peak	7515	2291	35
Mt. Hagan	6800+	2073+	70
Haig Mountain	7865	2397	180
Hai Tower	est. 7850	2393	241
Half Moon	7960+	2426+	239
Mt. Hardy	8080+	2463+	277
Hatchethead Mountain (B.C.)	6391	1947	166
Hayden Peak	6400+	1951+	43
Haystack Mountain	7303	2226	170
Haystack Mountain (B.C.)	8541	2603	191
Mt. Herman	6285	1916	312
Mt. Hewitt Bostock (B.C.)	7100+	2164+	202
Himmelhorn	est. 7800	2377	92
Hock Mountain	7750	2362	223
Holliway Mountain	8000+	2438+	277
Holman Peak	7550	2301	169
Holy Cross Mountain (B.C.)	6810	2076	118
Hoodoo Peak	8464	2580	218
Hope Mountain (B.C.)	6026	1837	195
Horseshoe Mountain	8000	2438	303
Horton Butte	6834	2083	303

Peak	Elevation Feet	Meters	Page
Hozomeen Mountain	8066	2459	162
Hurley Peak	7820	2384	179
Ibex Peak (B.C.)	6600+	2011+	199
Icy Peak	est. 7070	2155	52
Ike Mountain	7186	2190	178
Illusion Peaks (B.C.)	6900+	2103+	127
Indian Mountain	7131	2174	103
Inspiration Peak	7840+	2390+	84
International Peak	8478	2584	111
Isolillock Mountain (B.C.)	6810	2076	118
Jackass Mountain (B.C.)	6588	2008	202
Jackita Peak	7350	2240	162
Jack Mountain	9066	2763	157
Jagged Ridge			66
Jaw's Tooth	est. 6400	1951	43
Jeffrey Peak (B.C.)	6729	2051	117
Jim Peak	7033	2144	169
Joe Mills Mountain	7716	2352	179
Joker Mountain	7603	2317	168
Jorgenson Peak (B.C.)	6000+	1829+	195
July Mountain (B.C.)	6973	2125	202
Juno-Jupiter Tower	7920+	2414+	237
Kanaka Mountain (B.C.)	6200+	1890+	202
Kangaroo Ridge			237
Kangaroo Temple	7572	2308	241
Klesilkwa Mountain (B.C.)	6800+	2073+	117
Knight Peak (B.C.)	7200+	2195+	120
Lady Peak (B.C.)	7100+	2164+	119
Mt. Lago	8745	2666	172
Lake Mountain	8371	2552	172
Lakeview Mountain (B.C.)	8622	2628	190
Mt. Larrabee	7868	2398	47
Last Chance Point	7046	2148	170
Last Tooth	8000+	2438+	227
Mt. Laughington (B.C.)	5800+	1768	305
Lexington Tower	7560+	2304+	257
Liberty Bell	7720	2353	259
Lincoln Butte	7065	2153	313
Lincoln Peak	9096	2773	36
Mt. Lindeman (B.C.)	7578	2310	122
Mt. Ling (B.C.)	6472	1973	118
Little Finger	7400+	2256+	245
Little Sister	6524	1989	43
Liumchen Mountain (B.C.)	6000+	1829+	138

Peak	Elevation Feet	Meters	Page
Llama Peak (B.C.)			201
Mt. Lockwood (B.C.)	6700+	2042+	117
Lone Goat Mountain (B.C.)	6575	2004	309
Lone Mountain (B.C.)	5900	1798	309
Lonesome Peak	6720+	2048+	72
Loomis Mountain	5587	1703	36
Lost Peak	8464	2580	173
Luna Peak	8285	2525	96
Mt. Lytton (B.C.)	6706	2044	202
Macabre Tower (B.C.)	est. 8500	2591	190
Macdonald Peak (B.C.)	7300+	2225+	122
Mt. MacFarlane (B.C.)	6885	2099	136
MacLeod Peak (B.C.)	7100+	2164+	192
Mad Eagle Peak	8080+	2463+	115
Majestic Mountain	7510	2289	278
Many Trails Peak	8241	2512	174
Marmot Mountain (B.C.)	6800+	2073+	193
Martin Peak	8375	2553	218
Matriarch Mountain (B.C.)			190
McAlester Mountain	7928	2416	222
McGregor Mountain	8122	2476	223
Mt. McGuire (B.C.)	6620	2018	138
McKay Ridge	7000+	2134+	278
McLeod Mountain	8099	2469	174
McMillan Spire	8000+	2438+	81
Melted Tower	7920+	2414+	239
Mt. Mercer (B.C.)	5500	1676	305
Mt. Meronuik (B.C.)	5900+	1798+	117
Methow Pinnacles	7564	2306	277
Middle Peak	7464	2275	124
Midnight Mountain	7595	2315	224
Mineral Mountain	6781	2067	51
Minuteman Tower	est. 7000	2134	258
Molar Tooth	7547	2300	274
The Monk			186
Monument Peak	8592	2619	172
Mox Peaks	8480+	2585+	105
Mushroom Tower	8180+	2493+	238
Nak Peak (B.C.)	6700+	2042+	202
Nancy Peak	5900+	1798+	44
Nanny Goat Mountain	7700	2347	175
Needle Peak (B.C.)	6900+	2103+	196
The Needles	8140	2481	274

Peak	Elevation Feet	Meters	Page
Nepopekum Mountain (B.C.)	6357	1938	165
Nodoubt Peak	7290	2222	116
Nooksack Tower	8268	2520	64
North Early Winter Spire	7760+	2366+	253
North Gardner Mountain	8956	2730	225
Mt. Northgraves (B.C.)	6900+	2103+	117
North Navarre Peak	7963	2427	218
North Twentymile Peak	7437	2067	178
North Twin	6570	2003	39
Mt. Nowell (B.C.)	6000+	1829+	117
Oakes Peak	5696	1736	306
Obstruction Peak	7940	2420	178
Ogilvie Peak (B.C.)	5900+	1798+	195
Old Baldy	7844	2391	178
Old Brownie	7082	2159	72
Old Maid Mountain	7882	2403	218
Orthodox Mountain (B.C.)	8224	2507	187
Osceola Peak	8587	2617	171
Ottohorn	est. 7700	2347	92
Mt. Outram (B.C.)	8000+	2438+	192
Outrigger Peak	7680+	2341+	96
Oval Peak	8795	2681	221
Ovis Mountain (B.C.)			190
Paisano Pinnacle	est. 7900	2408	236
Paleface Mountain (B.C.)	5800+	1767+	117
Pasayten Peak	7850	2393	169
Pass Butte	8140	2481	174
Mt. Payne (B.C.)	8100+	2469+	194
Peak 5800+	5800+	1768+	43
Peak 6561	6561	2000	70
Peak 6585	6585	2007	72
Peak 6914	6914	2107	77
Peak 7100+ (B.C.)	7100+	2164+	194
Peak 7126 (B.C.)	7126	2172	195
Peak 7153	7153	2180	109
Peak 7200+ (B.C.)	7200+	2194+	192
Peak 7200+ (U.S.)	7200+	2194+	76
Peak 7400+ (B.C.)	7400+	2256+	202
Peak 7680+	7680+	2341+	116
Peak 7718 (B.C.)	7718	2352	176
Peak 7800+	7800+	2377+	246
Peak 7821	7821	2384	176
Peak 7895	7895	2406	109
Peak 7905	7905	2409	223
Peak 7949	7949	2423	177
Peak 7970+ (B.C.)	7970+	2429+	180

Peak	Elevation Feet	Meters	Page
Peak 8000+ (B.C.)	8000+	2438+	180
Peak 8142	8142	2482	222
Peak 8200+	8200+	2499+	112
Peak 8211	8211	2503	174
Peak 8392	8392	2558	221
Peak 8824	8824	2690	109
Pearrygin Peak	6644	2025	178
Peepsight Mountain	8146	2483	177
Pernod Spire	8441	2573	233
Phantom Peak	8045	2452	99
Pica Peak	7565	2306	246
Pick Peak	7620	2323	303
Picket Range			77
Mt. Pierce (B.C.)	6426	1959	136
Pinnacle Peak	6805	2074	87
Pioneer Ridge	7020	2140	72
Pi Pillar (B.C.)			127
Pistol Peaks	7802	2378	173
The Platypus	est. 7200	2195	245
The Pleiades	7360+	2243+	47
Pocket Peak	7040+	2146+	129
Point Defiance	7403	2256	308
Point 6495	6495	1980	311
Point 6728	6728	2051	311
Point 7002	7002	2134	246
Point 8025	8025	2446	177
Point 8080+	8080+	2463+	115
Point 8183	8183	2494	239
The Pope	8264	2519	187
Porcupine Peak	7762	2366	269
Mt. Potter (B.C.)	6200+	1890+	193
Powder Mountain	7714	2351	169
Preston Ridge	7845	2391	177
Mt. Prophet	7640+	2329+	77
Ptarmigan Peak	8614	2626	174
Purple Mountain	7161	2183	222
The Pyramid	7920+	2414+	86
Quartz Mountain	7539	2298	176
Radium Peak (B.C.)	7097	2163	122
Mt. Raeburn	6863	2092	111
Mt. Rahm	8478	2584	111
The Rake	est. 7700	2347	88
Rampart Ridge	7941	2420	174
Rapid Peak	7059	2152	128
Raven Ridge	8580+	2615+	219
Red Face Mountain	7174	2187	103
Red Mountain (B.C.)	6633	2022	309
Mt. Redoubt	8956	2730	113
Red Tooth	8240+	2512+	227
Reh Peak (B.C.)	5800+	1768+	199
Mt. Remmel	8685	2647	177
Rennie Peak	7742	2360	222
Mt. Rexford (B.C.)	7600+	2317+	124

Peak	Feet	Meters	Page
Rexford-Illusion Crags (B.C.)			127
Reynolds Peak	8512	2594	222
Mt. Rideout (B.C.)	8029	2447	194
Robinson Mountain	8726	2660	170
Rock Mountain	7617	2322	180
Mt. Rolo	8096	2468	171
The Roost	6705	2044	76
Mt. Ross	6052	1845	76
Rustic Peak	7732	2357	104
Ruth Mountain	7106	2166	50
Saddle Slab Peak	5700+	1737+	43
Sauk Mountain	5537	1688	67
Seahpo Peak	7429	2264	66
Mt. Sefrit	7191	2192	49
Mt. Sentinel (B.C.)	8000+	2438+	187
Serna Peak (B.C.)	5800+	1768+	199
Setting Sun Mountain	7255	2311	174
Seward Peak	8005	2440	37
Shawatum Mountain (B.C.)	7081	2158	165
Sheep Mountain	8274	2522	176
Sherman Peak	8204	2501	175
Shirley Peak	5836	1779	43
Mt. Shuksan	9127	2782	52
Shull Mountain	7830	2387	169
Silverdaisy Mountain (B.C.)	6700+	2042+	166
Silver Horn	8351	2545	230
Silver Peak (B.C.)	6400+	1951+	118
Silver Star Mountain	8876	2705	228
Silvertip Mountain (B.C.)	8500+	2591+	193
Skagit Peak	6800+	2073+	162
Skaist Mountain (B.C.)	6300+	1920+	309
Skookum Peak	6500+	1981+	42
Skookum Puss Mountain	7240+	2207+	221
Slate Peak	7440	2268	170
Slesse Mountain (B.C.)	7800+	2377+	129
Smokey the Bear (B.C.)			190
Smoky Mountain	7580	2310	168
Snagtooth Ridge			225
Snass Mountain (B.C.)	7580	2310	191
Snazzy Peak (B.C.)	est. 7300	2225	191
Mt. Snider (B.C.)	6700	2042	192
Snow Camp Mountain (B.C.)	6497	1980	309
Snowshoe Mountain	7823	2384	180

Peak	Feet	Meters	Page
Snowy Mountain (B.C.)	8507	2593	179
Soda Peak	7762	2366	168
Sourdough Mountain	5985	1824	310
South Early Winter Spire	7807	2380	246
South Navarre Peak	7870	2399	218
South Twentymile Peak	6670	2033	178
South Twin	6932	2113	41
Mt. Spickard	8879	2706	107
Spider Mountain (B.C.)	5200+	1585+	196
Splawn Mountain	7450	2271	221
Split Tooth	est. 8000	2438	227
Spratt Mountain	7258	2212	298
Squeah Mountain (B.C.)	5900+	1798+	195
Star Peak	8690	2649	221
State Crag	7560+	2304+	274
Steinbok Peak (B.C.)	6500+	1981+	199
Stewart Peak (B.C.)	7300+	2225+	120
Stiletto Peak	7660	2335	223
The Still (B.C.)	7500+	2286+	120
Stone City Mountain (B.C.)	8570	2612	190
Storey Peak	7821	2384	225
Stoyoma Mountain (B.C.)	7486	2282	202
Stoyoma's Widow (B.C.)	7400+	2256+	202
Sun Mountain	7492	2284	221
Sunrise Peak	8002	2439	218
Sunrise Peak	8144	2482	175
Swiss Peak	7840+	2390+	97
Switchback Peak	8321	2536	218
Tamarack Peak	7307	2227	297
Tamarack Ridge	7748	2362	174
Tatie Peak	7386	2251	297
Tatoosh Buttes	7245	2208	174
Teapot Dome	7608	2319	180
The Temple	7572	2308	241
Mt. Terror	8151	2484	88
Thompson Peak (B.C.)	7000+	2134+	116
Thornton Peak	6911	2106	76
Three AM Mountain	7180	2188	224
Three Brothers (B.C.)	7453	2272	191
Three Fools Peak	7920+	2414+	169
Three Pinnacles	8124	2476	173
Thunder Mountain	7073	2156	179
Mt. Thurston	5335	1626	305

Peak	Elevation		Page
	Feet	Meters	
Tiffany Mountain	8242	2512	179
The Tomahawk	7320+	2231+	245
The Tomb	est. 7800	2377	241
Tomyhoi Peak	7451	2271	44
Tower Mountain	8444	2574	274
Trappers Peak	5964	1818	76
Trisolace Peak	5800+	1768+	43
Mt. Triumph	7270	2216	74
Twin Moles (B.C.) est.	5700	1737	166
Twin Needles	7840+	2390+	91
Twin Peaks	7686	2343	221
Twin Sisters Range			37
Twin Spires	8480+	2585+	105
Two Point Mountain	7955	2425	176
Tulameen Mountain (B.C.)	7499	2286	192
Uno Peak	7640+	2329+	218
Van Peak	7665	2336	177
Vasiliki Ridge			236
Vasiliki Tower	7920+	2414+	236
Vicuna Peak (B.C.)	6900+	2103+	201
Vie Mountain	7777	2370	308
Wallaby Peak	7995	2437	241
Wamihaspi Peak	7800+	2377+	246
Mt. Watson	6234	1900	68
Mt. Webb (B.C.)	7097	2163	122
Welch Peak (B.C.)	7800+	2377+	120
Wells Peak (B.C.)	6000+	1829+	195
Whatcom Peak	7574	2309	102
Whistler Mountain	7790	2374	269
Whitworth Peak (B.C.)	7525	2294	116
Wildcat Mountain	7958	2426	171
Williams Peak (B.C.)	6965	2123	122
Willow Tooth	8330	2539	227
Winchester Mountain	6521	1988	314
Windy Peak	8334	2540	179
Mt. Winthrop	7850	2393	168
Mt. Wittenberg (B.C.)	6100+	1859+	117
Wolframite Mountain	8137	2480	180
Wright Peak (B.C.)	6700	2042	301
Yak Peak (B.C.)	6600+	2012+	201
Yellow Aster Butte	6145	1873	303
Mt. Zakwaski (B.C.)	6703	2043	203
Zupjok Ridge (B.C.)	6000+	1829+	201

NOTES

NOTES

ABOUT THE AUTHOR

Fred Beckey has achieved enduring recognition as the most imaginative, persistent, and thorough explorer, and mountain investigator of the Cascade Range wilderness. His intimate knowledge of the topography has been gained through many years of personal experience, including the ascent of hundreds of peaks — many of them first ascents — in all parts of the range, and the study of an untold number of maps and aerial photographs.

This knowledge is reflected in his other guidebooks, and a personal narrative, *Challenge of the North Cascades*.

In addition to becoming a legendary personality, Beckey has also earned a reputation as a student of human history, where he has made his own scholarly contributions. In addition he has carefully perused the body of natural history, ecology, glaciology, and geology, and added his own contributions. Beckey has served as an advisor to Washington State Board on Geographic Names, and has indirectly contributed many feature names in the Cascades, including For-

Author Beckey packs up for yet another journey into the mountains. (Photo by Russell D. Lamb)

bidden Peak, Crooked Thumb, Phantom Peak, and Cruel Finger.

Through keeping abreast of published literature, seeking out and interviewing other climbers and explorers, and investigating documents in various libraries throughout North America, Beckey has become widely acknowledged as an authority on Cascade history. Many of his findings have been published in the literature of the region.

"The kids up here (Vancouver) talk about you (Fred Beckey) in a legendary way — in the same breath as Buffalo Bill — got to watch out for that! Don't let old age creep up on you.
LES MacDONALD, 1971

OTHER BOOKS FROM THE MOUNTAINEERS

The ABC of Avalanche Safety
Across the Olympic Mountains
Animal Tracks of the Pacific Northwest
The Ascent of Denali
Bicycling the Backroads of Northwest Washington
Bicycling the Backroads of Southwest Washington
Bicycling the Backroads Around Puget Sound
Bicycling Notes
Canoe Routes/British Columbia
Canoe Routes/Yukon
Cascade Alpine Guide: Climbing and High Routes
— Columbia River to Stevens Pass
— Stevens Pass to Rainy Pass
The Challenge of the North Cascades
The Challenge of Rainier
Climber's Guide to the Olympic Mountains
Climbing Notes
Cloud Walkers
The Coffee Chased Us Up
Cross-Country Skiing
Cross-Country Ski Gear
Discover Southeast Alaska with Pack and Paddle
Emergency Survival Handbook
Everest: The West Ridge
Expeditions to Nowhere
Exploring Manning Park
Exploring Purcell Wilderness
Exploring the Yukon River
Fire & Ice: The Cascade Volcanoes
First Aid Pamphlet
Footsore 1, 2, 3 and 4: Walks and Hikes Around Puget Sound
Gervasutti's Climbs
Give Me the Hills
High Drama
High Mountains, Cold Seas: A Biography of H.W. Tilman
Hiking Notes
K2-The Savage Mountain
Land of Mountains
The Last Blue Mountain

The Last Step: The American Ascent of K2
Many People Come, Looking, Looking
Medicine for Mountaineering
Men Against the Clouds
Men for the Mountains
Men, Mules and Mountains
Mexico's Volcanoes: A Climbing Guide
Monte Cristo
Mountain Flowers
Mountaineering and Its Literature
Mountaineering First Aid
Mountaineering: The Freedom of the Hills
Mountains of Canada
Mountains of the World
Mt. McKinley: The Pioneer Climbs
Northwest Trees
Rock Climbing
The Rogue I Remember
The San Juan Islands, Afoot and Afloat
Sivalaya
Snowshoeing
Snow Trails
Switchbacks
Tales of a Western Mountaineer
Tatoosh
Trekking in Nepal
Trips and Trails 1
Trips and Trails 2
Unknown Mountain
Welzenbach's Climbs
A Year in Paradise
50 Hikes in Mt. Rainier National Park
55 Ways to the Wilderness in Southcentral Alaska
100 Hikes in the Alps
101 Hikes in the North Cascades
102 Hikes in the Alpine Lakes
103 Hikes in British Columbia
109 Walks in Lower British Columbia

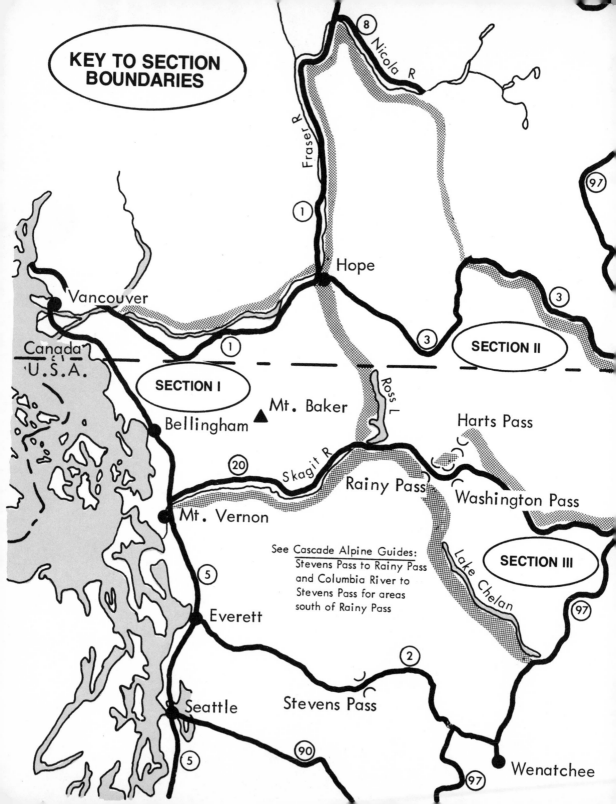

KEY TO SECTION BOUNDARIES

8

Nicola R

Fraser R

1

97

Hope

Vancouver

3

1

SECTION II

3

Canada
U.S.A.

SECTION I

Mt. Baker

Ross L

Harts Pass

Bellingham

20

Skagit R

Rainy Pass

Washington Pass

Mt. Vernon

See Cascade Alpine Guides:
Stevens Pass to Rainy Pass
and Columbia River to
Stevens Pass for areas
south of Rainy Pass

SECTION III

Lake Chelan

97

5

Everett

2

97

Seattle

Stevens Pass

5

90

Wenatchee

97